■ Parenting and Substance Abuse

Parenting and Substance Abuse

Developmental Approaches to Intervention

EDITED BY

Nancy E. Suchman
Marjukka Pajulo

AND

Linda C. Mayes

OXFORD
UNIVERSITY PRESS

OXFORD
UNIVERSITY PRESS

Oxford University Press is a department of the University of Oxford.
It furthers the University's objective of excellence in research, scholarship,
and education by publishing worldwide.

Oxford   New York
Auckland   Cape Town   Dar es Salaam   Hong Kong   Karachi
Kuala Lumpur   Madrid   Melbourne   Mexico City   Nairobi
New Delhi   Shanghai   Taipei   Toronto

With offices in
Argentina   Austria   Brazil   Chile   Czech Republic   France   Greece
Guatemala   Hungary   Italy   Japan   Poland   Portugal   Singapore
South Korea   Switzerland   Thailand   Turkey   Ukraine   Vietnam

Oxford is a registered trademark of Oxford University Press in the UK and certain other
countries.

Published in the United States of America by
Oxford University Press
198 Madison Avenue, New York, NY 10016

Library of Congress Cataloging-in-Publication Data
    Parenting and substance abuse : developmental approaches to intervention / edited by
Nancy E. Suchman, Marjukka Pajulo, Linda C. Mayes.
      p. cm.
Includes bibliographical references and index.
ISBN 978-0-19-974310-0
1. Parents—Substance use—United States.   2. Parents—Substance use—United States—
Prevention.   3. Substance abuse—Treatment—United States.   4. Children of drug addicts—
United States.   I. Suchman, Nancy E.   II. Pajulo, Marjukka.   III. Mayes, Linda C.
HV4999.P37P37 2013
362.29085—dc23
2012042599

9 8 7 6 5 4 3 2
Printed in the United States of America
on acid-free paper

To my mother, Fay Binenkorb Krawchick, whose intelligence and commitment I will cherish always.

—NS

To my daughters, Anna, Helena and Sonja, for reminding me of what is essential in life.

—MP

To my mother, Marion Mayes, whose courage, lively curiosity, and strength are enduring gifts.

—LM

CONTENTS

■ ACKNOWLEDGMENTS

First and foremost, we would like to express our deep gratitude to the mothers and fathers struggling with addiction who have shared their experience with clinicians and researchers so that we may learn how to better support their development and their children's. Second, we are grateful to our colleagues and collaborators who shared their enthusiasm and support often, and reminded us of the exceptional scholarship, creativity, and clinical work taking place in the trenches every day.

■ CONTRIBUTORS

Tessa Baradon
The Anna Freud Centre
London, England

Charles Beekman
Department of Psychology
The Pennsylvania State University

Ritva Belt
Department of Child Psychiatry
University of Tampere, Finland
Tampere City Child Welfare,
    Finland

Kristin Bernard
Department of Psychology
University of Delaware

Susan Bers
Department of Psychiatry
Yale University School of Medicine

Johanna Bick
Child Study Center
Yale University

Zack Boukydis
Department of Pediatrics
Semmelweis Medical School &
    Institute of Psychology
Eotvos Lorand University
Budapest, Hungary Department
    of Pediatrics
University of Turku, Finland

Tara M. Chaplin
Department of Psychiatry
Yale University School of Medicine

Minna Daum
The Anna Freud Centre
London, England

Cindy DeCoste
Department of Psychiatry
Yale University School of Medicine

Mary Dozier
Department of Psychology
University of Delaware

Philip A. Fisher
Oregon Social Learning Center
Center for Research to Practice
University of Oregon

Hiram E. Fitzgerald
Department of Psychology
University Outreach and Engagement
Michigan State University

Marjo Flykt
Department of Child Psychiatry
Small Children Open-Care Unit
Helsinki University Central Hospital
Department of Psychology
University of Tampere

Jessica L. Garber
Department of Psychology
Center for Addictions, Personality and
    Emotion Research
University of Maryland, College Park

William H. Gottdiener
John Jay College of Criminal Justice
City University of New York
St.Luke's-Roosevelt Medical Center

Therese M. Grant
Department of Psychiatry and
    Behavioral Sciences
Fetal Alcohol and Drug Unit
University of Washington School of
    Medicine

Leila Guller
Department of Psychology
University of Kentucky

Cynthia V. Healey
Oregon Social Learning Center
Center for Research to Practice

James M. Henson
Department of Psychology
Old Dominion University

Janet E. Huggins
Department of Psychiatry and
  Behavioral Sciences
Fetal Alcohol and Drug Unit
University of Washington School of
  Medicine

Lauren M. Jansson
Johns Hopkins University
School of Medicine

Mirjam Kalland
Faculty of Social Science
University of Helsinki, Finland
Folkhälsan Research Center
Mannerheim League for Child Welfare

Karol Kaltenbach
Departments of Pediatrics and
  Psychiatry and Human Behavior
Jefferson Medical College
Thomas Jefferson University

Michelle L. Kelley
Department of Psychology
Old Dominion University

Keith Klostermann
Department of Psychology
Old Dominion University

C. W. Lejuez
Department of Psychology
Center for Addictions, Personality and
  Emotion Research
University of Maryland, College Park

Hannah M. Lyden
University College London
Yale Child Study Center

Richard J. Macatee
Department of Psychology
Florida State University

Jessica F. Magidson
Department of Psychology
Center for Addictions, Personality and
  Emotion Research
University of Maryland, College Park

Alexis K. Matusiewicz
Department of Psychology
Center for Addictions, Personality, and
  Emotion Research
University of Maryland, College Park

Linda C. Mayes
Yale Child Study Center
Yale University School of Medicine

Thomas J. McMahon
Department of Psychiatry
Yale Child Study Center
Yale University School of Medicine

Susan Minear
Department of Pediatrics
Boston Medical Center/Boston
  University School of Medicine

Jenae M. Neiderhiser
Department of Psychology
The Pennsylvania State University

Monica Roosa Ordway
Yale University School of Nursing

Marjukka Pajulo
Department of Child Psychiatry
University of Turku, Finland
Turku University Hospital

Marc N. Potenza
Department of Psychiatry
Yale University School of Medicine

Raija-Leena Punamäki
School of Social Sciences and
Humanities/Psychology
University of Tampere, Finland

Angela M. Relling
Oregon Social Learning Center
Center for Research to Practice

Helena J. V. Rutherford
Yale Child Study Center
Yale University School of
Medicine

Saara Salo
Department of Child Psychiatry
Small Children Open-Care Unit
Helsinki University Central Hospital

Rajita Sinha
Department of Psychiatry
Yale University School of Medicine

Jari Sinkkonen
Department of Child Psychiatry
University of Turku, Finland
Save the Children, Finland

Nancy E. Suchman
Department of Psychiatry
Yale Child Study Center
Yale University School of Medicine

Amanda van Scoyoc
Department of Psychology
University of Oregon

Martha L. Velez
Johns Hopkins University
School of Medicine

Maria M. Wong
Department of Psychology
Idaho State University

Robert A. Zucker
Departments of Psychiatry and
Psychology
Addiction Research Center
University of Michigan

Barry Zuckerman
Department of Pediatrics
Boston Medical Center/Boston
University School of Medicine

■ INTRODUCTION

Within every addicted parent, there is a child who experienced a relationship with a parent. And in every child of an addicted parent, there is an enduring reflection of the parent.

■ THE LONGSTANDING GAP BETWEEN ADDICTION AND DEVELOPMENTAL SCIENCE AND PRACTICE

Historically, there has been little integration of theoretical or applied research on addiction treatment and parenting intervention development. Rather, addiction and developmental research relating to parenting have progressed on largely separate trajectories, even though their focus powerfully, and often tragically, intersects each time a parent is diagnosed with a substance-use disorder. This gap is perpetuated in clinical practice, where we often recognize that one complicates the other—addiction makes it difficult to parent a child, and being a parent often adds additional complications and stressors for addicted adults already struggling with their day-to-day lives. Moreover, drug use by a parent is sometimes viewed by professionals as a willful act rather than a psychiatric illness, making a parent's difficulties with caregiving at least incomprehensible and at the worst reprehensible. Sadly, these views can lead to fatalistic beliefs and punitive attitudes among healthcare providers and can also trigger hurried and ill-conceived responses to parental substance abuse (e.g., immediate and enduring changes in custody) that bode poorly for the long-term well-being of the dyad. The perpetual cycles of substance abuse and concomitant psychosocial maladjustment across generations is not likely to be interrupted for families until its inevitability is no longer assumed by their healthcare providers.

As a result of poor integration between addiction and developmental science, few developmental investigators have ventured into conceptualizing and evaluating treatments targeting parent–child relationships involving substance-abusing parents, even though developmental research has the potential to influence and improve treatments currently offered to drug-dependent parents and their children. Likewise, although a handful of interventions to date have been developed by addiction and health professionals, the absence of developmentally informed perspectives may limit their long-term efficacy in terms of sustained abstinence and improved psychosocial functioning, a handicap that has been reflected in empirical findings of these interventions. Finally, very little has been written to guide professionals in their decisions about designing and evaluating new interventions for substance-using parents. Illuminating the special considerations and decisions involved in treatment development and evaluation can serve an important heuristic for developing relevant, timely, and effective approaches that address each population's unique characteristics.

■ WHY BRING ADDICTION AND PARENTING TOGETHER IN ONE VOLUME?

Both addiction and parenthood are conditions and states of being that impact many others—families, friends, children, and communities—and bring profound transformative changes in a person's life, sometimes for the worse in both instances, sometimes for the positive in one and negative in the other. The interdependence between addiction and parenthood is complex and involves mechanisms and processes that are not yet well understood. For example, knowing that parenting stress triggers cravings and relapses (see Chaplin & Sinha, this volume) would help drug treatment providers tailor interventions to parents.

Most parents who become addicted to substances express a strong desire to become better parents and worry about the impact of their addiction on their children. But still they struggle with the often crushing impact of their addiction conflicting with the needs of their children. Understanding the neurobiological, developmental, and environmental mechanisms that derail these intentions can inform the development of better interventions for parents who are also struggling with addiction. For example, knowing that chronic substance abuse offsets reward systems in the brain, making parenting a more stressful and less rewarding experience (see Rutherford & Mayes, this volume) can help clinicians maximize emotional reward in parenting interventions (see Bick, Bernard, & Dozier, this volume).

Bringing the child into the treatment focus is highly feasible and can add richness and meaning to a parent's life and the parent–child relationship. This has been the experience of many parents participating in the interventions described in this volume (see Pajulo & Kalland, this volume; Suchman, DeCoste, Ordway, & Bers, this volume). Within every addicted parent, there is a child who experienced a relationship with a parent. And in every child of an addicted parent, there is an enduring reflection of the parent. Understanding how the addicted parent's childhood influences her parenting (see Lyden & Suchman, this volume) and how a child experiences his or her parent's addiction at different ages (see Fitzgerald, Wong, & Zucker, this volume) can help inform efforts to prevent the transmission of psychosocial risk across generations.

Given the strong continuity between a parent's experience as a child and how she brings this experience to bear as a parent, childhood and parenting are relevant treatment issues long before a baby arrives (see Boukydis, this volume; Gottdiener, this volume; Lyden & Suchman, this volume). How these issues are addressed in treatment can strongly impact an adult's transition into the parenting role. The development and evaluation of early intervention before the baby arrives (see Boukydis, this volume; Pajulo & Kalland, this volume; Punamäki & Belt, this volume; Velez & Jansson, this volume) are critical in this regard.

Parenting-focused interventions starting during pregnancy serve a crucially important preventive function when they target the child's prenatal biophysiological exposure to substance effects, maternal prenatal representations about the baby and parenting, and maternal attachment to the fetus. Problems in the mother–child relationship are most often rooted in pregnancy and can become identified and focused on well before the baby arrives. Preventive work during pregnancy, however, requires improvement in identification and treatment-referral systems for mothers and families in conjunction with intervention development.

The transition to parenthood around the time of pregnancy is a critical developmental hurdle that is often overlooked in addiction-treatment settings where patients are identified more often as "addicts" than as "parents with addiction problems." This is typically the case even though a strong parental identity is often what motivates individuals to seek treatment for addiction. Adult development in the parenting role can potentially and profoundly modify the course of an addiction, yet this potential has received little attention in empirical studies.

▪ FOCUS ON MOTHERS

Most research and interventions targeting parents with substance-use disorders focus on mothers, who are most often the primary caregivers. Consequently, the work described herein focuses largely on mothers as parents. Two chapters, however, focus exclusively on fathers. There is a great need for researchers and interventionists to recognize the unique issues linking fatherhood and addiction. Unfortunately, the fields of addiction and development lag behind in this regard.

▪ THE PURPOSE OF THIS BOOK

Recently, there has been a growing interest in collaboration across the fields of addiction and developmental science to address and close an increasingly recognizable gap. *Parenting and Substance Addiction: Developmental Approaches to Intervention* is the first book to report on pioneering efforts to move the treatment of substance-abusing women forward by embracing their roles and experiences as mothers directly and continually across the course of their treatment. The chapters in this volume represent important new strides among researchers and clinicians to bridge the gap between addiction and developmental science. International experts were invited to share their recent work with an eye toward understanding its implications for intervention.

▪ FOR WHOM IS THIS BOOK WRITTEN?

The principal audience for the book includes professionals working in applied research settings in medical schools and centers (e.g., primary care, pediatric care, psychiatry); university-based and public mental health care and addiction clinics (e.g., outpatient mental health centers, outpatient and residential drug treatment centers); and community-based addiction treatment programs. We expect the readership to include physicians, nurses, social workers, psychologists, parent educators, addiction specialists, and graduate-level trainees. The book will also be appropriate as a text in graduate-level training seminars on addiction treatment.

■ IN CONCLUSION

This volume represents a diverse sampling of work that we believe begins to embrace the complexity of how addiction impacts parenting and how addiction reflects a developmental process for both parent and child. In the organization and content of the chapters, we intend to underscore a different way to think about the relationship between parenting and addiction. First, we wish to convey the importance of thinking about individuals as parents (rather than as addicts). Second, we wish to emphasize the parallel circumstances of parent and child and to promote developmental thinking of parenthood as well as childhood. Like any developmental transition, parenthood is a time of vulnerability to disorder and psychological distress. Third, focusing on parenting in addicted adults provides another perspective for understanding the intergenerational transmission of risk for addictive disorders. And finally, we suggest that attending to the parenting responsibilities and parental development of adults potentially changes treatment approaches in the instance of addiction. It is our hope that this volume will raise questions and stimulate future investigation and intervention development that will embrace the complexity and richness that characterize these very important and critical topics. Most of all, we hope that any new interventions stimulated by this volume will bring new hope for parents struggling to care for their children under the burden of their addiction.

June 13, 2012
Nancy E. Suchman, Ph.D.   Marjukka Pajulo, M.D., Ph.D.
Linda C. Mayes, M.D.   *Turku, Finland*
New Haven, Connecticut

PART I

Understanding Substance Abuse and its Implications for Parenting

1 The Neurobiology of Addiction and Attachment

HELENA J. V. RUTHERFORD,
MARC N. POTENZA, AND
LINDA C. MAYES

Substance use and abuse in women is of significant interest when considering the transition to motherhood. In 2007, it was found that 5.2% of pregnant women reported current or recent use of illicit drugs, with 11.6% reporting alcohol use and 16.4% reporting tobacco use (Substance Abuse and Mental Health Services Administration, SAMHSA, 2008). Teratogenic substances may have a negative impact on fetal and infant development, including increasing the rates of pre-term delivery, low birth weight, and multiple congenital abnormalities (Jansson & Velez, 2011). From 2002 to 2007, 11.9% of children were living with a parent who abused or was dependent upon alcohol or other illicit substances (SAMHSA, 2008). Accordingly, substance use may significantly impact the postpartum environment. Maternal substance use is associated with increased rates of child maltreatment, including neglect and abuse (Cash & Wilke, 2003), and a twofold increase in the incidence of removal of a child from a family (U.S. Department of Health and Human Services, 1999). Furthermore, substance abuse has been reported as being associated with two-thirds of child maltreatment fatalities (Reid, Macchetto, & Foster, 1999). For mothers who do abstain from substance use during pregnancy, relapse rates are high postpartum (Park et al., 2009), suggesting this time as a specific period of vulnerability to substance use and abuse. Importantly, this may reflect the processes related to addiction, the demands of caring for a new child, as well as other factors that may put significant demands on the person's capacity to parent (including availability of resources, physical and mental health, and social support).

In this chapter, we adopt a neurobiological perspective to understand the mechanisms that may underscore the impact of addiction on parenting. We will present the evidence that suggests the neural systems recruited in parenting are the same neural systems that are compromised by addiction, and that this notion presents a neurobiological pathway through which substance use may impact the capacity to parent.

A NEUROBIOLOGICAL MODEL OF ADDICTION AND PARENTING

The parental brain appears to undergo significant neurobiological changes throughout the postpartum period (Swain, 2011; Swain, Lorberbaum, Kose, & Strathearn, 2007). For instance, a recent study found that gray matter volume

3

significantly increased in mothers from two to four weeks postpartum to three to four months postpartum, particularly in the prefrontal, parietal, and mid-brain regions (Kim et al., 2010). These findings are consistent with the notion of cortical reorganization over the postpartum period that may serve to facilitate parenting behavior and the orientation of attention and perception toward the infant. Interestingly, in the Kim et al. (2010) study, changes in gray matter volume were predicted by positive perceptions of parenting. In keeping with this, recent work has also found differences in gray matter volume when examining structural magnetic resonance imaging (MRI) data between substance-using and non-substance-using mothers, with substance-using mothers having significantly less gray matter volume, particularly in frontal cortical regions, at approximately three months postpartum (Rutherford, Gerig, Gouttard, Mayes, & Potenza, submitted). Critically in the latter study, increasing gray matter volume in the substance-using mothers was associated with greater insight into mother-infant bonding (Rutherford et al., submitted).

Importantly, if becoming a parent represents a neurobiological shift to facilitate caregiving, there should be measurable differences in the neural response elicited by infant cues (i.e., photographs of infant faces, recordings of infant vocalizations) in parents compared to non-parents. Supporting this notion, both functional MRI (fMRI) and electrophysiological studies have reported differences in the neural response to infant cues while comparing parents and non-parents (Proverbio, Brignone, Matarazzo, Del Zotto, & Zani, 2006; Seifritz et al., 2003). Consequently, the neurobiological response to infant cues has received significant attention in recent years in understanding both the normative neurobiological transition to parenthood as well as sensitivity to infant cues in non-parents (Glocker et al., 2009; Montoya et al., 2012), in addition to the situations where parenting may be compromised. This has included conditions such as depression (Laurent & Ablow, 2011), mothers that have a history of substantiated neglect of their child (Rodrigo et al., 2011), and the focus of the present discussion, addiction (Landi et al., 2011). Critically, in bringing together the literature on the neurobiology of parenting in this chapter, it is hoped that the model of parenting that is later presented can account for variations in clinical disorders as well as for differences between addicted and non-addicted parents.

Broadly, addiction can be conceptualized as the dysregulation between stress and reward neural systems; although it is important to recognize that other neuroanatomical regions are important to addiction, such as the insula (Naqvi & Bechara, 2009). The hedonic effects of drugs link reward circuitry to substance use, particularly in relation to rewarding responses to initial and early substance use that reinforces repeated future use (i.e., positive reinforcement). Consistent with this is the finding that the majority of drugs of abuse stimulate reward neural circuitries (Di Chiara & Imperato, 1988). Critically, though, and as described below, studies recruiting addicted adults show evidence that the reward response to drugs of abuse is blunted relative to healthy controls, with an increased reward response observed instead to conditioned cues associated with substance use (Volkow, Fowler, Wang, Baler, & Telang, 2009; Volkow, Wang, Fowler, Tomasi, & Telang, 2011). Therefore, it has been hypothesized that it is the expectation of reward from learned cues (i.e., habitual behavior) that may drive repeated drug use in addiction.

Recent theoretical and empirical work has also focused on the role of the stress circuitry in addiction. Specifically, in substance-dependent individuals, the rewarding value of drugs is through relief from the negative affective states in the face of withdrawal or other distressing situations (i.e., negative reinforcement). That is, continued substance use is reinforcing in allowing the user to return to a feeling of normality that is counter to the distress being experienced. Thus the addictive process may involve transitions from positive to negative reinforcement mechanisms in guiding behavior, and preclinical studies have suggested an important role for the basal circuitry of the extended amygdala in mediating this transition (Koob & Volkow, 2009). Consistent with this model, there is a well-documented relationship between stress and substance use, where increases in stress are associated with increases in craving in substance-using adults (Sinha, 2001). Throughout this chapter, consideration of both stress and reward neural circuitries and their involvement in addiction will be described with a view to unifying their involvement in parenting.

Although there is much discussion about the impact of drugs on reward processing, other, more normative, rewards stimulate reward neural circuitries and serve to alleviate negative affect states, including social-affiliative relationships. Here we focus on the parent–child relationship, with it being widely held that caring for an infant is an inherently rewarding process and with there existing a specific motivation to care for infants. Consistent with this, Lorenz (1943) proposed that certain features of infant faces (including large eyes and rounded cheeks) serve to elicit positive affective responses from caregivers as an evolutionary mechanism to facilitate the baby's survival. In support of this proposal, recent empirical work has demonstrated that these baby schema primarily activate the nucleus accumbens in nulliparous women (Glocker et al., 2009), a critical component of the reward neural circuitry that will be described more below. Although these findings support the notion of the pleasurable elements of parenting, it is also important to recognize that the demands of caring for an infant can also be stressful to parents (Webster-Stratton, 1990). Therefore, when bringing together the literature related to the neurobiology of addiction and the emerging literature on the neurobiology of parenting, there is a clear overlap in the recruitment of reward and stress neural circuitries (Rutherford, Williams, Moy, Mayes, & Johns, 2011). Accordingly, the purpose of this chapter is to document the emerging evidence that the neural circuitries underscoring parenting and attachment appear to overlap with the neural systems that are dysregulated in addiction. Furthermore, it is proposed that this dysregulation of stress-reward neural circuits in addiction represents a neurobiological mechanism to understand how addiction may impact the capacity to parent.

In the following sections, we will consider how the neural circuits of stress and reward have been adapted to support parenting, and how addiction may impact this. We propose to bring together the stress and reward literatures within an integrated framework of addiction and attachment. Notably, the studies discussed here focus on human parenting and addiction research, although some evidence from preclinical studies is discussed.[1] We end our discussion with considering the implications of this work for intervention and future research.

■ THE REWARD CIRCUIT: SUBSTANCE USE AND PARENTING

Preclinical work has identified the key neural regions underscoring responding to reward, and these regions include the ventral tegmental area (VTA), nucleus accumbens (NAcc), and medial prefrontal cortex (medial PFC). Specifically, dopaminergic projections connect the VTA to the NAcc and PFC, with information converging in the NAcc to drive responding to reward (Koob & Volkow, 2009). Functional MRI studies of reward processing in humans have identified comparable neural regions, which include the orbitofrontal cortex (OFC), amygdala, NAcc, as well as the PFC and anterior cingulate cortex (ACC; McClure, 2004). In humans, the NAcc mediates the anticipation and prediction of reward (Knutson & Cooper, 2005), and NAcc activity has been found to be modulated by reward magnitude (Haber & Knutson, 2009). These "reward regions" are primarily innervated by the neurotransmitter dopamine, although it is important to note that other neurotransmitters may play a role in both their modulation of, as well as in isolation from, dopamine. Consistent with this notion, Kalivas (2009) has proposed that addiction may represent a homeostatic imbalance of the neurotransmitter glutamate, and other neurotransmitter systems, including opioids and serotonin, may influence dopaminergic function within the mesolimbic dopamine pathway (Leeman & Potenza, 2012).

It is well established that increases in the neurotransmitter dopamine are critical in determining the relative rewarding value of a stimulus, including the rewarding response to substances of abuse (Volkow et al., 2009). In preclinical work for instance, increases in dopamine are seen in limbic brain regions, primarily in the NAcc, in response to licit and illicit substances that are used by humans, including cocaine, nicotine, and amphetamine (Di Chiara & Imperato, 1988). Similarly in humans, increases in dopamine in the ventral striatum (the region to which the NAcc belongs) are typically observed following drug administration. For instance, positron emission tomography (PET) has been used in healthy participants to evidence that the administration of dextroamphetamine increases levels of dopamine in the ventral striatum (relative to the caudate), with this increased dopaminergic response correlating with self-reported levels of euphoria (Drevets et al., 2001). Converging with this, fMRI studies have also explored changes in the hemodynamic response within the NAcc following exposure to drugs. Consistent with this PET finding, one study found that there was an increase in activity in the NAcc following acute cocaine administration in cocaine-dependent adults (Breiter et al., 1997). However, in this latter study, activity in the NAcc peaked early and was sustained in duration, correlating with self-reported craving rather than the euphoria associated with the administration of the drug. This was somewhat surprising

---

1. For an extensive review of human and preclinical studies of addiction and parenting, see Rutherford et al. (2011).

given the evidence described above that suggests NAcc involvement in the reward response to drugs, and findings from more recent fMRI studies that instead report a decreased response in the NAcc following cocaine administration, where NAcc activity correlated with a self-reported high rather than craving (Kufahl et al., 2005; Risinger et al., 2005).

How can we understand these differential findings of the NAcc response and differential craving and euphoric self-reports? Recent work has transitioned into conceptualizing the role of reward in addiction as being more critical in motivating drug-seeking behaviors rather than as positive reinforcement following drug consumption (Volkow et al., 2009; 2011). Specifically, in the addicted individual, it is the conditioned response associated with the drug that is rewarding, serving to motivate drug-seeking behavior. Consistent with this notion, one study showed that when cocaine-addicted adults watched films related to cocaine consumption (relative to a neutral condition), there was an increase in dorsal striatal activity that correlated with self-reports of craving (Volkow et al., 2006). This finding is noteworthy because the dorsal striatum is associated with habitual learning, and finding an increased response in this region that is related to craving identifies the importance of cue-conditioned responses in promoting drug-seeking behaviors. Thus, while positive reinforcement of the pharmacological effects of drugs may be important during initiation of use, chronic use leads to a shift in reward responsivity such that the role of reward neural circuits to addiction is in motivating drug-seeking behavior (Volkow et al., 2011). However, one should also consider sex differences in these processes, as cocaine-addicted women tend to show greater corticolimbic-striatal activation to stress conditions, and cocaine-addicted men tend to show greater corticolimbic-striatal activation to drug-cue conditions (Potenza et al., 2012).

It is also important to note that changes in subcortical reward circuits may have consequences further upstream in prefrontal cortical function that underscores decision-making and executive control functions more generally where impairments may contribute to increased vulnerability to substance use. Indeed, reductions in striatal dopamine receptors in cocaine-addicted adults are associated with decreased glucose metabolism in the OFC, ACC, and dorsolateral prefrontal cortex (DLPFC; Volkow et al., 1993). These regions contribute importantly to executive functions (e.g., inhibitory control, regulation, and decision-making) and led to the proposal that impaired innervations of these regions by dopamine may underscore the increased impulsivity, compulsivity, and heightened salience of drugs that are common in addiction (Dalley, Everitt, & Robbins, 2011; Jentsch & Taylor, 1999; Volkow et al., 2011).

Other studies have also examined the neural response to reward in substance-dependent individuals, but focusing on sources of reward other than the drug. Specifically, researchers have explored sensitivity to monetary reward during cognitive tasks to investigate whether there is a more generalized reduction in reward sensitivity in addiction. In these studies, it has generally been reported that there is a decrease in the hemodynamic response measured in the ventral striatum in addicted adults, relative to healthy controls, during the anticipation of monetary reward (Balodis et al., 2012; Beck et al., 2009; Wrase et al., 2007; although see also Bjork, Smith, & Hommer, 2008). Such findings appear to extend to adults vulnerable to addictions (e.g., those with familial histories of alcoholism, Andrews et al., 2011), as well as to adolescents (Bjork, Smith, Chen, & Hommer, 2010), particularly those who use substances like tobacco (Peters et al., 2011). These studies are important because they suggest that the anticipation of non-drug rewards in addicted adults and adolescents do not engage key regions of the reward neural circuitry to the same extent as in non-addicted individuals, unlike the studies described earlier that indicate anticipation of drug use may be more rewarding than the consumption of the drug itself. Extrapolating these findings to the context of the present discussion on addiction and attachment suggests that the anticipation or motivation to parent may be diminished in addiction, if infant cues and caretaking are imbued with reward. We will now discuss the evidence consistent with this notion.

Accumulating research supports the recruitment of reward neural circuits in mothers when they are engaged with infant cues. In one study, 28 first-time mothers viewed photographs of either their own infant or an unfamiliar infant smiling, crying, or showing a neutral expression (Strathearn, Li, Fonagy, & Montague, 2008). The hemodynamic response in key dopaminergic innervated regions, including the left lateral OFC, ventral striatum, putamen, head of the caudate nucleus, VTA, and substantia nigra, significantly increased when mothers viewed their own infant compared to viewing an unknown infant. This increased response was observed most when the infant faces were smiling. Regions typically associated with emotion processing, including the amygdala, insula, and ACC, showed a similar increase in activation. Following up on this work, Strathearn and colleagues (2009) investigated whether the neural response to smiling infant faces may be modulated by attachment style (secure, insecure). For instance, securely attached mothers showed increased activity in the OFC, as well as the mPFC, and ventral striatum, while viewing their happy infant, with insecure mothers instead showing decreased activity in the ventral striatum (and increased activity in the DLPFC). Taken together, these studies support the recruitment of reward responsive regions in parenting and suggest that there may be important individual differences that mediate this response.

Converging with these studies of maternal responding to infant cues, the OFC has proven important in other studies of parenting as well. Increased activity in the right OFC is observed when mothers listen to infants' cries compared to white noise (Lorberbaum et al., 1999; Lorberbaum et al., 2002). Moreover, bilateral OFC activity increases when mothers view photographs of their own infant's face compared to unknown infants' faces (Nitschke et al., 2004), with OFC activity correlating with self-reported mood states (Nitschke et al., 2004; Noriuchi, Kikuchi, & Senoo, 2008). Activity in lateral OFC (as well as the periaqueductal gray) also appears to distinguish maternal from romantic attachment, although neural circuits of maternal and romantic attachment appear to overlap, including regions such as the striatum, insula, and dorsal ACC (Bartels & Zeki, 2000, 2004). Medial OFC activity may also modulate the temporal dynamics of infant cue perception, prioritizing the perception of infant as compared to adult faces (Kringelbach et al., 2008). Notably, the OFC is important in the representation of reward (O'Doherty,

2004), as well as in updating and maintaining the value of a reward (Gallagher, McMahan, & Schoenbaum, 1999). Moreover, the OFC also plays a critical role in decision-making more generally (Bechara, Damasio, & Damasio, 2000). Consequently, these studies suggest that the neural correlates of reward processing overlap with those that are recruited when processing infant cues in mothers.

Considering that normative rewards may be devalued in the presence of addiction, it could be hypothesized that in addicted adults, the rewarding value of infant cues may be depreciated, and this may impact parenting behavior as a consequence. Observational studies have provided some initial support for this. For instance, substance-using mothers may respond more passively and be less engaged with their infants as early as 48 hours postpartum (Gottwald & Thurman, 1994). Furthermore, examining mother–infant interactions later in the postpartum (three and six months postpartum), it has been observed that cocaine use was associated with decreased attentiveness and responsiveness to infants and fewer interactions between mothers and their infants (Mayes et al., 1997). Therefore, from a neurobiological perspective, the motivation to engage and respond to infants may be compromised in the presence of addiction, and this may be owing to infant signals holding less reward value. In the first fMRI study to test this notion (Landi et al., 2011), substance-using mothers and non-substance-using mothers listened to infant cries and viewed photographs of infant faces. In response to both cries and faces, substance-using mothers evidenced significantly less brain activity in sensory processing, prefrontal and limbic (parahippocampal and amygdala) regions, compared to non-substance-using mothers. These findings are consistent with the decreased saliency of infant cues in addiction and may represent the neurobiological underpinnings to maternal engagement during dyadic interactions in substance-using women (Gottwald & Thurman, 1994; Mayes et al., 1997).

Further support for this notion can be drawn from a recent electrophysiological study in substance-using and non-substance-using mothers (Rutherford, Landi, et al., submitted), also viewing photographs of infant faces and listening to infant cries. Here, the N170 event-related potential (ERP) component that marks face perception was significantly delayed in substance-using mothers viewing infant faces compared to healthy controls. Moreover, this was observed in the absence of any slowing of other markers of visual perception, suggesting that perceptual processing in general is not compromised by addiction or chronic drug use. Taken together, this emerging research supports the potential for a reduction in the saliency of infant cues in addiction, and is consistent with the reduction in neural responses to reward in other studies of addiction (Balodis et al., 2012; Beck et al., 2009; Peters et al., 2011; Wrase et al., 2007).

▪ THE STRESS CIRCUIT: SUBSTANCE USE AND PARENTING

While parenting is an inherently rewarding experience, it is also a time that is accompanied by increased levels of stress (Webster-Stratton, 1990). Parenting also requires enhanced regulatory strategies, especially in response to infant distress. Stress contributes significantly to addiction as well. Therefore, in addition to considering the neural circuitry of reward as it pertains to addiction and parenting, it is also important to consider the neural circuitry of stress. Indeed, the role of negative reinforcement suggests habitual behaviors that afford relief of negative affect states are reinforced and maintained in addiction. Accumulating evidence in human and preclinical studies supports the notion that increased exposure to stress increases vulnerability for addiction (Goeders, 2004). Moreover, a substantive body of research has demonstrated that exposure to stress increases the level of craving for substances of abuse (Sinha, 2001). In all individuals, irrespective of addiction status, stress can have detrimental effects on prefrontal cortical function (Mayes, 2006), which underscores executive and cognitive control functions that may be important to parenting. Indeed the capacity to parent probably demands a range of executive control functions, including inhibitory control, planning, and regulation, although this notion has received less recognition in empirical work (Deater-Deckard, Sewell, Petrill, & Thompson, 2010). For instance, in response to infant affect (such as crying), parents may have to try multiple behaviors to soothe their infant, finding that past successful behaviors may not be effective. Therefore, addiction may have an impact on parenting in a number of ways, given data suggestive of diminished reward sensitivity (Balodis et al., 2012; Beck et al., 2009; Peters et al., 2011; Wrase et al., 2007), prefrontal cortical function impairments (Volkow et al., 1993), as well as there being additional, heightened vulnerability to stress (Goeders, 2004; Sinha, 2008). Moreover, increased levels of stress and its association with craving during the postpartum period may explain increased relapses to substance use during this time, identifying the postpartum period as a time of particular vulnerability to substance use.

The neurocircuitry of the stress response system has been well established. In response to a stressor, the sympathetic nervous system and hypothalamic-pituitary-adrenal (HPA) axis are activated (Stratakis & Chrousos, 1995). Typically, the sympathetic nervous system responds by increasing norepinephrine and facilitating fight-or-flight responding. With respect to the HPA axis, in response to an internal or external stressor, the paraventricular nucleus (PVN) of the hypothalamus secretes corticotrophin releasing factor (CRF) to the pituitary gland (as well as to the central amygdala and bed nucleus of the stria terminalis). The pituitary gland secretes adrenocorticotrophic hormone (ACTH) into the blood, which goes to the adrenal gland. In response to this, the adrenal gland releases cortisol (in humans; corticosterone in rodents) into the blood, which has widespread neurophysiological and physiological effects. Critically, cortisol acts as part of a negative feedback loop that acts on the PVN and pituitary gland to prevent further release of CRF and ACTH, allowing the restoration of homeostasis.

Converging preclinical and human research has been important in understanding the relationship between stress and addiction. One approach that has been taken to understand the relationship between stress and addiction is to examine the influence of substance use on the stress response. Exposure to a variety of drugs activates the HPA axis, resulting in the increased secretion of cortisol (Lovallo, 2006). Administration or release of cortisol leads to increases in craving in substance-dependent adults, with subsequent administration of drugs relieving craving and increasing euphoria in these same individuals (Elman, Lukas,

Karlsgodt, Gasic, & Breiter, 2003). Thus, cortisol may contribute importantly to the relationship between stress reactivity and substance use. Consistent with this, when the adrenal glands are removed from rodents, self-administration of cocaine is abolished; with this effect being partially reversed with the administration of corticosterone (Goeders & Guerin, 1996). Also noteworthy here is that the central amygdala and basal nucleus of the stria terminalis (BNST) connect reciprocally with the PVN of the hypothalamus and produce CRF (Alheid, 2003). In response to stress, CRF-driven activity in the amygdala and BNST is increased with exposure to cocaine (Corominas, Roncero, & Casas, 2010). This therefore suggests another neurobiological route through which addiction may affect stress reactivity. Interestingly, exposure to drug cues has been associated with reduced amygdala volume (as well as hippocampal and ventral striatal volume) in alcohol-dependent adults relative to healthy controls (Wrase et al., 2008). Moreover, in this latter study, decreases in amygdala volume were associated with increased craving and likelihood of relapse at follow-up. Therefore, it is important to consider both the HPA axis as well as the circuits that project onto the HPA axis when understanding the relationship between substance use and the stress response.

A complementary approach taken to understand the relationship between stress and addiction is to examine the role of stress on substance use. Exposure to a variety of stressors increases self-administration of cocaine in rats; moreover, when the stressor is uncontrolled, the dose response curve of cocaine self-administration shifts such that rats are more sensitive to lower levels of cocaine than when the stress is controlled, or in the absence of a stressor (Goeders, 2003). While these findings are consistent with negative reinforcement accounts of maintained substance use, they also highlight the significance of the controllability of the stressor in determining substance use.

A substantial body of research has examined the relationship between stress symptomatology and addiction in human adults, and has also demonstrated the role stress plays in relapse rates in abstinent adults (Sinha, 2008). Specifically, the neural circuitry recruited in response to stress differentiates addicted from non-addicted participants, and in addicted adults relates to self-reported craving. For instance, when listening to personalized stressful situations, cocaine-addicted patients evidence reduced activity in the ACC, extending into medial and frontal regions, as well as left hippocampal/parahippocampal regions, right fusiform and postcentral gyri, relative to healthy controls (Sinha et al., 2005). The anterior cingulate has previously been identified as being important to self-regulation, and the authors proposed that this decreased activity in the ACC might reflect an impairment in stress regulation. Notably, in this same study with exposure to stress, relative increases in the dorsal striatum and caudate were observed in cocaine-addicted patients compared to healthy controls, and this increased activity correlated with self-reported craving. This converges with the findings described earlier of the role of the dorsal striatum in the motivation to seek drugs (Volkow et al., 2011) and suggests that stress may be an antecedent to the striatal response in driving drug-seeking behaviors that have past associations with the relief of negative affect. As noted above, sex differences are important to consider in this regard, with cocaine-dependent women appearing particularly different from non-addicted women with respect to their responses to stress cues (Potenza et al., 2012).

These findings together suggest that in the presence of stress, while activity in regions involved in self-regulation may be diminished, reward-related regions show increased activity that is related to craving and thus drug-seeking behavior. This further exemplifies the dysregulation of stress and neural circuitries in addiction. Furthermore, other regions implicated in the reward neural circuitry that are innervated by dopamine also show increases in regional activity correlating with craving in response to drug-induced cues, including the OFC, VTA, and striatum (Sinha & Li, 2007). Importantly, though, stress-induced craving, rather than drug cue-induced craving, has been found to significantly predict relapse in currently abstinent patients (Sinha, 2006). Taken together, these studies demonstrate the role of stress in addiction and its relationship to craving, substance use, and relapse.

Stress has significant influences on parenting behavior (Webster-Stratton, 1990), and a wide variety of stressors may contribute to impairments in parenting, including poverty, poor physical and mental health, domestic violence, and decreased social support (Wells, 2009). Furthermore, parenting stress may mediate the relationship between maternal risk factors (e.g., sociodemographic risks, psychological maladjustment) and their impact on caregiving (Suchman & Luthar, 2001). Consequently, individuals who may be more vulnerable to stress may be more reactive to stressors inherent in the parenting role, such as responding to infant distress. This may increase craving for substances of abuse, triggering drug-seeking behaviors in currently using mothers and relapse in abstinent parents. Consistent with this notion, substance-using mothers report higher levels of stress than do non-substance-using mothers (Kelley, 1998), with one study reporting that nicotine-addicted women described episodes of infant crying and irritability triggering smoking-related cognitions and smoking behaviors (Gaffney, Beckwitt, & Friesen, 2008). A number of studies have specifically examined the role of negative affect and smoking behaviors in mothers. For instance, one study reported that 67% of nicotine-addicted mothers who relapsed reinitiated smoking when experiencing a high-energy, negative affect state that included stress and anxiety (Park et al., 2009). Similarly, amongst a group of women who were abstinent from smoking in their final month of pregnancy, mothers who relapsed by 24 weeks postpartum had higher composite scores of anxiety, stress, and depression than mothers who did not relapse (Mullen, Quinn, & Ershoff, 1990). While these studies evidence the demands of parenting, it is also important to acknowledge that stress may not just be focally related to the demands of caregiving, but that stress related to insufficient resources (e.g., income, housing, social support) may also contribute to heightened levels of stress reported in substance-using parents.

Research specifically designed to understand the importance of the HPA axis to parenting is in its early stages. In preclinical studies, reductions in maternal behavior are observed if rodents are exposed to stress during pregnancy (Champagne & Meaney, 2006), and administration of corticosterone to pregnant or lactating rats increases neglectful behaviors to pups and decreases nursing behaviors (Bosch,

Müsch, Bredewold, Slattery, & Neumann, 2007). In human mothers, activity of the HPA axis as indexed by salivary cortisol during the strange-situation procedure has been related to the neural response to infant cry in subsequent assessment (Laurent, Stevens, & Ablow, 2011). Specifically, mothers with lower HPA trajectory of cortisol response during their child's strange situation evidenced a greater neural response when listening to their child's cry (relative to a control sound) in prefrontal regions, including bilateral OFC, medial PFC, and ACC, as well as in limbic regions, including the right insula and periaqueductal gray.

Emerging research has focused on the role of oxytocin in parenting behavior. Oxytocin is a neuropeptide produced in the PVN of the hypothalamus that is important in both the initiation and the maintenance of maternal behavior (Gordon, Zagoory-Sharon, Leckman, & Feldman, 2010). Importantly, while oxytocin has been traditionally associated with triggering critical aspects of maternal care (specifically lactation), as well as being believed important for affiliative relationships more broadly (MacDonald & MacDonald, 2010), recent evidence suggest that oxytocin may play a role in modulating the stress response. There is a bi-directional relationship between oxytocin and HPA activity, with a reduction in responding to acute stress in rodents following chronic oxytocin administration (Uvnäs-Moberg, Arn, & Magnusson, 2005). Other studies have also reported the release of oxytocin by the heart and vasculature, which may be important in modulating cardiac activity and vascular tone (Jankowski et al., 1998; Jankowski et al., 2000). Extrapolating from these studies to the present discussion, oxytocinergic effects on the cardiac and vascular system may serve a beneficial role in modulating the physiological response to stressful parenting situations. In human mothers, a reduction in maternal sensitivity is observed during the postpartum period if these mothers have a low-functioning oxytocin receptor allele (Bakermans-Kranenburg & van IJzendoorn, 2008). Notably, securely attached mothers have a stronger oxytocin response following a play interaction with their child compared to insecurely attached mothers (Strathearn et al., 2009). In this same study, this oxytocin response correlated with activity in the hypothalamus and pituitary regions, as well as the ventral striatum, while mothers viewed photographs of their own infants during a separate neuroimaging session.

Initial work has also begun to examine to the impact of substance use on maternal oxytocin levels. In one study, mothers taking cocaine during pregnancy evidenced lower-levels of blood plasma oxytocin than non-exposed mothers in the postpartum period; moreover, these oxytocin levels further decreased in mothers taking cocaine following a stress induction with there being no reliable change in the levels of oxytocin in the non-exposed mothers (Light et al., 2004). Another study focused on the oxytocin response following exposure to stress. While plasma oxytocin levels did not increase following two stress inductions in a sample of recent mothers, the amount of oxytocin was related to lower cardiac and vascular reactivity, as well as increased levels of norepinephrine (Grewen & Light, 2011). Taken together, these studies suggest that oxytocin may have a wider regulatory function than previously thought in modulating the stress response in parents.

■ BRIDGING THE NEUROBIOLOGY OF ADDICTION AND ATTACHMENT

The apparent relationship between reward, stress, and craving in addiction has significant implications for addicted parents. Specifically, the body of work highlighted here suggests that addiction reduces the rewarding value of caregiving, and that addicted adults are particularly vulnerable to stress. The postpartum period and caring for a child is generally stressful for all parents; however, addicted parents may be more vulnerable to the increased levels of stress associated with parenting. Stress, addiction, and their interactions may have an impact on prefrontal cortical function that may have detrimental effects on executive function as it relates to parenting and non-parenting behavior. The putative relationship between stress and craving is implicated in increased drug-seeking behaviors in addicted parents and in relapse for previously abstinent parents. This may have detrimental consequences for the infant, with caregivers not responding to infant cues (in the case of neglect), responding inappropriately to infant cues (in the case of abuse), or a combination of both response types. This can have a significant impact on the child's physical and emotional development, particularly given proposals that infants learn to regulate their emotions through early dyadic interactions with their mothers (e.g., Fonagy, Gergely, Jurist, & Target, 2006).

A proposed model of the overlapping reward and stress neural circuits and how they are related to parenting is presented and described in Figure 1.1. This model is informative for both addicted and non-addicted parents, and highlights the key neural regions and their involvement in parenting that have been reviewed in this chapter. Furthermore, this model of parenting may be applicable to multiple clinical disorders, not just addiction, in their modulation of parenting behavior.

We have presented here the notion that addicted parents may find caregiving more stressful than do non-addicted parents, and that the stress of caring for a child may increase their craving for substances of abuse. In order to test this hypothesis, it will be necessary to measure and assess stress in both substance-using and non-substance-using parents as it pertains to caregiving and non-caregiving situations. This will serve to help us understand whether substance-using parents face heightened levels of stress more generally, as well as whether this is exacerbated when caregiving. Furthermore, it will be necessary to carefully characterize the sources of stress in these parents' lives to identify other converging stressors, including the availability of services for them as well as their socioeconomic status and psychological adjustment. In addition to measuring levels of stress, it will also be necessary to establish whether the stress experienced with caregiving increases craving as outlined in the model presented here (Figure 1.1).

Although examining group differences is a concrete first step in this area of work, it will also be necessary to understand individual differences in the capacity to parent and manage stress in the face of addiction. This may also provide valuable insight into potential protective factors that could be the focus of intervention. It is clear from our own and others' experiences of working with addicted parents that their capacity as caregivers varies tremendously; that is, addiction does not necessarily negatively affect parenting. Moreover, pregnancy and the postpartum period

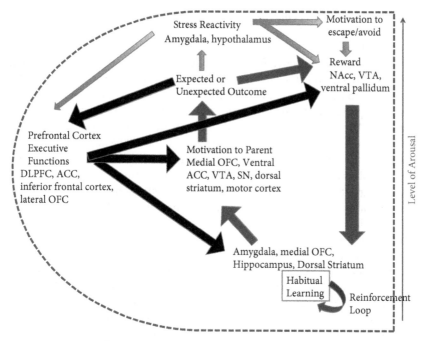

Figure 1.1 A proposed model of the neural circuitry that underscores parenting, highlighting the reward (dark gray arrows), prefrontal (black arrows), and stress (light gray arrows) circuits. When an infant cries, the motivation to parent elicits a behavioral response to soothe the infant. This can be rewarding if the infant stops crying, and this behavior is positively reinforced and will be added to the parent's behavioral repertoire for the future. If the infant continues to cry, functions of the prefrontal cortex serve to facilitate decision making and inhibitory control to support additional parenting behaviors. Stress reactivity may decrease prefrontal cortical function and motivate behaviors to find relief elsewhere (i.e., negative reinforcement). In the substance using parent, it is hypothesized that the reward of parenting and motivation to parent are diminished, and that increased stress reactivity results in increased craving, with substance use affording one means of stress regulation. This prevents the involvement of prefrontal cortical functions, and therefore parenting is instead mediated through the reward neural circuits that have been co-opted for addiction. This model is also applicable to other aspects of parent–infant interactions, where a parenting behavior that elicits a positive response from the infant (smiling, cooing, laughing) will be positively reinforced both motivating further parenting behavior as well as forming part of the parenting behavioral repertoire in the future. Note, the current level of arousal may impact each part of the neural circuitry.

may represent an important time for intervention efforts. Many women report their role as a mother as being highly valued (Wells, 2009), and clinicians could work with expecting and recent mothers to enhance and promote this value in caretaking. As described in both observational and neuroimaging studies, sensitivity to infant cues appears diminished in addiction, and this may serve to explain the high rates of neglect observed in addicted parents. Intervention work could focus on increasing sensitivity to infant signals with at-risk parents, during pregnancy as well as into the postpartum period, to facilitate improved understanding of infants' expressions of affect. Such interventions may help decrease rates of child abuse. Moreover, identifying protective factors that promote increased sensitivity and understanding in the mother–infant dyad are critical. Current intervention work is focusing on reflective functioning capacity and its importance to parenting (Suchman, Decoste, Castiglioni, Legow, & Mayes, 2008; Suchman et al., 2010), and other empirical work on maternal tolerance of distress converges with this as a potential protective factor (Rutherford, Goldberg, Luyten, Bridgett, & Mayes, submitted). However, understanding the broader framework of mitigating factors where addiction does not affect the capacity to parent will be important.

Many of the neurobiological studies presented here in human parents do not relate neural activity to parental function. Therefore, future work must bridge the neurobiology of parenting and addiction to observational measures of the capacity to parent, as well as child physical and psychological outcomes. For instance, what does the relative increase (or absence of an increase) in reward neural circuitries in response to infant cues mean for in vitro parenting behaviors, particularly as infants mature? Furthermore, many of the studies described here report the perception of infant cues in passive paradigms, and therefore more functional paradigms tapping other mechanisms of parenting will be important. In keeping with the literature reviewed here, identifying the potential relationship between oxytocin and stress reactivity, empirical work designed to understand the role of oxytocin in parenting (both in substance-using and non-substance-using populations) would be beneficial. Some recent work has shown that intra-nasal administration of oxytocin to non-mothers modulates the neural response to infant cry (Riem et al., 2011), and this could be an interesting avenue to explore in addicted samples.

Finally, in the review presented here, we have considered more discretely the role of the stress and reward neural circuits as they pertain to the neurobiology of addiction and attachment. However, as can be seen in Figure 1.1, this work also needs to consider how these systems interact in their functions in underscoring behavior. Indeed, while exposure to a stressor activates the stress neural circuitry, increasing activity in reward neural circuitry may also result. For instance, increases in dopaminergic activity have been observed in response to stress exposure in mesolimbic regions (e.g., NAcc [Thierry, Tassin, Blanc, & Glowinski, 1976]). Therefore, it is necessary to keep in mind that these systems do not exist in isolation but operate complexly, possibly in competing or synergistic fashions, in circuits underscoring cognition and behavior.

■ CONCLUSIONS

Substance use has a detrimental effect on both parental and infant health, and it is important to understand specific periods of vulnerability for relapse and/ or worsening of substance-using behavior among addicted parents to effectively target intervention. Early postpartum represents such a period, when becoming a new parent places significant demands on mothers that would not be typical in other periods of adulthood. Thus, the work presented here serves to recognize the parent–child relationship as a potential stressor in substance-using behavior and in triggering relapse, and suggests that addiction interventions need to address the demands of parenting, in addition to the addiction itself. Furthermore, recognizing that there may be a neurobiological basis underscoring inattentive or withdrawn dyadic encounters will be important for clinicians in focusing intervention work on the meaning of the infant and their affective signals to parents. This may have the added benefit of reducing the incidences of, and in time the potential for preventing, child neglect and abuse associated with substance use.

■ AUTHOR NOTE

We wish to acknowledge our ongoing grant support from the National Institutes of Health (R01 DA026437, P01 DA022446, K05 DA020091, R01 DA017863).

■ REFERENCES

Alheid, G. F. (2003). Extended amygdala and basal forebrain. *Annals of the New York Academy of Sciences, 985*(1), 185–205. doi: 10.1111/j.1749-6632.2003.tb07082.x

Andrews, M. M., Meda, S. A., Thomas, A. D., Potenza, M. N., Krystal, J. H.,... Pearlson, G. D. (2011). Individuals family history positive for alcoholism show functional magnetic resonance imaging differences in reward sensitivity that are related to impulsivity factors. *Biological Psychiatry, 69*(7), 675–683.

Bakermans-Kranenburg, M. J., & van IJzendoorn, M. H. (2008). Oxytocin receptor (OXTR) and serotonin transporter (5-HTT) genes associated with observed parenting. *Social Cognitive and Affective Neuroscience, 3*(2), 128–134. doi: 10.1093/scan/nsn004

Balodis, I. M., Kober, H., Worhunsky, P. D., Stevens, M. C., Pearlson, G. D., & Potenza, M. N. (2012). Diminished frontostriatal activity during processing of monetary rewards and losses in pathological gambling. *Biological Psychiatry, 71*(8), 749–757.

Bartels, A., & Zeki, S. (2000). The neural basis of romantic love. *Neuroreport, 11*(17), 3829–3834.

Bartels, A., & Zeki, S. (2004). The neural correlates of maternal and romantic love. *Neuroimage, 21*(3), 1155–1166.

Bechara, A., Damasio, H., & Damasio, A. R. (2000). Emotion, decision making and the orbitofrontal cortex. *Cerebral Cortex, 10*(3), 295–307. doi: 10.1093/cercor/10.3.295

Beck, A., Schlagenhauf, F., Wüstenberg, T., Hein, J., Kienast, T.,... Wrase, J. (2009). Ventral striatal activation during reward anticipation correlates with impulsivity in alcoholics. *Biological Psychiatry, 66*(8), 734–742. doi: 10.1016/j.biopsych.2009.04.035

Bjork, J.M., Smith, A.R., Hommer, D.W. (2008) Striatal sensitivity to reward deliveries and omissions in substance dependent patients. *NeuroImage, 42*(4): 1609–1621.

Bjork, J. M., Smith, A. R., Chen, G., & Hommer, D. W. (2010). Adolescents, adults and rewards: Comparing motivational neurocircuitry recruitment using fMRI. *PLoS ONE, 5*(7), e11440. doi: 10.1371/journal.pone.0011440

Bosch, O. J., Müsch, W., Bredewold, R., Slattery, D. A., & Neumann, I. D. (2007). Prenatal stress increases HPA axis activity and impairs maternal care in lactating female offspring: Implications for postpartum mood disorder. *Psychoneuroendocrinology, 32*(3), 267–278. doi: 10.1016/j.psyneuen.2006.12.012

Breiter, H. C., Gollub, R. L., Weisskoff, R. M., Kennedy, D. N., Makris, N.,... Hyman, S. E. (1997). Acute effects of cocaine on human brain activity and emotion. *Neuron, 19*(3), 591–611. doi: 10.1016/s0896-6273(00)80374-8

Cash, S. J., & Wilke, D. J. (2003). An ecological model of maternal substance abuse and child neglect: Issues, analyses, and recommendations. *American Journal of Orthopsychiatry, 73*(4), 392–404. doi: 10.1037/0002-9432.73.4.392

Champagne, F. A., & Meaney, M. J. (2006). Stress during gestation alters postpartum maternal care and the development of the offspring in a rodent model. *Biological Psychiatry, 59*(12), 1227–1235. doi: 10.1016/j.biopsych.2005.10.016

Corominas, M., Roncero, C., & Casas, M. (2010). Corticotropin releasing factor and neuroplasticity in cocaine addiction. *Life Sciences, 86*(1–2), 1–9. doi: 10.1016/j.lfs.2009.11.005

Dalley, J. W., Everitt, B. J., & Robbins, T. W. (2011). Impulsivity, compulsivity, and top-down cognitive control. *Neuron, 69*(4), 680–694. doi: 10.1016/j.neuron.2011.01.020

Deater-Deckard, K., Sewell, M. D., Petrill, S. A., & Thompson, L. A. (2010). Maternal working memory and reactive negativity in parenting. *Psychological Science, 21*(1), 75–79. doi: 10.1177/0956797609354073

Di Chiara, G., & Imperato, A. (1988). Drugs abused by humans preferentially increase synaptic dopamine concentrations in the mesolimbic system of freely moving rats. *Proceedings of the National Academy of Sciences, 85*(14), 5274–5278.

Drevets, W. C., Gautier, C., Price, J. C., Kupfer, D. J., Kinahan, P. E., Grace, A. A.,... Mathis, C. A. (2001). Amphetamine-induced dopamine release in human ventral striatum correlates with euphoria. *Biological Psychiatry, 49*(2), 81–96. doi: 10.1016/s0006-3223(00)01038-6

Elman, I., Lukas, S. E., Karlsgodt, K. H., Gasic, G. P., & Breiter, H. C. (2003). Acute cortisol administration triggers craving in individuals with cocaine dependence. *Psychopharmacology bulletin, 37*(3), 84089.

Fonagy, P., Gergely, G., Jurist, E. L., & Target, M. (2006). *Affect Regulation, Mentalization, and the Development of the Self.* London: H. Karnac (Books) Ltd.

Gaffney, K. F., Beckwitt, A. E., & Friesen, M. A. (2008). Mothers' reflections about infant irritability and postpartum tobacco use. *Birth, 35*(1), 66–72. doi: 10.1111/j.1523-536X.2007.00212.x

Gallagher, M., McMahan, R. W., & Schoenbaum, G. (1999). Orbitofrontal cortex and representation of incentive value in associative learning. *Journal of Neuroscience, 19*(15), 6610–6614.

Glocker, M. L., Langleben, D. D., Ruparel, K., Loughead, J. W., Valdez, J. N., Griffin, M. D.,... Gur, R. C. (2009). Baby schema modulates the brain reward system in nulliparous women. *Proceedings of the National Academy of Sciences, 106*(22), 9115–9119. doi: 10.1073/pnas.0811620106

Goeders, N. E. (2003). The impact of stress on addiction. *European Neuropsychopharmacology, 13*(6), 435–441. doi: 10.1016/j.euroneuro.2003.08.004

Goeders, N. E. (2004). Stress, motivation, and drug addiction. *Current Directions in Psychological Science, 13*(1), 33–35. doi: 10.1111/j.0963-7214.2004.01301009.x

Goeders, N. E., & Guerin, G. F. (1996). Effects of surgical and pharmacological adrenalectomy on the initiation and maintenance of intravenous cocaine self-administration in rats. *Brain research, 722*(1), 145–152.

Gordon, I., Zagoory-Sharon, O., Leckman, J. F., & Feldman, R. (2010). Oxytocin and the development of parenting in humans. *Biological Psychiatry, 68*(4), 377–382.

Gottwald, S. R., & Thurman, S. K. (1994). The effects of prenatal cocaine exposure on mother–infant interaction and infant arousal in the newborn period. *Topics in Early Childhood Special Education, 14*(2), 217–231. doi: 10.1177/027112149401400206

Grewen, K. M., & Light, K. C. (2011). Plasma oxytocin is related to lower cardiovascular and sympathetic reactivity to stress. *Biological Psychology, 87*(3), 340–349. doi: 10.1016/j.biopsycho.2011.04.003

Haber, S. N., & Knutson, B. (2009). The reward circuit: Linking primate anatomy and human imaging. *Neuropsychopharmacology, 35*(1), 4–26.

Jankowski, M., Hajjar, F., Kawas, S. A., Mukaddam-Daher, S., Hoffman, G.,... Gutkowska, J. (1998). Rat heart: A site of oxytocin production and action. *Proceedings of the National Academy of Sciences, 95*(24), 14558–14563. doi: 10.1073/pnas.95.24.14558

Jankowski, M., Wang, D., Hajjar, F., Mukaddam-Daher, S., McCann, S. M., & Gutkowska, J. (2000). Oxytocin and its receptors are synthesized in the rat vasculature. *Proceedings of the National Academy of Sciences, 97*(11), 6207–6211. doi: 10.1073/pnas.110137497

Jansson, L. M., & Velez, M. L. (2011). Infants of drug-dependent mothers. *Pediatrics in Review, 32*(1), 5–13. doi: 10.1542/pir.32-1-5

Jentsch, J. D., & Taylor, J. R. (1999). Impulsivity resulting from frontostriatal dysfunction in drug abuse: implications for the control of behavior by reward-related stimuli. *Psychopharmacology (Berlin), 146*(4), 373–390.

Kalivas, P. W. (2009). The glutamate homeostasis hypothesis of addiction. [10.1038/nrn2515]. *Nature Reviews. Neuroscience, 10*(8), 561–572.

Kelley, S. J. (1998). Stress and coping behaviors of substance-abusing mothers. *Journal for Specialists in Pediatric Nursing, 3*(3), 103–110. doi: 10.1111/j.1744-6155.1998.tb00215.x

Kim, P., Leckman, J. F., Mayes, L. C., Feldman, R., Wang, X., & Swain, J. E. (2010). The plasticity of human maternal brain: Longitudinal changes in brain anatomy during the early postpartum period. *Behavioral Neuroscience, 124*(5), 695–700.

Knutson, B., & Cooper, J. C. (2005). Functional magnetic resonance imaging of reward prediction. *Current Opinion in Neurology, 18*(4), 411–417.

Koob, G. F., & Volkow, N. D. (2009). Neurocircuitry of addiction. *Neuropsychopharmacology, 35*(1), 217–238.

Kringelbach, M. L., Lehtonen, A., Squire, S., Harvey, A. G., Craske, M. G.,... Stein, A. (2008). A Specific and Rapid Neural Signature for Parental Instinct: *PLoS One, 3*(2), e1664.

Kufahl, P. R., Li, Z., Risinger, R. C., Rainey, C. J., Wu, G., Bloom, A. S., & Li, S.-J. (2005). Neural responses to acute cocaine administration in the human brain detected by fMRI. *Neuroimage, 28*(4), 904–914. doi: 10.1016/j.neuroimage.2005.06.039

Landi, N., Montoya, J., Kober, H., Rutherford, H. J. V., Mencl, E., Worhunsky, P.,... Mayes, L. C. (2011). Maternal neural responses to infant cries and faces: Relationships with substance use. [Original research]. *Frontiers in Psychiatry, 2*(32). doi: 10.3389/fpsyt.2011.00032

Laurent, H. K., & Ablow, J. C. (2011). A cry in the dark: Depressed mothers show reduced neural activation to their own infant's cry. *Social Cognitive and Affective Neuroscience.* doi: 10.1093/scan/nsq091

Laurent, H. K., Stevens, A., & Ablow, J. C. (2011). Neural correlates of hypothalamic-pituitary-adrenal regulation of mothers with their infants. *Biological Psychiatry, 70*(9), 826–832. doi: 10.1016/j.biopsych.2011.06.011

Leeman, R. F., & Potenza, M. N. (2012). Similarities and differences between pathological gambling and substance use disorders: A focus on impulsivity and compulsivity. *Psychopharmacology (Berlin), 219*(2), 469–490. doi: 10.1007/s00213-011-2550-7

Light, K. C., Grewen, K. M., Amico, J. A., Boccia, M., Brownley, K. A., & Johns, J. M. (2004). Deficits in plasma oxytocin responses and increased negative affect, stress, and blood pressure in mothers with cocaine exposure during pregnancy. *Addictive Behaviors, 29*(8), 1541–1564. doi: 10.1016/j.addbeh.2004.02.062

Lorberbaum, J. P., Newman, J. D., Dubno, J. R., Horwitz, A. R., Nahas, Z.,... George, M. S. (1999). Feasibility of using fMRI to study mothers responding to infant cries. *Depression and Anxiety, 10*(3), 99–104.

Lorberbaum, J. P., Newman, J. D., Horwitz, A. R., Dubno, J. R., Lydiard, R. B.,... George, M. S. (2002). A potential role for thalamocingulate circuitry in human maternal behavior. *Biological Psychiatry, 51*(6), 431–445.

Lorenz, K. (1943). Die angeborenen Formen möglicher Erfahrung [The innate forms of potential experience]. *Zeitschrift fur Tierpsychologie, 5*, 233–519.

Lovallo, W. R. (2006). Cortisol secretion patterns in addiction and addiction risk. *International Journal of Psychophysiology, 59*(3), 195–202. doi: 10.1016/j.ijpsycho.2005.10.007

MacDonald, K., & MacDonald, T. (2010). The peptide that binds: A systematic review of oxytocin and its prosocial effects in humans. *Harvard Review of Psychiatry, 18*(1), 1–21.

Mayes, L. C. (2006). Arousal regulation, emotional flexibility, medial amygdala function, and the impact of early experience. *Annals of the New York Academy of Sciences, 1094*(1), 178–192. doi: 10.1196/annals.1376.018

Mayes, L. C., Feldman, R., Granger, R. H., Haynes, O. M., Bornstein, M. H., & Schottenfeld, R. (1997). The effects of polydrug use with and without cocaine on mother–infant interaction at 3 and 6 months. *Infant Behavior and Development, 20*(4), 489–502. doi: 10.1016/s0163-6383(97)90038-2

McClure, S. M., York, M. K., & Montague, P. R. (2004). The neural substrates of reward processing in humans: the modern role of fMRI. *Neuroscientist, 10*, 260–268.

Montoya, J. L., Landi, N., Kober, H., Worhunsky, P., Rutherford, H. J. V.,... Potenza, M. N. (2012). Regional brain responses in nulliparous women to emotional infant stimuli. *PloS one, 7*(5), e36270.

Mullen, P. D., Quinn, V. P., & Ershoff, D. H. (1990). Maintenance of nonsmoking postpartum by women who stopped smoking during pregnancy. *American Journal of Public Health, 80*(8), 992–994. doi: 10.2105/ajph.80.8.992

Naqvi, N. H., & Bechara, A. (2009). The hidden island of addiction: The insula. *Trends in Neurosciences, 32*(1), 56–67. doi: 10.1016/j.tins.2008.09.009

Nitschke, J. B., Nelson, E. E., Rusch, B. D., Fox, A. S., Oakes, T. R., & Davidson, R. J. (2004). Orbitofrontal cortex tracks positive mood in mothers viewing pictures of their newborn infants. *Neuroimage, 21*(2), 583–592.

Noriuchi, M., Kikuchi, Y., & Senoo, A. (2008). The functional neuroanatomy of maternal love: Mother's response to infant's attachment behaviors. *Biological Psychiatry, 63*(4), 415–423.

O'Doherty, J. P. (2004). Reward representations and reward-related learning in the human brain: Insights from neuroimaging. *Current Opinion in Neurobiology, 14*(6), 769–776.

Park, E. R., Chang, Y., Quinn, V., Regan, S., Cohen, L., Viguera, A.,… Rigotti, N. (2009). The association of depressive, anxiety, and stress symptoms and postpartum relapse to smoking: A longitudinal study. *Nicotine & Tobacco Research, 11*(6), 707–714. doi: 10.1093/ntr/ntp053

Peters, J., Bromberg, U., Schneider, S., Brassen, S., Menz, M.,… Buchel, C. (2011). Lower ventral striatal activation during reward anticipation in adolescent smokers. *American Journal of Psychiatry, 168*(5), 540–549. doi: 10.1176/appi.ajp.2010.10071024

Potenza, M. N., Hong, K. I., Lacadie, C. M., Fulbright, R. K., Tuit, K. L., & Sinha, R. (2012). Neural correlates of stress-induced and cue-induced drug craving: Influences of sex and cocaine dependence. *American Journal of Psychiatry, 169*(4), 406–414. doi: 10.1176/appi.ajp.2011.11020289

Proverbio, A. M., Brignone, V., Matarazzo, S., Del Zotto, M., & Zani, A. (2006). Gender and parental status affect the visual cortical response to infant facial expression. *Neuropsychologia, 44*(14), 2987–2999.

Reid, J., Macchetto, P., & Foster, S. (1999). *No Safe Haven: Children of Substance-Abusing Parents.* National Center on Addiction and Substance Abuse at Columbia University. New York.

Riem, M. M. E., Bakermans-Kranenburg, M. J., Pieper, S., Tops, M., Boksem, M. A. S.,… Rombouts, S. A. R. B. (2011). Oxytocin modulates amygdala, insula, and inferior frontal gyrus responses to infant crying: A randomized controlled trial. *Biological Psychiatry, 70*(3), 291–297. doi: 10.1016/j.biopsych.2011.02.006

Risinger, R. C., Salmeron, B. J., Ross, T. J., Amen, S. L., Sanfilipo, M.,… Stein, E. A. (2005). Neural correlates of high and craving during cocaine self-administration using BOLD fMRI. *Neuroimage, 26*(4), 1097–1108. doi: 10.1016/j.neuroimage.2005.03.030

Rodrigo, M. J., León, I., Quiñones, I., Lage, A., Byrne, S., & Bobes, M. A. (2011). Brain and personality bases of insensitivity to infant cues in neglectful mothers: An event-related potential study. *Development and Psychopathology, 23*(01), 163–176. doi: doi:10.1017/S0954579410000714

Rutherford, H. J. V., Gerig, G., Gouttard, S., Mayes, L., & Potenza, M. N. (submitted). The impact of substance use on the maternal brain and postpartum bonding.

Rutherford, H. J. V., Landi, N., Greger-Moser, M., Mayes, M., Holcomb, K. R., Potenza, M. N., & Mayes, L. (submitted). Investigating the relationship between maternal substance use and neural responses to infant cues: An event-related potential study.

Rutherford, H. J. V., Goldberg, B., Luyten, P., Bridgett, D. J., & Mayes, L. C. (submitted). Examining the contribution of parental reflective functioning to tolerance of infant distress.

Rutherford, H. J. V., Williams, S. K., Moy, S., Mayes, L. C., & Johns, J. M. (2011). Disruption of maternal parenting circuitry by addictive process: rewiring of reward and stress systems. [Review]. *Frontiers in Psychiatry, 2.* doi: 10.3389/fpsyt.2011.00037

Seifritz, E., Esposito, F., Neuhoff, J. G., Lüthi, A., Mustovic, H.,… Di Salle, F. (2003). Differential sex-independent amygdala response to infant crying and laughing in parents versus nonparents. *Biological Psychiatry, 54*(12), 1367–1375.

Sinha, R. (2001). How does stress increase risk of drug abuse and relapse? *Psychopharmacologia, 158,* 343–359.

Sinha, R., Lacadie, C., Skudlarski, P., Fulbright, R. K., Rounsaville, B. J., Kosten, T. R., & Wexler, B. E. (2005). Neural activity associated with stress-induced cocaine craving: a functional magnetic resonance imaging study. *Psychopharmacology, 183*(2), 171–180.

Sinha, R., Garcia, M., Paliwal, P., Kreek, M. J., & Rounsaville, B. J. (2006). Stress-induced cocaine craving and hypothalamic-pituitary-adrenal responses are predictive of cocaine relapse outcomes. *Archives of General Psychiatry, 63*(3), 324.

Sinha R, & Li, CS. (2007). Imaging stress- and cue-induced drug and alcohol craving: association with relapse and clinical implications. *Drug and Alcohol Review, 26*, 25–31.

Sinha, R. (2008). Chronic stress, drug use, and vulnerability to addiction. *Annals of the New York Academy of Sciences, 1141*, 105–130. doi: 10.1196/annals.1441.030

Stratakis, C. A., & Chrousos, G. P. (1995). Neuroendocrinology and pathophysiology of the stress system. *Annals of the New York Academy of Sciences, 771*(1), 1–18. doi: 10.1111/j.1749-6632.1995.tb44666.x

Strathearn, L., Fonagy, P., Amico, J., & Montague, P. R. (2009). Adult attachment predicts maternal brain and oxytocin response to infant cues. *Neuropsychopharmacology, 34*(13), 2655–2666.

Strathearn, L., Li, J., Fonagy, P., & Montague, P. R. (2008). What's in a smile? Maternal brain responses to infant facial cues. *Pediatrics, 122*(1), 40–51. doi: 10.1542/peds.2007-1566

Substance Abuse and Mental Health Services Administration (SAMHSA). (2008). Results from the 2007 National Survey on Drug Use and Health: National Findings (Office of Applied Studies, NSDUH Series H-34, DHHS Publication No. SMA 08-4343). Rockville, MD.

Suchman, N. E., Decoste, C., Castiglioni, N., Legow, N., & Mayes, L. (2008). The Mothers and Toddlers Program: Preliminary findings from an attachment-based parenting intervention for substance-abusing mothers. *Psychoanalytic Psychology: The Official Journal of the Division of Psychoanalysis, American Psychological Association, Division 39, 25*(3), 499–517.

Suchman, N. E., DeCoste, C., Castiglioni, N., McMahon, T. J., Rounsaville, B., & Mayes, L. (2010). The Mothers and Toddlers Program, an attachment-based parenting intervention for substance using women: Post-treatment results from a randomized clinical pilot. *Attachment & Human Development, 12*(5), 483–504. doi: 10.1080/14616734.2010.501983

Suchman, N. E., & Luthar, S. S. (2001). The mediating role of parenting stress in methadone-maintained mothers' parenting. *Parenting: Science & Practice, 1*(4), 285–315.

Swain, J. E. (2011). The human parental brain: In vivo neuroimaging. *Progress in Neuro-Psychopharmacology and Biological Psychiatry, 35*(5), 1242–1254. doi: 10.1016/j.pnpbp.2010.10.017

Swain, J. E., Lorberbaum, J. P., Kose, S., & Strathearn, L. (2007). Brain basis of early parent–infant interactions: Psychology, physiology, and in vivo functional neuroimaging studies. *Journal of Child Psychology and Psychiatry, 48*(3–4), 262–287. doi: 10.1111/j.1469-7610.2007.01731.x

Thierry, A. M., Tassin, J. P., Blanc, G., & Glowinski, J. (1976). Selective activation of the mesocortical DA system by stress. *Nature, 263*(5574), 242–244. doi: 10.1038/263242a0.

U.S. Department of Health and Human Services, National Center for Health Statistics, and National Health Interview Survey. (1999). ICPSR version. Hyattsville, MD: U.S. Dept. of

Health and Human Services, National Center for Health Statistics 1999; Ann Arbor, MI: Inter- university Consortium for Political and Social Research 2002.

Uvnäs-Moberg, K., Arn, I., & Magnusson, D. (2005). The psychobiology of emotion: The role of the oxytocinergic system. *International Journal of Behavioral Medicine, 12*(2), 59–65. doi: 10.1207/s15327558ijbm1202_3

Volkow, N. D., Fowler, J. S., Wang, G. J., Baler, R., & Telang, F. (2009). Imaging dopamine's role in drug abuse and addiction. *Neuropharmacology, 56, Supplement 1*(0), 3–8. doi: 10.1016/j.neuropharm.2008.05.022

Volkow, N. D., Fowler, J. S., Wang, G. J., Hitzemann, R., Logan, J.,… Wolf, A. P. (1993). Decreased dopamine D2 receptor availability is associated with reduced frontal metabolism in cocaine abusers. *Synapse, 14*(2), 169–177. doi: 10.1002/syn.890140210

Volkow, N. D., Wang, G. J., Fowler, J. S., Tomasi, D., & Telang, F. (2011). Addiction: Beyond dopamine reward circuitry. *Proceedings of the National Academy of Sciences, 108*(37), 15037–15042. doi: 10.1073/pnas.1010654108

Volkow, N. D., Wang, G. J., Telang, F., Fowler, J. S., Logan, J.,… Wong, C. (2006). Cocaine cues and dopamine in dorsal striatum: Mechanism of craving in cocaine addiction. *The Journal of Neuroscience, 26*(24), 6583–6588. doi: 10.1523/jneurosci.1544-06.2006

Webster-Stratton, C. (1990). Stress: A potential disruptor of parent perceptions and family interactions. *Journal of Clinical Child Psychology, 19*(4), 302–312.

Wells, K. (2009). Substance abuse and child maltreatment. *Pediatric Clinics of North America, 56*(2), 345–362. doi: 10.1016/j.pcl.2009.01.006

Wrase, J., Makris, N., Braus, D. F., Mann, K., Smolka, M. N., Kennedy, D. N.,… Heinz, A. (2008). Amygdala volume associated with alcohol abuse relapse and craving. *The American Journal of Psychiatry, 165*(9), 6.

Wrase, J., Schlagenhauf, F., Kienast, T., Wüstenberg, T., Bermpohl, F.,… Heinz, A. (2007). Dysfunction of reward processing correlates with alcohol craving in detoxified alcoholics. *Neuroimage, 35*(2), 787–794. doi: 10.1016/j.neuroimage.2006.11.043

2 Stress and Parental Addiction

TARA M. CHAPLIN AND
RAJITA SINHA

In the present chapter, we discuss the role of stress in addictive behaviors in adults, explore how stress affects parenting in addicted individuals and how this may subsequently affect children's development of psychopathology and substance use.

■ ADDICTION AND STRESS

Stress has long been known to increase vulnerability to addiction development and relapse to addictive behaviors and may play an important role in the parenting of addicted individuals. Here we define *stress* as processes involving perception, appraisal, and response to harmful, threatening, or challenging events or stimuli (Lazarus, 1999). Stress experiences can be emotionally or physiologically challenging, and activate stress responses and adaptive processes to regain homeostasis (Cohen, Kessler, et al., 1995; Charmandari, Tsigos, et al., 2005; McEwen, 2007). Examples of stressors common for addicted individuals include emotional stressors such as interpersonal conflict, loss of relationship, and loss of a child; physiological stressors such as sleep deprivation/insomnia and drug withdrawal states; and pharmacological stressors such as regular and binge use of many psychoactive drugs.

There is a substantial literature on the association between acute and chronic stress and the motivation to abuse addictive substances (see Sinha, 2001, for review). Many of the major theories of addiction also identify an important role of stress in addiction processes. For example, psychological models of addiction (such as the "self-medication hypothesis") posit that addicts use drugs as a strategy to cope with stressors, to reduce tension, to self-medicate, and to decrease withdrawal-related distress (Baker, Piper, et al., 2004; Khantzian, 1985; Marlatt & Gordon, 1985). Also, neurobiological models of addiction propose incentive sensitization and stress allostasis concepts to explain how neuroadaptations in reward, learning, and stress pathways may increase craving, loss of control, and compulsion, which then lead individuals to move from casual use of substances to addiction (Koob & Le Moal, 1997; Hyman & Malenka, 2001; Robinson & Berridge, 2003).

Chronic Stressors and Vulnerability to Drug Use

There is considerable evidence from population-based and clinical studies supporting an association between psychosocial stress or adversity and addiction. First, prospective studies have found links between greater negative life events in adolescence and future increases in drug use and abuse (Johnson & Pandina, 1993;

Johnson & Pandina, 2000; Sher, Gershuny, et al., 1997; Turner & Lloyd, 1995; Wills & Cleary, 1996). Second, a large body of research finds that substance abusers are more likely than non-abusers to report a history of sexual and physical abuse (two severe stressors) in childhood (e.g., Clark, Lesnick, et al., 1997, Widom et al., 1999). Some prospective studies also find a link between child abuse and future drug use and abuse (Breslau, Davis, et al., 2003; Dembo et al., 1988, but see Widom et al., 1999). Third, recent research finds links between lifetime exposure to stressors and the impact of cumulative adversity on addiction vulnerability after accounting for a number of control factors such as race/ethnicity, gender, socioeconomic status, prior drug abuse, prevalence of psychiatric disorders, family history of substance use, and behavioral and conduct problems. (Turner & Lloyd, 2003; Lloyd & Turner, 2008). This literature shows that the cumulative number of stressful events predicts alcohol and drug dependence in a dose-dependent manner.

Acute Laboratory Stress and Response in Addicted Individuals

Bio-behavioral studies. In our laboratory studies, we have examined the effects of stress and drug-related cues on drug craving, emotions, and HPA-axis response in alcoholics, cocaine-dependent individuals, and naltrexone-treated opiate-dependent individuals in recovery. Drug craving and stress responses were assessed using personalized guided-imagery procedures as the induction method (Sinha, Talih, et al., 2003). We have found that cocaine-dependent individuals show increased negative emotions, behavioral arousal, heart rate, salivary cortisol levels, plasma ACTH, plasma norepinephrine (NE) and epinephrine (EPI) levels, and, importantly, drug craving, in response to stress exposure as compared to a neutral control exposure (and as compared to healthy controls) (Chaplin et al., 2010; Fox, Hong, et al., 2008; Sinha, Catapano, et al., 1999; Sinha, Fuse, et al., 2000; Sinha, Talih, et al., 2003). And, we have some evidence that these stress responses (particularly ACTH, NE, and EPI) persist over an hour after the five-minute imagery exposure, suggesting that these elevated stress responses are not being regulated.

Alcoholics and naltrexone-treated opiate-addicted individuals also show increased craving, negative emotions, and physiological responses to stress imagery as compared to neutral imagery and healthy controls (Fox, Bergquist, et al., 2007; Hyman, Fox, et al., 2007; Sinha, Fox, et al., 2009). On the other hand, recently abstinent alcoholics and nicotine users show altered basal HPA responses and a suppressed HPA response as measured by cortisol to stress compared to their non-addicted counterparts (Lovallo, Dickensheets, et al., 2000; Al'absi, Hatsukami, et al., 2005; Badrick, Kirschbaum, et al., 2007).

Brain imaging studies. We have recently examined brain activation in response to stress (vs. neutral) imagery in addicted versus healthy individuals in a functional magnetic resonance imaging (fMRI) study. Although healthy controls and cocaine-dependent individuals showed similar levels of distress and pulse changes during stress exposure, brain response to emotional stress in paralimbic regions such as the anterior cingulate cortex, hippocampus, and parahippocampal regions was greater in healthy controls during stress, while cocaine patients showed a striking absence of such activation (Sinha, Lacadie, et al., 2005). In contrast, cocaine-dependent subjects had increased activity in the caudate and dorsal striatum region during stress, activation that was significantly associated with stress-induced cocaine craving ratings. PET studies have also shown correlations between the dorsal striatum and drug-cue-induced cocaine craving (Volkow, Wang, et al., 2006; Wong, Kuwabara, et al., 2006). And imaging studies with alcoholic patients have shown association between dorsal striatum regions and alcohol craving in response to alcohol-related stimuli (Wrase, Grusser, et al., 2002; Grusser, Wrase, et al., 2004). Together, these findings indicate that increased stress in addicted individuals is associated with greater activity in the striatum, but decreased activity in specific regions of the cingulate and prefrontal cortex, regions involved in controlling impulses and emotions.

Stress and relapse. Indeed, our laboratory and others have found links between elevated responses to stress in the laboratory and future relapse to drug use. In our studies of cocaine-dependent individuals, stress-induced craving predicted time to relapse, and ACTH and cortisol responses to stress predicted the amounts of cocaine consumed during relapse (Sinha, Garcia, et al., 2006). In alcoholics, negative mood and stress-induced alcohol craving and blunted stress and cue-induced cortisol responses have been associated with alcohol relapse outcomes (e.g., Adinoff, Junghanns, et al., 2005; Breese, Chu, et al., 2005). Nicotine-deprived smokers who were exposed to a series of stressors showed blunted ACTH, cortisol, and blood pressure responses to stress, but increased nicotine withdrawal and craving scores, and these responses predicted nicotine relapse outcomes (Al'absi, Hatsukami, et al., 2005). Thus, for alcoholic, cocaine-dependent, and smoking samples, it appears that the drug craving state marked by increasing distress and compulsive motivation for drug (craving) along with poor stress regulatory responses (altered glucocorticoid feedback or increased noradrenergic arousal) results in an enhanced susceptibility to addiction relapse.

Implications for parenting. Parents with addiction may show elevated (or, in the case of alcoholics or smokers, perhaps blunted) emotional, hormonal, and/or physiological arousal responses to stress, including stress related to parenting. If this emotional/physiological arousal is not regulated, addicted parents may be particularly reactive and negative in stressful parenting situations (e.g., when a child is hurt, ill, or emotionally upset). Likewise, brain imaging studies suggest that parents with addiction who are experiencing parenting stress may have difficulty regulating their emotions and impulses and a strong concomitant motivation to use substances. Finally, in parents with addiction, increased motivation, or craving for drugs, coupled with poor stress regulation—in the presence of ongoing parenting stress—is likely to increase vulnerability to relapse. A relapse, in turn, would likely have serious consequences for the parent's ability to care for children.

Stress Exposure Increases Drug Self Administration

Animal studies. There is some evidence from animal studies to support the notion that acute exposure to stress increases initiation and escalation of drug use and abuse (see Sinha, 2001, for review). For example, in animals models, social defeat stress, social isolation, tailpinch and footshock, restraint stress, and novelty stress are known to enhance acquisition of opiates, alcohol, and psychostimulant self-administration, with caveats relating to stressor type, genetic background of animals, and variations by drug type (see Miczek, Covington, et al., 2004; Le, Harding, et al., 2005; Lu & Shaham, 2005; Cleck & Blendy, 2008, for reviews). Also, although there are some negative findings, other evidence indicates that early life stress, using procedures such as neonatal isolation or maternal separation, and prolonged and repeated stressors representing chronic stress experiences, enhances self-administration of nicotine, psychostimulants and alcohol, and/or their acute behavioral effects (Higley, Hasert, et al., 1991; Kosten, Miserendino, et al., 2000; Lu, Shepard, et al., 2003; Boyce-Rustay, Cameron et al., 2007; Moffett, Vicentic, et al., 2007; Park, Belluzzi, et al., 2007).

Human studies. Human studies examining the effects of stress exposure on drug use have begun to show evidence that acute stress increases drinking and nicotine smoking (see Sinha, 2005, for review), but the effects of drinking history, history of adversity, social stress, and expectancies may moderate this effect.

Implications for parenting. For parents with addiction, exposure to ongoing parenting stress may not only trigger a relapse but also increase frequency and quantity of substance use.

Chronic Drug Use as a Biological Stressor

In addition to having greater life stressors and greater responsiveness to stressors (acute and chronic)—which could be a consequence of adaptations in stress and reward pathways—addicted individuals have the unique added stress of being exposed to psychoactive drugs that act as a pharmacological stressor on biological circuitry involved in stress, emotional arousal/regulation, and reward. There is substantial evidence that drugs of abuse activate or suppress the stress axis and, by their effects on learning and adaptation mechanisms, also play a role in escalating drug use, drug craving, compulsive drug-seeking, and relapse. For example, it is well known that alcohol activates the CRF-HPA axis and the autonomic nervous system pathways involved in emotional and stress-related arousal and responding to challenge states. Other data from animal studies find that chronic cocaine use is associated with alterations in central noradrenergic pathways in the ventral and dorsal striatum and other areas of the forebrain and the ventromedial prefrontal cortex (Beveridge, Smith, et al., 2005; Porrino, Smith, et al., 2007). Human research with alcohol- and cocaine-addicted individuals similarly finds reduced D2 receptors and dopamine transmission in the frontal and ventral striatum regions during acute withdrawal and protracted withdrawal (up to 3–4 months) (Volkow, et al., 1993, 1996, 1997). Regular, binge, and high levels of alcohol consumption result in tolerance and adaptation in stress and in dopaminergic learning and motivation brain pathways that in turn compromise the individual's ability to regulate emotions and stressful situations and use cognitive and executive control functions towards long-term goals (Sinha, 2008). Individuals who consume substances are then susceptible to increased and persistent drug craving under personal stressful situations that often include stressors related to family and children. Such increases in drug craving increase the risk of continued drug use and relapse, promoting a cyclical pattern involving greater dysregulation and increased drug craving and drug use.

Children as Stressors for Addicted Parents

Interestingly, having a child, the associated responsibilities of parenthood, and the behaviors of children may themselves be stressors to an addicted individual who is a parent. For example, infant cries activate the sympathetic nervous system in both the infant and the parent and, thus, hearing their infant cry may elicit a stress response in parents (LaGasse, Neal, & Lester, 2005), particularly addicted parents who are sensitive to stress. These parents may respond to infant cries in non-adaptive ways—by either distancing themselves from the child or by being overly reactive or even abusive to the child, as in the case of "shaken baby" syndrome. In one study, cocaine-using mothers were more likely to rate recordings of a newborn infant's hunger cries as less arousing and aversive, were less likely to report that they would pick up or feed the crying infant, and were more likely to give the infant a pacifier or just "wait and see" (Schuetze, Zeskind, & Eiden, 2003). This suggests that cocaine-using mothers are less responsive to infants' crying. This lower responsiveness could have negative consequences for child development.

As children grow older, they may show other behaviors that are stressful or aversive to parents, particularly parents with addiction. For example, one study found that parents who were exposed to a confederate child exhibiting deviant behaviors consumed more alcohol than parents exposed to normal child behavior (Pelham & Lang, 1999), potentially because they were stressed by the deviant child behaviors. Unfortunately, children of substance abusers may be more likely to have behavior problems and so may place more stress on addicted parents, who are less prepared to respond effectively. This may create a loop between parental addiction, poor parenting, and child behavior problems (Leonard & Eiden, 2007). In the context of the stress–addiction relationship, one would conceptualize this as parental addiction being a compromised stress-regulation state that is associated with high craving and relapse risk in the face of personal stressors. Thus a vicious cycle is set in motion, with low stress-regulatory capacity leading to poor parenting, poor parenting exacerbating child behavior problems, and behavior problems leading to greater stress for parents and potentially greater substance use and subsequent poorer outcomes for the child (and parent).

Sex Differences in Stress–Addiction Associations

Sex plays an important role in stress-related arousal and craving in addicted individuals. There are sex differences in the effects of early trauma and maltreatment on the increased risk of addiction, with women showing a stronger association between early maltreatment and addiction (Simpson & Miller, 2002; Hyman, et al., 2006). Also, there are sex differences in stress-related sensitivity to the reinforcing effects of drugs and in stress enhancement of drug self-administration (Lynch, 2006; Park, Belluzzi, et al., 2007), with females showing a stronger effect of stress on drug administration than males. Finally, in our laboratory studies, we have also found sex differences in effects of stress imagery on arousal in addicted populations. Cocaine-addicted women (and women social drinkers) report greater stress-induced sadness and anxiety than men (Chaplin et al., 2008; Fox et al., 2008). And comorbid alcohol and cocaine-dependent women show increased cortisol and ACTH response to stress as compared to men (Fox et al., 2009).

Implications for parenting women. If women are more susceptible to the effects of stress on addiction, this could have important implications for parenting, as women are more likely than men to be primary caregivers for children. Interventions to decrease stress and addictive behaviors must then be appropriate and effective for women in order to have a strong impact on parenting and child outcomes.

Summary

In sum, the experience of chronic life stressors and acute in-the-moment stressors may lead to alterations in the HPA axis and autonomic system basal tone and responsivity that, in turn, affect the emotional, behavioral, and stress-regulatory responses as well as drug craving in addicted parents. A heightened emotional behavioral and craving response combined with an altered biological stress response results in an inability in the addicted individual to regulate emotions, stress, and arousing situations. This pattern of responses may lead these individuals to be emotionally reactive, impulsive, and motivated to find and use drugs when under stress. As parents, addicted individuals who are faced with stressors (as many are) may be: 1) overly emotionally reactive to children's misbehavior (as this may be a stressor for them), 2) neglectful/ignoring of children's behavior and needs due to being overwhelmed by their own life stressors, and 3) likely to use substances, which would then lead to greater emotional dysregulation.

■ PARENTING IN ADDICTED INDIVIDUALS

As stated earlier, addicted individuals may experience higher levels of stress and may show problems in regulation of this stress, leading them to be impulsive, reactive, and likely to seek out drugs when under stress. This could lead addicted individuals to have compromised parenting, particularly under stressful conditions (Leonard & Eiden, 2007). In addition, substance abusers also show comorbid stress-related psychopathology (e.g., depression or antisocial behavior) and problematic family processes (e.g., marital discord), which have been linked to negative parenting and poor outcomes for children (Finger et al., 2010; Luthar & Sexton, 2007).

There are a few specific parenting deficits that have been found in addicted parents. Addicted parents have been found to show reduced attention to children, high negative reactivity to their children, and greater rates of abuse of their children. Furthermore, addicted parents may model use of substances as a method of coping with stress. We review the literature on parenting in addicted individuals below, and then discuss how stress may affect the relationship between addiction and compromised parenting.

Decreased Responsiveness in Addicted Parents

Several studies have shown that addicted parents may show decreased responsiveness to their children in parent–child interactions. For example, mothers with a history of cocaine use have been found to display less emotional engagement and responsiveness than non-cocaine-using mothers with their infants and toddlers during laboratory-based tasks such as separation tasks and feeding (Minnes, Singer, Arendt, & Satayathum, 2005; Molitor, Mayes, & Ward, 2003). This lack of response has been specifically related to mothers' current amount of cocaine use and current depressive symptoms (Eiden, et al., 2006). This suggests that current cocaine use may lead mothers to be neglectful of children. Cocaine-using mothers may be preoccupied with their own negative, depressed, affect (perhaps as a side effect of cocaine use or of withdrawal) and may therefore not have the resources to engage in parenting. Interestingly, Eiden (2001) found that cocaine-using mother's use of marijuana and alcohol was related to lowered maternal responsiveness to infants during feeding. Research has also found that alcoholic fathers displayed lower synchrony and engagement with their infants than non-alcoholic fathers (Eiden, Chavez, & Leonard, 1999). So, use of cocaine, marijuana, and alcohol may all place parents at risk for showing lower responsiveness to their infants.

In parents of toddlers and preschoolers, similar findings have been revealed. In our work, we examined mothers with a history of cocaine use during pregnancy versus mothers without cocaine-use history in an emotion-eliciting task (a toy wait task) with their 2½-year-old children. We coded toddlers' displays of negative emotions during the task and then coded mothers' behaviors immediately following toddler's negative emotion displays. Mothers with a history of cocaine use showed less contingent responding to their toddler's in-the-moment expressions of negative emotion, particularly with girls (Chaplin, Sinha, & Mayes, 2009). Similarly, in another study, fathers with an alcohol-use disorder showed lower parental warmth (which may include attention to child emotion) with children at age two, and lower parental warmth in turn predicted lower child social competence at age three (Eiden, Edwards, & Leonard, 2007; Eiden, Colder, et al., 2009). Research with preschool-aged children has shown similar findings. For example, Whipple and colleagues (1995) found that alcoholic families showed lower dyadic synchrony and made less of an effort to engage their preschool-aged sons in a family play task than non-alcoholic families.

Less work has been conducted with school-aged children or adolescents, in particular observational studies of parenting interactions. One observational study found that alcoholic fathers (and depressed fathers) showed lower congeniality and also fewer problem-solving behaviors than non-distressed fathers in parent–adolescent problem-solving discussions (Jacob, Krahn, & Leonard, 1991). This lack of response to children's emotions and behaviors may lead to fewer opportunities to teach children good emotional regulation and social skills, leading to lower social and emotional competence as children develop (Denham, 2007; Gottman, Katz, & Hooven, 1997).

Increased Negative Parenting in Addicted Parents

In addition to showing less responsiveness, addicted parents may also be overly negatively reactive to children. In general, substance-using mothers use more punitive parenting, rely on more severe disciplinary practices, and show higher levels of "authoritarian involvement" in parenting in which they are likely to exclude outside influences on their parenting in an attempt to control the child or his/her development than non-substance-using mothers (Hien & Honeyman, 2000; Miller, Smyth, & Mudar, 1999; Wellisch & Steinberg, 1980). Maternal cocaine use has been associated with more angry and intrusive behavior (and less supportive/positive behavior) with infants (Eiden et al., 2006) and toddlers (Bauman & Dougherty, 1983; Johnson et al., 2002). Related to this, maternal drug use and parental alcohol problems have been associated with insecure mother–infant attachment (Edwards, Eiden, & Leonard, 2004; Rodning et al., 1991).

Longitudinal studies further suggest that parental drinking predicts future problematic parenting. For example, fathers' heavy drinking when children were one year old predicted greater observed negative parental behavior (more negative affect and behavior in a parent–child interaction) at 24 months of child age (Eiden et al., 2004) and more self-reported "over-reactive" parenting over time from child age of 18 months to six years (Edwards, Homish, Eiden, Grohman, & Leonard, 2009).

Studies (although fewer in number) have also examined addiction and the parenting of older children. El-Sheikh and colleagues have found that parent problem-drinking is associated with greater mother-reported parent–child conflict, and father drinking is linked to less secure child-reported attachment with parents in 6–12-year-olds (El-Sheikh & Flanagan, 2001; El-Sheikh & Buckhalt, 2003).

Increased Abuse by Addicted Parents

At an extreme level, addicted individuals' tendencies to be unresponsive to and/or overly punitive of their children may lead them to be neglectful or abusive. Studies both of court samples and of cohorts of substance abusers have established a robust relationship between parents' substance abuse and their maltreatment of children (Chaffin, Kelleher, & Hollenberg, 1996; Magura, Laudet, Kang, & Whitney, 1999). Children whose parents abuse substances may be twice as likely to experience physical or sexual abuse (Walsh, MacMillan, & Jamieson, 2003). Many children of drug abusers also face neglect as their parents fail to care for their basic needs (e.g., food, appropriate housing) due to active substance use or related stressors.

Due to child-abuse behaviors, addicted parents may have children removed from their custody. Eiden et al. (1999) found that cocaine-using mothers' children spent a greater amount of time in foster care compared with children of non-cocaine using mothers. This disruption to the parent–child relationship can further impact the well-being of children of addicted parents. Also, addicted parents who have a child removed from their custody show a worsening of addiction severity and an increase in stressors such as homelessness (Meier, Donmall, & McElduff, 2004). As noted above, many addicted parents were themselves abused and neglected as children and thus did not learn alternate ways of regulating their high-stress states. They are thus perpetuating the same behaviors that they were subjected to in a victim-perpetrator cycle. As we know, victims of child abuse are at elevated risk for being abusive towards their own children (Oliver, 1993).

Modeling of Addictive Behavior

Addicted parents may model use of drugs as a way to deal with stress, which may increase children's likelihood of developing addictions themselves later in life. Andrews, Hops, and Duncan (1997) found that adolescents modeled their parents' cigarette smoking and marijuana use, and adolescents also modeled their fathers' drinking behavior if they had a close or moderately close relationship with the father (but not if they had a distant relationship: see Fitzgerald et al., Chapter 7, this volume). Studies have shown that parents' beliefs about drugs are related to adolescents' drug use, with parents who disapprove of alcohol use (or are perceived as disapproving by youth) having adolescents who are less likely to use alcohol (e.g., Jackson, Henriksen, & Dickinson, 1999; Koning, Engels, et al., 2010; Sawyer & Stevenson, 2008).

■ STRESS EFFECTS ON PARENTING IN ADDICTED INDIVIDUALS

Taken together, these findings suggest that, as a group, alcoholic and drug-abusing parents are less responsive to, more negatively reactive to, more likely to abuse or neglect, and more likely to model drug-using behavior with their children. The increased life stressors and altered stress response of addicted individuals may help explain the pathway from addiction to poor parenting (see Figure 2.1 for description of conceptual model of stress effects on parenting in addicted individuals).

First, as stated above, addicted individuals have higher levels of chronic life stressors (e.g., worries about housing and money) and have the additional physiological stressor of exposure to bingeing and high levels of drug use, including overstimulation of stress and reward pathways, tolerance and adaptation, and withdrawal-related effects. This accumulation of stressors may lead addicted individuals to be emotionally overwhelmed, leading them to lack the resources and energy to pay attention to and respond appropriately to their children's needs and problems. For example, perceived stress in opiod-addicted mothers has been linked to poorer mother-reported parenting (Suchman & Luthar, 2001).

Second, as stated above, substance abusers show alterations in the HPA axis and autonomic system basal tone and responsivity to stress and drug cues, with heightened emotional, behavioral, and craving responses combined with a heightened or blunted biological stress response. Furthermore, chronic use of substances directly affects brain circuitry involved in inhibition of impulsive behavior and emotion or stress regulation. This altered stress system shown by addicted individuals could

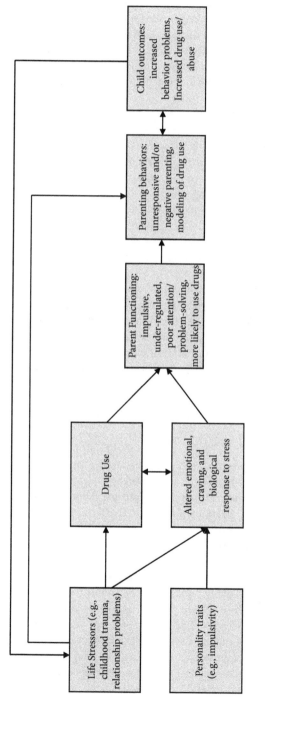

Figure 2.1 Integrated Bio-Psycho-Social Model of Stress Effects on Parenting in Addicted Individuals.

lead them as parents to show heightened (and impulsive or under-regulated) emotional reactions to children's behaviors in daily interactions. Even relatively minor child behaviors (such as whining) could be stressful to addicted individuals, given their heightened sensitivity to stressors. Heightened sensitivity to stressors in the parent–child relationship could, in turn, lead addicted parents to become negative and overly punitive of children—or lead them to shut down and neglect or avoid their children. Thus, addicted individuals may respond to challenging child behaviors with heightened emotional reactivity, similar to the ways they respond to stressors in the laboratory.

In addition to having altered stress systems from the use of substances, addicted individuals may also have greater impulsivity and poorer emotion regulation at a trait level—before they began using substances. This reactivity may also be evident in interactions with their children. Such reactivity may be genetically linked and may be passed on to their children (who may themselves be more temperamentally "difficult" or reactive, making parenting a particular challenge).

Third, as stated above, addicted individuals are more likely to have a history of child abuse themselves. This abuse, and its effects on stress systems, could help explain the greater rates of abuse and neglect by addicted parents as research has documented an inter-generational transmission of abuse behaviors (Oliver, 1993).

Fourth, as shown in laboratory studies of stress imagery, stress increases craving for and a motivation to use drugs and alcohol. Thus, when under stress, addicted parents may be more likely to use substances, and children may be exposed to watching their parents get intoxicated. While under the influence, parents are then likely to show even greater emotional lability and may be more likely to be abusive. Also, parents' use of substances increases the modeling of drug-using behavior for their children.

■ SUMMARY AND IMPLICATIONS

In sum, addicted individuals have greater levels of life stressors (including child-abuse histories); are exposed to the pharmacological stressor of drug use itself; and show altered, under-regulated, and impulsive responses to stress, including responding to stress by craving and using drugs. Furthermore, female addicts may be more sensitive to stress than males. Perhaps due to their under-regulated and heightened responses to stress, their greater levels of life stress, and possibly their comorbid personality traits and psychopathology, addicted individuals show decreased responsiveness and increased negative parenting compared with non-addicted parents. These parenting deficits may be most pronounced in stressful situations. Unfortunately, many typical child behaviors (such as crying in infancy) may be seen as stressful by addicted parents, and many children of addicted individuals may show higher levels of aversive behaviors, such as crying and temper tantrums, which can also act as stressors. Stressors (child-related or otherwise) may not only lead to compromised parenting, but may also lead addicted parents to crave and use drugs, which may further adversely affect their stress-reward systems and promote emotional dsyregulation, further negatively affecting their parenting while at the same time leading to increased chances of modeling drug use behavior for children.

Implications for child development. The unresponsive and punitive parenting often observed in addicted parents almost always has negative consequences for children's social and emotional development. This type of parenting, particularly in the context of the chaotic family life associated with active drug use by a parent, can lead children to have problems with their own emotion regulation and impulsivity, which can lead them to be at greater risk for the development of behavior problems and, in adolescence and young adulthood, addictive behaviors. A family history of alcohol abuse, for example, predicts youth's externalizing psychopathology and major depression at age 11 (King, Iacono, & McGue, 2004) and also predicts youth's substance abuse in young adulthood and greater heavy drinking/heavy drug use from adolescence to young adulthood (Chassin, Pitts, DeLucia, & Todd, 1999; Chassin, Flora, & King, 2004). Of course, the transmission of addictive behaviors could be due in part to genetic risk factors for addiction that are passed from parent to child (such as behavioral disinhibition: King et al. 2005, Iacono, McGue, 2009). However, the compromised parenting practices of addicted individuals, combined with increased stress in the family environment, would suggest poor stress-regulation and coping-modeling also play an important role in mediating the effects of parental addiction on children's development.

Implications for intervention. Given the consequences of stress for parenting of addicted individuals and subsequent child development, it will be important for future treatments and interventions with addicted parents to focus on regulating stress. A primary intervention target would be addiction treatment. As active drug use further debilitates the stress-regulatory systems, leading to more compromised parenting, addiction intervention for parents is critical to break the intergenerational cycle of stress and addiction. Motivational enhancement strategies may be used to strengthen internal motivation to seek out addiction treatment. To further motivate parents to seek treatment for their addiction, parents could receive education about the negative impact of drug use on stress systems in order to better understand that drug use makes their response to stress worse, and also functions to model drug use in their children. Specific family-based positive contingencies may also be offered to promote drug abstinence and support positive parenting.

In the context of addiction treatment, addicted parents could be taught relaxation strategies to remain calm in the face of negative child behaviors (e.g., whining) or other stressors so that they can respond to their children in sensitive ways. Novel stress-reduction strategies such as mindfulness-based relapse prevention (Hendershot et al., 2011) that focus on stress reduction to prevent relapse could be of particular use to those who are in early recovery and need immediate support to cope with parenting stress.

Finally, there is a greater emphasis on addressing the stress-related pathophysiology in addiction with novel medications (Sinha et al., 2011). For example, recent data on Prazosin, an old anti-hypertensive agent, indicates its benefit in decreasing traumatic symptoms in PTSD (Raskind, et al., 2007) and also decreasing stress and cue-induced alcohol craving in alcohol-dependent individuals (see Fox et al., 2011). Additional evidence indicates its benefit in decreasing alcohol use in a pilot study of alcohol-dependent individuals (Simpson et al., 2009). While these data need further support from larger clinical trials of Prazosin in substance-abusing patients, they point to the active development of specific interventions to address stress-related addiction pathophysiology with potential implications for improving parenting.

Implications for future research. More research on the basic mechanisms by which stress affects parenting in addicted individuals would be helpful to inform the development and refinement of interventions. For example, there is a need for research on parents' stress responses to negative child behaviors, particularly in middle childhood and during adolescence, a time when stressful parent–child conflicts increase in frequency. It would be interesting to understand how parents respond to conflict with their children, and, in turn, how that affects their attitudes toward parenting, their parenting behaviors, and their use of substances. It would be interesting to see if treatments to reduce parents' addictive behavior (both psychological and pharmacological) have an impact on how parents respond to in-the-moment stressful parent–child and parent–adolescent interactions. In addition, it would be interesting to understand more fully which stress-related mechanisms are the most important in the transmission of addictive behaviors from parents to children—including genetic factors, shared family stress, modeling of drug use, and negative parenting;—and how these factors interact over time to lead to risk for the child. Through understanding stress-related factors in the parenting of addicted individuals, we can hopefully prevent this intergenerational transmission of stress response and addiction.

■ **AUTHOR NOTE**

Work on this chapter was supported in part by the National Institute on Drug Abuse through Grant K01-DA-024759 (PI: Chaplin) and through a grant from ABMRF/The Foundation for Alcohol Research (PI: Chaplin).

■ **REFERENCES**

Adinoff, B., Junghanns, K., Kiefer, F., & Krishnan-Sarin, S. (2005). Suppression of the HPA axis stress-response: implications for relapse. *Alcoholism: Clinical and Experimental Research, 29,* 1351–1355.

Al'absi, M., Hatsukami, D., & Davis, G. L. (2005). Attenuated adrenocorticotropic responses to psychological stress are associated with early smoking relapse. *Psychopharmacology (Berlin), 181,* 107–117.

Andrews, J. A., Hops, H., & Duncan, S. C. (1997). Adolescent modeling of parent substance use: The moderating effect of the relationship with the parent. *Journal of Family Psychology, 11,* 259–270.

Badrick, E., Kirschbaum, C., & Kumari, M. (2007). The relationship between smoking status and cortisol secretion. *Journal of Clinical Endocrinology & Metabolism, 92,* 819–824.

Baker, T. B., Piper, M. E., McCarthy, D. E., Majeskie, M. R., & Fiore, M. C. (2004). Addiction motivation reformulated: An affective processing model of negative reinforcement. *Psychological Review, 111,* 33–51.

Bauman, P. S., & Dougherty, F. E. (1983). Drug-addicted mothers' parenting and their children's development. *Substance Use & Misuse, 18*, 291–302.

Beveridge, T. J., Smith, H. R., Nader, M. A., & Porrino, L. J. (2005). Effects of chronic cocaine self-administration on norepinephrine transporters in the nonhuman primate brain. *Psychopharmacology, 180*, 781–788.

Boyce-Rustay, J. M., Cameron, H. A., & Holmes, A. (2007). Chronic swim stress alters sensitivity to acute behavioral effects of ethanol in mice. *Physiology & Behavior, 91*, 77–86.

Breese, G. R., Chu, K., Dayas, C. V., Funk, D., Knapp, D. J., Koob, G. F., et al. (2005). Stress enhancement of craving during sobriety and the risk of relapse. *Alcoholism: Clinical and Experimental Research, 29*, 185–195.

Breslau, N., Davis, G., & Schultz, L. R. (2003). Posttraumatic stress disorder and the incidence of nicotine, alcohol, and other drug disorders in persons who have experienced trauma. *Archives of General Psychiatry, 60*, 289–294.

Chaffin, M., Kelleher, K., & Hollenberg, J. (1996). Onset of physical abuse and neglect: Psychiatric, substance abuse, and social risk factors from prospective community data. *Child Abuse & Neglect, 20*, 191–203.

Chaplin, T. M., Hong, K., Fox, H. C. Siedlarz, K. M., Bergquist, K., & Sinha, R. (2010). Behavioral arousal in response to stress and drug cue in alcohol and cocaine addicted individuals versus healthy controls. *Human Psychopharmacology: Clinical and Experimental, 25*, 368–376.

Chaplin, T. M., Hong, K. A., Bergquist, K., & Sinha, R. (2008). Gender differences in response to emotional stress: An assessment across subjective, behavioral, and physiological domains and relations to alcohol craving. *Alcoholism: Clinical and Experimental Research, 32*, 1242–1250.

Chaplin, T.M., Sinha, R., & Mayes, L. C. (2009, April). Emotion Socialization of Prenatally Cocaine Exposed Children. Poster presented at the biennial meeting of the Society for Research on Child Development in Denver, Colorado.

Charmandari, E., Tsigos, C., et al. (2005). Endocrinology of the stress response. *Annual Review of Physiology 67*, 259–284.

Chassin, L., Flora, D. B., & King, K. M. (2004). Trajectories of alcohol and drug use and dependence from adolescence to adulthood: The effects of familial alcoholism and personality. *Journal of Abnormal Psychology, 113*, 483–498.

Chassin, L., Pitts, S. C., DeLucia, C., & Todd, M. (1999). A longitudinal study of children of alcoholics: Predicting young adult substance use disorders, anxiety, and depression. *Journal of Abnormal Psychology, 108*, 106–119.

Clark, D. B., Lesnick, L., & Hegedus, A. M. (1997). Traumas and other adverse life events in adolescents with alcohol abuse and dependence. *Journal of the American Academy of Child & Adolescent Psychiatry, 36*, 1744–1751.

Cleck, J. N., & Blendy, J. A. (2008). Making a bad thing worse: adverse effects of stress on drug addiction. *Journal of Clinical Investigation, 118*, 454–461.

Cohen, S., R. C. Kessler, et al. (1995). Strategies for measuring stress in studies of psychiatric and physical disorders. In S. Cohen, R. C. Kessler and L. U. Gordon, *Measuring Stress: A Guide for Health and Social Scientists*, pp. 3–26. New York, Oxford University Press.

Dembo, R., Dertke, M., Borders, S., Washburn, M., & Schmeidler, J. (1988). The relationship between physical and sexual abuse and tobacco, alcohol, and illicit drug use among youths in a juvenile detention center. *International Journal of Addictions, 23*, 351–378.

Denham, S. A. (2007). Dealing with feelings: How children negotiate the worlds of emotions and social relationships. *Cognitie, Creier, Comportament* [Cognition, Brain, Behavior], *11*, 1–48.

Edwards, E. P., Eiden, R. D., & Leonard, K. E. (2004). Impact of fathers' alcoholism and associated risk factors on parent-infant attachment stability from 12 to 18 months. *Infant Mental Health Journal, 25*, 556–579.

Edwards, E. P., Homish, G. G., Eiden, R. D., Grohman, K. K., & Leonard, K. E. (2009). Longitudinal prediction of early childhood discipline styles among heavy drinking parents. *Addictive Behaviors, 34*, 100–106.

Eiden, R. D., Leonard, K. E., Hoyle, R. H., & Chavez, F. (2004). A transactional model of parent-infant interactions in alcoholic families. *Psychology of Addictive Behaviors, 18*, 350–361.

Eiden, R. D., Chavez, F., & Leonard, K. E. (1999). Parent–infant interactions among families with alcoholic fathers. *Development and Psychopathology, 11*, 745–762.

Eiden, R. D., Stevens, A., Schuetze, P., & Dombkowski, L. E. (2006). Conceptual model for maternal behavior among polydrug cocaine-using mothers: The role of postnatal cocaine use and maternal depression. *Psychology of Addictive Behaviors, 20*, 1–10.

Eiden, R. D. (2001). Maternal substance use and mother-infant feeding interactions. *Infant Mental Health Journal, 22*, 497–511.

Eiden, R. D., Edwards, E. P., & Leonard, K. E. (2007). A conceptual model for the development of externalizing behavior problems among kindergarten children of alcoholic families: Role of parenting and children's self-regulation. *Developmental Psychopathology, 43*, 1187–1201.

Eiden, R. D., Colder, C., Edwards E. P., & Leonard, K. E. (2009). A longitudinal study of social competence among children of alcoholic and nonalcoholic parents: Role of parental psychopathology, parental warmth, and self-regulation. *Psychology of Addictive Behaviors, 23*, 36–46.

Eiden, R. D., Peterson, M., & Coleman, T. (1999). Maternal cocaine use and the caregiving environment during early childhood. *Psychology of Addictive Behaviors, 13*, 293–302.

El-Sheikh, M., & Flanagan, E. (2001). Parental problem drinking and children's adjustment: Family conflict and parental depression as mediators and moderators of risk. *Journal of Abnormal Child Psychology, 29*, 417–432.

El-Sheikh, M., & Buckhalt, J. A. (2003). Parental problem drinking and children's adjustment: Attachment and family functioning as moderators and mediators of risk. *Journal of Family Psychology, 17*, 510–520.

Finger, B., Kachadourian, L. K., Lorig, K., Molnar, D. S., Eiden, R. D., Edwards, E. P., et al. (2010). Alcoholism, associated risk factors, and harsh parenting among fathers: Examining the role of marital aggression. *Addictive Behaviors, 35*, 541–548.

Fox, H.C., Anderson, G. M., Tuit, K., Hansen, J., Kimmerling, A., Siedlarz, K. M., et al. (2011). Prazosin effects on stress- and cue-induced craving and stress response in alcohol-dependent individuals: Preliminary findings. *Alcoholism: Clinical and Experimental Research, 36*, 351–360.

Fox, H. C., Bergquist, K. L., Hong, K. I., & Sinha, R. (2007). Stress-induced and alcohol cue-induced craving in recently abstinent alcohol dependent individuals. *Alcoholism: Clinical and Experimental Research, 31*, 395–403.

Fox, H. C., Hong, K. I., Siedlarz, K., & Sinha, R. (2008). Enhanced sensitivity to stress and drug/alcohol craving in abstinent cocaine-dependent individuals compared to social drinkers. *Neuropsychopharmacology, 33*, 796–805.

Fox, H. C., Hong, K. I., Siedlarz, K. M., Bergquist, K. L., Anderson, G. M., Kreek M. J., et al. (2009). Sex-specific dissociations in autonomic and HPA responses to stress and cues in alcohol dependent patients with cocaine abuse. *Alcohol and Alcoholism, 44*,575–585.

Gottman, J., Katz, L. F., & Hooven, C. (1997). *Meta-Emotion: How Families Communicate Emotionally.* Hillsdale, NJ: Erlbaum.

Grusser, S. M., Wrase, J., Klein, S., Hermann, D., Smolka, M. N., Ruf, M., et al. (2004). Cue-induced activation of the striatum and medial prefrontal cortex is associated with subsequent relapse in abstinent alcoholics. *Psychopharmacology (Berlin), 175*, 296–302.

Hendershot, C.S., Witkiewitz, K., George, W. H., & Marlatt, G. A. (2011). Relapse prevention for addictive behaviors. *Substance Abuse Treatment, Prevention, and Policy, 6*, 1–17.

Hien, D., & Honeyman, T. (2000). A closer look at the drug abuse–maternal aggression link. *Journal of Interpersonal Violence, 15*, 503–522.

Higley, J. D., Hasert, M. F., Suomi, S. J., & Linnoila, M. (1991). Nonhuman primate model of alcohol abuse: Effects of early experience, personality, and stress on alcohol consumption. *Proceedings of the National Academy of Sciences of the United States of America, 88*, 7261–7265.

Hyman, S. M., Fox, H., Hong, K. I., Doebrick, C., & Sinha, R. (2007). Stress and drug-cue-induced craving in opioid-dependent individuals in naltrexone treatment. *Experimental and Clinical Psychopharmacology, 15*, 134–143.

Hyman, S. M., Garcia, M., & Sinha, R. (2006). Gender specific associations between types of childhood maltreatment and the onset, escalation and severity of substance use in cocaine dependent adults. *The American Journal of Drug and Alcohol Abuse, 32*, 655–664.

Hyman, S. E., & Malenka, R. C. (2001). Addiction and the brain: The neurobiology of compulsion and its persistence. *Neuroscience 2*, 695–703.

Jackson, C., Henriksen, L., & Dickinson, D. (1999). Alcohol-specific socialization, parenting behaviors and alcohol use by children. *Journal of Studies on Alcohol, 60*, 362–367.

Jacob, T., Krahn, G. L., & Leonard, K. (1991). Parent-child interactions in families with alcoholic fathers. *Journal of Consulting and Clinical Psychology, 59*, 176–181.

Johnson, A. L., Morrow, C., Accornero, V. H., Xue, L., Anthony, J. C., & Bandstra, E. S. (2002). Maternal cocaine use: Estimated effects on mother—child play interactions in the preschool period. *Journal of Developmental and Behavioral Pediatrics, 23*, 191–20.

Johnson, V., & Pandina, R. J. (1993). A longitudinal examination of the relationships among stress, coping strategies, and problems associated with alcohol use. *Alcoholism: Clinical and Experimental Research, 17*, 696–702.

Johnson, V., & Pandina, R. J. (2000). Alcohol problems among a community sample: longitudinal influences of stress, coping, and gender. *Substance Use Misuse 35*, 669–686.

Khantzian, E. J. (1985). The self-medication hypothesis of addictive disorders: Focus on heroin and cocaine dependence. *American Journal of Psychiatry, 142*, 1259–1264.

King, S. M., Keyes, M., Malone, S. M., Elkins, I., Legrand, L. N., Iacono, W. G., et al. (2009). Parental alcohol dependence and the transmission of adolescent behavioral disinhibition: A study of adoptive and non-adoptive families. *Addiction, 104*, 578–586.

King, S. M., Iacono, W. G., & McGue, M. (2004). Childhood externalizing and internalizing psychopathology in the prediction of early substance use. *Addiction, 99,* 1548–1559.

Koning, I. M., Engels, R. C. E., Verdurmen, J. E. E., & Vollebergh, W. A. M. (2010). Alcohol-specific socialization practices and alcohol use in Dutch early adolescents. *Journal of Adolescence, 33,* 93–100.

Koob, G. F., & Le Moal, M. (1997). Drug abuse: Hedonic homeostatic dysregulation. *Science, 278,* 52–58.

Kosten, T. A., Miserendino, M. J., & Kehoe, P. (2000). Enhanced acquisition of cocaine self-administration in adult rats with neonatal isolation stress experience. *Brain Research, 875,* 44–50.

LaGasse, L. L., Neal, A. R., & Lester, B. M. (2005). Assessment of infant cry: Acoustic cry analysis and parental perception. *Mental Retardation and Developmental Disabilities, 11,* 83–93.

Lazarus, R. S. (1999). *Stress and Emotion: A New Synthesis.* New York, NY, Springer Publishing Company.

Le, A. D., Harding, S., Juzytsch, W., Funk, D., & Shaham, Y. (2005). Role of alpha-2 adrenoceptors in stress-induced reinstatement of alcohol seeking and alcohol self-administration in rats. *Psychopharmacology (Berlin) 179,* 366–373.

Leonard, K. E., & Eiden, R. D. (2007). Marital and family processes in the context of alcohol use and alcohol disorders. *Annual Review of Clinical Psychology, 3,* 285–310.

Lloyd, D. A., & Turner, R. J. (2008). Cumulative lifetime adversities and alcohol dependence in adolescence and young adulthood. *Drug and Alcohol Dependence, 93,* 217–226.

Lovallo, W. R., Dickensheets, S. L., Myers, D. A., Thomas, T. L., & Nixon, S. J. (2000). Blunted stress cortisol response in abstinent alcoholic and polysubstance-abusing men. *Alcoholism: Clinical and Experimental Research, 24,* 651–658.

Lu, L., & Shaham, Y. (2005). The role of stress in opiate and psychostimulant addiction: evidence from animal models. *Techniques in the Behavioral and Neural Sciences, 15,* 315–332.

Lu, L., Shepard, J. D., Hall, F. S., & Shaham, Y. (2003). Effect of environmental stressors on opiate and psychostimulant reinforcement, reinstatement and discrimination in rats: a review. *Neuroscience & Biobehavioral Reviews, 27,* 457–491.

Luthar, S. S., & Sexton, C. C. (2007). Maternal drug abuse versus maternal depression: Vulnerability and resilience among school-age and adolescent offspring. *Development and Psychopathology, 19,* 205–225.

Lynch, W. (2006). Sex differences in vulnerability to drug self-administration. *Experimental Clinical Psychopharmacology, 14,* 34–41.

Magura, S., Laudet, A., Kang, S. Y., & Whitney, S. A. (1999). Effectiveness of comprehensive services for crack-dependent mothers with newborns and young children. *Journal of Psychoactive Drugs, 31,* 321–338.

Marlatt, G. A., & Gordon, J. R. (1985). *Relapse Prevention: Maintenance Strategies in the Treatment of Addictive Behaviors.* New York, Guilford Press.

McEwen, B. S. (2007). Physiology and neurobiology of stress and adaptation: central role of the brain. *Physiological Reviews, 87,* 873–904.

Meier, P. S., Donmall, M. C., & McElduff, P. (2004). Characteristics of drug users who do or do not have care of their children. *Addiction, 99,* 955–961.

Miczek, K. A., Covington, H. E. III, Nikulina, E. M. Jr., & Hammer, R. P. (2004). Aggression and defeat: persistent effects on cocaine self-administration and gene expression in peptidergic and aminergic mesocorticolimbic circuits. *Neuroscience & Biobehavioral Reviews, 27,* 787–802.

Miller, B. A., Smyth, N. J., & Mudar, P. J. (1999). Mothers' alcohol and other drug problems and their punitiveness toward their children. *Journal of Studies on Alcohol, 60,* 632–642.

Minnes, S., Singer, L. T., Arendt, R., & Satayathum, S. (2005). Effects of prenatal cocaine/ polydrug use on maternal-infant feeding interactions during the first year of life. *Journal of Developmental & Behavioral Pediatrics, 26,* 194–200.

Moffett, M. C., Vicentic, A., Kozel, M., Plotsky, P., Francis, D. D., & Kuhar, M. J. (2007). Maternal separation alters drug intake patterns in adulthood in rats. *Biochemical Pharmacology, 73,* 321–330.

Molitor, A., Mayes, L. C., & Ward, A. (2003). Emotion regulation behavior during a separation procedure in 18-month-old children of mothers using cocaine and other drugs. *Development and Psychopathology, 15,* 39–54.

Oliver, J. E. (1993). Intergenerational transmission of child abuse: rates, research, and clinical implications. *American Journal of Psychiatry, 150,* 1315–1324

Park, M. K., Belluzzi, J. D., Han, S. H., Cao, J., & Leslie, F. M. (2007). Age, sex and early environment contribute to individual differences in nicotine/acetaldehyde-induced behavioral and endocrine responses in rats. *Pharmacology Biochemistry and Behavior, 86,* 297–305.

Pelham, W. E., & Lang, A. R. (1999). Can your children drive you to drink? *Alcohol Research & Health, 23,* 293–298.

Porrino, L. J., Smith, H. R., Nader, M. A., & Beveridge, T. J. (2007). The effects of cocaine: a shifting target over the course of addiction. *Progress in Neuropsychopharmacology & Biological Psychiatry, 31,* 1593–1600.

Raskind, M.A., Peskind, E.R., Hoff, D.J., Hart, K.L., Holmes, H.A., Warren, D., Shofer, J., O'Connell, J., Taylor, F., Gross, C., Rohde, K., & McFall, M.E. (2007). A parallel group placebo controlled study of prazosin for trauma nightmares and sleep disturbance in combat veterans with post-traumatic stress disorder. *Biological Psychiatry, 61,* 928–934.

Robinson, T. E., & Berridge, K. C. (2003). Addiction. *Annual Review of Psychology, 54,* 25–53.

Rodning, C., Beckwith, L., & Howard, J. (1991). Quality of attachments and home environments in children prenatally exposed to PCP and cocaine. *Developmental and Psychopathology, 3,* 351–366.

Sawyer, T. M., & Stevenson, J. F. (2008). Perceived parent and peer disapproval toward substances: Influences on adolescent decision-making. *The Journal of Primary Prevention, 29,* 465–477.

Schuetze, P., Zeskind, P. S., & Eiden, R. D. (2003). The perceptions of infant distress signals varying in pitch by cocaine-using mothers. *Infancy, 4,* 65–83.

Sher, K. J., Gershuny, B. S., et al. (1997). The role of childhood stressors in the intergenerational transmission of alcohol use disorders. *Journal of Studies on Alcohol and Drugs, 58,* 414–427.

Simpson, T. L., & Miller, W. R. (2002). Concomitance between childhood sexual and physical abuse and substance use problems: A review. *Clinical Psychology Review, 22,* 27–77.

Simpson, T. L., Saxon, A. J., Meredith, C. W., Malte, C. A., McBride, B., Ferguson, L. C., Gross, C. A., Hart, K. L., & Raskind, M. (2009). A pilot trial of the alpha-1 adrenergic antagonist, prazosin, for alcohol dependence. *Alcoholism: Clinical and Experimental Research, 33,* 255–263.

Sinha, R. (2001). How does stress increase risk of drug abuse and relapse? *Psychopharmacology (Berlin) 158,* 343–359.

Sinha, R. (2008). Chronic stress, drug use, and vulnerability to addiction. *Annals of the New York Academy of Sciences, 1141,* 105–130.

Sinha, R. (2011). New findings on biological factors predicting addiction relapse vulnerability. *Current Psychiatry Reports, 13,* 398–405.

Sinha, R., Catapano, D., & O'Malley, S. (1999). Stress-induced craving and stress response in cocaine dependent individuals. *Psychopharmacology (Berlin), 142,* 343–351.

Sinha, R., Garcia, M., Paliwal, P., Kreek, M. J., & Rounsaville, B. J. (2006). Stress-induced cocaine craving and hypothalamic-pituitary-adrenal responses are predictive of cocaine relapse outcomes. *Archives of General Psychiatry, 63,* 324–331.

Sinha, R., Fox, H. C., Hong, K. I., Bergquist, K., Bhagwager, Z., & Siedlarz, M. (2009). Enhanced subjective, behavioral and physiological sensitivity to stress and alcohol craving during abstinence from chronic alcohol abuse. *Neuropsychophamacology, 34,* 1198–1208.

Sinha, R., Fuse, T., Aubin, L. R., & O' Malley, S. (2000). Psychological stress, drug-related cues and cocaine craving. *Psychopharmacology (Berlin) 152,* 140–148.

Sinha, R., Lacadie, C., Skudlarski, P., Fulbright, R. K., Rounsaville, B. J., Kosten, T. R., et al. (2005). Neural activity associated with stress-induced cocaine craving: A functional magnetic imaging study. *Psychopharmacology (Berlin), 183,* 171–180.

Sinha, R., Talih, M., Malison, R., Cooney, N., Anderson, G. M., & Kreek, M. J. (2003). Hypothalamic-pituitary-adrenal axis and sympatho-adreno-medullary responses during stress-induced and drug cue-induced cocaine craving states. *Psychopharmacology (Berlin) 170,* 62–72.

Suchman, N. E., & Luthar, S. S. (2001). The mediating role of parenting stress in methadone-maintained mother's parenting. *Parenting: Science and Practice, 1,* 285–315.

Turner, R. J., & Lloyd, D. A. (1995). Lifetime traumas and mental health: the significance of cumulative adversity. *Journal of Health and Social Behavior, 36,* 360–376.

Turner, R. J., & Lloyd, D. A. (2003). Cumulative adversity and drug dependence in young adults: racial/ethnic contrasts. *Addiction, 98,* 305–315.

Volkow, N. D., Fowler, J. S., Wang, G. J., Hitzemann, R., Logan, J., Schlyer, D. J., et al. (1993). Decreased dopamine D2 receptor availability is associated with reduced frontal metabolism in cocaine abusers. *Synapse, 14,* 169–177.

Volkow, N. D., Wang, G. J., Fowler, J. S., Logan, J., Gatley, S. J., Hitzemann, R., et al. (1997). Decreased striatal dopaminergic responsiveness in detoxified cocaine-dependent subjects. *Nature, 386,* 830–833.

Volkow, N. D., Wang, G. J., Fowler, J. S., Logan, J., Hitzemann, R., Ding, Y. S., et al. (1996). Decreases in dopamine receptors but not in dopamine transporters in alcoholics. *Alcoholism: Clinical & Experimental Research, 20,* 1594–1598.

Volkow, N. D., Wang, G. J., Telang, F., Fowler, J. S., Logan, J., Childress, A. R., et al. (2006). Cocaine cues and dopamine in dorsal striatum: mechanism of craving in cocaine addiction. *Journal of Neuroscience, 26,* 6583–6588.

Walsh, C., MacMillan, H. L., & Jamieson, E. (2003). The relationship between parental substance abuse and child maltreatment: Findings from the Ontario health supplement. *Child Abuse & Neglect, 27,* 1409–1425.

Wellisch, D. K., & Steinberg, M. R. (1980). Parenting attitudes of addict mothers. *Substance Use & Misuse, 15,* 809–819.

Whipple, E. E., Fitzgerald, H. E., & Zucker, R. A. (1995). Parent-child interactions in alcoholic and nonalcoholic families. *American Journal of Orthopsychiatry, 65,* 153–159.

Widom, C. S., Weiler, B. L., & Cottler, L. B. (1999). Childhood victimization and drug abuse: A comparison of prospective and retrospective findings. *Journal of Consulting & Clinical Psychology, 67,* 867–880.

Wills, T. A., & Cleary, S. D. (1996). How are social support effects mediated? A test with parental support and adolescent substance use. *Journal of Personality and Social Psychology, 71,* 937–952.

Wong, D. F., Kuwabara, H., Schretlen, D. J., Bonson, K. R., Zhou, Y., Nandi, A., et al. (2006). Increased occupancy of dopamine receptors in human striatum during cue-elicited cocaine craving. *Neuropsychopharmacology, 31,* 2716–2727.

Wrase, J., Grusser, S. M., Klein, S., Diener, C., Hermann, D., Flor, H., et al. (2002). Development of alcohol-associated cues and cue-induced brain activation in alcoholics. *Journal of the Association of European Psychiatrists, 17,* 287–291.

3 | Impulsivity and Addiction in Parents

ALEXIS K. MATUSIEWICZ,
RICHARD J. MACATEE,
LEILA GULLER, AND
C. W. LEJUEZ

Parenting difficulties are often described in terms of either maladaptive parenting behaviors, or emotional and relational problems in the parent–child relationship (Suchman, Mayes, Conti, Slade, & Rounsaville, 2004). The former approach emphasizes the development of behavioral management skills to reduce negative parenting practices and increase positive parenting practices (Kumpfer & Alvarado, 1998; Sanders, 1999; Hinshaw, Owens, Wells, Kraemer, Abikoff, et al., 2000). The latter approach focuses on enhancing the parent's emotional sensitivity and responsiveness to the child (Suchman, et al., 2004; Suchman, McMahon, Zhang, Mayes, & Luthar, 2006). As a compliment to these perspectives, many problematic parenting behaviors may be understood through the lens of *impulsivity*, which is defined as the tendency to act rapidly without forethought or apparent regard for the consequences (Moeller, Barratt, Dougherty, Schmitz, & Swann, 2001; Dawe & Loxton, 2004). Impulsive behaviors often fulfill fleeting, short-term aims without apparent regard for the longer-term problems that they create. Abusive parenting behaviors may be considered impulsive because the short-term relief brought on by harsh discipline (i.e., termination of a child behavior the parent wants to stop) may come at the expense of long-term consequences, including threats to the mental well-being of the child, damage to the parent–child emotional bond, or even loss of child custody (Barnard & McKeganey, 2004; Chang, Schwartz, Dodge, & McBride-Chang, 2003). Impulsive parenting may also take less extreme forms: A parent who capitulates to a child's tantrum may avoid the embarrassment of making a scene, yet rewarding the tantrum increases the likelihood that the unwanted behavior will recur. Similarly, a parent who does not set or enforce clear house rules, but sporadically reacts when the child violates an unspoken rule, may create a general sense of unpredictability for the child, which may produce anxiety, fear, or oppositional behavior (Ross & Gill, 2002; Feehan, McGee, Stanton, & Silva, 1991). The framework of impulsivity may be especially relevant for substance-using parents, given that substance use itself is often conceptualized as an impulsive behavior (DeWit, 2008), and the precipitating factors for one type of impulsive behavior may make the parent vulnerable to other forms of impulsive behavior (Baumeister, Vohs, & Tice, 2007; Tice, Bratslavsky & Baumeister, 2001; Dawe & Loxton, 2004). The goal of this chapter is to provide a framework for understanding the role of impulsivity in problematic parenting, with a particular emphasis

44

on the collateral impact of substance use. The chapter begins with a definition of impulsivity and its potential role in parenting, followed by a review of individual difference and situational factors that may engender diverse forms of impulsive parenting behavior. The chapter concludes with a discussion of implications for intervention with vulnerable, substance-using parents.

■ DEFINING IMPULSIVITY

Impulsivity is considered a broad and complex trait that is thought to underlie many types of problematic behavior (e.g., substance use, aggression, overeating, overspending; cf. Evenden, 1999; DeYoung, 2010). Most conceptualizations of impulsivity emphasize behavior that occurs rapidly, without forethought or without apparent regard for the consequences (Moeller et al., 2001; Dawe & Loxton, 2004). When a behavior is labeled "impulsive," it usually suggests a conflict between a person's short-term desires and longer-term goals, such that their behavior ultimately favors the immediate goal (Magen & Gross, 2010; Vohs, Baumeister, & Ciarocco, 2005; Fishbach & Trope, 2005). Recent conceptualizations of impulsive behavior have expanded this definition to encompass not only the element of time but also the notion of priorities among goals (Fishbach, Friedman, & Kruglanski, 2003). In other words, impulsive behavior may reflect a preference for short-term over long-term goals, as well as the dominance of relatively low-priority goals over relatively high-priority goals. Often, though not always, short-term goals are relatively lower-priority and more concrete (e.g., get high, feel better, eat dessert); whereas long-term goals are relatively higher in priority and more abstract (e.g., live a healthy life, have a close relationship with my child, look attractive). Impulsive behavior is thought to occur because people tend to overvalue immediate, concrete rewards and underestimate the value of delayed, abstract rewards; likewise, people often underestimate the aversiveness of distal negative events (Rachlin, Raineri, & Cross, 1991; Liberman & Trope, 2002; Trope & Liberman, 2000). Finally, although functional forms of impulsive behavior certainly exist (Dickman, 1990), impulsive behavior is generally characterized by negative, or at least suboptimal, outcomes (DeYoung, 2010).

Impulsive behavior occurs when a person experiences an urge or impulse to act in line with a short-term, low-priority goal and then fails to control or inhibit that urge (DeYoung, 2010). Urges, which are triggered by different motivational states (i.e., goals), are habitual, automatic, and reflect the strategy that has been most effective in meeting that specific goal in the past. Urges may occur in or out of conscious awareness and pertain to basic cognitive processes such as attention and perception, emotional experiences, thoughts, and overt behavior. For instance, when a mother hears her child crying, she will orient her attention to the child without awareness of the specific urge to redirect her attention. Likewise, both her interpretation and emotional response to the child's cries arise automatically based on the mother's previous experiences. The appraisal that the child "just wants attention" might evoke anger, whereas the interpretation that the child is lonely or afraid might evoke an empathic emotional response. In turn, these interpretations and emotional responses trigger behavioral urges—to ignore, scold, or comfort the child. These impulses unfold rapidly and virtually without effort, which makes responding according to impulse extremely efficient. For most people, most of the time, this type of automatic, habitual responding is consistent with longer-term goals and values and results in appropriate and effective behavior. However, in certain situations, the automatic response (i.e., urge) may be inconsistent with higher-priority goals and values. For example, generally, it is appropriate for a parent to be vigilant about her child's emotional state, and to turn her attention toward the child when the child seems upset. However, if the parent is driving 75 miles per hour, her urge to look to the backseat to check on the child might create a safety hazard. In such cases, if the urge cannot be restrained, it may result in impulsive behavior, including substance use or problematic parenting behavior.

The ability to inhibit impulses is critical to resisting temptation in all forms (e.g., drugs, alcohol, food, sex, parental abuse), making difficult decisions, controlling the content of one's thoughts, and modulating emotional experiences and expression (cf. Baumeister et al., 2007). Inhibitory control also serves an important interpersonal function: it allows people to respond kindly to others' difficult, demanding, or aggressive behavior; promotes fidelity in relationships; and aids in impression management (i.e., acting in an uncharacteristic way to convey a certain image; Baumeister, 2005; Gailliot & Baumeister, 2007; Baumeister et al., 2007). However, just as acting according to impulse is efficient, inhibiting urges is an active, effortful process, which is only possible under certain circumstances.

Impulsive behavior occurs when a person experiences an urge and then fails to inhibit that urge. Thus, impulsive behavior is most likely to occur when urges are very strong or when the ability to inhibit the urge is low. Many factors influence urge-strength, and others affect inhibitory capacity, which means that it is extremely difficult to tell, simply by observing an impulsive behavior, *why* the behavior occurred. Historically, impulsive behavior has been understood as the product of stable, trait-like tendencies. From this perspective, certain people are considered particularly likely to engage in impulsive behavior because they are impulsive or have enduring vulnerabilities that predispose them to behave impulsively, relatively independent of context (Barratt & Patton, 1983; Dickman, 1990; Whiteside & Lynam, 2001; Depue & Collins, 1999). Another approach has been to understand impulsive behavior as the product of contextual and environmental factors that predispose people to behave impulsively. From this perspective, everyone has the capacity to behave impulsively under the right circumstances (Coyne & Clack, 1981). An integrative approach demands consideration of both individual difference and contextual factors, acknowledging that there are traits that confer risk for impulsive behavior, as well as particular contexts that increase the likelihood of impulsive action (cf. Lazarus & Launier, 1978). The following sections seek to identify and discuss several individual difference and contextual factors that serve to create strong urges and diminish inhibitory capacity, and that, therefore, increase impulsive behavior.

■ FACTORS INFLUENCING IMPULSIVE BEHAVIOR

Reward Sensitivity

Reward sensitivity, which refers to the tendency to experience more frequent and stronger urges to pursue opportunities for reward and to actively avoid punishment, is one factor associated with impulsive behavior. People with high reward sensitivity experience greater pleasure in the presence of reward and exhibit more rapid conditioning (i.e., learn more quickly) when rewards are available (Gullo & Dawe, 2008). Clearly, people differ in the things that bring them pleasure; the specific form taken by preferred rewards is shaped over time, through classical and operant conditioning processes (Corwin & Hajnal, 2005). In the context of addiction, people with elevated reward sensitivity enjoy the subjective effects of the substance more than others and experience greater craving when exposed to drug-related cues (Franken & Muris, 2006; Franken, 2002). In terms of parenting, parents who are highly reward-sensitive exhibit greater positive affectivity, warmth, nurturance, and sensitivity to their children's emotional cues (Belsky, Cmic, & Woodworth, 1995; Desjardins, Zelenski, & Coplan, 2008; Weiss, 2000), and are described as more assertive and dominant in interactions with their children (Clark, Kochanska, & Ready, 2000; Desjardins, et al., 2008). The downside is that, when reward-sensitive parents are dissatisfied or unfulfilled in their parenting role, they are likely to neglect their parenting responsibilities in favor of other sources of gratification and pleasure (Desjardins et al., 2008). The affinity for reward and the parallel tendency to experience strong urges and impulses when rewards are available corresponds to variations in functioning in the mesolimbic dopaminergic system. Higher dopaminergic activity is related to impulsive and risk-taking behaviors and features of clinical disorders including attention-deficit/ hyperactivity disorder and borderline personality disorder (Cardinal & Everitt, 2004; Stuettgen, Hennig, Reuter, & Netter, 2005; Depue, 1995; Depue & Collins, 1999; Spoont, 1992; Zald & Depue, 2001; Spear, 2000; Friedel, 2004). Reward sensitivity, which encompasses the hedonic experience and reinforcing value of reward, is thought to stem from hyper-responsiveness of the dopaminergic pathways from the ventral tegmental area to the nucleus accumbens and amygdala (Jentsch & Taylor, 1999; Robinson & Berridge, 2008).

However, despite evidence of the association between heightened reward sensitivity, elevated dopamine, and some impulsive behaviors, it seems that certain impulsive behaviors, including substance use, may result *not* from over-sensitivity to reward but rather from *dampened* sensitivity to reward (Beauchaine, 2001; Verdejo-Garcia, Lawrence, & Clark, 2008; Volkow et al., 2003). Recent research suggests that an extreme orientation to reward may reflect an effort to compensate for dopaminergic *hypo*activation in response to reward cues (Blum, Braverman, Holder, Lubar, Monastra et al., 2000; Beauchaine & Neuhaus, 2008). In this way, one's insensitivity to reward is characterized by blunted dopamine response to reward, resulting from lower D2 dopamine receptor density in the striatum (Stice, Spoor, Bohon, & Small, 2008; Noble, 2000). Individuals who are insensitive to reward may fail to experience normal, day-to-day contingencies as subjectively rewarding (Johnson & Kenny, 2010), prompting more extreme or excessive forms of behavior (e.g., drug use, overeating) to stimulate the dopaminergic pathways, repair mood, and create the experience of satiety (Blum et al., 2000; Bowirrat & Oscar-Berman, 2005). Extreme behavior persists because it is effective; thus, when a particular motivation arises, the strongest impulse will be to repeat the extreme or excessive behavior. In addition, a person characterized by reward insensitivity may experience diminished incentive motivation and may neglect unrewarding, difficult, or challenging tasks, including those related to his child and parenting role (Brinkmann, Schupbach, Joye, & Guido, 2009). A parent with reward insensitivity may experience urges to avoid interactions with the child, potentially leading to insensitive or unresponsive parenting, and even neglect.

Low sensitivity to reward may be particularly problematic among parents with a history of substance use. Prolonged substance use dysregulates the endogenous reward system that underlies subjective reward (Leckman & Mayes, 1998); as a consequence, substance-using parents may not perceive non-substance reinforcers, including those related to parenting (e.g., playing with his child) as enjoyable or rewarding (Dackis & Gold, 1985; Adinoff, 2004). Furthermore, prenatally drug-exposed children may be emotionally reactive and more difficult to care for (O'Connor, Sigman, & Kasari, 1992; 1993). For reward-insensitive parents, the enjoyable aspects of the interactions or gratification in the parenting role may not balance the strain of caring for a reactive child. Therefore, the parent may be highly motivated to avoid interactions with and withdraw from with her child. Taken together, current findings seem to suggest that both hyper- and hypo-responsive dopaminergic functioning can contribute to a tendency to develop strong motivational states (i.e., urges), which, in turn, may be associated with a number of problematic, impulsive behaviors.

Negative Affect

Negative affect plays an important motivational role for behavior in general, and for impulsive behavior in particular. Affect is part of a feedback loop that helps people maintain balance among their goals and priorities (Carver & Scheier, 2010). Negative affect signals a discrepancy between the present condition and the desired or intended state (i.e., a goal). Negative affect triggers behavior aimed at reducing this discrepancy, which, in turn, reduces negative affect (Powers, 1973). On the other hand, positive affect signals that a goal has been surpassed, indicating that it is no longer necessary to expend effort on that goal, and that continuing toward that goal may actually detract from other goals. Essentially, the presence of affect signals a need for reprioritization of goals, with stronger affect denoting greater need for reprioritization (Carver & Scheier, 2010). Negative affect signals a need to interrupt effort toward the current goal and redirect energy toward the source of negative emotions. Positive affect indicates that the current goal has been met, indicating that this goal can be deprioritized, allowing another goal to become active (Carver, 2003).

Affect signals a discrepancy between a person's current state and their goal state, which informs goal prioritization and subsequent goal pursuit. Within this framework, reduction in negative affect is not the primary goal per se, but rather denotes the need for goals to be rearranged. Goal attainment is often accompanied by a reduction in negative affect, even if the goal is not directly related to modification of affect. However, there are cases in which the reduction or avoidance of negative affect is an end in itself; in other words, the focal goal becomes emotion regulation. Goals oriented toward decreasing negative affect and/or increasing positive affect are inherently focused on the present moment (Koole &

Rothermund, 2011) and frequently lead to behavior that conflicts with other, longer-term goals. For instance, Tice and colleagues (2001) conducted a series of experiments examining the effect of negative (vs. happy) mood on involvement in various forms of impulsive behavior. Participants who underwent a negative mood induction ate more junk food, procrastinated more, and were less likely to delay gratification on a behavioral task, relative to participants in a happy mood. However, this effect was only present among participants who were highly motivated to change their negative mood *and* believed the impulsive behavior was likely to improve their mood.

These findings suggest impulsive behavior that occurs in the context of distress is used strategically as a way to meet a particular emotion-regulation goal. For instance, a parent in early abstinence might return home from his job to find that the house is a mess, his child is inconsolable, and there are neither groceries nor money to go buy more. Up to that moment, the long-term, high priority goals may have included maintaining sobriety and spending some time playing with the child. However, as the chaotic scene unfolds, these priorities, which may have been firm in his mind minutes before, are rearranged. The parent might think that he can't begin to manage the situation until he calms down. The short-term goal of reducing anxiety becomes the priority, accompanied by the immediate urge to do what has worked previously to relieve stress (e.g., have a drink), while the significance of his other goals fades. This example illustrates the importance of negative affect in creating urges that are aimed at reducing distress, potentially at the expense of other values and goals.

Cognitive Resources and Dispositional Capacity for Inhibition of Urges

Impulsive behavior results when people fail to inhibit urges that are incompatible with their longer-term objectives. Inhibiting these urges requires temporary mobilization of cognitive resources, a form of mental energy necessary for all goal-directed activities. Cognitive resources are colloquially referred to as willpower, ego strength, or self-control, and are associated with various executive functions (e.g., working memory capacity, inhibitory control; Baumeister et al., 2007; Shah & Kruglanski, 2008). An individual's supply of cognitive resources is limited, exhaustible, and cannot be restored immediately, which necessarily limits the ability to interrupt unwanted impulses (Shah & Kruglanski, 2008). There is considerable individual variation in people's baseline levels of cognitive resources and, consequently, in their dispositional capacity for inhibition of urges.

People with dispositionally low cognitive resources are more likely to engage in a range of problematic behaviors, including substance abuse, crime, violence, overeating, overspending, and relationship difficulties (Baumeister, Heatherton, & Tice, 1994; Tangney, Baumeister, & Boone, 2004; Vohs & Farber, 2004). People with relatively more resources experience benefits throughout the lifespan and across domains of functioning (Shoda, Mischel, & Peake, 1990; Tangney et al., 2004; Gailliot & Baumeister 2007). They experience stronger, healthier interpersonal relationships, manage stress more effectively, and generally engage in less impulsive and self-defeating behavior (Finkel & Campbell, 2001; Shoda et al., 1990; Tangney et al., 2004; Bensley & Wu, 1991; Collins & Lapp, 1992).

The ability to inhibit urges corresponds primarily to activity in the lateral prefrontal cortex (LPFC) and anterior cingulate cortex (ACC; Heatherton & Wagner, 2011). The LPFC is associated with planning and maintaining behaviors, as well as inhibition of distracting, goal-irrelevant information (Heatherton & Wagner, 2011). Under-activation of the LPFC is associated with poorer executive function and working memory capacity (Miller & Cohen, 2001; Vendrell, Junque, Pujol, & Jurado, 1995) and difficulties with day-to-day activities that involve multi-step sequences or require inhibitory control (Shallice & Burgess, 1991). The role of the ACC is to detect conflict among potential responses and to identify discrepancies between intended and actual behavior. The ACC is involved in identifying situations in which additional cognitive resources should be allocated and, with the LPFC, works to align behavior with high-priority goals (Botvinick, Braver, Barch, Carter, & Cohen, 2001; Ridderinkhof, Ullsperger, Crone, & Nieuwenhuis, 2004). Neuroimaging studies implicate hypoactivity and poor connectivity in the LPFC and ACC as vulnerability factors for substance use initiation and progression to substance dependence (Perry, Joseph, Jiang, Zimmerman, Kelly, et al., 2011), Chronic substance use may further compromise functioning in these areas (Volkow, Fowler, & Wang, 2003) producing lasting deficits in inhibitory capacity (e.g., cognitive resources).

Demands for Inhibition and Cognitive Resource Depletion

Although the level of cognitive resources may function as an individual-difference variable, repeated demands for inhibition and self-restraint can lead to depletion of these resources, thereby increasing the likelihood of impulsive behavior (Gailliot & Baumeister, 2007). Specifically, each person's reserve of cognitive resources can be depleted over repeated instances of inhibition, making subsequent attempts at inhibition less successful (Muraven & Baumeister, 2000). Put another way, when resources are depleted, people are more likely to act according to their initial impulse, leading to greater impulsive behavior.

The effects of cognitive resource depletion can be observed across many domains of behavior, including eating junk food, drinking alcohol, smoking cigarettes, suppressing emotions, and persisting on demanding tasks (Baumeister, Bratslavsky, Muraven, & Tice, 1998; Muraven, Tice, & Baumeister, 1998; Baumeister et al., 2007). For instance, in one experiment, comparing chronic dieters to non-dieters, participants were seated either next to or far away from a candy bowl while they completed another task (Vohs & Heatherton, 2000). Later, all subjects were asked to complete a demanding cognitive task and were offered ice cream. Dieters who sat next to the candy bowl were less persistent on the cognitive challenge and ate more ice cream than non-dieters or dieters who sat far away from the candy. Presumably, dieters seated next to the candy faced the greatest goal conflict: the strongest urge (due to the proximity of the candy) and the strongest motivation to inhibit that urge (due to their dieting goal). Inhibiting the urge to eat the candy led to resource depletion and, eventually, more impulsive behavior. On the other hand, dieters who sat further from the candy did not experience a strong urge to eat it, and non-dieters had no motivation to inhibit the candy-eating urge; as a result, no inhibition was necessary, and these groups were more self-controlled on subsequent tasks.

In similar experiment (Muraven & Shmueli, 2006), social drinkers were either asked to smell, but not drink, their favorite alcoholic beverage, or smell, but not drink, water. They were then asked to complete a cognitive inhibition task and perform in a physical challenge. As in the previous paradigm, participants who smelled alcohol experienced an urge to drink it, which then had to be inhibited to conform to the experimenter's request. By expending cognitive resources in this domain, they were less able to inhibit urges during subsequent tasks that required inhibition. Because participants who smelled water did not experience a strong urge to drink water, they did not have to deploy resources to inhibit the urge, and did not exhibit decrements in performance on subsequent tasks that required self-control.

The phenomenon of resource depletion has been demonstrated repeatedly, across many forms of behavior, including aggression, overspending, sexual impulses, and careful decision-making (Vohs et al., 2005; Baumeister et al., 2007). Notably, performance on simple, straightforward tasks (e.g., simple arithmetic) does not suffer from the effects of cognitive resource depletion. The effects of cognitive resource depletion can be observed only during other tasks that specifically require inhibition of a response, whether this involves control of attention, regulation of emotion, reappraisal or restructuring of ideas or beliefs, or behavior.

The effects of resource depletion on behavior may be especially important for substance-using parents, because achieving and maintaining sobriety is highly demanding in terms of resources. Recovery involves making changes in every life area. People in recovery must overcome craving, which itself requires resources, but they must also modulate uncomfortable feelings (which previously may have been managed through substance use), seek support rather than "isolating," pursue new, healthy relationships, confront uncomfortable truths, and alter their routines. These activities demand that the person inhibit his initial responses and, instead, respond to triggers in a manner consistent with abstinence-related goals. These efforts are critical to the person's recovery, but are likely to deplete cognitive resources, which may make it more difficult to inhibit subsequent urges, including impulses to use drugs or alcohol. For instance, a parent who overcomes craving all day may have fewer resources available to inhibit irritable responses to her child's difficult behavior, or may be less able to resist a strong temptation or pressure to use.

Summary

There are numerous factors that may produce strong urges, as well as factors that moderate the effectiveness of inhibitory efforts. Reward sensitivity and negative affect are both associated with increased intensity of urges. Reward sensitivity may cause people to respond in extreme or excessive ways to reward, including substance use. Negative affect has a unique relationship with urge strength. The experience of negative affect signals a need for goal reprioritization and creates urges to address the source of dissatisfaction. In addition, negative affect may generate goals specifically focused on the reduction or avoidance of negative affect. In addition, people are at greater risk for impulsive behavior when their ability to inhibit impulses is compromised. Individuals with dispositionally low levels of cognitive resources are more likely than those with higher levels of cognitive resources to engage in a range of problematic behaviors. Furthermore, even individuals with high levels of cognitive resources may experience problems with inhibitory capacity when cognitive resources are depleted, which occurs after repeated efforts to inhibit impulses. Cognitive resource depletion weakens inhibitory control and therefore increases the likelihood of impulsive behavior.

■ **TREATMENT IMPLICATIONS**

Impulsive behavior takes many forms and may pose a serious threat to the health and well-being of parents and their children. The problem of impulsive behavior may be of particular concern when the parent is engaging in substance use. Despite clear theoretical and empirical links between impulsivity and substance use, current research on impulsive behavior has yet to be applied to intervention efforts for substance-using parents. Towards the development of a translational research approach, we suggest several general considerations that may be incorporated into existing interventions and may provide a useful starting point for understanding clients' difficulties with impulsive behavior.

Reward Sensitivity

Parents high in reward sensitivity are often characterized by enthusiasm, extraversion, and positive affectivity (Carver 2004; Gullo & Dawe, 2008). High reward sensitivity is also associated with greater parental sensitivity, warmth, and nurturance, and parents characterized by high reward sensitivity may be more likely to engage with their child emotionally and in play (Belsky et al., 1995; Desjardins et al., 2008). Although reward sensitivity may be an asset for some parents, reward sensitivity may also cause difficulties if the parent is distressed or dissatisfied in the parental role, as his attention turns to alternate sources of reinforcement (e.g., substance use) and he becomes neglectful. Prolonged substance use may also dysregulate the endogenous reward system that underlies reward processing (Leckman & Mayes, 1998). As a consequence, substance-using parents may not perceive non-substance reinforcers as enjoyable or rewarding, especially in the early stages of abstinence and recovery (Dackis & Gold, 1985; Adinoff, 2004). Engaging the parent in his parenting role is a critical challenge early in treatment. To this end, parenting interventions might seek to create positive, mutually rewarding experiences for the parent and child.

Addressing Negative Affect

Given the prominent relationship between negative affect and impulsive behavior, a clear target for intervention is helping parents reduce and manage negative affect, which may in turn help reduce emotion-focused impulsive behavior. There are many ways negative affect can be addressed, including addressing co-occurring affective psychopathology and helping clients respond more effectively to negative affect. One potential treatment target involves helping individuals manage extreme forms of negative affect related to psychopathology. Among substance users, rates of co-occurring mood and anxiety disorders are extremely high (Chen, Banducci, Guller, Macatee, Lavelle, et al., 2011), suggesting that substance-using parents may benefit from a comprehensive psychiatric evaluation and appropriate psychological and pharmacological treatment of psychiatric comorbidity. Of course, even clients without mood-related psychopathology will encounter stressors and experience negative affect throughout the process of recovery. In addition to addressing major sources of stress, clients are likely to benefit from learning to manage and respond adaptively to negative affect. Mindfulness-based interventions, which promote non-judgmental awareness of thoughts, urges, sensations, and emotions, appear to enhance emotion regulation and diminish emotion-focused impulsive behaviors such as substance use, self-harm, aggression, and binge eating, as well as avoidance behaviors characteristic of depression and anxiety (Hayes & Feldman, 2004; Bowen, Witkiewitz, Dillworth, & Marlatt, 2007; Linehan, Dimeff, Reynolds, Comtois, Welch, et al., 2002; Lynch, Chapman, Rosenthal, Kuo, & Linehan, 2006; Baer, 2003; Bishop, 2002; Singh, Lancioni, Winton, Adkins, Wahler, Sabaawi, & Singh, 2007). Addressing mood-related psychopathology and emotion regulation difficulties, either prior to or concurrently with parenting and substance use interventions, may facilitate parents' participation in all aspects of treatment and may decrease impulsive behavior.

Understanding Resource Depletion

Research on cognitive resource depletion has important implications for substance-using parents in the process of recovery. A fundamental assumption of many parenting interventions is that the client lacks a skill[1] or ability and must be fortified in some way to help them interact more effectively with their children. Whether parenting interventions target behavior management skills or relational quality, they generally encourage the parent to replace their typical way of relating to the child with new strategies. This process requires inhibition and is therefore demanding of cognitive resources. Likewise, managing craving (i.e., inhibiting the urge to use) also demands, and therefore depletes, cognitive resources. The fact that inhibiting urges in one domain makes later inhibitory efforts more difficult may mean that parents who are trying to manage urges in one domain may be less successful in their subsequent attempts to inhibit habitual patterns of behavior. For instance, newly abstinent parents who expend resources to manage craving may have fewer resources available to inhibit their typical way of responding to their children as they attempt to integrate new parenting skills.

---

1. We use the term "skill" very broadly to refer to many types of parenting behaviors, including practices taught in behavioral management training and those targeted by relationally focused interventions.

Cognitive resource depletion may diminish inhibitory capacity, and therefore increases the likelihood of impulsive behavior. However, research suggests that the adverse impact of cognitive resource depletion can be attenuated through automatization of behavior. Automatization is the process by which a new behavior is gradually learned, practiced, and reinforced until it becomes a standard response and no longer requires conscious choice or intention (Bargh & Ferguson, 2000). In other words, the habitual, dominant response (i.e., the urge) changes if the new behavior is more effective, on the whole, than the old behavior. When a positive behavior is automatized, cognitive resources are less critical because the new urge is compatible with longer-term goals, and therefore does not require inhibition or cognitive resources. After some time, the recovery/abstinence goal may eventually demand fewer cognitive resources, freeing up resources to devote to other goal-directed activities, such as the development of new parenting skills.

Along these lines, Fishbach and colleagues (2003) showed that chronic dieters automatically responded to potential dietary temptations by refocusing attention on their weight-loss goal. Because this process unfolded automatically, there was no toll on cognitive resources and no negative impact on attempts to inhibit subsequent urges. Similarly, it is expected that people in the early stages of recovery will encounter substance-related cues, experience craving, inhibit these urges through deployment of cognitive resources, and engage in another behavior that is more compatible with the abstinence goal (e.g., going to an Alcoholics Anonymous or Narcotics Anonymous meeting). Over time, the association between substance-related cues and the new behavior is strengthened, until it becomes the new habitual, automatic response to substance-related cues. Accordingly, the abstinence goal may demand many cognitive resources during early recovery, and increasingly few resources later in the process. Likewise, a parent who is learning new ways of interacting with and responding to her child may require relatively more resources to identify opportunities to use the new skill, inhibit the dominant behavior, and replace it with the new behavior; however, as the new behavior is reinforced, it will eventually become more automatic and habitual. Automatization has the benefit of increasing the likelihood of self-controlled behavior (i.e., because fewer resources are required, inhibition will be successful in a greater variety of situations) and freeing up cognitive resources to devote to other goals that require them.

A similar pattern should emerge as parents adopt new parenting behaviors. For example, one problematic parenting practice involves misattribution of the child's affective state, which may result in insensitive or hostile interactions with the child (Suchman et al., 2004; Sanders, Pidgeon, Gravestock, Connors, Brown, & Young, 2004; Iwaniec, 1997). Therefore, some parenting interventions aim to help parents make less hostile and more accurate attributions of their child's intent, a process that may involve a combination of psychoeducation, modeling, and cognitive restructuring. However, the complexity of this task and its corresponding demands on cognitive resources must be acknowledged. Given a long history of hostile attributions, the parent's automatic, habitual attribution of the child's behavior is likely to be similarly hostile. A more accurate interpretation of the child's intentions requires the parent to inhibit the first attribution and generate a new response, both of which demand cognitive resources. If the parent has few cognitive resources available to devote to this effort, this process is less likely to succeed, resulting in behavior that appears to be impulsive. That is, the parent's failure to use the new skill may be interpreted as a lack of commitment to improving his relationship with the child, but may actually reflect the effects of resource depletion—given the demands on the parent at that moment, it may have been extremely difficult to implement that skill. Fortunately, as the parent practices identifying and correcting inaccurate attributions, this process will become automatic and will require fewer and fewer resources. Eventually, the parent may begin to generate non-hostile attributions as an automatic response to the child's behavior.

The practical implications of this research have to do with the parent's and the clinician's understanding of the behavior-change process (Rothman, Baldwin, Hertel, & Fuglestad, 2010). Early attempts at a new behavior are predicted by people's confidence in their ability to perform a new behavior and their faith that the new behavior will improve their lives (Rothman & Salovey, 2007; Taylor & Gollwitzer, 1995). Thus, early in the intervention, treatment should focus on building optimism about the new skills and confidence in the parent's abilities to implement them. During this phase, the goal of performing the new behavior is important and salient, so the parent is likely to devote more cognitive resources to implementing the new skill. As soon as the parent reliably performs the new behavior, she shifts into the second stage, which involves continued use of the behavior. This stage is characterized by tension between the parent's motivation to perform the behavior and the reality of performing the new behavior (Rothman et al., 2010). The parent may find that the new behavior requires a great deal of effort, is difficult to incorporate in day-to-day life when there are other demands on her time and energy, or does not always work as expected. During this phase, the parent should be supported through the inevitable challenges and lapses into the old way of doing things. The behavior change is most likely to "stick" if the parent is able to maintain a sense of confidence and optimism about the new behavior, even if his experiences are at times disappointing and frustrating (Rothman et al., 2010). Finally, the third phase of behavior change, maintenance, is characterized by consistent, automatic use of the new behavior, which requires relatively few cognitive resources.

■ CONCLUSIONS

Impulsive behavior can take many forms, including parenting problems and substance use, yet the traits and circumstances that elicit impulsive behavior are largely consistent. In other words, the factors that predispose people to one form of impulsive behavior may confer risk for other forms of impulsive behavior. The chapter aimed to apply current theoretical and empirical accounts of impulsive behavior to better understand the parenting difficulties encountered by substance-using parents. To this end, we reviewed research on several factors that serve to increase, and in some cases, decrease the likelihood of impulsive behavior. In addition, we suggested some ways in which these variables may affect substance-using parents as they work toward abstinence, positive parenting, and stronger relationships with their children. Finally, we considered the implications of this work for understanding clients' parenting difficulties and mitigating their vulnerability to impulsive behavior in the course of parenting and/or substance use treatment.

We believe that the current framework represents a novel and compelling conceptualization of the challenges faced by substance-using parents. However, a clear limitation of this work is the absence of empirical data that directly links risk factors for impulsive behavior to parenting problems. Likewise, there is little clinical research to show that addressing (or accommodating) risk factors for impulsive behavior may improve outcomes for substance-using parents and their children. Continued work is clearly needed to understand the challenges faced by this vulnerable clinical population.

■ AUTHOR NOTE

This work was supported by R01 DA19405. The authors wish to thank Dr. Catalina Kopetz for her invaluable comments and suggestions.

■ REFERENCES

Adinoff, B. (2004). Neurobiological processes in drug reward and addiction. *Harvard Review of Psychiatry, 12*(6), 305–320.

Baer, R. A. (2003). Mindfulness training as a clinical intervention: A conceptual and empirical review. *Clinical Psychology, 10*(2), 125–143.

Bargh, J. A., & Ferguson, M. J. (2000). Beyond behaviorism: On the automaticity of higher mental processes. *Psychological Bulletin, 126*(6), 925–945.

Barnard, M., & McKeganey, N. (2004). The impact of parental problem drug use on children: what is the problem and what can be done to help? *Addiction, 99*(5), 552–559.

Barratt, E. S., & Patton, J. H. (1983). Impulsivity: Cognitive, behavioral and psychophysiological correlates. In M. Zuckerman (Ed.), *The Biological Basis of Sensation Seeking, Impulsivity and Anxiety* (pp. 77–116). Hillsdale, NJ: Erlbaum.

Baumeister, R. F. (2005). *The Cultural Animal: Human Nature, Meaning, and Social Life.* New York: Oxford University Press.

Baumeister, R. F., Bratslavsky, E., Muraven, M., Tice, D. M. (1998). Ego depletion: Is the active self a limited resource? *Journal of Personality and Social Psychology, 74*(5), 1252–1265.

Baumeister, R. F., Heatherton, T. F., Tice, D. M. (1994). *Losing Control: How and Why People Fail at Self-Regulation* (pp. xi, 307). San Diego, CA: Academic Press.

Baumeister, R. F., Vohs, K. D., & Tice, D. M. (2007). The strength model of self-control. *Current Directions in Psychological Science, 16*(6), 351–355.

Beauchaine, T. P., & Neuhaus, E. (2008). Impulsivity and vulnerability to psychopathology. In T. P. Beauchaine & S. P. Hinshaw (Eds.), *Child and Adolescent Psychopathology* (pp. 129–156). Hoboken, NJ: John Wiley & Sons.

Beauchaine, T. (2001). Vagal tone, development, and Gray's motivational theory: Toward an integrated model of autonomic nervous system functioning in psychopathology. *Development and Psychopathology, 13*(2), 183–214.

Belsky, J., Cmic, K., & Woodworth, S. (1995). Personality and parenting: Exploring the mediating role of transient mood and daily hassles. *Journal of Personality, 63,* 905–929.

Bensley, L. S., & Wu, R. (1991). The role of psychological reactance in drinking following alcohol prevention messages. *Journal of Applied Social Psychology, 21*(3), 1111–1124.

Bishop, S. R. (2002). What do we really know about mindfulness-based stress reduction? *Psychosomatic Medicine, 64*(1), 71–83.

Blum, K., Braverman, E. R., Holder, J. M., Lubar, J. F., Monastra, V. J., et al. (2000). Reward deficiency syndrome: A biogenetic model for the diagnosis and treatment of impulsive, addictive, and compulsive behaviors. *Journal of Psychoactive Drugs, 32,* 1–68.

Botvinick, M. M., Braver, T. S., Barch, D. M., Carter, C. S., & Cohen, J. D. (2001). Conflict monitoring and cognitive control. *Psychological Review, 108*(3), 624–652.

Bowen, S., Witkiewitz, K., Dillworth, T. M., & Marlatt, G. A. (2007). The role of thought suppression in the relationship between mindfulness meditation and alcohol use. *Addictive Behaviors, 32*(10), 2324–2328.

Bowirrat, A., & Oscar-Berman, M. (2005). Relationship between dopaminergic neurotransmission, alcoholism, and reward deficiency syndrome. *American Journal of Medical Genetics. Part B, Neuropsychiatric Genetics, 132,* 29–37.

Brinkmann, K., Schupbach, L., Joye, I. A., & Guido, H. E. (2009). Anhedonia and effort mobilization in dysphoria: Reduced cardiovascular response to reward and punishment. *International Journal of Psychophysiology, 74*(3), 250–258.

Cardinal, R. N., & Everitt, B. J. (2004). Neural and psychological mechanisms underlying appetitive learning: links to drug addiction. *Current opinion in neurobiology, 14*(2), 156–162.

Carver, C. S. (2003). Pleasure as a sign you can attend to something else: Placing positive feelings within a general model of affect. *Cognition and Emotion, 17,* 241–261.

Carver, C. S. (2004). Negative affects deriving from the behavioral approach system. *Emotion, 4,* 3–22.

Carver, C. S., & Scheier, M. F. (2010). Self-regulation of action and affect. In R. F. Baumeister & K. D. Vohs (Eds.), *Handbook of Self-Regulation: Research, Theory and Applications* (pp. 3–21). New York: Guilford Press.

Chang, L., Schwartz, D., Dodge, K. A., & McBride-Chang, C. (2003). Harsh parenting in relation to child emotion regulation and aggression. *Journal of Family Psychology, 17*(4), 598–606.

Chen, K. W., Banducci, A. N., Guller, L., Macatee, R. J., Lavelle, A., Daughters, S. B., & Lejuez, C. W. (2011). An examination of psychiatric comorbidities as a function of gender and substance type within an inpatient substance use treatment program. *Drug and Alcohol Dependence, 118*(2–3), 92–99.

Clark, L. A., Kochanska, G., & Ready, R. (2000). Mothers' personality and its interaction with child temperament as predictors of parenting behavior. *Journal of Personality and Social Psychology, 79,* 274–285.

Collins, R. L., & Lapp, W. M. (1992). The temptation and restraint inventory for measuring drinking restraint. *British Journal of Addiction, 87,* 625–633.

Corwin, R. L., & Hajnal, A. (2005). Too much of a good thing: Neurobiology of non-homeostatic eating and drug abuse. *Physiology & Behavior, 86,* 5–8.

Coyne, R. K., & Clack, J. R. (1981). *Environmental Assessment and Design: A New Tool for the Applied Behavioral Scientist.* New York: Praeger. Dackis & Gold.

Dawe, S., & Loxton, N. J. (2004). The role of impulsivity in the development of substance use and eating disorders. *Neuroscience and Biobehavioral Reviews, 28*, 343–351.

Depue, R. A., Collins, P. F. (1999). Neurobiology of the structure of personality: Dopamine, facilitation of incentive motivation, and extraversion. *Behavioral and Brain Sciences, 22*(3), 491–517.

Dackis, C. A., & Gold, M. S. (1985). New concepts in cocaine addiction: the dopamine depletion hypothesis. *Neuroscience & Biobehavioral Reviews, 9*(3), 469–477.

Depue, R. A. (1995). Neurobiological factors in personality and depression. *European Journal of Personality, 9*, 413–439.

Desjardins, J., Zelenski, J. M., & Coplan, R. J. (2008). An investigation of maternal personality, parenting styles, and subjective well-being. *Personality and Individual Differences, 44*, 587–597.

De Wit, H. (2008). Impulsivity as a determinant and consequence of drug use: a review of underlying processes. *Addiction Biology, 14*(1), 22–31.

DeYoung, C. G. (2010). Impulsivity as a personality trait. In R. F. Baumeister & K. D. Vohs (Eds.), *Handbook of Self-Regulation: Research, Theory and Applications* (pp. 3–21). New York: Guilford Press.

Dickman, S. J. (1990). Functional and dysfunctional impulsivity: personality and cognitive correlates. *Journal of Personality and Social Psychology, 58*, 95–102.

Evenden, J. L. (1999). Varieties of impulsivity. *Psychopharmacology, 146*(4), 348–361.

Feehan, M., McGee, R., Stanton, W. R., & Silva, P. A. (1991). Strict and inconsistent discipline in childhood: Consequences for adolescent mental health. *British Journal of Clinical Psychology, 30*(4), 325–331.

Finkel, E. J., & Campbell, W. K. (2001). Self-control and accommodation in close relationships: An interdependence analysis. *Journal of Personality and Social Psychology, 81*(2), 263–277.

Fishbach, A., Friedman, R. S., & Kruglanski, A. W. (2003). Leading us not unto temptation: Momentary allurements elicit overriding goal activation. *Journal of Personality and Social Psychology, 84*, 296–309.

Fishbach, A., & Trope, Y. (2005). The substitutability of external control and self-control. *Journal of Experimental and Social Psychology, 41*(3), 256–270.

Franken, I. H. A. (2002). Behavioral approach system (BAS) sensitivity predicts alcohol craving. *Personality and Individual Differences, 32*, 349–355.

Franken, I. H. A., & Muris, P. (2006). Gray's impulsivity dimension: A distinction between reward sensitivity versus rash impulsiveness. *Personality and Individual Differences, 40*, 1337–1347.

Friedel, R. O. (2004). Dopamine dysfunction in borderline personality disorder: A hypothesis. *Neuropsychopharmacology, 29*(6), 1029–1039.

Gailliot, M. T., & Baumeister, R. F. (2007). Self-regulation and sexual restraint: Dispositionally and temporarily poor self-regulatory abilities contribute to failures at restraining sexual behavior. *Personality and Social Psychology Bulletin, 33*(2), 173–186.

Gullo, M. J., & Dawe, S. (2008). Impulsivity and adolescent substance use: Rashly dismissed as "all bad?" *Neuroscience and Biobehavioral Reviews, 32*, 1507–1518.

Hayes, A. M., & Feldman, G. (2004). Clarifying the construct of mindfulness in the context of emotion regulation and the process of change in therapy. *Clinical Psychology, 11*(3), 255–262.

Heatherton, T. F., & Wagner, D. D. (2011). Cognitive neuroscience of self-regulation failure. *Trends in Cognitive Sciences, 15*(3), 132–139.

Hinshaw, S. P., Owens, E. B., Wells, K. C., Kraemer, H. C., Abikoff, H. B., et al. (2000). Family processes and treatment outcome in the MTA: Negative/ineffective parenting practices in relation to multimodal treatment. *Journal of Abnormal Child Psychology, 28*(6), 555–568.

Iwaniec, D. (1997). Evaluating parent training for emotionally abusive and neglectful parents: Comparing individual versus individual and group intervention. *Research on Social Work Practice, 7*(3), 329–349.

Jentsch, J. D., & Taylor, J. R. (1999). Impulsivity resulting from frontostriatal dysfunction in drug abuse: Implications for the control of behavior by reward-related stimuli. *Psychopharmacology, 146*, 373–390.

Johnson, P. M., & Kenny, P. J. (2010). Dopamine D2 receptors in addiction-like reward dysfunction and compulsive eating in obese rats. *Nature Neuroscience, 13*, 635–641.

Koole, S. L., & Rothermund, K. (2011). "I feel better but I don't know why": The psychology of implicit emotion regulation. *Cognition and Emotion, 25*(3), 389–399.

Kumpfer, K. L., & Alvarado, R. (1998). *Effective Family Strengthening Interventions. Juvenile Justice Bulletin Family Strengthening Series.* Washington, DC: U.S. Department of Justice, Office of Justice Programs, Office of Juvenile Justice and Delinquency Prevention.

Lazarus, R. S., & Launier, R. (1978). Stress-related transactions between persons and environment. In L. A. Pervin & M. Lewis (Eds.), *Perspectives in interactional psychology* (pp. 287–327). New York: Plenum.

Leckman, J. F., & Mayes, L. C. (1998). Understanding developmental psychopathology: How useful are evolutionary accounts? *Child and Adolescent Psychiatry, 37*, 1011–1020.

Liberman, N., & Trope, Y. (2002). The role of feasibility and desirability considerations in near and distant future decisions: A test of temporal construal theory. *Journal of Personality and Social Psychology, 75*(1), 5–18.

Linehan, M. M., Dimeff, L. A., Reynolds, S. K., Comtois, K. A., Welch, S. S., Heagerty, P., & Kivlahan, D. R. (2002). Dialectical behavior therapy versus comprehensive validation therapy plus 12-Step for the treatment of opioid dependent women meeting criteria for borderline personality disorder. *Drug and Alcohol Dependence, 67*(1), 13–26.

Lynch, T. R., Chapman, A. L., Rosenthal, M. Z., Kuo, J. R., & Linehan, M. M. (2006). Mechanisms of change in dialectical behavior therapy: Theoretical and empirical observations. *Journal of Clinical Psychology, 62*(4), 459–480.

Magen, E., & Gross, J. J. (2010). The cybernetic process model of self-control. Situation- and person-specific considerations. In R. H. Hoyle (Ed.), *Handbook of Personality And Self-Regulation* (pp. 353–374). Oxford, UK: Blackwell Publishing, Ltd.

Miller, E. K., & Cohen, J. D. (2001). An integrative theory of prefrontal cortex function. *Annual Review of Neuroscience, 24*, 167–202.

Moeller, F. G., Barratt, E. S., Dougherty, D. M., Schmitz, J. M., & Swann, A. C. (2001). Psychiatric aspects of impulsivity. *American Journal of Psychiatry, 158*, 1783–1793.

Muraven, M., & Baumeister, R. F. (2000). Self-regulation and depletion of limited resources: Does self-control resemble a muscle? *Psychological Bulletin, 126*(2), 247–259.

Muraven, M., & Shmueli, D. (2006). The self-control costs of fighting the temptation to drink. *Psychology of Addictive Behaviors, 20*(2), 154–160.

Muraven, M., Tice, D. M., & Baumeister, R. F. (1998). Self-control as limited resource: Regulatory depletion patterns. *Journal of Personality and Social Psychology, 74*(3), 774–789.

Noble, E. P. (2000). Addiction and its reward process through polymorphisms of the D2 dopamine receptor gene: a review. *European Psychiatry, 15*(2), 79–89.

O'Connor, M. J., Sigman, M., & Kasari, C. (1992). Attachment behavior of infants exposed prenatally to alcohol: Mediating effects of infant affect and mother–infant interaction. *Development and Psychopathology, 4*, 243–256.

O'Connor, M. J., Sigman, M., & Kasari, C. (1993). Interactional model for the association among maternal alcohol use, mother-infant interaction, and infant cognitive development. *Infant Behavior and Development, 16*(2), 177.

Perry, J. L., Joseph, J. E., Jiang, Y., Zimmerman, R. S., Kelly, T. H., et al. (2011). Prefrontal cortex and drug abuse vulnerability: Translation to prevention and treatment interventions. *Brain Research Reviews, 65*(2), 124–149.

Powers, W. T. (1973). *Behavior: The Control of Perception.* Chicago: Aldine.

Rachlin, H., & Raineri, A. (1992). Irrationality, impulsiveness and selfishness as discount reversal effects. In G. Loewenstein & J. Elster (Eds.), *Choice Over Time* (pp. 93–118). New York: Russell Sage Foundation.

Rachlin, H., Raineri, A. & Cross, D. (1991). Subjective delay and probability. *Journal of the Experimental Analysis of Behavior, 55*(2), 233–244.

Ridderinkhof, K. R., Ullsperger, M., Crone, E. A., & Nieuwenhuis, S. (2004). The role of the medial frontal cortex in cognitive control. *Science, 5695*, 443–446.

Robinson, T. E., & Berridge, K. C. (2008). The incentive sensitization theory of addiction: some current issues. *Philosophical Transactions of the Royal Society of Biological Sciences, 363*(1507), 3137–3146.

Ross, L. T., & Gill, J. L. (2002). Eating disorders: Relations with inconsistent discipline, anxiety and drinking among college women. *Psychological Reports, 91*, 289–298.

Rothman, A. J., Baldwin, A. S., Hertel, A. W., Fuglestad, P. T. (2010). Self-regulation and behavior change: Disentangling behavioral initiation and behavioral maintenance. In R. F. Baumeister & K. D. Vohs (Eds.), *Handbook of Self-Regulation: Research, Theory, and Applications* (pp. 106–124). New York: Guilford Press.

Rothman, A. J., & Salovey, P. (2007). The reciprocal relation between principles and practice: Social psychology and health behavior. In A. W. Kruglanski & T. E. Higgins (Eds.), *Social Psychology: Handbook of Basic Principles* (2nd ed., pp. 826–849). New York: Guilford Press.

Sanders, M. R., Pidgeon, A. M., Gravestock, F., Connors, M. D., Brown, S. & Young, R. W. (2004). Does parental attributional retraining and anger management enhance the effects of the triple p-positive parenting program with parents at risk of child maltreatment? *Behavior Therapy, 35*(3), 513–536.

Sanders, M. R. (1999). Triple p-positive parenting program: Towards an empirically validated multilevel parenting and family support strategy for the prevention of behavior and emotional problems in children. *Clinical Child and Family Psychology Review, 2*(2), 71–90.

Shah, J. Y., & Kruglanski, A. W. (2008). Structural dynamics: The challenge of change in goal systems. In J. Y. Shah & W. L. Gardner (Eds.), *Handbook of Motivation Science* (pp. 217–234). New York: Guilford Press.

Shallice, T. I. M., & Burgess, P. W. (1991). Deficits in strategy application following frontal lobe damage in man. *Brain, 114*(2), 727–741.

Shoda, Y., Mischel, W. & Peake, P. K. (1990). Predicting adolescent cognitive and self-regulatory competencies from preschool delay of gratification: Identifying diagnostic conditions. *Developmental Psychopathology, 26,* 978–986.

Singh, N. N., Lancioni, G. E., Winton, A. S. W., Adkins, A. D., Wahler, R. G., Sabaawi, M., & Singh, J. (2007). Individuals with mental illness can control their aggressive behavior through mindfulness training. *Behavior Modification, 31*(3), 313–328.

Spear, L. (2000). Modeling adolescent development and alcohol use in animals. *Alcohol Research and Health, 24*(2), 115–123.

Spoont, M. R. (1992). Modulatory role of serotonin in neural information processing: implications for human psychopathology. *Psychological Bulletin, 112*(330), 50.

Stice, E., Spoor, S., Bohon, C., & Small, D. M. (2008). Relation between obesity and blunted striatal response to food is moderated by *TaqIA* A1 allele. *Science, 322*(5900), 449–452.

Stuettgen, M. C., Hennig, J., Reuter, M., & Netter, P. (2005). Novelty seeking but not BAS is associated with high dopamine as indicated by a neurotransmitter challenge test using mazindol as a challenge substance. *Personality and Individual Differences, 38*(7), 1597–1608.

Suchman, N. E., Mayes, L., Conti, J., Slade, A., & Rounsaville, B. (2004). Rethinking parenting interventions for drug dependent mothers: From behavior management to fostering emotional bonds. *Journal of Substance Abuse Treatment, 27,* 179–185.

Suchman, N. E., McMahon, T. J., Zhang, H., Mayes, L. C., & Luthar, S. (2006). Substance-abusing mothers and disruptions in child custody: An attachment perspective. *Journal of Substance Abuse Treatment, 30,* 197–204.

Tangney, J. P., Baumeister, R. F., & Boone, A. L. (2004). High self-control predicts good adjustment, less pathology, better grades, and interpersonal success. *Journal of Personality, 72,* 271–322.

Taylor, S. E., & Gollwitzer, P. M. (1995). Effects of mindset on positive illusions. *Journal of Personality and Social Psychology, 69*(2), 213.

Tice, D. M., Bratslavsky, E., & Baumeister, R. F. (2001). Emotional distress regulation takes precedence over impulse control: If you feel bad, do it! *Journal of Personality and Social Psychology, 80*(1), 53–67.

Trope, Y., & Liberman, N. (2000). Temporal construal. *Psychological Review, 110*(3), 403–421.

Vendrell, P., Junque, C., Pujol, J., & Jurado, M. A. (1995). The role of prefrontal regions in the Stroop task. *Neuropsychologica, 33*(3), 341.

Verdejo-Garcia, A., Lawrence, A. J., & Clark, L. (2008). Impulsivity as a vulnerability marker for substance-use disorders: Review of findings from high-risk research, problem gamblers and genetic association studies. *Neuroscience and Biobehavioral Reviews, 32,* 777–810.

Vohs, K. D., Heatherton, T. F. (2000). Self-regulatory failure: A resource-depletion approach. *Psychological Science, 11*(3), 249–254.

Vohs, K. D., & Faber, R. J. (2004). To buy or not to buy? Self-control and self-regulatory failure in purchase behavior. In R. F. Baumeister & K. D. Vohs (Eds.), *Handbook of Self- Regulation: Research, Theory, and Applications* (pp. 509–524). New York: Guilford Press.

Vohs, K. D., Baumeister, R. F., & Ciarocco, N. J. (2005). Self-regulation and self-presenta-tion: Regulatory resource depletion impairs impression management and effortful self-presentation depletes regulatory resources. *Journal of Personality and Social Psychology*, *88*, 632–657.

Volkow, N. D., Fowler, J. S., & Wang, G. J. (2003). The addicted human brain: Insights from imaging studies. *Journal of Clinical Investigation*, *111*(10), 1444–1452.

Weiss, M. (2000). ADHD in parents. *Journal of the American Academy of Child & Adolescent Psychiatry*, *39*, 1059–1061.

Whiteside, S., & Lynam, D. (2001). The Five Factor Model and impulsivity: Using a structural model of personality to understand impulsivity. *Personality and Individual Differences*, *30*(4), 669–689.

Zald, D. H., & Depue, R. A. (2001). Serotonergic functioning correlates with positive and negative affect in psychiatrically healthy males. *Personality and Individual Differences*, *30*, 71–86.

4 Behavioral Genetic Perspectives on Substance Abuse and Parenting

CHARLES BEEKMAN AND
JENAE M. NEIDERHISER

Understanding the intergenerational transmission of drug abuse has been the focus of an enormous body of research. Based on existing literature in this and related areas, there are at least three ways this transmission may operate: 1) via *genetic transmission*; 2) via *disruption of parenting and family processes*; and 3) via *prenatal drug exposure*. This chapter will consider these three possible transmission mechanisms, and their possible interrelatedness, through a review of the literature for each of the possible mechanisms, with a focus on the implications for child development. The importance of understanding and accounting for genetic influences is highlighted in regard to studies examining the effects of prenatal exposure to drugs on child development. The final section of the chapter describes a number of novel strategies for disentangling genetic influences from prenatal exposure to drugs and the role of parenting and family environments.

■ GENETIC AND ENVIRONMENTAL INFLUENCES ON DRUG USE AND ABUSE

The importance of genetic influences for drug, alcohol, and tobacco use and abuse has been indicated through family, twin, sibling, and adoption studies and, more recently, through studies of specific genes. The most common design for disentangling genetic and environmental influences on behavior, including drug use behaviors, is the twin design. Twin studies are a natural experiment that capitalizes on the fact that monozygotic (MZ; "identical") twins share 100 percent[1] of their genes, while dizygotic (DZ; "fraternal") twins share 50 percent, on average, of their segregating genes.[2] Genetic influences on drug abuse, for example, can be estimated by comparing the extent to which MZ twins are similar for drug abuse

---

1. *Because of epigenetic influences—environmental factors that impact gene expression—MZ twins may be less than 100 percent genetically identical. Recent reports have found that there are more epigenetic differences in DZ twins than MZ twins, thus the logic of the twin method remains the same (Kaminsky et al., 2009).*

2. Approximately 85 percent of genes are shared between mice and humans, and 96 percent between humans and chimpanzees. Within human populations, only 0.1 percent of our genes vary, or are "segregating." It is this one-tenth of one percent that accounts for the vast number of genetically influenced differences in people.

with the extent to which DZ twins are similar. If MZ twins are twice as (or more) similar as DZ twins or full siblings, then there is evidence for genetic influences. These models also provide estimates of the extent to which the shared environment (nongenetic influences that make siblings similar) and non-shared environment (nongenetic influences that are uncorrelated for family members, also including measurement error) influence drug use and abuse. Thus, through the use of twin studies, important information about genetic *and* environmental influences can be obtained, including a clarification of which types of environmental influences are operating.

Genetic contributions to many drug and alcohol use and abuse disorders are substantial, with genetic influence explaining as much as 70 percent of the total variance (Lynskey, Agrawal, & Heath, 2010; Kendler, Myers, & Prescott, 2007; Kendler et al., 2003). These findings have led to three interrelated questions about how genetic and environmental factors contribute to drug use behaviors. First: To what extent are genetic influences on the use and abuse of specific drugs distinct from, and to what extent do they overlap with, environmental influences? Second, and relatedly: Are the same genetic and environmental influences responsible for the initiation of use as well as the continued use and abuse of and dependence on drugs and alcohol? Third: How do specific shared and non-shared environmental influences affect the development of substance use and abuse, and where does rearing environment fall in this categorization? Answers to these questions can directly inform drug prevention and intervention efforts by identifying commonalities in the etiologies of drug use and abuse and environments that may be appropriate targets for preventive interventions. In addition, by taking a developmental approach to work in this area—both the individual development and progression of drug use—the timing of interventions for optimal effectiveness may be clarified.

Common and Specific Genetic Influences

Do children whose parents abuse drugs inherit a genetic risk for drug use and abuse in general, or are there unique genetic influences for use and abuse of specific types of drugs? A growing body of literature points to both: a common genetic influence for drug abuse as well as specific genetic influences for specific drugs or classes of drugs. Merikangas and colleagues (1998) found that there was an eightfold increase in the risk for having any drug disorder for the first-degree relatives of drug-dependent individuals, suggesting a general inherited risk for drug abuse and dependence. In the same study, there was also evidence for genetic influences on the abuse of specific drug classes across generations, suggesting separate genetic influences for specific drugs (Merikangas et al., 1998). Similarly, findings from a large population-based twin study estimated that the abuse of any type of drug increased the probability of abusing all other categories of drugs, suggesting a common drug genetic risk factor, with each drug category (except psychedelics) also showing unique genetic influences (Tsuang, et al., 1998). More recently, Kendler and colleagues (2007) found that two distinct, yet highly related, genetic factors (one for illicit and one for licit drugs) were required to best explain genetic influences on drug dependence, and that caffeine and nicotine had significant drug-specific genetic effects. A meta-analysis of genetically informed studies of adolescent drug use and abuse supported the findings reported above, with evidence for both common genetic influences across different drugs and specific genetic and environmental influences, depending on the drug of interest (Hopfer et al., 2003). Additional research has, in general, supported the existence of common genetic influences for drug abuse, along with smaller, inconsistent, specific genetic effects for individual drugs (Fu et al., 2002; Kendler et al., 2003). There is also evidence for common shared and non-shared environmental influences on illicit drug use in men, indicating that, at least for men's use of illicit drugs, the effects of the environment are not specific to the type of illicit drug use, although there are also specific non-shared environmental influences (Kendler et al., 2003). In other words, the inherited risk for drug use and abuse is, at least in part, not specific to the type or class of drug, although there are also drug-specific genetic and environmental influences.

The extent of environmental and genetic influences that are common to multiple drugs may also depend on developmental timing, with genetic influences increasing in magnitude as children move from adolescence to young and middle adulthood (Kendler et al., 2008). Specifically, the associations among the use of different drugs were explained more by shared environmental influences during adolescence, but more by genetic influences in middle adulthood. In a sample of adolescent twins, tobacco use was more heritable than illicit drug use, with significant and substantial shared environmental influences for both (McGue et al., 2000). The authors interpreted these findings to indicate that the availability of the drug is likely to have an impact on whether or not genetically influenced tendencies to use it are activated. Heritability of illicit drug use has been shown to be comparable to that reported for tobacco use in samples of adults (see, e.g., Kendler, Karkowski, Neale, & Prescott, 2000; Kendler et al., 2007; Kendler, Thornton, & Pedersen, 2000) which lends some support to this interpretation. Although the difference in genetic influences on tobacco and illicit drug use for adolescents and adults may not be a true developmental effect, but rather an artifact of availability that is age-related, this is another clear indication of the complexities facing drug-abuse researchers. There are probably developmental differences in genetic and environmental influences on drug use and dependence such that the magnitude of influences may be different, depending on where in the time course of development is of interest.

Taken together, these findings support a significant and surprisingly consistent pattern of genetic and environmental influences on risk for drug use and abuse. Specifically, there are both general and drug-specific genetic influences, while shared environmental influences tend to be more general for drug use and dependence. Non-shared environmental influences, on the other hand, also tend to have both general and drug-specific influences on drug use. The developmental, or at least age-related, differences in genetic and environmental influences on drug use that have been found highlight that genetic influences are not static, and also suggest particular opportunities for interrupting a trajectory towards continued drug use and dependence. During adolescence, when shared environmental influences are greater, the possibility of preventing the progression from initiation to dependence is greater. More focused work in this area is described in the next section, below.

Genetic and Environmental Influences on Initiation of Drug Use, Continued Use, and Dependence

Another important question facing drug abuse researchers is whether the same genetic influences are responsible for both the initiation of use and the continued use and abuse of drugs, including alcohol and tobacco. These questions have been addressed primarily in the smoking literature, as smoking initiation and nicotine dependence have been well studied within a genetic framework (Heath et al., 2002). Genetic and shared environmental factors are both important for smoking initiation, while primarily genetic and non-shared environmental influences contribute to nicotine dependence (Hardie et al., 2006; Madden et al., 2004; Rhee et al., 2003; Vink et al., 2005), cessation (Morley et al., 2007), and smoking during pregnancy (Agrawal et al., 2008). The biggest difference, then, in genetic and environmental influences on initiation and continuing to dependence in smoking is in environmental influences. Specifically, shared environmental influences, which may include siblings' initiating smoking together, influence initiation but are not important in explaining individual differences in nicotine dependence. Additional studies have found that the covariation between smoking initiation and dependence is due to common genetic influences, but shared environmental influences are significant only for initiation, not dependence (Kendler et al., 1999; Maes et al., 2004). In other words, parents who smoke in the home may increase the chances that their children try cigarettes, but genetic influences may be the primary factor affecting smoking persistence and dependence.

Fewer studies have examined the distinction between initiation and dependence for other drugs. Genetic and environmental influences on the stage of use (initiation, occasional use, regular use, and disordered use) may depend on the drug being studied and the stage of use that is of interest (Tsuang et al., 1999). For example, a review of genetically informative research on cannabis use and dependence suggested there may be specific genetic influences for use, abuse, and dependence (Agrawal & Lynskey, 2006). Some studies have found evidence for distinct patterns of influence for certain drugs, or certain stages of use. In a study of adult twins, genetic, shared and non-shared environmental factors were associated with the initiation of use of cannabis or stimulants, but only non-shared environmental factors contributed to subsequent abuse of either (Kendler et al., 1999). Shared environmental influences may be strongest for the *early* use of alcohol, nicotine, and cannabis, while genes may more significantly influence levels of use later in life (Kendler, Schmitt, Aggen, & Prescott, 2008). A study of serious alcohol problems found that shared environmental influences were the most impactful in the initiation of alcohol use, although genetic influences best explained actual alcohol problems in young adulthood (Pagan et al., 2006). Two meta-analyses and a large-scale twin study of adolescent drug initiation and continued use and abuse of drugs suggest that, overall, findings are consistent with those regarding smoking initiation and nicotine dependence that were presented above. Specifically, while genetic and shared environmental factors are important for initiation of drug use, genetic factors account for more variance in any continued use and abuse of drugs (Hopfer et al., 2003; Rhee et al., 2003).

A handful of studies have sought to understand the shared environmental influences on early substance use, with a particular focus on environmental risk factors within and outside the family. Low levels of environmental risk (peers, school, family conflict) were found to buffer the effects of high familial risk (biological parents' substance-related diagnosis), while familial risk became prominent when environmental risk was also high (Legrand, McGue, & Iacono, 1999). A second report from the same research group found that a majority of the variance in early substance use could be explained by variance shared between parent–child relationship problems and peer deviance, with additional variance accounted for by peer deviance alone (Walden et al., 2004). As the overlap among these three constructs was due entirely to shared environmental influences, these findings indicate that a majority of the shared environmental influences on early substance use can be explained by peer deviance and parent–child relationship problems, at least in this sample of 14-year-old twins.

Taken together, the literature on initiation, use, and abuse of drugs suggests that shared environmental factors, like availability and acceptance of drugs in the home and/or deviant peer influence, may play a large role in initial use of drugs by children. Continued use and drug abuse problems later in life may be more strongly influenced by genes. These findings highlight the importance of focusing on the rearing environment as an important domain for interventions, as aspects of that environment may serve as important risk or protective factors for initial drug use.

■ SUMMARY

These findings underscore the importance of genetic influences on the intergenerational transmission of drug use and abuse problems. At the same time, genetically informative studies on drug abuse often show modest to moderate influences for both the shared and non-shared environment, underscoring the importance of the environment and helping to clarify the type of environmental influences likely to be operating. The bulk of evidence on the differing etiologies of initiation and abuse of drugs and alcohol converges on a developmental pathway that can directly inform prevention and intervention efforts; common environmental influences may be more important for initiation of use, whereas genetic influences may contribute more to continued abuse and dependence. These findings suggest drug abuse interventions aimed at curbing drug use initiation should be targeted in aspects of the environment that can act to make children in a family more similar (e.g., siblings, neighborhood factors, availability and acceptance of drugs in the home). A critical next step in genetically informative studies of drug abuse is to clarify further the specific shared and non-shared environmental influences on child development, especially in regard to the development of drug use and abuse. The rearing environment within a household with a drug-abusing parent provides an example of the second possible mechanism for the intergenerational transmission of drug abuse: disruption of parenting and family processes.

■ DRUG ABUSE AND FAMILY DISRUPTION

A sizable literature shows that, in families in which one or both parents are using drugs, family process (e.g., parent–child interactions, marital and partner relationships, general family climate) is often disrupted. Parental drug abuse has been associated with an increased risk for child maltreatment, especially if both parents are abusing drugs (Walsh, MacMillan, & Jamieson, 2003). Young adult children of an alcohol-dependent parent are more likely to be heavy drinkers and show more symptoms of alcohol dependence, with the most important predictive factors being exposure to parental alcoholism, abusive punishment, and psychological symptoms in the parent (Hill, Nord, & Blow, 1992). In a study of families who had previous cases with child protective services, drug abuse by parents was directly predictive of subsequent child protective service reports' being filed, and it also predicted future reports *through* the negative impact drug abuse had on family functioning (Wolock & Magura, 1996). These findings highlight how drug abuse in the family can lead to adverse outcomes both directly and indirectly, through family disruption.

The disruptive impact of an alcoholic father is evident as early as infancy, and has been associated with lower levels of effortful control in young children (Eiden, Edwards, & Leonard, 2004). Paternal alcoholism is also related to lower levels of maternal warmth with the child, poorer marital attachment, and poorer quality of infant attachment to both mother and father, independent of mothers' own alcohol use and depression (e.g., Edwards, Eiden, & Leonard, 2004; Eiden, Edwards, & Leonard, 2002; Eiden et al., 2004; Keller et al., 2005). Longitudinal analysis of the links between parent behavior and infant behavior from 12 to 24 months indicates that fathers with alcohol problems and their spouses behaved more negatively when their child was one year old, and had less positive involvement with their child at age two (Eiden et al., 2004). Eiden, Edwards, and Leonard (2007) provided evidence that highlights a possible pathway for the development of child externalizing problems in children of parents with alcohol problems. Paternal alcohol diagnosis when children were one year old was linked with poorer parenting (e.g., less warmth and sensitivity) at 18 months. Increases in poorer parenting were associated with lower levels of self-regulation when children were three years of age, and poorer self-regulation was linked with increases in externalizing behavior problems and poorer social competence outcomes in kindergarten (Eiden, Edwards, & Leonard, 2007; Eiden, Colder, Edwards, & Leonard, 2009). This set of findings shows, in the same sample, a developmental progression where paternal alcohol problems when a child is an infant may operate to disrupt parenting practices and, through those disruptions, negatively affect subsequent child development. In sum, there is clear evidence that alcohol problems within a family can negatively affect family functioning on a variety of levels, and that these disruptions may mediate the association between parental alcohol problems and maladaptive child functioning.

Fewer studies have examined the effects of parental drug use on family functioning and subsequent associations with child outcomes. Children of drug-abusing fathers were found to have more internalizing and externalizing problems at ages eight to twelve, compared to children with non-drug-abusing fathers. This association was mediated by increases in parental conflict and parenting dysfunction, which were associated with paternal drug abuse (Fals-Stewart, Kelley, et al., 2004). Similarly, a study of cocaine- and opiate-dependent parents showed that unhealthy family functioning and parental social problems were predictive of child internalizing and externalizing symptoms. Drug-dependent mothers in those families indirectly influenced increases in child problems through their association with more family problems and higher levels of dysfunction (Stanger et al., 2002). Drug abuse by parents can pervasively impact child development by creating a maladaptive rearing environment for their children. Consistent with the literature on parents with alcohol problems, family disruptions are often marked by increased conflict and dysfunction, and these disruptions are often association with maladaptive child developmental outcomes.

■ PARENTING RESPONSES TO CHILD BEHAVIOR

There are several factors that may impair a drug-using parent's ability to respond appropriately to his or her child. For example, one study showed that drug-using mothers tended to lack vital, basic parenting information, which may then lead to their inability to respond appropriately to their child (Velez et al., 2004). Cocaine-using mothers may also experience their interactions with their children differently. One study found that cocaine-using mothers were less attentive and created more interruptions in their interactions with their young infants than non-drug-using mothers (Mayes et al., 1997).

Drug use by parents may also affect the way parents respond to their children in certain developmental contexts. For example, in one study, maternal drug use was related to unresponsive and negative parenting during middle childhood, and drug-dependent women had more problems than mothers without drug dependence in responding appropriately to their children on tasks requiring interpersonal connection, coordination, and attunement (Hans, Bernstein, & Henson, 1999). In a second study, mothers who were using cocaine used harsher parenting practices, and their children faced increased environmental risks, such as more frequent changes in primary caregivers and less frequent contact with male caregivers (Eiden, Peterson, & Coleman, 1999). Similarly, in other studies, mothers using cocaine responded less sensitively to children at one, six, and 18 months, and infants were more likely to have a disorganized/disoriented attachment (Espinosa et al., 2001; Molitor, Mayes, & Ward, 2003; Swanson, Beckwith, & Howard, 2000). Interestingly, in another study, mothers who were using cocaine also responded less sensitively when they rated their infants as being more reactive (Eiden, Schuetze, & Coles, 2011), suggesting that cocaine use by mothers may be associated with poorer parenting when appropriate responses are needed most.

■ GENETIC INFLUENCES ON PARENTING

Until fairly recently, parenting behaviors have been almost exclusively considered to be environmental influences in the direction from the parent to the child (e.g., Maccoby, 1992; Collins, Maccoby, Steinberg, Hetherington, & Bornstein, 2000; but see Bell, 1968, for an exception). Over the past few decades, genetically informative studies have shown that parenting behaviors, and their associations with child development, are also due to genetic influences (Deater-Deckard, 2000; McGue, Elkins, Walden, & Iacono, 2005; Neiderhiser et al., 2004; Neiderhiser et al., 2007; Plomin & Bergman, 1991; Rowe, 1994; Pike et al., 1996). When parents in a family are abusing drugs, there is a potential for extensive disruption of family processes and relationships, and genetic influences on parenting are likely to be associated with drug abuse in one of two ways: First, genetic influences on the development of drug use and related behaviors in children may also influence parenting behavior. For example, a harsher or more punitive parenting style may be due, in part, to the same genetic influences that contribute to an increased likelihood to use drugs. Second, parents may react to their child's genetically influenced behavior. For example, a reactive infant may elicit a harsher response from their parent than an easy-to-soothe infant, especially if their parent is also using drugs. Each of these possible processes has specific implications for understanding drug abuse and parenting.

■ SUMMARY

It is clear that drug abuse can have a profoundly maladaptive effect on both parenting and family functioning in general. However, the effects of drug abuse and family disruption on the developing child are complex and involve aspects of fit, reactivity, and genetic influences, as discussed above. None of the studies reviewed above can clearly estimate *to what extent* parental drug use and family disruptions affect the developing child, because the child is (typically) being reared by his or her biological parents. If drug abuse is genetically influenced, then it stands to reason that genetic influences on parents' drug abuse behavior may also be influenced by the family disruptions associated with such behavior. This potential confound of rearing environment with genetic influences makes identifying specific, direct environmental influences a challenge in studies of biological families and their children. To fully understand the role of the environment in influencing child behavior and risk and/or protection, a genetically informed design is necessary.

The first two sections of this chapter have presented two messages that are intended to be complementary but may seem contradictory. First, drug use and abuse are genetically influenced, but more research on specific environmental influences is needed. Second, studies that report on the direct impact of drug use on family dysfunction and parenting (specific environmental influences) and child development are typically confounded with genetic influences passed from parent to offspring. This difficulty underscores the complexity that drug-abuse researchers face as they try to clearly elucidate the mechanisms involved in the impact of parenting on the development of drug use in children. The next sections will focus on another possible mechanism for the intergenerational transmission of drug abuse—the prenatal environment, where there are again challenges with disentangling direct environmental effects from genetic influences as well as from parenting influences. The final section will focus on innovative research designs used in prenatal drug-abuse research that have begun to tackle these etiological obstacles.

■ PRENATAL DRUG USE AND CHILD BEHAVIOR PROBLEMS

The intergenerational transmission of drug abuse also involves what is perhaps the first true "rearing" environment, the prenatal environment. There have been many studies of how the use of drugs during pregnancy is associated with maladaptive child developmental outcomes, and many studies show direct effects of prenatal exposure to drugs on the developing fetus and on the later development and adjustment of the exposed child. For example, three studies of children who were exposed to cocaine prenatally showed that exposed children had altered stress responses, poorer inhibitory control at age 7.5, and language deficits at age 10 (Bauer et al., 2011; Bridgett & Mayes, 2011; Lewis et al., 2011). Similar long-term problem outcomes have been found for children of mothers who used marijuana (Day et al., 2011) or drank alcohol (Richardson et al., 2002), and children of mothers who smoked during pregnancy (Wakschlag et al., 2011). One question that researchers have been struggling with is whether associations found between drug use during pregnancy and child outcomes are attributable to the child's prenatal exposure to the drug, or whether the associations are a proxy for genetic influences conferred by parents on child outcomes. Given that prenatal drug use has itself been shown to be genetically influenced (Agrawal et al., 2008), as is drug use, especially persistent and problematic use and abuse (Hopfer et al., 2003; Rhee et al., 2003), the need to consider the role of possible genetic influences becomes apparent.

One of the most extensively studied prenatal exposures is smoking during pregnancy. Smoking during pregnancy has been linked to a variety of child behavior problems, with the majority of studies indicating problems along the externalizing spectrum with some associations extending into adulthood. For example, children of mothers who smoked during pregnancy were more likely to have escalating externalizing problems and difficulty regulating their behavior during toddlerhood (Wakschlag et al., 2006). Smoking during pregnancy has also been linked with disruptive behavior problems (Wakschlag et al., 2011) and increased rates of psychiatric symptoms for conduct disorder, drug abuse, and depression in adolescence (Ferguson, Woodward, & Horwood, 1998). Children of mothers who were serious smokers during pregnancy (more than 10 cigarettes almost daily) showed greater risks for prepubertal-onset of conduct disorder in boys and adolescent-onset drug dependence in girls (Weissman, Warner, Wickramaratne, & Kandel, 1999). The associations between smoking during pregnancy and a wide range of child externalizing and internalizing problems have persisted even when proxies for possible genetic influences like antisocial behaviors in parents are consistently controlled for (see Wakschlag et al., 2002, for a review). Interestingly, children may be at the highest risk when mothers smoke during their pregnancy and continue to smoke in the home, suggesting that the mechanism of effect may be behavioral rather than from prenatal exposure per se (Maughan et al., 2001).

The use of cocaine during pregnancy has similarly been associated with a wide array of maladaptive child-developmental outcomes. Cocaine use by mothers during pregnancy probably affects the neurological arousal systems of children, such that they have more difficulty regulating their arousal, effects that can persist if exposure continues (Mayes, 2002, 2006). Similarly, children exposed to cocaine prenatally may also have more difficulty regulating their attention, which can be a risk factor for the later development of attentional and/or anxiety disorders (Mayes et al., 1993). Use of cocaine during pregnancy has been linked to flatter affect and decreased levels of executive functioning in children (Bridgett & Mayes, 2011; Espy, Kaufmann, & Glisky, 1999). Multiple studies have also pointed to the possibility of gender differences in the effects of cocaine exposure, showing that exposed boys, but not girls, were twice as likely as control children to have behavior problems. Cocaine exposure was also related to challenging behavior in boys but not girls in two studies of young children (Delaney-Black et al., 2000; Delaney-Black et al., 2004). Unlike studies of smoking during pregnancy, there have been no studies of prenatal cocaine exposure that have attempted to control for genetic influences. Given the infant and child behaviors that have been associated with prenatal cocaine exposure, it may be that parental executive functioning and attention-related problems would be appropriate variables to consider as controls.

The negative impact of prenatal alcohol use is well established, especially in regard to fetal alcohol syndrome (FAS), which is beyond the scope of this chapter (Mattson & Riley, 1998; Mattson et al., 1999; Riley & McGee, 2005; Sowell et al., 2008; Spohr, 1993). Children diagnosed with attention deficit hyperactive disorder (ADHD), without FAS, have been found to be 2.5 times more likely to have been exposed to alcohol prenatally, an effect that persists even after controlling for familial ADHD, parental antisocial behavior, and socioeconomic status (SES) (Mick, Biederman, Faraone, Sayer, & Kleinman, 2002). Alcohol use during pregnancy, even at low levels, has been associated with increases in child behavior problems, and a dose response was also evident, such that greater alcohol exposure was associated with increased risk (Sood et al., 2001). With regard to the intergenerational transmission of substance use, the development of alcohol problems in young adulthood has been associated with exposure to alcohol prenatally after controlling for parental alcohol and other drug use (Baer et al., 2003). Verbal deficits have also been found in children exposed to alcohol prenatally (Richardson et al., 2002), and, in one study, these deficits were not detected until age 14, suggesting possible long-term effects on the development of the central nervous system in children exposed to alcohol prenatally (Willford et al., 2004). There is also evidence that patterns of drinking during pregnancy (e.g., occasional binge drinking) may also predict child behavior problems independent of prediction from daily average drinking levels (Sayal et al., 2009).

The use of marijuana and other drugs during pregnancy has also been associated with maladaptive child outcomes, although less extensively. The two main domains of findings on pregnancy cannabis use and child outcomes are those related to impulsivity and attention and executive functioning. Use of cannabis during pregnancy has been associated with increases in child inattention and impulsivity at age 10 (Richardson et al., 2002). Similarly, children exposed to cannabis prenatally had higher levels of impulsivity at age six (Leech, Richardson, Goldschmidt, & Day, 1999). At age 10, children who had been exposed to cannabis prenatally were more hyperactive, impulsive, and inattentive (Goldschmidt, Day, & Richardson, 2000). With regard to executive functioning, Fried and Watkinson (2000) found executive functioning deficits in children from 10 to 12 years of age who were exposed to cannabis prenatally. Similar deficits in executive functioning were also found in six- and 10-year-old children who were exposed to marijuana prenatally (Goldschmidt, Richardson, Willford, & Day, 2008; Richardson et al., 2002). Most recently, a study of 580 mother-child dyads found that children exposed to one or more joints per day during pregnancy were 1.76 times more likely to exhibit delinquent behavior at age 14; this effect was mediated by child depressive symptoms and attention problems at age 10 (Day, Leech, & Goldschmidt, 2011).

Although not explicitly discussed, many of the studies reviewed above that focused on child behavioral outcomes have shown convincing evidence that prenatal exposure to drugs is associated with a wide range of birth problems, specifically low birth weight; these findings suggest that any use of drugs should be avoided during pregnancy. Consistent with these findings, a recent report provides evidence that young children of mothers who smoked during pregnancy had both thicker and less elastic arterial walls at age five than children of mothers who did not smoke, suggesting possible long-term structural and functional damage of the vascular walls (Geerts et al., 2012).

The pervasive maladaptive physical effects associated with substance use during pregnancy highlight the importance of continuing to consider the possible effects on child behavior. Because a majority of studies on the impact of prenatal drug use on child behavior are not genetically informative, there are unresolved issues with regard to whether prenatal exposure to drugs directly leads to the development of child behavior problems or whether these behavior problems are due to genetic influences. Specifically, the genetic factors in parents that influence their likelihood of using drugs during pregnancy may also influence the development of behavior problems in their children.

The majority of the studies discussed above attempted to disentangle the effects of prenatal drug use from possible genetic effects by using covariates (e.g., parents' antisocial behavior) to control for possible genetic confounds. These efforts should be applauded, as early research on the effects of prenatal drug use on child behavior all but ignored the possibility that these same effects could be explained by genetic influences. More recently, however, novel and genetically informative research designs have allowed researchers to better disentangle whether effects are due to prenatal drug use specifically, or are due to genetic transmission.

■ SEPARATING EFFECTS OF PRENATAL EXPOSURE TO DRUGS FROM GENETIC INFLUENCES

Novel genetically informative research designs have allowed for a more accurate investigation of the possible effects of the prenatal use of drugs on child behavior. The design methods, strengths, and limitations of the innovative genetically informative designs covered here can be found in Table 4.1. One such technique is to compare siblings within families who are differentially exposed to drugs prenatally (Lahey & D'Onofrio, 2010). An example of how this strategy works with regard to pregnancy drug use and child outcomes can be found in the research of D'Onofrio and colleagues (2010), who used the sibling comparison design in a large population-based sample of Swedish youth to test whether smoking during pregnancy was a causal environmental predictor of child-conduct problems. A cross-family analysis suggested the risk for conviction of a violent crime was three times higher for children of mothers who smoked during pregnancy than for children of mothers who did not. However, within families, there were no significant differences in conviction risk between children who were exposed to smoking prenatally and those who were not. If smoking during pregnancy was a causal predictor of violent crime conviction, then one would expect children who were exposed to smoking prenatally within families to have higher risk than those who were not. In the same sample of Swedish adolescents, associations were found between smoking during pregnancy and poorer academic achievement in unrelated children, but again, there were no significant differences for siblings who were differentially exposed to prenatal smoking (D'Onofrio et al., 2010). An additional strength of the sibling comparison design is that it is a more feasible strategy for accounting for within-family effects as compared to studies that require the (relatively infrequent) birth of twins (Rutter, 2007; Lahey, D'Onofrio, & Waldman, 2009). In addition, twins are not differentially exposed prenatally, as twins share the prenatal environment. These findings highlight how a relatively simple yet powerful quasi-experimental study design has been used to suggest that specific exposure to smoking during pregnancy does not account for the associations between nicotine use during pregnancy and adolescent criminality or academic achievement.

The study design described above can be extremely useful in its potential to eliminate pregnancy drug use as a causal predictor of child outcomes. However, it is limited in its potential to provide alternative explanations for the associations commonly found between pregnancy drug use and child outcomes. Another novel, genetically informative research design that has been used to disentangle the effects of drug use during pregnancy from inherited influences is the "Children of Twins" (COT) design (see Row 2 of Table 4.1). The COT design compares the children of twins who are discordant on a given behavior or trait. By assessing twins and their children, the COT design can be used to estimate genetic influences (e.g., parental alcoholism), direct environmental influences (e.g., drug use during pregnancy), and environmental influences shared by both parents (such as SES) (D'Onofrio, Turkheimer, Eaves et al., 2003; Jacob et al., 2003). Jacob and colleagues (2003) used the COT design with twin parents who had histories of alcohol abuse or alcohol dependency, or were non-alcoholics. Children of twins who

TABLE 4.1 *Genetically Informative Research Designs Used to Study Drug Abuse*

Method	How Is It Done?	What Can We Learn?	Limitations
Twin Studies	Compare siblings who vary in their genetic relatedness	Percentage of variance in an outcome that is explained by genetic or environmental influences Correlations between respective genetic and environmental influences for a given outcome	Difficult to determine specific environmental influences Non-shared environment also includes measurement error Although twin studies are becoming more common, birth of twins is still a relatively infrequent event
Children of Twins (COT)	Compares twins as well as their offspring	All of the above Additionally, the extent of influence for certain specific environments can be estimated	Assessing twins and their children can be logistically difficult Measurement is often retrospective
In-Vitro Fertilization (IVF)	Compares children of IVF who are related either to both parents, a single parent, or neither parent	In certain cases, allows for the disentangling of genetic influences from those of the prenatal and/or postnatal environment Especially useful if studying the effects of the prenatal environment	IVF is relatively infrequent (although becoming less so) and can be a difficult population to access and assess
Adoption Studies	Compare adopted children, their adopted parents, and their birth parents	Can estimate effects of the rearing environment that are unbiased by genetic influences Can estimate genetic influences that are unbiased by environmental influences	Adoptions are infrequent, and following birth parents as well as adoptive family units can be difficult logistically

had histories of alcohol abuse or dependency (i.e., had genetic risk for drug use) were, as hypothesized, more likely to exhibit alcohol abuse or alcohol dependency themselves. Interestingly, children of twins who were non-alcoholic but whose co-twin had histories of alcohol dependence (i.e., genetic risk) showed no greater propensity for alcohol problems than children of nonalcoholic twins (Jacob et al., 2003). This study used a COT design to provide evidence for the protective power of the familial environment (the non-alcoholic parent) for risk for alcohol problems even in the face of genetic influences (the parent's co-twin with a history of alcohol dependence). D'Onofrio and colleagues (2003) used the COT design with twins discordant for maternal smoking during pregnancy and found evidence for a direct effect of smoking during pregnancy on low infant birth weight, with no support for alternative genetic or shared environmental explanations, further supporting the association between prenatal nicotine exposure and maladaptive birth outcomes. The importance of genetic influences on the development of ADHD was illustrated in a different study that used the COT design. Specifically, associations between smoking during pregnancy and ADHD were non-significant once maternal alcohol-use disorders (for twin mothers) were considered (Knopik et al., 2006; Knopik et al 2009). Specifically, these findings suggest that the association between pregnancy smoking and ADHD may be a proxy for genetic influences.

Another exciting research design involves taking advantage of the natural experiment of children conceived using in-vitro fertilization (IVF; Table 4.1, Row 3). IVF can be used to disentangle prenatal and genetic influences because the prenatal environment of children who are conceived using this method can be related to both parents, to the mother only (egg donation), to the father only (sperm donation), or to neither parent (embryo donation). Thus, in the case of an embryo donation, the prenatal environment is provided by an individual who is not biologically related to the fetus; thus the effects of the prenatal environment cannot be attributed to genetic influences (Thapar et al., 2007; Rice et al., 2009). IVF studies are strengthened by their ability to not only disentangle the prenatal environment from genetic influences, but, in the case of embryo donation, to also disentangle the subsequent rearing environment from both prenatal and genetic influences. Rice and colleagues (2009) used the IVF design to examine prenatal smoking effects in unrelated (embryo donation) and related (sperm or egg donation) pregnancies on infant birth weight and child antisocial behavior. Prenatal smoking was associated with low birth weight in both the related and unrelated children, suggesting a direct effect of prenatal smoking on low birth weight. However, the association between pregnancy smoking and child antisocial behavior was only present in related offspring, suggesting genetic influences as opposed to a direct effect of pregnancy smoking (Rice et al., 2009). Similar results were found in an IVF study of pregnancy smoking and child ADHD (Thapar et al., 2009). Taken together, these findings have provided further evidence for a direct effect of pregnancy smoking on low birth weight but have suggested that there may not be a causal link between pregnancy smoking and child antisocial behavior or child ADHD.

■ SUMMARY

Comparing differentially exposed siblings, COT designs, and prospective samples of children conceived with IVF are just three examples of innovative research strategies that can better tease apart prenatal effects from those that are passed down genetically from parents to children. Evidence from these studies has provided support for direct links between smoking during pregnancy and low birth weight, which is associated with a plethora of maladaptive developmental outcomes. At the same time, being able to adequately tease out genetic influences from prenatal influences has called into question whether prenatal drug use is directly associated with more downstream child behavioral outcomes. This is not to say that prenatal drug use does not have an impact on maladaptive child development outcomes. Rather, the trajectories of intergenerational transmission of drug abuse are likely to be more complex and also influenced by genetic transmission.

■ INTEGRATING THE MECHANISMS OF DRUG ABUSE TRANSMISSION: A PROSPECTIVE ADOPTION DESIGN

This chapter has reviewed three mechanisms through which the intergenerational transmission of drug abuse behaviors may operate: a) via genetic transmission; b) via disruption of parenting and family processes; and c) via prenatal drug exposure. It is likely that all three of these mechanisms are operating on the development of a child's risk for drug use. Drug use is highly heritable, with initiation showing substantial shared environmental influences. The quantitative genetic literature is limited in that the measurement of the specific environments that may be impactful has, until fairly recently, been relatively poor. Family-based research designs that have been used to investigate parental drug abuse have provided evidence for the direct impact of parental drug abuse on family relationships, child functioning, and subsequent drug use behaviors of the children. These studies are often limited by a lack of consideration of genetic factors, which may also explain, at least in part, associations between heritable behaviors of parents and their offspring. Studies of pregnancy drug use have shown convincing evidence for effects of prenatal drug exposure on infant birth weight, child conduct problems, and deficits in executive functioning; even when controlling for inherited influences. In contrast, some research indicates attenuation of pregnancy drug use effects when genetic influences are controlled for (Maughan et al., 2001). Molecular genetics strategies have also been used to disentangle prenatal substance-use effects from genetic influences. For example, Wakschlag and colleagues (2010) found that the interaction between gender, having a risky genotype variant monoamine oxidase A (MAO-A), and being exposed to smoking prenatally, predicted increased adolescent antisocial behavior. These studies are excellent examples of how researchers are adapting by including genetics in their models of pregnancy substance use and the development of child problem behavior. A recent and accumulating set of studies using innovative quasi-experimental research designs that allow different aspects of risk to be "controlled" have provided new evidence that the effects of prenatal exposure to drugs may not be a direct effect of the prenatal exposure itself, but rather due to other environmental influences and/or genetic influences. These designs often rely on retrospective reporting or are limited in their ability to adequately disentangle the effects of specific postnatal rearing environments from inherited influences.

The Early Growth and Development Study (EGDS; Leve et al., 2008) is a prospective longitudinal adoption design that can be used to consider simultaneously the three mechanisms for intergenerational transmission of drug use and abuse discussed in this chapter (Table 4.1, Row 4). The EGDS follows children adopted at birth by non-relatives and their linked biological parent(s) from infancy to middle childhood using a multi-agent, multi-measure assessment strategy. Detailed assessments of birth and adoptive parent mental health, drug use and related behaviors, contextual factors, parenting and marital relationships, and developmentally appropriate child outcomes are obtained at regular intervals. By assessing birth parents, adoptive parents, and adopted children longitudinally, the EGDS can: a) estimate the genetic risk conferred by drug-using birth parents on their offspring independent of rearing environment confounds; b) disentangle the effects of postnatal rearing environments from effects of genetic and prenatal influences; and c) estimate the effects of prenatal drug exposure independent of genetic influences, and, when birth-father data are available, independent of prenatal exposure effects. Most importantly, EGDS allows for the effects of genetic, prenatal environmental, and postnatal environmental influences to be considered together as well as estimated "free of" the effects of the other influences (although prenatal and genetic influences are confounded in birth mothers, birth fathers do not provide the prenatal environment and thus contribute only genetic influences).

The EGDS is in the beginning stages of considering the effects of prenatal environment on child development of risk for drug use. There is at least one published report from this study that found, in the final model, that genetic influences (birth mother depressive symptoms) influenced child behavior problems at 18 months indirectly through a general index of pre- and perinatal risk factors (e.g., prenatal care, pregnancy complications, drug and alcohol use, toxin exposure; Pemberton et al., 2010). Consistent with the findings of Agrawal et al. (2008), this report found that there were genetic influences on the pre- and perinatal risk index, which included pregnancy drug use. More interesting, however, was the finding that the pre- and perinatal risk factors had a direct effect on toddler functioning and that genetic and prenatal risk worked together. In other words, it is possible that the mechanism through which genetic influences have an effect on toddler behavior problems is the pre- and perinatal environment. Analyses are currently underway to examine how prenatal drug exposure may influence child development in the EGDS.

■ CONCLUSIONS

Parental drug abuse problems can disrupt family processes through affecting parent–child relationships, relationships with spouses, or general family functioning. Unfortunately, drug use and abuse issues can span generations within families with a variety of manifestations of problems. In this chapter we have reviewed three possible mechanisms for the intergenerational transmission of drug use and abuse. We have highlighted the importance of considering genetic influences, as many drug-abuse disorders and related behaviors are heritable, and much of the research on the intergenerational transmission of drug use and abuse does not use genetically informed designs. The literature on prenatal exposure to drugs and alcohol has also typically not accounted for genetic influences, although there is a recent shift in this area to incorporate such strategies. These efforts have produced findings that strengthen the support for the direct effects of prenatal exposure on child outcomes in some areas (e.g., smoking during pregnancy and low birth weight), while tempering support for others (e.g., smoking during pregnancy and child behavior problems). It is clear that drug use and abuse is a damaging and pervasive problem, one that can be exacerbated by a combination of the three mechanisms of transmission covered in this chapter. By integrating across multiple disciplines and approaches—family, genetic, prenatal exposure—we will advance our understanding of *how* disorders are transmitted across generations. There is a need for the use of novel research designs and strategies and for replication in order to continue to clarify the mechanisms involved. Parenting has been shown to be an integral part of the equation and is likely to provide one of the best opportunities for intervention and prevention.

■ AUTHOR NOTE

Work on this chapter was supported by Pr/Award R305B090007 IES Training Program Grants to Charles Beekman (Principal Investigators: Tom Farmer and Karen Bierman) and by grant R01 DA020585 from the National Institute on Drug Abuse, the National Institute on Mental Health, and the Office of Behavioral and Social Science Research, NIH, U.S. PHS (Principal Investigator: Jenae Neiderhiser, Ph.D.).

■ REFERENCES

Agrawal, A., & Lynskey, M. T. (2006). The genetic epidemiology of cannabis use, abuse and dependence. *Addiction, 101*(6), 801–812. PMID: 16696624

Agrawal, A., Knopik, V. S., Pergadia, M. L., Waldron, M. Bucholz, K. K., Martin, N. G., et al. (2008). Correlates of cigarette smoking during pregnancy and its genetic and environmental overlap with nicotine dependence. *Nicotine Tobacco Research, 10*(4), 567–578. PMID: 18418779.

Baer, J. S., Sampson, P. D., Barr, H. M., Connor, P. D., & Streissguth, A. P. (2003). A 21-year longitudinal analysis of the effects of prenatal alcohol exposure on young adult drinking. *Archives of General Psychiatry, 60*, 377–385.

Bauer, C. R. Lambert, B. L., Bann, C. M., Lester, B. M., Shankaran, S., Bada, H. S., et al. (2011). Long-term impact of maternal substance use during pregnancy and extrauterine environmental adversity: Stress hormone levels of preadolescent children. *Pediatric Research, 70*(2), 213–219.

Bell, R. Q. (1968). A reinterpretation of the direction of effects in studies of socialization. *Psychological Review, 75*, 81–95.

Bridgett, D. J., & Mayes, L. C. (2011). Development of inhibitory control among prenatally cocaine exposed and non-cocaine exposed youths from late childhood to early adolescence: the effects of gender and risk and subsequent aggressive behavior. *Neurotoxicology & Teratology, 33*, 137–144.

Collins, W. A., Maccoby, E. E., Steinberg, L., Hetherington, E. M., & Bornstein, M. H. (2000). Contemporary research on parenting: The case for nature and nurture. *American Psychologist, 55*(2), 218–232.

Day, N. L., Leech, S. L., & Goldschmidt, L. (2011). The effects of prenatal marijuana exposure on delinquent behaviors are mediated by measures of neurocognitive functioning. *Neurotoxicology & Teratology, 33*, 129–136.

Deater-Deckard, K. (2000). Parenting and child behavioral adjustment in early childhood: a quantitative genetic approach to studying family processes. *Child Development, 71*(2), 468–484. PMID: 10834478

Delaney-Black, V., Covington, C., Templin, T., Ager, J., Nordstrom- Klee, B., Martier, S., et al. (2000). Teacher-assessed behavior of children prenatally exposed to cocaine. *Pediatrics, 106*(4), 782–791. PMID: 11015523.

Delaney-Black, V., Covington, C., Nordstrom, B., Ager, J., Janisse, J., Hannigan, J. H., et al. (2004). Prenatal cocaine: quantity of exposure and gender moderation. *Journal of Developmental Behavioral Pediatrics, 25*(4), 254–263. PMID: 15308926.

D'Onofrio, B. M., Turkheimer, E. N., Eaves, L. J., Corey, L. A., Berg, K., Solaas, M. H., et al. (2003). The role of the children of twins design in elucidating causal relations between parent characteristics and child outcomes. *Journal of Child Psychology & Psychiatry, 44*(8), 1130–1144. PMID: 14626455.

D'Onofrio, B. M., Singh, A. L., Iliadou, A., Lambe, M., Hultman, C. M., et al. (2010). A quasi-experimental study of maternal smoking during pregnancy and offspring academic achievement. *Child Development, 81*(1), 80–100. doi: 10.1111/j.1467-8624.2009.01382.x

Edwards, E. P., Eiden, R. D., & Leonard, K. E. (2004). Impact of fathers' alcoholism and associated risk factors on parent-infant attachment stability from 12 to 18 months. *Infant Mental Health, 25*(6), 556–579. PMID: 19436769.

Eiden, R. D., Peterson, M., & Coleman, T. (1999). Maternal cocaine use and the caregiving environment during early childhood. *Psychology of Addictive Behaviors, 13*(4), 293–302. doi: 10.10370893-164X.13.4.293.

Eiden, R. D., Edwards, E. P., & Leonard, K. E. (2002). Mother-infant and father-infant attachment among alcoholic families. *Developmental Psychopathology, 14*(2), 253–278. PMID: 12030691.

Eiden, R. D., Edwards, E. P., & Leonard, K. E. (2004). Predictors of effortful control among children of alcoholic and nonalcoholic fathers. *Journal of Studies on Alcohol, 65*(3), 309–319. PMID: 15222587.

Eiden, R. D., Edwards, E. P., & Leonard, K. E. (2007). A conceptual model for the development of externalizing behavior problems among kindergarten children of alcoholic families: role of parenting and children's self-regulation. *Developmental Psychology, 43*(5), 1187–1201. PMID: 17723044.

Eiden, R. D., Colder, C., Edwards, E. P., & Leonard, K. E. (2009). A longitudinal study of social competence among children of alcoholic and nonalcoholic parents: role of parental psychopathology, parental warmth, and self-regulation. *Psychology of Addictive Behaviors, 23*(1), 36–46. PMID: 19290688.

Eiden, R. D., Schuetze, P., & Coles, C. D. (2011). Maternal cocaine use and mother-infant interactions: Direct and moderated associations. *Neurotoxicology & Teratology, 33*(1), 120–128. PMID: 21256426.

Espinosa, M., Beckwith, L., Howard, J., Tyler, R., & Swanson, K. (2001). Maternal psychopathology and attachment in toddlers of heavy cocaine-using mothers. *Infant Mental Health, 22*(3), 316–333. doi: 10.1002/imhj.1004.

Espy, K. A., Kaufmann, P. M., & Glisky, M. L. (1999). Neuropsychological function in toddlers exposed to cocaine in utero: A preliminary study. *Developmental Neuropsychology, 15*(3), 447–460. doi: 10.1080/87565649909540761.

Fals-Stewart, W., Kelley, M. L., Fincham, F. D., Golden, J., & Logsdon, T. (2004). Emotional and behavioral problems of children living with drug-abusing fathers: comparisons with children living with alcohol-abusing and non-substance-abusing fathers. *Journal of Family Psychology, 18*(2), 319–330. PMID: 15222839.

Ferguson, D. M., Woodward, L. J., & Horwood, L. J. (1998). Maternal smoking during pregnancy and psychiatric adjustment in late adolescence. *Archives of General Psychiatry, 55*(8), 721–727. PMID: 9707383.

Fried, P. A., & Watkinson, B. (2000). Visuoperceptual functioning differs in 9- to 12-year olds prenatally exposed to cigarettes and marijuana. *Neurotoxicology & Teratology, 22*(1), 11–20.

Fu, Q., Heath, A. C., Bucholz, K. K., Nelson, E., Goldberg, J., Lyons, M. J., et al. (2002). Shared genetic risk of major depression, alcohol dependence, and marijuana dependence. *Archives of General Psychiatry, 59*(12), 1125–1132.

Geerts, C. C., Bots, M. L., van der Ent, C. K., Grobbee, D. E., & Uiterwaal, C. S. P. M. (2012). Parental smoking and vascular damage in their 5-year-old children. *Pediatrics, 129*(1), 45–54. doi: 10.1542/peds.2011-0249.

Goldschmidt, L., Day, N. L., & Richardson, G. A. (2000). Effects of prenatal marijuana exposure on child behavior problems at age 10. *Neurotoxicology & Teratology, 22*(3), 325–335. PMID: 100840176.

Goldschmidt, L., Richardson, G. A., Willford, J., & Day, N. L. (2008). Prenatal marijuana exposure and intelligence test performance at age 6. *Journal of the American Academy of Child & Adolescent Psychiatry, 47*(3), 254–263. doi: 10.1097CHI.0b013e318160b3f0

Hans, S. L., Bernstein, V. J., & Henson, L. G. (1999). The role of psychopathology in the parenting of drug-dependent women. *Developmental Psychopathology, 11*(4), 957–977. PMID: 10624734.

Hardie, T. L., Moss, H. B., & Lynch, K. G. (2006). Genetic correlations between smoking initiation and smoking behaviors in a twin sample. *Addictive Behaviors, 31*(11), 2030–2037. PMID: 16675152.

Heath, A. C., Martin, N. G., Lynskey, M. T., Todorov, A. A., & Madden, P. A. (2002). Estimating two-stage models for genetic influences on alcohol, tobacco or drug use initiation and dependence vulnerability in twin and family data. *Twin Research, 5*(2), 113–124. PMID: 11931689.

Hill, E. M., Nord, J. L., & Blow, F. C. (1992). Young-adult children of alcoholic parents: protective effects of positive family functioning. *British Journal of Addiction, 87*(12), 1677–1690. PMID: 1490082.

Hopfer, C. J., Crowley, T. J., & Hewitt, J. K. (2003). Review of twin and adoption studies of adolescent substance use. *Journal of the American Academy of Child & Adolescent Psychiatry, 42*(6), 710–719. PMID: 12921479.

Jacob, T., Waterman, B., Heath, A., True, W., Bucholz, K. K., Haber, R., et al. (2003). Genetic and environmental effects on offspring alcoholism: new insights using an offspring-of-twins design. *Archives of General Psychiatry, 60*(12), 1265–1272. PMID: 14662559.

Kaminsky, Z. A., Tang, T., Wang, S.-C., Ptak, C., Oh, G. H. T., Wong, A. H. C., et al. (2009). DNA methylation profiles in monozygotic and dizygotic twins. *Nature Genetics, 41*, 240–245.

Keller, P. S., Cummings, E. M., & Davies, P. T. (2005). The role of marital discord and parenting in relations between parental problem drinking and child adjustment. *Journal of Child Psychology & Psychiatry & Allied Disciplines, 46*, 943–951.

Kendler, K. S., Neale, M. C., Sullivan, P., Corey, L. A., Gardner, C. O., & Prescott, C. A. (1999). A population-based twin study in women of smoking initiation and nicotine dependence. *Psychological Medicine, 29*(2), 299–308. PMID: 10218922.

Kendler, K. S., Karkowski, L. M., Neale, M. C., & Prescott, C. A. (2000). Illicit psychoactive substance use, heavy use, abuse, and dependence in a U.S. population-based sample of male twins. *Archives of General Psychiatry, 57*(3), 261–269.

Kendler, K. S., Thornton, L. M., & Pederson, N. L. (2000). Tobacco consumption in Swedish twins reared apart and reared together. *Archives of General Psychiatry, 57*, 886–892.

Kendler, K. S., Prescott, C. A., Myers, J., & Neale, M. C. (2003). The structure of genetic and environmental risk factors for common psychiatric and substance use disorders in men and women. *Archives of General Psychiatry, 60*, 929–937.

Kendler, K. S., Myers, J., & Prescott, C. A. (2007). Specificity of genetic and environmental risk factors for symptoms of cannabis, cocaine, alcohol, caffeine, and nicotine dependence. *Archives of General Psychiatry, 64*(11), 1313–1320.

Kendler, K. S., Schmitt, E., Aggen, S. H., & Prescott, C. A. (2008). Genetic and environmental influences on alcohol, caffeine, cannabis, and nicotine use from early adolescence to middle adulthood. *Archives of General Psychiatry, 65*(6), 674–682. PMID: 18519825.

Knopik, V. S., Heath, A. C., Jacob, T., Slutske, W. S., Bucholz, K. K., Madden, P. A., et al. (2006). Maternal alcohol use disorder and offspring ADHD: disentangling genetic and environmental effects using a children-of-twins design. *Psychological Medicine, 36*(10), 1461–1471. PMID: 16734942.

Knopik, V. S., Jacob, T., Haber, J. R., Swenson, L. P., & Howell, D. N. (2009). Paternal alcoholism and offspring ADHD problems: a children-of-twins design. *Twin Research & Human Genetics, 12*(1), 53–62. PMID: 19210180.

Lahey, B. B., D'Onofrio, B. M., & Waldman, I. D. (2009). Using epidemiological methods to test hypotheses regarding causal influences on child and adolescent mental disorders. *Journal of Child Psychology & Psychiatry, 50*(1–2), 53. doi: 10.1111j.1469-7610.2008.01980.x.

Lahey, B. B., & D'Onofrio, B. M. (2010). All in the family: Comparing siblings to test causal hypotheses regarding environmental influences on behavior. *Current Directions in Psychological Science, 19*(5), 319–323. doi: 10.11770963721410383977.

Leech, S. L., Richardson, G. A., Goldschmidt, L., & Day, N. L. (1999). Prenatal substance exposure: effects on attention and impulsivity of 6-year-olds. *Neurotoxicology & Teratology, 21*(2), 109–118. PMID: 10192271.

Legrand, L. N., McGue, M., & Iacono, W. G. (1999). Searching for interactive effects in the etiology of early onset substance use. *Behavior Genetics, 29*(6), 433–440. PMID: 10857248.

Leve, L. D., Neiderhiser, J. M., Scaramella, L. V., & Reiss, D. (2008). The Early Growth and Development Study: using the prospective adoption design to examine genotype-environment interplay. *Acta Psychologica Sinica., 40*, 1106–1115.

Lewis, B. A., Minnes, S., Short, E., Weishampel, P., Satayathum, S., Min, M. O., et al. (2011). The effects of prenatal cocaine on language development at 10 years of age. *Neurotoxicology & Teratology, 33*, 17–24.

Lynskey, M. T., Agrawal, A., & Heath, A. C. (2010). Genetically informative research on adolescent substance use: Methods, findings, and challenges. *Journal of the American Academy of Child & Adolescent Psychiatry, 49*(12), 1202–1214.

Maccoby, E. E. (1992). The role of parents in the socialization of children: An historical overview. *Developmental Psychology, 28*(6), 1006–1017.

Madden, P. A., Pedersen, N. L., Kaprio, J., Koskenvuo, M. J., & Martin, N. G. (2004). The epidemiology and genetics of smoking initiation and persistence: cross-cultural comparisons of twin study results. *Twin Research, 7*(1), 82–97. PMID: 15053857.

Maes, H. H., Sullivan, P. F., Bulik, C. M., Neale, M. C., Prescott, C. A., Eaves, L. J., et al. (2004). A twin study of genetic and environmental influences on tobacco initiation, regular tobacco use and nicotine dependence. *Psychological Medicine, 34*(7), 1251–1261. PMID: 15697051.

Mattson, S. N., & Riley, E. P. (1998). A review of the neurobehavioral deficits in children with fetal alcohol syndrome or prenatal exposure to alcohol. *Alcoholism: Clinical & Experimental Research, 22*(2), 279–294. DOI: 10.1111/j.1530-0277.1998.tb03651.x.

Mattson, S. N., Goodman, A. M., Caine, C., Delis, D. C., & Riley, E. P. (1999). Executive functioning in children with heavy prenatal alcohol exposure. *Alcoholism: Clinical and Experimental Research, 23*(11), 1808–1815. DOI: 10.1111/j.1530-0277.1999.tb04077.x

Maughan, B., Taylor, C., Taylor, A., Butler, N., & Bynner, J. (2001). Pregnancy smoking and childhood conduct problems: A causal association? *Journal of Child Psychology & Psychiatry, 42*(8), 1021–1028. doi: 10.11111469-7610.00800

Mayes, L. C., Granger, R. H., Frank, M. A., Schottenfield, R., & Bornstein, M. H. (1993). Neurobehavioral profiles of neonates exposed to cocaine prenatally. *Pediatrics, 91*(4), 778–783. PMID: 8464666.

Mayes, L. C., Feldman, R., Granger, R. H., Haynes, O. M., Bornstein, M. H., & Schottenfield, R. (1997). The effects of polydrug use with and without cocaine on mother–infant interaction at 3 and 6 months. *Infant Behavior & Development, 20*(4), 489–502.

Mayes, L. C. (2002). A behavioral teratogenic model of the impact of prenatal cocaine exposure on arousal regulatory systems. *Neurotoxicology & Teratology, 24*, 385–395.

Mayes, L. C. (2006). Arousal regulation, emotional flexibility, medial amygdale function, and the impact of early experience. *Annals of the New York Academy of Sciences, 1094*, 178–192.

Merikangas, K. R., Stolar, M., Stevens, D. E., Goulet, J., Preisig, M. A., Fenton, B., et al. (1998). Familial transmission of substance use disorders. *Archives of General Psychiatry, 55*(11), 973–979. PMID: 9819065.

McGue, M., Elkins, I., & Iacono, W. G. (2000). Genetic and environmental influences on adolescent substance use and abuse. *Neuropsychiatric Genetics, 96*, 671–677.

McGue, M., Elkins, I., Walden, B., & Iacono, W. G. (2005). Perceptions of the parent-adolescent relationship: A longitudinal investigation. *Developmental Psychology, 41*, 971–984.

Mick, E., Biderman, J., Faraone, S. V., Sayer, J., & Kleinman, S. (2002). Case-control study of attention-deficit hyperactivity disorder and maternal smoking, alcohol use, and drug use during pregnancy. *Journal of the American Academy of Child & Adolescent Psychiatry, 41*(4), 378–385. PMID: 11931593.

Molitor, A., Mayes, L. C., & Ward, A. (2003). Emotion regulation behavior during a separation procedure in 18-month-old children of mothers using cocaine and other drugs. *Development & Psychopathology, 15*(1), 39–54. PMID: 12848434.

Morley, K. I., Lynskey, M. T., Madden, P. A., Treloar, S. A., Heath, A. C., & Martin, N. G. (2007). Exploring the interrelationship of smoking age-at-onset, cigarette consumption and smoking persistence: genes or environment? *Psychological Medicine, 37*(9), 1357–1367. PMID: 17466111.

Neiderhiser, J. M., Reiss, D., Pedersen, N. L., Lichtenstein, P., Spotts, E. L., Hansson, K., et al. (2004). Genetic and environmental influences on mothering of adolescents: a comparison of two samples. *Developmental Psychology*, 40(3), 335–351. PMID: 15122961.

Neiderhiser, J. M., Reiss, D., Lichtenstein, P., Spotts, E. L., & Ganiban, J. (2007). Father-adolescent relationships and the role of genotype-environment correlation. *Journal of Family Psychology*, 21(4), 560–571. PMID: 18179328

Pagan, J. L., Rose, R. J., Viken, R. J., Pulkkinen, L., Kaprio, J., & Dick, D. M. (2006). Genetic and environmental influences on stages of alcohol use across adolescence and into young adulthood. *Behavioral Genetics*, 36(4), 483–497. PMID: 16586152.

Pemberton, C. K., Neiderhiser, J. M., Leve, L. D., Natsuaki, M. N., Shaw, D. S., & Reiss, D. (2010). Influence of parental depressive symptoms on adopted toddler behaviors: An emerging developmental cascade of genetic and environmental effects. *Development & Psychopathology*, 22, 803–818. PMID: 20883583.

Pike, A., McGuire, S., Hetherington, E. M., Reiss, D., & Plomin, R.(1996). Family environment and adolescent depressive symptoms and antisocial behavior: A multivariate genetic analysis. *Developmental Psychology*, 32(4), 590–604.

Plomin, R., & Bergman, C. S. (1991). The nature of nurture: Genetic influence on "environmental" measures. *Behavioral & Brain Science*, 14(3), 373–427.

Rhee, S. H., Hewitt, J. K., Young, S. E., Corley, R. P., Crowley, T. J., & Stallings, M. C. (2003). Genetic and environmental influences on substance initiation, use, and problem use in adolescents. *Archives of General Psychiatry*, 60(12), 1256–1264. PMID: 14662558.

Rice, F., Harold, G. T., Boivin, J., Hay, D. F., van den Bree, M., & Thapar, A. (2009). Disentangling prenatal and inherited influences in humans with an experimental design. *Proceedings of the National Academy of Sciences of the United States of America*, 106(7), 2464–2467. PMID: 19188591.

Richardson, G. A., Ryan, C., Willford, J., Day, N. L., & Goldschmidt, L. (2002). Prenatal alcohol and marijuana exposure: Effects on neuropsychological outcomes at 10 years. *Neurotoxicology & Teratology*, 24, 309–320.

Riley, E. P., & McGee, C. L. (2005). Fetal alcohol spectrum disorders: An overview with emphasis on changes in brain and behavior. *Experimental Biology & Medicine*, 230(6), 357–365.

Rowe, D. C. (1994). *The Limits of Family Influence: Genes, Experience, and Behavior*. New York: Guilford Press.

Rutter, M. (2007). Proceeding from observed correlation to causal inference: The use of natural experiments. *Perspectives on Psychological Science*, 2, 377–395.

Sayal, K., Heron, J., Golding, J., Alati, R., Smith, G. D., Gray, R., & Emond, A. (2009). Binge pattern of alcohol consumption during pregnancy and childhood mental health outcomes: longitudinal population-based study. *Pediatrics*, 123(2), 289–296. PMID: 19171582.

Sood, B., Delaney-Black, V., Covington, C., Nordstrom-Klee, B., Ager, J., Templin, T., et al. (2001). Prenatal alcohol exposure and childhood behavior at age 6 to 7 years: I. dose-response effect. *Pediatrics*, 108(2), e34. doi: 10.1542/peds.108.2.e34.

Sowell, E. R., Mattson, S. N., Kan, E., Thompson, P. M., Riley, E. P., & Toga, A. W. (2008). Abnormal cortical thickness and brain behavior correlation patterns in individual with heavy prenatal alcohol exposure. *Cerebral Cortex*, 18(1), 136–144. doi: 10.1093/cercor/bhm039.

Spohr, H. L. (1993). Prenatal alcohol exposure and long-term developmental consequences. *The Lancet, 341*(8850), 907–910.

Stanger, C., Kamon, J., Dumenci, L., Higgins, S. T., Bickel, W. K., Grabowski, J., et al. (2002). Predictors of internalizing and externalizing problems among children of cocaine and opiate dependent parents. *Drug & Alcohol Dependence, 66*(2), 199–212. PMID: 11906807.

Swanson, K., Beckwith, L., & Howard, J. (2000). Intrusive caregiving and quality of attachment in prenatally drug-exposed toddlers and their primary caregivers. *Attachment & Human Development, 2*(2), 130–148. PMID: 11707907.

Thapar, A., Harold, G., Rice, F., Ge, X., Boivin, J., Hay, D., et al. (2007). Do intrauterine or genetic influences explain the foetal origins of chronic disease A novel experimental method for disentangling effects. *Medical Research Methodology, 22*, 7–25. PMID: 17587444

Thapar, A., Rice, F., Hay, D., Boivin, J., Langley, K., van den Bree, M., et al. (2009). Prenatal smoking might not cause attention-deficit/hyperactivity disorder: evidence from a novel design. *Biological Psychiatry, 66*(8), 722–727. PMID: 19596120.

Towers, H., Spotts, E. L., & Neiderhiser, J. M. (2003). Genetic and environmental influences on parenting and marital relationships. *Marriage & Family Review, 33*(1), 11–29. doi:10.1300/J002v33n01_03

Tsuang, M. T., Lyons, M. J., Meyer, J. M., Doyle, T., Eisen, S. A., Goldberg, J., et al. (1998). Co-occurrence of abuse of different drugs in men: the role of drug-specific and shared vulnerabilities. *Archives of General Psychiatry, 55*(11), 967–972. PMID: 9819064.

Tsuang, M. T., Lyons, M. J., Harley, R. M., Xian, H., Eisen, S., Goldberg, J., et al. (1999). Genetic and environmental influences on transitions in drug use. *Behavior Genetics, 29*(6), 473–479. PMID: 10857252.

Vink, J. M., Willemsen, G., & Boomsma, D. I. (2005). Heritability of smoking initiation and nicotine dependence. *Behavior Genetics, 35*(4), 397–406. PMID: 15971021.

Wakschlag, L. S., Pickett, K. E., Cook, E. Jr., Benowitz, N. L., & Leventhal, B. L. (2002). Maternal smoking during pregnancy and sever antisocial behavior in offspring: a review. *American Journal of Public Health, 92*(6), 966–974.

Wakschlag, L. S., Leventhal, B. L., Pine, D. S., Pickett, K. E., & Carter, A. S. (2006). Elucidating early mechanisms of developmental psychopathology: the case of prenatal smoking and disruptive behavior. *Child Development, 77*(4), 893–906. PMID: 16942496.

Wakschlag, L. S., Kistner, E. O., Pine, D. S., Biesecker, G., Pickett, K. E., Skol, A. D., et al. (2010). Interaction of prenatal exposure to cigarettes and MAOA genotype in pathways to youth antisocial behavior. *Molecular Psychiatry, 15*(9), 928–937. PMID: 19255579.

Wakschlag, L., Henry, D. B., Blair, J. R., Burns, J., Pickett, K. E., & Dukic, V. (2011). Unpacking the association: Individual differences in the relation of prenatal exposure to cigarettes and disruptive behavior phenotypes. *Neurotoxicology & Teratology, 33*, 145–154.

Walden, B., McGue, M., Iacono, W. G., Burt, S. A., & Elkins, I. (2004). Identifying shared environmental contributions to early substance use: the respective roles of peers and parents. *Journal of Abnormal Psychology, 113*(3), 440–450. PMID: 15311989.

Walsh, C., MacMillan, H. L., & Jamieson, E. (2003). The relationship between parental substance abuse and child maltreatment: findings from the Ontario Health Supplement. *Child Abuse & Neglect, 27*(12), 1409–1425. PMID: 14644059.

Weissman, M. M., Warner, V., Wickramaratne, P. J., & Kandel, D. B. (1999). Maternal smoking during pregnancy and psychopathology in offspring followed to adulthood. *Journal of the American Academy of Child & Adolescent Psychiatry, 38*(7), 892–899. PMID: 10405508.

Willford, J. A., Richardson, G. A., Leech, S. L., & Day, N. L. (2004). Verbal and visuospatial learning and memory function in children with moderate prenatal alcohol exposure. *Alcoholism, Clinical & Experimental Research, 28*(3), 497–507. PMID: 15084908.

Wolock, I., & Magura, S. (1996). Parental substance abuse as a predictor of child maltreatment re-reports. *Child Abuse & Neglect, 20*(12), 1183–1193. PMID: 8985609

5 Understanding, Treating, and Preventing the Development of Substance Use Disorders

A Psychodynamic Perspective

WILLIAM H. GOTTDIENER

Substance use disorders (SUD) are complex public health problems that affect millions of people worldwide (Coombs, 2005; Frances, Miller, & Mack, 2005). Important advances in understanding and treating SUD have been made by a broad range of people working in an array of scholarly disciplines (Frances et al., 2005). The field of psychoanalysis has made its own strides in understanding SUD and in developing treatments for it (Dodes; 1996; Gottdiener & Suh, 2012; Johnson, 1999; Khantzian & Albanese, 2008; Levin & Weiss, 1994; Weegman & Cohen, 2002; Petrucelli & Stuart, 2001; Wurmser, 1995; Yalisove, 1997). This chapter serves as an introduction to a complicated area of psychodynamic theories, clinical treatment, and empirical research. My goal is to provide a basic description of the psychopathology, treatment, and prevention of SUD from a psychodynamic perspective so that clinicians can use this information in clinical practice. In addition, this chapter will also be useful for teachers and researchers who are interested in learning about psychodynamic views of SUD. I have organized the chapter into three sections: "Causes of SUD," "Treatment of SUD," and "Prevention of SUD."

■ CAUSES OF SUD FROM A PSYCHODYNAMIC VIEWPOINT

Multi-determined causes of psychopathology have long been a hallmark of psychodynamic theories (Meissner, 2005). Psychodynamic theories, like a number of theories about the causes, treatment, and prevention of SUD, employ a bio-psycho-social perspective, which views SUD as a set of psychological problems that have complex interacting biological, psychological, and social determinants (Frances, Miller, & Mack, 2005; Washton & Zweben, 2006).

Central, though, to a psychodynamic position, and what distinguishes it from other theoretical models of SUD, is the view that the motivation to abuse psychoactive drugs is largely unconscious and is caused by problems in a variety of mental functions (Gottdiener, Murawski, & Kucharski, 2008; Juni & Stack, 2005; Khantzian & Albanese, 2008; Wilson & Khantzian, 1993).[1] The psychodynamics

1. There is, however, wide variation among psychodynamic theoreticians on which ego functions are believed to be most responsible for the development of an SUD; how to provide treatment; and even

of SUD involve three related dynamical processes: defense mechanisms, object relations, and drives (Johnson, 1999).

Psychodynamic theories posit that deficits in psychological functions lead to the development of an SUD. The major consequence of these problems is that they leave people unable to cope effectively with negative emotions, and drug use aids coping by enabling people to alter at will what they feel (see Gottdiener & Suh, 2012; Khantzian & Albanese, 2008). The self-medication hypothesis is the most prominent example of a psychodynamic-deficit model of SUD (Khantzian & Albanese, 2008).

The Self-Medication Hypothesis

The self-medication hypothesis of SUD is the most widely used psychodynamic model of SUD, in addition to being widely employed outside of psychoanalysis (Khantzian & Albanese, 2008). The self-medication hypothesis states that people develop an SUD because they are unable to cope with psychological pain, and that psychoactive drug use helps them medicate or defend against that pain (Khantzian & Albanese, 2008). Furthermore, people cope with specific psychological discomfort with specific classes of drugs, and if one type of discomfort predominates, then specific classes of drugs will become someone's drug of choice: such as, opiate abuse being reported as a salve for calming rage.

The notion of self-medicating is commonplace. The businesswoman who needs a drink at the end of a hard day's work; the man who snorts lines of cocaine in the bathroom of a nightclub to enhance the festive mood; the teenager who smokes blunts and drinks beer while relaxing with friends after school; the laid-off worker who cannot stop drinking wine in the evening after the loss of a job; and so on. These stories are known to most people, and most people understand that sometimes psychological pain is too much to deal with and a little help in the form of a drug can help a person feel better, or at least not feel as badly as they feel now.

Defense Mechanisms

The mind copes with negative psychological affects (dysphoria, anxiety, threats to the self) via automatic unconscious coping mechanisms called *defense mechanisms* (Brenner, 1982; Cramer, 2006; Shapiro, 2000; Vaillant, 1993). Defense mechanisms can be crudely organized into two groups called *maladaptive defenses* and *adaptive defenses*. Maladaptive defenses tend to provide immediate and short-term relief of psychological pain. Adaptive defenses tend to provide delayed and long-term relief of psychological pain. Maladaptive defenses are motivated by the pleasure principle wherein people seek immediate, albeit short-lived, gratification, and adaptive defenses are motivated by the reality principle, wherein people seek delayed, albeit long-lasting, gratification (Ainslie, 1982).

how to prevent an SUD from developing. Each psychodynamic school emphasizes different aspects of ego functions and each emphasizes different clinical interventions (see Gottdiener & Suh, 2012, for important scholarship on the wide range of psychodynamic approaches to SUD).

People who mostly use maladaptive defenses cannot effectively cope with negative affects. Clinical observation and empirical research has found that people with an SUD primarily use maladaptive defense mechanisms (Bornstein, Gottdiener, & Winarick, 2010; Soldz & Vaillant, 1998; see also Khantzian & Wilson, 1993). Denial is a common maladaptive defense seen in people with an SUD. The person who thinks he drives better when drunk is an example. Anticipation, on the other hand, is a common adaptive defense seen in people who have fully recovered from an SUD. This is seen in the person who plans ahead of time how to deal with offers for drinks from colleagues at a cocktail party. The planning includes imagining the types of situations that might arise, how to respond diplomatically, and how to cope with the temptation to drink alcohol when and if it arises.

Defense mechanisms do not just help people cope with negative emotions, they have interpersonal implications, too. Maladaptive defenses tend to put distance between the person using them and others (Vaillant, 1993). It is hard to tolerate the company of a person who constantly uses denial—a maladaptive defense (the drunkard with liver problems who claims his drinking is minimal compared with his friends'), but it is not hard to tolerate the company of a person who uses sublimation—an adaptive defense—because sublimation enables people to turn psychological pain into behavior that produces something that benefits the self and others (former drug abusers who become drug abuse counselors; turning the pain of their past to the benefit of others).

Furthermore, maladaptive defenses aim to rid the person's consciousness of psychological pain as quickly as possible, but adaptive defenses aim to keep that pain in conscious awareness to some extent because being aware of it longer can help the person cope more effectively. In fact, the adaptive defense of anticipation works precisely because a person tries to expect the kinds of possible experiences that might occur in the future from certain activities, which might include imagining the pain that could be experienced from behaving badly.

Object Relations

Why might maladaptive defense mechanisms create interpersonal distance? This distancing process might be related to poor object relations. In psychodynamic terms, internal representations of others are called *objects* (Gabbard, 2000). Object relations theories have in common the core notion that people are motivated from infancy onwards to relate to other people, and that aggressive and libidinal drives are directed toward others (Gabbard, 2000). Object relations contrast with defense mechanisms in that the main motivation of defenses is to seek pleasure and to avoid pain, whereas in object relations the main motivation is to relate to other people.

An SUD develops in a person who experiences him- or herself as having been deprived of a nurturing, loving, supportive relationship with parental figures according to an object-relations perspective (Johnson, 1999; Potick et al., 2007). Hence, there is a deficit in the way a substance abuser experiences his or her mental representations of significant others. Furthermore, the person who develops an

SUD has been previously thwarted in his or her attempts to relate to significant others. Psychoactive drugs are thought to play the role of a symbolic "object" in the substance abuser's mental life. Psychoactive drugs are thought to provide a positive emotional experience with a reliable object that is always giving and does so with consistently predictable results (Johnson, 1999; Silverman, Lachmann, & Milich 1982). The relationship with the drug is, therefore, an idealized one. The person who has had poor experiences of significant others is likely to find being with others painful, and a drug can be experienced as perfect "companionship."

Clinical observation and empirical research have found that people with an SUD have deficits in object relations (Johnson, 1999; Juni & Stack, 2005). People manifest problems in their ability to form meaningful relationships with others (Bornstein et al., 2010; Sprohg, Handler, Plant, & Wicker (2002). Furthermore, object relationship quality is positively correlated with SUD psychopathology (Rutherford et al., 1996).

Drives

A person who cannot be with others comfortably because of poor object relations might nonetheless still hunger to be with others. Longing to be with others, to be able to rely on them, is to be able to depend on them. The need to depend on others can be conceptualized, in part, as an expression of the libidinal drive. Research has found that people with an SUD are more pathologically dependent on other people (Bornstein et al., 2010; Sprohge et al., 2002). Either they express their need for others in a clingy way, or they deny needing others altogether. This need for others has been conceptualized in psychoanalytic theory as *oral dependency* or more simply as *interpersonal dependency* (Bornstein et al., 2010). A clingy dependency or the denial of dependency needs can also express aspects of the aggressive drive, because people who cling to others and those who deny needing others are angry at other people for not meeting their dependency needs. According to psychoanalytic theory, drives are psycho-biological processes that must be gratified (Brenner, 1982).

A contemporary view of the role that drives play in SUD comes from neuropsychoanalysis (Johnson, 1999; Zellner, Watt, Solms, & Panskepp, 2011). According to Zellner et al. (2011), dopamine is responsible for almost all motivated goal-directed behavior, and the dopaminergic neural circuitry is called "the Seeking System" (Solms & Turnbull, 2002). The Seeking System is a general motivational system that is thought to underlie libidinal and aggressive behavior. Dopamine is involved in all SUD behavior and is largely the cause of the pleasure provided by drug intoxication (Kosten, George, & Kleber, 2005; Zellner et al., 2011). Thus, rather than viewing drug abuse as a function of libidinal and aggressive drives per se, drug abuse is seen as a function of the general Seeking System. The development of an SUD can be further understood as the development of a *new* biological drive for a drug, and that new drive—like all drives—needs to be gratified (Johnson, 2001), thus, increasing the motivational valence for drug use. Drives for drugs can therefore be seen as the result of a deficit in the ability to gratify basic drive needs. Drug use compensates for the lack of earlier gratification.

▪ DEFENSE MECHANISMS, OBJECT RELATIONS, AND DRIVES IN SUD: CLINICAL IMPLICATIONS

The discussion about the psychodynamics of SUD paints a picture of a person whose drug-abusing behavior aims to (a) seek relief from negative affects; (b) seek the company of others, and (c) seek pleasure. The motivations to abuse drugs are therefore psychologically, socially, and biologically based. The clinical implications are profound.

The most common goal of SUD treatment is to enable people to become "sober"—meaning that they will never use psychoactive drugs again for the remainder of their lives. Initial abstinence is sought in most treatment programs (Frances et al., 2005; Khantzian & Albanese, 2008). This is a difficult challenge for patients and clinicians because there is so much motivation for patients to continue to use drugs. Imagine having to relinquish the behaviors that you have relied on to (a) seek relief from negative affects; (b) seek the company of others (especially if the drug is experienced as a reliable "other"); and (c) seek pleasure. That is a tough row to hoe. Nonetheless, people do relinquish or considerably reduce their drug use, and clinicians find ways of helping people with their SUD. How can clinicians use psychodynamic treatments to help people with an SUD?

Psychodynamic Treatment of SUD

Psychodynamic psychotherapies have been found to benefit a wide range of individuals with a wide range of psychological problems, and this finding has been empirically supported for decades (Shedler, 2010). Clinical reports and empirical research on the benefits of psychodynamic treatments for people with an SUD is, however, considerably more limited in scope than the findings on other psychological problems (see Gottdiener & Suh, 2012). The reported clinical case studies and the extant clinical research on psychodynamic treatments for SUD do not reflect the breadth of psychodynamic theorizing on SUD. Nonetheless, the empirical research consistently shows that psychodynamic treatments produce positive outcomes for people with an SUD (Gottdiener & Suh, 2012).

A number of manualized psychodynamic psychotherapies have been developed and tested with patients who have an SUD. These include Supportive-Expressive Therapy (Crits-Christoph et al., 2008; Luborsky & Luborsky, 2006); Combined Psychiatric and Addictive Disorders treatment (Rosenthal, 2002), and Dynamic Deconstructive Psychotherapy (Gregory, DeLucia-Deranja, & Mogle, 2010; Gregory, Remen, Soderberg, & Ploutz-Snyder, 2009; Gregory, Chlebowski, Kang, Remen, Soderberg, Stepkovitch, et al., 2008). These treatments have been found to improve symptoms of opiate, cocaine, and alcohol abuse, including helping patients with a variety of comorbid problems such as schizophrenia and borderline personality disorder.

Empirical psychotherapy process research has not determined why psychodynamic psychotherapies can help people with an SUD. Nonetheless, it is possible to describe how a clinician can use the ideas and information discussed in this chapter and to apply them in clinical practice.

First, it is important that the clinician understand that no treatment abruptly halts and cures an SUD. Most patients who start psychotherapy attend for only eight sessions, usually leaving well before they have resolved their problems (Garfield, 1994). Hence, the clinician has to approach treatment of people with an SUD realistically. This is particularly so in SUD treatment, where newer models of treatment emphasize treatment flexibility (Gottdiener, in press; Mee-Lee, MacLellan, & Miller, 2010).

Second, as implied in this chapter, it can be useful to conceptualize defense mechanisms, object relations, and drives as working together in a patient's psychopathology, and that any treatment will affect all three dynamic components. Defense mechanisms serve their function via self-deception—by making people unaware of various aspects of themselves (Shapiro, 2000; Vaillant, 1993). A patient who loudly tells his therapist, "I had to drink!" can be understood via the perspective of his defenses. Having to drink and stating so loudly could suggest that the patient is unaware of wanting to drink and of needing to disown that desire. In addition, stating loudly that he had to drink could suggest that he sees the therapist as a potentially disapproving person (object) and that the only way to tell him this is to do so in a way that clearly removes any responsibility from his actions, thereby, trying to preserve a positive object relationship with his therapist. Last, the patient's loud statement of "having to" drink could suggest that drinking has become a biological drive in need of gratification. Failing to drink would be like intentionally ceasing to breathe, and it is that need that the patient is trying to convey to his therapist.

As noted earlier in this chapter, a psychodynamic view of SUD is a bio-psycho-social model of SUD. As a bio-psycho-social model, it recognizes that the act of excessive alcohol drinking is a multi-determined, caused event. It also underscores that there are many contributing factors to a substance abuser's poor ability to cope with psychological pain. For clinicians, knowing that there are many contributing factors to SUD symptoms means that clinical interventions need to be flexible; they need to address various aspects of the patient's bio-psycho-social SUD behavior, and that at any one time the clinician might focus on one or another aspect of the dynamics of the patient's substance abuse. A clinician responding to the above patient might make any one of a number of replies to that patient, such as, "Saying you 'had to drink?' You mean you didn't want to drink?" That statement might address the defensive functioning of the drinking because it suggests that the patient was willfully, albeit unconsciously, ignoring the desire to drink. Another clinician might say, "You sound like you want to make sure that I know that you are not to blame for your drinking," thus capturing the object-relations aspect of the drinking. Yet another therapist might say, "It sounds like you really needed a drink—like it was something you couldn't live without," thus highlighting the person's need to gratify a drive to drink.

It is important that clinicians remind themselves to be flexible in their therapeutic interventions. Although a clinician might intervene to address the patient's defenses, object relations, and drives, it is important to understand that exclusive use of individual psychotherapy of a person with an SUD might be insufficient to help any one person (see Khantzian & Albanese, 2008; Gottdiener, 2012).

■ THE IMPORTANCE OF RECOGNIZING AND RESOLVING NEGATIVE COUNTER-TRANSFERENCE REACTIONS

A difficult stumbling block in treating patients with an SUD is the tendency for therapists to experience negative counter-transference reactions to their SUD patients that undermine the treatment (Wurmser, 1995). Patients with an SUD differ from other patients in that their SUD problem is viewed by most people in society as immoral. Even the most accepting psychotherapists can harbor this attitude of immorality, but defend against it, thereby ignoring it.

It is not uncommon to find therapists lecturing their patients about the problems they will encounter in life if they continue to abuse drugs and alcohol; to scold their patients when they relapse; or to refer them to various other treatment programs that will "straighten them out" and get them sober so that they can continue therapy after sobriety has set in. Many psychotherapists who treat people with an SUD refuse to see them if they attend a therapy session while intoxicated. Therapists usually establish these rules because they believe that if they see the patient when the patient is intoxicated, they are tacitly endorsing the patient's substance abuse. Or, they believe that if they see an intoxicated patient there is no way that a quality psychotherapy session can occur because they will be talking to a patient whose cognitive processes are clouded by drug effects. They do not tell their anxious patients to stop being anxious or even consider how anxiety clouds cognitive processes, but they believe that psychoactive drugs do so in an untoward and untreatable manner. Other therapists refuse to treat patients because they believe that all substance abusers lie and cannot be trusted. Still other therapists can be notoriously insensitive:

> A patient who had been in individual psychodynamic psychotherapy for over one year was referred by his individual psychotherapist for a consultation for psychiatric medication from a psychiatrist. The patient told the psychiatrist that medication was sought to cope with symptoms of depression and anxiety related to severe post-traumatic stress disorder. The patient also disclosed that he was abusing alcohol and tranquilizers to cope with his trauma symptoms, but that, despite the substance abuse and an interest in using medication to boost the effects of his therapy, individual psychotherapy had been helpful in getting the patient back on his feet again. The psychiatrist told the patient to stop therapy immediately because it was contraindicated for people who were active substance abusers; to get sober by going into an inpatient treatment program, and to attend Alcoholic Anonymous meetings daily or else the patient would not recover from his trauma or SUD problems. The patient was highly offended by the psychiatrist's recommendation. As a result, he never returned to that psychiatrist; never filled the prescription that he was given, continued in individual psychotherapy, but refused to again seek psychiatric assistance despite having severe enough symptoms for the next six months that warranted a psychiatric medication consultation.

The psychiatrist's behavior, driven in part by negative counter-transference attitudes, had an untoward effect on the patient's treatment because the patient refused to seek another psychiatric consultation, potentially experiencing more misery than it was necessary for him to experience.

There are no absolute solutions to resolving negative counter-transference problems. Good supervision is essential, though (see Gottdiener, 2008). In addition, it is also useful for therapists to hold two ideas in mind. First, rather than seeing drug-seeking as a problem, it is useful to see it as "an interest" that the patient has. Most psychotherapists do not see a patient who reads extensively as having a problem. Most psychotherapists would see it as an interest that is intellectually gratifying and stimulating, but it is also possible that extensive engagement in reading could be a way of avoiding uncomfortable feelings that are aroused when socializing. As a result of doing so much reading, the person has a diminished social life and feels increasingly lonely as time moves on. In this case, an interest in reading might be pursued to the detriment of interpersonal relationships.

Similarly, drug abuse can be seen as an intense interest in getting high that is pursued potentially to the detriment of many areas of life. The defensive, object relations, and drive aspects of SUD enable a person to have an increasing interest in seeking drugs and getting high. This means that an overarching goal of treatment is to help people (a) recognize that they are interested in getting high and (b) that getting sober or becoming a "social user" requires losing or reducing an interest in getting high. It is not uncommon for SUD patients to enter psychotherapy or any drug treatment and say that they have no interest in drugs; that the drugs do nothing for them, and that they have to stop using. Noticeable in these statements, however, are the patient's denial of interest in using and the lack of interest in stopping using. "Having to stop using" is a considerably different attitude to have than "wanting to stop using." It is the difference between someone who is in the pre-contemplation stage of change versus someone who is in the action stage of change (Prochaska, DiClemente, & Norcross, 1992; see also Dodes & Khantzian, 2005).

A second way to cope with counter-transference problems is to use an old actor's technique called "the magical 'What if?'" (Stanislavski, 1964/1936). When actors have trouble understanding the motivation that a character has to say or do what is written in the text, they can try to gain understanding by asking themselves, "What if I were to say these words and do these actions—why would I do so?" I have found with my own clinical work and with that of my supervisees that using this actor's technique can help create not only psychological understanding of the patient's possible motives, but also empathy for the patient's situation. If a patient relapses, and the therapist cannot understand why, it can help to ask, "Why would *I* relapse? What would motivate *me* to relapse when all seemed to be going so well?" The "magical what if" will not guarantee successful understanding of a patient's motivation or empathy for the patient's plight, nor will it resolve negative counter-transference reactions, but it can be a helpful technique to enable positive engagement with patients to occur, and it can be a useful source of clinical hypotheses to enable treatment to move forward.

Prevention of SUD from a Psychodynamic Viewpoint

A patient I reported on in a previous publication (Gottdiener, 2001) was a mother in her twenties who was in treatment in a residential therapeutic community program. She was a single parent who had lost her child to foster care when she was arrested and entered a jail diversion program. She also entered treatment in the early part of her first trimester of pregnancy with her second child. The patient was volatile and was nearly dismissed from the treatment program several times due to her aggressive behavior and failure to participate in group treatment during the orientation phase of treatment.

I treated the patient with weekly individual psychodynamic psychotherapy that enabled her to discuss her history of child abuse; the shame she felt over it and over having lost her first child to foster care. She was a thin-skinned person who was easily insulted and who responded aggressively. Nonetheless, I helped her recognize that when she was insulted or threatened, her emotions went from anger to violent rage nearly instantly, to which she agreed. Although she was able to gain insight into the connections between her emotions and her behavior, that insight was not always enough to prevent rage and aggression from occurring. Simply telling her to walk away from people she felt insulted by helped her. Enabling her to safely speak with me about her shame also emboldened her to participate in the group activities of the treatment program.

During her second trimester, I gave her a copy of Benjamin Spock's book on baby and child care because she knew little about child development or child-rearing despite being the mother of a young child (Spock & Needleman, 2012). She appreciated receiving the book and later told me reading it helped her to calm herself down when she was able to determine that her contractions were not premature labor, but instead were Braxton-Hicks contractions. She eventually transferred to a mother and child therapeutic community program where she was to receive treatment and parenting education while living with her child.

Although I do not know the ultimate fate of this patient, the treatment I provided combined individual psychodynamic psychotherapy with a therapeutic community milieu treatment, and with psychoeducation on child care and child-rearing. Ultimately, she was able to participate effectively enough in the therapeutic community to qualify as a good candidate for the mother and child program she entered, where one focus of the program was to help prevent her second child from developing an SUD.

To date, there is no literature I am aware of that discusses how to use psychodynamic theories or techniques in the service of primary prevention of an SUD. There is, however, literature on relapse prevention in people who have achieved abstinence (Khantzian, Halliday, & McAullife, 1990), and on the psychodynamic treatment of substance-abusing parents in which treatment also helps prevent the development of an SUD in their children (Suchman et al., 2008; 2010).

Relapse prevention and use of individual psychotherapy to help prevent the development of an SUD in the child of a parent with an SUD was evident in my patient's treatment. Although I do not know if my patient ever relapsed, she did not while she was in treatment with me, even though she could have done so because the therapeutic community was an unlocked facility. And, although I do not know if her second child ever developed an SUD, my patient's treatment helped put her into a position that decreased the likelihood of her child developing one. Problematic parenting has been associated with later development of an SUD in children (Shedler & Block, 1990; Suchman et al., 2008; 2010). If parenting can be improved, then it appears as if the children of people with an SUD have a better chance at avoiding developing an SUD themselves. New research is being conducted to address this very issue (Suchman et al., 2008; 2010).

■ SUMMARY AND CONCLUSION

Psychodynamic models of SUD are bio-psycho-social models of psychopathology. Defense mechanisms, object relations, and drives commingle to create SUD symptoms, and they reflect the behavioral and mental manifestations of the bio-psycho-social view. Each of these psychodynamic processes can be understood as contributing to the development and maintenance of an SUD, and each component can be worked with psychotherapeutically to help people with an SUD. Individual psychodynamic psychotherapy can be combined with other treatments in a therapeutic approach to SUD that is flexible and humane. Thinking and approaching patients psychodynamically can expand a psychotherapist's clinical purview and enable the therapist to help a wide range of patients.

■ REFERENCES

Ainslie, G. (1982). A behavioral economic approach to the defense mechanisms: Freud's energy theory revisited. *Social Science Information, 21*(6), 735–779.

Bornstein, R. F., Gottdiener, W. H., Winarick, D. (2010). Construct validity of the relationship profile test: Links with defense style in substance abuse patients and comparison with non-clinical norms. *Journal of Psychopathology and Behavioral Assessment, 32*(3), 293–300.

Brenner, C. (1982). *The Mind in Conflict*. New York: International Universities Press.

Coombs, R. H. (2005). *Addiction Counseling Review: Preparing for Comprehensive, Certification, and Licensing Examinations*. Mahwah, NJ: Lawrence Erlbaum.

Crits-Christoph, P., Connolly-Gibbons, M. B., Gallop, R., Ring-Kurtz, S., Barber, J. P., Worley, M., Present, J., & Hearon, B. (2008). Supportive-expressive psychodynamic therapy for cocaine dependence: A closer look. *Psychoanalytic Psychology, 25*(3), 483–498.

Cramer, P. (2006). *Protecting the Self: Defense Mechanisms in Action*. New York: Guilford.

Dodes, L. (1996). Compulsion and addiction. *Journal of the American Psychoanalytic Association, 44*(3), 815–835.

Dodes, L. M., & Khantzian, E. J. (2005). Individual psychodynamic psychotherapy. In R. J. Frances, S. I. Miller, & A. H. Mack (Eds.), *Clinical Textbook of Addictive Disorders* (pp. 457–473). New York: Guilford.

Frances, R. J., Miller, S. I., & Mack, A. H. (2005). *Clinical Textbook of Addictive Disorders* (3rd ed.). New York: Guilford.

Gabbard, G. O. (2000). *Psychodynamic Psychiatry in Clinical Practice* (3rd ed.). Washington, DC: American Psychiatric Publishing.

Garfeld, S. L. (1994). Research on client variables in psychotherapy. In S. L. Garfield & A. E. Bergin (Eds.), *Hand- book of psychotherapy and behavior change* (pp. 190–228). New York: John Wiley.

Gottdiener, W. H. (2001). The utility of individual supportive psychodynamic psychotherapy for substance abusers in a therapeutic community. *Journal of the American Academy of Psychoanalysis, 29*(3), 469–482.

Gottdiener, W. H. (2008). Sexual boundary violations in residential drug-free therapeutic community treatment. *The International Journal of Applied Psychoanalytic Studies, 5*(4), 257–272.

Gottdiener, W. H. (in press). Assimilative Dynamic Addiction PsychoTherapy (ADAPT). *Journal of Psychotherapy Integration.*

Gottdiener, W. H., Murawski, P., & Kucharski, L. T. (2008). Using the delay discounting task to test for failures in ego-control in substance abusers: A meta-analysis. *Psychoanalytic Psychology, 25*(3), 533–549.

Gottdiener, W. H., & Suh, J. (2012). *Psychodynamic approaches to understanding and treating substance use disorders: Theory, research, treatment.* In P. Luyten, L. Mayes, P. Fonagy, M. Target, & S. Blatt (Eds.), *Handbook of Contemporary Psychodynamic Approaches to Psychopathology.* New York: Guilford.

Gregory, R. J., DeLucia-Deranja, E., & Mogle, J. A. (2010). Dynamic deconstructive psychotherapy versus optimized community care for borderline personality disorder co-occurring with alcohol use disorders: A 30-month follow-up. *Journal of Nervous and Mental Disease, 198*(4), 292–298.

Gregory, R. J., Remen, A. L., Soderberg, M., & Ploutz-Snyder, R. J. (2009). A controlled trial of psychodynamic psychotherapy for co-occurring borderline personality disorder and alcohol use disorder: Six-month outcome. *Journal of the American Psychoanalytic Association, 57*(1), 199–205.

Gregory, R. J., Chlebowski, S., Kang, D., Remen, A. L., Soderberg, M. G., Stepkovitch, J., et al. (2008). A controlled trial of psychodynamic psychotherapy for co-occurring borderline personality disorder and alcohol use disorder. *Psychotherapy: Theory, Research, Practice, Training, 45*(1), 28–41.

Johnson, B. (2001). Drug dreams: A neuropsychoanalytic hypothesis. *Journal of the American Psychoanalytic Association, 49*(1), 75–96.

Johnson, B. (1999). Three perspectives on addiction. *Journal of the American Psychoanalytic Association, 47*(3), 791–815.

Juni, S., & Stack, J. E. (2005). Ego function as a correlate of addiction. *American Journal on Addictions, 14,* 83–93.

Khantzian, E. J., & Albanese, M. J. (2008). *Understanding Addiction as Self-Medication: Finding Hope Behind the Pain.* New York: Rowman & Littlefield.

Khantzian, E. J., Halliday, K. S., McAuliffe, W. E. (1990). *Addiction and the Vulnerable Self. Modified Dynamic Group Therapy for Substance Abusers.* New York: Guilford.

Khantzian, E. J., & Wilson, A. (1993). Substance abuse, repetition, and the nature of addictive suffering. In A. Wilson & J. Gedo (Eds.), *Hierarchical Concepts in Psychoanalysis: Theory, Research and Clinical Practice* (pp. 263–283). New York: Guilford.

Kosten, T. R., George, T. P., & Kleber, H. D. (2005). The neurobiology of substance dependence: Implications for treatment. In R. J. Frances, S. I. Miller, & A. H. Mack, (Eds.), *The Clinical Textbook of Addictive Disorders* (pp. 3–15). New York: Guilford.

Levin, J. D., & Weiss, R. H. (1994). *The Dynamics and Treatment of Alcoholism: Essential Papers.* Northvale, NJ: Jason Aronson.

Luborsky, L., & Luborsky, E. (2006). *Research and Psychotherapy: The Vital Link.* Lanham, MD: Jason Aronson.

Mee-Lee, D., MacLellan, T. A., & Miller, S. D. (2010). What works in substance abuse treatment. In B. L. Duncan, S. D. Miller, B. E. Wampold, & M. A. Hubble (Eds.), *The Heart* and Soul of Change: Delivering What Works in Psychotherapy (pp. 393–417). Washington, DC: American Psychological Association.

Meissner, W. J. (2005). The dynamic unconscious: Psychic determinism, intrapsychic conflict, fantasy, dreams, and symptom formation. In E. S. Person, A. M. Cooper, and G. O. Gabbard (Eds.), Textbook of Psychoanalysis (pp. 21–37). Washington, DC: American Psychiatric Publishing.

Petrucelli, J., & Stuart, C. (2001). Hungers and Compulsions: The Psychodynamic Treatment of Eating Disorders & Addictions. Northvale, NJ: Jason Aronson.

Potick, D., Adelson, M., & Schreiber, S. (2007). Drug addiction from a psychodynamic perspective: Methadone maintenance treatment (MMT) as a transitional phenomena. Psychology and Psychotherapy: Theory, Research, and Practice, 80, 311–325.

Prochaska, J. O., DiClemente, C. C., & Norcross, J. C. (1992). In search of how people change: Applications to addictive behaviors. American Psychologist, 47, 1102–1114.

Rosenthal, R. N., (2002). Group treatment for patients with substance abuse and schizophrenia. In D. W. Brook & H. I. Spitz (Eds.), The Group Therapy of Substance Abuse (pp. 327–349). New York: Haworth.

Rutherford, M. J., McKay, J. R., Alterman, A. I., Cacciola, J. S., & Cook, T. G. (1996). The relationship between object relations and reality testing deficits to outcome status in methadone maintenance patients. Comprehensive Psychiatry, 37(5), 347–354.

Shapiro, D. (2000). Dynamics of Character: Self-Regulation in Psychopathology. New York: Basic Books.

Shedler, J. (2010). The efficacy of psychodynamic therapy. American Psychologist, 65(2), 98–109.

Shedler, J., & Block, J. (1990). Adolescent drug use and psychological health: A longitudinal inquiry. American Psychologist, 45(5), 612–630.

Silverman, L. H., & Lachmann, F. M., & Milich, R. H. (1982). The Search for Oneness. New York: International Universities Press.

Soldz, S., & Vaillant, G. E. (1998). A 50-year longitudinal study of defense use among inner city men: A validation of the DSM-IV defense axis. Journal of Nervous and Mental Disease, 186(2), 104–111.

Solms, M., & Turnbull, O. (2002). The Brain and the Inner World: An Introduction to the Neuroscience of Subjective Experience. New York: Other Press.

Spock, B., & Needleman, R. (2012). Dr. Spock's Baby and Childcare. New York: Gallery Books.

Sprohg, E., Handler, L., Plant, D., & Wicker, D. (2002). A Rorschach study of oral dependence in alcoholics and depressives. Journal of Personality Assessment, 79(1), 142–160.

Stanislavski, C. (1964/1936). An Actor Prepares. New York: Routledge.

Suchman, N., DeCoste, C., Castiglioni, N., Legow, N., & Mayes, L. (2008). The mothers and toddlers program: Preliminary findings from an attachment-based parenting intervention for substance-abusing mothers. Psychoanalytic Psychology, 25(3), 499–517.

Suchman, N. DeCoste, C., Castigilioni, N., McMahon, T. J., Rounsaville, B., & Mayes, L. (2010). The mothers and toddlers program, an attachment-based parenting intervention for substance using women: Post-treatment results from a randomized clinical pilot. Attachment and Human Development, 12(5), 483–504.

Suchman, N., McMahon, T., DeCoste, C., Castigilioni, N., & Luthar, S. (2008). Ego development, psychopathology, and parenting problems in substance-abusing mothers. American Journal of Orthopsychiatry, 78(1), 20–28.

Vaillant, G. E. (1993). *The Wisdom of the Ego*. Cambridge, MA: Harvard University Press.

Washton, A. M., & Zweben, J. E. (2006). *Treating Alcohol and Drug Problems in Psychotherapy Practice: Doing What Works*. New York: Guilford.

Weegman, M., & Cohen, R. (2002). *The Psychodynamics of Addiction*. London: Whurr.

Wurmser, L. (1995). *The Hidden Dimension: Psychodynamics of Compulsive Drug Use*. New York: Jason Aronson.

Yalisove, D. (1997). *Essential Papers on Addictions*. New York: New York University Press.

Zellner, M. R., Watt, D. F., Solms, M., & Panksepp, J. (2011). Affective neuroscientific and neuropsychoanalytic approaches to two intractable psychiatric problems: Why depression feels so bad and what addicts really want. *Neuroscience and Biobehavioral Reviews*, 35(9), 2000–2008.

6 Transmission of Parenting Models at the Level of Representation

Implications for Mother–Child Dyads Affected by Maternal Substance Abuse

HANNAH M. LYDEN AND
NANCY E. SUCHMAN

The robust continuity of substance abuse across generations can be explained on many different levels. Epidemiological and etiological studies have shown a large genetic component involved in substance abuse transmission (Tsuang, Lyons, Eisen, Goldberg, True, Lin, et al., 1996). Similarly, investigations of the environmental factors involved in the intergenerational continuity of substance abuse have shown that children in alcoholic or drug abusing families are more likely to experience marital conflict and interpersonal violence between parents (Fitzgerald & Eiden, 2007; Floyd, Cranford, Daugherty, Fitzgerald, & Zucker, 2006; Schumm, O'Farrell, Murphy, & Fals-Stewart; 2009; Stanley, 2008), as well as financial instability and low socio-economic status (Fitzgerald, Zucker, & Yang, 1995). Each of these experiences further promotes vulnerability to substance abuse (Fitzgerald & Zucker, 2005). At the behavioral level, problems have been observed in children of drug abusing parents in the domains of emotion regulation (Sher, 1991; Zucker, Chermack, & Curran, 2000) and interpersonal relationships (Whipple, Fitzgerald, & Zucker, 1995).

Vulnerability to substance abuse within a substance abusing parent–child dyad can also be explored at the representational level (see Fitzgerald, Wong, & Zucker, this volume). The representational level involves the mental structures in the mind of the mother as well as representations that are transmitted to the mind of the child. These representations are thought to underlie behaviors and interactions (such as those observed in the investigations mentioned above). Although any one level of investigation does not fully encompass the intergenerational continuity of substance abuse across generations, each level adds a layer of understanding to the dynamic processes involved in vulnerabilities to substance abuse disorders.

In order to examine the vulnerability to substance abuse disorders conferred by mental processes at the representational level, this chapter will focus on early mother–infant interactional processes and the subsequent development of representations that may increase vulnerability to substance abuse. Normative early mother–infant interaction processes and the concomitant formation of representations and reflective functioning are reviewed first. Next, the role of maternal substance use in the formation of maladaptive attachment relationships and representations is considered. Finally, potential implications for intervention development and future research within a developmental framework are explored.

■ FORMATION OF ATTACHMENT REPRESENTATIONS

Mental Representations

Mental representations, a central construct in the psychoanalytic literature on parent–infant relationships (see Bowlby, 1960, 1973, 1980; Breuer & Freud, 1895; Winnicott, 1960), have been defined as internalized features of the external world that, taken together, construct the internal world. In the context of self–object relationships, they are an intrapsychically produced component of the relationship with the other. The *representational level* is the level of inquiry directed toward the study of mental representations. In the context of mother–child dyads, the representational level involves a specific focus on mental representations of the mother and their transmission to the child. Although the transmission of representations involves behavioral interactions between mother and child, behavioral interactions are thought to be guided by the internal mental representations of the mother. Maternal behaviors are then thought to form as representations in the mind of the child (for further discussion, see Fonagy, Gergely, Jurist, & Targey, 2002).

The concept of mental representations has been examined and recapitulated in many psychoanalytical dialectics. Breuer and Freud (1885) initially conceptualized the internal world as an internalized copy of the external world constructed from actual early experiences. Hartmann (1927) later contended that higher organisms increasingly displace activity toward the external world into internal activity. Object relations theorists have conceived of representations of self and other as internalized "pieces" of actual experienced relationship patterns (e.g., Fairbairn, 1952; Kernberg, 1975; Sandler & Sandler, 1978; Sullivan, 1953). What these definitions share is the expectation that, in the context of the parent–infant relationship, an infant will internalize interactions as they happen and form representations of these interactions, and these internal representations will guide how the infant feels and behaves in future interactions. Thus, for example, an infant who experienced and internalized a parent's punishment is likely to carry forward a sense of self-loathing in subsequent interactions with that parent and with others.

Internal Working Models—Representations of Attachment

The discourse on mental representations became more dynamic and constructivist with Bowlby's (1960) notion of *internal working models* in Attachment Theory. Bowlby (1960) defined the *internal working model* as not simply an internalized version of the external reality but instead as a fluid blend of real and perceived events. Bowlby (1960) included representations of self and the attachment figure within the model and suggested that the interaction of these two representations allows the infant to interpret and anticipate the attachment figure's behavior as well as plan for or guide their own behavior in the attachment relationship. In referring to them as internal *working* models of self and attachment figure, he emphasized the *dynamic* and *functional* aspects of these attachment models (Greenberg & Mitchell, 1983). Rejecting the *static* nature implied in earlier definitions of mental representations, Bowlby (1969) emphasized that internal working models are constructed not only from real external events, but also from the infant's *perceptions* of these external events.

Bowlby (1973) identified two key features of internal working models of attachment: (a) whether or not the *attachment figure* is judged to be generally responsive to calls for support and protection, and (b) whether or not the *self* is judged to be responded to in a helpful way. Bartholomew and Horowitz (1991) have since suggested that the dual representations of self and other interact to form underlying expectancies associated with specific attachment classifications. For example, a *secure* classification would correspond to a an internal working model of the caregiver as responsive and the self as worthy of being responded to; a *preoccupied* classification would correspond to a working model of the caregiver as generally responsive but the self as unworthy of responsiveness; and an *avoidant* classification would correspond to a working model of the caregiver as generally unresponsive and the self as unworthy of any responsiveness.

Bowlby (1973) suspected that internal working models—as constructed internal models for relationship—are appropriated to other current and future relationships. Bowlby (1973) also suggested that the construction of internal expectations through contingent interactions with the attachment figure was a dynamic process that continued throughout development, an idea that allows for the possibility of *change* in representations as new interpersonal experiences are processed internally. Depending on developmental experiences across the lifespan, then, Bowlby believed that internal working models may remain stable *or* adapt and change. In fact, a central tenet of Bowlby's (1960, 1973, 1980) theory of attachment development across the lifespan was that internal working models change.

Stability and Malleability of Attachment Classification Throughout Development

Bowlby (1988) hypothesized, and a number of studies have confirmed, a continuity suggesting that an individual's experience with his or her parents strongly influences later attachments (Hazan & Shaver, 1987; Main, Kaplan, & Cassidy, 1985); adult social networks (Flaherty & Richman, 1986; Sarason, Sarason, & Shearin, 1986); mother and infant bonding (Parker & Barnett, 1988); and adult intimate relationships (Truant, Herscovitch, & Lohrenz, 1987). At the same time, Bowlby's (1973, 1980) theory was deeply rooted in the idea that internal working models are persistent yet open to revision based on new interpersonal experiences (Bowlby, 1973, 1980; Waters, Weinfield, & Hamilton, 2000). For example, individuals with insecure attachment classifications in early childhood may gain access to corrective relationships later in life that allow them to move from insecure to secure attachment styles. Conversely, events that are detrimental to development may transform a secure attachment style into an insecure one (Ammaniti, Van Ijzendoorn, Speranza, & Tambelli, 2000; Waters, Weinfield, & Hamilton. 2000).

Findings regarding the continuity of attachment classifications over time remain equivocal (Waters et al., 2000; Waters, Merrick, Treboux, Crowell, & Albersheim, 2000; Weinfield, Sroufe, & Egeland, 2000). For example, Waters, Merrick, Treboux, Crowell, and Albersheim (2000) conducted a 20-year longitudinal study to investigate the stability of attachment classifications assessed using the "Strange Situation" in childhood and the Berkeley "Adult Attachment Interview" (AAI) in adulthood. Overall, 72 percent of the infants received the same secure versus insecure attachment classification in adulthood. For the 27 percent whose attachment classifications changed, some studies suggest that attachment-related life experience is an important change agent. For example, negative life events such as maternal depression may assault a child's already established attachment patterns and force change in the representations of self or the attachment figure over the course of development. In support of this idea, Waters, Merrick, et al. (2000) found that negative life events, defined as the loss of a parent, parental divorce, life-threatening illness of parent or child, parental psychiatric disorder, and physical or sexual abuse by a family member, were important factors in the change of attachment classification over time. The assault on these representations might come either from changes in the caregiver's behavior (e.g., decreased sensitivity to the child's affect), or from changes in the child's expectations for the caregiver.

The internal working model, whether characterized by continuity or change, is a critical mechanism in the intergenerational transmission of attachment (Hamilton, 2000; Waters, Merrick, Treboux, Crowell, & Albersheim, 2000; Weinfield, Sroufe, & Egeland, 2000). Guiding relational activities throughout development, internal working models are also activated during the development of the parental mind. *It is in this parental mind state that internal working models of early attachment confer expectancies and behaviors upon the relationship between caregiver and infant.*

The Potential Role of Subjective Experience

Although Bowlby's (1973, 1980) claims about the stability and malleability of attachment classifications have been supported by attachment research, the question remains: What causes classifications to change when no negative life event is experienced? One possible mechanism of change may be a perceived but undocumented negative life event, one that is unsubstantiated by family members but is nevertheless evident in the subjective experience of the individual. This emphasis on the importance of individual subjective experiences of external events is an important contribution to attachment by psychoanalytic theorists (Breuer & Freud, 1885). Individual differences in perceptions of attachment relationships lend an important new avenue for investigating differential outcomes associated with attachment classification, such as personality development and other forms of competence. If these internal subjective working models do guide interpersonal interactions throughout development, as Bowlby (1969) has suggested, then the transmission of these models may be explained in part by the transmission of subjective experience (as well as documented events).

Theories of Intergenerational Transmission

There are many theoretical and empirical investigations of the mechanisms of the intergenerational transmission of working models and parenting. Fraiberg, Adelson, and Shapiro (1975) coined the phrase *ghosts in the nursery* to illustrate the implications of *ghosts* from the past (i.e., early trauma for the mother), and their effects on the relationship between mother and child in the present. Fraiberg and colleagues (1975) claimed that not all–past intruders plague mother-infant relationships, and even some of the most horrific pasts are not transmitted into the present functioning of the parent. After reviewing clinical cases, Fraiberg and colleagues (1975) concluded that the presence of traumatic memories in the absence of experienced negative affective states determined the pervasiveness of "ghosts" in the mother–child relationship as well as maternal identification with the aggressor and her inability to access negative affective states in the present (Freud, 1936). The mechanism, then, that allows repetition of past relationships in the present is the inability to work through negative events from the past so that negative and positive affective states can be integrated. Although not in the same language as internal working models, Fraiberg and colleagues' formulation implies that representations of past parent–child relationships form in childhood and, if not consciously worked through, will pervade interactions between parent and child in the present.

George and Solomon (1996) also proposed a mechanism of transmission of parenting models at the representational level. This *caregiving system* originates with the same representations of self, other, and relationship that compose internal working models of attachment. In addition, it involves a representation of self-as-caregiver. The representations in the model are derived from the mother's own working model of attachment (Bowlby, 1982; Main & Goldwyn, 1991; Slade & Aber, 1992). The childhood attachment working models and the caregiver models share the same goal (i.e., proximity to the attachment-figure) and function (i.e., protection or protecting the attachment-figure). Therefore, differential responsiveness from attachment figures during development allows mental representations to change in response to formation of new attachments (Solomon & George, 1996). The internal working models of caregiving are then thought to represent the mature transformation of the attachment system (Solomon & George, 1996).

Research on Intergenerational Transmission

Transmission of Parenting Practices

Numerous research investigations have documented the intergenerational continuity of parenting practices, demonstrating that present-day parents tend to use parenting strategies similar to those used by their own parents (Putallaz, Costanzo,

Grimes, & Sherman, 1998; van Ijzendoorn, 1992). Empirical studies from the child abuse literature especially have reported an association between early experiences of parental abuse and individuals' later abusive treatment of their own children (Belsky, 1984; Egeland, Jacobvitz, & Papatola, 1987; Straus, Gelles, & Steinmetz, 1980). Importantly, this association did not disappear even after controlling for socioeconomic status, personality, psychological well-being, and parenting beliefs (Whitbeck et al.,1992; Simons, Beaman, Conger, & Chao, 1993). Early exposure to harsh or abusive parenting is probably the most consistent predictor of later use of coercive parenting practices toward one's own children (Steinmetz, 1987). Similar patterns of parenting across generations have been found in the normal range of parenting practices (Belsky, 1984).

Transmission of Attachment Classification

Although research indicates a robust continuity between the quality of a parent's childhood experiences and their own child's attachment, the child's attachment is not necessarily the same classification as the parents' (Aber, Slade, Cohen, & Meyer, 1989; Ainsworth & Eichberg, 1991; George & Solomon, 1996; Main & Goldwyn, 1991; Main, Kaplan, & Cassidy, 1985; Oppenheim, Nir, Warren, & Emde, 1997; Slade et al., 1995; Steele, Steele, & Fonagy, 1996; Ward, Botyanski, Plunket, & Carlson, 1989). For example, a secure mother may have insecure children, and vice versa. Discontinuities in classification support Bowlby's (1973, 1980) assertion that internal working models are pervasive throughout development, yet are open to revision due to experience. A handful of researchers have investigated intergenerational discontinuity of attachment and proposed catalysts for change to secure attachment, including psychotherapy, a supportive partner, and the birth of the baby (Bowlby, 1982; Egeland, Jacobvitz, & Sroufe, 1988; George & Solomon, 1991; Slade et al., 1995; Ward et al., 1989).

Summary

Early interactions between infant and mother precipitate the construction of beliefs about the caregiver and self that eventually form the internal working models, or mental representations of attachment. Through interpersonal interactions, these models morph and change and are eventually reactivated during the time of impending motherhood (George & Solomon, 1996). In the intergenerational transmission of internal working models, representations in the parental mind are transmitted to the child and define interactional processes throughout the child's development.

■ FORMATION OF AFFECT REPRESENTATIONS

The primary interactions between infant and mother are also the birthplace of emotional understanding and emotional development for the infant (Fonagy et al., 2002). A foundation for emotional understanding and affect regulation is forming at the same time that mental representations of attachment are being transmitted.

These interactional processes between mother and infant in constructing emotional understanding in the infant are outlined by Fonagy and colleagues (2002), and will now be discussed.

Interactional Processes Between Mother and Infant

When an infant is born, its initial contact with the external world arrives in the form of the mother. During the early post-partum phases, mother and child are involved in a symbiotic relationship ideally unaffected by the external world (Winnicott, 1956). The infant's dependency on the mother dictates a necessity for extreme preoccupation by the mother—called *primary maternal preoccupation* (Winnicott, 1956)—to attune fully to her baby's physiological and emotional needs. Fonagy and colleagues (2002) proposed that, through contingent interactions with the mother, the child learns to identify and tolerate his/her own emotions. The process begins with internal-state cues felt by the infant that are expressed as emotion states (e.g., when the baby is frightened) but are not yet perceived consciously by the infant. Fonagy and colleagues (2002) proposed that, through a repetitive pattern of emotional displays from the infant to the caregiver and a consequent reaction from the caregiver to the infant, the infant eventually becomes sensitized to the internal-state cues and learns to identify the correct set of internal-state cues that corresponds to a distinctive emotional category.

Evidence for this process of an externally induced sensitization to internal states is proposed in the form of biofeedback training procedures (Fonagy et al., 2002). In biofeedback training procedures, such as blood-pressure regulation, the subject learns to identify internal cues associated with high blood pressure and, through repeated exposure to the external representation, or pulse, of the internal state eventually attains sensitization to and in some cases control over the internal state. Fonagy and colleagues (2002) proposed that the psychological mechanism involved in affect mirroring involves this same process, or recognizing an internal state as associated with external stimuli.

Construction of Affect Representations

Ordinarily, when a baby expresses an emotion derived from an internal-state cue, the mother registers and demonstrates the emotion through her emotional facial expressions. The infant is initially unaware of the emotion category corresponding to the behaviorally expressed internal-state cue and must therefore rely on the mother's empathic reflection of the emotion to begin organizing (and recognizing) emotional states. Fonagy and colleagues (2002) have hypothesized that, while perceiving the empathic reflection from the mother, the infant uses its contingency-detection capacities to associate the internal and behavioral cues with the parental empathic reflection and to understand which internal-state cue and own behavioral expression preceded the empathic reflection of the parent (for further discussion, see Fonagy et al., 2002). Based on these two associations, the infant is able to understand which internal-state cues and own behavioral expressions caused the parental empathic reaction (see Gergely & Watson, 1999).

A foundation for emotional understanding is constructed in this way over time through repetitive contingent interactions with the mother. Fonagy and colleagues (2002) refer to the maternal behavior in this process as "mirroring" since the mother is mirroring the emotion the infant is feeling back to the infant.

Once the infant has a general understanding of the affect expression, seeing the mother with the same expression may produce errors in attribution. The infant may not know if the mother is simply registering the infant's affect or if the affect is originating within the mother. Fonagy and colleagues (2002) have proposed that a mother will ordinarily reflect affect back to the infant in an exaggerated or "marked" manner similar enough to the infant's emotional expression for the infant to recognize and yet marked enough by exaggeration to prevent misattribution of the emotion to the mother (Fonagy et al., 2002). In this way, the infant develops a representation of the marked emoted response from the mother as a representation of the felt internal-state cues and calls upon this representation to understand the internal state. Over time, the infant will learn to detect and group together internal-state cues that signify distinct emotional states and construct secondary symbolic representations of each emotional state that can be cognitively accessed for the purpose of affect regulation (for further discussion, see Fonagy et al., 2002).

Four Developmental Functions of Affect Mirroring

Fonagy and colleagues (2002) conceived the process just described as the four developmental functions served by parental affect mirroring. These include:

1. The *Sensitization Function* whereby the infant learns to detect and group together sets of internal-state cues that signify distinct emotional categories;
2. The *Representation-Building Function* whereby the infant develops separate representations for the mother's "marked" emotive expressions and establishes secondary representations associated with primary affective states;
3. The *State-Regulation Function* whereby marked mirroring allows the infant to experience positive arousal (associated with the newfound efficacy in eliciting maternal empathy) that helps regulate negative affect state; and
4. The *Communicative and Mentalizing Function* whereby secondary representations associated with primary affective states give the infant a new means to express and communicate about his/her and others' emotions.

Effects of Dysfunctional Interactional Processes on Affect Representations

Fonagy and colleagues (2002) have also described less optimal affect mirroring that involves deviations in mirroring and/or markedness. If, for example, a mother has unresolved intrapsychic conflicts and is not able to contain or becomes overwhelmed by the infant's affect, the mirrored affect will be congruent to the affect displayed by the infant but will lack markedness. In this case, the infant will probably attribute the expressed affect to the mother instead of recognizing it as a reflection of its own. Similarly, mothers who are capable of marked yet incongruent emotional displays may end up promoting misattribution of affect. For example, when a mother misinterprets her crying baby's cues as anger or aggression, the infant is likely to misidentify the mirrored emotional display (e.g., aggression) with his internal-state cues (i.e., sadness) and wrongly categorize the internal-state cues (as well as attribute the parental emotional reflection to his affective state), which does not reflect his actual emotional state.

In the first instance involving unmarked mirroring, the infant will be unable to group together its own internal-state cues into discrete emotions (sensitization function), and secondary representations of these emotions will not be formed (representation function). In both instances, the infant's capacity to regulate (state-regulation function) and communicate about emotion (communicative and mentalizing function) will also be compromised.

Affect Representations and Attachment Classification

Contingent interactions between mother and child are the necessary mechanisms for the infant's emotional development. They are also central to the formation and solidification of attachment classification. In the formative interactions between mother and infant, the infant builds representations of the self and the caregiver in constructing internal working models of attachment. When mirroring is unmarked or incongruent, over time, insecure or disorganized attachment patterns are more likely to ensue. For example, if a mother has unresolved intrapsychic conflicts such as a conflict-ridden representations of her own mother, she may not be able to tolerate the infant's affect, causing her contingent response to be unmarked (expressing her own affective response to the infant rather than reflecting the infant's own affect). She may also retreat from the infant or be unable to soothe the infant in that moment. The infant may then begin to form a representation of the caregiver as unsoothing and unavailable and of the self as undeserving of an available caregiver. Representations acquired in this way, through contingent caregiver–infant interactional processes in early life, further consolidate as 1) secondary, symbolic representations of marked emotive responses from the mother that may be cognitively called upon to reflect and rationalize about affect; and as 2) mental representations of attachment that can serve as prototypes for other and future attachment relationships.

Mentalization and Reflective Functioning

The attachment and affective representations that form in early life are important for two mental processes: *mentalization* and *reflective functioning* (Soderstrom & Skarderud, 2009). Although these two terms are sometimes used interchangeably, they are independently important for interactional capacities between mother and child. Fonagy, Target, and colleagues (Fonagy et al., 1991; Fonagy & Target, 1996) have developed and defined the concept of mentalization as *an individual's competence in envisioning mental states of the self and other in order to understand behaviors in terms of mental states; i.e., thoughts, feelings, desires, beliefs, and intentions.* Stated differently, mentalization implies an ability *to understand the mental states of the self and of the other during interactional processes.*

The concept of reflective functioning is usually used to indicate the *degree of a mentalizing capacity* (Fonagy, Target, Steele, & Steele, 1998). Reflective functioning, in the context of parent–infant relationships, refers to the parent's ability to understand the mental states of the infant and attend to these mental states in a timely and appropriate manner. The concept of "parental reflective function" was introduced by Slade and colleagues (Slade, 2005; Slade, Grienenberger, et al., 2005), who define it as the "... parent's capacity to make sense of her/his child as a separate, differentiated person with thoughts, feelings, and a mind of his own...." (Slade, 2006, p. 640). Slade and her colleagues have viewed this parental capacity as critical to the child's ability to develop adaptive means of affect regulation, (i.e., affect representations) and establish productive relationships, (i.e., secure attachment classifications).

Reflective functioning can be understood as the functional constituent bringing together attachment representations and the development of affect representations (see Soderstrom and Skarderud, 2009). During the earliest interactions between mother and infant, the infant constructs representations of affect and attachment, and it is in the efficient construction of these representations that the abilities in reflective functioning arise.

Summary

Early constructed affect representations may be cognitively called upon by the infant in emotional situations in order to regulate and act appropriately in new situations. Similarly, the attachment patterns formed during early mother–child interactions are eventually appropriated to other and future relationships and guide an individual's behavior in assessing and reacting to all important attachment situations. The development of reflective functioning may be the important mechanism by which each of these representations is transmitted across generations (Slade, Grienenberger et al., 2005; Soderstrom & Skarderud, 2009). Reflective functioning is the primary mental process necessary for appropriate attunement to one's own infant and thus for construction of the infant's own affect and attachment representations. We now focus on interactive processes in the mother–child dyad when the mother is a substance abuser, to understand how contingent interactional processes might break down at the representational level.

■ DEVELOPMENTAL VULNERABILITIES TO ADULT SUBSTANCE ABUSE BASED ON EARLY REPRESENTATION DEVELOPMENT

The representations that consolidate during early life are vitally important for later emotional and relational functioning, and deficits in these processes can lead to extreme vulnerability to psychological dysfunction, emotion dysregulation, antisocial behaviors, and, most importantly for this chapter, substance abuse (Soderstrom & Skarderud, 2009). In this section we consider how adult addiction disorders may arise in response to early deficits in representation development. Several psychodynamic writers have conceived of substance abuse as an effort to compensate for the early developmental deficits and losses. We now review some of these psychodynamic observations and explanations for the initiation of substance abuse. We then suggest how these psychodynamic perspectives echo failures in the early development of affect representations described previously, setting the stage for compulsive substance use and substance use disorders.

Failures to Recognize, Represent, and Regulate Affect

Krystal and Raskin (1970) were among the first to characterize the affective experiences of drug addicts as undifferentiated, global, primarily somatic, and by having great difficulty in tolerating painful affects. They also reported drug abusers describing subjective affective states in vague and unspecific terms, such that distinct feelings of anxiety and depression were not discernable (Krystal, 1962; Krystal & Raskin, 1970). Wurmser (1984) used the term *hyposymbolization* to capture the inability to articulate feelings, which, in turn, limits the ability to experience one's own affects or to empathize with others.

Krystal (1982) has further suggested that an inability to verbalize affect or use affect as a signal of feeling states causes substance abusers to become preoccupied with bodily sensations of emotional arousal and use the drug to block these bodily sensations. Krystal and Raskin (1970) have linked the substance abuser's experience of withdrawal from substances with the inability to understand and thus regulate emotions. The "primitive sensorimotor form" of affective states in the drug abuser seems to amplify the pain of withdrawal, in that the bodily reactions from the withdrawal threaten to overwhelm the individual both emotionally and physically.

Greenspan (1977) has delineated specific mechanisms by which the drug of choice acts on specific developmental vulnerabilities related to attachment and affect representations garnered through early relationships with the primary caregiver. More specifically, Greenspan (1977) has described developmental problems stemming from an absence of affect representations and the lack of cognitive capacities to use these representations in emotional regulation and affective control, due to a lack of psychological structures "necessary for experiencing organized feeling states" (Greenspan, 1977, p. 89).

Greenspan has suggested that many substance abusers experience an anhedonic feeling of "nothing inside." Clinical interviews conducted by Greenspan (1977) have indicated that many substance abusers do in fact experience this emptiness, which may, as Greenspan suggested, originate from undifferentiated feeling states and unknowable emotional responses within the individual. The drug of choice in producing bodily sensations may allow the individual to feel distinct feelings, of pleasure or pain, which may be initially undifferentiated and unfelt.

The drug of choice may also make the emptiness more tolerable. Importantly, the drug can never replace or compensate for deficits in emotional development, so the maladaptive compulsive behaviors associated with drug seeking persist and magnify, while the developmental issues fail to be resolved. Neurological changes also reinforce the compulsive drug seeking behavior, making it increasingly difficult to stop (see Volkow et al., 2003).

Based on the collective psychodynamic observations of the undifferentiated and somatic understanding of emotions in substance abusers outlined above, Khantzian (1985) proposed the *self-medication hypothesis*, stating that individuals are compelled to depend on alcohol and drugs to manage painful affective states of which they have no symbolic understanding or means to regulate. The individual who 1) does not recognize internal-state cues as emotions, 2) cannot call upon these representations for cognitive control over his emotions, 3) views the world as unable to soothe him, and 4) lacks the ability to self-soothe, and uses drugs to compensate for these deficits. The drug acts as a consistent and reliable treatment for the overwhelming affects he experiences in everyday life. The addict is self-medicating in order to function in a world where affects are overwhelming and he lacks the ability to control or regulate them.

Allen, Fonagy & Bateman (2008) have described a two-way process between substance abuse and reflective functioning in the substance-abusing adult: Addiction and intoxication can impair reflective functioning both in relation to her own internal states and in perceiving the internal states of others. Impaired reflective functioning then leads to an inability to regulate her own or others' emotions, which can, in turn, cause high levels of conflict and stress in close relationships and potentially precipitate episodes of drug abuse to assuage heightened arousal.

Failures in the Development of Attachment Representations

Greenspan (1977) has also suggested that the initial contact between mother and infant ordinarily provides a homeostatic situation for the infant in that its basic needs are met and a primary human attachment is formed. In the case of a substance abuser, when the mother is emotionally unavailable, the infant will never experience a basic stable homeostatic experience, developing instead a disrupted (e.g., insecure or disorganized) attachment. Greenspan (1977) tied this absence of homeostatic experience to the substance abuser's description of a need to obtain a "basic and primitive kind of homeostatic experience" (Greenspan, 1977, p. 87). The substance is thought to work at the physiological and psychological representational levels to attain this basic homeostatic experience. The drug creates the calming or stimulating effect, depending on its active ingredient, that the substance abuser is unable to achieve independently.

The lack of a representation of the ability to self-soothe or of the other as soothing confers another vulnerability to the development of substance abuse. In some drug-dependent individuals, there is a disturbance of what Krystal (1977) has described as a "walling off" of maternal object representations along with representations of self-helping and self-comforting abilities (similar to the attachment representation of a mother as unavailable or unable to soothe, described earlier). Krystal has suggested that this absence of self-soothing representations leads the addict toward drugs to take over the mothering functions that s/he is unable to perform otherwise (e.g., comforting, relaxing, going to sleep).

Krystal and Raskin (1970) have also suggested that the child's ability to maintain sleep is the first developmental milestone in exercising self-care functions and may also be an indicator of the child's own self-representation as being soothable. Conroy, Armitage, and Hoffman (2009) found that children of alcoholics slept less and took longer to fall asleep than children of non-alcoholics. Tarokh and Carskadon (2009) also found that children of alcoholics had lower non-rapid eye movement brain delta wave power than children of non-alcoholics, waves that are suggested to play a role in protecting sleep by blocking sensory thalamic input into the cortex (De Gennaro & Ferrara, 2003; Yamadori, 1971). Although these studies do not directly measure underlying representations, they do support the link between children's inability to self-soothe and a possible vulnerability to developing a substance abuse disorder later in life. Further exploring the relationship between a child's inability to sleep and early representation formation will be an important research direction.

As a substitute for a human attachment object, the substance itself can take on the maternal role in its constant availability to the individual. As the unmarked emotive responses from the mother have led to the individual's inability to determine the source of emotion, he is unable to distinguish a sense of himself distinct from the other. This lack of differentiation causes anxiety in the infant about being completely merged or completely separated from the mother (Krystal, 1977). The ingestion of the substance allows him to be completely merged with the maternal object, now symbolized by the drug, yet does not lead to a complete loss of himself, as the drug is not the actual object (Krystal & Raskin, 1970).

Origins of Psychodynamic Observations in Affect Representation and Attachment Deficits

Many of the observations noted above can be understood in light of the processes of affect representations described earlier in this chapter. For instance, the undifferentiated internal state-cues within the mind of the individual precipitate vague and primarily somatic understanding of discrete emotions. The lack of acquisition of the representations of affective states also precludes the individual from entering into a mentalistic understanding of the emotions of himself and others. The individual who has not developed categorical representations of internal-state cues or a symbolic understanding of the meaning of the sensation will only experience felt emotions as bodily sensations. Similarly, the individual who lacks a representation of discrete emotional categories will only be able to verbalize his emotions as vague and unclear bodily sensations.

Attachment-related deficits may originate with a substance user's experience of her affect as "overwhelming" to an early caregiver (and hence the outside world) when the caregiver retreated from the infant during times of distress. The self-representation of affect as too overwhelming may have caused the individual to experience her affect as uncontainable and uncontrollable, and any effort to do so as unnecessary and possibly dangerous. In this case, the overwhelming affect threatens to take over the individual just as it pushed away her mother.

■ MATERNAL SUBSTANCE ABUSE AND INFANT REPRESENTATIONS

Deficits in affect recognition, representation, and regulation, and in attachment representation development are likely to precipitate a compensatory response that leads to addiction, as described above. In addition, deficits in representation development in the mother are likely to precipitate impairment in her interactions with the child—especially in her ability to mirror affect and foster a secure attachment. In this section, we consider the implications of maternal substance abuse—and its accompanying representational deficits—for the development of healthy affect and attachment representations in the young child (Smyke, Dumitrescu, & Zeanah, 2002); Zeanah & Zeanah, 1989).

Infant Attachment Representations

Within the context of the mother–infant dyad, when the infant feels an internal state-cue (e.g., hunger) and begins to express this state behaviorally (e.g., crying), the mother ordinarily acknowledges his behavior and reacts with her own marked emotive expression. When the mother's mind is co-opted by drug dependence, the mother–infant relationship is at risk of suffering from maternal emotional unavailability, incongruent mirroring, and dyadic dysregulation (Soderstrom & Skuderad, 2009). If the mother is preoccupied by her addiction or intoxicated, she may be impaired in her reflective function and therefore be either 1) overwhelmed by the affect of her infant and therefore express a contingent but unmarked display of the affect, or 2) compelled to retreat from the infant without displaying any emotive expression (returning to drugs to regulate her own affect).

The infant is consequently confronted with either an unmarked contingent emotion or a lack of contingent interaction from his caregiver (Bauman & Dougherty, 1983; Bernstein, Jeremy, Hans, & Marcus, 1984; Jeremy & Bernstein, 1984). The infant may then develop a representation of the mother as unavailable based on either neglect of his emotional needs or her inability to soothe him. The infant may also form a representation of himself as unworthy of attention and soothing. Because the mother is not available to soothe the infant, the infant may develop a representation of the outside world as unable to soothe internal states, and of internal states as overwhelming to the outside world. If he is unable to successfully attach to his mother, he is left with disturbed representations of the outside world as unavailable and of himself as unworthy of attachment.

Infant Affect Representations

Based on the four functions Fonagy et al. (2002) proposed as influenced by representations during early interactional processes, the following four deficits may be found at the representational level of an infant with a substance abusing mother.

The Sensitization Function

The lack of contingent interaction from a mother who has neglected her infant during episodes of the infant's emotional display will prevent the infant from developing the capability of detecting and grouping together sets of internal-state cues that signify distinct emotions. For example, if the infant is frightened and the mother is unavailable to mirror his emotion, the different internal-state cues or bodily reactions that signify fright will not be grouped together in the infant's mind and understood as a discreet emotion. This lack of contingency will therefore deter his construction of emotional representations.

The Representation-Building Function

When the substance abusing mother is overwhelmed by her infant's affect and displays a contingent yet unmarked emotional display, the infant is unable to establish secondary representations that become associated with her primary affective states. The infant may recognize his own internal state as reflected by the mother, but, because the emotive display is unmarked, the infant cannot identify the emotion as his own. The infant will therefore lack the cognitive means for accessing and attributing emotional states to himself. These secondary representations form the bases of controlling and understanding affective states later in development.

The State-Regulation Function

In normative processes, the mother's emotive display is contingent on the behavioral display of the infant, enabling the infant to see the temporal relationship between his own and his mother's behaviors. This coupling leads to the infant's belief that he is controlling his mother's affective-reflective displays during soothing interactions, and thus leads to a sense of omnipotence that gradually decreases the felt negative affect. This representation supports the infant's ability to use the external world to soothe his own affective states while also allowing him to develop a representation of the ability to self-soothe (see Fonagy et al., 2002). Therefore, in situations where the mother is not contingently responding to the infant, the infant will not develop positive arousal from causal contingency, and the negative affect will not be assuaged. Similarly, the infant will not develop the ability to use the external world to be soothed, nor build a representation of the ability to self soothe.

The Communicative and Mentalizing Function

If the infant is able to achieve the previous three developmental points, the infant is able to internalize the "marked" secondary representations associated with the primary affective states and begin to develop a means to communicate and reason about affective states. The child will then be able to use the acquired affect representations in relationships with others and when reasoning about himself, marking the beginning of mentalization and reflective functioning. If the three previous developmental points are either nonexistent or dysfunctional, the infant will be barred from entry into a mentalistic understanding of emotions in the relational context. This final step is important in the development, or in this instance non-development, of reflective functioning.

The Child's Mental Representations of the Drug

Through early interactional processes with a substance-abusing mother, representations constructed within the mind of the child may lead to vulnerabilities to substance abuse in later life. How, though, might the drug itself becomes the "fix" for the individual's underlying deficits in both affect representations and attachment? An individual's motivation to turn to the drug for self-soothing or regulatory processes, beyond the chemical properties of the drug and its concomitant neurobiological effects, may be explained in part through the representation of the drug itself within the mind of the child who is exposed to his parent's drug use during his early years.

As Fitzgerald, Wong, and Zucker (this volume) have reported, children as young as preschool age have mental representations of alcohol use composed of sensory and perceptual sensitivities, cognitive/cultural rules for use, and expectations about their own use (Zucker & Fitzgerald, 1991; Zucker, Kincaid, Fitzgerald, & Bingham, 1995). The study by Zucker et al. (1995), described in the chapter by Fitzgerald and colleagues (this volume) is of particular interest here. Zucker and colleagues (1995) found that children of alcoholics were more likely to be able to identify an alcoholic beverage than children of non-alcoholics, and by kindergarten age attributed more alcoholic beverage use to drinkers. This finding illustrates that, at least by preschool age, the child who has been exposed to parental alcohol use has already developed underlying perceptual representations of alcohol and has an understanding of a relationship between the alcoholic and the beverage itself. In other words, there seems to be a mental representation of the substance itself within the mind of the child.

Similarly, Gottdiener (this volume) has suggested that an individual with a drug-abusing parent has a superego (the internalized version of the parental objects that works as a rule-maker for the individual) that will contain mental images of parents who use drugs. These mental images might provide rules that permit the individual to use drugs and a message that being a drug-abusing parent is acceptable. The work presented by both authors illustrates a potential mentalistic process at work within the mind of the child involving the parent's drug of choice. It may then be inferred that, during early interactional processes between the substance-abusing mother and the infant, the drug itself may be involved in the child's representational understanding of its attachment to its mother.

The ideas of Jacques Lacan (1977) suggest a third possible mechanism by which the mental representation of the drug interacts with the deficient attachment and affect representations also within the mind of the child. Like Bowlby (1969), Fonagy and colleagues (2002), and Winnicott (1956), Lacan (1977) proposed an all-encompassing dyadic relationship between mother and child in early life. The concept of "Mother," according to Lacan (1977), is the baby's first act of symbolization. All things related to the mother (e.g., comfort, soothing, feeding) are symbolized by the ideation of a person (e.g., the mother). The mother, however, is not always available. The leaving and returning of the mother is what Lacan (1977) thought determines the infant's understanding of object permanence (that an object can disappear but also reappear). However, with this understanding come questions such as: "Where has my mother gone?" "Where is she when she is not with me?" (Bailly, 2009). Lacan (1977) stated that these questions are in their proto-conceptual form even in pre-language infants (Bailly, 2009).

The father, Lacan (1977) thought, represents the most obvious answer to these proto-conceptual questions. Before the infant can understand such things as "chores" or "work," it can understand and *see* the father as a probable distraction for the mother. This distraction, Lacan (1977) thought, is communicated by the mother to the infant via language in statements such as "It's time to sleep. Mommy and Daddy must have their dinner now."

Lacan (1977) proposed that the infant designs a hypothesis that determines why the mother chooses the father over the infant; namely, that "father has something that I do not." This unqualified "something" that the mother wants is the object of the mother's desire. However, due to the fact that the mother is sometimes with the infant, the infant begins to think that maybe he has this quality as well. The infant's understanding that there exists another entity that is desired by the mother (i.e., the paternal metaphor) is the beginning of the infant's understanding of the external world. The paternal metaphor allows the child to enter into a triadic environment and understand that there exists a world outside the Mother. This allows the child to enter into a symbolic understanding, where other things or events (e.g., work and chores) may be substituted for Father as the distraction for the mother, and the child can mentalistically understand the motivations and actions of the other. Importantly, Lacan (1977) thought that a symbolic understanding may only be attained through an internalization of the paternal metaphor or a symbolic understanding of "something else" occupying the mind of the mother. Likewise, Lacan (1977) warned that an inability to enter the symbolic world, or a late entrance into it, can result in psychotic structures of the mind.

The object of the mother's desire, according to Lacan (1977), can maintain a strong influence in the unconscious of the child. The idea that the mother is seeking the object when it is away from the child makes it the ultimate object of desire for the child, who thinks, "It must be a wonderful thing if she spends so much time on it," so the child's desire forms also around the object. The child also thinks, "Maybe if I can get it, then mother will want to be with me, and I will not have to face her absences" (Bailly, 2009).

The child begins to think of the object as an attainable object and a possible defense against the anxiety of losing the mother. Moreover, the child can retain hope that it itself has the object, as evidenced by the Mother's presence. However, if acceptance of the paternal metaphor is complete, then the object is symbolized as something else that the mother desires (e.g., the father).

This symbolization allows the child to seek the lost object through other symbols of the object of desire. Importantly, what the child supposes the object to be for its mother depends on her actual, real desires. For example, a mother who is sociable and is constantly holding parties may have a child who determines that the object of her desire is "sociability" or "popularity" (Bailly, 2009). In an attempt to gain the object of her desire, the child then sets out to be popular. In this way, Lacan (1977) suggested, the desire to possess the object of the mother's desire is the motivation behind much human activity in that it assuages the anxiety that comes from recognizing that one lacks the object. The constant search to possess the object of the mother's desire is an unending battle to assuage the anxiety that comes from not having the desired object and thus being undesirable.

In the case of the substance-abusing mother, the object may be interpreted by the child as the mother's drug of choice. The infant may see the mother using the drug instead of attending to its needs, or the mother may communicate to the infant that taking the drug is what the mother desires at that moment. In either instance, it is the drug itself that is occupying space in the mother's mind and what the child must compete with for attention from the mother. The symbolized object in the mind of the child will be the drug of choice, precipitating an unquenchable desire to possess the drug-object.

The idea of "the object" is ultimately used by Lacan (1977) to portray how desire shapes one's sense of self. The unconscious desire to possess this object is transmitted through one's relationship to others and becomes a significant part of the other's self-definition. This dynamic conflict within the mind of the child to become as absorbing as the drug may precipitate future interactions with the drug in order to do just that—become the absorbing object of its mother's desire. If the symbolized object in the mind of the child is the mother's drug of choice, this representation will become a determining point in the child's self-concept and will guide future actions and choices.

Summary

Infants who are confronted with a substance-abusing mother who is either neglectful or overwhelmed by the infant's affect are at risk of developing representations of the outside world as unavailable and unsoothing, representations of themselves as unworthy of attention and attachment, and representations of their own internal-state cues as overwhelming to the outside world. They will probably lack representations of the ability to self-soothe; lack representations of emotional categories; and lack secondary representations of primary affective states that may be called upon for self-regulation. Finally, they are likely to lack internalized representations of affective categories that lead to a mentalistic understanding of emotions of themselves and others and reflective function. Disturbed affect representations and attachment patterns coupled with intrapsychic motivation to seek out the drug provide a potential explanatory mechanism for the intergenerational transmission of substance abuse from substance-abusing mother to child.

Implications for Treatment

Although other factors in the transmission of substance abuse disorders exist (e.g., genetics, neurobiology, and social environment), understanding the representational world of the substance-abusing mother and the child affected by her substance abuse provides important new avenues for developing effective parenting treatments for this population. Earlier in this chapter, we presented an attachment-based explanation of the development of cognitive structures (e.g., symbolic representation of affective experiences, mental representations of attachment) that promote emotional regulation and mentalization. We then reviewed psychodynamic observations of adults with addictions and suggested that adult characteristics seem to echo problematic representation-formation with early caregivers. Finally, we considered how maternal addiction influences the formation of affect and attachment representations in children, directly through dyadic interactions and indirectly through the symbolic meaning the child ascribes to the abused substance. We now turn to a discussion of the potential treatment implications of these patterns of representation development and transmission in mothers and their young children.

The mother is the first and most critical point of entry for treatment. There is a need for development and evaluation of interventions that target maternal development at the representational level, including the mother's capacity to recognize simple affective experience (her own and her infant's) and develop cognitive structures that enable her to symbolically represent and organize her affective experiences so that they are no longer overwhelming and unknowable and can be better regulated. In this way, affect representations may be rebuilt, beginning with the foundations of discrete emotions, so that secondary representations of these emotions will have a more distinct quality, and a mentalistic understanding of these discrete emotions may be utilized in therapy (Suchman et al., 2011).

This focus on the mother's own affective experience is also critical to the infant's regulation, not only because it enables the mother to mirror the infant's affect appropriately but also because the infant's affect may itself be a source of considerable affective distress for the mother. Interventions also need to provide support and guidance for the mother to learn about her infant's needs for a secure attachment and affect mirroring in order to promote the infant's cognitive and emotional development, self-organization, and affect regulation.

There is an equally critical need for interventions that provide the mother with an opportunity to modify her own attachment representations that perpetuate her experience of herself as unworthy of care, the world as a dangerous place where needs go unmet, relationships as untrustworthy, and the infant as a potential adversary. Fortunately, adult attachment representations can change in the context of a consistent and caring relationship (see Waters et al., 2000).

Even if affect regulation issues and attachment models are addressed and restructured, the unquenchable need to "become" the drug, or the object of the mother's desire, may still be a motivating factor in the individual's need for the drug. Therefore, addressing the intrapsychic relationship the individual may have with the drug may release him from the desire for the drug and allow for a more successful treatment.

Each of these closely related intervention foci requires the involvement of a well-trained professional clinical team with whom the mother can form a reliable, long-term, trusting alliance and maintain a firm yet supportive presence that can withstand her setbacks over the course of her recovery. Research on attachment, mentalization, and the intervention process has shown that improvement in any targeted outcome (e.g., attachment status and mentalization) occurs only within the context of a carefully developed, secure and consistent therapeutic relationship (Lieberman & Van Horn, 2008; Sadler, Slade, & Mayes, 2006; Shedler, 2010).

Promoting change at the representational level involves a careful assessment of attachment history (past and present), personality organization, interpersonal and parental functioning, and potential psychiatric disorders. It takes time (years, in most cases), and requires ongoing clinical training, supervision, and support from well-informed colleagues. Interventions targeting the more immediate aims of improving abstinence and relapse-prevention (including motivational enhancement) and harm reduction are critical complementary interventions that can help restore the neurological reward systems to premorbid states while providing early reinforcing experiences of success in the struggle to overcome addiction. Over time, the development of new cognitive capacities at the representational level (e.g., to symbolically represent affect, maintain secure attachment representations, and appropriately mirror the infant's affect) may further reduce dependency on addictive substances by replacing it with a steady reliance on internal representational stability.

There is also a need for carefully coordinated wrap-around services for most mothers with addictive disorders, because they often have difficulty in many aspects of daily life, including meeting basic family needs (e.g., safety, housing, food, supplies, employment, transportation, and medical needs) and finding and sustaining supportive relationships (with partners, family, friends, and co-workers). They may also be involved with a wide range of social and legal services (e.g., state welfare programs, child welfare services, criminal court systems). Carefully-coordinated and timed case management and supportive services to address concomitant problems related to addiction, maternal responsibilities, and the mother-child relationship is imperative. Three such interventions for mothers with addictive disorders are in the process of being developed and evaluated (see Pajulo & Kalland, this volume; Punamaki & Belt, this volume; Suchman, DeCoste, Ordway, & Bers, this volume).

■ IMPLICATIONS FOR RESEARCH

From a developmental standpoint, focusing on mental representations may add to an understanding of the pathways to substance use disorders. Specifically, considering mental processes at the representational level as potential contributors to substance use disorders may help clarify instances of equifinality and multifinality in pathological developmental trajectories resulting in substance abuse disorders (see Cichetti & Rogosch, 1996). *Equifinality* (Moyer, 1974) involves the notion that, in an open system, many different risk factors, or starting points, may lead to the same outcome or disorder. *Multifinality* (Wilden, 1980) refers to the notion that one risk factor or starting point may lead to many different end points or disorders. While developmental inquiries into psychopathology may be bolstered by genetic trends or common experiential factors between individuals, it is within the level of representation that the individual's subjective understanding of certain processes may be explored and the problems of multifinality and equifinality may be more closely answered. The subjective understanding, or the individual's unique perception and representations of events, may be what better explains why one individual develops a substance abuse disorder while another does not within similar developmental trajectories. Therefore, exploring the relationship between mother and child affected by substance abuse on the level of representation may allow for a broader understanding of the individual's development and may lead to different avenues in which to intervene in the development of a substance abuse disorder.

Developmental psychologists (Fonagy, Gyorgy, Jurist, & Target, 2002; Greenspan, 1977) have proposed that the initial interactions between mother and child form the foundation of mental representations in the mind of the child. Therefore, if for example, in the case of substance-abusing mothers, dyadic interactional processes between mother and child are dysfunctional, the representations constructed within the mind of the child may not be developmentally sound for future relational and emotional development. The underdeveloped or dysfunctional representations may then lead to future vulnerabilities associated with substance abuse and thus explain one mechanism in the intergenerational continuity of the disorder. In order to fully explore this relationship between mother and child, the purpose of this chapter has been to delineate the processes by which both attachment representations as well as affect representations are constructed in the mind of the child, and to explore the implications of this perturbed interaction in the case of mothers and children affected by substance abuse.

■ REFERENCES

Aber, J. L., Slade, A., Cohen. L., & Meyer, J. (1989). *Parental Representation of Their Toddlers: Their Relationship of Parental History and Sensitivity and Toddler Security*. Paper presented at the biennial meeting of the Society for Research in Child Development, Kansas City, MO.

Ainsworth, M. D. S., & Eichberg, C. (1991). Effects on infant-mother attachment of mother's unresolved loss of an attachment figure, or other traumatic experience. In C. M. Parkes, J. Stevenson-Hinde, & P. Manis (Eds.), *Attachment Across the Life Cycle* (pp. 160–186). New York: Routledge.

Allen, J. G., Fonagy, P., & Bateman, A. W. (2008). *Mentalizing in Clinical Practice*. Washington, DC: American Psychiatric Publishing.

Ammaniti, M., Van Ijzendoorn, M. H., Speranza, A. M., & Tambelli, R. (2000). Internal working models of attachment during late childhood and early adolescence: an exploration of stability and change. *Attachment & Human Development, 2*(3), 328–346.

Bailly, L. (2009). *Lacan: A Beginner's Guide*. London: Oneworld Publications, Ltd.

Bartholomew, K., & Horowitz, L. M. (1991). Attachment styles among young adults: A test of a of a four-category model. *Journal of Personality and Social Psychology, 61*(2), 226–244.

Bauman, P. S., & Dougherty, F. E. (1983). Drug-addicted mothers' parenting and their children's development. *International Journal of the Addictions, 18*, 291–302.

Belsky, J. (1984). The determinants of parenting: A process model. *Child Development, 55,* 83–96.

Bernstein, V., Jeremy, R. J., Hans, S. L., & Marcus, J. A. (1984). A longitudinal study of off-spring born to methadone-maintained women: II. Dyadic interaction and infant behavior at four months. *American Journal of Drug and Alcohol Abuse, 10,* 161–193.

Bowlby, J. (1960). Separation Anxiety. *International Journal of Psycho-Analysis, 39,* 89–113.

Bowlby, J. (1973). *The Making and Breaking of Affectional Bonds.* London: Tavistock Publications.

Bowlby, J. (1980). *Attachment and Loss: Vol. 3: Loss, Sadness and Depression. The International Psycho-Analytical Library,* 109: 1–462. London: The Hogarth Press and the Institute of Psycho-Analysis.

Bowlby, J. (1982). *Attachment and Loss. Vol. 1: Attachment* (2nd Ed.). New York: Basic Books.

Bowlby, J. (1988). *A Secure Base.* New York: Basic Books.

Breuer, J., & Freud, S. (1885). Studies on hysteria. In S. Freud, A. Freud, & J. Strachey (Eds.), *The Standard Edition of the Complete Psychological Works of Sigmund Freud. Vol. 2.* London: Hogarth Press.

Cichetti, D., & Rogosch, F. A. (1996). Equifinality and multifinality in developmental psychopathology. *Developmental and Psychopathology, 8,* 597–600.

Conroy, D. A., Armitage, R., & Hoffman, R. (2009). Children with substance abusing parents show a mismatch between sleep in the laboratory and subjective sleep in an age and sex matched sample. *Alcoholism: Clinical & Experimental Research, 33*(6 Suppl), 121A.

De Gennaro, L., & Ferrara, M. (2003). Sleep spindles: An overview. *Sleep Medicine Reviews, 7,* 423–440.

Egeland, B., Jacobvitz D., & Papatola, K. (1987). Intergenerational continuity of abuse. In R. J. Gelles & J. B. Lancaster (Eds.), *Child Abuse and Neglect: Bio-social Dimensions* (pp. 255–276). New York: Aldine de Gruyter.

Egeland, B., Jacobvitz. D., & Sroufe. L. A. (1988). Breaking the cycle of abuse: Relationship predictors. *Child Development, 59,* 1080–1088.

Fairbairn, W. R. D. (1952). *An Object Relations Theory of Personality.* New York: Basic Books.

Fitzgerald, H. E., & Eiden, R. A. (2007). Paternal alcoholism, family functioning, and infant mental health. *Zero to Three, 27*(4), 11–18.

Fitzgerald, H. E., & Zucker, R. A. (2005). Pathways of risk and aggregation for alcohol use disorders. In H. E. Fitzgerald, R. Zucker, & K. Freeark (Eds.), *The Crisis in Youth Mental Health* (Vol. 3, p. 1488). Santa Barbara, CA: Greenwood Publishing Group.

Fitzgerald, H. E., Zucker, R. A., & Yang, H.-Y. (1995). Developmental systems theory and alcoholism: Analyzing patterns of variation in high-risk families. *Psychology of Addictive Behaviors, 9*(1), 8–22.

Flaherty, J. A., & Richman, J. A. (1986). Childhood relationships, adult coping resources and depression. *Social Science & Medicine, 23*(7), 709–716.

Floyd, F. J., Cranford, J. A., Daugherty, M. K., Fitzgerald, H. E., & Zucker, R. A. (2006). Marital interaction in alcoholic and nonalcoholic couples: Alcoholic subtype variations and wives' alcoholism status. *Journal of Abnormal Psychology, 115*(1), 121–130.

Fonagy, P., Gergely, G., Jurist, E. L., & Target, M. (2002). *Affect Regulation, Mentalization, and the Development of the Self.* New York: Other Press.

Fonagy, P., Steele, M., Steele, H., Moran, G. S., & Higgitt, A. C. (1991). The capacity for understanding mental states: The reflective self in parent and child and its significance for security of attachment. *Infant Mental Health Journal, 12*(3), 201.

Fonagy, P., & Target, M. (1996). Playing with reality: I. Theory of mind and the normal development of psychic reality. *International Journal of Psychoanalysis, 77* (Pt 2), 217–233.

Fonagy, P., Target, M., Steele, H., & Steele, M. (1998). Reflective Functioning Manual, Version 5. Unpublished manuscript.

Fraiberg, S., Adelson, E., & Shapiro, V. (1975). Ghosts in the nursery. A psychoanalytic approach to the problems of impaired infant–mother relationships. *Journal of the American Academy of Child & Adolescent Psychiatry, 14*(3), 387–421.

Freud, A. (1936). *Collected Writings.* New York: International Universities Press.

George, C., & Solomon, J. (1996). Representational models of relationships: Links between caregiving and attachment. *Infant Mental Health, 17*, 198–216.

Gergely, G., & Watson, J. S. (1999). Early socio-emotional development: Contingency perception and the social-biofeedback model. In P. Rochat (Ed.), *Early Social Cognition: Understanding Others in the First Months of Life* (pp. 101–136). Hillsdale, NJ: Erlbaum.

Greenberg, S. M., & Mitchell, S. A. (1983). *Object Relations in Psychoanalytic Theory.* Cambridge, MA: Harvard University Press.

Greenspan, S. I. (1977). *Substance Abuse: An Understanding from Psychoanalytic Developmental Learning Perspectives.* Psychodynamics of Drug Dependence. National Institute on Drug Abuse: Washington D.C.

Hartmann (1927). Concept formation in psychoanalysis. *Psychoanalytic Study of the Child, 19*, 11–47.

Hazan, C., & Shaver, P. (1987). Romantic love conceptualized as an attachment process. *Journal of Personality and Social Psychology, 52*, 511–524.

Lacan, J. (1977). *The Signification of the Phallus. Ecrits: A Selection.* New York: W.W. Norton & Co.

Jeremy, R. J., & Bernstein, V. B. (1984). Dyads at risk: methadone-maintained women and their 4-month old infants. *Child Development, 55*, 1141–1154.

Khantzian, E. J. (1985). The self-medication hypothesis of addictive disorders: Focus on heroin and cocaine dependence. *American Journal of Psychiatry, 142*, 1259–1264.

Kernberg, O. (1975). *Borderline Conditions and Pathological Narcissism.* New York: Jason Aronson.

Krystal, H. (1962). The opiate withdrawal syndrome as a state of stress. *Psychiatric Quarterly, 36*, 53–65.

Krystal, H. (1977). Self and object-representation in alcoholism and other drug dependence: Implications for therapy. In J. D Blaine, & D.A. Julius (Eds.), *Psychodynamics of drug dependence, NIDA Research Monograph, 12* (pp. 300–309). Rockville, MD: Levin & Weiss.

Krystal, H. (1982). Adolescence and the tendencies to develop substance dependence. *Psychoanalytic Inquiry, 2*, 581–617.

Krystal, H., & Raskin, H. (1970). *Drug Dependence.* Detroit, MI: Wayne State University Press.

Lieberman, A. F., & Van Horn, P. (2008). *Psychotherapy with infants and young children: Repairing the effects of stress and trauma on early attachment.* NY: The Guilford Press.

Main, M., & Goldwyn, R. (1991). Interview-based adult attachment classifications: Related to infant–mother and infant–father attachment. Unpublished manuscript, Department of Psychology, University of California, Berkeley.

Main, M., Kaplan, N., & Cassidy, J. (1985). Security in infancy, childhood, and adulthood: A move to the level of representation. *Monographs of the Society for Research in Child Development, 50*, 1–2.

Moyer, K. E. (1974). Sex differences in aggression. In: R. C. Friedman, R. M. Richart, and R. L. Wiele, Vande (Eds.), *Sex Differences in Behavior* (pp. 335–372). New York: Wiley.

Oppenheim, D., Nir, A., Warren, S., & Emde, R. N. (1997). Emotion regulation in mother-child narrative co-construction: Associations with children's narratives and adaptation. *Developmental Psychology 33*(2), 284–294.

Parker, G. B., & Barnett, B. (1988). Perceptions of parenting in childhood and social support in adulthood. *American Journal of Psychiatry, 145*, 479–482.

Putallaz, M., Costanzo, P. R., Grimes, C. L., & Sherman, D. M. (1998). Intergenerational continuities and their influences on children's social development. *Social Development, 7*, 389–427.

Sadler, L. S., Slade, A., & Mayes, L. C. (2006). Minding the Baby: A mentalization-based parenting program. In J. G Allen and P. Fonagy (Eds.). *Handbook of Mentalization-Based Treatment* (pp. 271–288). Hoboken, NJ: John Wiley and Sons.

Sandler, J. (1978). On the development of the object relationships and affects. *International Journal of Psychoanalysis, 59*, 285–296.

Sarason, J. G., Sarason, B. R., & Shearin, E. N. (1986). Social support as an individual difference variable: Its stability, origins, and relational aspects. *Journal of Personality and Social Psychology, 50*, 845–855.

Schumm, J. A., O'Farrell, T. J., Murphy, C. M., & Fals-Stewart, W. (2009). Partner violence before and after couples-based alcoholism treatment for female alcoholic patients. *Journal of Consulting and Clinical Psychology, 77*(6), 1136–1146.

Shedler, J., (2010). The efficacy of psychodynamic psychotherapy, *American Psychologist, 65*, 98–109.

Sher, K. J. (1991). Psychological characteristics of children of alcoholics: Overview of research methods and findings. In M. Galanter, H. Begleiter, R. Deitrich, D. M. Gallant, D. Goodwin, E. Gottheil, et al. (Eds.), *Recent Developments in Alcoholism, Vol. 9: Children of Alcoholics* (pp. 301–326). New York: Plenum Press.

Simons, R. L., Beaman, J., Conger, R. D., & Chao, W. (1993). Childhood experience, conceptions of parenting, and attitudes of spouse as determinants of parental behavior. *Journal of Marriage and the Family, 55*, 91–106.

Slade, A. (2005). Parental reflective functioning: An introduction. *Attachment & Human Development, 7*(3), 269.

Slade, A. (2006). Reflective parenting programs: Theory and development. *Psychoanalytic Inquiry, 26*(4), 18.

Slade, A., & Aber, J. L. (1992). Attachments, drives and development: Conflicts and convergences in theory. In J. Barron, M. Eagle, & D. Wolitzky (Eds.), *Interface of Psychoanalysis and Psychology* (pp. 154–186). Washington, DC: APA Publications.

Slade, A., Firmer, M., Gerber, J., Gibson, L., Graf, F., & Siegel, N. (1995). *Prenatal Representations, Dyadic Interaction and Quality of Attachment.* Paper presented at the biennial meeting of the Society for Research in Child Development, Indianapolis, IN.

Slade, A., Grienenberger, J., Bernbach, E., Levy, D., & Locker, A. (2005). Maternal reflective functioning, attachment, and the transmission gap: A preliminary study. *Attachment & Human Development, 7*(3), 283.

Smyke, A. T., Dumitrescu, A., & Zeanah, C. (2002). Attachment disturbance in young children, 1: The continuum of caretaking casualty. *Journal of the American Academy of Child and Adolescent Psychiatry, 41*(8), 972–982.

Soderstrom, K., & Skarderud, F. (2009). Minding the baby: Mentalization-based treatment in families with parental substance use disorder: Theoretical framework. *Nordic Psychology, 61*(3), 47–65.

Solomon, J., & George, C. (1996). Defining the caregiving system: Toward a theory of caregiving. *Infant Mental Health, 17*, 183–197.

Stanley, S. (2008). Interpersonal violence in alcohol-complicated marital relationships (A study from India). *Journal of Family Violence, 23*(8), 767–776.

Steele, H., Steele, M., & Fonagy, P. (1996). *Child Development, 67*(2), 541–555.

Steinmetz, S. K. (1987). Family violence. In M. B. Sussman & S. K. Steinmetz (Eds.), *Handbook of Marriage and the Family* (pp. 725–765). New York: Plenum Press.

Straus, M. A., Gelles, R. J., & Steinmetz, S. K. (1980). *Behind Closed Doors: Violence in the American Family*. Beverly Hills, CA: Sage.

Suchman, N., DeCoste, C., McMahon, T., Rounsaville, B., & Mayes, L. (2011). The Mothers and Toddlers Program, an attachment-based parenting intervention for substance-using women: Results at 6-week follow up in a randomized clinical pilot. *Infant Mental Health Journal, 32*, 427–449.

Sullivan, H. S. (1953). *The Interpersonal Theory of Psychiatry*. New York: Norton.

Tarokh, L., & Carskadon, M. A. (2009). Sleep electroencephalogram in children with a parental history of alcohol abuse/dependence. *Journal of Sleep Research, 11*, 65–69.

Truant, G. S., Herscovitch, J., & Lohrenz, J. G. (1987). The relationship of childhood experience to the quality of marriage. *Canadian Journal of Psychiatry, 32*, 87–93.

Tsuang, M. T., Lyons, M. J., Eisen, S. A., Goldberg, J., True, W., Lin, N., et al. (1996). Genetic influences on *DSM-III-R* drug abuse and dependence: A study of 3,372 twin pairs. *American Journal of Medical Genetics, 67*: 473–477.

van Ijzendoorn, M. H. (1992). Intergenerational transmission of parenting: A review of studies in non-clinical populations. *Developmental Review, 12*, 76–99.

Volkow, N. D., Fowler, J. S., Gene-Jack, W. (2003). The addicted human brain: Insights from imaging studies. *The Journal of Clinical Investigation, 111*(10), 1444–1451.

Ward, M. J.. Botyanski, N. C., Plunket, S. W., & Carlson. E. A. (1989). *Identity in Pregnant Adolescents*. Paper presented at the biennial meeting of the Society for Research in Child Development, Kansas City, MO.

Waters, E., Weinfield, N. S., & Hamilton, C. E. (2000). The stability of attachment security from infancy to adolescence and early adulthood: general discussion. *Child Development, 71*, 703–706.

Weinfield, N. S., Sroufe, L. A., & Egelund, B. (2000). Attachment from infancy to early adulthood in a high-risk sample. Continuity, discontinuity and their correlates. *Child Development, 71*, 695–702.

Whipple, E. E., Fitzgerald, H. E., & Zucker, R. A. (1995). Parent–child interactions in alcoholic and non-alcoholic families. *American Journal of Orthopsychiatry, 65*(1), 153–159.

Whitbeck, L. B., Hoyt, D. R., Simons, R. L., Conger, R. D., Elder, G. H. Jr., Lorenz, E. O., et al. (1992). Intergenerational continuity of parental rejection and depressed affect. *Journal of Personality and Social Psychology, 63,* 1036–1045.

Wilden, A. (1980). *System and Structure.* London: Tavistock.

Winnicott, D. W. (1956). Primary maternal preoccupation. *Collected Papers.*

Winnicott, D. W. (1960). The theory of the parent–infant relationship. *International Journal of Psychoanalysis, 41,* 585–595.

Wurmser, L. (1984). More respect for the neurotic process: Comments on the problem of narcissism in severe psychopathology, especially the addictions. *Journal of Substance Abuse Treatment*(1), 37–45.

Yamadori, A. (1971). Role of the spindles in the onset of sleep. *Kobe Journal of Medical Sciences, 17,* 97–111.

Zeanah, C., & Zeanah, P. D. (1989). Intergenerational transmission of maltreatment: Insights from attachment theory and research. *Psychiatry: Interpersonal and Biological Processes, 52*(2), 177–196.

Zucker, R. A., Chermack, S. T., & Curran, G. M. (2000). Alcoholism: A lifespan perspective on etiology and course. In A. J. Sameroff, M. Lewis, & S. M. Miller (Eds.), *Handbook of Developmental Psychopathology* (2nd ed.), (pp. 569–587). Dordrecht, Netherlands: Kluwer Academic Publishers.

Zucker, R. A., & Fitzgerald, H. E. (1991). Early developmental factors and risk for alcohol problems. *Alcohol Health and Research World, 15,* 18–24.

Zucker, R. A., Kincaid, S. B., Fitzgerald, H. E., & Bingham, C. R. (1995). Alcohol schema acquisition in preschoolers: Differences between children of alcoholics and children on nonalcoholics. *Alcoholism: Clinical and Experimental Research, 19*(4), 1011–1017.

7 Early Origins of Alcohol Use and Abuse

Mental Representations, Relationships, and the Challenge of Assessing the Risk–Resilience Continuum Very Early in the Life of the Child

HIRAM E. FITZGERALD,

MARIA M. WONG, AND

ROBERT A. ZUCKER

■ INTRODUCTION

Alcoholism is the most common form of substance dependence disorder in the United States, affecting approximately 17 million adults. Approximately one in four children in the United States has been exposed to alcohol abuse/alcohol dependence at some point in his/her life before reaching 18 years of age (Grant, 2000), resulting in an estimated 15 to 19.9 million children of alcoholics (COAs) (Eigen & Rowden, 1996). Prospective longitudinal studies, beginning when children of alcoholics are infants and preschoolers, suggest that it is no longer adequate to view adolescent drinking onset as the baseline for understanding the etiological risk for problem drinking. For example, nearly 10 percent of fourth graders, 16 percent of fifth graders, and 29 percent of sixth graders report having had more than just a sip of alcohol (Donovan, 2007), and by eighth grade (early adolescence), slightly more than 19 percent report having been drunk at least once in their lifetime.

Prospective longitudinal studies suggest that risk for problem drinking shows itself even in infancy and early childhood and unfolds in a cascade of interplay between biological and experiential factors (Zucker & Gomberg, 1986; Zucker, 2006; Eiden, Leonard, Hoyle, & Chavez, 2004), particularly in families where co-occurring psychopathology exacerbates the negative impact of parental alcoholism. In this chapter, we focus on evidence pointing to early dysregulatory functioning of COAs reared in high-risk environments consisting of paternal alcoholism. We highlight evidence suggesting that children as young as preschool age have mental representations of alcohol use that include sensory and perceptual sensitivities, cognitive/cultural rules for use, and expectancies about self-use, and are exposed to affective relationship disturbances within the family. We propose that these early expectancies for alcohol use, emergent from parent–child relationships in the earliest years, can be linked to various developmental processes that organize mental representations of self, others, and self–other relationships, as well as to the synergistically developing neurobiological stress management and behavioral self-regulation systems. In addition, we also point to the role that temperament, dyadic relationships, and the child's expanding social network can play in structuring internal resilience that may enable some children to ward off the negative effects of being reared in an environment surrounded by parental alcoholism, comorbid psychopathology, and conflictual relationship dynamics. Finally, we offer some comments concerning the difficulties of conducting research with high-risk families where there is parental substance abuse, comorbid psychopathology, high interpersonal conflict, and family disorganization.

Children of Alcoholics

It is beyond the scope of this chapter to summarize all the research in what is now a substantive prospective literature on children being reared in families with alcoholic parents (Eiden, Edwards, & Leonard, 2006; Fitzgerald, Puttler, Refior, & Zucker, 2007; Zucker, Donovan, Masten, Mattson, & Moss, 2009). Our goal is to (a) identify major challenges faced by COAs in early childhood (birth to 5 years of age), (b) show how these challenges are related to literature involving older COAs, and (c) comment on early childhood factors that are predictive of both risk and protection from alcohol abuse and related problem behaviors. After describing the context in which many COAs are reared and summarizing known behavioral and neurobiological outcomes that have been identified as arising as early as infancy and early childhood, we propose that children's mental representations about alcohol use, including their beliefs, expectations (Zucker et al., 2009), and internalization of family codes and values (Sameroff, 1995) shift them toward the risk side of the risk–resilience continuum for subsequent problem drinking and comorbid psychopathology.

▪ FACTORS IN EARLY CHILDHOOD PREDICTING RISK FOR ALCOHOL PROBLEM BEHAVIOR

Past research has consistently shown that COAs are more likely than non-COAs to develop psychopathology and substance-related problems (Sher, 1991; Windle & Searles, 1990). Many COAs are exposed to risk factors early in life that predispose them to becoming canalized into pathways leading to high risk for psychological and substance-use disorders (Fitzgerald & Zucker, 2005). Among those at highest risk, these pathways are infused with regulatory problems, relationship problems, and environmental stress, all of which are components of the early etiology for alcohol use disorders.

Regulatory Problems

Self-regulation has been defined as "the exercise of control over oneself, especially with regard to bringing the self into line with preferred standards" (Vohs & Baumeister, 2004, p. 2). It refers to the capacity to regulate one's behaviors, attention, and emotions (McCabe, Cunnington, & Brooks-Gunn, 2004). COAs are at risk for a number of problems related to the dysregulation of behavioral, cognitive, and physiological processes. As early as the preschool years, COAs, especially boys, are more likely to have externalizing problems than non-COAs (Fitzgerald, Puttler, Mun, & Zucker, 2000; Puttler, Zucker, Fitzgerald, & Bingham, 1998; Zucker, Heitzeg, & Nigg, 2011). COAs also have more internalizing problems than non-COAs, although the differences related to internalizing problems become more prominent during adolescence and young adulthood (Sher, 1991; Zucker, Chermack, & Curran, 2000).

Two- and three-year-old COAs are more likely than non-COAs to be impulsive and to have a difficult temperament and negative mood states (Eiden, Edwards, & Leonard, 2002; Eiden, Leonard, & Morrisey, 2001; Fitzgerald, Sullivan, Zucker, et al., 1993). They also appear to have a shorter attention span, higher externalizing behavior, and hyperactivity (Alterman & Tarter, 1986; Loukas, Fitzgerald, Zucker, & von Eye, 2001) than non-COAs. Moreover, early problem behaviors are often identifiable as precursors of conduct disorder, aggressiveness, and delinquency in childhood (Pihl & Peterson, 1991) and adolescence (Mayzer, Fitzgerald, & Zucker, 2009).

Sleep Patterns as Indicators of Dysregulation

In addition to behavioral and attention problems, there is preliminary evidence to suggest that young COAs have problems regulating basic physiological processes such as sleep. During infancy and early childhood, the amount of time that children sleep ranges from 18 hours for newborns (National Sleep Foundation, 2011) to 12 hours for preschoolers (Iglowstein, Jenni, Molinari, & Largo, 2003). Sleep plays an important restorative function for human beings at all age levels (Sheldon, 2005). Evidence suggests that COAs exhibit a deficit in the neural circuitry responsible for protecting sleep (Tarokh & Carskadon, 2009). Disturbances in sleep appear to have negative impacts on the child's mental, emotional, and physical stability (Goldstein, Bridge, & Brent, 2008; Wong, Brower, & Zucker, 2009; Wong, Brower, Nigg, & Zucker, 2010). Therefore, it seems plausible that various aspects of sleep can provide an indication of the extent to which very young children are stressed by exposure to family conflict, parent emotional and/or physical abuse, or parental psychopathology.

The hypothalamic-pituitary-adrenal axis system (HPA axis; McEwen & Wingfield, 2003; Ganzel, Morris, & Wethington, 2010) plays a key role in regulating emotions and is known to be negatively affected by both acute (Dickerson & Kemeny, 2004) and chronic stress, causing an imbalance in the individual's ability to self-regulate stress and increasing the allostatic load (McEwen & Stellar, 1993). *Allostatic load* refers to the physiological consequences of stress exposure; and posits that persistent exposure to high stress has a negative effect on the individual's ability to self-regulate.

The HPA axis in the neuroendocrine system helps individuals cope with stress. In response to stress, the human body quickly increases the production of corticotrophin-releasing hormone, adrenal corticotrophin, and cortisol (McEwen, 1998). When stress is terminated, the neuroendocrine system stops producing these hormones, and the hormones in the body quickly return to pre-stress levels (Dai, Thavundayil, Santella, & Gianoulakis, 2007). Among alcoholics, the question is the extent to which these stress regulatory systems no longer function to restore balance (Adinoff, Iranmanesh, Veldhuis, & Fisher, 1998). The developmental question concerns how early in the life cycle the homeostatic HPA-axis regulatory system becomes disorganized and what factors solidify or modify its functional status over the life course (Dickerson & Kemeny, 2004; Zucker et al., 2009).

Chronic stress, which is often present in alcoholic families, is likely to lead to chronic arousal of the HPA-axis among some COAs. Past research has shown a dysfunction of the HPA-axis in adult sons of alcoholics prior to the development of alcohol dependence (Gianoulakis, Thavundayil, & Brown & Dai, 2005; Dai et al., 2007). In addition to exposure to chronic stress, genetic differences in HPA-axis response to stress may interact with environmental triggers (Waltman, McCaul, & Wand, 1994; Dai, Thavundayil, & Gianoulakis, 2002; Zimmerman, Spring, Koller, Holsboer, & Soyka, 2004), predisposing COAs to stress-management dysfunction and increasing their vulnerability for the development of psychological and substance-related problems.

Everhart and Emde (2006) draw attention to a variety of stressors during infancy and early childhood that increase allostatic load and therefore increase the likelihood of dysregulation. Examples of dysregulation include problems controlling one's behavior (externalizing behaviors), retreat from social interactions (internalizing behavior), or problems with endogeneous or internal biorhythms such as sleep–wake cycles. For example, in prospective studies using sleep measures based on parental ratings, investigators have found no differences in the prevalence of sleep problems among three- to five-year-old COAs compared with non-COAs (Wong, Brower, Fitzgerald, & Zucker, 2004; Wong, Brower, & Zucker, 2009; Wong, Brower, Nigg, & Zucker, 2010). However, studies using actigraphy (assessment of body movements during sleep) and polysomnography (multi-measure assessment of biophysiological activities during sleep) indicate that COAs between the ages of eight and 12 show different patterns of sleep and different physiological activity during sleep compared to non-COAs (Conroy, Hairston, Heitzeg, Gower, & Zucker, 2009; Tarokh & Carskadon, 2009). One study comparing actigraphy and sleep diary data between the two groups showed that eight- to 12-year-old COAs slept less and took longer to fall asleep than did non-COAs (Conroy et al., 2009). Sleep diaries on the same children indicated that COAs not only took longer to fall asleep, they also had lower "sleep efficiency" (a measure of the time sleeping divided by time in bed) than non-COA children.

Another study compared sleep electroencephalograms (EEG) of children nine to 10 years old with or without a parental history of alcohol abuse or dependence (Tarokh & Carskadon, 2009). Sleep researchers distinguish between two types of sleep, that with rapid eye movement (REM) activity (most often associated with dreaming), and that without rapid eye movements. Non-rapid eye movement sleep has various levels of depth, marked by different patterns (theta and delta waves) of electrical activity as measured by an electroencephalogram (EEG). Often, one observes bursts of activity, called *spindles*, in these recordings of brain waves. Tarokh and Caraskadon (2009) found that there were no signs of sleep disruption in sleep stages in nine- to 10-year-old children whose parents had no history of alcohol abuse or dependence. However, children with parents who had alcohol abuse histories had lower non-rapid eye movement (NREM) brain delta wave activity than comparison children, a finding that is consistent with other sleep studies comparing adult alcohol-dependent and abstinent alcoholics with non-alcoholics (Gillin, Smith, Irwin, & Kripke, 1990; Irwin, Miller, Gillin, Demodena, & Ehlers, 2000). The reduced delta wave activity among children with alcohol abusing parents may reflect a failure of the neurobiological structures responsible for protecting sleep. Children with alcohol abusing parents also exhibited less activity in the spindle range than comparison children. Some researchers have suggested that spindles play a role in protecting sleep by blocking the flow of sensory information from the thalamus to the cortex (De Gennaro & Ferrara, 2003; Yamadori, 1971) and therefore keeping the sleeper in deeper stages of sleep and maximizing the restorative aspects of sleep, such as the release of growth hormone.

Relationship Problems

Marital conflict and rates of interpersonal violence are high in many alcoholic families (Fitzgerald & Eiden, 2007; Floyd, Cranford, Daugherty, Fitzgerald, & Zucker, 2006; Schumm, O'Farrell, Murphy, & Fals-Stewart, 2009; Stanley, 2008), and contribute to allostatic load in the form of persistent parent–child relationship difficulties. In one study, higher paternal alcohol consumption at 12 months of child's age predicted negative parental behavior at 24 months (e.g., high negative affect, low warmth, and low sensitivity). Negative parental behavior in turn predicted high negative affect and low responsiveness in COAs. Another study showed that low parental warmth in the toddler years predicted low internalization of rules of conduct and poor effortful control among COAs in the preschool years (Eiden, Edwards, & Leonard, 2004, 2006).

Paternal alcoholism has been associated with elevated rates of father–son conflict. Loukas et al. (2001) found that both family conflict and father–son conflict partially accounted for the relationship between father's antisocial behavior and his three- to eight-year-old son's externalizing problems. Evidence supports the conclusion that the poor quality of parent–child interactions in alcoholic families has a negative impact on children's behavior. Whipple, Fitzgerald, and Zucker (1995) found that during parent-directed play and clean-up, alcoholic fathers were less able to keep their preschool age sons on task than were non-alcoholic fathers. Alcoholic fathers and their sons also were less able to interpret each other's nonverbal cues and less likely to respond to each other appropriately. These fathers were less skillful at facilitating compliance in their children. As a result, more time was required to complete clean-up and children showed increasing levels of negative affect toward their fathers.

Another study also reported non-compliant behavior among the preschool-age sons of alcoholic fathers during clean-up sessions after free play (Eiden et al., 2001). When compared to sons of non-alcoholic fathers, sons of alcoholic fathers showed higher rates of non-compliance. When both parents were alcoholic, higher rates of noncompliance were found among boys and lower rates were found among girls. Moreover, there was little mutual affect between the girls and their parents. These findings suggest that in response to insensitive parental attempts to achieve compliance, girls were more likely to comply and withdraw from their parents, whereas boys were more likely to engage in aggressive and oppositional behavior.

Environmental Stress

Environmental stress is associated with heavy drinking and alcoholism (Dawson, Grant, & Ruan, 2005; Linsky, Straus, & Colby, 1985; King, Bernardy, & Hauner, 2003) and contributes to family and individual allostatic stress and the inability to maintain normative regulatory processes. Alcoholics are more likely than others to have trouble in job-related, financial, and legal matters, and they are more likely to have lower socio-economic status (Fitzgerald & Zucker, 1995). These adjunctive influences to family and person dynamics combine to expose alcoholics to persistent stress (Fitzgerald, Zucker, & Yang, 1995). As might be expected, these adult stress experiences also have an impact on stress within the family. Across several longitudinal studies, alcoholic parents systematically reported more family stressors than did non-alcoholics. Many of these events were related to family crises, such as eviction, job loss, being cut off from welfare, and being in financial trouble (Hussong, Bauer, Huang, et al., 2008). All of these experiences not only engender acute crises, but to the extent that they exist over time, they also lead to a sense of chaos and unpredictability of the environment and of the future, factors that have been linked to high levels of cortisol production (Dickerson & Kemeny, 2004).

■ PROTECTIVE FACTORS

Even though COAs are exposed to multiple risk factors and are therefore vulnerable to the development of multiple problems, there is considerable heterogeneity in developmental outcomes, suggesting that some COAs are more resilient than others (Wong, Zucker, Puttler, & Fitzgerald, 1999; Zucker, Wong, Puttler, & Fitzgerald, 2003). Compared to the vast literature on risk factors for alcohol problem behavior, research on protective factors is scarce. Nevertheless, there are some indications that protective factors are embedded in the child's temperament, mother–child relationships in early development, and in sibling relationships later in childhood and adolescence.

Temperament

Resilient COAs appear to have more easy-going temperaments than do non-resilient COAs. One longitudinal study found that resilient COAs were more "cuddly and affectionate" during the first year of life than non-resilient COAs (Werner, 1986). By grade 12, the resilient COAs in the same study appeared to show more self-control, more caring toward others, and more tolerance of individual differences. Another study found that, over a longitudinal time frame of three to 14 years, vulnerable COAs, defined by individual and family risk, were more reactive and had a shorter attention span than children from a low-risk background (Zucker et al., 2003). Reactivity is a core component of temperament and is related to the individual's stress management system, thus providing, at the least, a connection to allostatic processes (Rothbart, Derryberry, & Posner, 1994; Strelau, 1998).

Secure Mother–Child Attachment

A core tenet of the interdisciplinary field of infant mental health is that early relationships matter. For COAs, studies of relationship dynamics during the early years are consistent with the infant mental health dictum. A secure relationship with the non-alcoholic parent (mother) appears to moderate the relationship between father's alcoholism and externalizing problems in COAs (Edwards, Eiden, & Leonard, 2006). COAs who had a secure mother–infant attachment at 12 months had significantly fewer externalizing problems at 24 months and 36 months of age compared with COAs with insecure attachment. The same pattern of findings was reported for internalizing problems at 36 months of age. Another study also reported similar findings among COAs under the age of six (Kittmer, 2005). The extant literature on social-emotional development provides ample evidence to support the contention that the quality of the mother–infant relationship provides a powerful moderating influence on development of the HPA-axis stress regulating system (Fonagy, Luyten, & Strathearn, 2011a,b).

It is important to note that children may develop secure relationship with caregivers other than their mothers. Such relationships also appear to be associated with good outcomes. One longitudinal study of children of alcoholics showed that children who received a great deal of attention and affection from their primary caregivers had better developmental outcomes, regardless of who their primary caregivers were (Werner, 1986; Werner & Johnson, 2000).

Sibling Relationships

Very little research is available on how sibling relationships may be related to positive outcomes in young COAs. Existing research on adolescents shows that siblings influence each other's behavior, including their drinking and drug use (Trim, Leuthe, & Chassin, 2006). Support from siblings was positively related to adolescent COA's (mean age = 12.7 years) self-esteem and negatively related to father ratings of externalizing problems (Barrera, Chassin, & Rogosch, 1993). In contrast, conflict with siblings was positively related to self-report and maternal ratings of externalizing problems. In retrospective reports, resilient adult COAs reported that they had strong relationships with their siblings in childhood (Kittmer, 2005).

Enjoyment of School and Achievement Scores

COAs who are resilient are more likely to enjoy school, regardless of whether they do well academically (Werner & Johnson, 2000). Resilient COAs appear to have higher achievement scores than non-resilient COAs. One study found that there were significant differences on a measure of educational progress between resilient COAs and non-resilient COAs (Werner, 1986). Another study reported that resilient COAs had higher scores on a measure of math, reading, and spelling than non-resilient COAs (Zucker, Wong, Puttler, & Fitzgerald, 2003). There is also some evidence showing that resilient COAs have a stronger achievement orientation than non-resilient COAs (Werner, 1986).

■ **SUMMARY**

COAs are at greater risk for alcohol abuse and alcohol-related problems than children without an alcoholic parent. Although some of the risk may be transmitted genetically, there also is strong evidence for significant interactions between adverse environments and vulnerable neurobiological risk, underlying the contemporary understanding of the interplay between genetic and experiential organizers of behavior (Sun & Zhao, 2010). Moreover, a considerable body of work indicates that the familial and other environmental adversity is evident during early childhood and contributes to heightened difficulties with stress management as evidenced by the early appearance of behavior problems. This is especially the case when the father is the alcoholic.

Mental Representations, Expectancies, and Alcoholism Etiology

Overwhelming evidence supports the conclusion that behavioral and neurobiological dysregulation very early in the life course are part of the etiological pathway toward alcohol problem behaviors (Zucker et al., 2009). Such behaviors may become manifest as early as the preschool years. Advances in brain science and understanding of hormone regulatory systems have opened new approaches for understanding the individual's mental representations of events and for exploring how such representations formed early in the life course affect decision processes later in development. Of particular interest to the etiology of alcoholism are the experiential triggers that may evoke specific expectancies at critical decision points guiding the individual towards decisions to engage in risky behavior. In the study of risk development in childhood, there is considerable literature on alcohol expectancies, but little attention has been paid to the mental representations that children of alcoholics form concerning parental drinking and problem behaviors. Of particular interest is how such representations may be mediated by neurobiological structures that were organized in relation to the child's experiential world, including the inner world of self-development as well as the relational world of self–other interaction. One area of potential research concerns the extent to which mental representations of experience are homologous to the structure-function organization of the prefrontal cortex and HPA axis, each of which plays a critical role in self-regulation.

Over twenty years ago, we presented evidence that many COAs have mental representations of alcoholic beverages as substances, and that COA's "ability to recognize and name these substances, to recognize the cultural rules of their use, and to formulate expectancies about the cognitive and behavioral effects of use can occur well before adolescence" (Zucker & Fitzgerald, 1991; Zucker, Kincaid,

Fitzgerald, & Bingham, 1995). We noted that mental representations or schemas about alcohol use have their origins during the preschool years, and that schemas include aspects of context, motivation, emotion, and normative characteristics of use (Zucker et al., 1995).

Investigators asked a community sample of preschool- to kindergarten-age children to engage in a series of tasks designed to determine whether they could discriminate and identify a variety of substances by their smell (Noll, Zucker, & Greenberg, 1990). The smell task included alcoholic beverages and a variety of non-alcoholic substances that were likely to be familiar to the children (Play-Doh, apple juice, popcorn, etc.). Children were first asked to identify a smell through recall; a subsequent trial used a photograph of the substances as a prompt to recognition memory. After the identification task, children were then asked to provide information about who used the substance, whether the child liked the substance, and if the child expected to use it in the future.

Noll and his colleagues found that older children did better on the recall and recognition tasks than younger children, and that prompting improved their ability to recognize the smells. Children were better able to identify familial substances than they were alcohol or tobacco. The children who correctly identified the alcoholic beverages also attributed their use to adults, not to children. Of specific interest was the finding that success at odor identification was related to heavier parental drinking (especially by fathers) and to parental use of alcohol for purposes of escape. Thus, in a community sample of very young children, there was a connection between parental alcohol use and young children's sensory and perceptual representations about alcoholic beverages.

Mental representations refer to the encoding of experience into memory. Such encoding comes from self-reflections about experience (sensory and perceptual identification of objects in the individual's experiential world), and from the self–other relationship experiences about events (parental labeling of objects, descriptions of events, comments about others). In infancy and early childhood, the construction of mental representations occurs in a relationship context, in which significant others interpret internal feeling states ("You are certainly a very happy baby today!" "Your father is a drunk and doesn't care about us!"), and shape the child's intersubjective world of shared meaning (Trevarthen, 1980).

In a high-risk population-based sample, three- to six-year-old children were shown 10 photographs of beverages (5 non-alcoholic and 5 alcoholic) in a random order, and were asked to identify each of the beverages, first by recall ("What is this?") and then by recognition ("Show me the milk bottle!") (Zucker et al., 1995). Ten drawings of adults and/or children in various contexts were presented, and the children were asked to name the beverage that each person in each drawing was drinking. The vast majority of the sample correctly identified at least one alcoholic beverage, including three-year-olds. COAs were seven times more likely to be able to identify at least one alcohol beverage. Kindergarten-age children attributed more alcoholic beverage use to drinkers, especially male drinkers.

Overall, children in the study attributed alcohol beverage use to adult males more than to adult females, and considerably more than to children. Fathers' consumption, reported separately by the fathers, was correlated with their sons' attributions of adult male consumption, and mothers' reported consumption (not fathers') predicted their children's attributions of alcohol use to adult women. These findings suggest that, by age five, children reared in high-risk alcoholic families have schemas that include sensory, perceptual, and expected use dimensions of alcoholic beverages that are more organized than those of children reared in non-alcoholic families. This led Zucker et al. (1995, p. 1016) to conclude that the "presence of such schemas, nested in an environment that sustains their development and encourages the development of non-alcohol-specific risks, is the breeding ground within which the most severe alcohol problems are likely to emerge and then crystallize."

However, the cognitive and sensory-perceptual components of an emergent schema are only part of the story. Missing are the social-emotional components, the affective load that underlies problem behavior and, we contend, completes the nesting structures that can cascade children of alcoholics into early onset smoking, drinking, sexual, and antisocial behavior.

■ MENTAL REPRESENTATIONS, FAMILIAL ALCOHOLISM, AND CO-OCCURRING PSYCHOPATHOLOGY

Mentalization refers to the ability to recognize mental states in oneself and in others, including the ability to reflect on one's own thoughts, emotions, wishes, desires, and needs as well as those of others. It is a mother's inference that her infant is thinking and feeling ("You sure love little teddy bear and he makes you so happy!"). It also is an ability that gradually organizes in infancy and early childhood with respect to children's ability to disconnect their feelings from their behavior. For example, parents and preschool teachers spend considerable time helping their children understand that they can feel angry, but must learn not to express angry feelings in self-destructive or other-destructive behaviors.

Mental representations involve the encoding of events into autobiographical narratives about self, others, and self–other relationships. Autobiographical memory for events develops during the second and third postnatal years, roughly at the same time that children develop "a knowledge structure whose features serve to organize memories of experiences that happened to 'me'" (Howe & Courage, 1997, p. 499). As events merge over the life course, autobiographical memories become part of one's "autobiographical reasoning" (Habemas & Bluck, 2000) and merge into a coherent narrative that is organized from familial and cultural experiences (Atran, Medin, & Ross, 2005).

With the exception of the Buffalo and Michigan longitudinal studies (see Fitzgerald & Eiden, 2008), discussion of relationship disorders (Zeanah et al., 1999) in connection with mental representations and very early life course narratives does not appear in the alcoholism literature. Other researchers, however, have repeatedly demonstrated that early relationship disorders and traumatic events influence the narratives that children construct over time (Conway & Pleydell-Pearce, 2000). For example, three- to five-year-old children who are exposed to repeated parental use of aggression in response to frustration themselves have high levels of aggression, externalizing, and antisocial behavior (Muller, Fitzgerald, Sullivan, & Zucker, 1994).

Mental representations of events are also linked to the neurobiological responses triggered by stressful and traumatic experiences in infancy and early childhood. Stress responses increase glucosteroid release, which has a negative effect on the hippocampus and medial temporal lobe networks (Markowitsch, Thiel, Kessler, von Stockhausen, & Heiss, 1997) that affect memory and stress regulation. The hippocampus and related limbic structures of the medial temporal lobe mature relatively early in postnatal life and are involved in the development of explicit memory (Nelson, 1995), a component of memory that reaches its near-adult level by the preschool years. Thus, damage to the hippocampus and the neural networks it is associated with would have direct effects on impulse control and self-regulation of behavior. In their studies of borderline personality disorder and the attachment system, Fonagy et al. (2011a, 2011b) stress the connections between behavioral indicators of emotion dysregulation, impulsivity, and disturbed interpersonal functioning, and the dopaminergic and oxytocinergic systems, both of which play key roles in the regulation of emotional and social behavior.

In the early-childhood literature, emphasis on mental representations has been twofold; development of mental representations of attachment objects in children (the initial love objects in the child's life) (Bowlby, 1969; Spitz, 1965), and the influence of such representations on one's parenting abilities (Fraiberg, Adelson, & Shapiro, 1975). The representations of adults who have unresolved conflicts with their parents subsequently affect their parenting abilities. Thus, memory for familiar events during early development (mother–infant or father–infant relationships) is related to the development of a working model of self and relationships that is hypothesized to carry over into adulthood and to be evoked when the adult is placed in the parenting context. Búrgin (2011) refers to representations as "intrapsychic entities" that symbolize meaning to external events, and posits that they are evoked from self–other interactions and are unconsciously activated during subsequent interpersonal interactions. Stern (1985) describes the progression of self, beginning with self–other differentiation, moving to intersubjective relatedness, and ending with a sense of self coming into being, a sort of existential affirmation that "I am!" Fraiberg et al. (1975) used the "ghosts in the nursery" metaphor in an effort to capture the mother's intrapsychic entities created by her own rearing that interfere with her ability to form nurturing relationships with her baby. Some evidence suggests that similar "ghosts" may exist for fathers as well (Fuller, Chermack, Cruise, et al., 2003; Grossman & Fremmer-Bombik, 1994, Shears, Robinson, & Emde, 2002).

An explicit assumption of attachment theory (Lyons-Ruth, 1996) is that memory for familiar events (mother–infant interactions) is related to the development of a working model of self as well as a working model for relationships (Verschuren, Marcven, & Schoefs, 1996). The bulk of this literature suggests that children as young as three years of age already have working models or schemas about familiar events. Autobiographical memories are only partially based on experience, however, because they are constructed from experience and are influenced by exposure to others' constructions of experience, particularly those of parents (Schneider & Bjorklund, 1998). Mothers who elaborate their stories and challenge their toddlers with high rates of memory questions tend to have toddlers with richer autobiographical memories (Harley & Reese, 1999). Toddlers who were developmentally more advanced in self recognition also tended to have richer autobiographical memories of shared events. "Therefore, to understand the relations among the attachment system and the hidden traumas that produce dysregulation of the HPA axis during the first year, it is necessary to elucidate how attachment processes during the first year are embedded within a matrix of intersubjective communications" (Schuder & Lyons-Ruth, 2004, p. 90).

Infancy and early childhood provide numerous occasions for children to model sex-role behavior and to construct their initial working models of what it is to be a father, mother, spouse, or parent. These mental representations incorporate adult behavior and interpersonal dynamics, including such behaviors as drinking and smoking, and such dynamics as marital conflict. Children remember events that are consistent with gender role stereotypes better than those that are inconsistent, and, remarkably, when events are not consistent with these stereotypes, preschool-age children distort the information to make it consistent (Davidson, 1996). "Like father, like son" is driven as much by the son's identification processes as it is by the father's modeled behavior.

When considered in the context of a broader developmental literature, therefore, alcohol expectancies of preschool age children are complex organizational structures. Moreover, they are unique to the individual child's experiences, the autobiographical structures of mind (Schneider & Bjorklund, 1998). The question is, do these early mental structures strengthen over the elementary-school years so that when children transition to adolescence, the mental models or expectancies related to alcohol and interpersonal relationships play a regulatory role in decisions about drinking, smoking, sexual activity, or other risky behaviors? Evidence from longitudinal studies of externalizing behavior suggests that an affirmative answer to this question is a reasonable hypothesis. According to Lorber and Egeland (2009, p. 912), "Infancy is characterized by rapid development of emotion regulatory capacity, patterns of relating to others, and internal representations of relationships; each is surmised to be important to the development of externalizing problems. Maladaptive infancy parenting may negatively impact these capacities and behaviors during a period in which they are thought to be highly sensitive to environmental input, thus setting the stage for the development of persistent externalizing psychopathology."

Studies of the early years of life that are related to the development of memory for events provide some support for the hypothesis that early mental representations play a critical role in subsequent decision processes. Figure 7.1 captures this process in the context of children exposed to high levels of parental psychopathology and marital conflict. As the self and self–other systems organize during the first three postnatal years, children consolidate expectancies and create and co-create (through parenting and other relationships) mental representations about the self and interpersonal relationships and consciously or unconsciously evoke representations as their social and affective networks expand and they become increasingly independent actors in constructing their own life narratives. As the

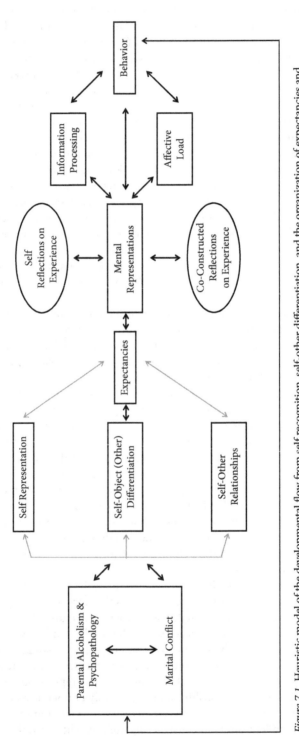

Figure 7.1 Heuristic model of the developmental flow from self recognition, self-other differentiation, and the organization of expectancies and mental representations of events during infancy and early childhood. Fitzgerald, H. E. (2010). Origins of alcohol use disorders: Mental representations, relationships, and the risk-resilience continuum. Presented at the biennial meeting of the World Association for Infant Mental Health, Leipzig, Germany. Reprinted with permission of H. E. Fitzgerald.

children move through childhood and into adolescence, various experiences will maintain, enhance, facilitate, or dampen cumulative risk. What seems increasingly clear is that movement along the risk–resilience continuum apropos of the etiology of alcohol problem behavior and associated co-active psychopathology is driven in part by the mental representations about drinking and interpersonal relationships that have their origins in infancy and early childhood.

▪ RESEARCH CHALLENGES WORKING WITH HIGH-RISK ALCOHOLIC FAMILIES

Problems associated with longitudinal studies appear in the literature frequently, beginning with introductory textbooks in psychology, where they are contrasted with cross-sectional approaches. However, some literature does exist to assist investigators who want to plan long-term and large-scale studies, particularly where there is interest in etiological pathways and the influence of risk factors as organizing constructs (Stouthamer-Loeber, van Kammen, & Loeber, 1992). Working with high-risk, substance abusing families presents a number of challenges for participants and researchers. For participants, the challenges are best understood in the context of daily life events related to addictive behavior, family conflict, parent–child relationships, and interaction with social agencies. For participants working with researchers, the challenge also is to be able to describe their lives and in so doing become more aware of them. This is often a challenging task when one's life has been heavily burdened by trauma and stress. For researchers, the challenges encompass issues related to the ethical conduct of research, adherence to scientific rigor, scheduling data collection sessions, unpredictable participant behavior, staff selection, recruitment, training, and continuity.

Subject Recruitment

Assembling evidence that risk aggregation for alcoholism begins at least as early as the preschool years, Zucker and his colleagues began a recruitment process that involved a search through 18,359 court files in order to recruit an alcoholic family sample, and 18,889 residences to recruit a community comparison sample (Zucker et al., 2000). This effort produced 159 court alcoholic families and 91 community families that met the recruitment criteria. Families recruited into the study were informed that researchers would have to report instances of suspected child abuse or personal harm. Because family dynamics within the high-risk court-recruited sample were fragile, it was imperative that we used a contact strategy that would build trust and compliance for the planned 30-year multiple contact, intense data-collection study. We found our trust builder when we hired an individual with a master's degree in social work (MSW) as our field coordinator, whose responsibilities included conducting the recruitment interview and sustaining family contacts throughout the (now 26) years of the study. We note this explicitly to illustrate the critical importance that trust-building plays in sustaining relationships with high-risk families. Indeed, when focusing on individual and family relationship dynamics to understand etiology and the flow of risk over time, it is important to learn as much as possible about life course pathways that may or may not be tapped by standardized assessment tools. Many investigators use narratives to achieve this depth of understanding. In other instances, trust building may allow personal disclosure to occur naturally, but over time. For example, in one instance a mother informed the assessor that the target child's father was not in fact his biological father. This revelation required us to code all data related to that family as suspect for biological-father parenthood.

Thus, maintaining a personal and consistent relationship with each family meant that family members were more willing to share intimate information about their personal and family life. In addition to our field coordinator, we also discovered it was essential to use clinically sophisticated data collectors, individuals who were at ease with blue-collar families, sometimes quite poor, and sometimes troubled by personal and family difficulties in addition to paternal alcoholism. Evidence that relationships matter was demonstrated by the fact that after five to ten years in the study, many participants included the Longitudinal Study staff among key social supports, whereas we were not listed in the initial assessment of social support networks.

Data Collection

Because initially all participants lived within 50 miles of Michigan State University most data collection took place on campus. This enabled us to include structured videotape observation sessions, as well as to have controlled settings in which to assess children and parents. As the study moved into the third data collection wave (child aged 9–12), many families had moved considerably further from campus, including out of state. Therefore, we began to shift toward home visits for data collection. Data collection from teachers has always been conducted by mailing research packets with return envelopes.

Home visits introduced new complications to the assessment process. On some occasions, when home visitors arrived for scheduled sessions, participants were intoxicated and therefore data collection could not take place. This required rescheduling and another round trip. When done at a distance (some participants now reside over a thousand miles from Michigan), rescheduling is done on the spot because the data collector is staying at a hotel in the area. Some homes are located in unsafe neighborhoods, and occasionally dogs are not people-friendly and dog bites can occur. In other instances, guns are plentiful and in very open display. Female data collectors sometimes may be in uncomfortable situations with male participants. We advise female data collectors about their appearance and how to gently but firmly deal with propositioning from adult male participants. We are always in need of more male assessors.

Assessors also need to be trained in how to deal appropriately, and legally, with events such as child abuse and anything that suggests that a participant may be suspect for self-harm. They also are trained to deal with family trauma resulting from death, illness, or separation/divorce. Such events can be especially difficult for young children.

Marital and Partner Conflict

Family conflict also presents challenges to assessors. When step-parents are involved, assessors need to be prepared to interact with jealous spouses who do not want "investigators hanging around," or do not want their partner talking with female interviewers even on the telephone. Occasionally, we interact with family members who have become involved with fundamental religious sects whose religious leaders advise them not to share personal or family information with "outsiders."

Maximizing Retention and Participant Mobility

From one perspective, all of our strategies for preparing data collectors are focused on assuring their safety and the quality of the data obtained. From another perspective, our strategies are to maximize retention, a constant challenge when working with high-risk families (Cotter, Burke, Loeber, & Navratil, 2002; Navratil, Green, Loeber, & Lahey, 1994). For a planned over-thirty-year study, paying attention to participant retention is essential. In addition to trust building and staff consistency, we use multiple family informants to track highly mobile families.

High mobility requires use of multiple strategies for tracking and locating families over long periods of time, stressing financial resources that otherwise could be invested in other aspects of the research project. Peripatetic residence and the inability to keep schedules and appointments negatively impact financial resources committed to data collection; the assessor may travel considerable distances to meet with families, only to return empty-handed. Life styles are also peripatetic, sometimes to avoid the law (e.g., child protective services being about to remove a child from the home), sometimes to get a new job, sometimes to avoid paying the rent.

Among very-low-income families, practices such as leaving forwarding addresses are less likely to be routine. We send cards for nearly every occasion possible, including birthdays and secular and religious holidays, and we send child and adult newsletters. All are sent with postal return codes so that we know within a relatively short time whether a family has moved. When that occurs, we kick in our family informant contacts to locate the participant family. We sometimes have hired private detectives to track families, and we collate visits in local areas for drop-ins, even if a particular family is not scheduled for assessment. The use of home data collections and phone assessments also provides information about family mobility and continued interest in the study. Without question, our decision to move from university-based to home-based data collection was critical to the continued success of the longitudinal aspects of the study.

Multi-University Partnerships

Originally, the study was located at one university. When it relocated to the University of Michigan and became a two-university site, new administrative issues surfaced. Because the universities are only about one hour's driving distance apart, we scheduled project meetings at each site on alternate months. Modern forms of electronic communication also assist in keeping a sense of connectedness between the sites. Social gatherings for project staff also help build rapport and project spirit. One problem, however, carries a real administrative burden, and that concerns project oversight by two institutional review boards (IRBs). What is acceptable to one IRB may not be acceptable to the other. In our case, the project is reviewed by a Medical IRB at one site and by a Community IRB at another site. One IRB may request specific changes to a consent letter, whereas another IRB may find the requested changes problematic. While we have managed to negotiate the two IRBs, it frequently requires considerable administrative time to secure joint agreement. Having multiple sites also means more coordination and thus more work. For instance, managing two biweekly payrolls may mean that an administrator has to do payroll-related paperwork every week.

Aging of Participants, Researchers, Review Panels, and the Scientific Zeitgeist

Everyone in the study deals with all of the issues related to life-course changes. Our three-year-olds have moved through puberty, into adulthood, and in some instances into parenthood. Parents who originally were in their 20s to 40s are now 26 years older, as are the researchers who have been with the study from its inception. Compliant preschool- and elementary-age children become less compliant teenagers, and as assent forms turn to consent forms when participants reach age 18, we have discovered that earlier study involvement, primarily negotiated with the parents, is of no particular interest to a late adolescent or young adult who has other things on his or her mind than sitting down to fill out some forms and answer questions that require reflection. Family composition changes with step-parent and single parent configuration. Parents and teens become involved with the criminal justice system, with some serving prison time. The problems associated with reconnecting with teenagers are especially challenging, particularly with teens that drop out of school and leave home.

At a different level, there is a contact challenge to staff, because when a study like this is initiated, one typically has expertise with subject functioning and important/relevant variables within a specific developmental window. Long-term, as subjects become older, investigators need to educate themselves about development and functioning in order to keep the study current. In some ways, the study outgrows the investigators' expertise. In addition, as study subjects grow older, they tend to become older than the young staff one typically hires for assessment. So the age differential can create rapport problems. Also, vis-à-vis engaging with families that are financially successful, study participants may no longer see the participation fees as worth the time required for data collection. We have used a sliding pay scale to attempt to deal with this issue.

An additional long-term challenge is to sustain funding for what has, over the years, been a very significant but also very expensive scientific undertaking. Even with five-year federal funding cycles, keeping a study alive over five federal funding cycles (our earliest period was supported by local and state resources) has always been a significant hurdle. Review panels have no interest in supporting and monitoring important risk variables for a very expensive scientific undertaking, just so that a decade or more later the study will (probably) be able to examine long-term predictors of adult disorder. If the study is to be sustained, one must uncover important intermediary questions. And even then, non-longitudinal researchers tend not to have patience for the large cost and long span of time involved in characterizing a long-term story.

Perhaps the biggest challenge of all is that the science changes while the study is being conducted. State-of-the-art measures in one decade are *passé* in the next. A focus on one domain of function, considered central to understanding the development of risk at one time point may be regarded as of secondary, or even of trivial importance at another. Only by sustaining a broad network of relationships with a multidisciplinary group of colleagues can these challenges be effectively met.

The Human Story

When one examines the descriptive statistics on families participating in the high risk for alcoholism prospective studies, it is clear that there are numerous environmental experiences that flood children in the highest-risk homes. In the Michigan Longitudinal Study, to date, five percent of parents have died, with 1.4 percent of the total having been suicides or probable suicides (an annual rate approximately 100 times higher than the national average), and another 1.0 percent of the deaths have involved accidents (most often vehicular) and drug overdoses.

Other indicators point to a kaleidoscope of negative imagery surrounding earlier life in the highest-risk families. Marital assortment (Thiessen & Gregg, 1980) is substantial for drinking, rule breaking, and inattention to social achievement. There are strong relationships between mothers' and fathers' age of first drunkenness, their level of delinquency, and their antisocial behavior in their own childhoods. There also is assortment on the level of education each parent has achieved. These experiences form the background history of the child-rearing environment. It is most negative among the families at highest risk for the evolution of early risk, and for the subsequent development of substance use disorder among the children (Zucker et al., 1996; Buu et al., 2009).

At the individual level, the life stories of these families is heartrending; parental conflict is the norm, and physical violence between parents is not uncommon; adults come and go because they have multiple, usually sequential relationships, but also multiple sexual partners. Unemployment is often present, either within the immediate family or among relatives, who then spend time just hanging around; children are shipped to a grandparent when a parent is incarcerated or sent to a detoxification center; learning difficulties and attentional problems for the children are not unusual, and although initial involvement in school is looked forward to, by late middle childhood, there is too much going on outside the school setting to allow a sustained focus. School performance deteriorates, or there are conflicts with the teacher. Peer involvement with friends is commonly with others coming from like kinds of families, and the peer network becomes the quasi-support group and home away from home. Early involvement with alcohol and cigarettes is frequent, and it is an easy jump to engage in such life-course decisions when access and use is so common among one's friends. Often parents do not care. Sometimes they even offer the children alcohol or other drugs, thinking it is cute, or they are being friendly. Earlier sexual involvement often occurs, and teen pregnancies are more common. Among the offspring who have already had a child by age 20, the overwhelming majority come from families with an alcoholic parent.

Not all individuals nor all families have such a bleak picture. Some children, even within such disorganized homes, manage to stay disengaged from their parents and siblings. Sometimes they, for whatever reason, come to the conclusion that the substance involvement leads only downward, and they make a personal resolution to not use. Not uncommonly, a friend's parents take an interest in the youngster, or a minister does, and the child responds to the interest and attention and begins to spend more and more time at the other family's home. Significant involvement in church activity is sometimes an escape, and school performance is good. Functioning in young adulthood, to the extent we have information on this, suggests such a trajectory of disconnection can be maintained, including steady employment, sometimes pursuit of a college education, and advancement from minimum wage to supervisory/managerial jobs. At the same time, health problems (acid reflux, problems with weight control) and psychological indicators of distress, such as phobias, fears of public speaking, or bouts of depression, are often present. Unfortunately, wherever there has been this history of exposure to negative contexts and negative images, a residue of psychological or interpersonal scars shows itself, albeit playing a minor role in day-to-day functioning.

Although this continuity picture of incremental risk across childhood is the worst-case scenario, a more common, albeit also troubling, pattern of adaptation is more the norm. This is the pattern of moving into and out of damaged functioning and traumatic exposure to high stress at irregular intervals; that is, a period of time exists where a number of these negative experiences are occurring, which then subside. Thereafter, a period of time of irregular duration occurs, when problems are manageable and life appears to return to normal, and then another wave of difficulties shows up.

For staff who are involved in interviewing and other data collection, the burden of observing these life difficulties is a hard one to carry. Frequent discussions among staff, the proffering of referrals whenever requested, and urging attention and treatment for serious troubles that are mentioned only in passing or on a questionnaire (e.g., suicidal thoughts) all ease the burden a little, but not much, especially when such advice is ignored. (Child abuse is another matter entirely, and is reported when there are signs it is happening.) This work has sent an undercurrent message to all of us, repeatedly: it is that preventive intervention is essential for this population, and the blindness about its need, the lack of awareness about its early appearance, and the lack of funding for sustained and/or periodic intervention effort are roadblocks that are essential to remove.

■ FUTURE DIRECTIONS

If one includes the time when the early pilot work was being done for the Michigan Longitudinal Study, it has been in the field and under scientific stewardship for 30 years; if one counts the time since the formal start of the regular data collection, the duration is 25 years at this writing. Over that interval, a series of major collaborations have been developed that extend our scientific inquiry biologically deeper—by way of collaborations with neuroscientists (Heitzeg et al., 2008, 2010) and molecular geneticists (Villafuerte et al., 2011; Strumba et al., 2011), and environmentally broader—by way of extensive examination of the neighborhood context and its effects upon development for both generations of these families (Buu et al., 2007, 2009, 2010). These collaborations also have allowed us, by means of trajectory analysis, to characterize developmental variation and individual differences in a much more differentiated way (Shedden & Zucker, 2008; Jester, Nigg, et al., 2008; Jester, Puttler, et al., 2008) than we had at the study's outset.

Currently, the project is integrated with, and participates in, five other National Institutes of Health (NIH) projects focused on:

(a) neuroimaging (functional magnetic resonance imaging, fMRI) of late adolescents and young adults;
(b) a parallel neuroimaging project examining the emergence of risk in children in middle childhood who have not yet begun alcohol or other drug use;
(c) the role of the dopaminergic system in addiction in young adults (examined via positron-emission tomography, PET);
(d) the role of sleep problems as a mediator of externalizing and internalizing risk prior to the onset of substance use;
(e) the genes mediating precursive behavioral risk;
(f) the components of neurocognitive risk that are precursive to alcohol use as well as those that develop as a result of heavy consumption.

Four other projects were previously funded to examine:

(a) the neurophysiological components of precursive risk for smoking;
(b) marital interactions as protectors or enhancers of problem alcohol use and relapse over time;
(c) the roles of stress and internalizing risk on drug abuse; and
(d) the relationship between sleep problems, alcohol/other drug abuse, and related comorbidity (e.g., suicidality) in adolescence and young adulthood.

Although NIH funding has ended for these latter projects, the integrative work with the core study continues.

This array of projects, assessing multiple levels of functioning simultaneously and also developmentally, has given us an extraordinarily broad playing field on which to explore relationships, both over time and across levels of analysis. It is not an accident that these collaborations have developed. They were a direct result of the initial nature of the study design, and also of the very carefully constructed, albeit very broad, measurement structure of the data collection. The availability of these multiple probes is of special relevance to the hypothesis we proposed at the beginning of the chapter; namely, that it is mental representations about self and social context (one component of which is representations about alcohol), along with the internalization of family codes and values, that shift the child toward the risk side of the risk–resilience continuum for subsequent problem drinking and comorbid psychopathology. This is a complex set of relationships to parse, because it involves relationships between conscious self-experience, presence of a set of environments or risky contexts, and some kind of internal processing that consolidates these interactions. Such processing does not all take place at a "conscious" level, but rather involves substructures of the brain that monitor feeling and action tendencies, suppress some, and allow others to be expressed. At the neural level, this is the core mechanical structure, but at the same time, the brain is assessing meaning and assimilating what the context is conveying about support, opposition, reward, punishment, etc. A number of recent project activities have focused on these issues (e.g., Heitzeg et al., 2008; Weiland et al., in press; McAweeney et al., 2005, Fuller et al., 2003).

This is not the place to go into that work in any detail, but it forms the backbone of what we will be pursuing in the years ahead. That work will involve an extensive examination of:

— Gene X environment interactions, focusing on candidate genes known individually to relate to risky behavior, but where the interactions with environment leading to elevated risk are only meagerly charted (see, for example, Caspi et al., 2002).

— Developing a detailed characterization of the social environment, including development of a differentiated vocabulary about what environmental "types" are relevant to specific classes of behavior (internalizing behaviors/externalizing behaviors, inhibition, cognitive complexity, achievement, etc.)

— Characterizing the dynamics of resilience developmentally from early life to early adulthood, with a special focus on stability and instability/discontinuity of this adaptation.

Much of this work will take advantage of the multiple levels of function we have characterized, but not all are biological. Understanding the reciprocal relationship, developmentally, between facilitating environment and individual behavior, over long spans of time is already one specific item on our agenda.

■ SUMMARY

Children of alcoholics can be exposed to the full range of biological and experiential factors that organize, canalize, and structure life-course pathways. The heterogeneity of alcohol problem behavior indicates that there also are factors that contribute to resilience, although such factors are less well understood. Over the life course, many individuals slide from one side of the risk–resilience continuum to another in response to individual, familial, peer, and other influences. We suggest that mental representations about drinking and associated behaviors form as early as infancy and early childhood. Such representations influence expectancies and both decision and affective processes that are anchored in the neurobiology of executive and stress-regulatory systems that shift children of alcoholics toward the risk side of the risk–resilience continuum. These forces are particularly strong in families where parental addiction and comorbid psychopathology surround all facets of the child's rearing environment. Conducting longitudinal research in such families challenges the personal and relational resources of family members, and simultaneously challenges researchers to maintain constant vigilance over the changing dynamics of life-course transitions among research participants and themselves.

■ AUTHOR NOTE

Descriptions of individual and family functioning in this chapter are based on the Michigan Longitudinal Study interview accounts from multiple assessments of the same individuals over intervals as long as 25 years.

Preparation of this chapter was supported in part by grants from the National Institute on Alcohol Abuse and Alcoholism (R37 AA07065) (RAZ). We also want to recognize the extraordinary contributions that Susan Refior and Leon Puttler have made to the Michigan Longitudinal Study over the past 27 years.

■ REFERENCES

Adinoff, B., Iranmanesh, A., Veldhuis, J., & Fisher, L. (1998). Disturbances of stress response: The role of the HPA axis during alcohol withdrawal and abstinence. *Alcohol Health & Research World, 22*(1), 67–72.

Alterman, A. I., & Tarter, R. E. (1986). An examination of selected typologies: Hyperactivity, familial, and antisocial alcoholism. In M. Galanter (Ed.), *Recent Developments in Alcoholism* (Vol. 4, pp. 169–189). New York: Plenum Press.

Atran, S., Medin, D. L., & Ross, N. O. (2005). The cultural mind: environmental decision making and cultural modeling within and across populations. *Psychological Review, 112*, 744–776.

Barrera, M., Chassin, L., & Rogosch, F. (1993). Effects of social support and conflict on adolescent children of alcoholic and nonalcoholic fathers. *Journal of Personality and Social Psychology, 64*(4), 602–612.

Bowlby, J. (1969). *Attachment and Loss. Vol. 1: Attachment*. New York: Basic Books.

Burgin, D. (2011). From outside to inside to outside: Comments on intrapsychic representations and interpersonal interactions. *Infant Mental Health Journal, 32*, 95–114.

Buu, A., Mansour, M., Wang, J., Refior, S. K., Fitzgerald, H. E., & Zucker, R. A. (2007). Alcoholism effects on social migration and neighborhood effects on alcoholism over the course of 12 years. *Alcoholism: Clinical and Experimental Research, 31*(9), 1545–1551.

Buu, A., DiPiazza, C., Wang, J., Puttler, L. I., Fitzgerald, H. E., & Zucker, R. A. (2009). Parent, family, and neighborhood effects on the development of child substance use and other psychopathology from preschool to the start of adulthood. *Journal of Studies on Alcohol and Drugs, 70*(4), 489–498.

Buu, A., Wang, W., Wang, J., Puttler, L. I., Fitzgerald, H. E., & Zucker, R. A. (2010). Changes in women's alcoholic, antisocial, and depressive symptomatology over 12 years: A multilevel network of individual, familial, and neighborhood influences. *Development and Psychopathology, 23*, 325–337.

Caspi, A., McClay, J., Moffitt, T. E., Mill, J., Martin, J., Craig, I. W., et al. (2002). Role of genotype in the cycle of violence in maltreated children. *Science* Aug 2; *297*(5582), 851–854.

Conroy, D. A., Hairston, I. S., Heitzeg, M., Bower, K. H., & Zucker, R. A. (2009). Restless symptoms at night are associated with attention deficit symptoms during the day in children of alcoholics. *Alcoholism: Clinical and Experimental Research, 33*(6), Supplement, 236A.

Conway, M. A., & Pleydell-Pearce, C. (2000). The construction of autobiographical memories in the self-memory system. *Psychological Review, 107*, 261–288.

Cotter, R. B., Burke, J. D., Loeber, R., & Navratil, B. A. (2002). Innovative retention methods in longitudinal research: A case study of the developmental trends study. *Journal of Child and Family Studies, 22*, 485–498

Dai, X., Thavundayil, J., & Gianoulakis, C. (2002). Response of the hypothalamic-pituitary-adrenal axis to stress in the absence and presence of ethanol in subjects at high and low risk of alcoholism. *Neuropsychopharmacology, 27*, 442–452.

Dai, X., Thavundayil, J., Santella, S., & Gianoulakis, C. (2007). Response of the HPA-axis to alcohol and stress as a function of alcohol dependence and family history of alcoholism. *Psychoneuroendocrinology, 32*(3), 293–305.

Davidson, D. (1996). The role of schemata in children's memory. In H. Reese (Ed.), *Advances in Child Development and Behavior* (Vol. 26, pp. 35–58). New York: Academic Press.

Dawson, D. A., Grant, B. F., & Ruan, W. J. (2005). The association between stress and drinking: Modifying effects of gender and vulnerability. *Alcohol and Alcoholism, 40*(5), 453–460.

De Gennaro, L., & Ferrara, M. (2003). Sleep spindles: An overview. *Sleep Medicine Reviews, 7*, 423–440.

Dickerson, S. S., & Kemeny, M. E. (2004). Acute stressors and cortisol responses: A theoretical integration and synthesis of laboratory research. *Psychological Bulletin, 130*, 355–391.

Donovan, J. E. (2007). Really underage drinkers: The epidemiology of children's alcohol use in the United States. *Prevention Science, 8*, 192–205.

Edwards, E. P., Eiden, R. D., & Leonard, K. E. (2006). Behavior problems in 18- to 36-month-old children of alcoholic fathers: Secure mother–infant attachment as a protective factor. *Development and Psychopathology, 18*(2), 395–407.

Eiden, R. D., Edwards, E. P., & Leonard, K. E. (2002). Mother–infant and father–infant attachment among alcoholic families. *Development and Psychopathology, 14*, 253–278.

Eiden, R. D., Edwards, E. P., & Leonard, K. E. (2004). Predictors of effortful control among children of alcoholic and non-alcoholic fathers. *Journal of Studies on Alcohol, 65*, 309–319.

Eiden, R. D., Edwards, E. P., & Leonard, K. E. (2006). Children's internalization of rules of conduct: Role of parenting in alcoholic families. *Psychology of Addictive Behaviors, 20*, 305–315.

Eiden, R. D., Leonard, K. E., Hoyle, R. H., & Chavez, F. (2004). A transactional model of parent–infant interactions in alcoholic families. *Psychology of Addictive Behaviors, 18*(4), 350–361.

Eiden, R. D., Leonard, K. E., & Morrisey, S. (2001). Paternal alcoholism and toddler non-compliance. Alcoholism: Clinical and Experimental Research, 25(11), 1621–1633.

Eigen, L. D., & Rowden, D. W. (1996). A methodology and current estimate of the number of children of alcoholics in the United States. In S. Abbott (Ed.), *Children of Alcoholics, Selected Readings* (Vol. 2, pp. 1–21). Rockville, MD: National Association of Children of Alcoholics.

Everhart, K., & Emde, R. N. (2006). Perspectives on stress and self-regulatory processes. In H. E. Fitzgerald, B. M. Lester, & B. Zuckerman (Eds.), *The Crisis in Youth Mental Health: Critical Issues and Effective Programs, Vol. 1: Childhood Disorders* (pp. 1–24). Westport, CT: Praeger Publishers/Greenwood Publishing Group.

Fitzgerald, H. E., & Eiden, R. A. (2007). Paternal alcoholism, family functioning, and infant mental health. *Zero to Three, 27*(4), 11–18.

Fitzgerald, H. E., Puttler, L. I., Mun, E. Y., & Zucker, R. A. (2000). Prenatal and postnatal exposure to parental alcohol use and abuse. In J. D. Osofsky & H. E. Fitzgerald (Eds.), *WAIMH Handbook of Infant Mental Health, Vol. 4: Infant Mental Health in Groups at High Risk* (pp. 123–160). New York: John Wiley and Sons.

Fitzgerald, H. E., Puttler, L. I., Refior, S., & Zucker, R. A. (2007). Family responses to children and alcohol. *Alcoholism Treatment Quarterly: Families and Alcoholism. 25,* 11–25.

Fitzgerald, H. E., Sullivan, L. A., Zucker, R. A., Bruckel, S., Schneider, A. M., & Noll, R. B. (1993). Predictors of behavioral problems in three-year-old sons of alcoholics: Early evidence for onset of risk. *Child Development, 64,* 110–123.

Fitzgerald, H. E., & Zucker, R. A. (1995). Socioeconomic status and alcoholism: Structuring developmental pathways to addiction. In H. E. Fitzgerald, B. M. Lester & B. Zuckerman (Eds.), *Children of Poverty: Research, Health and Policy Issues* (pp. 125–148). New York: Garland Press.

Fitzgerald, H. E., & Zucker, R. A. (2005). Pathways of risk and aggregation for alcohol use disorders. In H. E. Fitzgerald, R. Zucker & K. Freeark (Eds.), *The Crisis in Youth Mental Health* (Vol. 3, p. 1488). Santa Barbara, CA: Greenwood Publishing Group.

Fitzgerald, H. E., Zucker, R. A., & Yang, H.-Y. (1995). Developmental systems theory and alcoholism: Analyzing patterns of variation in high-risk families. *Psychology of Addictive Behaviors, 9*(1), 8–22.

Floyd, F. J., Cranford, J. A., Daugherty, M. K., Fitzgerald, H. E., & Zucker, R. A. (2006). Marital interaction in alcoholic and nonalcoholic couples: Alcoholic subtype variations and wives' alcoholism status. *Journal of Abnormal Psychology, 115*(1), 121–130.

Fonagy, P., Lynton, P., & Strathern, L. (2011a). Borderline personality disorder, mentalization, and the neurobiology of attachment. *Infant Mental Health Journal, 32,* 47–69.

Fonagy, P., Lynton, P., & Strathern, L. (2011b). Mentalization and the roots of borderline personality disorder in infancy. In H. E. Fitzgerald, K. Puura, M. Tomlinson, & C. Paul (Eds.), *International Perspectives on Children and Mental Health: Development and Context.* (pp. 129–153). Santa Barbara, CA: Praeger.

Fraiberg, S., Adelson, E., & Shapiro, V. (1975). Ghosts in the nursery: A psychoanalytic approach to the problems of impaired infant-mother relationships. *Journal of the American Academy of Child Psychiatry, 14,* 387–421.

Fuller, B. E., Chermack, S. T., Cruise, K. A. Kirsch, E., Fitzgerald, H. E., & Zucker, R. A. (2003). Predictors of childhood aggression across three generations in children of alcoholics: Relationships involving parental alcoholism, individual and spousal aggression, and parenting practices. *Journal of Studies on Alcohol, 64*, 472–483.

Ganzel, B. L., Morris, P. A., & Wethington, E. (2010). Allostasis and the human brain: Integrating models of stress from the social and life sciences. *Psychological Review, 117*(1), 134–174.

Gianoulakis, C., Dai, X., Thavundayil, J., & Brown, T. (2005). Levels and circadian rhythmicity of plasma ACTH, cortisol, and β-endorphin as a function of family history of alcoholism. *Psychopharmacology, 181*(3), 437–444.

Gillin, J. C., Smith, T. L., Irwin, M., & Kripke, D. F. (1990). EEG sleep studies in "pure" primary alcoholism during subacute withdrawal: Relationships to normal controls, age, and other clinical variables. *Biological Psychiatry, 27*(5), 477–488.

Goldstein, T. R., Bridge, J. A., & Brent, D. A. (2008). Sleep disturbances preceding completed suicide in adolescents. *Journal of Consulting and Clinical Psychology, 76*, 84–91.

Grant, B. F. (2000). Estimates of U.S. children exposed to alcohol abuse and dependence in the family. *American Journal of Public Health, 90*(1), 112–115.

Grossman, F. K., & Fremmer-Bombik, E. (1994). Fathers' attachment representations and quality of their interactions with their children in infancy. Poster presented at the June meeting of the International Society for the Study of Behavioral Development, Amsterdam, The Netherlands.

Habemas, T., & Bluck, S. (2000). Getting a life: The emergence of the life story in adolescence. *Psychological Bulletin, 126*, 748–769.

Harley, K., & Reese, E. (1999). Origins of autobiographical memory. *Developmental Psychology, 35*, 1338–1348.

Heitzeg, M. M., Nigg, J. T., Yau, W-Y. W., Zubieta, J.-K., & Zucker, R. A. (2008). Affective circuitry and risk for alcoholism in late adolescence: Differences in frontostriatal responses between vulnerable and resilient children of alcoholic parents. *Alcoholism: Clinical and Experimental Research, 32*(3), 414–426.

Heitzeg, M. M., Nigg, J. T., Yau, W-Y., Zucker, R. A., Zubieta, J.-K. (2010). Striatal dysfunction marks preexisting risk and medial prefrontal dysfunction is related to problem drinking in children of alcoholics. *Biological Psychiatry, 68*(3), 287–295.

Howe, M. L., & Courage, M. L. (1997). The emergence and early development of autobiographical memory. *Psychological Review, 104*, 499–523.

Hussong, A. M., Bauer, D. J., Huang, W., Chassin, L., Sher, K. J., & Zucker, R. A. (2008). Characterizing the life stressors of children of alcoholic parents. *Journal of Family Psychology, 22*(6), 819–832.

Iglowstein, I., Jenni, O., Molinari, L., & Largo, R. (2003). Sleep duration from infancy to adolescence: Reference values and generational trends. *Pediatrics, 111*, 302–307.

Irwin, M., Miller, C., Gillin, J. C., Demodena, A., & Ehlers, C. L. (2000). Polysomnographic and spectral sleep EEG in primary alcoholics: An interaction between alcohol dependence and African-American ethnicity. *Alcoholism: Clinical and Experimental Research, 24*(9), 1376–1384.

Jester, J. M., Nigg, J. T., Buu, A., Puttler, L. I., Glass, J. M., Heitzeg, M. M., et al. (2008). Trajectories of childhood aggression and inattention/hyperactivity: Differential effects on substance abuse in adolescence. *Journal of the American Academy of Child and Adolescent Psychiatry, 47*(10), 1158–1165.

Jester, J. M., Puttler, L. I., Buu, A., & Zucker, R. A. (2008). Alcoholism symptom trajectory classes over the course of adolescence to middle adulthood: correlates and predictors of class membership. [Abstract]. *Alcoholism: Clinical & Experimental Research, 32*(Suppl. 6), 325A.

King, A. C., Bernardy, N. C., & Hauner, K. (2003). Stressful events, personality, and mood disturbance: Gender differences in alcoholics and problem drinkers. *Addictive Behaviors, 28*(1), 171–187.

Kittmer, M. S. (2005). *Risk and Resilience in Alcoholic Families: Family Functioning, Sibling Attachment, and Parent–Child Relationships.* Ann Arbor, MI: ProQuest Information & Learning, U.S.

Linsky, A. S., Straus, M. A., & Colby, J. P. (1985). Stressful events, stressful conditions and alcohol problems in the United States: A partial test of Bales's theory. *Journal of Studies on Alcohol, 46*(1), 72–80.

Lorber, M. F., & Egeland, B. (2009). Infancy parenting and externalizing psychopathology from childhood through adulthood: developmental trends. *Developmental Psychology, 45,* 909–912.

Loukas, A., Fitzgerald, H. E., Zucker, R. A., & von Eye, A. (2001). Parental alcoholism and co-occurring antisocial behavior: Prospective relationships to externalizing behavior problems in their young sons. *Journal of Abnormal Child Psychology: An official publication of the International Society for Research in Child and Adolescent Psychopathology, 29*(2), 91–106.

Lyons-Ruth, K. (1996). Attachment relationships among children with aggressive behavior problems: The role of disorganized attachment patterns. *Journal of Consulting and Clinical Psychology, 64,* 1245–1254.

Markowitsch, H. J., Thiel, A., Kessler, J., von Stockhausen, H. M., & Heiss, W. D. (1997). Ecphorizing semi-conscious episodic information via the right temporal polar cortex: A PET study. *Neurocase, 3,* 445–449.

Mayzer, R., Fitzgerald, H. E., & Zucker, R. A. (2009). Anticipating problem drinking risk from preschoolers' antisocial behavior: Evidence for a common delinquency-related diathesis model. *Journal of the American Academy of Child & Adolescent Psychiatry, 48*(8), 820–827.

McAweeney, M. J., Zucker, R. A., Fitzgerald, H. E., Puttler, L. I., & Wong, M. M. (2005). Individual and partner predictors of recovery from alcohol use disorder over a nine-year interval: Findings from a community sample of alcoholic married men. *Journal of Studies on Alcohol, 66*(2), 220–228.

McCabe, L. A., Cunnington, M., & Brooks-Gunn, J. (2004). The development of self-regulation in young children: Individual characteristics and environmental contexts. In R. F. Baumeister & K. D. Vohs (Eds.), *Handbook of Self-Regulation: Research, Theory, and Applications* (pp. 340–356). New York: Guilford Press.

McEwen, B. S. (1998). Stress, adaptation, and disease: Allostasis and allostatic load. In S. M. McCann, J. M. Lipton, E. M. Sternberg, G. P. Chrousos, P. W. Gold, & C. C. Smith (Eds.), *Annals of the New York Academy of Sciences, Vol. 840: Neuroimmunomodulation: Molecular Aspects, Integrative Systems, and Clinical Advances* (pp. 33–44). New York: New York Academy of Sciences.

McEwen, B. S., & Stellar, E. (1993). Stress and the individual. Mechanisms leading to disease. *Archives of Internal Medicine, 153,* 2093–2101.

McEwen, B. S., & Wingfield, J. C. (2003). The concept of allostasis in biology and biomedicine. *Hormones and Behavior, 43*(1), 2–15.

Muller, R. T., Fitzgerald, H. E., Sullivan, L. A., & Zucker, R. A. (1994). Social support and stress factors in child maltreatment among alcoholic families. *Canadian Journal of Behavioural Science, 26*, 438–461.

Navratil, J. L., Green, S. M., Loeber, R., & Lahey, B. B. (1994). Minimizing subject loss in a longitudinal study of deviant behavior. *Journal of Child and Family Studies, 3*, 89–106.

Nelson, C. A. (1995). The ontogeny of human memory: A cognitive neuroscience perspective. *Developmental Psychology, 31*, 723–738.

Noll, R. B., Zucker, R. A., & Greenberg, G. S. (1990). Identification of alcohol by smell among preschoolers: Evidence for early socialization about drugs occurring in the home. *Child Development, 61*, 1520–1527.

Pihl, R. O., & Peterson, J. B. (1991). Attention-deficit hyperactivity disorder, childhood conduct disorder, and alcoholism: Is there an association? *Alcohol Health & Research World, 15*(1), 25–31.

Puttler, L. I., Zucker, R. A., Fitzgerald, H. E., & Bingham, C. R. (1998). Behavioral outcomes among children of alcoholics during the early and middle childhood years: Familial subtype variations. *Alcoholism: Clinical and Experimental Research, 22*(9), 1962–1972.

Rothbart, M. K., Derryberry, D., & Posner, M. I. (1994). A psychobiological approach to the development of temperament. In J. E. Bates & T. D. Wachs (Eds.), *Temperament: Individual Differences at the Interface of Biology and Behavior* (pp. 83–116). Washington, DC: American Psychological Association.

Sameroff, A. J. (1995). General systems theories and developmental psychopathology. In D. Cicchetti & D. J. Cohen (Eds.), *Developmental Psychopathology* (pp. 659–695). New York: Wiley.

Schneider, W., & Bjorklund, D. F. (1998). Memory. In D. Kuhn & R. S. Siegler (Eds.), *Handbook of Child Psychology: Vol. 2. Cognition, Perception, and Language* (pp. 467–521). New York: Wiley.

Schuder, M. R., & Lyons-Ruth, K. (2004). "Hidden trauma" in infancy: Attachment, fearful arousal, and early dysfunction of the stress response system. In J. D. Osofsky (Ed.), *Young Children and Trauma: Intervention and Treatment* (pp. 69–104). New York: Guilford.

Schumm, J. A., O'Farrell, T. J., Murphy, C. M., & Fals-Stewart, W. (2009). Partner violence before and after couples-based alcoholism treatment for female alcoholic patients. *Journal of Consulting and Clinical Psychology, 77*(6), 1136–1146.

Shears, J., Robinson, J., & Emde, R. (2002). Fathering relationships and their associations with juvenile delinquency. *Infant Mental Health Journal, 23*, 79–87.

Shedden, K., & Zucker, R. A. (2008). Regularized finite mixture models for probability trajectories. *Psychometrika, 73*(4), 625–646.

Sher, K. J. (1991). Psychological characteristics of children of alcoholics: Overview of research methods and findings. In M. Galanter, H. Begleiter, R. Deitrich, D. M. Gallant, D. Goodwin, E. Gottheil, et al. (Eds.), *Recent Developments in Alcoholism, Vol. 9: Children of Alcoholics* (pp. 301–326). New York: Plenum Press.

Sheldon, S. H. (2005). Introduction to pediatric sleep medicine. In S. H. Sheldon, R. Ferber, & M. H. Kryger (Eds.), *Principles and Practices of Pediatric Sleep Medicine* (pp. 1–16). Philadelphia, PA: Elsevier Saunders.

Spitz, R. (1965). *The First Year of Life*. New York: International Universities Press.

Stanley, S. (2008). Interpersonal violence in alcohol complicated marital relationships (A study from India). *Journal of Family Violence, 23*(8), 767–776.

Stern, D. (1985). *The Interpersonal World of the Infant: A View from Psychoanalysis and Developmental Psychology.* New York: Basic Books.

Strelau, J. (1998). *Temperament: A Psychological Perspective.* New York: Plenum Press.

Strumba, V. S., Shedden, K., Zucker, R. A., & Burmeister, M. (2011). Heritability analysis of behavioral traits in children of alcoholics. *Alcoholism: Clinical and Experimental Research, 35*(Suppl. 6), 195A.

Stouthamer-Loeber, M., van Kammen, W., & Loeber, R. (1992). The nuts and bolts of implementing large-scale longitudinal studies. *Violence and Victims, 7,* 63–106.

Sun, J., & Zhao, Z. (2010). A comparative study of cancer proteins and in the human protein-protein interaction research. *BMG Genomics, 11* (Suppl 3), S5.

Tarokh, L., & Carskadon, M. A. (2009). Sleep electroencephalogram in children with a parental history of alcohol abuse/dependence. *Journal of Sleep Research, 11,* 65–69.

Thuessen, P., & Gregg, R. (1980). Human assortative mating and genetic equilibrium: an evolutionary perspective. *Ethology and Sociobiology, 1,* 111–140.

Trim, R. S., Leuthe, E., & Chassin, L. (2006). Sibling influence on alcohol use in a young adult, high-risk sample. *Journal of Studies on Alcohol, 67*(3), 391–398.

Trevarthen, C. (1980). The foundations of intersubjectivity: development of interpersonal and cooperative understanding in infants. In D. Olson (Ed.), *The Social Foundations of Language and Thought.* New York: W.W. Norton.

Verschuren, K., Marcven, A., & Schoefs, V. (1996). The internal working model of the self: Attachment and competence in five-year-olds. *Child Development, 67,* 2493–2511.

Villafuerte, S., Heitzeg, M. M., Foley, S., Yau, W., Majczenko, K., Zubieta, J.-K., et al. (2012). Impulsiveness and insula activation during reward anticipation are associated with genetic variants in GABRA2 in a family sample enriched for alcoholism. *Molecular Psychiatry, 17,* 511–519.

Vohs, K. D., & Baumeister, R. F. (2004). Understanding self-regulation: An introduction. In R. F. Baumeister & K. D. Vohs (Eds.), *Handbook of Self-Regulation: Research, Theory, and Applications* (pp. 1–9). New York: Guilford Press.

Waltman, C., McCaul, M. E., & Wand, G. S. (1994). Adrenocorticotropin responses following administration of ethanol and ovine corticotropin-releasing hormone in the sons of alcoholics and control subjects. *Alcoholism: Clinical and Experimental Research, 18*(4), 826–830.

Weiland, B. J., Nigg, J. T., Welsh, R., Yau, W., Zubieta, J.-K., Zucker, R. A., et al. (in press). Resiliency in adolescents at high-risk for substance abuse: flexible adaptation via subthalamic nucleus and linkage to drinking and drug use in early adulthood. *Alcoholism: Clinical and Experimental Research.*

Werner, E. (1986). Resilient offspring of alcoholics: A longitudinal study from birth to age 18. *Journal of Studies on Alcohol, 47*(1), 34–40.

Werner, E., & Johnson, J. (2000). The role of caring adults in the lives of children of alcoholics. In S. Abbott (Ed.), *Children of Alcoholics, Vol. 2: Selected Readings* (pp. 119–141). Rockville, MD: National Association for Children of Alcoholics.

Whipple, E. E., Fitzgerald, H. E., & Zucker, R. A. (1995). Parent–child interactions in alcoholic and nonalcoholic families. *American Journal of Orthopsychiatry, 65*(1), 153–159.

Windle, M., & Searles, J. S. (1990). *Children of Alcoholics: Critical Perspectives*. New York: Guilford Press.

Wong, M. M., Brower, K. J., Fitzgerald, H. E., & Zucker, R. A. (2004). Sleep problems in early childhood and early onset of alcohol and other drug use in adolescence. *Alcoholism: Clinical & Experimental Research, 28*, 578–587.

Wong, M. M., Brower, K. J., Nigg, J. T., & Zucker, R. A. (2010). Childhood sleep problems, response inhibition, and alcohol and drug outcomes in adolescence and young adulthood. *Alcoholism: Clinical & Experimental Research, 34*, 1033–1044.

Wong, M. M., Brower, K. J., & Zucker, R. A. (2009). Childhood sleep problems, early onset of substance use and behavioral problems in adolescence. *Sleep Medicine, 10*(7), 787–796.

Wong, M. M., Zucker, R. A., Puttler, L. I., & Fitzgerald, H. E. (1999). Heterogeneity of risk aggregation for alcohol problems between early and middle childhood: Nesting structure variations. *Development and Psychopathology, 11*, 727–744.

Yamadori, A. (1971). Role of the spindles in the onset of sleep. *Kobe Journal of Medical Sciences, 17*, 97–111.

Zimmerman, U., Spring, K., Koller, G., Holsboer, F., & Soyka, M. (2004). Hypothalamic-pituitary-adrenal system regulation in recently detoxified alcoholics is not altered by one week of treatment with acamprosate. *Pharmacopsychiatry, 37*(3), 98–102.

Zeanah, C. H., Danis, B., Hirschberg, L., Benoit, D., Miller, D., & Heller, S. S. (1999). Disorganized attachment associated with partner violence: A research note. *Infant Mental Health Journal, 20*, 77–86.

Zucker, R. A. (2006). Alcohol use and alcohol use disorders: A developmental biopsycosocial systems formulation covering the life course. In D. Cicchetti & D. J. Cohen (Eds.), *Developmental Psychopathology, Vol. 3: Risk, Disorder, and Adaptation* (2nd ed., pp 620–656). New York: Wiley.

Zucker, R. A., Donovan, J. E., Masten, A. S., Mattson, M. E., & Moss, H. B. (2009). Developmental processes and mechanisms, ages 0–10. *Alcohol Research and Health, 32*, 16–29.

Zucker, R. A., Chermack, S. T., & Curran, G. M. (2000). Alcoholism: A life span perspective on etiology and course. In A. J. Sameroff, M. Lewis, & S. M. Miller (Eds.), *Handbook of Developmental Psychopathology (2nd ed.*, pp. 569–587). Dordrecht, Netherlands: Kluwer Academic Publishers.

Zucker, R. A., Ellis, D. E., Fitzgerald, H. E., Bingham, C. R., and Sanford, K. P. (1996). Other evidence for at least two alcoholisms, II: Life course variation in antisociality and heterogeneity of alcoholic outcome. *Development and Psychopathology, 8*(4), 831–848.

Zucker, R. A., & Fitzgerald, H. E. (1991). Early developmental factors and risk for alcohol problems. *Alcohol Health and Research World, 15*, 18–24.

Zucker, R. A., Fitzgerald, H. E., Refior, S. K., Puttler, L. I., Pallas, D. M., & Ellis, D. A. (2000). The clinical and social ecology of childhood for children of alcoholics: Description of a study and implications for a differentiated social policy. In H. E. Fitzgerald, B. M. Lester, & B. Zuckerman (Eds.), *Children of Addiction: Research, Health, and Public Policy Issues* (pp. 109–141). New York: Garland.

Zucker, R. A., & Gomberg, E. S. (1986). Etiology of alcoholism reconsidered: The case for a biopsychosocial process. *American Psychologist, 41*(7), 783–793.

Zucker, R. A., Heitxzeg, M. M., & Nigg, J. T. (2011). Parsing the undercontrol-disinhibition pathway in substance use disorders: A multilevel developmental problem. *Child Development Perspectives, 5,* 248–255.

Zucker, R. A., Kincaid, S. B., Fitzgerald, H. E., & Bingham, C. R. (1995). *Alcoholism: Clinical and Experimental Research, 19*(4), 1011–1017.

Zucker, R. A., Wong, M. M., Puttler, L. I., & Fitzgerald, H. E. (2003). Resilience and vulnerability among sons of alcoholics: Relationship to developmental outcomes between early childhood and adolescence. In S. S. Luthar (Ed.), *Resilience and Vulnerability: Adaptation in the Context of Childhood Adversities (pp 76–103).* New York: Cambridge University Press.

8 Substance-Abusing Fathers

A Developmental Perspective

THOMAS J. MCMAHON

Over the past 20 years, a number of social and economic changes have converged in technologically oriented cultures to focus attention on the importance of fathering in the lives of men, women, and children (for further discussion, see Hobson, 2002). Believing that fathering is largely a social construct, scholars interested in family life (e.g., Pleck, 2004; Pleck & Pleck, 1997) have highlighted ways that social definitions of *good* versus *bad* fathering have changed over time in response to social, economic, and political forces. Concerned about social changes that leave fathers estranged from their children, researchers (e.g., Doherty, Kouneski, & Erickson, 1998; Dollahite, Hawkins, & Brotherson, 1997; Hawkins & Dollahite, 1997; Lamb, 1986; Palkovitz, 1997) have begun to outline contemporary definitions of *good* fathering in the context of rapidly changing ideas about men in family systems. Moving beyond deficit perspectives that focus on shortcomings in the parenting of men, these researchers have emphasized the need for new definitions of *good* fathering that acknowledge the ethical responsibility men have to care for their children, the interest they have in being a father, and the capacity they have for effective parenting.

Although there has been debate about the nature of the construct in North American culture (e.g., see Doherty, Kouneski, & Erickson, 1998, 2000 versus Walker & McGraw, 2000 and Silverstein & Auerbach, 1999, 2000 versus Blankenhorn, 2000; Daly & Wilson, 2000; Lykken, 2000; McDonagh, 2000; Popenoe, 2000), there appears to be agreement that *good* fathering involves (a) planning for the conception of children, (b) preparing for their birth, (c) acknowledging paternity, (d) building positive relationships with other caretakers, (e) being accessible to children, (f) contributing directly to their care, and (g) somehow contributing to their financial support (Doherty et al., 1998; Dollahite et al., 1997; Hawkins & Dollahite, 1997; Lamb, 1986; Palkovitz, 1997). Acknowledging that fathering has a profound impact on the psychosocial development of men (for a review, see McMahon & Spector, 2007), scholars (e.g., Palkovitz, 1997) have also begun to argue that any conceptualization of *good* fathering must move beyond concern for just mothers and children to include representation of the thoughts and feelings men have about themselves as a parent.

Ironically, in the context of increased attention to fatherhood as a social issue, fathering is not typically acknowledged as a psychological concern in the lives of substance-abusing men (McMahon & Rounsaville, 2002). At this time, relatively little is known about the nature of fathering occurring in the context of chronic substance abuse. As policymakers advocate programming designed to increase the presence of men in the lives of children (e.g., see Bronte-Tinkew, Bowie, &

156

Moore, 2007; Cabrera & Peters, 2000; McLanahan & Carlson, 2002; Mincy & Pouncy, 2002), there are only limited data to guide the development of clinical intervention designed to promote more effective parenting by substance-abusing men (McMahon & Rounsaville, 2002). In the absence of empirical data, the fathering of substance-abusing men continues to be defined by stereotypes that assume they are reproducing indiscriminately, woefully neglectful, psychological incapable, and potentially dangerous (for further discussion, see McMahon & Giannini, 2003). Unfortunately, it is not presently clear to what extent this is, in fact, true.

■ A DEVELOPMENTAL PERSPECTIVE ON FATHERING

When considered from the perspective of men, questions about fathering occurring in the context of chronic substance abuse are important because there is evidence that, contrary to ideas about social definitions of fathering, pathways to *good* and *bad* fathering appear to be defined by a complex interplay of genetic, psychological, interpersonal, and social influences as men move from childhood through adolescence and into early adulthood (for further discussion, see Belsky, 1997, 1999, 2000; Ellis, Figueredo, Brumbach, & Schlomer, 2009; Rowe, 2000a, 2000b). Since Belsky, Steinberg, and Draper (1991) first outlined a developmental theory of parenting grounded in evolutionary constructs, a number of scholars (e.g., Belsky, 1997, 1999, 2000; Chisholm, 1993, 1996; Kirkpatrick 1998; Simpson & Belsky, 2008) have begun to specify ways genetics and the quality of early relationships with primary caregivers interact with contextual factors to influence pair-bonding, production of children, and quality of parenting. Across generations, there is accumulating evidence that developmental pathways to *good* versus *bad* fathering may begin at birth, with the social circumstances of the family, the reproductive history of biological parents, and the quality of early relationships with primary caretakers (for further discussion, see Belsky et al., 1991). Relatively early in childhood, males, like females, typically develop increasingly complex psychological representations of themselves and others, including psychological representations of themselves as human beings with the capacity to create and parent children (for further discussion, see Ainsworth, 1989). Most boys begin to think of themselves as parents long before puberty (e.g., see Marsiglio & Hutchinson, 2002), and as boys move through childhood into adolescence, their pubertal development, age of first sexual intercourse, and number of early sexual partners become important developmental markers as young men move toward *good* versus *bad* fathering.

Working from different theoretical perspectives, researchers have begun to document the influence of genetic, psychological, interpersonal, and social factors on the reproductive and parenting behavior of men. Using the principles of behavioral genetics, researchers (Bailey, Kirk, Zhu, Dunne, & Martin, 2000; Bricker et al., 2006; Cherkas, Oelsner, Mak, Valdes, & Spector, 2004; Harden et al., 2007; Johansson et al., 2008; Lyons et al., 2004; Mustanski, Viken, Kaprio, Pulkkinen, & Rose, 2004; Varjonen et al., 2007) have shown that there is significant heritability in (a) markers of pubertal development, (b) attitudes toward sexuality, (c) age of first sexual intercourse, (d) specific sexual behaviors, (e) number of sexual partners, (f) quality of sexual partnerships, (g) marriage, and (h) divorce among men. They (e.g., Neiderhiser, Pike, Hetherington, & Reiss, 1998) have also shown that both positive and negative parenting behavior by men appear to have a heritable component. Citing complementary data documenting the heritability of personality, some researchers (e.g., Ganiban et al., 2009) have begun to argue that personality traits are the psychological phenotypes that account for much of the heritability of sexual and parenting behavior, and they (e.g., Ganiban et al., 2009; Spinath & O'Connor, 2003) have begun to show that, just as the heritability of substance abuse can be accounted for by the heritability of core personality traits (e.g., see Slutske et al., 2002), parenting behavior can also be accounted for by the heritability of core personality traits.

Moving beyond genetic contributions, researchers (e.g., Bakermans-Kranenburg, van IJzendoorn, Bokhorst, & Schuengel, 2004; Bokhorst et al., 2003; O'Connor & Croft, 2001) have begun to show that psychological representations of self and others that evolve out of early experience with primary caregivers relatively independently of genetic influence also seem to influence the production and parenting of children across generations. Although originally outlined to characterize mother–child relationships, there is evidence that, when fathers are present in the lives of children, psychological representations of relationships with fathers evolve concurrently with psychological representations of relationships with mothers (for a review, see Lamb, 2002). Although discussion continues about the organization and influence of different representations (e.g., see Howes & Spieker, 2008), psychological representations of early relationships become more elaborate during early to middle adolescence, and they become the foundation for complementary representations of self as a potential sexual partner and a potential parent (for further discussion, see George, 1996; George & Solomon, 2008; Solomon & George, 1996). While researchers measure residential status, child support payment, and frequency of the father's contact with his children, the most important dimension of early father–child relationships may be the psychological representation of the relationship men and women carry forward across generations as they become a sexual partner and then a parent.

Although an important developmental issue in the lives of men, fathering also occurs in a social context. Many scholars believe that it is useful to think of fathering as a developmental process that unfolds in a social ecology, because research indicates that contextual factors exert a great deal of influence on paternal involvement in the lives of children. For example, Dunne et al. (1997) have shown that the extent to which genetics influence reproductive behavior (like age of first sexual intercourse) may be attenuated as social norms concerning extramarital sexual activity change from more to less conservative. Similarly, Hetherington and Stanley-Morgan (1997) have shown that geographic proximity, employment status, quality of the co-parenting relationship, and the presence of another male in the household seem to mediate the impact of divorce on father–child relationships. Although contextual influences on the parenting of substance-abusing men have not been explored extensively, research done with substance-abusing mothers suggests that compromise of parenting otherwise attributable to psychopathology and substance abuse seems to be mediated and moderated by a number of contextual factors (Suchman & Luthar, 2000, 2001; Suchman, McMahon, Slade, & Luthar, 2005).

■ SCOPE OF THE PROBLEM

Epidemiological data indicate that substance use disorders are the most frequently occurring behavioral health problems among men. Approximately 42 percent of men over 18 years of age report a lifetime history of an alcohol, nicotine, or other substance use disorder (Kessler, Burgland, et al., 2005). Approximately 15 percent of men over 18 years of age also report a recent history of an alcohol, nicotine, or substance use disorder (Kessler, Chiu, Demler, Merikangas, & Walters, 2005). Unfortunately, there is currently only limited documentation of the parenting status of men with substance abuse problems, and the data that are available make it difficult to accurately estimate the number of alcohol- and drug-abusing fathers. Taken together, the data that are available do, however, suggest that a sizable portion of men with a substance-abuse problem are the biological or social father of at least one child.

For example, in a secondary analysis of data from the National Household Survey on Drug Abuse, the U.S. Department of Health and Human Services (1994) found that approximately eight percent of the 32 million fathers in this country with a minor biological child had used an illicit drug during the past 30 days. Moreover, although fathers (38.4%) with a recent history of illicit drug use were more likely than other fathers (20.7%) to be living away from all of their minor children, a substantial proportion (59%) of the fathers with a recent history of illicit drug use were living with at least one of their biological children. Unfortunately, this secondary analysis did not offer information about the use of alcohol or nicotine among fathers, and it did not distinguish between drug use and drug abuse.

Similarly, in a subsequent analysis of data from the same survey, the Substance Abuse and Mental Health Administration (2009) found that approximately 8.3 million (11.9%) of the minor children living with a biological, adoptive, step-, or foster parent were living with at least one substance-abusing parent. Approximately 5.4 million (65%) of those children were living with a substance-abusing father, most frequently an alcohol-abusing father. Most of them (77%) were living with two parents, and children less than five years of age were more likely to be affected. Unfortunately, the study did not provide information about the number of children separated from a substance-abusing father.

In a survey of opioid-dependent men seeking methadone maintenance treatment, McMahon, Winkel, Luthar, and Rounsaville (2005) found that approximately 60 percent of the men (versus 80% of the women) were the parent of at least one biological child. There were no significant gender differences in the number or age of the children. Men were, however, much more likely than women to be separated from all of their biological children. However, because there were far more men than women entering treatment, there were actually more fathers than mothers in the cohort, and nonresident fathers emerged as the largest group of parents seeking treatment.

■ DEVELOPMENTAL PRECURSORS TO FATHERING

Given the influence that developmental experiences in the family-of-origin seem to have across generations, it is important to note that very little is known about the ways developmental experiences in family-of-origin influence the fathering of substance-abusing men. The data that are available suggest that at least some substance-abusing men move toward early adulthood without the early developmental experiences thought to be important in determining the quality of parent–child relationships across generations. When compared with men who have no history of alcohol or drug abuse, substance-abusing men consistently report greater exposure to family adversity as a child and parenting behavior associated with poor developmental outcomes in children (Campo & Rohner, 1992; Duncan, Saunders, Kilpatrick, Hanson, & Resnick, 1996; Lisak & Luster, 1994; Wright, Garrison, Wright, & Stimmel, 1991). There is also evidence that developmental experiences thought to influence ability to parent the next generation may be different for individuals abusing alcohol that for those using illicit drugs (Bernardi, Jones, & Tennant, 1989). Taken together, the available data suggest that substance-abusing men consistently report greater exposure to early developmental experiences that other research has consistently associated with problems in parenting the next generation (Florsheim et al., 2003; Furstenberg & Weiss, 2000; Simons, Whitbeck, Conger, & Wu, 1991; Whitbeck, Yoder, Hoyt, & Conger, 1999).

Within the developmental literature, researchers have shown that there is consistency in patterns of pair bonding and reproduction across generations that seems to be influenced by early experiences with primary caregivers. However, this work has not, for the most part, been replicated with samples of men with social, psychiatric, and substance abuse problems. Researchers (e.g., Belsky et al., 1991) have argued that disruption of early family environments contributes to disturbance in psychological representations of self and caregiving relationships that influence reproductive strategy across generations. Unfortunately, it is not yet clear how developmental experiences, particularly early experiences with biological fathers, influence pair-bonding, reproduction, and parenting within populations of substance-abusing men.

■ DEVELOPMENTAL PATHWAYS TO CHRONIC SUBSTANCE ABUSE AND FATHERHOOD

Research done with cohorts of children followed forward into adolescence and early adulthood does suggest that compromise of fathering in substance-using men may evolve out of a common developmental trajectory characterized by compromise of family environments, disturbance in early parent–child relationships, and exposure to childhood trauma that represent long-term risk for both chronic substance abuse and compromise of *good* fathering. Several longitudinal investigations have shown that (a) teens with early use of alcohol and drugs are at risk for early first sexual intercourse; (b) early first sexual intercourse represents risk for more sexual partners; and (c) having a number of early sexual partners represents risk for an early, unplanned pregnancy (Capaldi, Crosby, & Stoolmiller, 1996; Farrell, Danish, & Howard, 1992; Odgers et al., 2008; Santelli, Brener, Lowry, Bhatt, & Zabin, 1998; Whitbeck et al., 1999). Early, unplanned pregnancy often occurs in the context of ongoing substance use and other problem behavior (Christmon & Luckey, 1994; Elster, Lamb, & Tavare, 1987; Guagliardo, Huang, & D'Angelo, 1999; Stouthamer-Loeber & Wei, 1998). Other work suggests that early substance use and early sexual activity may evolve as young men move along a common developmental pathway involving genetic and environmental influences (Eisenberg et al., 2007; Laucht, Becker, Blomeyer, & Schmidt, 2007). The existing literature also suggests that relationships involving genetic and environmental risk for early substance use and early sexual activity may be mediated by the consolidation of specific personality traits, like sensation seeking, during adolescence and early adulthood (Brady & Donenberg, 2006; Laucht et al., 2007).

Early substance use that continues through the transition to adulthood is also associated with unstable sexual partnerships and a failure to accumulate the economic resources needed to support a family. Young, substance-abusing men are less likely to complete high school and less likely to have stable employment (Green & Ensminger, 2006). They are also more likely to demonstrate disturbance in romantic attachments (Vungkhanching, Sher, Jackson, & Parra, 2004); there is greater risk for psychological, physical, and sexual aggression within their sexual partnerships (for a review, see Foran & O'Leary, 2008; Moore et al., 2008); and they are more likely to cohabitate with a series of sexual partners than be involved in a legal marriage (McMahon, Winkel, & Rounsaville, 2008). Moreover, even when they do marry, many substance-abusing men are likely to marry very early (for a review, see Leonard & Eiden, 2007); they are more likely to choose a spouse who has her own personality, substance abuse, or psychiatric problems (for a review, see Leonard & Eiden, 2007); and there is likely to be more conflict and less satisfaction with the marriage, particularly if the spouse is not also actively using alcohol or illicit drugs (Homish & Leonard, 2007). Substance-abusing men who do marry are also more likely to pursue extramarital sexual activity with risk for an unplanned pregnancy (Hall, Fals-Stewart, & Fincham, 2008); and the couple is more likely to eventually divorce, particularly if the spouse is not also actively using alcohol or illicit drugs (Collins, Ellickson, & Klein, 2007; Ostermann, Sloan, & Taylor, 2005).

In a study done with opioid-dependent fathers, McMahon et al. (2008) also found that, when compared with men who have no history of alcohol or drug abuse, drug-abusing men who do have children tend to become fathers at an earlier age, typically in the context of ongoing drug abuse. They also appear to be at risk to have more children with more women within a briefer period of time without the social and economic capital to support a family (McMahon et al., 2008). Moreover, even if they make an initial effort to parent children in a socially desirable manner, they usually cannot sustain that effort over time (McMahon et al., 2008; McMahon, Winkel, Suchman, & Rounsaville, 2007).

■ PATERNAL SUBSTANCE ABUSE AND PARENTING BEHAVIOR

As *good* fathering has become a prominent social issue, researchers (e.g., Carlson & McLanahan, 2004; Fox & Benson, 2004; Nelson, Clampet-Lundquist, & Edin, 2002) have begun to examine attitudes toward parenting and parenting behavior within special populations of fathers, particularly overlapping populations of fathers struggling with social, economic, and psychological problems. Paternal substance abuse, particularly paternal alcoholism, has repeatedly been examined as a global risk factor for poor developmental outcomes in children (Clark et al., 1997; Hill, Locke, Lowers, & Connolly, 1999; Kelley & Fals-Stewart, 2004), but the parenting of alcohol- and drug-abusing men has, for the most part, not been the focus of much empirical investigation (McMahon & Rounsaville, 2002). That said, researchers have, on a limited basis, begun to show that, when compared with men without any history of alcohol or drug abuse, substance-abusing men demonstrate parenting behavior commonly associated with compromise of family environments, parental stress, dissatisfaction with parenting, and poor developmental outcomes in children.

For example, Eiden and her colleagues (Edwards, Eiden, & Leonard, 2004; Eiden, Chavez, & Leonard, 1999; Eiden, Edwards, & Leonard, 2002; Eiden & Leonard, 2000) found that, although a substantial number of alcoholic men were able to establish a positive emotional connection with their preschool child, paternal alcoholism was associated with (a) more negative attitudes toward children, (b) more negative emotion during father–child interactions, (c) less positive emotion during father–child interactions, and (d) more tenuous father–child attachment. El-Sheikh and her colleagues (El-Sheikh & Buckhalt, 2003; El-Sheikh & Flanagan, 2001) noted that paternal alcoholism was also associated with less cohesion, less adaptability, more conflict, and poorer father–child attachment in family systems with school-age children. Zhou, King, and Chassin (2006) found that paternal alcoholism was associated with less family harmony during adolescence, and Jacob, Kahn, and Leonard (1991) showed that, when compared with fathers with no history of alcoholism, fathers with a history of alcoholism demonstrated less positive affect and less problem-solving skill during interactions with their teenage children.

Although children with a drug-abusing father may be at even greater risk for poor developmental outcomes than children with an alcoholic father (Fals-Stewart, Kelley, Fincham, Golden, & Logsdan, 2004; Kelley & Fals Stewart, 2004), the parenting of drug-abusing men has received minimal attention in the substance abuse literature. McMahon et al. (2008) found that, when compared with fathers without a history of alcohol or drug abuse, drug-abusing fathers reported a narrower, more traditional conceptualization of fathering, and Ammerman, Kolko, Kirisci, Blackson, and Dawes (1999) found that paternal drug abuse was also associated with attitudes representing risk for physical abuse of children. McMahon et al. (2008) also found that drug-abusing fathers were less likely to be living with their youngest biological child, less likely to be a legal guardian for that child, and less likely to be contributing to the financial support of that child.

Blackson et al. (1999) found that, when compared with fathers who reported no history of substance abuse, fathers with a history of alcohol and drug abuse reported (a) relatively poorer father–child communication, (b) elevated risk for physical abuse of children, (c) poorer parent–child relationships, and (d) more parenting stress. There was, however, no significant difference in children's report of their father's parenting behavior.

Comparing drug-abusing fathers with fathers with no history of alcohol or drug abuse, Fals-Stewart et al. (2004) also found that the drug-abusing fathers reported more problematic disciplinary practices and less monitoring of their children. McMahon et al. (2008) found that drug-abusing fathers reported less involvement in all aspects of fathering without any significant difference in the frequency of positive or negative parenting behavior, probably because their sample included non-resident fathers, while the other samples were limited to fathers living with their children. Finally, it is important to note that Stanger, Dumenci, Kamon, and Burstein (2004) found that, when compared with drug-abusing mothers, drug-abusing fathers reported both less positive *and* less negative parenting behavior.

■ PATERNAL SUBSTANCE ABUSE AND QUALITY OF
CO-PARENTING RELATIONSHIPS

Over the past 10 years, researchers have begun to explore ways co-parenting relationships affect the psychosocial adjustment of parents and children (Feinberg, 2003; McHale et al., 2002). Within the existing literature, it is clear that, regardless of whether parents continue their sexual partnership, positive co-parenting relationships contribute directly to the psychological well-being of both parents and children (for further discussion, see Feinberg, 2003; McHale et al., 2002). Moreover, researchers (for a review, see Cummings & Davies, 2002; Feinberg, 2003; McHale et al., 2002; Zimet & Jacob, 2002) have repeatedly shown that conflict between parents, particularly conflict over parenting issues, directly and indirectly influences the psychosocial adjustment of both parents and children. Across varying circumstances, the quality of co-parenting relationships also seems to influence the parenting of men differently than the parenting of women. In general, when sexual partnerships become conflicted, men, more so than women, tend to withdraw from their children. Similarly, when sexual partnerships end, men's involvement with their children tends to decline, if not end, when non-resident fathers cannot maintain positive working relationships with the mothers of their children (for further discussion, see Carlson & McLanahan, 2004). Conversely, when men can maintain positive working relationships with mothers, they can be an important resource for both mothers and children, even when not living in the same household (for further discussion, see Carlson & McLanahan, 2004).

Within the substance abuse literature, there is fairly consistent evidence that substance abuse is associated with less cooperation and more aggression within sexual partnerships (for a review, see Foran & O'Leary, 2008; Moore et al., 2008). In a comparative study of drug-abusing fathers, Moore, Easton, and McMahon (2011) found that the drug-abusing fathers reported more aggressive behavior directed at the mother of their youngest child and more aggressive behavior directed at them by the mother of their youngest child over the course of their relationship. McMahon et al. (2008) also found less negotiation in the fathers' current relationship with the mother of their youngest child, and Moore et al. (2011) found more frequent aggression despite the fact that the drug-abusing fathers were much less likely to be living with the mother of their child.

Beyond risk for intimate partner violence within the sexual partnerships of substance-abusing fathers, there is relatively little additional information about other dimensions of co-parenting. When co-parenting was examined from the perspective of mothers and fathers, Waller and Swisher (2006) noted that, over time, unmarried couples seemed to respond to the substance abuse of fathers in several different ways. Some couples did not do anything in response to the substance abuse, primarily because the couple did not view the substance abuse as a problem. Some couples chose to continue their sexual partnership while developing a strategy to limit the impact of the substance abuse on the father–child relationship. That strategy often involved somehow establishing abstinence. Some mothers ended the sexual partnership and took steps to actively limit contact between father and child. Some fathers attempted to maintain a relationship with the child without working collaboratively with the mother, often after seeking treatment for their substance abuse. Some fathers withdrew from the father–child relationship and continued using substances. Some mothers simply chose to end the sexual partnership and end the father's access to the child without consulting him, particularly if the mother was herself striving to remain abstinent.

■ PATERNAL SUBSTANCE ABUSE AND QUALITY OF FAMILY ENVIRONMENTS

Although researchers typically focus on parenting behavior, family scholars (e.g., McHale, Kuersten, & Lauretti, 1996) have emphasized the importance of considering the quality of the broader family environment when examining different dimensions of family process. As might be expected, researchers have shown, on a limited basis, that parental substance abuse, particularly paternal alcoholism, is frequently linked with disruption of family functioning. In comparative research designs, paternal alcoholism has repeatedly been associated with (a) more family conflict, (b) less family cohesion, (c) disruption of daily routines, (d) more family adversity, and (e) disruption of family rituals (Fiese, 1993; Roosa, Dumka, & Tein, 1996; Sher, Gershuny, Peterson, & Raskin, 1997; Stanford, Bingham, & Zucker, 1999). In one of the few studies to examine paternal drug abuse and compromise of family environments, Moss, Lynch, Hardie, and Baron (2002) found that paternal drug abuse was associated with compromise of family functioning characterized by (a) more difficulty establishing family norms and rules, (b) poorer communication, (c) more problems with emotional expression, (d) less organization in day-to-day family life, and (e) poorer response to instrumental and emotional demands on the family.

■ PATERNAL SUBSTANCE ABUSE AND FAMILY PROCESS: WITHIN-GROUP DIFFERENCES

Although comparative research suggests that substance-abusing men are at risk for socially irresponsible production and parenting of children, there is some evidence that risk within populations of substance-abusing men may vary significantly. For example, Ichiyama, Zucker, Fitzgerald, and Bingham (1996) showed that personality disturbance accounts for differences in the quality of sexual partnerships established by alcoholic men. Fals-Stewart (2003) and Fals-Stewart, Golden, and Schumacher (2003) showed that continued use of alcohol and drugs seemed to have a direct impact on intimate partner violence among alcohol and drug-abusing men. El-Bassel et al. (2004) showed that psychological dominance accounted for both intimate partner violence and high-risk sexual behavior in drug-abusing men. Scheidt and Windle (1996) also found that personality disturbance, severity of daily alcohol use, the social context of alcohol use, and sexual history increased the probability of sexual activity outside an ongoing sexual partnership within a sample of alcoholic men.

Surprisingly, there has been very little consideration of within-population differences in the parenting behavior of substance-abusing men. Muller, Fitzgerald, Sullivan, and Zucker (1994) did, however, show that psychosocial stress and social support may contribute independently to risk for hostile-aggressive parenting behavior among alcoholic fathers. Several researchers have also shown that there may be important differences in family process associated with different drugs of abuse. For example, Fals-Stewart et al. (2004) showed that, when compared with alcoholic fathers, drug-abusing fathers reported more problematic disciplinary practices and less monitoring of their children. Disruption of family systems because of alcohol versus drug abuse may also be different, and risk for child abuse and neglect may vary with primary drug of abuse. For example, Famularo, Kinscherff, and Fenton (1992) found that, when parents lost custody of a child to the child welfare system, alcohol abuse seemed to be associated with greater risk for physical abuse of children and cocaine abuse seemed to be associated with greater risk for sexual abuse.

■ SUBSTANCE-ABUSINNG MEN: *GOOD FATHERS OR BAD FATHERS?*

As the nature of family life has changed in response to an array of social and economic forces that has left many fathers living away from their children, researchers (e.g., Carlson & McLanahan, 2004) have began to examine the fathering of men living outside traditional, two-parent, middle-income family structures. Although research examining the nature of attitudes toward fathering and parenting behavior within special populations has begun to characterize compromise of fathering, the findings sometimes also highlight efforts at socially responsible production and parenting of children inconsistent with popular stereotypes (Black, Dubowitz, & Starr, 1999; Coley & Chase-Lansdale, 1999; Grant et al., 2000;

Salem, Zimmerman, & Notaro, 1998; Way & Stauber, 1996; Zimmerman, Salem, & Maton, 1995). Furthermore, research done with special populations of fathers suggests that, even when they are not actively involved with their children, estranged fathers are often interested in being more involved but avoid making an effort to do so because of feelings, attitudes, stereotypes, and systemic issues that discourage greater involvement (e.g., see Furstenberg, 1995). Although relatively little is known about fathering occurring in the context of chronic substance abuse, it is important to acknowledge that empirical study of substance-abusing fathers may produce findings that contradict popular stereotypes and highlight socially desirable involvement that should be supported as much as possible (McMahon & Rounsaville, 2002).

Consistent with this notion, there is accumulating evidence suggesting that at least some substance-abusing men make an effort to father children in a socially responsible manner. In a comprehensive, descriptive study of fathers receiving methadone maintenance treatment, McMahon et al. (2007) noted that data on patterns of pair-bonding, reproduction, and parenting suggested that early efforts to father children in a socially responsible manner had, over time, been compromised by the chronic, recurring nature of the opioid dependence. Building upon that pilot study, McMahon et al. (2008) found that there were no significant differences in many markers of responsible fathering when drug-abusing fathers were compared with fathers without any history of alcohol or drug abuse. Similarly, Eiden et al. (2002) found that, even in the context of chronic alcoholism, a significant proportion of alcoholic fathers had still managed to establish a secure attachment with their preschool child.

■ A SPECIAL NOTE ON SOCIAL VERSUS BIOLOGICAL FATHERS

Although biological reproduction is the most common pathway to fatherhood, men also frequently serve as a father figure for children they did not conceive. Social fathering occurs formally through legal adoption and foster placement, and it occurs informally through affiliation with children as a member of their extended family or their mother's sexual partner. Although social fathers are frequently thought of as an asset in the lives of children, several authors (e.g., Hetherington & Henderson, 1997) have highlighted ways the presence of social fathers can complicate family relations, and there is evidence that, under some conditions, social fathers may represent a potentially negative influence in the lives of children (Radhakrishna, Bou-Saada, Hunter, Catellier, & Kotch, 2001). Although the existing literature highlights a number of consistent trends in the nature of social fathering within the general population, it is not clear to what extent substance-abusing men accept responsibility for the parenting of children they did not conceive. McMahon et al. (2008) found that, when compared with fathers confirming no history of alcohol or drug abuse, opioid-dependent fathers were more likely to have previously lived with children they did not conceive, but those father–child relationships did not seem to persist over time, probably because they ended as the opioid-dependent fathers moved through a series of cohabitating relationships with the mothers of those children.

■ PATERNAL SUBSTANCE ABUSE: CONSEQUENCES FOR CHILDREN

As social and economic changes have redefined the nature of *good* fathering, research on fathering and child development has expanded rapidly. Although much of this work has focused on ways fathers promote normative child development, some researchers have also begun, as Phares (1996) suggested, to consider ways *bad* fathering contributes to poor developmental outcomes in children. For a number of years, it has been clear that, as they move from childhood to early adulthood, children with an alcoholic father are at greater risk for psychopathology and substance abuse, particularly externalizing pathology and alcohol abuse (Chassin, Rogosch, & Barrera, 1991; Hill et al., 1999; Hill & Muka, 1996; Hill, Shen, Lowers, & Locke, 2000; Lieb et al., 2002; Loukas, Fitzgerald, Zucker, & von Eye, 2001; Noll, Zucker, Fitzgerald, & Curtis, 1992; Reich, Earls, Frankel, & Shayka, 1993; Rohde, Lewinsohn, Kahler, Seeley, & Brown, 2001; Schuckit, Smith, Radziminski, & Heyneman, 2000; Schuckit & Smith, 1996; Sher, Walitzer, Wood, & Brent, 1991).

Surprisingly, given the extensive literature on children with an alcoholic father, much less is known about the psychosocial development of children with a drug-abusing father (McMahon & Rounsaville, 2002). Although researchers often extrapolate from the literature on paternal alcoholism, Hogan (1998) has argued that there are important differences in the nature of alcohol and drug abuse that may limit the extent to which the literature on children with a father abusing alcohol generalizes to children with a father abusing illicit drugs. When researchers have broadly sampled children with an alcohol- or drug-abusing parent, they have consistently found substantial risk for both internalizing and externalizing pathology in children of all ages (Hoffmann & Cerbone, 2002; Merikangas, Dierker, & Szatmari, 1998; Stanger et al., 1999; Wilens, Biederman, Kiely, Bredin, & Spenser, 1995). Similarly, in one of the few investigations that focused specifically on children with a drug-abusing father, Moss and colleagues found that, when compared with boys whose father had no history of substance abuse, 10- to 12-year-old boys with a positive family history demonstrated more internalizing pathology, more externalizing pathology, and poorer academic achievement (Moss, Majumder, & Vanyukov, 1994; Moss, Mezzich, Yao, Gavaler, & Martin, 1995). In an expansion of that sample, Clark and colleagues found that boys with a positive family history had higher rates of anxiety disorders and disruptive behavior disorders (Clark, Kirisci, & Moss, 1998; Clark et al., 1997; Clark, Parker, & Lynch, 1999). They also demonstrated greater risk for substance use as they moved through middle childhood into adolescence.

Although paternal substance abuse undoubtedly represents risk for poorer developmental outcomes in children of all ages, there are significant limitations within the existing literature that make it difficult to clearly quantify that risk. Within broad samples that have included children with substance-abusing mothers and fathers, researchers (e.g., Merikangas et al., 1998) have generally not been able to clearly distinguish effects associated with gender of the affected parent. In other samples, they (e.g., Dawes, Tarter, & Kirisci, 1997) have not been able to distinguish effects associated with alcohol versus drug use, and they (e.g., Clark et al., 1997, 1998, 1999) have not yet been able to distinguish effects that may be associated with a specific drug of abuse. Similarly, in other investigations, a comparison group drawn from the same community has not been available (e.g., see Brook, Brook, Richter, et al., 2002; Brook, Brook, Whiteman, et al., 2002; Fals-Stewart, Kelley, Cooke, & Golden, 2002; Stanger et al., 1999), or subjects were originally recruited to participate in a family study of another developmental disorder (e.g., see Wilens et al., 2002). Moreover, only one comparative study has been done with a sizeable sample of children with a drug-abusing father, but girls have not been adequately represented in that work (e.g., see Clark et al., 1997, 1998, 1999; Moss et al., 2002). Children living away from a substance-abusing father have systematically been excluded from this research (e.g., see Fals-Stewart et al., 2002). These limitations in the existing database are important because there may be differences in risk associated with paternal versus maternal substance abuse, there appear to be differences in genetic liability for different forms of substance abuse (Tsuang et al., 1998), and children with a drug-abusing parent may be at greater risk when compared with children who have an alcoholic parent (Fals-Stewart et al., 2004). There may also be differences in risk for psychopathology and substance use associated with gender of the child (Stanger et al., 2002), and there is evidence that risk for children with a substance-abusing father may vary with residential status (Tarter, Schultz, Kirisci, & Dunn, 2001).

Although parental substance abuse represents risk for poorer developmental outcomes, the psychosocial adjustment of children tends to be variable, and researchers have explored ways protective and vulnerability factors interact across different levels of social organization to modify that risk. At this time, there appears to be agreement that genetic vulnerability and social circumstances interact in complex ways to influence which children actually develop substance abuse and other psychopathology over time. Within that literature, family process is consistently identified as a critical influence in pathways to poor developmental outcomes in children at risk because of a positive family history (for further discussion, see Tarter & Vanyukov, 1994; Fitzgerald, Davies, & Zucker, 2002). Unfortunately, surprisingly little is known about ways *bad* fathering contributes directly and indirectly to risk for poor developmental outcomes in children with a substance-abusing father. Because of a clear bias for researchers to focus on disruption of parenting and the maladjustment of children, even less is known about ways *good* fathering occurring despite the presence of chronic substance abuse may promote normative development in children with a substance-abusing father. Although family process consistently emerges as an important ingredient in the dynamics of resilience (for further discussion, see Masten, 2001), it is not presently clear how efforts at *good* fathering may promote normative development within this vulnerable population of children.

At this time, there is accumulating evidence that, after allowance for quality of mothering, quality of fathering can be an important influence on the psychosocial development of children (e.g., see Black et al., 1999; Salem et al., 1998). When examined from a family systems perspective, *good* and *bad* fathering occurring in the context of paternal substance abuse may both affect the psychosocial adjustment of children. The empirical data on the question are, however, rather limited and somewhat inconsistent. Within the existing literature, there is, for example, ambiguity concerning the potential impact of separation from a substance-abusing father. Tarter et al. (2001) found separation from an alcoholic father seemed to have a negative impact on the psychosocial adjustment of children; Carbonneau et al. (1998) found that separation from an alcoholic father did not seem to have any impact on the psychosocial adjustment of children; and Jaffee, Moffitt, Caspi, and Taylor (2003) found that separation from an antisocial father with or without substance abuse seemed to have a *positive* influence on the psychosocial adjustment of children. As might be expected, negative father–child relationships occurring in the context of paternal alcoholism probably negate protective influences and exacerbate risk for poor developmental outcomes (Barrera & Stice, 1998), but there is also presently ambiguity concerning the potential influence of positive father–child relationships when men have substance use problems. Although Brook and colleagues found that positive father–child relationships may promote positive adaptation in teenage children in the context of paternal substance abuse (Brook, Brook, Richter, et al., 2002; Brook, Brook, Whiteman, et al., 2002), other researchers have found that, under similar circumstances, positive father–child relationships may have relatively little influence or they may actually exacerbate risk for substance use during adolescence (Andrews, Hops, & Duncan, 1997; Foshee & Bauman, 1994; Zhang, Welte, & Wieczorek, 1999).

■ PATERNAL SUBSTANCE ABUSE: CONSEQUENCES FOR FATHERS

When considered from the perspective of fathers, questions about the relationship between substance abuse and compromise of fathering are also important because research indicates that family transitions have a significant effect on the psychosocial adjustment of men (for a review, see McMahon & Spector, 2007). Assuming that substance abuse contributes to compromise of fathering, it is not clear to what extent failure to fulfill this important social obligation contributes to affective distress in men that may represent risk for both continued substance use and further compromise of parenting. For more than 25 years, researchers have written about the guilt, shame, and depression that substance-abusing mothers experience when their substance use compromises their ability to care for their children (Baker & Carson, 1999; Kearney, Murphy, & Rosenbaum, 1994; Woodhouse, 1992). Family scholars have also repeatedly highlighted ways intense feelings of shame may cause men to withdraw from their children in the context of divorce and other perceived failures (for further discussion, see McMahon & Giannini, 2003). Because of both gendered assumptions about the nature of parenting (Phares, 1996) and concerns about the degree of sociopathy among substance-abusing men (Parke & Brott, 1999), the substance abuse treatment and research community does not acknowledge that, like mothers, fathers may be distressed about the difficulty they may have functioning as an effective parent.

Although women entering drug abuse treatment express more concern about parenting issues, some men do seek treatment concerned about their status as fathers (Gerstein, Johnson, Larison, Harwood, & Fountain, 1997). As changing definitions of fatherhood demand that men in this culture be more involved in the lives of their children, more and more men may present for substance abuse treatment distressed about their inability to function effectively as a father. Acknowledging that substance-abusing men may have feelings about their status as fathers, McMahon et al. (2008) recently showed that, when compared with fathers living in the same community with no history of substance abuse, drug-abusing fathers reported feeling less effective as a parent and less satisfied as a parent. More recently, McMahon et al., (2010) showed that, within a comparative study, drug-abusing fathers also demonstrated less guilt and more shame associated with their perceived failure to be a more effective parent. The heightened sensitivity to feelings of shame among the drug-abusing fathers is of concern because feelings of shame are likely to be associated with (a) dysphoric condemnation of self, (b) externalization of responsibility for their failures as a parent, (c) aggressive behavior directed at their children and the mothers of their children, (d) continued drug use to manage negative affect, and (e) flight from family intervention that heightens awareness of their failures as a parent (McMahon et al., 2010).

■ CONCLUSION

Although a number of socioeconomic forces have converged to make fathering one of the more prominent social issues in modern cultures, the status of substance-abusing men as fathers is still rarely acknowledged in the conceptualization of public policy, service delivery, or research focusing on the adverse consequences of alcohol and drug abuse (McMahon & Rounsaville, 2002). As social definitions of *good* versus *bad* fathering change in the context of ongoing debate about the presence of men in family life, research documenting the impact of substance abuse on fathering remains relatively limited. Given the impact fathering has on family systems across generations, there is a need to better understand how *good* and *bad* fathering occurring in the context of chronic substance abuse affects the psychosocial adjustment of fathers, mothers, and children. As suggested by McMahon and Rounsaville (2002), it is time to add fathering to the research agenda so there is an adequate database to inform the development of clinical and preventive interventions designed to minimize the harm associated with paternal substance abuse.

■ AUTHOR NOTES

Support for preparation of this chapter was provided by the National Institute on Drug Abuse (R01 DA020619).

The author would like to offer this chapter in memory of Bruce Rounsaville, M.D., who generously helped him begin a line of research designed to expand understanding of parenting as a treatment issue in the lives of substance-abusing men.

Correspondence concerning this chapter should be addressed to Thomas McMahon, Ph.D., Yale University School of Medicine, Connecticut Mental

Health Center, West Haven Mental Health Clinic, 270 Center Street, West Haven, Connecticut 06516. Electronic mail may be sent to thomas.mcmahon@yale.edu.

■ REFERENCES

Ainsworth, M. D. S. (1989). Attachments beyond infancy. *American Psychologist, 44,* 709–716.

Ammerman, R. T., Kolko, D. J., Kirisci, L., Blackson, T. C., & Dawes, M. A. (1999). Child abuse potential in parents with histories of substance use disorder. *Child Abuse and Neglect, 23,* 1225–1238.

Andrews, J. A., Hops, H., & Duncan, S. C. (1997). Adolescent modeling of parent substance use: The moderating effect of the relationship with the parent. *Journal of Family Psychology, 11,* 259–270.

Bailey, J. M., Kirk, K. M., Zhu, G., Dunne, M. P., & Martin, N. G. (2000). Do individual differences in sociosexuality represent genetic or environmentally contingent strategies? Evidence from the Australian twin registry. *Journal of Personality and Social Psychology, 78,* 537–545.

Baker, P. L., & Carson, A. (1999). "I take care of my kids": Mothering practices of substance-abusing women. *Gender and Society, 13,* 347–363.

Bakermans-Kranenburg, M. J., van IJzendoorn, M. H., Bokhorst, C. L., & Schuengel, C. (2004). The importance of shared environment in infant-father attachment: A behavioral genetic study of the attachment Q-sort. *Journal of Family Psychology, 18,* 545–549.

Barrera, M., & Stice, E. (1998). Parent-adolescent conflict in the context of parental support: Families with alcoholic and nonalcoholic fathers. *Journal of Family Psychology, 12,* 195–208.

Belsky, J. (1997). Attachment, mating, and parenting: An evolutionary interpretation. *Human Nature, 8,* 361–381.

Belsky, J. (1999). Modern evolutionary theory and patterns of attachment. In J. Cassidy & P. R. Shaver (Eds.), *Handbook of Attachment: Theory, Research, and Clinical Applications* (pp. 141–161). New York, NY: Guildford Press.

Belsky, J. (2000). Conditional and alternative reproductive strategies: Individual differences in susceptibility to rearing experiences. In J. L. Rodgers, D. C. Rowe, & W. B. Miller (Eds.), *Genetic Influences on Human Fertility and Sexuality: Theoretical and Empirical Contributions from the Biological and Behavioral Sciences* (pp. 127–146). Boston: Clair Academic Publishing.

Belsky, J., Steinberg, L., & Draper, P. (1991). Childhood experience, interpersonal development, and reproductive strategy: An evolutionary theory of socialization. *Child Development, 62,* 647–670.

Bernardi, E., Jones, M., & Tennant, C. (1989). Quality of parenting in alcoholics and narcotic addicts. *British Journal of Psychiatry, 154,* 677–682.

Black, M. M., Dubowitz, H., & Starr, R. H. (1999). African American fathers in low income, urban families: Development, behavior, and home environment of their three-year-old children. *Child Development, 70,* 967–978.

Blackson, T. C., Butler, T., Belsky, J., Ammerman, R. T., Shaw, D. S., & Tarter, R. E. (1999). Individual traits and family contexts predict sons' externalizing behavior and preliminary relative risk ratios for conduct disorder and substance use disorder outcomes. *Drug and Alcohol Dependence, 56,* 115–131.

Blankenhorn, D. (2000). This article isn't serious. *American Psychologist, 55,* 682–683.

Bokhorst, C. L., Bakermans-Kranenburg, M. J., Fearon, R. M. P., van IJzendoorn, M. H., Fonagy, P., & Schuengel, C. (2003). The importance of shared environment in mother-infant attachment security: A behavioral genetic study. *Child Development, 74,* 1769–1782.

Brady, S. S., & Donenberg, G. R. (2006). Mechanisms linking violence exposure to health risk behavior in adolescence: Motivation to cope and sensation seeking. *Journal of the American Academy of Child and Adolescent Psychiatry, 45,* 673–680.

Bricker, J. B., Stallings, M. C., Corley, R. P., Wadsworth, S. J., Bryan, A., Timberlake, D. S., et al. (2006). Genetic and environmental influences on age at sexual initiation in the Colorado Adoption Project. *Behavior Genetics, 36,* 820–832.

Bronte-Tinkew, J., Bowie, L., & Moore, K. (2007). Fathers and public policy. *Journal of Applied Developmental Science, 11,* 254–259.

Brook, D. W., Brook, J. S., Richter, L., Whiteman, M., Arencibia-Mireles, O., & Masci, J. R. (2002). Marijuana use among the adolescent children of high-risk drug-abusing fathers. *American Journal on Addictions, 11,* 95–110.

Brook, D. W., Brook, J. S., Whiteman, M., Arencibia-Mireles, O., Pressman, M. A., & Rubenstone, E. (2002). Coping in adolescent children of HIV-positive and HIV-negative substance-abusing fathers. *Journal of Genetic Psychology, 163,* 5–23.

Cabrera, N., & Peters, H. E. (2000). Public policies and father involvement. *Marriage and Family Review, 29,* 295–314.

Carbonneau, R., Tremblay, R. E., Vitaro, F., Dobkin, P. L., Saucier, J., & Pihl, R. O. (1998). Paternal alcoholism, paternal absence and the development of problem behaviors in boys from age six to twelve years. *Journal of Studies on Alcohol, 59,* 387–398.

Campo, A. T., & Rohner, R. P. (1992). Relationships between perceived parental acceptance-rejection, psychological adjustment, and substance abuse. *Child Abuse and Neglect, 16,* 429–440.

Capaldi, D. M., Crosby, L., Stoolmiller, M. (1996). Predicting the timing of first sexual intercourse for at-risk adolescent males. *Child Development, 67,* 344–359.

Carlson, M. J., & McLanahan, S. S. (2004). Early father involvement in fragile families. In R. D. Day & M. E. Lamb M. E. (Eds.), *Conceptualizing and Measuring Father Involvement* (pp. 241–271). Mahwah, NJ: Lawrence Erlbaum Associates.

Chassin, L., Rogosch, F., & Barrera, M. (1991). Substance use and symptomatology among adolescent children of alcoholics. *Journal of Abnormal Psychology, 100,* 449–463.

Cherkas, L. F., Oelsner, E. C., Mak, Y. T., Valdes, A., & Spector, T. D. (2004). Genetic influences on female infidelity and number of sexual partners in humans: A linkage and association study of the role of the vasopressin receptor gene (AVPR1A). *Twin Research, 7,* 649–658.

Chisholm, J. S. (1993). Death, hope, and sex: Life-history theory and the development of reproductive strategies. *Current Anthropology, 34,* 1–24.

Chisholm, J. S. (1996). The evolutionary ecology of attachment organization. *Human Nature, 7,* 1–38.

Christmon, K., & Luckey, I. (1994). Is early fatherhood associated with alcohol and other drug use? *Journal of Substance Abuse, 6,* 37–43.

Clark, D. B., Kirisci, L., & Moss, H. B. (1998). Early adolescent gateway drug use in sons of fathers with substance use disorders. *Addictive Behaviors, 23,* 561–566.

Clark, D. B., Moss, H. B., Kirisci, L., Mezzich, A. C., Miles, R., & Ott, P. (1997). Psychopathology in preadolescent sons of fathers with substance use disorders. *Journal of the American Academy of Child and Adolescent Psychiatry, 36,* 495–502.

Clark, D. B., Parker, A. M., & Lynch, K. G. (1999). Psychopathology and substance-related problems during early adolescence: A survival analysis. *Journal of Clinical Child Psychology, 28,* 333–341.

Coley, R. L., & Chase-Lansdale, P. L. (1999). Stability and change in paternal involvement among urban African American fathers. *Journal of Family Psychology, 13,* 416–435.

Collins, R. L., Ellickson, P. L., & Klein, D. J. (2007). The role of substance use in young adult divorce. *Addiction, 102,* 786–794.

Cummings, E. M., & Davies, P. T. (2002). Effects of marital conflict on children: recent advances and emerging themes in process-oriented research. *Journal of Child Psychology and Psychiatry, 43,* 31–63.

Daly, M., & Wilson, M. (2000). Not quite right. *American Psychologist, 55,* 679–680.

Dawes, M. A., Tarter, R. E., & Kirisci, L. (1997). Behavioral self-regulation: Correlates and 2 year follow-ups for boys at risk for substance abuse. *Drug and Alcohol Dependence, 45,* 165–176.

Doherty, W. J., Kouneski, E. F., & Erickson, M. F. (1998). Responsible fathering: An overview and conceptual framework. *Journal of Marriage and Family, 60,* 277–292.

Doherty, W. J., Kouneski, E. F., & Erickson, M. F. (2000). We are all responsible for responsible fathering: A response to Walker and McGraw. *Journal of Marriage and Family, 62,* 570–574.

Dollahite, D. C., Hawkins, A. J., & Brotherson, S. E. (1997). Fatherwork: A conceptual ethic of fathering as generative work. In A. J. Hawkins, & D. C. Dollahite (Eds.), *Generative Fathering: Beyond Deficit Perspectives* (pp. 17–35). Thousand Oaks, CA: Sage Publications.

Duncan, R. D., Saunders, B. E., Kilpatrick, D. G., Hanson, R. F., & Resnick, H. S. (1996). Childhood physical assault as a risk factor for PTSD, depression, and substance abuse. *American Journal of Orthopsychiatry, 66,* 437–448.

Dunne, M. P., Martin, N. G., Statham, D. J., Slutske, W. S., Dinwiddie, S. H., Bucholz, K. K., et al. (1997). Genetic and environmental contributions to variance in age at first sexual intercourse. *Psychological Science, 8,* 211–216.

Edwards, E. P., Eiden, R. D., & Leonard, K. E. (2004). Impact of fathers' alcoholism and associated risk factors on parent-infant attachment stability from 12 to 18 Months. *Infant Mental Health Journal, 25,* 556–579.

Eiden, R. D., Chavez, F., & Leonard, K. E. (1999). Parent-infant interactions among families with alcoholic fathers. *Development and Psychopathology, 11,* 745–762.

Eiden, R. D., Edwards, E. P., & Leonard, K. E. (2002). Mother-infant and father-infant attachment among alcoholic families. *Development and Psychopathology, 14,* 253–278.

Eiden, R. D., & Leonard, K. E. (2000). Paternal alcoholism, parental psychopathology, and aggravation with infants. *Journal of Substance Abuse, 11,* 17–29.

Eisenberg, D. T. A., Campbell, B., MacKillop, J., Modi, M., Beauchemin, J., Dang, D., et al. (2007). Polymorphisms in the dopamine D2 and D4 receptor genes and reproductive and sexual behaviors. *Evolutionary Psychology, 5,* 696–715.

El-Bassel, N., Gilbert, L., Golder, S., Wu, E., Chang, M., Fontdevila, J., et al. (2004). Deconstructing the relationship between intimate partner violence and sexual HIV risk among drug involved men and their female partners. *AIDS and Behavior, 8*, 429–439.

El-Sheikh, M., & Buckhalt, J. A. (2003). Parental problem drinking and children's adjustment: Attachment and family functioning as moderators and mediators of risk. *Journal of Family Psychology, 17*, 510–520.

El-Sheikh, M., & Flanagan, E. (2001). Parental problem drinking and children's adjustment: Family conflict and parental depression as mediators and moderators of risk. *Journal of Abnormal Child Psychology, 29*, 417–432.

Ellis, B. J., Figueredo, A. J., Brumbach, B. H., & Schlomer, G. L. (2009). Fundamental dimensions of environmental risk: The impact of harsh versus unpredictable environments on the evolution and development of life history strategies. *Human Nature, 20*, 204–268.

Elster, A. B., Lamb, M. E., & Tavare, J. (1987). Association between behavioral and school problems and fatherhood in a national sample of adolescent youths. *Journal of Pediatrics, 111*, 932–936.

Fals-Stewart, W. (2003). The occurrence of partner physical aggression on days of alcohol consumption: A longitudinal diary study. *Journal of Consulting and Clinical Psychology, 71*, 41–52.

Fals-Stewart, W., Golden, J., & Schumacher, J. A. (2003). Intimate partner violence and substance abuse: A longitudinal day-to-day examination. *Addictive Behaviors, 28*, 1555–1574.

Fals-Stewart, W., Kelley, M. L., Cooke, C. G., & Golden, J. C. (2002). Predictors of the psychosocial adjustment of children living in households in which fathers abuse drugs: The effects of postnatal parental experience. *Addictive Behaviors, 27*, 1–19.

Fals-Stewart, W., Kelley, M. L., Fincham, F. D., Golden, J. C., & Logsdan, T. (2004). The emotional and behavioral problems of children living with drug-abusing fathers: Comparisons of children living with alcohol-abusing and non-substance-abusing fathers. *Journal of Family Psychology, 18*, 319–330.

Famularo, R., Kinscherff, R., & Fenton, T. (1992). Parental substance abuse and the nature of child maltreatment. *Child Abuse and Neglect, 16*, 475–483.

Farrell, A. D., Danish, S. J., & Howard, C. W. (1992). Relationship between drug use and other problem behaviors in urban adolescents. *Journal of Consulting and Clinical Psychology, 60*, 705–712.

Feinberg, M. E. (2003). The internal structure and ecological context of co-parenting: A framework for research and intervention. *Parenting: Science and Practice, 3*, 95–131.

Fiese, B. H. (1993). Family rituals in alcoholic and nonalcoholic households: Relations of adolescent health symptomatology and problem drinking. *Family Relations, 42*, 187–192.

Fitzgerald, H. E., Davies, W. H., & Zucker, R. A. (2002). Growing up in an alcoholic family: Structuring pathways for risk aggregation and theory-driven intervention. In R. J. McMahon & R. D. Peters, (Eds.), *The Effects of Parental Dysfunction on Children* (pp. 127–146). New York: Kluwer Academic/Plenum Publishers.

Florsheim, P., Sumida, E., McCann, C., Winstanley, M., Fukui, R., Seefeldt, T., et al. (2003). The transition to parenthood among young African American and Latino couples: Relational predictors of risk for parental dysfunction. *Journal of Family Psychology, 17*, 65–79.

Foran, H. M., & O'Leary, K. D. (2008). Alcohol and intimate partner violence: A meta-analytic review. *Clinical Psychology Review, 28*, 1222–1234.

Foshee, V., & Bauman, K. E. (1994). Parental attachment and adolescent cigarette smoking initiation. *Journal of Adolescent Research, 9*, 88–104.

Fox, G. L., & Benson, M. L. (2004). Violent men, bad dads?: Fathering profiles of men involved in intimate partner violence. In R. D. Day & M. E. Lamb (Eds.), *Conceptualizing and Measuring Father Involvement* (pp. 359–384). Mahwah, NJ: Lawrence Erlbaum Associates.

Furstenberg, F. F. (1995). Fathering in the inner city. In W. Marsiglio (Ed.), *Fatherhood: Contemporary Theory, Research, and Social Policy* (pp. 119–147). Thousand Oaks, CA: Sage Publications.

Furstenberg, F. F., & Weiss, C. C. (2000). Intergenerational transmission of fathering roles in at risk families. *Marriage and Family Review, 29*, 181–201.

Ganiban, J. M., Ulbricht, J. A., Spotts, E. L., Lichtenstein, P., Reiss, D., Hansson, K., et al. (2009). Understanding the role of personality in explaining associations between marital quality and parenting. *Journal of Family Psychology, 23*, 646–660.

Gerstein, D. R., Johnson, R. A., Larison, C. L., Harwood, H. J., & Fountain, D. (1997). *Alcohol and Other Drug Treatment for Parents and Welfare Recipients: Outcomes, Costs, and Benefits.* Washington, DC: U. S. Department of Health and Human Services, Office of the Assistant Secretary for Planning and Evaluation.

Grant, K. E., O'Koon, J. H., Davis, T. H., Roache, N. A., Poindexter, L. M., Armstrong, M. L., et al. (2000). Protective factors affecting low-income urban African American youth exposed to stress. *Journal of Early Adolescence, 20*, 388–417.

Green, K. M., & Ensminger, M. E. (2006). Adult social behavioral effects of heavy adolescent marijuana use among African Americans. *Developmental Psychology, 42*, 1168–1178.

Guagliardo, M. F., Huang, Z., & D'Angelo, L. J. (1999). Fathering pregnancies: Marking health-risk behaviors in urban adolescents. *Journal of Adolescent Health, 24*, 10–15.

George, C. (1996). A representational perspective of child abuse and prevention: Internal working models of attachment and caregiving. *Child Abuse and Neglect, 20*, 411–424.

George, C., & Solomon, J. (2008). The caregiving system: A behavioral systems approach to parenting. In J. Cassidy & P. R. Shaver (Eds.), *Handbook of Attachment: Theory, Research, and Clinical Applications* (2nd ed.; pp. 833–856). New York, NY: Guildford Press.

Hall, J. H., Fals-Stewart, W., & Fincham, F. D. (2008). Risky sexual behavior among married alcoholic men. *Journal of Family Psychology, 22*, 287–292.

Harden, K. P., Turkheimer, E., Emery, R. E., D'Onofrio, B. M., Slutske, W. S., Heath, A. C., et al. (2007). Marital conflict and conduct problems in children of twins. *Child Development, 78*, 1–18.

Hawkins, A. J., & Dollahite, D. C. (1997). Beyond the role inadequacy perspective on fathering. In A. J. Hawkins & D. C. Dollahite (Eds.), *Generative Fathering: Beyond Deficit Perspectives* (pp. 3–16). Thousand Oaks, CA: Sage Publications.

Hetherington, E. M., & Henderson, S. H. (1997). Fathers in stepfamilies. In M. E. Lamb (Ed.), *The Role of the Father in Child Development* (3rd ed.; pp. 212–226). New York: John Wiley & Sons.

Hetherington, E. M., & Stanley-Morgan, S. H. (1997). The effects of divorce on fathers and their children. In M. E. Lamb (Ed.), *The Role of the Father in Child Development* (3rd ed.; pp. 191–211). New York: John Wiley & Sons.

Hill, S. Y., Locke, J., Lowers, L., & Connolly, J. (1999). Psychopathology and achievement in children at high risk for developing alcoholism. *Journal of the American Academy of Child and Adolescent Psychiatry, 38*, 883–891.

Hill, S. Y., & Muka, D. (1996). Childhood psychopathology in children from families of alcoholic female probands. *Journal of the American Academy of Child and Adolescent Psychiatry, 35*, 725–733.

Hill, S. Y., Shen, S., Lowers, L., & Locke, J. (2000). Factors predicting the onset of adolescent drinking in families at high risk for developing alcoholism. *Biological Psychiatry, 48*, 265–275.

Hobson B. (Ed.). (2002). *Making Men into Fathers: Men, Masculinities, and the Social Politics of Fatherhood.* Cambridge, UK: Cambridge University Press.

Hoffmann, J. P., & Cerbone, F. G. (2002). Parental substance use disorder and the risk of adolescent drug abuse: An event history analysis. *Drug and Alcohol Dependency, 66*, 255–264.

Hogan, D. M. (1998). Annotation: The psychological development and welfare of children of opiate and cocaine users: Review and research needs. *Journal of Child Psychology and Psychiatry, 39*, 609–620.

Homish, G. G., & Leonard, K. E. (2007). The drinking partnership and marital satisfaction: The longitudinal influence of discrepant drinking. *Journal of Consulting and Clinical Psychology, 75*, 43–51.

Howes, C., & Spieker, S. (2008). Attachment relationships in the context of multiple caregivers. In J. Cassidy & P. R. Shaver (Eds.), *Handbook of Attachment: Theory, Research, and Clinical Applications* (2nd ed.; pp. 317–332). New York, NY: Guildford Press.

Ichiyama, M. A, Zucker, R. A., Fitzgerald, H. E., & Bingham, C. R. (1996). Articulating subtype differences in self and relational experience among alcoholic men using Structural Analysis of Social Behavior. *Journal of Consulting and Clinical Psychology, 64*, 1245–1254.

Jacob, T., Kahn, G. L., & Leonard, K. (1991). Parent-child interactions in families with alcoholic fathers. *Journal of Consulting and Clinical Psychology, 59*, 176–181.

Jaffee, S. R., Moffitt, T. E., Caspi, A., & Taylor, A. (2003). Life with (or without) father: The benefits of living with two biological parents depend on the father's antisocial behavior. *Child Development, 74*, 109–126.

Johansson, A., Santtila, P., Harlaar, N., von der Pahlen, B., Witting, K., Algars, M., et al. (2008). Genetic effects on male sexual coercion. *Aggressive Behavior, 34*, 190–202.

Kearney, M. H., Murphy, S., & Rosenbaum, M. (1994). Mothering on crack: A grounded theory analysis. *Social Science and Medicine, 38*, 351–361.

Kelley, M. L., & Fals- Stewart, W. (2004). Psychiatric disorders of children living with drug-abusing, alcohol-abusing, and non-substance-abusing fathers. *Journal of the American Academy of Child and Adolescent Psychiatry, 43*, 621–628.

Kessler, R. C., Berglund, P. A., Demler, O., Jin, R., Merikangas, K. R., & Walters, E. E. (2005). Lifetime prevalence and age-of-onset distributions of DSM-IV disorders in the National Comorbidity Survey Replication (NCS-R). *Archives of General Psychiatry, 62*, 593–602.

Kessler, R. C., Chiu, W. T., Demler, O., Merikangas, K. R., & Walters, E. E. (2005). Prevalence, severity, and comorbidity of twelve-month DSM-IV disorders in the National Comorbidity Survey Replication (NCS-R). *Archives of General Psychiatry, 62*, 617–627.

Kirkpatrick, L. A. (1998). Evolution, pair-bonding, and reproductive strategies: A reconceptualization of adult attachment. In J. A. Simpson & W. S. Rholes (Eds.), *Attachment Theory and Close Relationships* (pp. 353–393). New York: Guilford Press.

Lamb, M. E. (1986). The changing roles of fathers. In M. E. Lamb (Ed.), *The Father's Role: Applied Perspectives* (pp. 3–27). New York: John Wiley & Sons.

Lamb, M. E. (2002). Infant-father attachments and their impact on child development. In C. S. Tamis-LeMonda, & N. Cabrera (Eds.), *Handbook of Father Involvement: Multidisciplinary Perspectives* (pp. 93–1175). Mahwah, NJ: Lawrence Erlbaum Associates.

Laucht, M., Becker, K., Blomeyer, D., & Schmidt, M. H. (2007). Novelty seeking involved in mediating the association between the dopamine D4 receptor gene exon III polymorphism and heavy drinking in male adolescents: Results from a high-risk community sample. *Biological Psychiatry, 61,* 87–92.

Leonard, K. E., & Eiden, R. D. (2007). Marital and family processes in the context of alcohol use and alcohol disorders. *Annual Review of Clinical Psychology, 3,* 207–232.

Lieb, R., Merikangas, K. R., Hofler, M., Pfister, H., Isensee, B., & Wittchen, H. U. (2002). Parental alcohol use disorders and alcohol use and disorders in offspring: A community study. *Psychological Medicine, 32,* 63–78.

Lisak, D., & Luster, L. (1994). Educational, occupational, and relationship histories of men who were sexually and/or physically abused as children. *Journal of Traumatic Stress, 7,* 507–523.

Loukas, A., Fitzgerald, H. E., Zucker, R. A., & von Eye, A. (2001). Parental alcoholism and co-occurring antisocial behavior: Prospective relationships to externalizing behavior problems in their young sons. *Journal of Abnormal Child Psychology, 29,* 91–106.

Lykken, D. T. (2000). Reconstructing fathers. American Psychologist, 55, 681–682.

Lyons, M. J., Koenen, K. C., Buchting, F., Meyer, J. M., Eaves, L., Toomey, R., et al. (2004). A twin study of sexual behavior in men. *Archives of Sexual Behavior, 33,* 129–136.

Marsiglio, W., & Hutchinson, S. (2002). *Sex, Men, and Babies: Stories of Awareness and Responsibility.* New York: New York University Press.

Masten, A. S. (2001). Ordinary magic: Resilience processes in development. *American Psychologist, 56,* 227–238.

McDonagh, J. (2000). Science without a degree of objectivity is dead. *American Psychologist, 55,* 678.

McHale, J., Khazan, I., Erera, P., Rotman, T. DeCourcey, W., & McConnell, M. (2002). Co-parenting in diverse family systems. In M. H. Bornstein (Ed.), *Handbook of Parenting. Volume 3: Being and Becoming a Parent* (2nd ed.; pp. 75–107). Mahwah, NJ: Lawrence Erlbaum Associates.

McHale, J. P., Kuersten, R., & Lauretti, A. (1996). New directions in the study of family-level dynamics during infancy and early childhood. In J. P. McHale & P. A. Cowan (Eds.), *Understanding How Family-Level Dynamics Affect Children's Development: Studies of Two-Parent Families* (pp. 5–26). San Francisco: Jossey-Bass.

McLanahan, S. S., & Carlson, M. J. (2002). Welfare reform, fertility, and father involvement. In R. E. Behrman (Ed.), Children and welfare reform. *Future of Children, 12*(1), 147–165.

McMahon, T. J., Connell, C. M., Winkel, J. D., Giannini, F. D., Suchman, N. E., & Ball, S. A. (2010). Guilt, Shame, and Compromise of Fathering: Multiple Mediation of Differences Associated with Chronic Drug Abuse. Manuscript submitted for publication.

McMahon, T. J., & Giannini, F. D. (2003). Substance-abusing fathers in family court: Moving from popular stereotypes to therapeutic jurisprudence. *Family Court Review*, *41*, 337–353.

McMahon, T. J., & Rounsaville, B. J. (2002). Substance abuse and fathering: Adding poppa to the research agenda. *Addiction*, *97*, 1109–1115.

McMahon, T. J., & Spector, A. Z. (2007). Fathering and the mental health of men. In J. E. Grant & M. N. Potenza (Eds.), *Clinical Guide to Men's Mental Health* (pp. 259–282). Arlington, VA: American Psychiatric Publishing.

McMahon, T. J., Winkel, J. D., Luthar, S. S., & Rounsaville, B. J. (2005). Looking for poppa: Parenting responsibilities of men versus women seeking drug abuse treatment. *American Journal of Drug and Alcohol Abuse*, *31*, 79–91.

McMahon, T. J., Winkel, J. D., & Rounsaville, B. J. (2008). Drug-abuse and responsible fathering: A comparative study of men enrolled in methadone maintenance treatment. *Addiction*, *103*, 269–283.

McMahon, T. J., Winkel, J. D., Suchman, N. E., & Rounsaville, B. J. (2007). Drug-abusing fathers: Patterns of pair-bonding, reproduction, and paternal involvement. *Journal of Substance Abuse Treatment*, *33*, 295–302.

Merikangas, K. R., Dierker, L. C., & Szatmari, P. (1998). Psychopathology among offspring of parents with substance abuse and/or anxiety disorders: A high-risk study. *Journal of Child Psychology and Psychiatry*, *39*, 711–720.

Mincy, R. B., & Pouncy, H. W. (2002). The responsible fatherhood field: Evolution and goals. In C. S. Tamis-LeMonda, & N. Cabrera (Eds.), *Handbook of Father Involvement: Multidisciplinary Perspectives* (pp. 555–597). Mahwah, NJ: Lawrence Erlbaum Associates.

Moore, B. C., Easton, C. J., & McMahon, T. J. (2011). Drug abuse and intimate partner violence: A comparative study of opioid-dependent fathers. *American Journal of Orthopsychiatry*, *81*, 218–227.

Moore, T. M., Stuart, G. L., Meehan, J. C., Rhatigan, D., Hellmuth, J. C., & Keen, S. M. (2008). Drug abuse and aggression between intimate partners: A meta-analytic review. *Clinical Psychology Review*, *28*, 247–274.

Moss, H. B., Lynch, K. G., Hardie, T. L., & Baron, D. A. (2002). Family functioning and peer affiliation in children of fathers with antisocial personality disorder and substance dependence: Associations with problem behaviors. *American Journal of Psychiatry*, *159*, 607–614.

Moss, H. B., Majumder, P. P., & Vanyukov, M. (1994). Familial resemblance for psychoactive substance use disorders: Behavioral profile of high risk boys. *Addictive Behaviors*, *19*, 199–208.

Moss, H. B., Mezzich, A., Yao, J. K., Gavaler, J., & Martin, C. S. (1995). Aggressivity among sons of substance-abusing fathers: Association with psychiatric disorder in the father and son, paternal personality, pubertal development, and socioeconomic status. *American Journal of Alcohol Abuse*, *21*, 195–208.

Muller, R. T., Fitzgerald, H. E., Sullivan, L. A., & Zucker, R. A. (1994). Social support and stress factors in child maltreatment among alcoholic families. *Canadian Journal of Behavioural Science*, *26*, 438–461.

Mustanski, B. S., Viken, R. J., Kaprio, J., Pulkkinen, L., & Rose, R. J. (2004). Genetic and environmental influences on pubertal development: Longitudinal data from Finnish twins at ages 11 and 14. *Developmental Psychology, 40,* 1188–1198.

Neiderhiser, J. M., Pike, A., Hetherington, E. M., & Reiss, D. (1998). Adolescent perceptions as mediators of parenting: Genetic and environmental contributions. *Developmental Psychology, 34,* 1459–1469.

Nelson, T. J., Clampet-Lundquist, S., & Edin, K. (2002). Sustaining fragile fatherhood: Father involvement among low-income, noncustodial African-American fathers in Philadelphia. In C. S. Tamis-LeMonda, & N. Cabrera (Eds.), *Handbook of Father Involvement: Multidisciplinary Perspectives* (pp. 525–553). Mahwah, NJ: Lawrence Erlbaum Associates.

Noll, R. B., Zucker, R. A., Fitzgerald, H. E., & Curtis, W. J. (1992). Cognitive and motoric functioning of sons of alcoholic fathers and controls: The early childhood years. *Developmental Psychology, 28,* 665–675.

O'Connor, T. G., & Croft, C. M. (2001). A twin study of attachment in preschool children. *Child Development, 72,* 1501–1511.

Odgers, C. L., Caspi, A., Nagin, D., Piquero, A. R., Slutske, W. S., Milne, B., et al. (2008). Is it important to prevent early exposure to drugs and alcohol among adolescents? *Psychological Science, 19,*1037–1044.

Ostermann, J., Sloan, F. A., & Taylor, D. H. (2005). Heavy alcohol use and marital dissolution in the USA. *Social Science and Medicine, 61,* 2304–2316.

Palkovitz R. J. (1997). Reconstructing "involvement": Expanding conceptualizations of men's caring in contemporary families. In A. J. Hawkins & D. C. Dollahite (Eds.), *Generative Fathering: Beyond Deficit Perspectives* (pp. 200–216). Thousand Oaks, CA: Sage Publications.

Parke, R. D., & Brott, A. A. (1999). *Throwaway Dads: The Myth and Barriers That Keep Men from Being the Fathers They Want to Be.* Boston: Houghton Mifflin.

Phares, V. (1996). *Fathers and Developmental Psychopathology.* New York: John Wiley & Sons.

Pleck, E. H. (2004). Two dimensions of fatherhood: A history of the good dad–bad dad complex. In M. E. Lamb (Ed.), *The Role of the Father in Child Development* (4th ed.; pp. 32–57). New York: Wiley.

Pleck, E. H., & Pleck, J. H. (1997). Fatherhood ideals in the United States: Historical dimensions. In M. E. Lamb (Ed.), *The Role of the Father in Child Development* (3rd ed.; pp. 33–48). New York: Wiley.

Popenoe, D. (2000). Ideology trumps social science. *American Psychologist, 55,* 678–679.

Radhakrishna, A., Bou- Saada, I. E., Hunter, W. M., Catellier, D. J., & Kotch, J. B. (2001). Are father surrogates a risk factor for child maltreatment? *Child Maltreatment, 6,* 281–289.

Reich, W., Earls, F., Frankel, O., & Shayka, J. J. (1993). Psychopathology in children of alcoholics. *Journal of the American Journal of Child and Adolescent Psychiatry, 32,* 995–1002.

Rohde, P., Lewinsohn, P. M., Kahler, C. W., Seeley, J. R., & Brown, R. A. (2001). Natural course of alcohol use disorders from adolescence to young adulthood. *Journal of the American Academy of Child and Adolescent Psychiatry, 40,* 83–90.

Roosa, M. W., Dumka, L., & Tein, J. Y. (1996). Family characteristics as mediators of the influence of problem drinking and multiple risk status on child mental health. *American Journal of Community Psychology, 24*, 607–624.

Rowe, D. C. (2000a). Death, hope, and sex: Steps to an evolutionary ecology of mind and morality. *Evolution and Human Behavior, 21*, 352–364.

Rowe, D. C. (2000b). Environmental and genetic influences on pubertal development: Evolutionary life history traits? In J. L. Rodgers, D. C. Rowe, & W. B. Miller (Eds.), *Genetic Influences on Human Fertility and Sexuality: Theoretical and Empirical Contributions from the Biological and Behavioral Sciences* (pp. 147–168). Boston: Clair Academic Publishing.

Salem, D. A., Zimmerman, M. A., & Notaro, P. C. (1998). Effects of family structure, family process, and father involvement on psychosocial outcomes among African American adolescents. *Family Relations, 47*, 331–341.

Santelli, J. S., Brener, N. D., Lowry, R., Bhatt, A., & Zabin, L. S. (1998). Multiple sexual partners among U. S. adolescents and young adults. *Family Planning Perspectives, 30*, 271–275.

Scheidt, D., & Windle, M. (1996). Individual and situational markers of condom use and sex with non-primary partners among alcoholic inpatients: Findings from the ATRISK Study. *Health Psychology, 15*, 185–192.

Schuckit, M. A., & Smith, T. L. (1996). An 8-year follow-up of 450 sons of alcoholic and control subjects. *Archives of General Psychiatry, 53*, 202–210.

Schuckit, M. A., Smith, T. L., Radziminski, S., Heyneman, E. K. (2000). Behavioral symptoms and psychiatric diagnoses among 162 children in nonalcoholic or alcoholic families. *American Journal of Psychiatry, 157*, 1881–1883.

Sher, K. J., Gershuny, B. S., Peterson, L., & Raskin, G. (1997). The role of childhood stressors in the intergenerational transmission of alcohol use disorders. *Journal of Studies on Alcohol, 58*, 414–427.

Sher, K. J., Walitzer, K. S., Wood, P. K., & Brent, E. E. (1991). Characteristics of children of alcoholics: Putative risk factors, substance use and abuse, and psychopathology. *Journal of Abnormal Psychology, 100*, 427–448.

Silverstein, L. B., & Auerbach, C. F. (1999). Deconstructing the essential father. *American Psychologist, 54*, 397–407.

Silverstein, L. B., & Auerbach, C. F. (2000). Continuing the dialogue about fathers and families. *American Psychologist, 55*, 683–684.

Simons, R. L., Whitbeck, L. B., Conger, R. D., & Wu, C. I. (1991). Intergenerational transmission of harsh parenting. *Developmental Psychology, 27*, 159–171.

Simpson, J. A., & Belsky, J. (2008). Attachment theory within a modern evolutionary framework. In J. Cassidy & P. R. Shaver (Eds.), *Handbook of Attachment: Theory, Research, and Clinical Applications* (2nd ed.; pp. 131–157). New York: Guilford Press.

Slutske, W. S., Heath, A. C., Madden, P. A. F., Bucholz, K. K., Statham, D. J., & Martin, N. G. (2002). Personality and the genetic risk for alcohol dependence. *Journal of Abnormal Psychology, 111*, 124–133.

Solomon, J., & George, C. (1996). Defining the caregiving system: Toward a theory of caregiving. *Infant Mental Health Journal, 17*, 183–197.

Spinath, F. M., & O' Connor, T. G. (2003). A behavioral genetic study of the overlap between personality and parenting. *Journal of Personality, 71*, 785–808.

Stanford, K., Bingham, C. R., & Zucker, R. A. (1999). Validity issues with the Family Environment Scale: Psychometric resolution and research application with alcoholic families. *Psychological Assessment, 11,* 315–325.

Stanger, C., Dumenci, L., Kamon, J., & Burstein, M. (2004). Parenting and children's externalizing problems in substance-abusing families. *Journal of Clinical Child and Adolescent Psychology, 33,* 590–600.

Stanger, C., Higgins, S. T., Bickel, W. K., Elk, R., Grabowski, J., Schmitz, J., et al. (1999). Behavioral and emotional problems among children of cocaine- and opiate-dependent parents. *Journal of the American Academy of Child and Adolescent Psychiatry, 38,* 421–428.

Stanger, C., Kamon, J., Dumenci, L., Higgins, S. T., Bickel, W. K., Grabowski, J., et al. (2002). Predictors of internalizing and externalizing problems among children of cocaine and opiate dependent parents. *Drug and Alcohol Dependence, 66,* 199–212.

Stouthamer-Loeber, M., & Wei, E. H. (1998). The precursors of young fatherhood and its effects on delinquency of teenage males. *Journal of Adolescent Health, 22,* 56–65.

Substance Abuse and Mental Health Services Administration, Office of Applied Studies. (2009, April). *Children Living with Substance-Dependent or Substance-Abusing Parents: 2002 to 2007.* Rockville, MD: SAMHSA.

Suchman, N. E., & Luthar, S. S. (2000). Maternal addiction, child maladjustment, and sociodemographic context: Implications for parenting behaviors. *Addiction, 95,* 1417– 1428.

Suchman, N. E., & Luthar, S. S. (2001). The mediating role of parenting stress in methadone-maintained mothers' parenting. *Parenting: Science and Practice, 1,* 285–315.

Suchman, N. E., McMahon, T. J., Slade, A., & Luthar, S. S. (2005). How early bonding, depression, illicit drug use, and perceived support work together to influence drug-dependent mothers' caregiving. *American Journal of Orthopsychiatry, 75,* 431–445.

Tarter, R. E., Schultz, K., Kirisci, L., & Dunn, M. (2001). Does living with a substance abusing father increase substance abuse risk in male offspring? Impact on individual, family, school, and peer vulnerability factors. *Journal of Child and Adolescent Substance Abuse, 10,* 59–70.

Tarter, R. E., & Vanyukov, M. (1994). Alcoholism: A developmental disorder. *Journal of Consulting and Clinical Psychology, 62,* 1096–1107.

Tsuang, M. T., Lyons, M. J., Meyer, J. M., Doyle, T., Eisen, S. A., Goldberg, J., et al. (1998). Co-occurrence of abuse of different drugs in men: The role of drug-specific and shared vulnerabilities. *Archives of General Psychiatry, 55,* 967–972.

U.S. Department of Health & Human Services, Office of the Assistant Secretary for Planning and Evaluation. (1994, July). *Substance Abuse Among Women and Parents.* Washington, DC: US DHHS.

Varjonen, M., Santtila, P., Hoglund, M., Jern, P., Johansson, A., Wager, I., et al. (2007). Genetic and environmental effects on sexual excitation and sexual inhibition in men. *Journal of Sex Research, 44,* 359–369.

Vungkhanching, M., Sher, K. J., Jackson, K. M., & Parra, G. R. (2004). Relation of attachment style to family history of alcoholism and alcohol use disorders in early adulthood. *Drug and Alcohol Dependence, 75,* 47–53.

Walker, A. J., & McGraw, L. A. (2000). Who is responsible for responsible fathering? *Journal of Marriage and Family, 62,* 563–569.

Waller, M. R., & Swisher, R. (2006). Fathers' risk factors in fragile families: Implications for "healthy" relationships and father involvement. *Social Problems, 53,* 392–420.

Way, N., & Stauber, H. (1996). Are "absent fathers" really absent? Urban adolescent girls speak out about their fathers. In B. J. Leadbeater & N. Way (Eds.), *Urban Girls: Resisting Stereotypes, Creating Identities.* New York: New York University Press.

Whitbeck, L. B., Yoder, K. A., Hoyt, D. R., & Conger, R. D. (1999). Early adolescent sexual activity: A developmental study. *Journal of Marriage and the Family, 61,* 934–946.

Wilens, T. E., Biederman, J., Bredin, E., Hahesy, A. L., Abrantes, A., Neft, D.,… Spencer, T. J. (2002). A family study of the high-risk children of opioid- and alcohol-dependent parents. *American Journal on Addictions, 11,* 41–51.

Wilens, T. E., Biederman, J., Kiely, K., Bredin, E., & Spenser, T. J. (1995). Pilot study of behavioral and emotional disturbance in the high-risk children of parents with opioid dependence. *Journal of the American Academy of Child Adolescent Psychiatry, 34,* 779–785.

Woodhouse, L. D. (1992). Women with jagged edges: Voices from a culture of substance abuse. *Qualitative Health Research, 2,* 262–281.

Wright, L. S., Garrison, J., Wright, N. B., & Stimmel, D. T. (1991). Childhood unhappiness and family stressors recalled by adult children of alcoholics. *Alcoholism Treatment Quarterly, 8,* 67–80.

Zhang, L., Welte, J. W., & Wieczorek, W. F. (1999). The influence of parental drinking and closeness on adolescent drinking, *Journal of Studies on Alcohol, 60,* 245–251.

Zhou Q., King, K. M., & Chassin L. (2006). The roles of familial alcoholism and adolescent family harmony in young adults' substance dependence disorders: Mediated and moderated relations. *Journal of Abnormal Psychology, 115,* 320–331.

Zimet, D., & Jacob, T. (2002). Influences of marital conflict on child adjustment: Review of theory and research. *Clinical Child and Family Psychology Review, 4,* 319–335.

Zimmerman, M. A., Salem, D. A., & Maton, K. I. (1995). Family structure and psychosocial correlates among urban African-American adolescent males. *Child Development, 66,* 1598–1613.

PART II

Risk Assessment and Intervention

9 Bio-psychosocial Characteristics of Parenting Women with Substance Use Disorders

KAROL KALTENBACH

■ INTRODUCTION

Pregnant and parenting women who suffer from substance use disorders present a very complex and difficult challenge to those concerned with improving the environment of care for their children. At the micro-level, the foremost concern is the immediate safety of the child, whereas at a macro-level, one must understand both the breadth and the depth of issues that need to be considered in order for any necessary improvement to occur. Therefore, there is often a tension between systems such as child welfare, who are driven by a mission to protect the child from continued or imminent danger, whereas treatment for parenting women with substance use disorders is driven by the objective to address the myriad of bio-psychosocial factors that impact both her substance use and her parenting abilities in order to ensure she is capable of providing a responsive nurturing environment for her children.

A great deal of attention has been given to the fact that there is a high prevalence of substance use among families involved in child protective services. Studies suggest that 40% to 80% of families involved in the child welfare system are involved in alcohol or drug abuse (CWLA, 2010). The underlying assumption is that if a parent is abusing drugs, they cannot be a good parent. Although a child is certainly at risk when a parent is impaired from the use of psychoactive substances, the relationship between substance abuse and parenting is much more complex. The National Child Abuse and Data Systems (NCANDS) was created as a result of the Child Abuse Prevention and Treatment Act (CAPTA) and reports national child maltreatment data for each fiscal year based on State Child Protective Service (CPS) data. The latest report (Child Maltreatment, 2010), found that 81.3% of child victims were maltreated by a parent either acting alone or with someone else; 37.2% were maltreated by their mother alone, and 34% of the victims were younger than four years of age, with increased risk with decreasing age. *Maltreatment* is defined as abuse or neglect: 78.3% were neglected, 17.6 were physically abused, 9.2% were sexually abused, and 10.3% experienced "other'" types of maltreatment that include abandonment, threats of harm, or prenatal drug exposure. In 2010, a new category, "Children with a Drug Abuse Caregiver Risk Factor," was included for analysis. Twenty-eight states reported ranges of 63.7% to 3.2%, with a mean of

18%. These results do not necessarily contradict Child Welfare League of America data but rather reflect internal validity issues of the data, since each state independently defines what constitutes child abuse and neglect and determines the level of evidence needed to determine a disposition (Child Maltreatment, 2010). As such, given the aggregate types of data reporting and variability among state definitions, when a report is made that a child may be the victim of child abuse or neglect, it is difficult to establish that active substance use was a determinate factor. For example, a mother who is totally impaired due to active drug use and leaves her young infant unattended for an extended period of time maybe included in the same category as a mother who is in recovery receiving methadone-assisted treatment for opioid dependence but who is reported to CPS because her infant was prenatally exposed to methadone.

The child welfare system by definition focuses on the safety of the child, and while recognizing that there may be a number of factors in addition to impairment that may impede the parenting ability of parents with substance use disorders, the factors the system addresses tend to be limited to direct consequences of substance use such as a lack of funds due to drug purchases, frequent arrests, incarceration and court appearance, etc. (Child Welfare Information Gateway, 2009). The mandate to protect the child has also led to protection of the fetus, in which existing child abuse statutes in some states have been interpreted to apply to the fetus so that pregnant women could be arrested for "delivering drugs to a minor" or charged with "child abuse" (Scott, 2006). Implicit in this approach is the spurious assumption that, if faced with incarceration, pregnant women with substance use disorders will simply stop using drugs. It fails to recognize that addiction is a disease associated with a complex array of problems (Jones & Kaltenbach, in press).

Within recent years a distinctive bio-psychosocial profile of pregnant and parenting women with substance use disorders has emerged both from the experience of the substance abuse treatment system and from research focused on the characteristics of women in treatment. Included in this profile is family history, physical and sexual abuse, psychiatric comorbidity, caregiving environment, and parenting attitudes. Certainly not every woman with a substance use disorder fits a composite profile, but the data are overwhelmingly consistent across programs, geography, and time to support such generalization. (It should be noted, however, that these data do not include information from pregnant and parenting women who abuse prescription opioids. Although prescription opioid abuse has become a serious and growing problem, the widespread abuse is a relatively new phenomenon, and, to date, specific information about it is limited, despite the fact that women represent a significant proportion of this population [Kelly et al., 2008])

Initial understanding of the unique needs of pregnant and parenting women with substance use disorders emerged in the late 1970s and early 1980s with the implementation of a new paradigm that recognized a comprehensive model of care was essential if substance abuse treatment for pregnant women was to be effective (Reed, 1987). This led to major federal initiatives in the early 1990s to support specialized treatment services for pregnant and parenting women. These initiatives produced two separate streams of data: the Perinatal 20 projects, funded by the National Institute on Drug Abuse, National Institutes of Health (NIH), and the Residential Women and Children (RWC); and the Pregnant and Postpartum Women (PPW) demonstration programs funded by the Center for Substance Abuse Treatment, Substance Abuse Mental Health Services Administration, Department of Health and Human Services (DHHS). The data from these projects provide the foundation for the current understanding of the bio-psychosocial characteristics of pregnant and parenting women with substance use disorders.

■ FAMILY HISTORY

Women with substance use disorders frequently report family histories of alcohol and illicit drug abuse (Hans, 1999). Family history of substance abuse may include father, mother, or both; siblings; and grandparents. Numerous studies assessing histories of familial substance abuse disorders among parenting women in treatment report ranges from 20% to 75.2% (Bendersky et al., 1996; Comfort et al., 2003; Haller et al., 1993; Hutchins & Dipietro, 1997). Bendersky et al. (1996) assessed 105 pregnant women who abused cocaine, differentiating between familial histories of parental illicit drug abuse and parental alcoholism, and found a 20% rate of parental drug use, compared to a 40% rate of alcoholism. In a study that examined risk and protective factors related to treatment outcomes in 95 parenting women enrolled in substance abuse treatment, Comfort et al. (2003) found 63.3% of women in outpatient treatment and 48.6% of women in residential treatment reported having parents and/or grandparents with drug and alcohol problems. Similarly, one of the Perinatal 20 studies found rates of 53% for paternal substance abuse, 32% for maternal substance abuse, and 22% both paternal and maternal substance abuse (Haller et al., 1993). Hutchins and Dipietro (1997) sampled 237 pregnant women in an urban prenatal clinic and identified 102 cocaine abusers. Of interest is that, although they found a very high rate of family drug history (75.2%) among the cocaine users, they also found a 44.1% family drug history among the 127 non drug users. These studies also reflect variability in how studies define and categorize familial histories of substance use and abuse. However, they clearly identify a serious issue in that parental substance abuse may influence the development of substance abuse disorders in their children, via several routes. Parents with substance abuse disorders may be unable to appropriately supervise their children and protect them from physical or sexual abuse; they may be emotionally unavailable to nurture their children; and/or their behavior may indicate to the child that using drugs is an acceptable coping mechanism (CSAT, 2009). In addition to the possible effect of intergenerational transmission of substance use (genetic and/or environmental), parental substance abuse may also have a negative impact on the woman's childhood development, thus limiting her own parenting abilities because of underdeveloped social and/or emotional development (Haller et al., 1993)

Physical, Emotional, and Sexual Abuse

One of the most troubling outcomes in the body of research examining the characteristics of pregnant and parenting women with substance use disorders is the overwhelming prevalence of lifetime victimization. A study by Comfort et al. (2003) reported an incidence of physical, emotional, or sexual abuse by family, partner, or friends of 76.7% of pregnant and parenting women in outpatient treatment and 82.9% in residential treatment, respectively. In this same sample, 56.7% of women in outpatient treatment and 60.0% of women in residential treatment also reported victimization that included domestic violence, rape, robbery, and assault. A study by Haller and Miles (2003) found 66% of pregnant women with substance use disorders reported experiencing one or more forms of abuse during childhood, with 48% reporting emotional abuse, 41% physical abuse, 44% sexual abuse, 26% both physical and sexual abuse, 28% both emotional and sexual abuse, and 35% both physical and emotional abuse. The combination of physical, sexual, and emotional abuse was reported by 23%. The Comfort et al. (2003) and Haller and Miles studies (2003) were relatively small with fewer than 100 participants.

A much larger study (Velez et al., 2006) of 715 pregnant women with substance use disorders found the lifetime prevalence of any type of violence; that is, physical, sexual, or emotional, was 84.9% for at least one type of abuse during their lifetime; 72.7% reported physical abuse, 71.3% emotional abuse, 44.5% sexual abuse, and 35.8% all three types of abuse. Moreover, the prevalence rate of exposure to any abuse during their current pregnancy was 45.3%. A very large nine-site study, the Women, Co-Occurring Disorders and Violence Study (Becker et al., 2005), comprised of 2,729 participants, provided a sobering portrait of the relationship between substance use disorders and interpersonal trauma. By design, participants had to have a DSM-IV Axis I and/or an Axis II psychiatric disorder, a DSM-IV substance use disorder, and a history of physical and/or sexual abuse. However, their early-life experiences were significant. Women were abused early in their lives and were abused repeatedly. The average age of the initial sexual and/or physical abuse was approximately 13 years of age, and the average age of emotional abuse and/or neglect was approximately nine years of age. Ninety-one percent of the women reported a history of physical abuse; 90% reported sexual abuse; 84% reported emotional abuse or neglect. Approximately 75% experienced multiple types of abuse as well as repeated abuse. A significant amount of sexual abuse has been identified as incest (Glover et al., 1996), but our understanding of this specific type of victimization is limited, as it is often not differentiated within the category of sexual abuse. The data discussed above are consistent with numerous studies that report very high rates of physical, sexual, and emotional abuse in pregnant and parenting women with substance use disorders (Root, 1989; Hutchins & Dipietro, 1997; Kissin et al., 2001; Medrano et al., 1999; Easton et al., 2000). Additionally, parental mental health problems, paternal under-education and unemployment, frequent changes in housing, and parental separation or divorce have been found to be more prevalent among women who were abused as children than among women who were not abused (Sacks et al., 2008).

Given the pervasive experience of victimization among pregnant and parenting women with substance use disorders, it is not unexpected that there would also be a high occurrence of post-traumatic stress disorder (PTSD).

It has been reported that between 33% and 59% of women with a substance use disorder have PTSD, most often the result of physical or sexual abuse during childhood (Najavits et al., 1997; Haller & Miles, 2003). In a study of 58 women enrolled in an outpatient substance abuse treatment program who also had PTSD (Najavits et al. 2004), the average age of first trauma was 8.7 years. Of particular concern was a 50% rate of physical assault by partners during the past year. These results are consistent with previous work that has established that, among women with histories of trauma and substance use disorders, there is a high likelihood to be involved in dangerous relationships (Najavits, 2002). Of particular relevance to the issue of parenting is the finding that PTSD in particular may precede substance use, and that substance use provides a means of managing/medicating painful affect (CSAT, 2009; Najavits, 2009; Kaysen et al., 2007).

■ PSYCHIATRIC COMORBIDITY

In addition to PTSD, which was discussed in the previous section due to its relationship to violence and trauma, women with substance use disorders have high rates of other psychiatric diagnoses. An evaluation of the 50 demonstration programs for pregnant and parenting women with substance use disorders funded by the Center for Substance Abuse Treatment, SAMHSA, DHHS, found that of the 5,110 women who received services, 60% had co-occurring psychiatric disorders (CSAT 2003). Anxiety disorders and depression are the most common co-occurring diagnoses (Agrawal et al., 2005). A study of pregnant cocaine-dependent women receiving outpatient or residential treatment assessed their lifetime history of depression and found psychiatric history in 45% of women in outpatient treatment and in 84% of women in residential treatment. In addition, rates of previous inpatient psychiatric treatment and previous outpatient psychiatric treatment were 22% and 32% for outpatient women, and 38% and 20% for residential women, respectively (Comfort & Kaltenbach, 1999). High rates of depression and anxiety have also been found in opioid-dependent women. A large national study that included 1,490 women who abused prescription opioids reported they had had psychiatric problems of depression (69.4%) and anxiety (78.7%) in the previous 30 days (Green et al. 2009). In one of the first studies to focus specifically on psychiatric disorders in pregnant opioid-dependent women, Fitzsimons et al. (2007) assessed 106 women and found 73% were diagnosed with co-occurring Axis I disorder. Of those, 37% had a primary mood disorder and 36% had a primary anxiety disorder. Moreover, of those with a primary mood disorder, 44% also had an anxiety disorder, and of those with a primary anxiety mood disorder, 37% also had a mood disorder. A study of 175 pregnant opioid-dependent women participating in a randomized controlled trial investigating the use of methadone and buprenorphine during pregnancy (Jones et al. 2010) found that, at study enrollment, 62% of the women had symptoms of a major depressive disorder, a generalized anxiety disorder, or both, as assessed by the Mini International Neuropsychiatric Interview (Benningfield et al., 2012). One would hope that engaging in substance abuse treatment would have positive implications for women with psychiatric morbidity, but an ever-present "Catch 22" challenge is that psychiatric disorders in women are often associated poor substance abuse treatment outcomes among the women, and with poor outcomes among their children (Benningfield et al., 2012; Comfort & Kaltenbach, 2000; Fitzsimons et al., 2007; Haller et al., 2002)

■ CAREGIVING ENVIRONMENT

Most pregnant and parenting women with substance use disorders women may have children living with them, but custody issues are frequent, with numerous configurations representing the dynamic flow of their child custody difficulties. They may have one or more children living with them while at the same time not have legal custody of one or more of their other children. They often have sole responsibility for the care of their children, as a high percentage of women with substance abuse disorders are not married or not involved in long-term relationships. Compounding the difficulty of their situation is that they usually have less than a high school education, receive public assistance, and have unstable living arrangements; e.g., are homeless and live with family or friends, or in shelters (Becker et al., 2005; Comfort & Kaltenbach, 1999; Kissin et al., 2001). Moreover, the majority of women living with family members, friends, or their sexual partners report living in homes where at least one other person had a substance use/abuse problem (Kissin et al., 2001). Legal issues are also common. In addition to involvement with child protective services, studies report high rates of legal problems in this population, including arrests and incarceration (Becker et al., 2005; Comfort & Kaltenbach, 1999; Kissin et al., 2001). Given the chaotic and transitory environment in which she lives and her experience with CPS, it is not surprising that pregnant and parenting women with substance use disorders may be reluctant to accept any types of services directed to her child and/or her interactions with her child for fear of being reported to CPS.

■ PARENTING ATTITUDES

Clinical observation of "discipline" techniques used by women in substance abuse treatment have been corroborated by research focused on attitudes and behaviors that found that a child's undesired behavior was often met with harshly punitive behavior, expressed by yelling, threatening, and physical punishment. Moreover, the definition that the child's behavior was "unacceptable" was often driven by a lack of understanding of basic developmental milestones, thus leading to unrealistic expectations of children's behavior (Kaltenbach et al., 1982; Lief, 1885; Sowder & Burt, 1980). In a study of abusive parents Azar and Rohrbeck (1986) found that parents frequently expected that a two- to three-year-old was capable of engaging in self-care and controlling their impulses, such as to stopping crying when told to do so. Such a lack of understanding is likewise expressed by perceiving infant crying as being demanding and inappropriate (Burns & Burns, 1988; Kaltenbach et al., 1982). Pregnant women with substance use disorders have also been found to have a range of emotions regarding their pregnancy. While the pregnancy is often viewed positively by women as a chance to "start over," these emotions may be accompanied by feelings of guilt related to their drug use, concern about their baby's health, general discontent with the state of pregnancy, and negative feelings regarding the circumstances of conception (Comfort & Kaltenbach, 1999; Kissin et al., 2001)

Overall, studies reporting parenting attitudes among pregnant and parenting women with substance use disorders indicate a lack of understanding about basic child development, a low capacity to reflect upon their children's emotional and cognitive experience, and ambivalent feelings about having and keeping their children (Mayes & Truman, 2002).

These components of a profile of bio-psychosocial characteristics of pregnant and parenting women with substance use disorders have been discussed independently for purposes of organization and presentation. They are, however, not mutually exclusive, but are multiple, complex, intersecting problems that reflect a continuum of genetic, environmental, and/or experiential risk factors that either preceded substance use or are a result of the chaotic lifestyle concomitant with substance abuse; and all, both singularly and collectively, have a significant role in the ongoing abuse disorder. Of additional import is that these risk factors are all associated with dysfunctional parenting, regardless of maternal substance use. This presents an extremely difficult challenge for those committed to developing effective parenting interventions. If we are to be successful in developing effective parenting intervention strategies for pregnant and parenting women with substance use disorders, we need to identify mechanisms that will mediate the interrelationships of these multiple risk factors on both substance abuse and dysfunctional parenting behaviors.

■ **REFERENCES**

Agrawal, A., Gardner, C. O., Prescott, C. A., & Kendler, K. S. (2005). The differential impact of risk factors on illicit drug involvement in females. *Social Psychiatry and Psychiatric Epidemiology, 40*, 454–466.

Azar, S. T., & Rohrbeck, C. A. (1986). Child abuse and unrealistic expectations: further validation of the Parent Opinion Questionnaire. *Journal of Counseling and Clinical Psychology, 54*, 876–868.

Becker, M. A., Noether, C. D., Larson, M. J., Gatz, M., Brown, V., et al. (2005). Characteristics of women engaged in treatment for trauma and co-occurring disorders: findings from a national multi-site study. *Journal of Community Psychology, 33*, 429–443.

Bendersky, M., Alessandri, S., Gilbert, P., & Lewis, M. (1996). Characteristics of pregnant substance abusers in two cities in the northeast. *American Journal of Drug and Alcohol Abuse, 22*, 349–362.

Benningfield, M. M., Dietrich, M. S., Jones, H. E., Kaltenbach, K., Heil, S. H., Stine, S. M., et al. (2012). Effects of depression and anxiety symptoms on treatment outcomes for opioid dependence during pregnancy. *Addiction, 107*(Suppl 1), 74–82.

Burns, W. J., & Burns, K. A. (1988). Parenting dysfunction in chemically dependent women. In I. Chasnoff (Ed.), *Drugs, Alcohol, Pregnancy and Parenting* (pp. 159–171). London: Kluwer.

Center for Substance Abuse Treatment. (2003). RWC/PPW Cross-Site Evaluation, Client Characteristics. Available at www.csat.samhsa.gov/publications [Accessed January (2012).]

Center for Substance Abuse Treatment. (2009). Substance Abuse Treatment: Addressing the Specific Needs of Women. Treatment Improvement Protocol (TIP) Series 51. HHS Publication No. (SMA) 09-446. Rockville MD: Substance Abuse Mental Health Service Administration.

Child Maltreatment (2010). Children's Bureau, Administration on Children, Youth and Families, Administration for Children and Families, U.S. Department of Health and Human Services. Available at www.acf.hhs.gov/programs/cb/pubs/cm10/ [Accessed January (2012).].

Child Welfare Information Gateway (2009). *Parental use and the child welfare system*, Children's Bureau, Administration on Children, Youth and Families, Administration for Children and Families, US Department of Health and Human Services. Available at www.childwelfare.gov/pub/factsheets/parentalsusabuse.cfm [Accessed January (2012).].

Child Welfare League of America (2010). *The Nation's Children (2010)*. Available at www.cwla.org/advocacy/statefactsheets/ (2010). /nationalfactsheet10pdf [Accessed January (2012).].

Comfort, M., & Kaltenbach, K. (1999). Biopsychosocial characteristics and treatment outcomes of pregnant cocaine-dependent women in residential and outpatient substance treatment. *Journal of Psychoactive Drugs, 31*, 279–289.

Comfort, M. L., & Kaltenbach, K. (2000). Predictors of treatment outcomes for substance abusing women: a retrospective study. *Substance Abuse, 21*, 33–45.

Comfort, M., Sockloff, A., Loverro, J., & Kaltenbach, K. (2003). Multiple predictors of substance-abusing women's treatment and life outcomes: a prospective longitudinal study. *Addictive Behaviors, 28*, 99–224.

Easton, C., Swan, S., & Sinha, R. (2000). Prevalence of family violence in clients entering substance abuse treatment. *Journal of Substance Treatment, 18*, 23–28.

Fitzsimons, H. E., Tuten, M., Vaidya, V., & Jones, H. E. (2007). Mood disorders affect drug treatment success of drug-dependent pregnant women. *Journal of Substance Treatment, 32*, 19–25.

Glover, N. M., Janikowski, T. P., & Benshoff, J. J. (1996). Substance abuse and past incest contact: a national perspective. *Journal of Substance Abuse Treatment, 13*, 185–193.

Green, T. C., Grimes Serrano, J. M., Licari, A., Budman, S. H., & Butler, S. F. (2009). Women who abuse prescription opioids: findings from the Addiction Severity Index–Multimedia Version Connect prescription opioid database. *Drug and Alcohol Dependence, 103*, 65–73.

Haller, D. L., Knisely, J. S., Dawson, K. S., & Schnoll, S. H. (1993). Perinatal substance abusers: psychological and social characteristics, *Journal of Nervous and Mental Disease, 181*, 509–513.

Haller, D. L., Miles, D. R., & Dawson, D. R. (2002). Psychopathology influences treatment retention among drug-dependent women. *Journal of Substance Abuse Treatment, 23*, 431–436.

Haller, D. L., & Miles, D. R. (2003). Victimization and perpetration among perinatal substance abusers. *Journal of Interpersonal Violence, 18*, 760–770.

Hans, S. L. (1999). Demographic and psychosocial characteristics of substance abusing pregnant women. *Clinics in Perinatology, 26,* 55–74.

Hutchins, E., & Dipietro, J. (1997). Psychosocial risk factors associated with cocaine use during pregnancy: a case control study. *Obstetrics & Gynecology, 90,* 142–147.

Jones, H. E., & Kaltenbach, K. *Treating Women with Substance Use Disorders During Pregnancy: A Comprehensive Approach to Caring for Mother and Child.* Oxford University Press, In Press.

Jones, H. E., Kaltenbach, K., Heil, S. H., Stine, S., Coyle, M., Arria, A. M., et al. (2010). Neonatal abstinence syndrome following methadone or buprenorphine exposure. *New England Journal of Medicine, 363,* 2320–2331.

Kaltenbach, K., Leifer, B., & Finnegan, L. P. (1982). Knowledge of child development in drug dependent mothers. *Pediatric Research, 16,* 87.

Kaysen, D., Dillworth, T. M., Simpson, T., Waldrop, A., Larimer, M. E., & Resick, P. A. (2007). Domestic violence and alcohol use: trauma-related symptoms and motives for drinking. *Addictive Behaviors, 32,* 1272–1283.

Kelly, J. P., Cook, S. F., Kaufman, D. W., Anderson, T., Rosenberg, L., & Mitchell, A. A. (2008). Prevalence and characteristics of opioid use in the US adult population. *Pain, 138,* 507–513.

Kissin, W. B., Svikis, D. S., Morgan, G. D., & Haug, N. A. (2001). Characterizing pregnant drug-dependent women in treatment and the children. *Journal of Substance Abuse Treatment, 21,* 27–34.

Lief, N. R. (1985). The drug user as a parent. *International Journal of the Addictions, 20,* 63–97.

Mayes, L., & Truman, S. (2002). Substance abuse and parenting. In M. Bornstein (Ed.), *Handbook of Parenting: Vol.4. Social Conditions and Applied Parenting* (2nd ed., 329–359). Mahwah, NJ: Lawrence Erlbaum.

Medrano, M. A., Zule, W. A., Hatch, J., & Desmond, D. P. (1999). Prevalence of childhood trauma in a community sample of substance-abusing women. *American Journal of Drug and Alcohol Abuse, 25,* 440–462.

Najavits, L. M. (2002). *Seeking Safety: A Treatment Manual for PTSD and Substance Abuse.* New York: Guilford.

Najavits, L. M. (2009). Seeking Safety: An implementation guide. In, A. Rubin & DW Springer (Eds.). *The Clinician's Guide to Evidence-Based Practice.* Hoboken, NJ: John Wiley.

Najavits, L. M., Weiss, R. D., & Shaw, S. R. (1997). The link between substance abuse and traumatic stress disorder in women: a research review. *American Journal on Addictions, 6,* 273–283.

Najavits, L. M., Sonn, J., Walsh, & Weiss, R. D. (2004). Domestic violence in women with PTSD and substance abuse. *Addictive Behaviors, 29,* 707–715.

Reed, B. G. (1987). Developing women-sensitive drug dependence treatment services: why so difficult? *Journal of Psychoactive Drugs, 19,* 151–164.

Root, M. D. (1989). Treatment failures: the role of sexual victimization in women's addictive behavior. *American Journal of Orthopsychiatry, 59,* 542–549.

Sacks, J. Y., McKendrick, K., & Banks, S. (2008). The impact of early trauma and abuse on residential substance treatment outcomes for women. *Journal of Substance Abuse Treatment, 34,* 90–100.

Scott, T. (2006). *Repercussions of the Crack Baby Epidemic: why a Message of Care Rather Than Punishment Is Needed for Pregnant Drug-Users. National Black Law Journal, 19,* 203–221.

Sowder, B. J., & Burt, M. R. (1980). *Children of Heroin Addicts: an Assessment of Health, Learning, Behavioral and Adjustment Problems.* New York: Praeger.

Velez, M. L., Montoya, I. D., Jansson, L. M., Walters, V., Svikis, D., Jones, H. E., et al. (2006). Exposure to violence among substance-dependent pregnant women and their children. *Journal of Substance Abuse Treatment, 30,* 31–38.

10 The Impact of Parental Addiction on Child Development

SAARA SALO AND MARJO FLYKT

■ INTRODUCTION

The lives of millions of children are affected by parental addiction. These children are at increased risk for abuse or neglect, as well as physical, academic, social, and emotional problems. Instead of attributing such developmental deficits directly to specific drug effects, however, a growing consensus suggests that these risks might actually arise from multiple medical and social factors that are cumulative in nature (Nair, Schuler, Black, Kettinger, & Harrington, 2003; Tronick & Beeghly, 1999). It is now recognized that searching for a singular effect or the location of effect is misdirected. Most substance users are polydrug users and parental addiction occurs in a context of multiple environmental risk factors. Although it is likely that different substances have also specific and dose-related effects independent of other factors, it is also feasible to consider the impact of parental addiction using a systemic, regulatory model of development. Transactional formulations of risk development for this population suggest, indeed, that it is not prenatal exposure to drugs per se, but also the early parenting environment that is of significance to children's developmental outcomes (Hans, 2002; Sameroff & Fiese, 1990). A predictable, consistent environment, together with positive caregiver relationships, is critical for normal emotional development of children. Parental addiction can cause home environments to become unpredictable, even leading to child maltreatment. The children's physical and emotional needs often take a back seat to their parents' activities related to obtaining, using, or recovering from the substance use. Consequently, focusing on child developmental issues and overall parental quality as well as reducing the potentially ongoing parental substance use seem all important interventive goals.

The Effects of Prenatal Substance Exposure

Exposure to alcohol during pregnancy can have serious effects on fetal development. Alcohol consumed by a pregnant woman is absorbed by the placenta and directly affects the fetus. A variety of birth defects to the major organs and the central nervous system can occur due to alcohol use during pregnancy. However, it is important to note that similar amounts of maternal alcohol consumption during pregnancy may not have the same outcomes, as the phenotype can differ according to critical periods of exposure (see Riley & McGee, 2005). Together, these defects emerging from different critical periods are called Fetal Alcohol Syndrome (FAS). Children with FAS may exhibit growth deficiencies, problems with central nervous system functioning, IQs in the mild to severely retarded range, small eye openings and poor development of the optic nerve, a small head and brain and joint, limb, ear, and heart malformations. (McCreight, 1997).

Alcohol-Related Neurodevelopmental Disorder (ARND) and Alcohol-Related Birth Defects (ARBD) are similar to FAS. ARND and ARBD refer to the functional and physiological problems associated with prenatal alcohol exposure, but are in a less severe form than FAS. Children with ARND can experience functional or mental impairments as a result of prenatal alcohol exposure, and children with ARBD can have malformations in the skeletal and major organ systems. Not all children who are exposed prenatally to alcohol develop FAS, ARND, or ARBD, but for those who do, these effects continue throughout their lives and at all the stages of development. (McCreight, 1997).

Similar to maternal alcohol use, use of other substances can have significant harmful effects on the developing fetus. These of course vary depending on the combination of substances used, their doses and the timing and duration of exposure. Most drug-abusers are polydrug-users who also use alcohol, smoke cigarettes and may have suboptimal nutrition and health care attendance during pregnancy, all of which have independent effects on child outcome (Bays, 1990; Brooks, Zuckerman, Bamforth, Cole, & Kaplan-Sanoff, 1994; Zuckerman & Brown, 1993). Maternal cigarette smoking during pregnancy is associated with reduced fetal growth, low birth weight, asthma and other respiratory problems, sudden infant death syndrome and many other medical disorders (Higgins, 2002). Marijuana, cocaine or opiate use during pregnancy may increase the risk for premature birth, low birth weight, decreased head circumference, or miscarriage. Opioid-exposed infants often show abnormalities in their neurobehavioral profiles (e.g., Finnegan, 1984; Lester et al., 2002). As newborns, these infants are at an increased risk for neonatal abstinence syndrome (NAS), usually occurring within 72 hours after birth and continuing for several weeks postpartum. NAS may include a number of symptoms such as tremors, irritability, mood swings, vomiting, weight loss, and diarrhea (Finnegan, 1984). These symptoms of newborn state may be associated with developmental or cognitive delays and can significantly interfere with the emotional bonding between the caregiver and the infant. It is also feasible that this biological vulnerability may be compensated for by sensitive and competent caregiving.

Child Developmental Outcomes

In addition to the direct fetal effects, exposure to parental addiction during childhood can also have multiple indirect consequences for children. Compared to children of parents who do not abuse alcohol or drugs, children of substance-abusing parents are more likely to experience physical, intellectual, social, and emotional problems and are also often customers of child welfare system. According to the transactional model of risk development, one pathway to later developmental problems among drug-exposed infants may be through proximal environmental factors such as the quality of mother-child interaction (Sameroff & Fiese, 1990).

Risks for Early Interaction and Attachment

The fundamental pre-requisite for the formation of healthy parent-child attachment is the caregiver's ability to pay attention to the child and to notice his/her signals for emotional communication. Enthusiasm and mutual enjoyment are essential components of the affectional bond between the parent and the infant. Within an emotionally available (EA) relationship, the mother's sensitive, structuring, nonhostile, and nonintrusive caregiving will facilitate the infant's ability to regulate emotion and behavior and to interact in a responsive and involving way (Biringen, & Easterbrooks, 2008). Drug-abusing parents may, however, bring their own problematic life style to the early interaction with their babies. When parents repeatedly miss their babies' cues, the babies eventually stop providing them, resulting in a combination of a disengaged mother with a disengaged baby.

The relational, holistic conceptualization of emotional communication may be of special relevance in a study of drug-exposed children where the risk for difficulties in early interaction may well lay in the child, in the parent, or in the parent-child dyad. Indeed, utilizing EA measure of parent-child interaction Swanson, Beckwith, and Howard (2000) found that maternal intrusiveness predicted disorganized attachment only in a group of drug-exposed infants. Their rationale was that maternal intrusiveness might be especially detrimental to drug-exposed infants because of the special vulnerability of these infants in the area of self-regulation. In line with this, it was found that opioid abusing mothers scored the lowest in maternal sensitivity, structuring and nonintrusiveness during the first year of baby's life as compared to normative and depressed mothers (Salo et al., 2010). Further, when children were 3 years of age, opioid abusing mothers scored lower on maternal sensitivity, and nonhostility than both normative as well as foster mothers (Salo et al., 2009). Also, compared to demographically matched non-abusers, polysubstance abusing mothers in drug-abuse treatment have shown lower sensitivity and general emotional availability with their 2–5 months old infants (Fraser, Harris-Britt, Thakkallapalli, Kurtz-Costes, & Martin, 2010; see also Chapter 17).

In line with the findings utilizing the EA framework, other studies on mother-infant interaction quality have yielded similar results. Observing a large sample of 4-month-old infants with their mothers, Tronick et al. (2005) did not find differences in the social-emotional behaviors between opiate-exposed infants and their mothers in the (face-to-face) still-face paradigm as compared to a nonopiate-exposure group. By contrast, differences were more evident among cocaine-exposed dyads, where mothers showed more negative engagement. In line with this, women whose primary drug is cocaine have also been shown to be less attentive and engaged during face-to-face interaction with their infants over the first 6 months (Mayes et al., 1997) as well as less enthusiastic and responsive during the first year of the infant's life than non-using mothers (Burns, Chethik, Burns, & Clark, 1997). Research on toddlers has indicated that these mothers are more likely to be intrusive and hostile and to engage in poorer quality of instruction with their 3-year -olds (Johnson et al., 2002). Women whose primary drug of abuse is opioids have been shown to be less positive with their newborns (Fitzgerald, Kaltenbach, & Finnegan, 1990) and less responsive throughout the first two years of life (Bernstein & Hans, 1994; Bernstein, Jeremy, & Marcus, 1986). Maternal polydrug use has been found to decrease of maternal contingent responsiveness and dyadic reciprocity during feeding interactions (Das Eiden, 2001).

Together these results show a consistently lower quality of early interaction patterns between drug-abusing parents and their children. There is also evidence that parental substance abuse negatively impacts the development of attachment relationships. Majority of substance exposed children may be insecurily attached or have disorganized attachment to their primary caregivers (O'Connor et al., 1987; Rodning, Beckwith, & Howard, 1989). However, although parental drug abuse seems to be detrimental to the parent-child interactions and the development of attachment, this association is not simply unidirectional one; it is a transactional system that evolves between the parents and children over time. Considering and delineating the transactional effects between parental, interactional and child characteristics which may act as buffering or vulnerability factors is especially important for designing interventions for this high-risk population. Child characteristics and behaviors affect responses from parents and vice versa, and therefore influence the future pattern of parent-child interactions. For example, difficult temperaments, which are frequently observed in children of drug abusers, have been linked with poor parenting practices (Mun et al., 2001).

Cognitive, Language and Motor Functions

Thus far, the literature suggests some systematic differences in child cognitive functioning among drug-exposed versus matched nonexposed comparisons throughout childhood (see Chiriboga, 2003; Tronick & Beeghly, 1999). Prenatal marijuana exposure does not seem to impact composite measures of global intelligence (Fried & Smith 2001), however, it does seem to impact academic achievement (Goldsmith, Richardson, Cornelius, & Day 2004). Studies that have focused on cocaine exposure, in turn, often report no significant main effects on general measures of developmental competence, such as the Bayley Scales' Mental Development Index (MDI) or other standardized intelligence tests (e.g., Azuma & Chasnoff, 1993; Frank et al., 2002). Still, other studies have shown for example that at the age of 7 years prenatally cocaine exposed children scored lower than comparison children on the Wechsler Intelligence Scale (3rd ed.) as well as on motor developmental measures such as Visual Motor Integration and Motor Coordination (Arendt et al., 2004). In line with this, results from a longitudinal study show that cocaine-exposed children show delayed mental performance from 3 to 36 months (Mayes et al., 2003). However, Mayes et al. also found that the developmental trajectories of cocaine exposed children were similar to those from noncocaine exposed comparison groups. In terms of language development, Bandstra and her colleagues have followed a sample of cocaine-exposed children from birth to 7 years, and report poorer language performance as compared to non-exposed children (Bandstra et al., 2002, 2004). Specifically,

Bandstra and her colleagues showed that greater severity of prenatal cocaine exposure was associated with greater deficits within the more stable aptitude for language performance.

On the other hand, opioid abuse has historically been linked with lower scores on the Bayley-II MDI, and Psychomotor Development Index (Hans & Jeremy, 2001) as well as on the McCarthy Scales of Children's Abilities (Lifschitz & Wilson, 1991), although the magnitude of differences is not large. More recently, infants of mothers who participated in buprenorphine-replacement therapy for their opiate addiction during their pregnancy were also shown to earn the lowest Bayley-III MDI scores as compared to normative infants as well as to infants of depressed mothers (Salo et al., 2010). Similarly, prenatal polysubstance exposure has been linked to lower performance on the Mullen Scale of Early Learning (Morrison, Cerles, Montaini-Klovdahl, & Skowron, 2000) as well as on Bayley-II MDI (Moe & Slinning, 2001).

In line with the transactional model proposition, however, the results have also indicated that the current environmental factors, such as the mother's vocabulary and quality of home environment may be even stronger developmental predictors than prenatal drug exposure per se (Arendt et al., 2004). Regardless of prenatal drug exposure, children living in poverty are at risk for cognitive delays (Petterson & Albers 2001) which becomes evident especially during toddlerhood and school years (e.g., Bradley & Corwyn, 2002) suggesting the general impact of impoverished environment on cognition. These environmental effects have already been demonstrated in intervention studies, such as the Kilbride, Castor, Hoffman, and Fuger study (2000) who found that among prenatally cocaine-exposed children who remained with their biological mothers, those who had received case management services had higher verbal scores at 36 months than those who had received routine management. Also, infants who lived with their substance abusing mothers in intensive residential care setting scored within normative range in Bailey-II at the age of 4 months (Pajulo et al., 2011). Thus, the existing evidence indicates that although prenatal exposure may confer some degree of developmental disadvantage, it frequently occurs in the inadequate rearing environment and disruptions in emotional parent-child relations or poverty which may be also strong determinants of the children's outcome.

Attention and Emotion Regulation

Parental addiction has also been shown to have an impact on the child neuropsychological mechanisms controlling for attention, memory, visuoperception and emotion regulation. Follow-up studies have consistently demonstrated that prenatal marijuana exposure has a negative influence on executive functioning, particularly on attentional behavior and visual analysis/hypothesis testing but not on overall measures of intelligence (Fried, 2002). Furthermore, some marijuana exposure effects have been associated with poorer regulation and higher excitability/impulsiveness during infancy (Lester et al., 2002) as well as in children of 6 up to 9 and 12 years old (Fried, O'Connell, & Watkinson 1992; Fried, Watkinson, & Gray 1998).

Prenatal cocaine exposure has likewise been associated with alterations in children's attention and emotion regulation systems (Mayes, 1999, Tronick & Beeghly, 1999). Early physiological regulation and autonomic stress indicators have been associated with prenatal cocaine exposure (Tronick et al., 2005) suggesting alterations in arousal regulation in response to stress. Cocaine exposed infants and preschoolers are found to be more excitable and to show greater irritability/frustration than non-exposed children in response to stressors (Chaplin, Fahy, Sinha, & Mayes, 2009). Likewise, children growing with persistently drug-using mothers at 7 years of age showed difficulties in sustained visual attention tasks (Ackerman et al., 2008). These self-regulation difficulties may occur either through direct teratogenic effects, through genetic transmission of arousal regulatory problems, or through chronic environmental stressors experienced postnatally by cocaine exposed children (Chaplin, Freiburger, Mayes, & Sinha, 2010). Recently, a study focusing on stress response in adolescents showed also that prenatally cocaine-exposed adolescents had higher cortisol levels before and after stress exposure (Chaplin et al., 2010). In a similar vein, some evidence suggests that prenatal opiate exposure is associated with greater impulsivity, and poorer attention (Mayes & Fahy, 2001) although research is much less sparse here.

The children of drug-abusing mothers show, furthermore, problematic emotion regulation patterns, probably due to both the effects of prenatal drug-exposure and deficits in maternal interactive behavior (Tronick et al., 2005). Cocaine-exposed children are often withdrawn and express less positive and more negative affect towards their mother (Bendersky & Lewis, 1998; Tronick et al., 2005). Further, infants exposed to heavier levels of cocaine showed more passive-withdrawn negative engagement and engaged in more negative affective matching with their mothers than other infants (Tronick et al., 2005). Several studies have also found associations between prenatal cocaine exposure and difficult temperament involving problems in reactivity and affect regulation (Alessandri, Sullivan, Bendersky, & Lewis 1995). These difficulties may persist beyond infancy. For example, it has been reported that cocaine-exposed children have deficits in emotional regulation, inhibitory control, and sustained attention measured at age 7 (Bandstra, Morrow, Anthony, Accornero, et al., 2001). Also, 3-year old children of Finnish buprenorphine-using mothers were found to show lower responsiveness and involvement than normative children (Salo et al., 2009).

All the above infant attention and emotion regulation characteristics can make parenting less awarding and compromise the developing attachment bond. It might also be that because attention regulation impacts children's abilities to perform on standardized measures of intelligence these children might be expected to show more delays in standard measures of development (Mayes, 2002). This makes the evaluation of neuropsychological profile among drug-exposed infants and children especially warranted.

Socioemotional Development

Parental addiction increases risk also for child abuse and neglect (Ammerman et al., 1999) which, in turn, may relate to poor socialization of emotion within these families. Neglected children who are unable to form secure attachments with their primary caregivers may suffer from many problems in understanding the emotions of others, or forming and maintaining relationships with others (Robinson et al., 2009; Shipman, Edwards, Brown, Swisher & Jennings, 2005). Abusive mothers have been found to respond to their child's noncompliance with more negative behavior (Borrego et al., 2004) which may lead to a cycle of negativeness. The parental anger-intensifying attributional style for especially negative child behavior (Pidgeon & Sanders, 2009) may cause the children to have a limited ability to feel remorse or empathy. For example Bennet, Bendersky and Lewis (2002) showed that cocaine exposed 5-year old boys living in high-risk environment were aggressive both behaviorally as well as in their self-report reactions to hypothetical interpersonal conflict situations. Impaired social cognition, which is awareness of oneself in relation to others as well as of others' emotions, can lead a person to view many social interactions as stressful and also mean that they could hurt others without feeling their actions were wrong. Indeed, maltreated children have been shown to demonstrate less understanding of negative emotions (Shipman et al., 2005), and to use fewer internal state words (Cicchetti & Begley, 1987). Also, drug-exposed toddlers' impaired symbolic functioning has been shown in a study demonstrating less representational play as compared to preterm toddlers (Rodning, Beckwith, & Howard, 1989). Overall the lack of social skills may prevent success in school adding to the cognitive and attention and emotion regulation difficulties evident in the children of addicted parents.

Risk for Substance Using Disorders and Other Psychiatric Disorders

There is an increased risk for psychiatric disturbances for children of substance abusing parents. In general, children of alcoholic parents are more likely to exhibit elevated levels of aggression, to meet the diagnostic criteria for conduct disorder and/or mood disorder, to engage in antisocial behaviors and to abuse alcohol and other psychoactive substances themselves later in life (see Kelley & Fals-Stewart, 2004). At this point, however, it is not known whether it is the exposure to illicit drugs in utero that is associated with vulnerability to drug abuse later in life rather than environmentally mediated effect or genetic risk (Glantz & Chambers, 2006). A gene-environment relationship has been considered to play a key role. On the one hand family, twin, and adoption studies have provided evidence that the intergenerational transmission of substance disorders can, in part, be attributed to genetic factors. Nonetheless substance use disorder will not be expressed in the absence of actual drug exposure, suggesting the role of environmental influences (see Kelley & Fals-Stewart, 2004).

As far as other psychiatric disorders are concerned, however, the results seem more clear. Luthar, Cushing, Merikangas and Rounsaville (1998) found that 66% of the children of cocaine and opiate-addicted mothers had at least one major psychiatric diagnosis by 12 years of age. Furthermore, 54% of children admitted to psychiatric hospital were found to have histories of parental substance abuse (Gabel & Shindledecker, 1993), and 53% of the children who lived with drug-abusing fathers at the age of 8- to 12-years were likely to have a lifetime psychiatric diagnosis as compared to 25% of matched children from homes with only alcohol abusing or 10% of non-substance abusing fathers. (Kelley & Fals-Stewart 2004). However, in addition to diagnosable disorders, more typically children of addicted parents suffer from both internalizing as well as externalizing behavioral and emotional problems. The severity of these problems vary but in many cases a strong positive home environment can significantly ameliorate the negative outcomes (Glantz & Chambers, 2006).

Abusive relationships and maternal emotional unavailability have been suggested to be the most important factors underlying later maladjustment and psychopathology (Weich, Patterson, Shaw, & Stewart-Brown, 2009). For example, Egeland, Yates, Appleyard and van Dulmen (2002) found that children physically abused in early childhood experienced more externalizing problems in elementary school; however, this relationship was mediated through alienation from a caregiver and emotional dysregulation. Also, the dysfunctional nature of parent-child interactions comprising negative emotionality, low levels of engagement, high coercion and little face-to-face contact has been shown to be a key factors in the emergence and maintenance of hostile-aggressive behavior beyond toddlerhood (Lyons-Ruth, Alpern, & Rapacholi, 1993). Parental psychopathology, which is highly common among substance abusing parents, is one important factor associated with later child outcome. Psychopathology in itself affects parenting negatively, but the parent's co-occurring substance use disorder may exacerbate the problems and increase the risks for the child's negative developmental outcome (Glantz and Chambers, 2006). The type of psychiatric problem may also be relevant. For example, it has been specifically shown that postnatal maternal somatic complaints, hostility and parainoa predicted the likelihood of the chid being placed in foster care after treatment in residential setting (Pajulo et al., 2011). Thus, in planning preventive and interventive strategies for children of parents with substance use disorders, it seems vital to consider also the presence of other comorbid psychiatric disorders in the parent.

Developmentally Based Interventions

When considering the many developmental risks children exposed to parental addiction may face, it seems clear that both drug exposure per se as well as adverse and disorganized postnatal caregiving environments inherent in substance abusing families place children at risk for maladaptive cognitive and emotional development (Arendt et al., 2004; Moe & Slinning, 2001; Tronick & Beeghly, 1999). As described in other chapters of this book, early clinic and home based intervention programs have been used with high-risk families with the goal to improve child development and parenting quality as well as to reduce parental drug use. The results have indicated improvement, especially from the child developmental perspective. For example, drug-exposed children who received family-based intervention have been shown to score higher in mental and psychomotor functioning than drug-exposed children who did not receive such family based intervention (e.g., Frank et al., 2002; Killbride et al, 2000; Schuler, Nair and Kettinger,

2003). Environmental effects have also been highlighted in a study where cocaine-exposed children growing up in non-kin foster care during the first two years perform better in several developmental domains, including cognitive status (Brown, Bakeman, Coles, & Platzman, & Lynch, 2004).

A conceptualization of cumulative effect of multiple risks for child developmental outcome may be helpful in understanding why there is also variability in the behavior and development of children receiving intervention. A number of psychosocial variables have been suggested to be of relevance such as family size, life events, psychological status of the parents, severity of drug abuse, domestic violence, parenting attitudes and early interaction quality. The results have also indicated that there may be age-related differences. Thus although Nair et al., (2003) found that through the first 18 months children of drug-abusing women with multiple risks were at no greater risk of mental, motor or language delay than were children of drug-abusing mothers with fewer risks, there are other studies suggesting the relevance of cumulative psychosocial risk at older ages. For example Carta et al. (2001) found that cumulative environmental risk accounted for more variance in development among children (3–57 months of age, followed over a 2-years period) than prenatal drug exposure. This suggests a need to have multiple targets in intervention models.

Also, the association between early emotional relationships and positive developmental trajectories among high-risk families argues in favor of intervention strategies focusing on the emotional aspects of parent-child relationships, namely sensitivity and responsiveness and relatedly, reflective capabilities of the parent (Bakermans-Kranenburg, van Ijzendoorn, & Juffer, 2005; Chapters 13 and 16). Consequently, keeping the developmental outcome of the child closely in mind, Tarabulsy et al., (2008) have outlined the most important components of attachment-based intervention with maltreating families. These consist of 1) improving parental mentalizing capabilities, that is, understanding of behaviors, emotions and signals of infants and children, 2) learning to give appropriate care in spite of past hardships and present preoccupations and 3) providing an interpersonal environment that encourages the child's development of emotional and behavioral regulatory abilities. Indeed, there is recent evidence showing that focusing on maternal reflective capabilities within an intensive residential treatment program for substance abusing mothers with their babies imporoved maternal reflective functioning significantly (Pajulo, Kalland, Suchman, & Mayes, 2006; Pajulo et al., 2012). Furthermore, mothers who showed lower postnatal reflective functioning relaped to substance use more often after treatment, and their children were more likely to be placed in foster care (Pajulo et al., 2012) further highlighting the importance of focusing on maternal mentalizing capabilities within treatment.

Finally, given that replacement therapy of pregnant opioid-dependent women using methadone, and more recently buprenorphine, has been shown to reduce the number of birth complications and us of street drugs during pregnancy (Fischer et al., 1998; Fischer et al., 2006), it becomes relevant to evaluate the effects from child developmental viewpoint. With methadone maintenance treatment, early studies have found differences on the Bayley Scales of Infant Development between exposed and comparison groups, differences which disappeared by 4 years of age (Kaltenbach & Finnegan, 1984). Other research indicates that methadone infants, as compared to nonexposed infants, have shown poorer motor coordination at 4 months and poorer attention at 12 months but this association was also shown to be moderated by various family factors (Marcus, Hans, & Jeremy, 1984). Evaluations of an antenatal surveillance program using buprenorphine replacement therapy at the Helsinki University Central Hospital (HUCH) have shown that there are still many problems for both the infant and mother after birth (Hytinantti et al., 2008, Kahila et al., 2007). First, not all mothers complied with the drug maintenance program offered during pregnancy. Second, many infants suffered from neonatal abstinence syndrome (NAS) after birth. Third, the psycho-social risk status of the group was evident in that less than 20% of the infants were discharged home with the mother after birth (Hytinantti et al., 2008). Finally, our studies have shown that from a child developmental perspective, a group of buprenorphine-exposed infants earned the lowest Bayley-II MDI scores during infancy as well as scored the lowest in infant involvement as compared to both normative and depressed mother sample. The role of environmental risk factors, in turn, was highlighted in that the mothers scored the lowest in maternal sensitivity, structuring and nonintrusiveness. (Salo et al., 2010). However, it has also recently been shown that mothers under medically supervised use of methadone presented as good-enough partners in dyadic interaction when the infants were six months old (Sarfi, Smith, Waal & Sundet, 2011). This may imply that whereas addicted women certainly have difficulties in some parenting domains, they are not necessarily seriously impaired in all aspects of how they relate to their children as also shown in other studies (see Luthar, Doyle, Suchman, & Mayes, 2001). Nevertheless, from a clinical point of view, it is important to recognize that mothers who are seeking recovery from drug addiction still need to overcome many personal challenges to maintain their sobriety and adjust to their parenting role. Involvement in drug rehabilitation may shift the maternal focus from the infant's needs because of the effects of drug withdrawal, underlying mental-health issues and dealing with other psychosocial stressors, complying with treatment programs in itself or the preoccupation with self that is required by the treatment process (Sarfi et al., 2011).

Summary

Children who experience either prenatal or postnatal exposure to parental addiction are at risk for a range of emotional, academic, and developmental problems. They are more likely to be at risk for disruptions on early interaction and insecure or disorganized attachment formation, to score lower on cognitive and other achievement tests especially after infancy, to experience difficulties in attentional control and emotion regulation, as well as in later social cognitive skills, and to suffer from psychiatric disorders. These children may from the very beginning behave in ways that are challenging for biological or foster parents to manage, which can lead to inconsistent caregiving and multiple alternative care placements. Positive social and emotional child development generally has been linked to family settings in which caregivers are nurturing and daily routines are predictable.

However, such circumstances are often missing in the homes of children living with parental addiction. As a result, extra supports and interventions are needed to help children to maximize their natural potential despite their home environments. Intervention strategies need to be developmentally tuned to specifically address the cognitive, motor as well as emotional delays evident in the children of substance using parents. They also need to focus on the emotional parent-child relationship as well as on other aspects of parental psychic well-being and family dynamics in order to increase the number of protective factors, such as the involvement of other supportive adults (e.g., extended family members, mentors, clergy, teachers, neighbors), that may help mitigate the impact of parental addiction on child developmental outcome.

■ REFERENCES

Ackerman, J. P., Llorente, A. M., Black, M. M., Ackerman, C., Mayes, L. A., Nair, P. (2008). The effect of prenatal drug exposure and caregiving contexts on children's performance on a task of sustained visual attention. *Journal of Developmental and Behavioral Pediatrics, 29,* 467–474.

Alessandri, S., M., Sullivan, M. W., Bendersky, M., & Lewis, M. (1995). Temperament in cocaine-exposed infants. In M. Lewis & M. Bendersky (Eds.), *Mothers, babies and cocaine: The role of toxins in development*(pp. 273–286). Hillsdale, NJ: Erlbaum.

Ammerman, R.T., Kolko, D., J., Kirisci, L., Blackson, T. C., & Dawes, M. A. (1999). Child abuse potential in parents with histories of substance use disorder. *Child Abuse & Neglect, 23,* 1225–1238.

Arendt, R. E., Short, E., Singer, L.T., Minnes, S., Hewitt, J., Flynn, S., Carlson, L., Min, M.O., Klein, N., & Flannery, D. (2004). Children prenatally exposed to cocaine: Developmental outcomes and environmental risks at seven years of age. *Developmental and Behavioural Pediatrics, 25,* 83–90.

Azuma, S.D. & Chasnoff, I.J. (1993). Outcome of children prenatally exposed to cocaine and other drugs: a path analysis of three-year data. *Pediatrics, 92,* 396–402.

Bakermans-Kranenburg, M.J., Van IJzendoorn, M- H., Juffer, F. (2005). Disorganized infant attachment and preventive interventions: A review and meta-analysis. *Infant Mental Health Journal, 26,* 191–216.

Bandstra, E. S., Morrow, C. E., Anthony, J. C., Accornero, V. H., & Fried, P. A. (2001). Longitudinal investigation of task persistence and sustaided attention in children with prenatal cocaine exposure. *Neurotoxicology and Teratotology, 23,* 545–559.

Bandstra, E.S., Morrow, C.E., Vogel, A.L., Fifer, R.C., Ofir, A.Y., Dausa, A.T., Xue, L., & Anthony, J. C. (2002). Longitudinal influence of prenatal cocaine exposure on child language functioning. *Neurotoxicology & Teratology, 24,* 297–308.

Bandstra, E. S., Vogel., A. L., Morrow, C. E., Xue, L., Anthony, J. C. (2004). Severity of prenatal cocaine exposure and child language functioning through are seven years: A longitudinal latent growth curve analysis. *Substance Use and Misuse 39,* 25–59.

Bays, J. (1990). Substance abuse and child abuse. *Pediatrics Clinics of North America, 37,* 881–904.

Bendersky, M., & Lewis, M. (1998). Prenatal cocaine exposure and impulse control at two years. *Annals of the New York Academy of Science, 846,* 365–367.

Bennet, D. S., Bendersky, M., & Lewis, M. (2002). Children's intellectual and emotional-behavioral adjustment at 4 years as a function of cocaine exposure, maternal character-istics and environmental risk. *Developmental Psychology, 38,* 648–658.

Bernstein, V.J., & Hans, S.L. (1994). Predicting the developmental outcome of two-year-old children born exposed to methadone: The impact of social-environmental risk factors. *Journal of Clinical Psychology, 23,* 349–359.

Bernstein, V.J., Jeremy, R.J., & Marcus, J. (1986). Mother-infant interaction in multiproblem families: Finding those at risk. *Journal of American Academy of Child Psychiatry, 25,* 631–640.

Biringen, Z. & Easterbrooks, A.E. (2008). Understanding relationships and relationship interventions. *Journal of Early Childhood and Infant Psychology, 4,* 1–3.

Bradley, R.H., Corwyn, R.F., 2002. Socioeconomic status and child development. *Annual Review Psychology, 53,* 371–399.

Brooks, C.S., Zuckerman, B., Bamforth, A., Cole, J., & Kaplan-Sanoff, M. (1994). Clinical issues related to substance-involved mothers and their infants. *Infant Mental Health Journal, 15,* 202–217.

Brown, J. V., Bakeman, R., Coles, C. D., Platzman, K. A., & Lynch, M. E. (2004). Prenatal cocaine exposure: A comparison of 2-year-old children in parental and nonparental care. *Child Development 75,* 1282–1295.

Burns, K. A., Chethik, L., Burns, W. J., & Clark, R. (1997). The early relationship of drug abusing mothers and their infants: as assessment at eight to twelve months of age. *Journal of Clinical Psychology 53,* 279–287.

Carta, J. J., Atwater, J. B., Greenwood, C. R., McConnell, S. R., McEvoy, M. A., & Williams, R. (2001). Effects of cumulative prenatal substance exposure and environmental risks on children's developmental trajectories. *Journal of Clinical Child Psychology, 30,* 327–337.

Chaplin, T.M., Fahy, R., Sinha, R., & Mayes, L. C. (2009). Emotional arousal and regula-tion in cocaine exposed toddlers: implications for behavior problems across a three-year follow-up. *Neurotoxicology and Teratology, 31,* 275–282.

Chaplin. T. M., Freiburger, M. B., Mayes, L. C., & Sinha, R. (2010). Prenatal cocaine exposure, gender, and adolescent stress response: a prospective longitudinal study. *Neurotoxicology and Teratology, 32,* 595–604.

Chiriboga, C. A., (2003). Fetal alcohol and drug effects. *The Neurologist 9,* 267–279.

Cicchetti, D., & Begley, M. (1987). Symbolic development in maltreated youngsters: An organizational perspective. *New Directions for Child Development, 36,* 5–29.

Das Eiden, R. (2001). Maternal substance abuse and mother-infant feeding interactions. *Infant Mental Health Journal 22,* 497–511.

Egeland, B., Yates, T., Appleyard, K., van Dulmen, M. (2002). The long-term consequences of maltreatment in the early years: a developmental pathway model to antisocial behav-ior. *Children's Services, 5,* pages 249–260.

Fischer, G., Etzerdorfer, P., Eder, H., Jagsch, R., Langer, M., & Weninger, M. (1998). Buprenorphine maintenance in pregnant opiate addicts. *European Addiction Research, 4(1),* 32–36.

Fischer G. Ortner R. Rohrmeister K. Jagsch R. Baewert A. Langer M. Aschauer H. (2006). Methadone versus buprenorphine in pregnant addicts: a double-blind, double-dummy comparison study. *Addiction. 101(2),* 275–81.

Finnegan, L.P. (1984). Neonatal abstinence. In: M. N. (Ed.). *Current therapy in neonatal and perinatal medicine* (pp. 314–320).Ontario: BC Decker Inc.

Fitzgerald, E., Kaltenbach, L., & Finnegan, L. (1990). Patterns of interaction among drug dependent women and their infants. *Pediatric Research, 10*, 24.

Frank, D. A., Jacobs, R. R., Beeghly, M., Augystyn, M., Bellinger, D., Cabral, H., & Heeren, T. (2002). Level of prenatal cocaine exposure and scores on the Bayley Scales of Infant Development: modifying effects of caregiver, early intervention, and birth weight. *Pediatrics, 110*, 1143–1152.

Fraser, J.G., Harris-Britt, A., Thakkallapalli, E.L., Kurtz-Costes, B., & Martin, S. (2010). Emotional Availability and Psychosocial Correlates among Mothers in Substance-Abuse Treatment and Their Young Infants. *Infant Mental Health Journal, 31*, 1–15.

Fried, P. A. (2002). Conceptual issues in bheavioral teratology and their application in determining long-term sequelae of prenatal marihuana exposure. *Journal of Child Psychology and Psychiatry and Allied Disciplines, 43*, 81–102.

Fried, P. A., O'Connell, C. M., Watkinson, B. (1992). 60- and 72-month follow-up of children prenatally exposed to marijuana, cigarettes, and alcohol: Cognitive and language assessment. *Journal of Developmental and Behavioral Pediatrics, 13*, 383–391.

Fried, P. A., & Smith, A. M. (2001). A literature review of the consequences of prenatal marijuana exposure. An emerging theme of a deficiency in aspects of executive function. *Neurotoxicology and Teratology, 23*, 1–11.

Fried, P. A., Watkinson, B., & Gray, R. (1998). Differential effects on cognitive functioning in 9- and 12-year olds prentally exposed to cigarettes and marijuana. *Neurotoxicology and Teratology, 25*, 427–436.

Gabel, S., & Shindledecker, R. (1993). Parental substance abuse and its relationship to severe aggression and antisocial behavior in youth. *American Journal of Addiction, 2*, 48–58.

Glantz, M. D., & Chambers, J. C. (2006). Prenatal drug exposure effects on subsequent vulnerability to drug abuse. *Development and Psychopathology, 18*, 893–922.

Goldsmith, L., Richardson, G. A., Cornelius, M. D., & Day, N. L. (2004). Prenatal marijuana and alcohol exposure and academic achievement at age 10. *Neurotoxicology and Teratology, 26*, 521–532.

Hans, S. L. (2002). Studies of prenatal exposure to drugs. Focusing on parental care of children. *Neurotoxicology and Teratology 24*, 329–337.

Hans, J., & Jeremy, R. J. (2001). Postneonatal mental and motor development of infants exposed in utero to opioid drugs. *Infant Mental Health Journal, 22*, 300–315.

Higgins, S. (2002). Smoking in pregnancy. *Current Opinion in Obstetrics and Gynecology 10*, 145–151.

Hytinantti, T., Kahila, H., Reblund, M., Järvenpää, A.-L., Halmesmäki, E., & Kivitie-Kallio, S. (2008). Neonatal outcome of 58 infants exposed to maternal buprenorphine in utero. *Acta Paediatrica, 97 (8)*, 1040–1044l

Johnson, A. L., Morrow, C. E., Accorno, V. H., Xue, L., Anthony, J. C., & Bandstra, E. S. (2002). Maternal cocaine use: estimated effects on mother-child play interactions in the preschool period. *Journal of Developmental and Behavioral Pediatrics, 23*, 191–20.

Kaltenbach, K., & Finnegan, L.P. (1984). Developmental outcome of children born to methadone maintained women: a review of longitudinal studies. *Neurobehavioral Toxigology & Teratology, 6(4)*, 271–275.

Kahila, H., Saisto, T., Kivitie-Kallio, S., Haukkamaa, M., & Halmesmaki E. (2007). A prospective study on buprenorphine use during pregnancy: effects on maternal and neonatal outcome. *Acta Obstetricia et Gynecologica Scandinavica, 86(2)*, 185–190.

Kelley, M., & Fals-Stewart, W. (2004). Psychiatric disorders of children living with drug-abusing, alcohol-abusing, and non-substance-abusing fathers. *Journal of the American Academy of Child and Adolescent Psychiatry, 43*, 621–628.

Kilbride, H., Castor, C. R. N., Hoffman, E., & Fuger, K. L. (2000). Thirty-six-month outcome of prenatal cocaine exposure for term or near-term infants: impact of early case management. *Journal of Developmental and Behavioral Pediatrics, 21*, 19–26.

Lester, B.M., Tronick, E.Z., LaGasse L., Seifer, R., Bauer, C. R., Shankaran, S., Bada, H. S., Wright, L. L., Smeriglio, V. L., Lu, J., Finnegan, L. P., & Maza, P. L. (2002). The maternal lifestyle study: effects of substance exposure during pregnancy on neurodevelopmental outcome in 1-month-old infants. *Pediatrics, 110*, 1182–1192.

Lifschitz, M.H., & Wilson, G.S. (1991). Patterns of growth and development in narcotic-exposed children. In: M.M. Kilbey, K. Asghar (Eds.). *Methodological Issues in Comparisonled Studies on Effects of Prenatal Exposure to Drug Abuse, NIDA Research Monographs, 114*, 323–339. Rockville, MD:

Luthar, S.S., Cushing, G., Merikangas, K. R., & Rounsaville, B. J. (1998). Multiple jeopardy: risk/protective factors among addicted mothers' offspring. *Developmental Psychopathology, 11*, 117–136.

Luthar, S. S., Doyle, K., Suchman, N. E., & Mayes, L. (2001). Developmental themes in women's emotional experiences of motherhood. *Development and Psychopathology, 13(01)*, 165–182.

Lyons-Ruth, K., Alpern, L., & Rapacholi, B. (1993). Disorganized infant attachment classification and maternal psychosocial problems as predictors of hostile-aggressive behavior in the preschool classroom. *Child Development, 64*, 572–585.

Marcus, J., Hans, S.L., & Jeremy, R.J. (1984). A longitudinal study of offspring born to methadone-maintained women. III. Effects of multiple risk factors on development at 4, 8, and 12 months. *American Journal of Drug & Alcohol Abuse. 10(2)*, 195–207.

Mayes, L.C. (1995). Substance abuse and parenting. In: M.H. Bornstein (Ed.), *Handbook of parenting*: vol. 4. *Applied and practical parenting* (pp. 101–126). Erlbaum, Mahwah, NJ.

Mayes, L. C. (1999). Developing brain and in utero cocaine exposure; Effects on neural ontogeny. *Development and Psychopathology, 11*, 685–714.

Mayes, L. C., Cicchetti, D., Acharyya, S., & Zhang, H. (2003). Developmental trajectories of cocaine-and-other-drug-exposed and non-cocaine-exposed children. *Journal of Developmental and Behavioral Pediatrics, 24*, 323–335.

Mayes, L., C., & Fahy, T. (2001). Prenatal drug exposure and cognitive development. In R. J. Sternberg & E. L., Grigorenko (Eds.), *Environmental effects on cognitive abilities* (pp.189–219). Mahwah, NJ: Erlbaum.

Mayes, L. C., Feldman, R., Granger, R. H., Haynes, O. M., Bornstein, M. H., & Schottenfeld, R. (1997). The effects of polydrug use with and without cocaine on mother-infant interaction at 3 and 6 months. *Infant Behavior and Development, 20*, 489–502.

McCreight, B. (1997). *Recognizing and managing children with fetal alcohol syndrome/fetal alcohol effects: A guidebook* (pp. 9–15). Washington, DC: Child Welfare League of America.

Mun, E. Y., Fitzgerald, H. E., Von Eye, A., Puttler, L. I. & Zucker, R. A., (2001). Temperamental characteristics as predictors of externalizing and internalizing child behavior problems in the contexts of high and low parental psychopathology. *Infant Mental Health Journal*, 2, 393–415.

Moe, V., & Slinning, K. (2001). Children prenatally exposed to substances: gender-related differences in outcome from infancy to 3 years of age. *Infant Mental Health Journal 22*, 334–350.

Morrison, D. C., Cerles, L., Montaini-Klovdahl, L., & Skowron, E. (2000). Prenatally drug-exposed toddlers: cognitive and social development. *American Journal of Orthopsychiatry*, 70, 278–283.

Nair, P., Schuler, M. E., Black, M. M., Kettinger L., & Harrington, D. (2003). Cumulative environmental risk in substance abusing women: early intervention, parenting stress, child abuse potential and child development. *Child Abuse and Neglect, 27*, 997–1017.

O'Connor, M.J., Sigman, M., & Brill, N. (1987). Disorganization of attachment in relation to maternal alcohol consumption. *Journal of Consulting and Clinical Psychology, 55*, 831–836.

Pajulo M, Suchman N, Kalland M, Mayes L.C. (2006). Enhancing the effectiveness of residential treatment for substance abusing pregnant and parenting women: focus on maternal reflective functioning and mother-child relationship. *Infant Mental Health Journal, 27(5)*, 448–65.

Pajulo M., Pyykkönen N., Kalland, M., Sinkkonen, J., Helenius, H., Punamäki R-L. (2011). Substance abusing mothers in residential treatment with their babies: postnatal psychiatric symptomatology and its association with mother-child relationship and later need for child protection actions. *Nordic Journal of Psychiatry, 65(1)*, 65–73.

Pajulo M, Pyykkönen N, Kalland M, Sinkkonen J, Helenius H, Punamäki R-L., Suchman N. (2012). Substance-abusing mother-baby pairs in residential treatment: importance of pre-and postnatal reflective functioning. *Infant Mental Health Journal, 33*(1),70–81.

Petterson, S. M., & Albers, A., B. (2001). Effects of poverty and maternal depression on early child development. *Child Development, 72*, 1794–1813.

Pidgeon, A. M., & Sanders, M. R. (2009). Attribution, parental anger and risk of maltreatment. *International Journal of Child Health and Human Development, 1*, 57–69.

Riley, E.P., & McGee, C.L. (2005). Fetal alcohol spectrum disorders: an overview with emphasis on changes in brain and behavior. *Experimental Biology and Medicine, 230*, 6, 357–365.

Robinson, L. R., Sheffield Morris, A., Scott Heller, A., Scheeringa, M. S., Boris, N. W., & Smyke, A. T. (2009). Relations between emotion regulation, parenting, and psychopathology in young maltreated children in out of home care. *Journal of Child and Family Studies, 18*, 421–434.

Rodning, C., Beckwith, L., & Howard, J. (1989). Characteristics of attachment organization and play organization in prentally drug-exposed toddlers. *Development and Psychopathology, 1*, 277–289.

Salo, S., Politi, J., Tupola, S.-M., Biringen, Z., Kalland, M., Halmesmäki, E., Kahila, H., & Kivitie-Kallio, S. (2010). Early development of opioid-exposed infants born to mothers in buprenorphine-replacement therapy. *Journal of Reproductive and Infant Psychology, 28*, 161–179.

Salo, S., Kivistö, K., Korja, R., Biringen, Z., Tupola, S.-M., Kahila, H., & Kivitie-Kallio, S. et al. (2009). Emotional availability, parental self-efficacy beliefs and child development in caregiver-child relationships with buprenorphine-exposed 3-year-olds. *Parenting, 9,* 244–259.

Sameroff, A.J., & Fiese, B. H. (1990). Transactional regulation and early intervention. In: S. J. Meisels & J.P. Shonkoff (Eds.), *Handbook of early childhood intervention.* (pp. 119–149). New York: Cambridge University Press.

Sarfi, M., Smith, L., Waal, H., & Sundet, J. M. (2011). Risks and realities: Dyadic interaction between 6-month-old infants and their mothers in opioid maintenance treatment. *Infant Behavior and Development, 34,* 578–589. Shipman, K., Edwards, A., Brown, A., Swisher, L., & Jennings, E. (2005). Managing emotion in maltreating context: A pilot study examining child neglect. *Child Abuse and Neglect, 29,* 1015–1029.

Schuler, M. E., Nair, P., & Kettinger, L. (2003). Drug-exposed infants and developmental outcome: effects of home intervention and ongoing maternal drug use. *Archives of Pediatrics and Adolescent Medicine 157,* 133–138.

Swanson, K., Beckwith, L., & Howard, J. (2000). Intrusive caregiving and quality of attachment in prenatally drug-exposed toddlers and their primary caregivers. *Attachment and Human Development, 2,* 130–148.

Tarabulsy, G. M., St-Laurent, D., Cyr, C., Pascuzzo, K., Moss, E., Bernier, A., & Dubois-Contois, K. (2008). Attachment-based intervention for maltreating families. *American Journal of Orthopsychiatry, 78,* 322–332.

Tronick, E., & Beeghly, M. (1999). Prenatal cocaine exposure, child development, and the compromising effects of cumulative risk. *Clinics in Perinatology 26,* 151–171.

Tronick, E.Z., Messinger, D.S., Weinberg, M.K., Lester, B.M., LaGasse, L., Seifer, R., Bauer, C.R., Shankaran S., Bada, H., Wright, L.L., Poole, K., & Liu, J. (2005). Cocaine exposure is associated with subtle compromises if infants' and mothers' social-emotional behavior and dyadic features of their interaction in the face-to-face still-face paradigm. *Developmental Psychology, 41,* 711–722.

Weich, S., Patterson, J., Shaw, R., & Stewart-Brown, S. (2009). Family relationships in childhood and common psychiatric disorders in later life: a systematic review of prospective studies. *The British Journal of Psychiatry, 194,* 392–398.

Zuckerman, B., & Brown, E.R. (1993). Maternal substance abuse and infant development. In: C.H. Zeanah (Ed.), *Handbook of infant mental health* (pp. 143–158). New York: Guilford Press.

11 Pre- and Perinatal Intervention for Substance Using Mothers

ZACK BOUKYDIS

■ INTRODUCTION

There has been increasing recognition that new models of substance abuse treatment are needed for women who are mothers (Finkelstein, 1996; Kerwin, 2005; Osterling & Austin, 2008) and especially for women in the pre- and peri-natal period (Jansson, Svikis, Lee, et al., 1996; Ashley, Marsden & Brady, 2003; Suchman, Mayes, Conti, Slade, & Rounsaville, 2004; Twomey, Soave, Gil, & Lester 2005; Suchman, Pajulo, DeCoste & Mayes, 2006; Armstrong, 2008). Fifteen years ago, in a paper titled "Keeping Mothers and Infants Together," my colleagues and I stated that, whenever possible, women involved in illegal substance use during pregnancy should not be separated from their infants following positive toxicology screens at birth but should instead be supported with adequate and comprehensive services (Lester, Affleck, Boukydis et al., 1996). The services that we advocated were innovations in treatment programs whose purpose was to transform existing models of drug treatment, support mothers and infants, and remove barriers to growth in the developing attachment relationship.

Over the years since our "Keeping Mothers and Infants Together" paper was published, there have been larger, more comprehensive studies of factors influencing the development of substance-exposed infants, including the caregiving environment and the early attachment relationship (Seifer et al., 2004; Mayes and Pajulo; 2006; Sheinkopf et al., 2006). Parallel to these studies with their developmental and attachment-based foci, there have been studies of different forms of treatment that include, not only examination of effects of maternal drug use status and psychological functioning, but also the concomitant effects on their children's developmental status over time (Jones, 2006). Accumulating evidence indicates that, when women are able to be in treatment with their children, there are lower rates of relapse (Roberts & Nishimoto, 1996). Furthermore, when treatment programs include a parenting component and services for children and families, there are higher rates of treatment success, better developmental status of the children, and other indicators of family stability (Roberts & Nishimoto, 1996; Szuster, Rich, Chung, & Bisconer, 1996; Kaltenbach & Finnegan, 1998; Jones, 2006).

This chapter focuses on the development of an intervention for substance abusing women in residential treatment. The intervention includes a prenatal and a postnatal component that together support the mother–infant relationship in the perinatal period. The intervention was established based on communication with parents, observations of parents and their at-risk infants, and assessment of infant neurobehavior. In this context, the neurobehavioral assessment combined traditional evaluation of infant reflexes and motor tone with observation and assessment of infant attentional and regulatory abilities (Lester & Tronick, 2004). The intervention was developed and then integrated into ongoing drug abuse treatment.

■ BACKGROUND

Teratogenic versus Transactional Models of Infant Development

Early on in the study of substance abuse and parenting, there were reports of the incidence of damage to organ and brain structures in substance-exposed infants. These findings were paralleled by a tendency in the public to envision substance-exposed infants as having moderate to severe organic damage. The stereotype included a morose picture of infants who were extremely irritable, underweight, and very difficult to soothe (Mayes, Granger, Bornstein, & Zuckerman, 1992).

The next generation of research (Lester, Tronick, LaGasse, et al., 2002) involved larger samples than those in the original reports and gave rise to a dialectic between what came to be known as *teratogenic* versus *transactional* models of behavior and development of substance-exposed infants (Hans, 2002; Sameroff, 2004; Mayes & Pajulo, 2005). (The teratogenic models assumed drugs in the bloodstream in pregnancy were most likely to injure cells and cell differentiation, while the transactional models assumed that drugs may affect neurotransmitter mechanisms and may or may not be compensated for by early environmental influences.) In addition to ongoing efforts to determine biological compromise in pregnancy (i.e., teratogenic effects), another focus (i.e., transactional) was on issues related to interactions between infants (sometimes with neurobehavioral vulnerabilities) and their early caregiving environment (Lester, Bagner, Liu, Lagasse, Seifer, Bauer et al., 2009). Here, too, there has often been a lag in perception and understanding from the public at large, treatment providers, and women themselves about the behavior, early development, and caretaking needs of substance-exposed infants (Kuecks-Morgan, 1999; Lester, Boukydis, & Twomey, 2000).

The interventions described in this chapter had to address the potential misperceptions not of only mothers about their infants, but also of treatment providers about what kinds of direct interventions and services were needed to treat and support women and their infants. The infants might have had needs that could be addressed by the healthcare and early intervention system but also had issues that were commonly referred to (by developmental specialists) as challenges in early regulation (Lester & Tronick, 1994).

The challenges in "early regulation" involved not only the infant's neurobehavior but also the infant's mother who was new to recovery and in some ways a neophyte in learning to recognize, hold, and attend to her own emotional reactions. Consequently, both members of the dyad were often having challenges in early regulation. A new treatment model had to respect what was known about regulation of the individuals in the dyad while also attending to and supporting the co-regulation of perceptions, interactions, and attachment.

Early Interaction Between Mothers and Infants

Many studies of mother–infant interaction in the population of substance using women and their infants indicate problems in maternal behavior—particularly with reading infant signals; effective soothing and management strategies; and successful management of daily cycles of feeding, sleep, and play (Kaltenbach & Finnegan, 1998;Pajulo, Savonlahti, & Piha, 1999; Pajulo, Savonlahti, Sourander, et al., 2001; Savonlahti, Pajulo, Ahlqvist, et al., 2005; Tronick et al., 2005). These early difficulties can lead to increased parental stress, maternal reactivity, lowered maternal self esteem, difficulty arranging the environment to meet the infant's needs for appropriate stimulation, and difficulty in the early formation of mother–child attachment (Egeland & Erikson, 1990). The perinatal period is a critical time for supporting women as they take on responsibilities of parenting while learning the emotional lessons necessary for themselves in treatment and recovery (Jannson, Svikis, Lee, Paluzzi, Rutigliano, & Hackerman, 1996; Pajulo, Suchman, Kalland, & Mayes, 2006; Mayes, Magidson, Lejuez, & Nicholls, 2009).

Clinical Understanding of the Mother's Representations

In a simple sense, an intervention must not only help a mother read and interpret her infant's states and requirements for soothing but also help her process and change her emotional reactions, which, at times, may prevent her from seeing her infant clearly. The representational processes of women who have used and abused substances are complex, especially because they involve the mother's view of herself in relation to her infant. In Stern's (2004) normative perspective on the "Motherhood Constellation," there are several central questions involving women's thoughts about themselves as they move through pregnancy and give birth:

1. "Will I be able to keep my baby alive and growing?" (*Life Growth* theme);
2. "Will I be able to have a satisfying and sustainable emotional engagement with my baby?"(*Primary Relatedness* theme);
3. "Am I capable of providing a nurturing environment, a home life for my baby?" (*Supporting Matrix* theme) and
4. "Will I be able to change or transform my self-identify to support the other three functions?" (*Identity Reorganization* theme).

There are potential variations to these themes with women who have had a long period of trauma and substance use. The following version of Stern's motherhood, called *Motherhood for Women in Recovery*, was developed accordingly:

1. Do I have the inner emotional resources (and who are my models of stable secure mothering?) to keep my baby alive and growing? (*Life Growth* theme);
2. As I heal the troubles of my own past, how will I be able to keep myself open to my baby's emotional signals and emotional needs and learn to be her secure base while I am learning to be a secure base for myself? (*Primary Relatedness* theme);

3. How can I, who survived in transitional, sometimes chaotic and dangerous, environments, learn to provide and maintain a stable "home" life for myself and my baby? (*Supporting Matrix* theme); and

4. When and how will I learn to love and respect myself enough (not denying but realistically accepting my addictive patterns) and see myself as an adequate and loving mother for this baby? (*Identity Reorganization* theme).

These modified themes are one example of how training for drug abuse treatment staff can be structured to introduce staff to important issues related to child development, mothering, and the fundamentals of infant mental health (see below). Importantly, these questions have formed the basis for staff reflection and discussion, including how accurate or representative the questions are; how they might be over-generalized (e.g., viewing all women who use substances during pregnancy this way); how they might serve to blind clinicians to a mother's true, often hidden, experience; and how they might help clinicians understand mother–baby interactions. Also central to this questioning is a model that views change in a woman's representational process as an important mediator of her developing ability to understand her infant's neurobehavior and engage in responsive interactions that are likely to promote her child's optimal development.

■ THE PERINATAL INTERVENTION

A Clinical Vignette: A Traumatic Event in a Baby's Life and His Mother's Changing Representations of Herself

In my capacity as a medical school and hospital-based applied researcher and clinician, I served as a consultant to a residential drug treatment program where women in recovery lived with their infants. The drug treatment program was in Providence, Rhode Island. Willie (pseudonym), at five days of age, appeared to his mother and the clinic staff very dusky in skin color and was very labored in his breathing. He and his mother were rushed to hospital, where, after repeated attempts to stimulate his heart and breathing, he was pronounced dead. I arrived at the hospital at this time to find his mother and family grieving. While we sat, a doctor entered the waiting room to say that, miraculously, Willie's heart had begun beating while he lay on the examining table, that he was being helped to breathe, and that he needed to be rushed to a larger hospital for emergency heart surgery. Although one can never truly know, some doctors believed that a duct in Willie's aorta that usually closes in the first days of life (permanently changing blood circulation from fetal circulation to post-birth, heart-pumped circulation) had reopened during the moments following the stoppage of heartbeat and breathing. There was probably a relaxation of muscle tone, the duct reopened, blood began to circulate, and Willie's heart somehow began to beat again. It's easy to imagine what an immensely powerful experience this was for Willie's mother, family, and all of us who were present.

Three months later, I waited with the staff and residents of the program for Willie and his mother to return from his second trip to the hospital for corrective surgery. When he arrived in his infant seat, Willie looked at everyone curiously, and then smiled the brightest smile. Most cried and everyone laughed and smiled. Here was this baby who had almost died, and who had since been through two major heart surgeries, beaming at us.

Months later, his mother spoke about this time with Willie as the turning point in her recovery from severe drug addiction. She was so deeply moved by Willie's will to live, and slowly realized that if he, who was in some ways so helpless and small, had the will to live, then she could only have a will to live also. As she loved Willie, she could begin to love herself. In a talk with me, she said that she had begun to identify with, hold, and nurture the willful, still alive, child in herself that survived all of her traumas. She no longer could see herself as just wounded, bad, guilty, and shameful.

While this story has unique elements, one central theme is that, as parents recognize (and hopefully identify with) key facets of newborn neurobehavioral functioning, their view of themselves as someone who produced a wounded child with a poor future may be genuinely challenged.

Intervention Objectives

Inherent in this intervention focusing on looking at the infant with mothers are the following touchstones for consultation:

1. *See aspects of the infant that are truly endearing;*
2. *Recognize aspects of the infant's behavior and functioning that are adaptive and organizing,* and
3. *Be realistic about concerns (not pathologies) in functioning,* but also
4. *Give the message that the infant will be caringly and intelligently watched and that the parent will be "teamed up with" by providers who will help the mother care for her baby* (Boukydis, 2012).

Developmental Principles

Multilevel Intervention

As drug treatment services for women advance, there is an ongoing need for differentiation among models of infant/child development, especially in terms of how they understand and address issues of risk and resiliency at multiple levels (e.g., individual, dyadic, triadic, and family) when substance use and abuse is a major disruptive influence (Lester, Masten, & McEwen, 2006). For example, in a review of six published reports of outpatient interventions aiming to enhance the caregiving skills of substance-abusing mothers caring for children between birth and five years of age, Suchman and colleagues (2006) found that only one intervention targeted change at multiple levels (e.g., women's emotional reactions to their infant as well as infant behavior; Field et al., 1998). The intervention described in this chapter also aimed to integrate advanced understanding of infant neurobehavior in the pre- and perinatal period with careful attention to changing women's representational and emotional reactions to their infant's behavior.

The Four A's of Infancy

In a paper titled "Four A's of Infancy," Lester and Tronick (1994) gave an important conceptual framework for the neurobehavioral functioning and development of substance-exposed infants. The Four A's are:

1. *Attention,* which refers to perceptual abilities that relate to the intake and processing of information from the environment,
2. *Arousal,* which includes control and modulation of behavioral states from sleep to waking to crying, ability to display the entire range of states, excitation, and inhibition of incoming stimuli,
3. *Affect,* which relates to the development of sociality and emotion, the mutual regulatory processes of social interaction and social relationships, and
4. *Action,* which indicates motor function, the development of fine and gross motor skills, and the acquisition of knowledge and social exchange through motor patterns.

The Four A's provide the basis for training interventionists to use neurobehavioral assessment to guide parents, who are often faced with learning to interpret the patterns of behavior of their infants while facing extra challenges in early parenting (e.g., managing crying, establishing functional and satisfying feeding, and developing a daily, predictable rhythm in infants' lives). A later-developed phase of the collaboration involved establishing referrals to a hospital-based Infant Crying Sleep and Behavior Clinic (Boukydis, High, Cucca, & Lester, 1997) to support women whose infants have excessive crying, colic, reflux, and early sleep and feeding concerns.

The Four A's framework is also integral to training drug treatment staff who are learning ways to view and support women new to recovery who are adapting to motherhood for the first time as "clean and sober" parents. The Four A's has been combined with a sensory processing framework (see Williamson & Anzalone, 2001) for use in early intervention and has been adapted into a training curriculum for protective service personnel who are required to screen substance-exposed infants in foster placements (Boukydis, 2012).

Early Intervention

Early parent–infant transactions are also considered to be major influences on the development of individuals and dyads (Waschlag & Hans, 1999; Sameroff, 2004; Seifer, Lester, LaGasse, et al., 2004). Therefore, if prevention and/or intervention are warranted, intervention is started as early as possible in the child's development to support the dyad.

Affect Regulation

At-risk infants face multiple vulnerabilities in their affect regulation and emotional arousal that can contribute to developing problems in dyadic interaction and regulation and contribute to possible attachment disorders later on (Lester, Bagner, Liu, et al., 2009). Infant affect regulation is therefore an important focus of assessment and intervention.

Sensitivity to Infant Cues

Parents who persistently misread their infant's signals (often called "mismatches in perception") have a higher likelihood of having children with developmental problems at later stages, including attention difficulties, learning problems, and lower cognitive attainment (Lester, Boukydis, Garcia-Coll, et al., 1995; Scheinkopf, Lester, LaGasse, Seifer, Bauer, Shankaran et al., 2006). The intervention therefore incorporates a focus on assessing and improving the parent's cue recognition and sensitivity.

Key Touchpoints

Touchpoints are periods during the first years of life in which children's spurts in development result in disruption in the family system (see Brazelton & Sparrow, 2006). For at-risk dyads, touchpoints can be critical points of intervention. Two key touchpoints in the developing parent–infant relationship are addressed in the current intervention model—prenatal and neonatal periods. A third touchpoint—the second- to third-month period that includes a "biobehavioral shift" in infant neurobehavioral regulation, was later incorporated into the collaboration with the drug treatment program.

Intervention Planning and Development

During initial intervention planning, there were several issues to address:

1. *Modifying existing services* (i.e., How to modify existing services provided by the drug treatment program to support development of the child and the mother–child relationship);
2. *Incorporating drug treatment professionals into the infant mental health service* (i.e., How to train drug treatment professionals, who had very little training in infant development, parenting of young infants, or infant mental health practice and supervision, to integrate this work into their drug treatment framework and practice);
3. *Integrating infant mental health and drug counseling* (e.g., How to integrate each woman's ongoing drug counseling with the dyadic observations and infant assessments; how to insure that women's reactions during mother–infant consults could be processed and integrated into drug counseling sessions, and how discoveries made in drug counseling might be brought into mother–infant consults); and
4. *Development of new services* (i.e., How to devise new services within and collateral to the program to support the child and the mother–child relationship).

The response to these questions during early planning and after the initial evaluation led to a number of innovations that had both a developmental focus and the intention to support the mother–infant relationship.

Perinatal Intervention

The perinatal intervention was developed first and involved consultants providing co-therapy for mother–infant dyads. Consultants also provided in-service training in infant development and principles of infant mental health for treatment program staff and drug counselors (Boukydis, 2002). The intervention also involved consultation on videotapes of mother–infant interaction and referral to a hospital-based clinic for crying, feeding, and sleep concerns.

Ultrasound Consultation

Following the development of the perinatal intervention, a prenatal ultrasound consultation was also established so that, for many mothers, the initial contact with the consultant during pregnancy included an ultrasound consultation that provided an opportunity to learn about mothers' reactions to seeing their baby during the ultrasound.

Intervention Description

Intervention Providers

The work described in this chapter involved enlisting the expertise of colleagues who studied the developmental outcomes of substance-exposed infants and the importance of developing effective models for supporting and consulting with parents of at-risk infants (Das Eiden & Reifman, 1996; Lester. Boukydis, & Twomey, 2000; Lester & Tronick, 2001). Expertise in the intervention was further enhanced through a collaboration with interested treatment providers in developing new ways to support women in their early interactions with their infants in treatment programs (Lester, Twomey, & Boukydis, 2000; Boukydis & Lester, 2008; Boukydis, 2012).

Intervention Format

The primary intervention began with a two-month series of mother–infant consultations provided during residential treatment following the birth of the infant. Consultants had expertise in infant mental health and infant neurobehavioral assessment. The consultants and drug counselors worked together in pairs as a co-therapeutic team for the mother.

Initial Contact

A consultant met initially with each mother during the month prior to the baby's birth. The purpose of this meeting was to explain the mother–baby sessions and the dual role of the consultant as a liaison between the mother and her drug counselor and between the treatment program and pediatricians who would be following her baby after the baby was born. The meeting provided an opportunity for the consultant to ask the mother how she had been doing with her pregnancy, how she understood and felt about her baby inside, and to insure that adequate prenatal care was being provided.

Intervention Modalities

In order to consult with mothers and their infants in the perinatal period, we used two interrelated modalities: 1) Neonatal Network Neurobehavioral Scale–based (NNNS; Lester & Tronick, 2004) parent–infant consultations (Boukydis & Lester, 2008) in a clinical intervention protocol (see Boukydis, 2012, for a detailed intervention description) and 2) Observing Infants Together with Parents (Boukydis, 2008). The intervention also derived from the Psychosocial Intervention with High Risk Infants and their Families program (Meyer, Lester, Boukydis, Garcia-Coll, & McDonough, 1994) which indicated that consultation in the perinatal period with parents including a neurobehavioral assessment and intensive case management can improve maternal reading of infant signals, as well as reduce maternal depression and costly rehopitalization.

Neonatal Network Neurobehavioral Scale-Based Parent-Infant Consults

The NNNS was originally developed by the NICHD NICU Network for use in a multisite study of the development of preterm/term substance-exposed infants (the Maternal Lifestyles Study; Lester et al., 2002; Lester & Tronick, 2004; Liu, Bann, Lester, et al., 2009). As a neurobehavioral assessment, the NNNS was designed to evaluate infant behavior on three major levels of functioning: 1) *behavioral* (e.g., attention to auditory and visual stimuli, states of consciousness, range of states, ability to be soothed, and irritability); 2) *neurological* (e.g., neonatal reflexes, motor tone and control); and 3) stress-abstinence (i.e., comprehensive checklist of 50 signs of stress in seven categories, including physiological, autonomic, CNS, skin, visual, gastrointestinal, and states of consciousness).

The NNNS was selected as a basis for the intervention for four major reasons:

1. The intervention team had extensive understanding of the value of the neurobehavioral assessment in working with caregivers of at-risk infants;
2. Use of the NNNS in a consultation emphasizes aspects of infant behavior that are closely related to maternal caregiving and attachment-related behavior;
3. The NNNS can be used to document change in infant functioning over time; and
4. The NNNS can be used both as a screen for substance-exposed infants whose mothers are in treatment programs *and* as a context for ongoing consultations with mothers about their infants' changes in neurobehavioral functioning and development based on their care.

The NNNS includes 45 items administered in packages (of similar items; e.g., "lower extremity reflex package" includes all reflex items administered to the feet and legs). In addition, there are 21 summary items that are intended to reflect overall functioning during the exam. The NNNS is appropriate for substance-exposed, pre-term and full-term at-risk infants 32 to 44 weeks' gestational age.

Using the NNNS (see Boukydis, 2012 for further details) as a context for watching the infant's response to handling allows the parent and consultant to observe and comment on the specific areas of functioning that can also be documented in the NNNS scoring system (e.g., efforts to achieve homeostasis, irritability and crying, unique ways of signaling stress, efforts to self-soothe, availability for interaction, emerging developmental steps, and so forth). After each session, these dimensions of infant functioning were jointly summarized by women and the consultant on the "What Happened Today" form (Boukydis, 2012) for the first month and the "My Baby's Development" form (Boukydis & Lester, 2008) for the second month.

Observing Infants Together with Parents

This part of the intervention involves observing an infant with its mother during regular caregiving and playful, nurturing interactions. The observational framework is derived from an understanding of infant neurobehavioral organization used in three neurobehavioral assessments (Neonatal Behavioral Assessment Scale [NBAS; Brazelton & Nugent, 1995], NICU Network Neurobehavioral Scale [NNNS; Lester & Tronick, 2004]; Assessment of Preterm Infant Behavior [APIB; Als, Lester, Tronick & Brazelton, 1982] described in Lester & Tronick, 2001]

During the intervention, infant behavior is observed on five levels simultaneously: 1) *physiological,* 2) *motor tone/motor control,* 3) *states of consciousness /state changes* 4) *interactive exchange with the personal and physical environment* and 5) *signs of stress and signs of regulation and self-soothing* (Boukydis, 2008). In training, consultants use the five levels to observe infants alone and then in typical interactions with parents and infants. In observing infants together with mothers, the consultant often:

1. Waits for the parent to comment and then reinforces or expands on the parent's comment;
2. Asks specific open-ended questions (e.g., "What do you think is going on for her right now?" or "What might she be telling us?");
3. Wonders out loud about specific infant behaviors (e.g., "When she saw your face, her eyes brightened, her breathing became steadier, and she kept her focus on you; I wonder what she is telling you right now?"); and
4. Comments directly on behavior based on the interrelationships of the five levels (e.g.: (a) physiological [breathing rate, skin color, etc.]; (b) motor tone and motor control [muscle tone and smoothness or jitteriness of physical movements]; (c) states and state control [deep sleep, light sleep. drowsy,

awake active awake; crying]; (d) interaction with personal and physical environment [responding to faces, voices, a red ball and rattle]; and (e) signs of stress and self soothing and regulatory behavior).

Women are also encouraged to attend to their own experience of their baby in play and caretaking situations and articulate their own observations (and reactions). The consultant serves as a collaborative observer who wonders aloud about what the baby may be telling the mother, as the mother might also be asking herself the same questions.

The second phase of the Observing Infants Together with Parents work involves taping caretaking and play interactions between mothers and their infants and reviewing them with mothers, and with mothers and their drug counselor. The framework for the video review and dyadic consultation was derived from Interaction Guidance (McDonough, 2004) and integrates the Observing Infants Together with Parents and a parenting group model into a video review format (for women who are receptive). Women observe each other's babies and young children in videotapes of caretaking and play interactions made at the program site and also filmed by the women themselves (during their play, and during caretaking time with their infants in the treatment program).

There were initially two essential elements involved in developing the video review aspect of the consultation: 1) Learning to select segments that reflected strengths in early interactions between mother and baby; and 2) Developing an atmosphere of trust that so that the mother could (a) have the right emotional distance (by seeing herself and her baby in the video segment), (b) explore and reflect on her immediate reactions to herself as mother and to her baby's behaviors), and (c) explore "deeper" reactions that might relate to her previous history of parenting and being parented.

Intervention Evaluation

The intervention was evaluated in a residential drug treatment program in Providence, Rhode Island (see Boukydis & Lester, 2008, for a detailed report). Women entered the treatment program in late pregnancy or with a young infant. The program offered drug treatment, parenting groups, on-site child care, health care for infants and mothers, life-management skills, job training, and extensive follow-up during post-residential treatment. The evaluation involved women who entered the program in the last trimester of pregnancy and who remained in treatment after their infant was born.

The format for the intervention involved two sessions (one Observing Infants with Mothers and one NNNS-based) per week during the first month postpartum and one session per week during the second month. Depending on the dyad's needs, the evaluated intervention phase was followed by a referral to a hospital clinic, Infant Behavior Sleep and Cry clinic, screening and referral to early intervention or ongoing observations and infant–mother dyadic consultation based on Interaction Guidance (McDonough, 2004).

Perinatal Intervention During the Evaluation Study

The sequence of sessions for mothers in the evaluation study was as follows:

(1) Introduction, establishing rapport, NNNS- based consultation, and joint completion of "My Baby's Day" form;
(2) Observing Infant Together with Parent with emphasis on managing feeding and soothing, follow-through on issues related to soothing, reading the infant's behavior on all five levels, joint completion of "My Baby's Day," and videotaping infant behavior for later review (and to show the infant to family and friends).
(3) Joint session with mother, consultant, and drug treatment counselor to provide an update on infant's response to input, handling and soothing.
(4) A consultation session called Observing and Documenting my Baby's Development.

Study Design

The evaluation consisted of analysis of group data from sequential cohorts of women who entered the program during the last trimester of pregnancy. The first three admissions were assigned to the Standard Care (no intervention) group, the next three to the Intervention, and so on. In order to fulfill screening and data collection requirements, the NNNS was completed on Day Five following delivery for all infants, but mothers in the Standard Care group did not observe the NNNS. (The screening using the NNNS was a requirement to make referrals, when necessary, to the pediatric practice that provided pediatric care to the infants in the program.) The Standard Care group received all services provided at the time except for the intervention.

Participants

Sixteen mother–infant pairs were assigned to the Standard Care condition and fifteen to the Intervention condition. Program staff did not know about the study per se; and infants in the Standard Care group received an NNNS screening and clinical status feedback, which took the place of the early intervention sessions with the women and infants. Program administrators selected counselors who would be involved in the standard care or intervention conditions with mothers. The ethnic composition for both groups was nearly identical (NNNS consultation 1st#; Standard care 2nd #: African American, 42%–45% Caucasian, 28%–30% and Hispanic 30%–25%). The groups did not differ significantly on maternal age (NNNS intervention $X = 27.9$ years; Standard care $X = 28.2$ years); or number of years of schooling (NNNS intervention $X = 10$ grades completed; Standard care $X = 10.2$ grades completed).

Parenting Stress Outcomes

The Parenting Stress Index (PSI; Abidin, 1990) was used to measure parenting stress when infants were 2 to 2.5 months old, and the PSI short version when infants were four months' gestational age. At 2 to 2.5 months, in both groups, total results of one-way ANOVAs showed that the Standard Care group (N = 15) had significantly higher scores (X = 151) than did the Intervention group (N = 16) of women (X = 134; P <.05). At 2 to 2.5 months, women in the Standard Care group had significantly higher scores on the Stress from Dysfunctional Parent–Child Interaction subscale of the PSI than did women in the Intervention group. At four months, the shortened 36-item version of the PSI was used (Abidin, 1990). The PSI shortened version yields a total score and 3 factor scores (Parental Distress, Parent–Child Dysfunctional Interaction, and Difficult Child). A sum of the Parental Distress and Parent–Child Dysfunctional Interaction scores were used for this study. Significant differences between the standard care and intervention groups were maintained, with the Intervention group mean average (X = 68.2) and the Standard care mean (X–73.1; P <.05). Based on the overall Parenting Stress Index comparisons, and the subscale Stress from Dysfunctional Parent–Child Interaction, we noted that women in the Intervention group were probably better able to read their infant's signals, help them soothe, and experienced less stress as a result of being able to manage their infant's crying and daily patterns of sleeping, feeding, and crying. Our analyses of NNNS summary scores at five days for both groups of infants indicated that the two groups of infants were similar in the neonatal period in overall neurobehavioral functioning, ranges of states, and irritability. It was probably not infant behavior per se that was contributing to parenting stress, but maternal ability to read and interpret significant aspects of infant behavior, and the "behavior reading" influence of the intervention (Boukydis & Lester, 2008).

Clinical Vignette: Consultation with a Mother and Her Substance-Exposed Infant

A unique strength of the intervention is having an early mother–infant consultation conducted by a professional trained in assessment of high-risk infants and ways to consult with parents using the NNNS and Observing Infants Together with Parents. Clinical training for the intervention consultants involves developing their capacity to read women's emotional availability and listen to their comments within a *representational* framework (common to work in infant mental health; Sameroff & McDonough, 2004). In the following vignette, a consultant responds to comments by focusing on infant behavior that is related to the physical reality of the mother's representation. This consultation was followed by a consultation with the drug treatment counselor about key representational comments that could be followed up on in subsequent treatment sessions.

What follows is part of a transcript of an early consultation with a mother and her infant that took place on the third day of the baby's life (details of the mother and baby have been altered to preserve confidentiality). The mother had entered residential treatment in the last trimester of pregnancy. She was estranged from the baby's father, a man with a history of substance abuse who was also the father of her first child (two years old). She had a lengthy history of involvement with illegal substances and indicated that she used primarily cocaine and alcohol during her current pregnancy. She had received no prenatal care at the time of her entry into the program. During her participation in the program (2½ months) she received prenatal care, daily participation in individual and group counseling, and had stable residence and daily nutrition in the context of the residential program.

Her daughter was born at 38–39 weeks gestational age after 14 hours of labor and a spontaneous vaginal birth. Her daughter was six pounds, 15 ounces (3090 grams), was stable after birth, had Apgar scores of 6 at one minute and 9 at 5 minutes. Mother and daughter left the hospital on the second day of the baby's life to return to the treatment program. The consultant had a consulting relationship with the treatment program that included meeting with mothers during pregnancy; regular consultations with mothers during the first three months of life; meetings with women's counselors and the mothers; and providing training and consultation in child development, infant mental health, and parenting to staff in the treatment program.

The transcript shows the kinds of exchanges that occur during the NNNS portion of the intervention with the mother watching, commenting, and participating. The beginning segment of the consultation is presented here to illustrate which maternal representational comments were noted, addressed, and referenced by the consultant during the joint session with the drug counselor. The transcript is from the first three to five minutes of the session. Representational comments noted by the consultant are underlined and subtle emphases by the consultant are in *italics*. The transcript begins one hour after the beginning of the consultation meeting, during which time the NNNS assessment had been completed (n.b.: not all NNNS items are noted in this segment). The segment begins with the baby dressed and lying on the bed beside the mother.

MOTHER (M): <u>She's *so precious*.</u>

CONSULTANT (C): *I'll say.*

M: *(to the baby?) God bless you.*

C: *(about the baby?) Some yawning.*

M: <u>Yep, one of my miracle babies.</u>

C: *I'll say. You said right after she was born you looked her all over to make sure she was all there?*

M: *Oh, yeah.*

C: *When she was awake, what was she doing?*

M: *She was smiling, she was looking all around. She was holding her head up.* <u>*I don't know what to expect, I'm just trying.*</u>

C: *Yeah you sure are. Well how about, if it's all right you could put her back in her crib, I'm going to look at her with you. You said you wanted to film her for your family, right? (Consultant puts baby in crib; and consultant and mother watch)*

M: *Yes*

[NNNS item: lower extremity, foot reflexes—basic reflexes of the feet and ankles]

C: *The first thing I do is just watch her foot and press on the balls of her toes. See, her toes curl in, then I go on the outside of her foot and her toes—are spreading out. See? Now I'm just sort of feeling the strength in her muscles while I do these things.*

M: *Okay.*

[NNNS item: leg extension and recoil: extending the infant's legs and seeing how they "rebound" or recoil]

C: *Okay. Now we can see she's got strength, strength in the legs. There we go.*

M: *Hmm Hmm.*

[NNNS item: popliteal angle—moving each leg upward toward the trunk, and noting how far the leg bends naturally]

C: *Now we're just going to undo a side of her diaper. And I'm going to just carefully put her leg up and see how it goes up. She fussed a little bit, but now while I'm handling her she seems to be okay and is settling down.*

M: Baby dear

[Scarf sign reflex; (pulling an arm slowly across the chest; to evaluate tone in the arm and shoulder); arm extension and recoil (extending the arms beside the body and letting go—to see the "bounce back" or recoil of the arms)]

C: *Mama's calling you, can you hear her voice? Yes, she settled when she heard your voice. I'm going to do that same kind of thing with her arms now. Just sort lift them up then stretch them down. Now with one hand I let go... and it comes back up... the other... and it comes back up.*

[NNNS item: Rooting and evaluation of sucking]

C: *Okay and I stroke your mouth on the side. Oh, okay you know how to root don't you?*

M: *Yeah. She's really pulling on the nipple of the bottle.*

C: *Oh boy, Okay now here we go. What's she doing she's playing games with me now. She is a really strong, steady sucker.*

M: *Oh yes.*

[NNNS item: pull to sit (carefully support infant sitting up) and trunkle tone (infant lying over the hand to see tone in the infant's trunk)]

C: *So we're going to watch while we sit her up. Oh, you're trying to get your head up aren't you? Baby, we are waking you up, yes we are.*

M: *Hey mama, wake up mama.*

[NNNS item; put infant down on front; observe crawling reflex]

C: *Okay, I'm going to put her down slowly on her front. See what she does. Wow, she can get her head up there. And she gets her head over to one side, to make sure that she can keep her nose and mouth clear. She's got her knees up underneath. She's already kind of trying to move her legs like early crawling motion... if I kind of press on her heels—there she sort of pushes up.*

M: <u>Wow, she's only three days old and she can do all of that!</u>

The NNNS-based consultation continues, with NNNS Orientation items: looking at consultant's (and mother's) face, watching face and voice; looking for voice, and so on.

Summary of the Assessment

What follows is the actual summary completed collaboratively between the consultant and mother on the "What Happened Today" form. The emphasis here is on finding a common language that reflects what the mother and consultant saw and commented on during the session. The objective is to have the mother contribute to the summary and endorse what is said. The consultant assures that the comments validate some of the mother's observations and concerns. The consultant also insures that the comments include implications for caregiving.

What Happened Today (Summary)

1. She is truly a joyful baby. She wakes up slowly without immediately crying. She moves her arms and legs smoothly.

2/3. Maybe she didn't appreciate being woken up and she fussed. This could be her way of saying, "If you do this, do it a little slowly and gently; or I will get more worked up."
   Right now, we agreed that she is a calm baby; and we will see if she stays that way in the next days.

4. You (mother) have said that when she fusses, you can hold her in your arms and she calms easily when she can feel you. We saw her fuss several times; but with your voice and once, my voice (consultant), she could calm down easily.

5. There were several times while we looked at her that she fussed; but she brought her fist to her mouth and settled down. You (mother) said; "already she can do this!"

6. During this time, she tried to wake up, but stayed a bit sleepy. We agreed this was probably a sign that she needed more rest. Tomorrow we will look at her again; and you agreed to watch when she wakes up what she likes looking at (in addition to you!).

7. She calmed to your (mother) voice; and looked for you; She did the same thing for me (consultant); and we saw her turn her head to find me, and my voice, several times.

8. She likes being held by you (mother); soothed by soft stroking on her back; and she likes your voice.

9. She is beginning to wake up and look at you (mother) more; she can lift her head; and when I (consultant) put her down; she turned her head to the side to keep her mouth and nose free.

10. I (infant) have shown that I am starting to wake up and will probably be more awake.

11. She (infant) says: "I am very good at eating from the bottle with a regular strong suck. You (mother) give me a break from sucking/eating every ounce or so put me on your shoulder and rub my back. Sometimes I burp; sometimes I don't." You (mother) are thinking about the "rhythm" of my day; when I wake up; when I eat; when I am awake; and when I need to sleep.

Salient Consultant Notes on Maternal Comments

This section highlights what the consultant kept track of in the mother's comments that had to do with representations of the baby.

One of my miracle babies. There are potentially several layers to this statement: It may be a miracle to the mother that baby appears alive and intact given her extensive drug use during this pregnancy. It may also be a miracle that this baby was the second child born while the mother was using drugs during pregnancy. One might wonder how miraculous this is given that there might be problems not evident now that will appear later. Might the mother also consider her a miracle because the baby is alive, with her own will and personality? Might the mother also be wondering, "Can I take care of this miraculous baby? Given how I was treated by my mother, will it take a 'miracle' for me to be able to care for her and help her grow?"

I don't know what to expect, I'm just trying. Earlier in the session, the mother had acknowledged that her first child had been taken into protective custody and placed with the mother's aunt following birth. (She saw her baby only once in the first three months of life). This statement may have several possible layers: "I genuinely don't know what to expect because my first child, a boy, was not with me after he was born," or "I am trying. I want to care for her, learn to care for her and be her mother, and I have many feelings, including joy, fear, doubt, guilt."

Wow, only three days old and she can do all that! There are many potential facets to this comment, including a genuine appreciation for what the mother saw her baby doing during the consultation, uncertainty about what her baby can do and what the developmental progression is, and the absence of a child to whom she can compare her baby (not having seen her first baby at all for the first two months of life).

Vignette Summary

In summary, this brief vignette illustrates how the NNNS-based consultation can elicit many reactions or representations from the mother, and the value of: 1) consultant attention to these comments, both immediately in response to the mother and in mental notes to address later during the session; and 2) following through on these representational comments to help the mother become aware of the many facets of feelings connected to the baby and her experience with the baby (while also holding a steady course in recovery and as a mother). Each of these comments formed the follow-up discussion between the consultant and the drug counselor. From this discussion, the drug counselor was more cognizant of ongoing issues that this mother had both about becoming a mother at the present time and about the influence of her mothering history and drug-taking history on her current functioning.

In this program, it was clear that each woman has her own internal emotional processing time course. Some responses could be responded to both verbally and "interactively" with the baby; and some reoccurred, for the mother, for many weeks and months.

Building Collaborations with Drug Counselors

The NNNS Consultation

A summary for each session (described above) was created for the woman's drug counselor and joint sessions occurred for follow-up. The drug counselor was given the summary and reviewed it with the consultant before her next session with the mother. Mother, drug counselor, and consultant (when invited) watched the tape.

In-Service Training on Child Development and Mothering Transactions

The drug counselors participated in an in-service training program based on an infant mental health curriculum (Boukydis, 2002) and reflective supervision (see below). An important experience gained from this intervention was the consideration of what women needed in early consultation and what it takes to integrate the early consultations with ongoing drug counseling.

Integrating Observing Together into Dyadic Therapy

The collaboration between the consultant and treatment staff led to three innovations:

1. We integrated models of child development and parenting with key issues in drug counseling. For example, when the treatment staff was reviewing Brazelton's Touchpoints (Brazelton & Sparrow, 2006) and learning about key changes in development that were "more likely" to be unbalancing or challenging to the woman's self confidence as a mother, they also considered whether and how these challenges might also trigger a relapse. In training this became known as the *Recovery Touchpoints* model.
2. (2) We combined *anticipatory guidance* and *anticipatory relapse prevention* (envisioning next developmental attainments and how they might be challenging, disruptive, and trigger anxious reactions that could lead to relapse).
3. (3) We used the collaborative model between consultant, mother, and drug counselor along with videotaping of mother–baby interactions to (a) explore the mother's emotional responses to the baby's crying as potential triggers for relapse and (b) define alternative self care strategies (and caretaking responses) when similar emotional responses occurred over time.

Our collaboration also anticipated the movement from essentially processing emotional content related to the mothers' own history of being parented *à la* Ghosts in the Nursery (Fraiberg, 1975) to also searching for who in the woman's life she could identify with as a role model for mothering and parenting *à la* Angels in the Nursery (Lieberman, Padron, VanHorn, & Harris, 2005). In the early stages, while the collaboration predated Lieberman's publishing of "Angels in the Nursery," women's search for mothering role models became a touchstone of the work and a common ground between the original intervention model and the evolving understanding of the drug treatment staff.

■ THE PRENATAL ULTRASOUND INTERVENTION

During the perinatal intervention, we were in the initial stages of developing an intervention for pregnant women in the second trimester of pregnancy. This intervention involved looking together with the woman at her baby during an ultrasound screen and became known as "ultrasound consultation" (Boukydis et al., 2006; Boukydis, 2006). Many of the influences on how the consultation was conducted were the same as for the perinatal consultation and included the same principles for watching fetal behavior as the Observing Infants Together with Parents and NNNS-Based Consultation.

At the time, with improvements in ultrasound technology, (Salisbury, Fallone, & Lester, 2005) it became possible to observe: 1) the appearance and physical features of the fetus, 2) fetal movement and activity, 3) fetal sensory exploration (e.g., stroking its own face; licking the uterine wall), and 4) response of the fetus to internal and external stimulation. In clinical publications there were also emerging accounts of women watching ultrasound screens and speculation as to how this might affect maternal–fetal attachment.

Women in the drug treatment program who entered during the second or third trimester of pregnancy participated voluntarily in the Ultrasound Consultation protocol. The protocol itself involved 1) watching the ultrasound with a trained sonographer; 2) immediately reviewing the ultrasound with women in the treatment program; 3) a post-ultrasound review with the consultant, mother, and drug counselor; and 4) ongoing processing with the drug counselor.

An initial evaluation of the ultrasound protocol itself using the Maternal–Fetal Attachment Scale (MFAS: Cranley, 1981) and the State-Trait Anxiety Index (STAI; Speilberger, Gorusch & Lushene, 1970) indicated that maternal–fetal attachment increased from pre- to post-ultrasound consultation; and state-related anxiety decreased significantly.

A subsequent randomized controlled trial in an inner-city prenatal clinic in Detroit, Michigan, comparing the experience of women who were in the Ultrasound Consultation versus the Standard Care condition, validated that those who participated in the ultrasound consultation compared with standard care had significant increases in maternal–fetal attachment and significant decreases in anxiety, and indicated the influence of the ultrasound consultation on their feelings for their baby and for attending to their own health during pregnancy (Boukydis et al., 2006).

Our clinical impression from using the ultrasound consultation and drug counselor follow-up was that women more frequently went through a process of coming to accept the pregnancy, including being able to invest in their own health care and prepare emotionally for the baby being born. The process was an emotionally challenging one for most women, but the women were "held" in residential treatment with individual counseling and groups. Many of the drug counselors, in surveys related to the new services, indicated that the ultrasound consultation helped to begin the type of recovery process for as many as 60% of women that had not typically occurred until well after the birth of their baby. This observation has yet to be confirmed in a prospective trial that implements the ultrasound consultation and perinatal intervention and follows women progress in treatment post-natally.

At the present time, the ultrasound consultation protocol is being developed for use with substance-using women in hospital prenatal clinics, combining the protocol with enhancements aimed at increasing maternal reflective function (Pajulo, Ekholm, & Boukydis, 2012).

■ SUMMARY

Over time, the "neurobehavioral assessment" approach to talking with parents and infants has evolved into a context for dyadic consultation. The intervention consultations presented in this chapter did not occur in isolation; rather, they were structurally integrated with each woman's "program," which included individual and group counseling. As the drug counselors participated in in-service training and reflective supervision of their own, they became more adept in a co-therapeutic modality that supported women in recovery, their early parenting, and the early attachment relationship.

The evaluation of the prenatal and perinatal interventions presented in this chapter gave some indication of possible benefits. In the past (Das Eiden & Reifman, 1996) neurobehavioral consultations in early infancy have been associated with improvement in mother–infant interaction. The next stage of evaluating these interventions that emphasize observing the infant and attending to evolving maternal representations should include ongoing observation and assessment of mother–infant interaction and the attachment relationship. Presently, two demonstration programs are being developed that expand on the current ultrasound consultation and neonatal consultation with substance-using women and their infants. Hopefully, both protocols will address unanswered questions about how, for whom, and under what circumstances the intervention is useful and effective.

■ REFERENCES

Abidin, R. R. (1990). *Parenting Stress Index–Manual* (3rd ed.). Charlottesville, VA: Pediatric Psychology Press.

Als, H., Lester, B. M., Tronick, E. Z., & Brazelton, T. B. (1982). Toward a research instrument for the assessment of preterm infants' behavior. (A.P.I.B.). In H. E. Fitzgerald, B. M. Lester, & M. Yogman (Eds.), *Theory and Research in Behavioral Pediatrics* (pp. 85–132). New York: Plenum Press.

Armstrong, M. (2008). Foundations for a gender based treatment model for women in recovery from chemical dependency. *Journal of Addictions Nursing, 19*(2), 77–82.

Ashley, O. S., Marsden, M. E., & Brady, T. M. (2003). Effectiveness of substance abuse treatment programming for women: A review. *The American Journal of Drug and Alcohol Abuse, 29,* 19–53.

Bagner, D., Sheinkopf, S., Miller-Loncar, C., et al. (2009).The effect of parenting stress on child behavior problems in children prenatally exposed to cocaine. *Child Psychiatry and Human Development, 40,* 73–84.

Boukydis, C. F. Z. (2002). The Infant Mental Health Training Program. C. F. Z. Boukydis, Principal Investigator. Federal DHHS/ACYF Head Start Award # 90FOO40/01, August, 2002.

Boukydis, C. F. Z. (2006).Ultrasound consultation to increase resiliency in pregnancy. *Annals of the New York Academy of Science, Resilience in Children, 1094,* 268–272.

Boukydis, C. F. Z. (2008). Working with parents and their infants in NICU settings: Use of joint observations and neurobehavioral assessment. *Early Childhood Services, 2*, 43–58.

Boukydis, C. F. Z. (2012). *Consultation with Parents and Infants in the Perinatal Period.* Baltimore, MD: Brookes Publishing Co.

Boukydis, C. F. Z., High, P., Cucca, J., & Lester, B. M. (1997). Treatment of infants and families: The infant crying and behavior clinic model. In B. M. Lester, & R. Barr (Eds.), *Colic and Excessive Crying, Proceedings from the 105th Annual Ross Conference on Pediatrics* (pp. 128–140). Columbus, OH: Ross Labs.

Boukydis, C. F. Z., Treadwell, M. C., Delaney-Black, V., Boyes, K., King, M., Robinson, T., et al. (2006). Women's response to viewing ultrasound during routine screens in an obstetric clinic. *Journal of Ultrasound in Medicine, 25*, 721–728.

Boukydis, C. F. Z., & Lester, B. M. (2008). Mother–infant consultation during drug treatment: Research and innovative clinical practice. *Harm Reduction Journal, 5*, 1–8.

Brazelton, T. B., & Nugent, J. K. (1995). *Neonatal Behavioral Assessment Scale* (3rd ed.). London: MacKeith Press.

Brazelton, T. B., & Sparrow, J. (2006). *Touchpoints: Birth to Three.* Cambridge MA: Dacapo Books.

Cranley, M. (1981). Development of a tool for the measurement of maternal attachment during pregnancy. *Nursing Research, 30*, 281.

Das Eiden, R., & Reifman, A. (1996). Effects of Brazelton demonstrations on later parenting: A meta-analysis. *Journal of Pediatric Psychology, 21*, 857–868.

Egeland, B., & Erikson, M. (1990). Rising above the past: Strategies for helping new mothers break the cycle of abuse and neglect. *Zero to Three, 11*, 29–35.

Field, T., Scafidi, F., Pickens, J., Prodromidis, M., Torquati, J., Wilcox, H, et al. (1998). Polydrug-using adolescent mothers and their infants receiving early intervention. *Adolescence, 33*, 117–144.

Finkelstein, N. (1996). Treatment programming for alcohol and drug-dependent pregnant women. *International Journal of the Addictions, 28*, 1275–1309.

Fraiberg, S. (1975). Ghosts in the nursery: A psychoanalytic approach to the problems of impaired infant–mother relationships. *Journal of American Academy of Child Psychiatry, 14*, 387–422.

Hans, S. (2002). Studies of prenatal exposure to drugs: Focusing on parental care of children. *Neurotoxicology and Teratology, 24*, 329–337.

Jansson, L., Svikis, D., Lee. J., Paluzzi, P., Rutigliano, P., & Hackerman, F. (1996). Pregnancy and addiction: A comprehensive care model. *Journal of Substance Abuse Treatment, 13*, 321–329.

Jones, H. E. (2006). Drug addiction during pregnancy. *Current Directions in Psychological Science, 15*, 126–130.

Kaltenbach, K., & Finnegan, L. (1998). Prevention and treatment issues for pregnant cocaine-dependent women and their infants. *Annals of the New York Academy of Sciences, 846*, 329–334.

Kerwin, M. E. (2005). Collaboration between child welfare and substance-abuse fields: Combined treatment programs for mothers. *Journal of Pediatric Psychology, 30*, 581–597.

Kuecks-Morgan R. (1999). *A Transactional Dyadic Intervention for Foster Providers and Infants Prenatally Exposed to Illegal Drugs.* Ph.D. dissertation. Boston: University of Massachusetts.

Lester, B. M., & Tronick, E. Z. (1994). The effects of prenatal cocaine exposure and child outcome. *Infant Mental Health Journal, 15,* 107–120.

Lester, B. M., Boukydis, C. F. Z., Garcia-Coll, C., Peucker, M., McGrath, M., Vohr, B., et al. (1995). Developmental outcome as a function of the goodness of fit between the infant's cry characteristics and the mother's perception of her infant's cry. *Pediatrics, 95,* 516–521.

Lester, B. M., Affleck, P., Boukydis, C. F. Z., Freier, K., & Boris, N. (1996). Keeping mothers and their infants together: Barriers and solutions. *New York University: Review of Law and Social Change, 22,* 425–440.

Lester, B. M., Boukydis, C. F. Z., & Twomey, J. (2000). Maternal substance abuse and child outcome. In C. H. Zeanah (Ed.), *Handbook of Infant Mental Health* (2nd ed., pp. 161–175). New York: Guilford Press.

Lester, B. M., &, Tronick, E. Z. (2001). Behavioral assessment scales: The NICU Network Neurobehavioral Assessment Scale, the Neonatal Behavioral Assessment Scale, and the Assessment of the Preterm Infant's Behavior. In L. Singer & P. S. Zeskind (Eds.), *Biobehavioral Assessment of the Infant* (pp. 363–380). New York: Guilford Press.

Lester, B. M., Tronick, E. Z., LaGasse, L., et al. (2002). The maternal lifestyle study: effects of substance exposure during pregnancy on neurodevelopmental outcome in 1-month-old infants. *Pediatrics, 110,* 1182–1192.

Lester, B. M., & Tronick, E. Z. (2004). The neonatal intensive care network neurobehavioral scale. *Pediatrics, 113,* 631–699.

Lester, B. M., Masten, A., & McEwen, B. (2006). Resilience in children. *Annals of the New York Academy of Sciences, 1094.* 1–368.

Lester, B. M., Bagner, D. M., Liu, J., La Gasse, L. L., Seifer, R., Bauer, C. R., et al. (2009). Infant neurobehavioral dysregulation: Behavior problems in children with prenatal substance exposure. *Pediatrics, 124,* 1355–1362.

Lieberman, A., Padron, E., Van Horn, P., & Harris, W. W. (2005). Angels in the nursery: The intergenerational transmission of benevolent parental influences. *Infant Mental Health Journal, 26,* 504–520.

Liu, J., Bann, C., Lester, B. M., Tronick, E. Z., Das, A., Lagasse, L., et al. (2009). Neonatal neurobehavior predicts medical and behavioral outcome. *Pediatrics, 125,* 123–129.

Mayes, L. C., Granger, R. H., Bornstein, M. H., & Zuckerman, B. (1992). The problem of prenatal cocaine exposure: A rush to judgment. *Journal of the American Medical Association, 267,* 406–408.

Mayes, L. C., & Pajulo, M. (2006). Neurodevelopmental sequelae of prenatal cocaine exposure. In: D. Bellinger (Ed.), *Human Developmental Neurotoxicology* (pp. 192–229). London, UK: Taylor and Francis Group.

Mayes, L., Magidson, J., Lejuez, C. J., & Nicholls, S. S. (2009). Social relationships as primary rewards: The neurobiology of attachment. In M. de Haan & M. R. Gunnar (Eds.), *Handbook of Developmental Neuroscience.* New York: Guilford.

Meyer, E., Lester, B. M., Boukydis, C. F. Z., Garcia-Coll, C., & McDonough, S. (1994). Family-based intervention improves maternal psychological well-being and feeding interaction of preterm infants. *Pediatrics, 93,* 241–246.

McDonough, S. M. (2004). Interaction guidance. In A. J. Sameroff, S. M. McDonough, & K. L. Rosenblum (Eds.), *Treating Parent–Infant Relationship Problems* (pp. 79–96). New York: Guilford Press.

Osterling, K. L., & Austin, M. J. (2008). Substance abuse interventions for parents involved in the child welfare system: evidence and implications. *Evidence-Based Social Work, 5,* 157–189.

Pajulo, M., Savonlahti, E., & Piha, J. (1999). Maternal substance abuse: Infant psychiatric interest: A review and hypothetical model of interaction. *American Journal of Drug and Alcohol Abuse, 25,* 761–769.

Pajulo, M., Savonlahti, E., Sourander, A., Ahlqvist, S., Helenius, H. & Piha, J. (2001). An early report on the mother-baby interactive capacity of substance-abusing mothers. *Journal of Substance Abuse Treatment, 20,* 143–151.

Pajulo, M., Suchman, N., Kalland, M., & Mayes, L. (2006). Enhancing the effectiveness of residential treatment for substance abusing pregnant and parenting women: Focus on maternal reflective functioning and mother–child relationship. *Infant Mental Health Journal, 27,* 448–452.

Pajulo, M., Ekholm, E., & Boukydis C. F. Z. (2012). Enhancing maternal reflective functioning in the context of ultrasound consultation (abstract from World Association for Infant Mental Health; Leipzig, Germany). *Infant Mental Health Journal,* in press.

Roberts, A. C., & Nishimoto, R. H. (1996). Predicting treatment retention of women dependent on cocaine. *American Journal of Drug and Alcohol Abuse, 31,* 313–333.

Salisbury, A., Fallone, M., & Lester, B. M. (2005). Neurobehavioral assessment from fetus to infant: The NICU network neurobehavioral scale and the fetal neurobehavior coding scale. *Mental Retardation and Developmental Disabilities Research Review, 11,* 14–20.

Sameroff, A. J. (2004). Ports of entry and the dynamics of mother–infant interactions. In A. J. Sameroff, S. M. McDonough, & K. L. Rosenblum (Eds.), *Treating Parent–Infant Relationship Problems* (pp. 3–28). New York: Guilford Press.

Savonlahti, E., Pajulo, M., Ahlqvist, S., Helenius, H., Korvenranta, H., Tamminen, T., et al. (2005).Interactive skills of high-risk infants and their mothers. *Nordic Journal of Psychiatry, 59,* 139–147.

Seifer, R., LaGasse, L. L., Lester, B. M., Bauer, C. R., Shankaran, S., Bada, H. S., et al. (2004). Attachment status in children prenatally exposed to cocaine and other substances. *Child Development, 75,* 850–868.

Sheinkopf, S. J., Lester, B. M., LaGasse, L. L., Seifer, R., Bauer, C. R., Shankaran, S., et al. (2006). Neonatal irritability, prenatal substance exposure, and later parenting stress. *Journal of Pediatric Psychology, 31,* 27–40.

Spielberger, C. D., Gorusch, R., & Lushene, T. (1970). *State-Trait Anxiety Inventory.* Palo Alto, CA: Consulting Psychologists Press.

Stern, D. (2004). The motherhood constellation: Therapeutic approaches to early relational problems. In A. J. Sameroff, S. M. McDonough, & K. L. Rosenblum (Eds.), *Treating Parent–Infant Relationship Problems* (pp. 29–42). New York: Guilford Press.

Suchman, N., Mayes, L., Conti, J., Slade, A., & Rounsaville, B. (2004). Rethinking parenting interventions for drug-dependent mothers: From behavior management to fostering emotional bonds. *Journal of Substance Abuse Treatment, 27,* 179–185.

Suchman, N., Pajulo, M., DeCoste, C., & Mayes, L. (2006). Parenting interventions for drug-dependent mothers and their young children: The case for an attachment-based approach. *Family Relations, 55,* 211–226.

Szuster, R. R., Rich, L. L., Chung, A., & Bisconer, S. W. (1996). Treatment retention in women's residential chemical dependency treatment: The effects of admission with children. *Substance Abuse and Misuse, 31,* 1001–1013.

Tronick, E. Z., Messinger, D. S., Weinberg, M. K., Lester, B. M., LaGasse, L., Seifer, R., et al. (2005). Cocaine exposure is associated with subtle compromises of infants' and mothers' social-emotional behavior and dyadic features of their interaction in the face-to-face still-face paradigm. *Developmental Psychology, 41,* 711–722.

Twomey, J. E., Soave, R., Gil, L., & Lester, B. M. (2005). Permanency planning and social service systems: A comparison of two families with prenatally substance exposed infants. *Infant Mental Health Journal, 26,* 250–267.

Wakschlag, L. S., & Hans, S. L. (1999). Relation of maternal responsiveness during infancy to the development of behavior problems in high-risk youths. *Developmental Psychology, 35,* 569–579.

Williamson, G., & Anzalone, M. E. (2001). *Sensory Integration and Self-Regulation in Infants and Toddlers: Helping Very Young Children Interact with Their Environment.* Washington, DC: Zero to Three Press.

12 Interventions for Children of Substance-Using Parents

SUSAN MINEAR AND
BARRY ZUCKERMAN

■ OVERVIEW

Over 20 percent of children in the United States are raised in drug-exposed environments, and in 2005, more than ten percent of American births involved prenatal exposure to alcohol or illicit drugs. Three percent of the 4.1 million women of childbearing age who abuse drugs are believed to continue drug use during pregnancy (SAMHSA, 2003) and more than one million children are affected per year when tobacco is added into the equation (Hamdan, 2010).

This chapter presents an approach to caring for pediatric and other child health professionals who work with children affected by parental substance use. The chapter is divided into two sections: 1) perinatal intervention for newborns exposed to alcohol and drugs *in utero* and 2) developmentally focused care for young children in the primary care setting. We stress the importance of relationships: mother and infant, clinician and mother, father to mother, and child to clinician. We will also explore the roles of extended family members, as they may have important protective or counterproductive influences on the child's development.

We will use the term "substance use" when referring to parental use of illicit drugs, abuse of alcohol, and prescribed use of psychoactive medications taken during pregnancy for maternal mental illness or opiate addiction. For the purpose of this chapter, "substance use" refers to current use as well as a positive past history.

This chapter is written for child health caregivers: doctors, nurses, nurse practitioners, social workers, early intervention providers, lactation specialists, day-care providers, child life specialists, and researchers, in hopes that the information presented here will stimulate ideas for intervention and further study. The term "clinician" refers to any one of these professionals. Our objectives are threefold: 1) to articulate the medical and developmental problems experienced by children of substance using parents; 2) to propose medically and developmentally appropriate interventions; and 3) to identify areas where additional research is required.

The authors' clinical experience working with families affected by substance abuse has been primarily at Boston Medical Center (BMC) (previously Boston City Hospital). BMC is a 580-bed multidisciplinary hospital that is located in an urban setting and serves families from local and international communities. BMC has a 32-bed postpartum unit and assisted in 2,400 deliveries in 2010.

Approximately 100 births were complicated by known prenatal substance abuse in 2010. To ensure safe and effective care, the BMC Nursery leadership created protocols for management of neonatal abstinence syndrome (NAS) and breastfeeding eligibility. A multidisciplinary perinatal NAS committee meets monthly to ensure that parents receive a unified approach to care.

■ PERINATAL INTERVENTIONS FOR NEWBORNS EXPOSED TO ALCOHOL AND DRUGS *IN UTERO*

Parenting is a special challenge for all mothers and fathers. Yet for substance using parents it is especially challenging as they are confronted with the conflict between their need to support their drug use, or their recovery, and their infant. Pediatric caregivers play a key role in promoting the success of these parents to help ensure that the intergenerational cycle of substance abuse is broken. Knowledgeable professionals can have a lifesaving effect on a family.

Illicit and Addictive Substances

The list of commonly used illicit and addictive substances and their effects on the newborn is given in Table 12.1. One of the most effective interventions for newborns is early identification and treatment of substance using women. Clinicians can intervene in three ways: 1) identify substance use in the prenatal period (Chasnoff, 2003; Seval Brooks & Fitzgerald Rice, 1997) (see Table 12.2); 2) help pregnant mothers access recovery programs and promote healthy behavior; 3) prepare mothers for what to expect during the postpartum hospital stay, including breastfeeding, length of stay, drug screening, infant monitoring, pharmacological treatment for drug withdrawal, and the institution's obligation regarding reports to child protection services (see Table 12.3). Honest and complete discussion with the mother prenatally will help her maintain a sense of control and active participation.

Maternal Mental Illness

More than 50 percent of women with substance abuse histories have psychiatric comorbidity such as depression, anxiety, or bipolar disorder (NIDA, 1994; Regier, JAMA 1990), and most women with addiction have a past history of physical and/or sexual abuse (Children of Alcoholics Foundation, 1994). People raised in alcoholic families experience physical, sexual or emotional abuse three times more often than those raised in non-alcoholic families (William Gladden Foundation, 2005). Within the last decade, an increasing number of pregnant women have received psychotropic medications, often in combination with medications such as methadone or buprenorphine, which are used to prevent opioid withdrawal during pregnancy. The possible effects of psychotropic medications on the newborn may complicate the long-term effects of prenatal substance exposure (see Table 12.4). This is an area where more research is required.

TABLE 12.1 *Common Illicit and Addictive Substances and Potential Neonatal Effects*

Substance Classification	Examples	Clinical Information
Narcotics	heroin, methadone, morphine, buprenorphine, codeine, fentanyl, meperidine, and oxycodone.	o Narcotics produce analgesia, lowered anxiety, improved mood, drowsiness, and a clouding of the sensorium. In sufficient doses they also cause respiratory depression, peripheral vasodilation, and decreased intestinal peristalsis. There is no evidence that narcotics increase the rate of congenital malformations. Their primary effects on the fetus are intrauterine growth retardation, pre-term birth (Wouldes, 2010; Lim, 2009; Dryden, 2009; Burgos & Burke, 2009), and neurobehavioral dysfunction. o The most common systems to be affected are the autonomic, gastrointestinal, and central nervous systems. o Fifty to 95 percent of babies exposed to opiates *in utero* will experience NAS symptoms, which include irritability, tremulousness, sweating, high-pitched cry, diarrhea, and vomiting, and should be monitored for weight loss, dehydration, and seizure (Hamdan, 2010; Chasnoff, 2003). Infants may have difficulty feeding due to uncoordinated and inefficient suckling (Kron, Litt, & Phoenix, 1976). Time of onset varies, depending upon the type and number of drug(s), frequency and duration of use. Heroin has a short half-life (4 hours), and withdrawal symptoms may appear on the first day. Methadone has a very long half-life of 32 hours in the newborn. Withdrawal symptoms may not occur before 24–48 hours of life or as late as seven to 10 days. Others suggest that NAS symptoms may peak at three to four days or not appear until 10–14 days (Hamdan, 2010; Burgos & Burke, 2009). Subacute opiate withdrawal includes restlessness, agitation, tremors, and sleep disturbance, and may persist for 3–6 months (Hutchings, 1982). In some infants, neurological irritability with abnormal moro reflex has been noted until 7–8 months (Burgos & Burke, 2009; Chasnoff, 2003).
Other Depressants	alcohol, barbiturates, benzodiazepines, tranquilizers, anesthetics, and opioids	o Approximately 20 percent of pregnant women drink alcohol, and 140,000 newborns in the United States are exposed to potentially teratogenic doses of alcohol each year (Stokowski, 2003). Alcohol exposure causes prematurity, symmetric IUGR, and hypotonia (Wang, 2009). The effects of poor nutrition, cigarette smoking, and other interrelated risk factors contribute to poor fetal growth and development (Zuckerman et al., 1986). o Unlike other substances, alcohol is teratogenic. Fetal alcohol syndrome (FAS), which can occur in 1%–2% of children of alcoholic women, is composed of physical, behavioral, and cognitive abnormalities and has three major criteria: prenatal or post-natal growth restriction, CNS involvement, and specific craniofacial dysmorphic features. Fetal alcohol effects (FAE) is a less severe result of alcohol exposure and includes growth deficiency, motor and speech delays, and behavior problems (Burgos & Burke, 2009). While there is no known safe amount of alcohol use during pregnancy, one large prospective study did not identify any problems among women who drank two or fewer drinks per day and were well nourished (Hingson & Zuckerman, 1986). o Barbiturate withdrawal can present with signs similar to those found with opiate-induced NAS, although onset is usually delayed until four to seven days after birth and lasts as long as four months (Burgos & Burke, 2009). o Benzodiazepine use during pregnancy may lead to withdrawal syndrome in the newborn, especially if used during the third trimester. Symptoms include poor suck, hypotonia, apnea, and seizure. Symptoms may persist for hours to months after birth (McElhatton, 1994).

(Continued)

TABLE 12.1 (Continued)

Substance Classification	Examples	Clinical Information
Stimulants	cocaine, methamphetamines, stimulants, MDMA ("Ecstasy" or XTC), nicotine, and caffeine	o Stimulants cause alertness, hypervigilance, and peripheral sympathetic arousal. Stimulant-exposed babies more commonly show direct effects of the stimulants such as tremors, high-pitched cry, irritability, excess suck, hyperalertness, apnea, and tachycardia. These effects are less common and less severe than those associated with methadone or heroin exposure. Symptoms can be seen in the first 72 hours after delivery (Burgos & Burke, 2009) and are more likely due to cocaine intoxication rather than withdrawal effect (Wang, 2009). o Cocaine's vasoactive effects cause placental abruption, spontaneous abortion, precipitous and preterm labor and delivery, poor fetal growth, congenital abnormalities, and hemorrhagic and cystic lesions in the CNS (Burgos & Burke, 2009; Chasnoff, 2003). Cocaine use during pregnancy is associated with decreased birth weight and head circumference (Zuckerman & Bresnahan, 1991; Bresnahan et al., 1991). However, poor growth is probably compounded by maternal undernutrition and polydrug abuse (Frank et al., 1988; Zuckerman et al., 1989). Infants exposed to cocaine showed a symmetrical pattern of growth retardation commonly associated with maternal malnutrition, suggesting decreased nutrient transfer (Frank et al., 1990) and growth typically catches up within two years (Wang, 2009). o Clinically, cocaine-exposed babies are poorly responsive and sleepy. When awake, they are easily overstimulated, become irritable, and quickly return to sleep. Newborns evaluated using the Neonatal Behavioral Assessment Scale (NBAS) have demonstrated increased tremulousness, startles, decreased interactive behaviors, and increased state lability (Chasonoff, Burns, Burns, & Schnoll, 1986; Chasnoff, Burns, Schnoll, & Burns, 1985). Infants whose mothers stopped using drugs in the first trimester showed impaired orientation, motor function, reflexes, and state regulation compared to infants whose mothers used no drugs (Chasnoff, Griffith, MacGregor, Dirkes, & Burns, 1989; Frank, Bresnahan & Zuckerman, 1993). Only four percent of methamphetamine-exposed babies (Smith L, 2003) and six percent of cocaine-exposed infants require pharmacological therapy (Fulroth, 1989). o Evidence indicates that nicotine causes more than 50% of all low birth-weight babies (Wang, 2009; Wang X et al., 2002). Infants have symmetrical decrease in all growth parameters but will catch up in growth (Wang, 2009). Some infants are genetically more vulnerable to cigarette smoke (Wang, 2007). Other risks include sudden infant death syndrome, respiratory infections, and difficulty self-soothing. Adverse outcomes beyond infancy include increased learning difficulties, hyperactivity, and short stature.
Hallucinogens	LSD, Phencyclidine (PCP), Mescaline, Datura (jimson weed), and Ketamine	o Distort emotions, perceptions, sensations.
Marijuana	Combined properties of depressant and hallucinogen	o The principal psychoactive chemical of marijuana is tetrahydrocannabinol (THC). In addition to its potentially direct effects, it has the indirect effect of decreasing fetal oxygenation and has been shown to cause fetal hypoxia in animals (Clapp, Wesley, & Cooke, 1986). Hypoxia also results from inhalation of carbon monoxide, which is present at higher levels than in cigarette smoke (Wu, Tashkin, & Djahed, 1988). Exposure to marijuana is associated with lowered birthweight and in some studies, neurobehavioral differences following birth.

TABLE 12.2 *Components of a Thorough Maternal History*

Drug and alcohol use	o Current and past use
	o Type and route
	o Method of obtaining medications (prescription vs. illegally acquired)
	o Reason for use
	o Recovery program(s) and compliance
	o Urine drug screen results through pregnancy
	o Previous relapse(s) and reason(s)
	o Previous successes in recovery
Maternal physical health	o Hepatitis C and B
	o Tuberculosis
	o STDs (gonorrhea, chlamydia, syphilis, HIV)
	o Compliance with prenatal visits
Mental illness	o Type(s), medications (past and present)
	o Past and/or present therapy
Family involvement	o Father—substance abuse, mental illness
	o Substance-using family members
	o Family support
	o Home environment—safety
Domestic violence/ legal history	o Past, current
	o Incarceration
Child protective services involvement	o Past, current
	o Previous loss of custody of children

The Newborn Nursery Stay

Obstetric and pediatric clinicians must collaborate to develop a consistent plan that the mother can anticipate and that also ensures safe care for the infant. The pediatric team should restate the plan that has been laid out in the prenatal period, obtain a thorough maternal and social history, and carefully explain the components of the newborn's care. The AAP Committee on [the] Fetus and Newborn (AAP, 2010) recommends that pediatric providers assess family, environmental, and social risk factors for every newborn. The parents should be screened for domestic violence, mental illness, and material stability. A social history (Kenyon et al., 2007) emphasizing food security, housing satisfaction, utility service, and other unmet basic needs is important. Discharge should be delayed until all concerns have been addressed and a safe plan has been established (AAP, 2010).

Honest and consistent communication using a nonjudgemental tone will help promote a positive relationship with the new mother. The best care is that which is given using a unified team approach. Pediatricians, obstetricians, midwives, lactation specialists, social workers, nurses, mental health professionals, child development specialists, substance abuse counselors, and all other consultants should understand the baby's plan of care and communicate a consistent message to the mother. To prevent conflict between mother and staff at BMC related to inconsistent information that mothers may have received prenatally,

TABLE 12.3 *Helping the Pregnant Substance-Using Mother Prepare*
for the Postpartum Hospital Stay

Breastfeeding	The Boston Medical Center criteria for breastfeeding for substance-using mothers (must meet all of the following).
	1. No positive urine toxicology screens for 10 weeks prior to birth
	2. Negative urine toxicology screen at time of birth
	3. Compliant in addiction recovery program for at least 12 weeks prior to birth
	Mothers should be given the above expectations during pregnancy where possible. Prenatal and postpartum staff should be clear and consistent in delivery of expectations and criteria. Staff should have a reliable method for screening urine and tracking recovery program attendance.
Neonatal abstinence scoring	Explain the process for objectively monitoring the newborn at risk for substance withdrawal. Be specific and use lay terms. Show the parent the scoring sheet. Partner with the parent where possible, allowing the parent to report symptoms such as sneezing, stooling frequency, and ease of feeding.
Length of hospital stay	Explain the criteria for discharge and possible need for extended stay. Do not make promises regarding length of stay. It is helpful to focus on the infant and not the drugs: "All babies are unique. We will let the baby tell us when he is ready to be discharged."
Urine and meconium testing of mother and baby	Explain the process of drug screening for mother and baby. Tell the parent(s) what tests will be conducted (urine, meconium drug screening). Be direct about reporting laws: "I have to report any positive test results to the state Child Protective Services Agency by law. I will let you know the test results as soon as I have them."
Medication for baby	Using positive language, explain indications for medicating the newborn who is experiencing withdrawal. "We want the baby to use her energy to grow. If she is irritable or jittery, we may start medicine to help her be calm. We'll continue to watch her closely and slowly decrease the medicine as she shows us she no longer needs it."
Involvement of Child Protection Services	Practitioners should be familiar with their state's regulations. Each practitioner is individually responsible for reporting suspected child neglect and abuse. The decision to file a report with CPS should not be delegated to one member of the team. Explain the role of Child Protection Services and how the mother can cooperate to help ensure that she retains custody of her child.
	1. Abstinence from substance use
	2. Compliance with recovery program
	3. Attention to the medical and social needs of the infant (e.g., housing, clothing)
	4. Cooperation with hospital staff

pregnant women who have a known history of substance use are given specific printed and verbal information prenatally (whenever possible), and again postnatally. The information tells them what to expect during their postpartum stay, including breastfeeding eligibility, neonatal abstinence scoring process, length of stay, drug screening, pharmacological treatment for NAS, and rules regarding reporting to child protection services (see Table 12.3). Successful collaboration has been achieved through multidisciplinary teams (represented by obstetrics, pediatrics, nursing, social work, and others who care for pregnant women and newborns), agreement on guidelines for management of substance abuse (such as those articulated in Tables 12.3 and 12.7), and by maintaining a consistent message to mothers.

TABLE 12.4 *Psychotropic Medications and Their Effect on the Newborn*

Medication	Examples	Potential Effects
Selective serotonin reuptake inhibitors (SSRIs)	Fluoxetine (Prozac), Sertraline (Zoloft), Citalopram (Celexa), and Paroxetine (Paxil)	SSRIs are the most commonly used antidepressants in postpartum mothers and cause NAS in up to one-third of neonates exposed *in utero* (Burgos & Burke, 2009). Signs include tremulousness, hypertonia, respiratory distress, high-pitched cry, sleep disruption, poor state regulation, and gastrointestinal disturbance. Symptoms present within 48 hours and usually resolve after 48 hours. Paroxetine (Paxil) has the greatest propensity to cause NAS (Burgos & Burke, 2009). Of all SSRIs studied, sertraline (Zoloft) has shown the safest neonatal clinical profile (Wang, 2009). Other authors have found no withdrawal syndrome associated with SSRIs (Sanz et al., 2005; Koren et al., 2005).
Antipsychotic medication	Second generation: Quetiapine (Seroquel) and Risperidone (Risperdal) Third generation: Aripiprazole (Abilify)	Antipsychotic medication use has dramatically increased over the past decade in patients with bipolar disorder (BPD) and for use as adjunctive medications for a variety of conditions such as depression, sleep disturbance, and agitation (Stowe, 2007). Second-generation (a) typical antipsychotics cross the placental barrier (Newport, 2007). An extensive and systematic review of the medical literature since 1950 regarding first- and second-generation antipsychotic therapy during early and late pregnancy was recently published (Gentile, 2010). Analysis of possible teratogenicity in many instances is complicated by concomitant use of other psychotropic medications. As of this writing, much of the evidence regarding perinatal complications and postnatal behavioral sequelae is inconclusive. Thus, in addition to providing informed consent when prescribing antipsychotics to pregnant and lactating women, clinicians should provide non-drug-related support programs and ensure that women with mental illness are provided with an opportunity for counseling.

The Newborn Physical Examination

The newborn should receive a thorough physical examination, including weight, length, and head circumference. The clinician should accurately assess gestational age and make appropriate adjustments in anthropometric measurements for the infant's corrected gestational age. Attention should be given to evidence of intrauterine growth retardation (IUGR), microcephaly, or congenital infections, as well as major and minor congenital malformations.

The infant should be monitored for signs of withdrawal (sleeping, feeding, and weight gain). Initial treatment strategies for infants showing signs of withdrawal include holding infant's skin directly to parent's skin, swaddling, breastfeeding if not contraindicated, minimizing noise, gentle handling, pacifier, rooming in with the mother as long as possible, and avoidance of abrupt changes in environment.

The Neurobehavioral Examination and Developmentally Appropriate Care

In addition to babies prenatally exposed to illicit substances, newborns who have been exposed prenatally to prescription antidepressants and antipsychotics (see Table 12.4) may demonstrate neurological signs and symptoms after birth depending upon the drug(s), dosage and duration of use during pregnancy. Neurobehavioral signs may be present at the time of birth, reflecting a direct effect of the psychoactive substance, and/or days later, reflecting withdrawal. Neurobehavioral assessment needs to be monitored over time. Substance-exposed babies may move unpredictably from one state to another or have difficulty maintaining or transitioning to a quiet alert state. They may show more tremulousness with even mild stimulation and may demonstrate other signs of stress, such as sneezing, hiccoughing, spitting up, skin mottling, and perioral cyanosis. Finally, they may only tolerate one mode of stimulation at a time and may decompensate with higher levels of stimulation such as loud noises, lights, and unpredictable movements.

Clinicians who are alert to the subtle developmental cues of the newborn will be able to identify their neurobehavioral vulnerabilities and help parents understand the baby's preferences as well as dysregulating stimuli, thus enabling parents to be better prepared to respond to their infant's needs at home. Every encounter offers an opportunity for teachable moments. For newborns of substance using mothers who have difficulty protecting their sleep (habituation), the practitioner can recommend limited stimulation (one modality at a time) and low levels of stimulation (soft sounds and indirect lighting). Substance using parents can be intrusive and overly stimulating. During the physical examination, the clinician can model gentle handling and a soft voice. Identifying the infant's cues as he sees them, the clinician can talk with parents about gaze aversion and signs of stress (hiccoughing, skin color changes, spitting up) that indicate the baby needs a rest.

Neonatal Drug Screening

Maternal self report underestimates *in utero* drug exposure by as much as 44 percent when compared with data from meconium analyses (Lester, 2001). Understandably, mothers who are afraid of legal consequences or losing custody may not report prenatal use. Indication for urine and meconium drug screening include known substance abuse, limited or no prenatal care, an intrauterine growth–retarded infant, pre-term delivery, placental abruption, cardiovascular accident in mother or child—especially when there is no other identifiable reason for these findings (Chasnoff, 2003).

Urine should be obtained from the mother and baby as soon as possible after delivery. Tetrahydrocannabinol (THC), the active ingredient in marijuana, remains in urine for seven days to one month in an adult, and possibly longer in an infant. Cocaine will be present for 24 to 48 hours in an adult and 72 to 96 hours in an infant. Benzodiazepines can be detected for three days. Heroin will remain for 24 hours in an adult and 24 to 48 hrs in an infant. Methadone can be detected for as long as 10 to 14 days after birth. Urine testing is an unreliable method to detect ethanol because immunoassays have low sensitivity for alcohol and because ethanol is rapidly eliminated (6–8 hours after last use).

At BMC, we conduct an expanded urine screen and meconium screen for all newborns whose mothers had fewer than three prenatal visits or who had known use of illicit substances in pregnancy. The expanded urine screen identifies amphetamines, barbiturates, benzodiazepines, cocaine, opiates, methadone, oxycodone, buprenorphine, and THC. Meconium analysis is currently the best method for detecting drug exposure in pregnancy, possibly as early as the second trimester when drugs begin to accumulate in meconium (Hamdan, 2010; Ryan, 1994).

Approach to Monitoring for Neonatal Drug Withdrawal

There are several scoring systems for evaluating the signs of NAS as they emerge in the neonate. The Finnegan Scoring System is the most commonly used and includes 21 different symptoms grouped into three categories: neurological, respiratory, and gastrointestinal (Finnegan, 1986, 1975) (see Table 12.5). Scoring takes place at two-hour intervals. Three consecutive scores greater than or equal to eight, or two consecutive scores greater than or equal to twelve, indicate severer withdrawal and the need to initiate pharmacological treatment. The scoring system is primarily used for withdrawal from narcotics (Wang, 2009). Other tools to evaluate neonatal withdrawal include the Neonatal Intensive Care Unit Network Neurobehavioral Scale (Lester, 2004), the Lipsitz Tool (Lipsitz, 1975), the Ostrea Criteria (Ostrea, 1997 and1976), the Neonatal Withdrawal Inventory (Zahorodny, 1998), and the Riley Infant Pain Scale (Schade, 1996). NAS scoring is complicated by subjectivity of the observer. More research is required to evaluate standardized scoring systems for management of infants exposed to narcotics.

To provide comprehensive care, the clinician must address the needs of the *whole* infant and family. Observing the infant with the parents is key. Substance using

TABLE 12.5 *Neonatal Abstinence Signs*

System	Components to Score	Qualities to Assess	To Ensure Accurate Score:
CNS	Cry Sleep Moro reflex Tremors Muscle tone Excoriatios Restlessness/activity Myoclonic jerks Seizure	High pitched/ continuous Note duration Hyperactive With or without stimulation Increased tone Increased activity, difficult to soothe	1. Recognize that all babies cry; distinguish normal vigorous cry from abnormal or prolonged cry. 2. Examine infant in various states and not just quiet sleep state.
Metabolic/ Vasomotor	Fever	99–101 or over 101	1. Recognize that all babies sneeze and all babies yawn.
Respiratory	Respiratory rate Sweating Yawning Nasal stuffiness Sneezing	Rate over 60 with or without retractions 3–4 times per interval	2. Recognize that normal babies frequently have nasal stuffiness.
Gastrointestinal	Excessive sucking Poor feeding Regurgitation Projectile vomiting Watery stools	Effectiveness of suck and swallow Is feeding well regulated?	Recognize that there are different reasons for poor feeding and reflux aside from withdrawal.

mothers may be reluctant to express their fears or ask questions because of guilt and fear of losing custody or appearing incompetent. Many mothers worry that exposure to drugs has harmed the baby. Some worry that the baby may become addicted, too. As the clinician examines the baby with the mother, he has the opportunity to discover her fears and understand her interpretation of her baby's behavior. Most mothers will then begin to express their concerns and provide a more complete social and family history. As the mother begins to trust, the clinician can begin to explore the mother's recovery status, her opportunities for treatment, counseling, and other critical issues such as safety, mental health, and resources for the family.

Pharmacotherapy

Medications should be initiated when supportive measures are not sufficient to keep the infant's NAS scores at appropriate levels. The clinician should discuss treatment plans with the infant's mother to update her about all changes in her infant's status. Some mothers are very reluctant to begin medication for their newborns because they believe their child may become addicted or because of concerns about prolonged hospital stays or losing custody. In addition, the decision to treat the newborn experiencing withdrawal symptoms often intensifies the mother's feelings of guilt. Clinicians can help relieve the mother's anxiety by explaining the benefits of pharmacotherapy for *her* baby, examining the infant with the mother and describing neurobehavioral signs in lay terms, and discussing the infant's medical plan and changes as they occur.

Medication Choices

The major drugs to treat narcotic withdrawal are neonatal morphine, deodorized tincture of opium (DTO), and phenobarbital (Burgos & Burke, 2009; Sarkar, 2006). Neonatal morphine and DTO may be better choices for infants exposed to narcotics only prenatally, since they are opiate agonists and directly address withdrawal. Neonatal morphine is gaining favor over DTO due to its safety profile (Wang, 2009). Phenobarbital is effective in controlling the central nervous system (CNS) symptoms through its sedative properties but does not control diarrhea and does not improve coordination of sucking and swallowing. Phenobarbital may be a better choice for infants exposed to multiple drugs in utero and for infants experiencing non-opiate withdrawal abstinence-related seizures, or inadequate response to maximum levels of morphine. Infants exposed to opiates may experience sedation, and infants given phenobarbital may have a poor sucking reflex. All infants being treated pharmacologically for substance abuse should have cardiorespiratory monitoring because of the potential for respiratory depression, and have an occupational therapist consultation to assess their oral muscular tone and neurobehavioral integrity.

No treatment has been found to be optimal, especially for polysubstance exposure. There are insufficient randomized studies evaluating the benefits of one pharmacological approach over another (Hamdan, 2010). There is some evidence that phenobarbital and DTO in combination result in a shorter hospital stay (Kassima,

2006). Morphine may be more effective when given with clonidine (Agthe, 2006). Sublingual buprenorphine has been investigated as a possible method of treatment for newborns. Benefits include limited hospitalization and less separation of mother and infant (Kraft, 2008). This is an area of research that requires more attention. There is no specific treatment plan for amphetamine, marijuana, tobacco, or alcohol (Wang, 2009).

Buprenorphine, a partial opiate agonist, is a newer drug being used instead of methadone for opiate-abusing pregnant women (Drug Addiction Treatment Act of 2000; Kacinko, 2008; Kraft 2008; Farid, 2008; Jones, 2005, 2010). Buprenorphine has a higher molecular weight than methadone and has a lower transference through the placenta (Wang, 2009). Its other benefits include a lower risk of respiratory depression, limited abuse liability, acceptable safety margin, and reduced treatment time and length of hospital stay (Kraft, 2008; Hamdan, 2010; Jones 2010). Other studies have evaluated neonatal withdrawal following exposure to buprenorphine in comparison to methadone exposure (Farid, 2008; Ebner, 2007; Jones, 2005). Eighty-five percent of infants exposed to buprenorphine experience withdrawal, but it is generally less severe than methadone withdrawal and not as long-lasting. More research is needed to explore the potential benefits of neonatal treatment with buprenorphine for management of NAS.

Differential Diagnosis and Identification of Comorbidities

The clinician should consider alternative diagnoses when presented with signs consistent with substance withdrawal or intoxication. Hyperthyroidism, hypocalcemia, hypoglycemia, sepsis, perinatal anoxia, and hypomagnesemia may present with similar features. Hyperviscosity can be associated with substance exposure and can cause intracranial hemorrhage. Congenital hypothyroidism can mask the signs of NAS. The maternal record should be reviewed for evidence of hepatitis C, chlamydia, gonorrhea, syphilis, and HIV.

The Newborn Behavior Observation (NBO)

Various tools have been developed to objectively evaluate newborn behavior (Brazelton & Nugent, 1995; Brazelton, 1973; Lester, 2004). Of these, the newborn behavior observation (NBO) is a brief, structured clinical tool for clinicians to use at the bedside in partnership with parents that goes beyond assessment to help build a relationship between clinician and parent. Observing the infant with the mother (and other family members if present), the clinician makes an objective assessment of the baby's behavior and provides appropriate anticipatory guidance (Nugent et al., 2007) (see Table 12.6). Clinician and parent joint observation can help ensure the accuracy of NAS scoring and newborn treatment.

The NBO consists of 18 newborn neurobehavioral items. Each of the items is linked to anticipatory guidance that can be shared with the parent at the time of the observation. As the mother and clinician observe the baby together, the clinician notices the strengths of the baby and affirms the mother's good efforts during her pregnancy. The clinician also elicits the mother's input. If the clinician

TABLE 12.6 *Newborn Behavior Observation Neurobehavioral Items*

Behavior	Anticipatory Guidance Checklist
Habituation to light	Sleep patterns
Habituation to sound	Sleep protection
Muscle tone	Neurodevelopment
Root	Feeding cues
Suck	Feeding cues
Hand grasp	Touch and contact
Shoulder and neck tone	"Tummy time," head control
Crawling response	Sleep position and safety
Response to face and voice	Social interaction
Visual response to face	Vision
Orientation to voice	Hearing
Orientation to sound	Hearing
Visual tracking	Communication cues
Crying	Crying and soothability
Soothability	Self-soothing
State regulation	State regulation
Autonomic response to stress	Stimulation threshold
Activity level	Cues for support

Source: adapted from Newborn Behavioral Observations (NBO) System Recording Form and Recording Guidelines. Copyright ©2007, Children's Hospital Boston, from *Understanding Newborn Behavior and Early Relationships; The Newborn Behavioral Observations (NBO) System Handbook* by J. Kevin Nugent, Constance H. Keefer, Susan Minear, Lise C. Johnson, and Yvette Blanchard. Copyright ©2007 Paul H. Brookes Publishing Co. All rights reserved.

observes autonomic signs of stress (e.g., tremulousness, sneezing, hiccoughing, skin mottling), he stops to ask the mother what she thinks, how often she has noticed them, and what she thinks makes them better or worse. He then gives the mother suggestions for minimizing these signs (swaddling, gentle rocking, indirect lighting, and low noise level).

In a similar manner, the clinician observes the infant's sleep protection (habituation), muscle tone, reflexes, responsiveness to face and voice, ability to track an object and turn to sound, state regulation, and activity. This five- to ten-minute process allows the clinician to create a partnership with the mother. Rather than simply giving information, the clinician enters into a dialogue with the mother. He elicits her interpretation of her baby's behavior, thus reinforcing her authority as the mother.

The clinician can identify the infant's behavioral cues (e.g., startles, yawns, sneezes, hiccoughs, spit ups, and tremors) and reframes those that have been misinterpreted by her (e.g., sneezing does not necessarily mean he has a cold), without appearing to correct her. A positive relationship emerges between clinician and parent as the clinician identifies the infant's strengths (e.g., ability to self-console) and needs for support (e.g., swaddling).

Over the next few visits, even when the infant is being treated pharmacologically, the clinician continues to apply the principles of the NBO, allowing space for the mother to identify areas where she needs support and referral. Using the NBO, the clinician can include fathers, who are often marginalized during the newborn nursery stay, and other family members (grandparents and siblings) who may be participating in the care of the newborn after discharge.

Infant Feeding

There is a plethora of evidence demonstrating the benefits of breastfeeding, including protection against ear infections, diarrhea, pneumonia, asthma, allergies, and leukemia in children, and protection against breast cancer in women. The American Academy of Pediatrics recommends exclusive breastfeeding for the first six months of life, continuing to at least one year or beyond with the addition of complimentary foods at approximately six months of life (AAP, 2005).

In 1991, in response to an alarming decrease in breastfeeding rates worldwide, the World Health Organization (WHO) and the United Nations Infant and Child Emergency Fund (UNICEF) launched the Baby-Friendly Hospital Initiative (BFHI). Baby-Friendly is a designation a hospital or birthing site can receive by demonstrating compliance with the Ten Steps to Successful Breastfeeding (Table 12.7). As of September 2009, there were approximately 20,000 Baby-Friendly sites throughout the world, with 84 in the United States.

The American Academy of Pediatrics has published a statement indicating that breastfeeding is safe for mothers on methadone maintenance programs (Jansson, 2008; AAP 2001). Because of the small amount of methadone present in breast milk (about 2.8% of maternal dose), breastfeeding may even decrease the severity of NAS (Abdel-Latif, 2006). Boston Medical Center has an institutional breastfeeding policy, including a subsection for mothers on a methadone maintenance program (see Table 12.3). Mothers are encouraged to breastfeed only if they have been in a structured rehabilitation therapy program for at least ten weeks prior to delivery, have been compliant with prenatal care visits, and have had negative (normal) urine drug screens during pregnancy. Breastfeeding is contraindicated if mother has HIV or is using illicit drugs.

Selective serotonin-reuptake inhibitors (SSRIs) are the most commonly used antidepressants in postpartum mothers (Burgos & Burke, 2009) and have been

TABLE 12.7 *Ten Steps to Successful Breastfeeding*

1. Have a written breastfeeding policy that is routinely communicated to all healthcare staff.
2. Train all healthcare staff in skills necessary to implement this policy.
3. Inform all pregnant women about the benefits and management of breastfeeding.
4. Help mothers initiate breastfeeding within one hour of birth.
5. Show mothers how to breastfeed and how to maintain lactation, even if they should be separated from their infants.
6. Give newborn infants no food or drink other than breast milk, unless *medically* indicated.
7. Practice "rooming-in"—allow mothers and infants to remain together 24 hours a day.
8. Encourage breastfeeding on demand.
9. Give no pacifiers or artificial nipples to breastfeeding infants.
10. Foster the establishment of breastfeeding support groups and refer mothers to them on discharge from the hospital or clinic.

Source: WHO/UNICEF, 1989.

widely studied in pregnant and breastfeeding women (Levinson-Castiel et al., 2006). Sertraline (Zoloft), paroxetine (Paxil), and fluvoxamine (Luvox) have the lowest degree of transfer into human milk and are therefore the first-choice drugs for treatment of maternal depression for breastfeeding mothers (Fortinguerra, 2009). Fluoxetine (Prozac) produces significant plasma concentrations in some breastfed infants, especially if exposure began *in utero* (Hale, 2004). These infants should be monitored for uneasy sleep, irritability, poor feeding, poor suckling (Burgos & Burke, 2009; Anthony, 2009; Hale, 2004).

To promote adequate growth, the baby should be breastfed eight to twelve times in 24 hours (if breastfeeding is not contraindicated), or fed hypercaloric formula (24 calories per ounce). High-calorie formula is indicated to promote growth in the face of irritability, poor state control, tremulousness, and hypertonicity (Hamdan, 2010; Chasnoff, 2003). Mothers who are breastfeeding should be offered lactation assistance.

Mother and infant should be kept together as much as possible following birth. Staff should facilitate skin-to-skin contact between mother and baby to help establish breastfeeding and to enable thermoregulation of the infant (Kennell & McGrath, 2003). Routine medical interventions (such as administration of eye ointment and vitamin K) should be delayed for at least one hour to promote mother–infant bonding and to establish breastfeeding if it is not contraindicated (Klaus & Kennell, 2002; Klaus et al., 1995; Klaus & Klaus, 1998).

Newborn Nursery Discharge

Prior to discharge, the newborn should be taking oral feeds, consistently gaining weight, physiologically stable, and showing neurobehavioral recovery (alert state, responsive to social stimuli, able to be consoled with reasonable measures) (Hamden, 2010). The clinician should ensure that parents and foster caregivers have all the information they need to safely care for the newborn. In addition to feeding, identification of jaundice, thermometers and temperature-taking, the clinician should focus on tummy time and sleep position. Sudden Infant Death Syndrome (SIDS) is significantly higher among infants who are exposed to drugs *in utero* (3.7-fold higher for methadone and 2.3-fold higher cocaine, compared to infants with no exposure) (Hamden 2010). However, like all babies, it is important for these infants to be placed on the abdomen when monitored to prevent plagiocephaly and to promote healthy development of shoulder and hip muscles.

The home environment should be carefully considered and screened for domestic violence (see Table 12.8) (Groves, Augustyn, Lee, & Sawires, 2004; Thackeray et al., 2010). In addition, depression is common and carries a lifetime risk of 10 to 25 percent in all women, with a peak prevalence occurring between the childbearing ages of 25 and 44 (Wisner et al., 1999). New mothers should be screened for postpartum depression and given appropriate evaluation, referrals, follow-up appointments, and telephone contacts prior to discharge.

The Patient Health Questionnaire–2 (PHQ-2) is an excellent two-question screen for adult depression. The brief screening tool inquires about the frequency of depressed mood and anhedonia over the past two weeks. Patients are asked,

TABLE 12.8 *Approach to Domestic Violence Inquiry*

Type of Inquiry/ Statement	Examples
Introductory statements or questions	• "I have begun to ask all of the women/parents/caregivers in my practice about their family life as it affects their health and safety, and that of their children. May I ask you a few questions?" • "Violence is an issue that unfortunately effects everyone today, and thus I have begun to ask all families in my practice about exposure to violence. May I ask you a few questions?"
Indirect questions	• "What happens when there is a disagreement with your partner/husband/boyfriend or other adults in your home?" • "Do you feel safe in your home and in your relationship?"
Direct questions	• "Have you ever been hurt or threatened by your partner/husband or boyfriend?" • "Do you ever feel afraid of (or controlled or isolated by) your partner/husband/boyfriend?" • "Has your child witnessed a violent or frightening event in your neighborhood or home?"

Examples from Groves, B. M., Augustyn, M., Lee, D., and Sawires, P., 2004: *Identifying and Responding to Domestic Violence: Consensus Recommendations for Child and Adolescent Health.* Produced by The Family Violence Fund, 383 Rhode Island Street, Suite 304, San Francisco, CA 94103–5133, (415) 252–8900. TTY (800) 595–4889. www.endabuse.org

"Over the past two weeks, how often have you been bothered by any of the following problems: 1) [loss of] interest or pleasure in doing things; 2) feeling down, depressed, or hopeless?" Scores range from 0 (not at all) to 3 (nearly every day). A score 3 had 83 percent sensitivity and 90 percent specificity for major depression (Kroenke et al., 2003).

Parents who have a trusting relationship with the medical community are more likely to confide sensitive information, which can lead to treatment and prevention of future morbidity. Parents who trust their child's clinician are more likely to comply with medical recommendations and return for outpatient care, especially if they understand the reason for their follow-up appointments.

Infants who are deemed to be eligible for early intervention (EI) should be referred at the earliest opportunity to avoid missing the opportunity for critical developmental intervention, and the primary care clinician should ensure that EI has been established. Identifying the family's non-medical needs (such as health insurance; car seats; financial, housing, immigration, employment, or day-care assistance; Women, Infant's and Children (WIC) support; food and other material needs), the health care team, especially social workers and case managers, can be a valuable link to crucial services.

Project HEALTH was founded at Boston Medical Center in 1996 (www.projecthealth.org). Recognizing that poverty creates a "double jeopardy" for infants and children with poor heath, Project HEALTH workers, volunteer Harvard University college students, work with families in the nursery to obtain assistance with housing, immigration, food security, jobs, child care, and a host of other nonmedical needs that threaten the health of the child. Project Health sites serve over 40,000 families annually in six cities: Baltimore, Boston, Chicago, New York City,

Providence, and Washington, D.C. Medical-Legal Partnerships, now practiced in over 180 clinical sites to address violations of legal protections (e.g., safe housing) and benefits such as access to food, health insurance, and supplemental security income (SSI), back up the healthcare team to insure material stability and reduce stress (Zuckerman et al., 2004; Zuckerman et al., 2008).

Multidisciplinary Follow-up Programs

Infants who are prenatally exposed to substances are at high risk for developmental problems and should be followed in a neonatal intensive care unit (NICU) follow-up program or similar multidisciplinary program for infants at risk. Infants should be monitored over time for developmental progress until their development is determined to have normalized or until they are enrolled in an appropriate early-intervention program or similar program that will follow the infant developmentally over time. Boston Medical Center has a program for infants at risk called Baby Steps for Healthy Infant Development. Infants are seen at approximately one month of age by a developmental pediatrician, occupational therapist, nutritionist, and family advocate. The infant's growth, neurobehavior, and motor development, as well as the family's needs, continue to be monitored; and infants are followed on an individual basis. Some programs follow infants at risk for up to 48 months (Vohr, 2001).

■ DEVELOPMENTALLY FOCUSED CARE IN THE PRIMARY CARE SETTING

Infant prognosis depends upon complex factors, including socioeconomic, family, and continued substance use (Hamden, 2010). One of the most important interventions for children of substance using parents is to identify pediatric primary care. Having a regular primary care clinician has been shown to improve the quality of preventive care for young children (Inkelas, 2008). Families affected by substance abuse are often chaotic. Children frequently miss appointments, have delayed immunizations, and are at higher risk for trauma, abuse, and neglect. The primary care clinician can best help families by establishing a medical "home" to intervene more effectively by ensuring that children are coming for routine appointments, up to date on immunizations, and maintaining appropriate growth for their age. Finally, continuity of care will give the clinician opportunity to learn more about the parents' history and style of parenting, while building a relationship with the family.

Clinicians provide essential anticipatory guidance regarding feeding and nutrition. The clinician should review the child's nutritional status and growth with parents at each routine health care visit and make appropriate recommendations. Laboratory testing for anemia and lead intoxication should be performed at regularly scheduled intervals, as recommended by the American Academy of Pediatrics

Children affected by substance abuse are at increased risk for developmental and behavioral disabilities because of the direct effects of drug exposure prenatally, poor maternal nutrition, and an impoverished postnatal environment, including parental mental health problems. The clinician should assess the child's level of development at each well-child visit (checkup) to ensure that the child is progressing appropriately and/or whether intervention is needed.

As children grow, they naturally demonstrate more autonomy. Substance using parents may use directive language, nonverbal commands, and limited vocabulary with their children. At each primary-care visit, the practitioner has an opportunity to model effective communication, observe development, ask about learning opportunities at home, and promote a desire for reading. Pediatricians in over 4,000 clinics nationally participate in Reach Out and Read (ROR), which gives children five years of age and under a book during their well-child visits. The program has been shown to increase children's language development, currently operates in all 50 states, and focuses on creating real-time learning experiences for children and parents during well-child visits. The clinician offers the child an age-appropriate book and assesses the child's development as he or she uses it. He talks about the importance of reading and learns whether or not there are books in the home. The book allows the practitioner an opportunity to model a positive communication style with the child and gives him a chance to affirm the child in front of the parent.

Infants of substance using parents should be considered for early intervention. After age three, the clinician can help families access appropriate educational opportunities, such as Head Start (Silverstein, 2004), and special education services if needed. Children with language delays should be referred to an audiologist for formal hearing evaluation and should be tested for anemia and high lead levels as part of a formal developmental evaluation. School-age children who are not functioning at a developmental level appropriate for their age should be referred for more intensive evaluation through the school system or through a developmental assessment program.

Safety

Pediatric clinicians see children more often than adult providers and have a critical opportunity to identify ongoing substance use in parents (SAMHSA, 2009; Smith, 2007). The clinician should assess the safety of the child's environment at each visit and look for evidence of domestic violence, ongoing substance abuse, failure to thrive, physical and sexual abuse, and neglect. Issues that should alert the clinician include missed medical appointments, emergency room visits, evidence of injuries, poor growth, and poor compliance with medical advice. The clinician should collaborate with the institution's child protection team or the state child protection agency to ensure that cases of suspected neglect or abuse are appropriately investigated and interventions implemented as needed.

Environmental Support

Poor living conditions threaten to compound the health risks of children affected by substance abuse. Mold in carpeting and rodent infestations may trigger asthma exacerbations, leading to extra hospital visits and missed school. Families with immigration problems may be afraid to seek medical care for their children, leading to immunization delays and undiagnosed medical illnesses. Developmental delays and school problems that go unaddressed by school systems may lead to school failure, delinquency, and eventual dropping out. The Medical Legal Partnership (MLP) provides free legal assistance to families for their children. The program partners with large legal firms who represent poor families who have issues concerning food, housing, immigration, school placement, and domestic abuse. The program operates out of 200 hospitals and clinics nationally and serves approximately 13,000 families per year.

■ SUMMARY

Effective intervention for children of substance using parents requires paying attention to the direct effects of drugs and to the child's environment. The most effective interventions may be to address the family's socioeconomic needs, maternal caregiving, and child development and safety.

■ AUTHORS' NOTE

The authors wish to thank Melissa Brennan for her assistance with preparation of this manuscript.

■ REFERENCES

Abdel-Latif, M. E., Pinner, J., Clews, S., Cooke, F., Lui, K., & Oei, J. (2006). Effects of breast milk on the severity and outcome of neonatal abstinence syndrome among infants of drug-dependent mothers. *Pediatrics, 117*, e1163–e1169. doi:10.1542/peds.2005–1561

Agthe, A. G., Mathias, K. B., Hendrix, C. W., et al. (2006). A blinded randomized clinical trial of clonidine in combination with diluted tincture of opium (DTO) versus DTO alone for opioid withdrawal in newborn infants. *European Journal Of Pediatrics, 165*(Suppl), 11–12.

American Academy of Pediatrics. (2001). Transfer of drugs and other chemicals into human milk. *Pediatrics, 108*(3), 776–789.

American Academy of Pediatrics Committee on Fetus and Newborn. (2010). Hospital stay for healthy term newborns. *Pediatrics, 125*, 405–409. doi: 10.1542/peds.2009–3119.

American Academy of Pediatrics Section on Breastfeeding. (2005). Breastfeeding and the use of human milk. *Pediatrics, 115*(2), 496–506.

Brazelton, T. B. (1973). Neonatal Behavioral Assessment Scale. *Clinics in Developmental Medicine*, No. 50. London, England: Spastics International Medical Publications.

Brazelton, T. B., & Nugent, J. K. (1995). Neonatal Behavioral Assessment Scale. *Clinics in Developmental Medicine*, No. 137. London, England: MacKeith Press.

Bresnahan, K., Brooks, C., Zuckerman, B. (1991). Prenatal cocaine use: Impact on infants and mothers. *Pediatric Nursing, 17*(2), 123–129.

Burgos, A. E., & Burke, B. L. (2009). Neonatal abstinence syndrome. *NeoReviews*, *10*(5), e222–e229. doi:10.1542/neo.10-5-e222.

Chasnoff, I. J. (2003). Prenatal substance exposure: maternal screening and neonatal identification and management. *NeoReviews*, *4*, 228. doi:10.1542/neo.4-9-e228

Chasnoff, I. J., Burns, W. J., Schnoll, S. H., & Burns, K. A. (1985). Cocaine use in pregnancy. *New England Journal of Medicine*, *313*, 666–669.

Chasnoff, I. J., Burns, K. A., Burns, W. J., & Schnoll, S. H. (1986). Prenatal drug exposure: Effects on neonatal and infant growth and development. *Neurobehavioral Toxicology & Teratology*, *8*, 357–362.

Chasnoff, I. J., Griffith, D. R., MacGregor, S., Dirkes, K., & Burnes, K. A. (1989). Temporal patterns of cocaine use in pregnancy. *Journal of the American Medical Association*, *261*, 1741–1744.

Children of Alcoholics Foundation. (1994). *Twice at Risk: A Forum on Children Affected by Family Violence and Parental Addiction*. New York: Children of Alcoholics Foundation.

Clapp, J., Wesley, M., & Cooke, R. (1986). The effects of marijuana smoke on gas exchange in bovine pregnancy. *Alcohol & Drug Research*, *7*, 85.

The Drug Addiction Treatment Act of 2000, Title XXXV, Section 3502 of the Children's Health Act of 2000.

Dryden, C., Young, D., Hepburn, M., & Mactier, H. (2009). Maternal methadone use in pregnancy: Factors associated with the development of neonatal abstinence syndrome and implications for healthcare resources. *BJOG*, *116*(5), 665–671.

Ebner, N., Rohrmeister, K., Winklbaur, B., et al. (2007). Management of neonatal abstinence syndrome in neonates born to opioid maintained women. *Drug & Alcohol Dependency*, *87*(2–3), 131–138.

Farid, W. O., Dunlop, S. A., Tait, R. J., & Hulse, G. K. (2008). The effects of maternally administered methadone, buprenorphine and naltrexone on offspring: A review of human and animal data. *Current Neuropharmacology*, *6*(2), 125–150.

Finnegan, L. P. (1986). Neonatal abstinence syndrome: Assessment and pharmacotherapy. In F. F. Rubaltelli, B. Granati, & B. Granti (Eds.), *Neonatal Therapy: An Update* (pp. 122–146). New York: Excerpta Medica.

Finnegan, L. P., Connaughton, J. F. Jr., Kron, R. E., & Emich, J. P. (1975). Neonatal abstinence syndrome: Assessment and management. *Journal of Addictive Diseases*, *2*, 141–158.

Fortinguerra, F., Clavenna, A., & Bonati, M. (2009). Psychotropic drug use during breastfeeding: A review of the evidence. *Pediatrics*, *124*, e547–e556; originally published online Sept. 7, 2009.

Frank. D, Bresnahan, K., & Zuckerman, B. (1993). Maternal cocaine use: Impact on child health and development. In Y. B. Barness (Ed.), *Advances in Pediatrics* (Vol. 40, pp. 65–99). St. Louis, MO: Mosby Yearbook.

Frank, D. A., Bauchner, H., Parker, S., Huber, A., Kyei-Aboagye K., Cabral, H., & Zuckerman, B. (1990). Neonatal body proportionality and body composition after *in utero* exposure to cocaine and marijuana. *Journal of Pediatrics*, *117*, 622–626.

Frank, D. A., Zuckerman, B., Reece, H., Amaro, H., Hingson, R., Fried, L., et al. (1988). Cocaine use during pregnancy: Prevalence and correlates. *Pediatrics*, *82*, 888–895.

Fulroth, R., Phillips, B., & Durand, D. J. (1989). Perinatal outcome of infants exposed to cocaine and/or heroin *in utero*. *American Journal of Diseases of Children*, *143*, 905–910.

Gentile, S. (2010). Antipsychotic therapy during early and late pregnancy: a systematic review. *Schizophrenia Bulletin, 36*(3), 518–544.

Groves, B., Augustyn, M., Lee, D., & Sawires, P. (2004). Identifying and responding to domestic violence: Consensus recommendations for child and adolescent health. *Family Violence Prevention Fund*, 3–94.

Hamdan, A. (2010). Neonatal abstinence syndrome. Available at http://emedicine.med-scape.com/article/978763-print. Accessed March 24, 2010.

Hutchings, D. E. (1982). Methadone and heroin during pregnancy: A review of behavioral effects in human and animal offspring. *Neurobehavioral Toxicology & Teratology, 4*, 429–434.

Inkelas, M., Newacheck, P. W., Olson, L. M., Zuckerman, B., & Schuster, M. (2008). Does having a regular primary care clinician improve quality of preventive care for young children? *Medical Care, 46*(3), 323–330.

Jansson, L. M., Choo, R., Celez, M. L., Harrow, C., Schroeder, J. R., & Shakleya, D. M. (2008). Methadone maintenance and breastfeeding in the neonatal period. *Pediatrics, 121*(1), 106–114.

Jones, H. E., Johnson, R. E., & Jasinski, D. R., et al. (2005). Buprenorphine versus metha-done in the treatment of pregnant opioid-dependent patients: Effects on the neonatal abstinence syndrome. *Drug & Alcohol Dependency, 79*(1), 1–10.

Jones, H. E., Kaltenbach, K., Heil, S. H., et al. (2010). Neonatal abstinence syndrome after methadone or buprenorphine exposure. *New England Journal of Medicine, 363*, 2320–2331.

Kacinko, S. L., Jones, H. E., Johnson, R. E., Choo, R. E., & Huestis, M. A. (2008). Correlations of maternal buprenorphine dose, buprenorphone, and metabolite concentrations in meconium with neonatal outcomes. *Clinical Pharmacology & Therapeutics, 84*(5), 604–612.

Kassima, Z., & Greenough, A. (2006). Neonatal abstinence syndrome: Identification and management. *Current Paediatrics, 16*, 172–175.

Kennell, J. H., & McGrath, S. K. (2003). Beneficial effects of postnatal skin-to-skin contact. *Acta Paediatrica, 92*, 272–273.

Kenyon, C., Sandel, M., Silverstein, M., Shakir, A., & Zuckerman, B. (2007). Revisiting the social history for child health. *Pediatrics, 120*(3), e734–e738.

Klaus, M. H., & Kennell, J. H. (2002). Commentary: Routines in maternity units: are they still appropriate for 2002? *Birth, 28*(4), 270–273.

Klaus, M. H., & Klaus, P. H. (1998). *Your Amazing Newborn*. Cambridge, MA: Perseus Books.

Klaus, M. H., Kennell J. H., & Klaus, P. H. (1995). *Bonding*. Reading, MA: Addison Wesley Longman.

Koren, G., Matsui, D., Einanson, A., Knopper, D., & Steiner, M. (2005). Using antidepres-sants during pregnancy. *Canadian Medical Association Journal, 173* (10), 1205–1206. doi:10.1503/cmaj.1050171.

Kraft, W. K., Gibson, E., Dysart, K., et al. (2008). Sublingual buprenorphine for treat-ment of neonatal abstinences syndrome: A randomized trial. *Pediatrics, 122*(3), e601–e607.

Kroenke, K., Spitzer, R., & Williams, J. (2003). The Patient Health Questionnaire–2: Validity of a two-item depression screener. *Medical Care, 41*(11), 1284–1292.

Kron, R. E. M., Litt, M., & Phoenix, M. D. (1976). Neonatal narcotic abstinence: Effects of pharmacotherapeutic agents and maternal drug usage on nutritive sucking behavior. *Journal of Pediatrics, 88*, 637–641.

Lester, B. M., & Tronick, E. Z. (2004). History and description of the neonatal intensive care unit network neurobehavioral scale. *Pediatrics, 113*(3 Pt 2), 634–640.

Lester, B. (2001). The maternal lifestyle study: Drug use by meconium toxicology and maternal self report. *Pediatrics, 107*, 309–317.

Levinson-Castiel, R., Merlob, P., Linder, N., Sirota, L., & Klinger, G. (2006). Neonatal abstinence syndrome after *in utero* exposure to selective serotonin reuptake inhibitors in term infants. *Archives of Pediatrics & Adolescent Medicine., 160*, 173–176.

Lim, S., Prasad, M. R., Samuels, P., Gardner, D. K., & Cordero, L. (2009). High dose methadone in pregnant women and its effect on duration of neonatal abstinence syndrome. *American Journal of Obstetrics & Gynecology, 200*(1): 70. e1–5.

Lipsitz, P. J. (1975). A proposed narcotic withdrawal score for use with newborn infants. A pragmatic evaluation of its efficacy. *Clinical Pediatrics, 14*, 592–594.

McElhatton, P. R. (1994). The effects of benzodiazepine use during pregnancy and lactation. *Reproductive Toxicology Review, 8*(6), 461–475.

National Institute on Drug Abuse. (1994). *Mental Health Assessment and Diagnosis of Substance Abusers* (Clinical Report Series, NIH Publication No. 94–3846). Bethesda, MD: National Institutes of Health.

Newport, D. J., Calameras, M. R., DeVane, C. L. et al. (2007). Atypical antipsychotic administration during late pregnancy: placental passage and obstetrical outcome. *American Journal of Psychiatry, 164*, 1214–1220.

Nugent, J. K., Keefer, C. H., Minear, S., Johnson, L., & Blanchard, Y. (2007). *Understanding Newborn Behavior and Early Relationships: The Newborn Behavioral Observations (NBO) System Handbook*. Baltimore, MD: Brookes Publishing Co.

Ostrea, E. M., Chavez, C. J., & Strauss, M. E. (1976). A study of factors that influence the severity of neonatal narcotic withdrawal. *Journal of Pediatrics, 88*, 642–645.

Ostrea, E. M., Ostrea, A. R., & Simpson, P. M. (1997). Mortality within the first 2 years in infants exposed to cocaine, opiate, or cannabinoid during gestation. *Pediatrics, 100*(1), 79–83.

Regier, D. A., Farmer, M. E., Rae, D. S., Locke, B. Z., Keith, S. J., Judd, L. L., et al. (1990). Comorbidity of mental disorders with alcohol and other drug abuse. *Journal of the American Medical Association, 264*(19), 2511–2518.

Ryan, R. M., Wagner, C. L., & Schultz, J. M., et al. (1994). Meconium analysis for improved identification of infants exposed to cocaine in utero. *Journal of Pediatrics, 125*(3), 435–440.

SAMHSA. (2009). *Substance Use Among Women During Pregnancy and Following Childbirth*. Rockville, MD.

SAMHSA Office of Applied Studies. (2003). National survey on drug use and health: Results. Available at http://www.drugabusestatistics.samhsa.gov/NHSDA/2k3NSDUH/2k3results.htm.

Sanz, E. J., De-las Cuevas, C., Kiuru, A., Bate, A., & Edwards, R. (2005). Selective serotonin reuptake inhibitors in pregnant women and neonatal withdrawal syndrome: A database analysis. *Lancet, 365*, 482–487.

Sarkar, S., & Donn, S. M. (2006). Management of neonatal abstinence syndrome in neonatal intensive care units: A national survey. *Journal of Perinatology, 26*(1), 7–15.

Schade, J. G., Joyce, B. A., Gerkensmeyer, J., & Keck, J. F. (1996). Comparison of three pre-verbal scales for postoperative pain assessment in a diverse pediatric sample. *Journal of Pain Symptom Management, 12*, 348–359.

Seval Brooks, C. S. and Rice, K. F. (1997). *Families in Recovery: Coming Full Circle.* Baltimore, MD: Brookes Publishing Company.

Silverstein, M., Mack, C., Reavis, N., et al.,(2004). Effect of a clinic-based referral system to head start: A randomized controlled trial. *Journal of the American Medical Association, 292*(8), 968–971.

Smith, D. K., Johnson, A. B., Pears, K. C., Fisher, P. A, and DeGarmo, D. S. (2007). Child maltreatment and foster care: Unpacking the effects of prenatal and postnatal parental substance use. *Child Maltreatment, 12*(2), 150–160.

Smith, L., Yonekura, M. I., Wallace, T., Berman, N., Kuo, J., & Berkowitz, C. (2003). Effects of prenatal methamphetamine exposure on fetal growth and drug withdrawal symptoms in infants born at term. *Journal of Developmental & Behavioral Pediatrics, 24*, 17–23.

Stokowski, L. A. (2003). Stemming the rising tide of prematurity. Available at: http://cme.medscape.com/viewarticle/465021_print.

Stowe, Z., & Newport, J. (2007). The management of bipolar disorder during pregnancy. Available at http://www.medscape.com/viewarticle/565128_print.

Thackeray, J., Hibbard, R., Dowd, M., and the Committee on Child Abuse and Neglect and the Committee on Injury, Violence and Poison Prevention. (2010). Intimate partner violence: The role of the pediatrician. *Pediatrics, 125*, 1094–1100.

Vohr, B. R. (2001). Neonatal follow-up programs in the new millennium. *Neoreviews, 2*, 241–248. doi: 10.1542/neo.2-11-e241.

Wang, M. (2009). Perinatal drug abuse and neonatal drug withdrawal. Available at: http://emedicine.medscape.com/article/978492-print.

Wang, X., Zuckerman, B., Pearson, C., et al. (2002). Maternal cigarette smoking, meta-bolic gene polymorphism, and infant birth weight. *Journal of the American Medical Association, 287*, 195–202.

William Gladden Foundation. (2005). *Children of Alcoholic Families.* Tallahassee, FL,

Wisner, K. L., Gelenberg, A. J., Leonard, H., Zarin, D., & Frank, E. (1999). Pharmacological treatment of depression during pregnancy. *Journal of the American Medical Association, 282*, 1264–1269.

Wouldes, T. A., & Woodward, L. J. (2010). Maternal methadone dose during pregnancy and infant clinical outcome. *Neurotoxicology Teratology, 32*(3), 406–413.

Wu, T., Tashkin, D., & Djahed, B. (1988). Pulmonary hazards of smoking marijuana as compared to tobacco. *New England Journal of Medicine, 318*, 347.

Zahorodny, W., Rom, C., & Whitney, W., et al. (1998). The Neonatal Withdrawal Inventory: a simplified score of newborn withdrawal. *Journal of Developmental & Behavioral Pediatrics, 19*, 89–93.

Zuckerman, B., Sandel, M., Lawton, E., & Morton, S. (2008). Medical-Legal Partnership: transforming health care. *Lancet, 372*(9650), 1615–1617.

Zuckerman, B., Sandel, M., Smith, L., & Lawton, E. (2004). Why pediatricians need lawyers to keep children healthy. *Pediatrics, 114*(1), 224–228.

Zuckerman, B., & Bresnahan, K. (1991). Developmental and behavioral consequences of prenatal drug and alcohol exposure. *Pediatric Clinics of North America, 83*, 1387–1407.

Zuckerman, B., Frank, D., Hingson, R., Amaro, H., Levenson, S. M., Kayne, H., et al. (1989). Effects of maternal marijuana and cocaine on fetal growth. *New England Journal of Medicine, 320,* 762–768.

Zuckerman, B. S., & Hingson, R. (1986). Alcohol consumption during pregnancy: a critical review. *Developmental Medicine & Child Neurology, 28*(5), 649–654.

13 The Substance-Exposed Dyad

Evaluation and Intervention in the Perinatal Period

MARTHA L. VELEZ AND
LAUREN M. JANSSON

The use and abuse of psychoactive substances during pregnancy remains a major public health and societal problem internationally, given its frequency, the potential adverse consequences on pregnancy and birth outcomes, and the effects on the mother's ability to provide care for a child with potential physiological and behavioral challenges. It is estimated that 16% to 30% of pregnant women ages 15 to 44 use tobacco, 10% to 15% use alcohol, 3% to 10% use cannabis, and 0.5% to 3% use cocaine during pregnancy (Lamy, 2010). Illicit opioid use is found in 0.1% of all pregnant women in the United States, and misuse of psychotherapeutic agents and pain relievers by pregnant women, including OxyContin®, is a significant problem. It is estimated that 4.4% of pregnant women used opioid analgesics without appropriate medical oversight in the past year, with 15- to 17-year-old pregnant females having the highest incidences of all age groups reported (15%). Another concerning issue for providers caring for pregnant, substance dependent women is the resumption of use following childbirth (SAMHSA, 2004; SAMHSA, 2005; SAMHSA, 2009).

The problems experienced by each substance-dependent pregnant woman are unique, usually complex, and each can have an individual or cumulative effect on her ability to parent and the child's development. Individualized and comprehensive care of the mother/fetal or mother/infant dyad, therefore, becomes an important and often challenging proposition, geared to the individual medical and psychosocial difficulties displayed by mother, the at-risk fetus/infant, and the combination of the two considered in the context of their environment.

The quality of the pregnancy and the early mother–infant relationship have been noted as important factors that may either exacerbate or soften the potentially adverse impact of prenatal substance exposure and associated negative perinatal outcomes, particularly concerning the infant's later competencies and development (Jansson, 1996; Suchman, 2008). This chapter will describe, based on a theoretical framework, review of the literature, clinical observations, and empirical data, the problems faced by the pregnant drug-dependent woman that can impact the relationship between mother and infant, and suggested interventions during the perinatal period.

■ **PROBLEMS FACED BY THE PREGNANT DRUG-DEPENDENT WOMAN AND EFFECTS ON THE DEVELOPING CHILD**

Complex health and social problems characterize perinatal substance abuse. These can include the direct effects of illicit substance use and/or licit substance misuse, indirect effects of the lifestyle associated with drug dependency (malnutrition, incarceration, homelessness, domestic violence); medical (HIV/AIDS, sexually transmitted diseases); and psychiatric complications (mood disorders, post-traumatic stress disorder, etc.) (Sales, 2000; Hans, 1999; LaGasse, 1999). It is well accepted that prenatal exposure to illicit and misuse of licit substances is a substantial and preventable risk factor for medical, developmental and behavioral problems in children. However, substance exposure is currently considered a marker or risk indicator in a contextual framework to explain the outcome of the prenatally substance exposed newborn. For these reasons, interventions with pregnant substance dependent women must integrate strategies to address the spectrum of biological and psychosocial risk factors that contribute to the poor perinatal outcomes associated with prenatal substance abuse, with consideration for the overall physical and mental health of the dyad.

Substance Abuse

Addiction affects adult brain function in ways that have direct implications for the achievement of maternal developmental tasks (e.g., appropriate prenatal care and nutrition, reduction of risky behaviors) that impact fetal and infant well-being. Preclinical and clinical studies indicate that addiction causes adaptations in various neurocircuitries and functions of several brain regions that mediate the transition from occasional, recreational drug use, to loss of control and chronic relapse even in the face of adverse consequences, such as the possibility of damaging the developing fetus or losing custody of the newborn. The transition to addiction entails reprogramming of neuronal circuits involved in 1) motivation and reward; 2) memory, attention, conditioning, and habituation; 3) executive function and inhibitory control; 4) interoception, insight, and self-awareness; and 5) reactivity to stress (Goldstein, 2009; Koob, 2010). Compromise in these functions affects the daily functioning of drug-dependent women and can explain many behaviors that put them at risk for being unable to provide care for themselves or their offspring.

Maternal drug use can also derail normal fetal and infant development directly and indirectly, through prenatal substance exposure and/or alterations in maternal care (Strathearn, 2010). Fetal exposure to drugs and other intrauterine stressors related to maternal addiction during critical periods can alter the fetal brain developmental processes and produce structural and/or functional changes resulting in an enhanced risk of medical, developmental, and emotional/behavioral disability in the developing infant (Salisbury, 2009). Epigenetic models of developmental theory, examining the intersecting influences of genes, physiology, and behavior with the physical, cultural, and social environment, have been implicated in the alteration of developmental trajectories in drug- and alcohol-exposed infants (Lester, 2009; Hellemans, 2010; Zhang, 2005), with consequences that can be seen at birth or that do not emerge until later life, and may be produced at drug levels that are insignificant for adults. Fetal programming theory suggests that fetal exposure to maternal illness and other intrauterine stressors that are probably mediated through the neurohormonal environment alters fetal hypothalamic-pituitary-adrenal (HPA) axis development with resulting vulnerability to medical and psychiatric disorders later in life (Salisbury, 2009). Most pregnant women suffering from addiction are aware of the potential negative effects of drug use for the pregnancy and fetus, and this awareness can be a motivation to seek treatment during pregnancy in an effort to maintain custody of the child (Howell, 1999). However, the transition to motherhood created by a pregnancy (planned or unplanned) and the process of recovery from active substance abuse and the attendant lifestyle involves physical, cognitive, emotional, and often spiritual changes that require serious personal commitment. The ability to commit to changes in one's lifestyle conducive to recovery from substance use and a healthy pregnancy depend on many factors, including the severity of the substance abuse and associated problems (Shieh, 2006).

Many substance-dependent women struggle between illicit drug use and the development of positive affiliative feelings toward the fetus, or maternal fetal attachment (MFA). Interventions that promote sobriety, preparation for motherhood during pregnancy, and a healthy MFA require evaluation of the maternal addiction history and neuropsychological status, and the effects of her substance use on her functioning in general and as a mother. Maternal awareness of the potential effects of her addiction and her associated lifestyle on the fetus/infant, and her efforts to stay emotionally and physically connected with her fetus, may be used as a motivator to make lifestyle changes needed to decrease intrauterine stressors and provide a nurturing developmental environment for the child (Shieh, 2006). Care providers need to consider the broad range of neurocognitive deficits and psychopathological symptoms associated with chronic substance abuse when addressing the barriers affecting maternal developmental tasks during pregnancy in this population.

Medical/Obstetrical Issues

In addition to symptoms associated with drug withdrawal or intoxication due to detoxification or relapse to drug use, there are several medical and obstetrical problems that are common in substance-dependent women, including infections (HIV/AIDS, hepatitis C and B, sexually transmitted diseases), hypertension, abruptio placenta, premature labor and delivery, chronic pain, and injuries due to physical or sexual abuse (Evans, 1991; Gyarmathy, 2009). The physical and emotional demands of these conditions, in addition to the physical and psychological changes related to the pregnancy, can compromise the functioning of the woman and additionally affect fetal and/or infant health.

The severity of medical problems may impact compliance with drug treatment and compromise other aspects of obstetric care. For example, testing for HIV is essential due to elevated risk related to unsafe sex practices and intravenous drug use, and for the interruption of mother-to-child transmission with antiretroviral therapy. However, healthcare providers need to be prepared to assess her feelings created by the diagnosis (e.g., fear of the partner's reaction, fear of the effect on the infant, shame, anger); the impact of the diagnosis as a stressor upon the woman and her pregnancy; and the adaptation processes she uses to manage her life, her relationship with partner(s) and children, and her disease. Frequently, stressful events can lead to inconsistent medical therapy and poor prenatal-care decision-making (Jones, 2008). Education regarding hepatitis B/C is important; knowledge of having these infections can increase feelings of guilt, weaken an already poor self-image, and create a sense of being unable to protect the child. In addition to the anxiety created by diagnoses such as these, the women, their partners, and their families frequently have questions, concerns, and mistaken beliefs that can create unnecessary stress, risky behaviors due to lack of knowledge, or detrimental effects on relationships. One anecdotal example involves a mother who was forbidden to see her children by their legal guardian grandmother after the mother was diagnosed with hepatitis C. Unintended, unwanted, and mistimed pregnancies, more common in substance-dependent women (Sinha, 2007), increase the risk for low birth weight and pre-term birth (Shah, 2011). Other factors that contribute to these neonatal conditions are maternal polysubstance abuse, stress, and poor nutrition. Infant medical problems can create additional demands that can increase difficulties with the postpartum attachment process and interactional mother/infant development (Johnson, 2001); further compounding the developmental and other difficulties with these vulnerable dyads.

Psychiatric Issues

Psychiatric disorders are particularly common coexistent conditions among substance-dependent pregnant women, with a prevalence rate of 45% to 73%. Depression and anxiety are the most common diagnoses; personality disorders are also frequent (Fitzsimons, 2007; Oei, 2009; Haller, 1993). The impact of psychiatric disorders on the well-being of the pregnancy and the developing fetus/infant relationship has received increased attention, reflecting a wider appreciation of the impact of the quality of caregiving during these developmental periods on the lasting mental health outcomes for the children (Hart, 2006).

Psychiatric comorbidity can affect substance abuse treatment enrollment and retention among pregnant women, and has been associated with less prenatal care, more domestic violence, and more previous pregnancies (Haller 2003; Fitzsimons, 2007; Oei, 2009). Prenatal anxiety has been associated with less optimal maternal–fetal quality of attachment, more negative attitudes towards motherhood and the self as mother, and those women having a low quality of attachment to the fetus report more symptoms of anxiety and depression (Hart, 2006). Both depression and low MFA are predictors of negative health practices during pregnancy (Hart, 2006; Lindgren, 2001).

The negative state of mind and poor affect regulation created by psychiatric disorders has been associated with poor health practices such as smoking, poor nutrition or overeating, sedentary lifestyle, and poor adherence to medical regimens (Katon, 2003; Carrico, 2007). These behaviors during pregnancy have been associated with poor maternal weight gain, pre-term labor, low birthweight, and preeclampsia.

Medications needed to treat psychiatric illness during pregnancy may have additional effects on fetal development and infant outcome, many of which are not completely known, making the choice to accept medical therapy of psychiatric illness during pregnancy an additional stressor. Women may attribute insomnia or appetite dysregulation to normal symptoms of pregnancy and overlook symptoms of depressed mood and anhedonia. In addition, the stigma associated with depression and the asynchrony between the woman's expectation of joy during pregnancy and her symptoms of sadness and irritability cause many women to under-report psychological symptoms (Marcus, 2008; Oberlander, 2009). Postpartum depression and anxiety are additional concerns for this population.

The interaction disturbances of depressed mothers and their infants are well known, and include depressed maternal sensitivity and reduced infant responsivity, increased maternal negative affect, and problematic infant–mother attachment (Martins, 2000; Field, 2010). Interventions to foster positive mother–infant attachment need to identify psychiatric problems and their impact in mother's adjustment to pregnancy, mental representations and affect about the fetus and becoming a mother, as well as her mood state.

Abuse, Trauma, and PTSD Issues

Exposure to childhood violence, abuse, and neglect is another important concurrent condition among drug-dependent pregnant women, with major implications for maternal, fetal, and infant health. In one study, among 803 patients who completed a violence-exposure questionnaire upon entering a drug treatment facility for substance-dependent pregnant women, 72% screened positive for lifetime history of physical abuse, 43% for sexual abuse, and 69% for emotional abuse; exposure to abuse during the current pregnancy ranged from 20% for physical abuse, 7% for sexual abuse, and 41% for emotional abuse. Violent encounters with partners were frequently mutual, with 30% of the pregnant women reporting physical fights, and 56% yelling and screaming fights with their current partner. These disputes were witnessed by the children in 29% of cases. Sexual partners were the primary perpetrators of lifetime physical (84%) and emotional (81%) abuse. Parents (especially mothers) were also frequent perpetrators of physical and emotional abuse (Velez, 2006). Sexual abuse during pregnancy was more frequently perpetrated by abusers other than the partners (e.g., distant relatives or strangers) but it was not uncommonly perpetrated by partners.

Women may seek treatment during pregnancy to escape an abusive or dangerous relationship over concern for the fetus. Abuse during pregnancy has been associated with physical injuries, miscarriage, early labor, increased smoking, relapse to drug use, sexually transmitted diseases, poor nutrition, low birthweight, and several psychological problems including depression, suicide, anxiety, and PTSD. Maternal history of cumulative interpersonal trauma has been associated with greater parental dissatisfaction, more parental aggression and physical punishment, less maternal confidence, less positive relationship with children, and other difficulties in caretaking abilities (Banyard, 2003; Roberts, 2004; Cohen, 2008).

It is suggested that the relationship between a maternal history of childhood sexual abuse, aspects related to her interaction with the child, parenting practices, and children's adjustment are mediated in part by aspects of the mother's mental health such as levels of anxiety, maternal confidence, anger, and deficits in emotional regulation (Roberts, 2004; DiLillo, 2000). Emotional regulation deficits have been consistently demonstrated in substance abusing populations (Hien & Honeyman, 2000; Hien & Miele, 2003). Difficulty regulating emotions is considered a risk factor underlying maternal aggressive behavior toward children (e.g., Hien, 2000) and partners (Hien, 2003) exceeding other factors, including psychiatric and substance use disorders.

Among substance-dependent women, pregnancies can be the product of rape by strangers, a family member, or a partner. Sexual violation can have profound effects on the woman's perception of her pregnancy, fetus, and infant, and it can be a very difficult topic for some women to address, creating great emotional instability. Difficulty in attaching to a fetus or infant conceived by rape, mental representations influenced by the sexual assault (i.e., the infant will be a reminder of the rapist), and difficulties with the partner relationship are among the problems associated with sexual violation. Pregnancies can also be the product of prostitution, or occur due to a sexual relationship that provides material needs in exchange for company and/or sex. Infants can complicate these relationships (i.e., become an additional burden to the provider) or be used to cement a situation that provides the mother with food, housing, or affection. Implications for the infant's safety and development can be profound and should be recognized by care providers. Many women may blame themselves for past or present violent encounters, and experience feelings of shame and guilt that they can then project onto their growing child. Sexual victimization can affect childrearing practices; for example, the desire to breastfeed and success of lactation (Kendall-Tackett, 1998; Kendall-Tackett, 2007).

Psychosocial Stress

When a woman starts using drugs, the decision does not occur in a vacuum, but usually occurs in the psychosocial context of a life with preexisting stressors occurring within a complicated social construct. Stressful and challenging psychosocial environments are often part of the developmental trajectories and/or current circumstances of the pregnant substance-dependent woman, and in both instances can negatively impact her ability to achieve and/or maintain abstinence, particularly if safe coping skills to handle stress are not incorporated in her treatment in tandem with assistance in identifying and reducing stressors.

Developmental stress exposure, or the experience of childhood adversity due to parental loss, neglect or abuse, domestic violence exposure and household

TABLE 13.1 *Perceived Needs Among Drug-dependent Pregnant Women with History of Exposure to Violence, Using the Needs Assessment Questionnaire (N = 129)*

Category	%
Housing	82.0
Individual therapy for abusive relationship	74.4
Group therapy for abusive relationship	69.0
Psychiatric evaluation or medication	63.7
Legal issues	33.3
Children's foster care issues	17.2
Children's problems	30.4
Parenting	70.9
Financial assistance	72.1
Medical issues	34.5
Intensive relapse prevention group	68.3
Suicide/self-harm	6.2

dysfunction, produces a cascade of physiological and neurohumeral events that alter trajectories of brain development (Andersen, 2003; Teicher, 2002), and has been postulated to play a very important role in the initiation and maintenance of drug abuse (Kreek, 1998; Andersen, 2009; Simmons, 2009), and be a powerful trigger for relapse, possibly through the activation of craving-related neural circuitry (Duncan, 2007). Additionally, dysregulation in HPA-axis function and/ or neurohormonal alterations are likely to participate in the enhanced sensitivity to stressors.

Stress negatively affects pregnancy outcome and fetal functioning and has been implicated in epigenetic mechanisms that may derail normal fetal and infant development (Salisbury, 2009). Stressors experienced by pregnant and postpartum drug-dependent women include poverty, violence, previous or potential loss of child custody, unemployment, crime, lack of stable housing, food, or protection for her children, chaotic lifestyle, lack of community support and stigmatization by her community and family.

Since substance abuse may be one way mothers cope with lack of social support or increased stress, it is essential to identify the types of stressors that exist and how they may be affecting the woman and/or her children. Using a Need Assessment Questionnaire (Velez, 2006) to determine perceived psychosocial needs, 129 women attending comprehensive substance abuse treatment provided the data in Table 13.1.

■ INTERVENTION DURING PREGNANCY

Treatment for the drug-dependent pregnant woman must be multidisciplinary in nature and comprehensive in scope (Lester, 2004). A comprehensive network of accessible, non-judgmental, non-punitive, culturally and gender-specific services that includes provisions for the care of her pending infant and other children is necessary to lower the barriers to care that often face this population. This comprehensive care needs to be drawn from the range of different disciplines, including addiction specialists, psychiatrists, obstetricians, and pediatricians, and it should include: individualized and group therapy sessions, psychosocial needs assessment and maternal case management, substance abuse treatment, psychiatric assessment and management, obstetrical and gynecological care, family planning, and pediatric care. Coordination between disciplines, communication between care providers and the patient, and ongoing care for the dyad are necessary.

The goals of comprehensive treatment for drug dependent pregnant woman should be to foster: 1) maternal understanding of herself (her history, her process of becoming a mother, the effects of addiction and other psychosocial problems on her health and the health of the infant); 2) identification of maladaptive coping mechanisms, and learning the practice of behaviors that help the woman feel competent as a parent; and 3) development of positive maternal concept of the pregnancy and the infant, and good mother–infant communication.

Although pregnancy is one of the biggest motivations for women to stop any substance use, each substance-dependent pregnant woman brings her own motivation and capabilities to remain abstinent and to practice healthy behaviors, depending on several factors that include:

1. genetic and epigenetic factors;
2. developmental life history;
3. addiction severity and associated impairments (e.g., loss of control over drug intake and compulsive drug-seeking, poor judgment, poor planning, and emotional dysregulation);
4. history of trauma;
5. psychiatric comorbidities;
6. medical problems;
7. obstetrical complications;
8. fetal/infant health concerns, or concerns regarding the health, development, or social-emotional and behavioral well-being of her other children;
9. social concerns; and
10. cognitive functioning.

Each of these aspects requires thorough and individualized assessment to create a treatment plan.

Interventions should be based on the premise that a comprehensive intervention needs to consider the biological, behavioral, and social issues of the patient (Leshner, 1999). Figure 13.1 summarizes the three aspects of an effective treatment for substance-dependent pregnant women, simultaneously providing pharmacological (e.g., methadone, buprenorphine, psychotropic medications), behavioral and social services interventions (Velez, 2008).

The interventions described below were developed at an urban, comprehensive care treatment facility developed in 1991, in an effort to meet the multiple needs of substance-dependent pregnant and postpartum women and their children in a comprehensive manner. The program incorporated the disciplines of mental health and substance abuse treatment, obstetrical and gynecological care, and

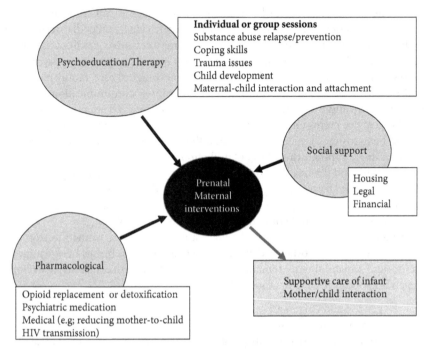

Figure 13.1 Components of Maternal Substance Abuse Treatment during Pregnancy. Comprehensive substance abuse treatment for drug-dependent pregnant women requires intervention that include pharmacological (e.g., opioid maintenance, psychiatric, and HIV medication), behavioral and psycho-educational therapy to treat symptoms related to addiction, while providing social support (e.g., case management to assist with legal, financial, and housing issues).

pediatrics at one site (for a description of the initial program, see Jansson, 1996). This chapter describes the programs developed under the initial theoretical framework and presents what the authors recommend for the comprehensive treatment of substance abusing pregnant and postpartum women.

Pharmacological Treatment

One of the most difficult decisions for women suffering from a chronic condition such as drug addiction is whether or not to start or continue taking maintenance treatment medications during pregnancy. Methadone maintenance, psychiatric medications, and medical treatment for infections (including HIV), asthma, and other conditions are frequently indicated in the treatment of pregnant substance-abusing women.

Medical, obstetrical, and psychiatric care should involve an agreed-upon and coordinated, individualized assessment and plan, including a thorough consideration and discussion of the balance between potential clinical benefit and the risk of possible negative consequences of any and all pharmacological treatments. For example, while a psychoactive medication may pose a risk to the developing fetus or infant, untreated maternal mental illness may do so as well; distinguishing the effects between medication exposure and maternal mental illness remains a key challenge for researchers (Oberlander, 2009).

Psychiatrists prescribing medications should do so in conjunction with obstetricians and pediatricians involved in the care of the dyad. Pediatricians recommending breastfeeding need to consider the maternal need for medications in the postpartum period, which may preclude lactation. Obstetricians providing prenatal care to high-risk women should consider the postpartum and pediatric requirements of the dyad. Addiction medicine specialists must consider the needs of all other providers in considering medical treatment for the woman's addiction and attendant effects on the health of the women, the fetus and the infant, and other children.

Opioid Replacement

Opioid replacement medications are indicated for the management of opioid-dependent pregnant women. Methadone and buprenorphine maintenance offer clear benefits to the pregnant and postpartum woman. Opioid replacement treatment aims to reduce the harm due to street opioid use and its associated lifestyle (e.g., prostitution, IV use, lack of prenatal care, poor nutrition, etc.), and improve the birth outcomes in offspring (Kandall, 1999). However, women and their care providers, partners, or relatives may have ideological objections to accepting methadone or buprenorphine as pharmacological treatments during pregnancy. It is well known that almost all opioid-exposed newborns will undergo symptoms of neonatal abstinence syndrome (NAS) which can result in significant neonatal morbidity and lengthy hospitalization; this reality makes the decision of accepting opioid replacement medications during pregnancy a painful and difficult one. As with psychiatric medications, the decision to accept these medications during pregnancy is a risk–benefit proposition, but it should be offered as one component of the multi-tiered and comprehensive treatment for this population of women in light of the consequences for the infant.

Behavioral and Psychoeducational Therapy

Drug-dependent women have a particular need for education regarding obstetrical issues, nutrition, addiction, relapse prevention, life-coping skills, trauma, care of the neonate, child development, parenting practices, and family planning. This education takes place in individual and group therapy. Mental health counseling and behavioral modification are critical in obtaining lasting cognitive, emotional, and behavioral transformations in substance-dependent patients. Specific cognitive and behavioral interventions can help her fight the urge for drug use (strengthen inhibitory control circuits), find alternative forms of gratification (by providing alternative reinforcers), develop the competency required to offset deficits and problems related to years of drug use, and stabilize her mood if disrupted (Volkow, 2004). Women who receive prenatal care, substance abuse treatment, parenting instruction, and mental health therapy during their pregnancy are more prepared to deal with the physical, emotional, and maternal demands of the post-partum period. Some aspects of the psychoeducational and behavioral component of treatment will be emphasized in this chapter, including the maternal developmental history, maternal–fetal attachment, trauma issues, parenting training, and preparation for the postpartum period. These aspects can greatly influence the mother–fetal-infant attachment and interaction.

Maternal History

There has been growing recognition of the need to consider the impact of psychosocial risk factors that women with substance abuse face that may directly or indirectly contribute to the quality of their parenting. A thorough developmental, medical, psychological, and social history is needed to create an individualized and comprehensive care plan. The lives of substance-dependent women are fraught with difficult past and present situations. These women are frequently raised by parents with substance abuse and psychiatric disorders and probably unable to provide continuous or adequate parental care. Often they were abandoned, neglected, or abused, creating no opportunities for internalization of appropriate parenting practices, caretaking techniques, or an adequate concept of child development. Due to their experiences during their childhood development, they are at higher risk for cognitive, emotional, and behavioral problems, including poor emotional regulation and social interaction, executive function deficits, exposure to violence within and outside the home, and higher rates of depression and post-traumatic stress disorder and substance abuse during adolescence (Conners, 2004; Clark, 2004; Simmons, 2009; SAMHSA, 2005).

Delineating the maternal history is usually complex due to the multiple difficult or extraordinary past events often experienced by the pregnant woman, frequently beginning during their infancy. It is beneficial to use a figure (see Figure 13.2) to describe the stages of development with the mother to elicit information about what she considers important events during her infancy, childhood, and adolescence, starting with her mother's pregnancy period. This exercise should result in a thorough maternal developmental and psychosocial history, and helps the woman understand how her history and her perceptions of life events affect her in the present, impact her ability to achieve and maintain sobriety, and her sense of competence in becoming a mother. This exercise helps to identify major negative or positive experiences and types of adaptive coping styles and patterns of behaviors she has adopted to manage negative events.

The same figure, with the addition of expected developmental tasks for each age period (see Figure 13.2), can be used later during individual and group parenting sessions to describe the stages of child development, expected milestones, behaviors and challenges of each stage, and the skills that mothers are encouraged to instill in their children at those specific stages. The dual use of this exercise can contribute to the mother's understanding of the importance of her effective parenting and her continued abstinence on her child's development.

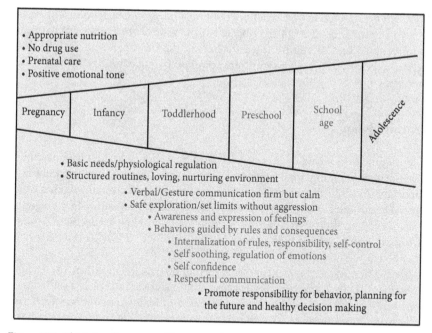

• Appropriate nutrition
• No drug use
• Prenatal care
• Positive emotional tone

Pregnancy   Infancy   Toddlerhood   Preschool   School age   Adolescence

• Basic needs/physiological regulation
• Structured routines, loving, nurturing environment
• Verbal/Gesture communication firm but calm
• Safe exploration/set limits without aggression
• Awareness and expression of feelings
• Behaviors guided by rules and consequences
• Internalization of rules, responsibility, self-control
• Self soothing, regulation of emotions
• Self confidence
• Respectful communication
• Promote responsibility for behavior, planning for the future and healthy decision making

Figure 13.2 Obtaining the maternal history in the context of her development. This figure describes lifetime developmental stages and the major skills developed in each stage. Used to gather relevant experiences in the mother's history that affected her in achieving those skills and may impact her current functioning. The figure can be also used during parenting education to illustrate the periods of child development.

Maternal-Fetal Attachment

The psychiatric, cognitive, or behavioral symptoms related to the life histories of this population of women may influence the way the woman relates to her pregnancy, the baby to be, and the choices she makes to foster fetal well-being. A solid maternal–fetal attachment (MFA) has been considered an important factor that may contribute to a successful mother–infant adaptation and postnatal attachment (Alhuse, 2008). The development of MFA among pregnant drug-dependent women seems to be characterized by conflicting feelings alternating between guilt, uncertainty, and concern for the fetus's health (Shieh, 2002). They often have difficulty in conceptualizing their gravid state as a precursor to caring for and parenting an infant.

Denial, hopelessness, or lack of readiness to accept the responsibility of motherhood or a life of abstinence is not uncommon in this population of women, some of whom have not experienced or conceptualized the opposites. In these cases, however, the healthcare provider can attempt to identify women with struggles in developing healthy representations of the fetus and the maternal–fetal relationship to facilitate any effort to decrease harm to herself and the child, whether by helping to improve her health practices or any nascent connection and willingness to protect the fetus. In addition,

MFA can be affected by maternal depression (Lindgren, 2001; Alhusen, 2008). Delay or avoidance of MFA may be self-protection from emotional pain due to unresolved loss of children, fear of having the newborn removed by child welfare services, depressive symptoms, poor self-image, and/or lack of social support.

Trauma Issues

Often, women who lived in chaotic or abusive households do not recognize abuse as abnormal. Defining what constitutes emotional, physical, or sexual abuse is important. Ideally, this can initiate a process of treating the woman who has experienced trauma in taking safety precautions, initiating measures to change the dynamic of her abusive relationships, receiving counseling to decrease psychological symptoms related to the abuse, and/or considering leaving the partner or other abusive relationships.

For women identified as being in a current abusive relationship, the Danger Assessment (DA) (Campbell 1986) can be administered. The DA is a self-administered 15-item yes/no questionnaire developed to help women assess their risk for lethality in an abusive intimate-partner relationship. This questionnaire helps some women recognize that they are in an abusive relationship that can affect her, her fetus, other children, and the pregnancy. For women who are at imminent risk, a safety plan is developed, and assistance with accessing shelter care is provided. Any decisions about staying with or leaving her partner are respected and supported if an imminent risk is not evident.

For women who are safe and are willing to explore how their substance abuse and their history of trauma, abuse, neglect, and negative parenting experiences are impacting their life and the lives of those around them, a series of assessments and individual and group sessions are offered. Improved understanding of how the combination of their history and addiction are impacting their thoughts, emotions, coping patterns, and ultimately their actions will help them understand how they came to the point where they are in their lives and what changes are required to heal and acquire new coping skills that might contribute to their development.

Maternal history of interpersonal trauma has been identified as important factor that can influence caretaking abilities (Banyard, 2003), and it is believed that the mother's understanding of her own life experiences and adaptations influence the way that she approaches her role as a mother (Siegel, 2004). Interventions that promote healing from traumatic experiences are an important component of the behavioral and psychoeducational component in the treatment of drug-dependent pregnant women. During the trauma assessment, special attention is given to the emotional states displayed by the woman while she is narrating her story and how she makes sense of her past experiences. Negative experiences are labeled and validated (e.g., emotional abuse, living with an alcoholic mother, abandonment) and protective factors (e.g., being cared by a loving and stable aunt) and strengths are pointed out.

Psychiatric Assessment

Two assessments are used to estimate the psychological functioning and impact of past and/or present traumatic events in the woman:

1. The *Symptom Checklist–90 Revised* (SCL-90R; Derogatis, 1973) is a relatively brief self-report questionnaire that measures current psychological symptom status (past 7 days) in the following categories: somatization, obsessive-compulsive, interpersonal sensitivity, depression, anxiety, hostility, phobic anxiety, paranoid ideation, psychotism; and three additional items, the Global Severity Index, the Positive Symptom Distress Index, and the Positive Symptom Total. Women usually display interest in these results and find that the test correlates well with the way they are feeling, and it can be used to follow the clinical evolution of the patients. Using the SCL-90R, among a sample of 223 drug-dependent women in comprehensive drug treatment, women in current abusive relationships with partners showed significantly higher levels of emotional distress than women without this situation in most of the domains and in the Global Severity Index (Velez, 2002).
2. The *Post-traumatic Stress Diagnostic Scale* (PDS; Foa, 1995) is administered to assess the presence and severity of PTSD. Using the PDS, one-half of substance-abusing pregnant women reporting violence exposure and accepting referral for violence-related counseling met criteria for comorbid PTSD, and the women with PTSD reported greater impairment across several domains of daily life functioning than women without PTSD (Velez, 2002). In addition, the majority of the women who report traumatic experiences and do not meet criteria for PTSD still report various symptoms or difficulties related to the traumatic experience that can impact their recovery, mental representations of the fetus and maternal role (i.e., re-experiencing trauma, numbness, emotional hyperarousal, problems with intimacy and self-image).

The questionnaires are administered and responses and results are discussed with the patient in the context of the formulation of the individualized plan regarding the need for psychiatric referral, individual counseling, or referral to focus groups. With these questionnaires, specific psychological symptoms or domains that need intervention are identified, and areas of specific behavioral and coping skills are selected for intervention (e.g., self-soothing, regulation of emotions, grounding, setting boundaries). Through individual and group sessions following curricula targeting specific trauma-related issues, it is expected that the woman can gain understanding of how her traumatic experiences may negatively affect her thoughts, emotions, and behaviors, including her interactions with her fetus and/or other children. Initial stages of treatment emphasize safety, identified as the critical first stage of recovery (Herman, 1992).

Evidence-Based Treatment Models

Seeking Safety (Najavits, 2002) and the Trauma Recovery and Empowerment Model (TREM) (Fallot, 2002) are two evidence-based program examples that take an integrated approach to supporting women with co-occurring trauma and substance use problems. Seeking Safety is a manualized treatment protocol for substance abuse and PTSD that uses cognitive, behavioral, and interpersonal approaches to help patients to replace substances and other destructive behaviors with "safe coping skills." TREM is a manualized group intervention designed for women with history of physical or sexual trauma with severe mental problems. This intervention program recognizes the complexity of long-term adaptation to trauma and addresses a range of difficulties common among survivors of sexual and physical abuse, focusing primarily on the development of specific recovery skills (i.e., self-awareness, emotional modulation, mutuality in relationships) and current functioning, Through these interventions, it is expected that the woman will redefine her self-concept and change distorted cognitions related to her trauma history; enhance her ability to recognize, label, modulate and/or tolerate emotions; develop a healthy pattern of bonding and relationships; and replace the use of high-risk behaviors as maladaptive attempts to numb the inner world or act out emotional pain, stress, or anger.

Parenting Training

Parenting training has been recommended as part of the comprehensive treatment of pregnant substance-dependent women. It is clear that the pervasive histories of poor parental role modeling, victimization, psychiatric comorbidity, high levels of stress, and difficulty in managing negative feelings may influence the way that a woman approaches the task of child rearing (Blunt, 2009). Additionally, studies have indicated that substance abusing mothers lack important parenting knowledge, and that knowledge can be improved after individual and group parenting training based on a curriculum developed to address the special needs of this population (Velez, 2004).

Maternal drug treatment programs need to focus on enhancing parental child-caring abilities, supporting parent–child attachment, and encouraging family support systems to improve children's health and developmental outcomes. A curriculum was developed to educate drug-dependent women regarding general parenting practices, but in particular to address situations related to maternal substance abuse (Velez, 1998). The manualized eight-week training curriculum was developed to conduct group and individual parenting instruction in the following areas: 1) basic infant care adapted to the specific needs of infants experiencing neurobehavioral problems due to the prenatal drug exposure (e.g., neonatal abstinence syndrome); 2) developmental milestones and challenges associated with each developmental stage; and 3) parenting topics oriented toward promoting skills that will prevent future drug abuse for the child, and emotional and behavioral problems among children of drug-dependent women. Self-awareness of thoughts and emotions triggered by the child's behavior and modulation of maternal feelings in tandem with response to the infants are at the core of the training. Each 90-minute weekly group therapy topic includes objectives, teaching points, conclusions, suggested activities, and references for further reading. The individual sessions involve the administration of developmental and behavioral assessment tools such as the Neonatal Behavioral Assessment Scale (Brazelton, 1984), and Denver Developmental Screening Test II (Frankenburg, 1967), to newborns and any other children in the mother's care. These tools are administered to the children in the presence of the mother to assess the individual child's developmental strengths and weaknesses, foster a better maternal understanding of the child's development, and to improve the mother's knowledge, expectations, and beliefs regarding appropriate child development, in addition to addressing the developmental needs of the child.

Preparation for the Postpartum Period

Maternal adjustment to the birth of a substance-exposed newborn is often marked by stress, guilt, anxiety, and concern about the child's distress, survival, and development. Preparation for the postpartum period should begin during pregnancy, particularly for women who experience difficulties in conceptualizing the pregnancy in terms of the resulting infant. This period can be overwhelming for many women, with not only physical demands, but interventions by children's welfare workers, hospital staff, and family members who may (overtly or covertly) condemn the mother's choices during pregnancy, and any other unexpected difficulties surfacing at a time when they are particularly vulnerable.

Ideally, drug-dependent women should be prepared for choices that will need to be made in this period, including: (a) maternal medication choices; (b) contraception; (c) postpartum obstetrical care; (d) the necessity of continued substance abuse treatment, opioid replacement maintenance, and mental health care; (e) pediatric care; (f) parenting instruction, including the emotional and educational information necessary to care for the newborn displaying symptoms related to substance exposure; and (g) breastfeeding. Women should be educated on medications and contraindications to breastfeeding, and supported to breastfeed if they are on maintenance medications and otherwise meet criteria (ABM, 2009).

Pregnant and postpartum women on opioid replacement medications have special needs that require close observation and treatment in the perinatal period. Pain control, changing requirements for dosing, and physical fatigue in the immediate postpartum period need to be differentiated from fatigue related to demands of the care of the baby, postpartum depression, or relapse for opioid replacement-medication-maintained women. These conditions may interfere with their ability to respond properly to the infant and to develop a nurturing interaction. Healthcare providers in different settings and of different disciplines caring for these dyads are in a crucial situation to assess and advocate for the mother and the infant. Maternal behaviors portending infant risk in the postpartum period (i.e., sedation, signs of relapse, postpartum depression) should be assessed by any provider involved with the dyad.

Discussions about the infant's experiencing signs and symptoms associated with maternal substance abuse, and provider-assisted maternal responses to the feelings that may be aroused, is useful in helping the women identify their feelings associated with seeing an infant with symptoms related to prenatal exposure, preparing them prenatally to understand the infant's experience and response to it. This preparation allows the women to understand NAS and other neo-natal problems related to prenatal substance exposure as a syndrome of infant dysfunction in four neurobehavioral domains: (state control regulation, motor and tone functioning, reactivity to sensory stimulation, and autonomic signs of stress). Demonstration of different comforting techniques and environmental modifications to ameliorate or prevent physiological or behavioral symptoms of withdrawal or neurobehavioral dysregulation can ensue. This systematic obser-vation of the infant is emphasized during pregnancy and the postpartum period, emphasizing the need of exploration and modulation of negative emotions (e.g., guilt) triggered by the newborn's behaviors (Velez, 2008). Prenatal or postnatal education of the partner or other person helping the mother with the care of the infant is very useful.

Social Support for the Dyad

Provision of social support via case management services has been found to be an effective strategy with pregnant, drug-dependent women, resulting in improved drug use status for mothers (Jansson, 2003; Velez, 2002) and greater treatment retention and participation (Velez, 2002). A comprehensive needs assessment, developed specifically for this population, is an effective tool for the comprehen-sive evaluation of the need for case management services. This assessment should explore the psychosocial needs of the woman during pregnancy in the following areas: material needs (clothes for the infant, infant supplies), drug treatment needs (if she is not currently in treatment), psychiatric service requirements, violence exposure, and housing, legal, financial, and medical needs (mother and children). Once the needs analysis is complete, a plan for assistance can be formulated. This plan should be accompanied by realistic support in the form of assisting women by allowing them phone use, transportation to appointments, and ideally, via home visitation.

Provider Education and Intervention with the Dyad

Pregnancy and the immediate postpartum period may present a unique oppor-tunity for intervention in the life of the pregnant drug-dependent woman. This period necessarily involves the administration of health care by multiple medical and social service disciplines, and each is poised to dramatically influence, posi-tively or negatively, the life of the woman, her newborn, and her other children. Prejudicial and stereotypically motivated attitudes have no place in the care of these high-risk dyads, and will serve to drive the pair away from vitally needed treatment at a critical juncture. Instead, a thoughtful and accepting attitude toward the woman is necessary. Trust is nearly universally impaired in this population, yet necessary for her to take part in treatment to obtain optimal pregnancy and infant outcomes. Abuse victims may have particular issues with male providers, and a female provider should be provided if this issue arises.

Education of all providers regarding substance abuse, and particularly the myriad issues faced by the drug-dependent woman and the drug-exposed neonate, is key to comprehensive care of the dyad. Knowledge of addictions, lacking in many providers outside of the field of addiction medicine, can overcome some of the difficulties that care providers typically face in treating this population. Understanding the woman's history and motivation for her choices and actions requires careful exploration of her history and feelings at a time that she is most vulnerable. Distressing topics, such as the loss of custody of other children or the experience of abuse, may require psychiatric assistance. The comprehensive care of these dyads, arguably the most vulnerable in our society, requires the extension of the boundaries of traditional health care in any arena, and involves interdisciplinary communication and coordination.

■ **SUMMARY**

As more experience has accumulated regarding the issues faced by pregnant women affected by addiction, better interventions have been adapted for some of their associated issues (e.g., trauma issues, evaluation and treatment of psychiatric comorbidities, HIV treatment). However, a gap remains regarding the psychosocial effects of substance abuse upon the pregnant woman's development of attachment with her unborn child, preoccupation with pregnancy, and preparation for a healthy mother–infant interaction. There is limited information regarding psychological and sociological effects of substance abuse on pregnancy, and vice versa; although there is sufficient indication of a relationship between the biological and psychosocial stressors related to each of these and the potential for a deleterious effect upon the pregnancy and fetus. Individualized interventions during pregnancy and postpartum (during neonatal hospitalization and transition to home) have been shown to reduce maternal stress and depression and increase maternal self-esteem and to improve positive early parent–infant interactions.

The link between maternal substance abuse, poor parenting skills, and child developmental risk has been clearly determined. It is important to note that drug abuse combined with the internal difficulties experienced by the drug-dependent mother results in deficiencies in emotional regulation, which probably play a role in most or all of the problems experienced by this population. Emotional-regulation difficulties have been associated with violence exposure and PTSD, mood and psychiatric disorders (Lovejoy, 2000), and with drug dependency (Hien, 2000; Hien, 2003), all of which can be comorbid in this population of women. These deficits in the ability to organize, integrate, and modulate the interplay between emotions, thoughts, and behavior interfere with behavioral controls, in particular limiting their ability to use effective coping strategies in times of stress (Hien, 2003). Altered maternal stress responses and dysregulation of the HPA axis may be markers for intergenerational transmission via parenting behavior (Schechter, 2004) or may affect the fetus through fetal programming or other epigenetic mechanisms (Salisbury, 2009).

The goal of any provider for this population of women and children should be to provide comprehensive and competent care in conjunction with all involved providers for the dyad in an effort to optimize the outcomes of the drug-dependent woman and her child(ren). Interventions with substance abusing women need to address the cognitive, social, and emotional deficits created by addiction, trauma, and psychiatric comorbidity (e.g., emotional dysregulation, deficits in executive functioning, distorted maternal self-image and representations of the fetus/infant) in tandem with interventions related to drug abstinence. Screening for substance abuse during pregnancy and through the early postpartum period can be accomplished at prenatal and pediatric visits. Once identified, interventions that target multi-risk factors associated with substance abuse should focus on substance abuse treatment, on minimizing psychological symptoms and impairment associated with other psychopathological conditions such as current or past trauma history, as well as on enhancing parenting efficacy. Such targeted interventions may minimize problems in MFA, maternal–infant attachment, parenting, early problem behaviors, and delays in the acquisition of developmental skills by the exposed infant or child. Comprehensively addressing the difficulties faced by the substance-exposed dyad will necessarily involve the adoption of empirically based research into clinical practice, and the willingness of all providers involved with the dyad to understand and treat the multiple difficulties and needs of this vulnerable population of women and children.

■ AUTHOR NOTE

The authors wish to acknowledge the support of NIH/NIDA Grant # RO1 DA031689

■ REFERENCES

Alhusen, J. L. (2008). A literature update on maternal-fetal attachment. *Journal of Obstetric, Gynecologic, & Neonatal Nursing, 37*, 315–328.

Andersen, S. L. (2003). Trajectories of brain development: point of vulnerability or window of opportunity? *Neuroscience & Biobehavioral Reviews, 27*, 3–18.

Andersen, S. L., & Teicher, M. H. (2009). Desperately driven and no brakes: developmental stress exposure and subsequent risk for substance abuse. *Neuroscience & Biobehavioral Reviews, 33*, 516–524.

Banyard, V. L., Williams, L. M., & Siegel, J. A. (2003). The impact of complex trauma and depression on parenting: an exploration of mediating risk and protective factors. *Child Maltreatment, 8*, 334–349.

Blunt, B. (2009). Supporting mothers in recovery: parenting classes. *Neonatal Network, 28*, 231–235.

Brazelton, T. B. (1984). *Neonatal Behavioral Assessment Scale* (Vol. 50). Philadelphia, PA: Lippincott.

Carrico, A. W., Johnson, M. O., Moskowitz, J. T., Neilands, T. B., Morin, S. F., Charlebois, E. D., et al. (2007). NIMH Healthy Living Project Team. Affect regulation, stimulant use, and viral load among HIV-positive persons on anti-retroviral therapy. *Psychosomatic Medicine, 69*, 785–792.

Campbell, J. (1986). Nursing assessment for risk of homicide with battered women. *Advances in Nursing Science, 8*, 36–51.

Cohen, L. R., Hien, D. A. &, Batchelder, S. (2008). The impact of cumulative maternal trauma and diagnosis on parenting behavior. *Child Maltreatment, 13,* 27–38.

Conners, N. A., Bradley, R. H., Mansell, L. W., Liu, J., Roberts, T. J., Burgdorf, K., et al. (2004). Children of mothers with serious substance abuse problems: an accumulation of risks. *American Journal of Drug & Alcohol Abuse, 30,* 85–100.

Clark, D. B., Cornelius, J., Wood, D. S. &, Vanyukov, M. (2004). Psychopathology risk transmission in children of parents with substance use disorders. *American Journal of Psychology, 161,* 685–691.

Derogatis, L. R., Lipman, R. S., & Covi, L. (1973). SCL-90: An outpatient psychiatric rating scale—preliminary report. *Psychopharmacology Bulletin, 9,* 13–28.

DiLillo, D., Tremblay, G. C., & Peterson, L. (2000). Linking childhood sexual abuse and abusive parenting: the mediating role of maternal anger. *Child Abuse & Neglect, 24,* 767–779.

Duncan, E., Boshoven, W., Harenski, K., Fiallos, A., Tracy, H., Jovanovic, T., et al. (2007). An fMRI study of the interaction of stress and cocaine cues on cocaine craving in cocaine-dependent men. *American Journal of Addiction, 16,* 174–182.

Evans, A. T., & Gillogley, K. (1991). Drug use in pregnancy: obstetric perspectives. *Clinics in Perinatology, 18,* 23–32.

Fallot, R. D., & Harris, M. (2002). The Trauma Recovery and Empowerment Model (TREM): conceptual and practical issues in a group intervention for women. *Community Mental Health Journal, 38,* 475–485.

Field, T. (2010). Postpartum depression effects on early interactions, parenting, and safety practices: a review. *Infant Behavior & Development, 33,* 1–6.

Fitzsimons, H. E., Tuten, M., Vaidya, V., & Jones, H. E. (2007). Mood disorders affect drug treatment success of drug dependent pregnant women. *Journal of Substance Abuse Treatment, 32,* 19–25.

Foa, E. B., Riggs, D. S., Dancu, C. V., & Rothbaum, B. O. (1993). Reliability and validity of a brief instrument for assessing post-traumatic stress disorder. *Journal of Traumatic Stress, 6,* 459–473.

Frankenburg, W., & Dodds, J. (1967). The Denver Developmental Screening Test. *Journal of Pediatriacs, 71,* 181–191.

Gyarmathy, V. A., Giraudon, I., Hedrich, D., Montanari, L., Guarita, B., & Wiessing, L. (2009). Drug use and pregnancy—challenges for public health. *Euro Surveillance, 5*(14), 33–36.

Goldstein, R. Z., Craig, A. D., Bechara, A., Garavan, H., Childress, A. R., Paulus, M. P., et al. (2009). The neurocircuitry of impaired insight in drug addiction. *Trends in Cognitive Science, 13,* 372–380.

Haller, D. L., Knisely, J. S., Dawson, K. S., & Schnoll, S. H. (1993). Perinatal substance abusers. Psychological and social characteristics. *Journal of Nervous & Mental Disease, 181,* 509–513.

Haller, D. L., Miles, D. R., & Dawson, K. S. (2003). Factors influencing treatment enrollment by pregnant substance abusers. *American Journal of Drug & Alcohol Abuse, 29,* 117–131.

Hans, S. L., Bernstein, V. J., & Henson, L. G. (1999). The role of psychopathology in the parenting of drug-dependent women. *Developmental Psychopathology, 11,* 957–977.

Hart, R., & McMahon, C. A. (2006). Mood state and psychological adjustment to pregnancy. *Archives of Women's Mental Health, 9*, 329–337.

Hellemans, K. G.C., Sliwowska, J., Verma, P., & Weinberg, J. (2010). Prenatal alcohol exposure: fetal programming and later life vulnerability to stress, depression and anxiety disorders. *Neuroscience & Biobehavioral Reviews, 34*, 791–807.

Herman, J. (1992). *Trauma and Recovery: The Aftermath of Violence—From Domestic Violence to Political Terror.* New York: Basic Books.

Hien, D., & Honeyman, T. (2000). A closer look at the drug abuse–maternal aggression link. *Journal of Interpersonal Violence, 15*, 503–522.

Hien, D. A., & Miele, G. M. (2003). Emotion-focused coping as a mediator of maternal cocaine abuse and antisocial behavior. *Psychology of Addictive Behaviors, 17*, 49–55.

Howell, E. M., & Chasnoff, I. J. (1999). Perinatal substance abuse treatment: findings from focus groups with clients and providers. *Journal of Substance Abuse Treatment, 17*, 139–148.

Jansson, L. M., Svikis, D. S., Lee, J., Paluzzi, P., Rutigliano, P., & Hackerman, F. (1996). Pregnancy and addiction. A comprehensive care model. *Journal of Substance Abuse Treatment, 13*, 321–329.

Jansson, L. M., Svikis, D. S., & Beilenson, P. (2003). Effectiveness of child case management services for offspring of drug dependent women. *Substance Use & Misuse, 38*, 1933–1952.

Jansson, L. M., Svikis, D. S., Velez, M., Fitzgerald, E., & Jones, H. E. (2007). The impact of managed care on drug dependent pregnant and postpartum women and their children. *Substance Use & Misuse, 42*, 1–14.

Jansson, L. M. (2009). Guidelines for breastfeeding and the drug-dependent woman. *Academy of Breastfeeding Medicine, 4*, 225–228.

Johnson, M. O. (2001). Mother-infant interaction and maternal substance use/abuse: an integrative review of research literature in the 1990s. *Online Journal of Knowledge Synthesis for Nursing, 8*, 2.

Jones, H. E., Kaltenbach, K., Heil, S. H., Stine, S. M., Coyle, M. G., Arria, A. M., et al. (2010). Neonatal abstinence syndrome after methadone or buprenorphine exposure *New England Journal of Medicine, 363*, 2320–2331.

Jones, T. B. (2008). Psychosocial dimensions of HIV infection in pregnancy. *Clinical Obstetrics & Gynecology, 51*, 456–466.

Kandall, S. R., Doberczak, T. M., Jantunen, M., & Stein, J. (1999). The methadone-maintained pregnancy *Clinics in Perinatology, 26*, 173–183.

Katon, W. J. (2003). Clinical and health services relationships between major depression, depressive symptoms, and general medical illness. *Biological Psychiatry, 54*, 216–226.

Kendall-Tackett, K. (1998). Breastfeeding and the sexual abuse survivor. *Journal of Human Lactation, 14*, 125–130.

Kendall-Tackett, K. A. (2007). Violence against women and the perinatal period: the impact of lifetime violence and abuse on pregnancy, postpartum, and breastfeeding. *Trauma, Violence & Abuse, 8*, 344–353. Review. Erratum in: *Trauma, Violence & Abuse*, 2007, vol. 8, Table of Contents.

Koob, G. F., & Volkow, N. D. (2010). Neurocircuitry of addiction. *Neuropsychopharmacology, 35*, 217–238.

Kreek, M. J., & Koob, G. F. (1998). Drug dependence: stress and dysregulation of brain reward pathways. *Drug & Alcohol Dependency, 51*, 23–47.

LaGasse, L. L., Seifer, R., & Lester, B. M. (1999). Interpreting research on prenatal substance exposure in the context of multiple confounding factors. *Clinics in Perinatology, 26*, 39–54.

Lamy, S., & Thibaut, F. (2010). Psychoactive substance use during pregnancy: A review. *L'Encephale, 36*, 33–38.

Leshner, A. I. (1999). Science-based views of drug addiction and its treatment. *Journal of the American Medical Association, 282*, (14), 1314–1316.

Leshner, A. I., & Koob, G. F. (1999). Drugs of abuse and the brain. *Proceedings of the Association of American Physicians, 111*, 99–108.

Lester, B., & Padbury, J. (2009). The third pathophysiology of prenatal cocaine exposure. *Developmental Neuroscience, 31*, 23–35.

Lester, B. M., Andreozzi, L., & Appiah, L. (2004). Substance use during pregnancy: time for policy to catch up with research. *Harm Reduction Journal, 1*, 5.

Lindgren, K. (2001). Relationships among maternal-fetal attachment, prenatal depression, and health practices in pregnancy. *Research in Nursing & Health, 24*, 203–217.

Lovejoy, M. C., Graczyk, P. A., O'Hare, E., & Neuman, G. (2000). Maternal depression and parenting behavior: a meta-analytic review. *Clinical Psychological Review, 20*, 561–592.

Marcus, S. M. (2009). Depression during pregnancy: rates, risks and consequences—Motherisk Update 2008. *Canadian Journal of Clinical Pharmacology, 16*, e15–e22.

Martins, C., & Gaffan, E. A. (2000). Effects of early maternal depression on patterns of infant-mother attachment: a meta-analytic investigation. *Journal of Child Psychology & Psychiatry, 41*, 737–746.

Muller, M. E. (1996). Prenatal and postnatal attachment: A modest correlation. *Journal of Obstetric, Gynecologic, & Neonatal Nursing, 25*, 161–166.

Najavits, L. M. (2002). *Seeking Safety: A Treatment Manual for PTSD and Substance Abuse.* New York: Guilford.

Oberlander, T. F., Gingrich, J. A., & Ansorge, M. S. (2009). Sustained neurobehavioral effects of exposure to SSRI antidepressants during development: molecular to clinical evidence. *Clinical Pharmacology & Therapeutics, 86*, 672–677.

Oei, J. L., Abdel-Latif, M. E., Craig, F., Kee, A., Austin, M. P., & Lui, K. (2009). Short-term outcomes of mothers and newborn infants with comorbid psychiatric disorders and drug dependency. *Australia & New Zealand Journal of Psychiatry, 43*, 323–331.

Roberts, R., O'Connor, T., Dunn, J., & Goldin, J. (2004). The effects of child sexual abuse in later family life; mental health, parenting and adjustment of offspring. *Child Abuse & Neglect, 28*, 525–545.

Sales, P., & Murphy, S. (2000). Surviving Violence: Pregnancy and Drug Use. *Journal of Drug Issues, 30*, 695–724.

Salisbury, A. L., Ponder, K. L., Padbury, J. F., & Lester, B. M. (2009). Fetal effects of psychoactive drugs. *Clinics in Perinatology, 36*, 595–619.

Sarkar, S., & Donn, S. M. (2006). Management of neonatal abstinence syndrome in neonatal intensive care units: a national survey. *Journal of Perinatology, 26*, 15–17.

Schechter, D. S., Coots, T., Zeanah, C. H., Davies, M., Coates, S. W., Trabka, K. A., et al. (2005). Maternal mental representations of the child in an inner-city clinical sample:

violence-related post-traumatic stress and reflective functioning. *Attachment & Human Development, 7*, 313–331.

Shah, P. S., Balkhair, T., Ohlsson, A., Beyene, J., Scott, F., & Frick, C. (2011). Intention to become pregnant and low birth weight and pre-term birth: A systematic review. *Maternal & Child Health Journal, 15*, 205–216.

Shieh, C., & Kravitz, M. (2002). Maternal–fetal attachment in pregnant women who use illicit drugs. *Journal of Obstetric, Gynecologic, & Neonatal Nursing, 31*, 156–164.

Shieh, C., & Kravitz, M. (2006). Severity of drug use, initiation of prenatal care, and maternal-fetal attachment in pregnant marijuana and cocaine/heroin users. *Journal of Obstetric, Gynecologic, & Neonatal Nursing, 35*, 499–508.

Siegel, D. J., & Hartzell, M. (2004). *Parenting from the Inside Out: how a Deeper Self-Understanding Can Help You Raise Children Who Thrive*. New York: Penguin Group.

Sinha, C., Guthrie, K. A., & Lindow, S. W. (2007). A survey of postnatal contraception in opiate-using women. *Journal of Family Planning & Reproductive Health Care, 33*, 31–34.

Simmons, L. A., Havens, J. R., Whiting, J. B., Holz, J. L., & Bada, H. (2009). Illicit drug use among women with children in the United States: 2002–2003. *Annals of Epidemiology, 19*, 187–193.

Strathearn, L., & Mayes, L. C. (2010). Cocaine addiction in mothers: potential effects on maternal care and infant development. *Annals of the New York Academy of Science, 1187*, 172–183.

Substance Abuse and Mental Health Services Administration. (2009). *Results from the 2008 National Survey on Drug Use and Health: National Findings* (Office of Applied Studies, NSDUH Series H-36, HHS Publication No. SMA 09-4434). Rockville, MD.

Substance Abuse and Mental Health Services Administration, Office of Applied Studies (2005). *The NSDUH Report: Mother's Serious Mental Illness and Substance Use Among Youths*. Rockville, MD: SAMHSA. May 13, 2005.

Substance Abuse and Mental Health Services Administration, Office of Applied Studies. (2005). *The NSDUH Report: Substance Use During Pregnancy: 2002 and 2003 Update*. Rockville, MD: SAMHSA. June 2, 2005.

Suchman, N., Decoste, C., Castiglioni, N., Legow, N., & Mayes L. (2008). The Mothers and Toddlers Program: Preliminary findings from an attachment-based parenting intervention for substance-abusing mothers. *Psychoanalysis & Psychology, 25*(3), 499–517.

Teicher, M. H., Andersen, S. L., Polcari, A., Anderson, C. M., & Navalta, C. P. (2002). Developmental neurobiology of childhood stress and trauma. *Psychiatric Clinics of North America, 25*, 397–426.

Velez, M., Peirce, J., Svikis, D., Walters, V., & Jansson, L. (2002). Clinical treatment-based research: Assessment and intervention for violence in pregnant women attending substance abuse treatment. In W. Kliewer & D. Svikis, Violence exposure and substance abuse. *NIDA Research Monograph*, 112–115.

Velez, M. L., Jansson, L. M., Montoya, I. D., Golden, A., & Svikis, D. (1998). Evaluation of a Parenting Curriculum for Mothers in Substance Abuse. Poster presented to the College on Problems of Drug Dependence, Scottsdale, Arizona.

Velez, M. L., Jansson, L. M., Montoya, I. D., Schweitzer, W., Golden, A., & Svikis D. (2004). Parenting knowledge among substance abusing women in treatment. *Journal of Substance Abuse Treatment, 27*, 215–222.

Velez, M. L., Montoya, I. D., Jansson, L. M., Walters, V., Svikis, D., Jones, H. E., et al. (2006). Exposure to violence among substance-dependent pregnant women and their children. *Journal of Substance Abuse Treatment, 30,* 31–38.

Velez, M., & Jansson, L. M. (2008). The opioid dependent mother and newborn dyad: non-pharmacologic care. *Journal of Addiction Medicine, 2,* 113–120.

Volkow, N. D., & Li, T. K. (2004). Drug addiction: the neurobiology of behaviour gone awry. *Nature Reviews. Neuroscience, 5,* 963–970.

Zhang, X., Sliwowska, J. H., & Weinberg, J. (2005). Prenatal alcohol exposure and fetal programming: effects on neuroendocrine and immune function. *Experimental Biology & Medicine, 230,* 376–388.

14 Mentalizing-Based Intervention with Mother–Baby Dyads

MARJUKKA PAJULO AND
MIRJAM KALLAND

■ CLINICAL BACKGROUND

The efforts to provide specialized treatment services for pregnant and parenting women with a substance abuse problem have increased during recent years. These developments have arisen from growing scientific findings on the negative effects of substance abuse on pregnancy and development of the child, estimated economic costs of those effects, and limited availability of substance abuse treatment services for this group (Daley, Argeriou, & McCarty, 1998; Mayes & Truman, 2002). The treatment approach described here has emerged from clinical experience in residential settings in which we have found that a woman's relationship with her children is a critical factor in her efforts toward abstinence.

Substance abuse is one of the most challenging risks to parent–infant relationships that clinicians encounter. Despite the magnitude of the problem, the topic has received inadequate attention in the infant mental health and substance abuse literatures, in part because of the professionals' cultural differences that define therapeutic approaches in the infant mental health and the substance abuse fields. We suggest that maternal abstinence and enhancing the parent–child relationship not only are seen as equally relevant aims to be worked on simultaneously, but also that abstinence may actually be related to effective parenting. That is, we propose that more persistent parental abstinence is achieved especially through intensive treatment focus on the parent–child relationship in addition to the converse, that abstinence facilitates more effective parenting. We suggest that this relates to the relationship between central reward pathways in the brain and the capacity to invest in another person as in parenting, or to become addicted. Many of the abused substances have been shown to affect the dopaminergic pathways in the brain, areas that are associated with initiation of behavior, hedonic reward, and motivation, and leading to selection of short-term rewards without consideration of consequences (Koob & Volkow, 2010). These central dopaminergic pathways are also critically involved in an adult's capacity to invest in the care of the new infant (Swain, Lorberbaum, Kose, & Strathearn, 2007; Mayes, Magidson, Lejuez, & Nicholls, 2009). Drug abuse may be seen as a co-optation or hijacking of this endogenous value system. As a consequence, once this system is co-opted by an addiction to a drug of abuse, the individual is less able to invest in caring for an infant or another person, and there is competition between investment in craving the drug and in caring for the infant (Leckman & Mayes, 1998).

In the treatment model described in this article, the mothers are helped to invest in their child instead of substances, and to "reset" the focus of the reward system by intensively facilitating and enhancing the mother's satisfaction with positive interaction experiences with her baby and with being a parent. The idea is that the individual becomes less focused on her relationship with and craving for the drug, and more on her preoccupation with and investment in the infant.

The Pychosocial Context of Mother–Infant Dyads Entering Treatment

Substance-abusing pregnant and parenting women are a group with exceptionally many risk factors on multiple levels. This often creates hopelessness and frustration in professionals, and has often led to their exclusion from studies within substance abuse field and infant psychiatry. The mothers typically have limited economic resources, are less educated, receive little social support, and have difficulties securing housing. Their pregnancy is often unplanned, and they suffer from depression, anxiety or more severe psychopathology, low self-esteem, and feelings of shame and guilt. They often have a history of childhood trauma, parental substance abuse, abusive relationships, negative representations of their childhood and the parental care they received, and hence, negative models for parenting (Grella, Joshi, & Hser, 2000; Pajulo 2001; Mayes & Truman, 2002; Suchman, McMahon, Slade, & Luthar, 2004). They also often have many difficulties in recognizing and dealing with emotions, and hence, have been accustomed to shutting down difficult feelings by using substances.

In addition to the direct, bio-physiological substance effects per se, all these factors have a cumulative negative effect on the well-being of the mother and the child and on the quality of their relationship. At the moment, quality of early care and the postnatal caregiving environment, combined with the neurophysiological vulnerability of the drug-exposed child, are considered most important for the prognosis of child development and psychosocial outcome in later years (Lester & Tronick, 1994; Carmichael, Olson, O'Connor, & Fitzgerald 2001; Mayes & Truman, 2002).

Despite the clear need for support in their parenting role, substance abusing women have special difficulties attending and staying in treatment. They often have experienced a lot of difficulties in their social relationships, have fear of authorities and little confidence and trust about their own maternity and parenting. At the same time, they often have high expectations for their children and for themselves, and easily get offended by their children and disappointed in their parenthood. They are in a situation where they have to make several great changes at the same time and in multiple areas in their life: make room for the child in their mind, take responsibility for the child, give up substances, reach for a new social network, and deal with practical life arrangements and authorities.

Substance-Abusing Mother with Her Baby

The substance-exposed mother and child are difficult regulatory partners for each other, as the exposed infant often has an impaired ability to regulate his states of wakefulness, sleep, or distress, and needs more parental help. At the same time, the mother usually has a reduced capacity to read the child's communicative signals (Beeghly & Tronick, 1994) and a reduced tolerance for coping with a distressed and difficult-to-soothe infant. This combination easily leads to a viciously negative cycle that culminates in both the mother's and the infant's withdrawal from interaction and increased risk for child neglect and abuse (Kalland, 2001).

Substance-abusing mothers have been found to be less sensitive in interaction with their children; less emotionally engaged; less attentive, resourceful, flexible, and contingent; experience less pleasure in the interaction; and more intrusive in their behavior (Eiden, 2001; Pajulo, Savonlahti, Sourander, Ahlqvist, Helenius, & Piha, 2001; Johnson, Morrow, Accornero, Lihua, Anthony, & Bandstra, 2002; Mayes & Truman, 2002; LaGasse, Messenger, Lester, Seifer, Tronick, Bauer, et al., 2003).

Substance-exposed children have been found to show less positive emotion during the interaction, more distress to novelty, a slower recovery from interruptions, an impaired response to stress, and a diminished ability to persist in a task or maintain an alert, attentive state (Bendersky & Lewis, 1998; Eiden, 2001; Eiden, Lewis, Croff, & Young, 2002; Johnson et al., 2002; Molitor, Mayes, & Ward, 2003). The pair shows fewer moments of dyadic interaction, the quality of the dyadic interaction lacks enthusiasm and mutual enjoyment, and it includes more dyadic conflict and less mutual arousal (Burns, Chetnik, Burns, & Clark, 1991, 1997; Mayes, Feldman, Granger, Haynes, Bornstein, & Schottenfeld, 1997; Eiden, 2001). Studies on child-attachment profiles have shown that a higher percentage of substance-exposed children have insecure and, in particular, disorganized attachment compared to normative samples (Rodning, Beckwith, & Howard, 1991; Swanson, Beckwith, & Howard, 2000; Espinosa, Beckwith, Howard, Tyler, & Swanson, 2001; Beeghly, Frank, Rose-Jacobs, Cabral, & Tronick, 2003).

From all of the existing risk factors found in the situations of substance-abusing mother-baby pairs, the most important one, from the point of view of the baby, is that the mother is not able to pay enough attention and keep the baby's experience and needs in her mind. The capacity to keep the experiences of the baby in mind has to do with maternal reflective functioning, which will be described later in this chapter.

Perinatal Period: A Time of Motivation, Upheaval, and Early Representations of the Baby

The basis for intensive treatment intervention for women who are pregnant is most fundamentally to protect the child, inasmuch as maternal substance use during pregnancy presents clear toxicological risks to fetal development. Often, the safety and well-being of her infant provide strong motivation for a woman to work towards abstinence. On the other hand, pregnancy can also be a period of increased fear, anxiety, and guilt regarding the health of the child, each of which may compromise a woman's full engagement in substance abuse treatment. The pregnancy is usually unplanned, and the guilt is often reinforced by societal stigmatization of addicted mothers (Daley et al., 1998), which in turn may make it difficult for pregnant substance using women to seek treatment.

The perinatal period is a time of enormous psychological change and upheaval, which makes it an especially important and difficult time from the intervention point of view (Raphael-Leff, 1991; Slade, 2002). In psychoanalytic theory and research, the importance of mental representations during this phase has become of growing interest. The mental representation about maternity and being a child becomes strongly activated during pregnancy and early motherhood (Stern, 1995; Ammaniti, Candelori, Pola, & Tambelli, 1995).

The relationship between representations of the experiences of being parented and current maternal behavior has special significance for high-risk populations such as substance-addicted mothers, since they so often have negative, fragile, or idealized representations of their own childhood and own parenting—and hence, of their own parenting capacities (Pajulo, Savonlahti, Sourander, Helenius, & Piha, 2001, Pajulo, Savonlahti, Sourander, Helenius, & Piha, 2004; Suchman, Mayes, Conti, Slade, & Rounsaville, 2004). Interventions aimed either toward abstinence or abstinence plus supportive guidance regarding expected infant and caregiver behavior do not seem to have an effect on the mothers' interactive behavior; that is, they do not show increased sensitivity to their children's needs. Change may often occur in the mother's attitude and perception of the child, but these changes are often not reflected in the behavior between mother and child. These modest changes in maternal attitudes may or may not be experienced by the child as any change in the parent's behavior.

Mentalizing Capacity/Reflective Functioning

During the last ten years, British psychoanalysts have increasingly drawn attention to the definition and importance of the concept of reflective functioning in human development. We propose that this concept has a strong relevance in the situation of substance abusing mother–baby couples and their treatment in a residential setting. *Mentalizing/reflective functioning* refers to the capacity to understand oneself and others in terms of mental states (feelings, beliefs, intentions, and desires), and to reason about one's own and others' behavior in relation to these (Fonagy, Gergely, Jurist, & Target, 2002; Fonagy, 2008). The concept is theoretically rooted in both object relations and attachment theory, and can be measured as a parent's capacity for mentalizing about himself/herself, about the child, and about relationships with the child.

Reflective functioning enables an individual to understand another's behavior as meaningful and predictable. A reflective parent is interested and able to think about the child's behavior and experience and her/his interests and feelings in terms of the child's mental states; i.e., in terms of the child's psychological reality. In addition to being a metacognitive capacity, *reflective functioning* refers to the ability to hold, regulate, and experience emotions.

The developmental roots for a capacity to understand and interpret affects lie in the early interaction between mother and child. Early interactions between a mother and her infant are based on the mother's contingently mirroring her infant's behavior and affect (e.g., smiling when the baby smiles or looking sad when the baby cries). At the same time, the mother expands upon these mirroring moments. For example, she comments on the baby's smile by adding a statement about the experience that has led to the infant's pleasure, or soothes the crying infant even as she initially looks sad herself. This ability to provide contingent mirroring of the child's emotions and behavior is the behavioral expression of a reflective ability, and high reflective functioning makes it possible for a mother to behave sensitively with her child.

The impact of reflective contingent mirroring is that it provides for the child a "mirror" of his own feelings; when the child looks into his mother's eyes, he sees there not only his mother, but the reflection of himself and his own feelings. Furthermore, mother often mirrors her child's behavior and emotions in a marked way; that is, with gently exaggerated mimicry (changes in the face and tone of the voice can, for example, be more intense, or more expanded in time or pitch than normally). When a mother reflects upon her child's distress or pleasure in a "marked" manner, this is a clear signal to the child that the mother understands his feelings and at the same time has a separate feeling herself. The mother is able to empathize with the child while showing her own individuality and separateness (Fonagy et al., 2002). Highly reflective parents also understand that mental states can be ambiguous, that they can change in valence or intensity over time, and that they can be hidden or disguised (Slade, 2002).

Reflective functioning is considered a mediator in the intergenerational transmission of attachment security, and to play a critical role in the shaping of maternal representations of an understanding, caring parent versus a distant, impervious one. Deprived and traumatized mothers who nonetheless are highly reflective are more likely to have securely attached children, whereas deprived mothers with low reflectiveness almost invariably have been found to have insecure children (Fonagy, Steele, & Steele, 1991; Fonagy et al., 1995).

Maternal reflective abilities also correlate positively with a child's better social skills, and negatively with a child's attention problems, tendency to withdraw from interaction, maternal distress, and dysfunctional mother–child interaction. When maternal reflective abilities are well developed, children are more pro-social, responsive, and better able to regulate their emotional state, and the dyadic relationship is more congruent, less frustrating, and less stressful (Fonagy et al., 2002).

Reflective functioning is considered a parental capacity that can be enhanced by accurate intervention (Schechter, Zeanah, & Myers, 2002; Schechter, Kaminer, Grienenberger, & Amat, 2003), and also in a group setting with at-risk (Goyette-Ewing et al., 2002) and drug-dependent women (Suchman, Altomare, Moller, Slade, & Mayes, 2003; Suchman, Mayes, Conti, Slade, & Rounsaville, 2004). There are a few data showing that among substance using mothers' reflective abilities toward their children are generally low (Suchman et al., 2003; Suchman, McMahon, Slade, & Luthar, 2004; Truman, Levy, & Mayes, 2004). It seems a promising avenue for substance abuse treatment programs to incorporate the concept of reflective functioning in clinical interventions with substance abusing parents, and we focus here on the incorporation of such an emphasis in a residential treatment approach.

■ PROGRAM DESCRIPTION

Treatment Units

Since 1990, six residential treatment units, designed for pregnant and parenting women who have a severe substance abuse problem, have been established in different parts of Finland. The units are part of the child protection field in the social welfare sector (Federation of Mother and Child Homes and Shelters), and they all share the same approach and way of working. The personnel in the units represent different educational backgrounds and working experience, as they come from the substance abuse field, family and infant work, the child protection field, and psychiatry. A typical unit has a leader (who is usually a social worker), one social worker, one special worker (e.g., a social worker, occupational therapist, or psychologist), and eight clinical counselors, who work in three shifts.

The treatment staff of each unit receives an intensive initial training as a group during the first six months, which concentrates on early parent–child interaction, attachment, and child development within the context of maternal substance abuse. The units have the capacity to serve, on average, five mother-baby couples, and one place for a whole family to live-in, and are situated within the ordinary city-area with their own house and garden. The treatment occurs throughout each day on all days of the week.

The average duration of stay has been eight months, and the treatment usually starts two to four months before delivery. The referral to the unit is made by a social welfare agency, delivery hospital, well-baby clinic, or by the mother herself, due to her primary problem with alcohol and/or other drugs. The use of a residential facility gives the mothers a substance-free environment and model of healthy living, which are important intervention areas in themselves. Mothers are supported to make healthy food, take care of themselves personally, improve their physical health, and organize their daily lives, rhythm, and use of leisure time. Another important task is, together with the mother/family, to establish the outpatient treatment and follow-up plan for the time after the residential treatment period. Accumulated clinical experience suggests that most of these mothers benefit from this highly structured and holding environment in the beginning.

Structure of Intervention

In the units, each mother and each baby has their own individual counselor as well as working familiarity with all of the staff. All mothers and all staff participate in weekly group meetings focusing on a specific parenting theme; for example, on different roles in being a parent, feelings evoked by parenting, or how to deal with child's tantrums. Each mother participates in planning her living, treatment aims and work with her family and social network, and has responsibilities for helping with the daily routines in the unit. When needed, detoxification and other medical or mental health treatment are provided outside the unit. The mother is supported in her participation in those, and openness of the collaboration between the unit, social welfare agency, and well-baby clinic is emphasized. Mothers are expected to stay substance-free, but one to two relapses are allowed during the treatment period. All relapses are also discussed together in the group meetings.

Content of Intervention

The core idea in treatment is to create a holding environment at three levels: helping the mother hold the baby and her relationship with the baby in her mind (Winnicott, 1957); helping the mother's social network and the unit personnel hold the mother in mind, and through supervision, evaluation, and research work, showing continuous interest in development of the work, that is, holding the treatment units in the researchers' mind. The two main aims in the treatment are to intensively support the mother in her efforts toward abstinence and simultaneously to support her relationship with the child. This is based on the clinical finding that the specific challenges and most worrisome deficiencies found in parenting of these mothers include their inability to keep their baby in mind and to stay emotionally connected and present to the baby. The mother often cannot adjust her own needs, rhythm, and behavior in ways that are responsive and sensitive to the baby, and the baby is not able to follow the mother in her actions. The mother often has great difficulties anticipating and following the child in her/his next developmental stage and new skills, in part because of her unrealistic expectations for the child and in part because of her difficulty in differentiating the child's needs from her own.

Parenting is supported through discussions and support in daily situations with the child, through weekly group meetings around a parenting theme, and through setting small, concrete aims for each week. The mothers are also helped in dealing with authorities, repairing and building up new social network during the treatment period, which in turn is felt to increase their own psychological resources and makes it possible for them to focus on their child. The residential format of treatment makes intensive support possible, as daily situations between the mother and the baby form a natural and rich working arena. There are multiple moments each day to work on interaction experiences, to help parents shift from a negative to a positive attitude toward their own parenting and their child, to effect change in maternal representations, to enhance reflective capacity in the mother, and to facilitate change in mother's interaction behavior. Additionally, the residential setting affords more concentrated therapeutic time for a mother to reveal and explore her perceptions of her relationships with her own parents and to understand how those perceptions play out in her current relationship with her child.

The relationship work is considered most important for the outcome of the treatment, both for the mother and the child. It is also an area of the work that requires most careful and ongoing training, clinical experience and regular supervision.

Enhancing Reflective Functioning During Pregnancy

Usually the substance dependent pregnant mother's mind is so much preoccupied by craving for substances and worries related to life-situation, that she does not spontaneously express her thoughts or feelings regarding the baby and parenting (Jaskari, 2008). She must be stopped to concentrate and think of the baby. When the mother talks about her own problems and behavior, etc., the clinician can ask her to think about it from the baby's perspective: "What do you think it means for the baby that you are short-tempered/sad/angry to your husband/find it hard to be alone? Do you think the baby notices? What have you observed?" The pregnant mother may be asked to tell her baby about how she herself feels and experiences things. Talking to the baby enhances the mother's experience of having already a real relationship with the child; a separate person to talk to.

The mother is also helped to think of what the baby may wish to tell the mother -a message from the baby. One mother described how she imagined the baby saying to her: "Mom, remember to stop cigarette smoking." The clinician wanted to pay attention to this and started to work around it with the mother: how the baby may feel when the mother smokes, what is his/her experience of it, how does the mother feel when thinking about the baby's experience, and how this, again, affects the mother. At first, the mother found it too difficult to think of the baby's experience. Gradually, however, with the clinician's support, she was able to think about it and face her own feelings of guilt.

Mentalizing can give a different perspective to the issue of guilt. Feelings of guilt are a healthy reaction in a situation where one's own behavior causes harm to the other person. By our supporting the mother to think about her child's perspective and experience, she can begin to feel empathy for the baby, to protect her child from further harm, and become more sensitive to the baby's point of view. This kind of work must, however, always be done within a safe treatment context, individually tailored and monitored according to each mother's capacity to tolerate difficult feelings. We as clinicians are also different in our capacity to tolerate feelings of guilt and shame.

During pregnancy, the mother is also helped to imagine different future situations with the baby: feeding, soothing, and playing together, what might be especially enjoyable or difficult moments to deal with; how tiredness may affect one's capacity to tolerate baby's fussiness or crying, and how to seek help (Jaskari, 2008). Prenatal work is especially critical and facilitative because negative perceptions toward the infant and the derailment of mother–child relationship almost always begin in pregnancy.

Enhancing Reflective Functioning After Birth: Specific Techniques

After the birth of the child, the mother is supported to reflect on the intentions of her child and to see the child's actions and affects as meaningful. Equally important is that the clinician is able to do the same: to be interested in the intentions of the mother, to help the mother to focus on experiences, and give them value and meaning. The containing relationship between the clinician and the mother also emphasizes that the negative feelings of the mother are to be tolerated and attuned, not avoided, distanced, or criticized.

"Growing: Birth to Three"

The personnel of the units are trained in the "Growing: birth-to-three" method (Doan-Sampon, Wollenberg, & Campbell, 1993), in which the parent–child interaction is considered the primary way to support and promote child growth and development. The training provides techniques for supporting mutually satisfying interactions between parent and child and also offers strategies for enhancing communication between the clinician and the caregiver. Throughout the process, the development of the child is carefully documented. The intervention includes discussions with the mother on her child's development, picking up the areas of most concern for her, discussions on normal development, on the steps to be next expected in this child's development, the role of a parent in enhancing development, the importance of gaining new skills for the child, and the amount of help the child needs from the parent at different ages. The method is also used specifically as the vehicle for enhancing maternal reflective functioning. Generally, the clinician shows interest in and asks mothers about their feelings and is careful not to interpret conflict or ambivalence too early. In Bion's words (Bion, 1962), the clinician provides the "alpha-function," a state in which the mother is able to think about what she is thinking—which is the beginning of the reflective functioning. The task for the clinician is to help the mother focus on important and often difficult feelings, which is often opposite to what they are used to: avoiding painful thoughts and using substances for this purpose.

Interpreting the Baby's State of Mind

One important aspect of supporting reflective functioning in the mother is to interpret the state of the baby for the mother when she is unable to do that herself. This does not automatically mean inadequate caregiving in terms of feeding or other basic care. The mother is often "technically" adequate, but may be silent, withdrawn, or intrusive in her interaction behavior. The clinician can use the "voice of the infant" to help the mother to understand her baby. This is often not threatening for the mother, and leads to the mother doing what needs to be done. Each developmental step of the child can also be described from the point of view of the baby, like a letter or message sent by the baby to her/his mother.

Use of Videotaping

Different situations between the mother and baby are videotaped: playing, getting to sleep, feeding, comforting the baby. The tapes are then watched together with the mother, noting moments when the mother feels that she is "clicking" with the child or other positive moments that she feels good about. Also these videotaped interactions may usefully highlight moments when the baby is signaling that she/

he is becoming tired, or beginning to withdraw from interaction. The mother is helped through watching the tapes to "read" her child, and also to recognize her own feelings at that particular moment. The mother is supported in searching for the cues, specific for this baby, from which the mother can conclude how he is feeling.

For example, when watching a situation in which the baby is getting tired and turns his face and gaze away from the mother, the tape is stopped, and the mother is asked what she feels seeing that particular moment and behavior of the child. Often the mother may interpret the child's signals of getting tired as dislike or rejection by the child towards her. The mother feels distressed about this and tries to get more of the child's attention towards herself by stimulating him more. The child becomes even more distressed and starts to cry, the mother feels helpless, and becomes disappointed in herself and the child, and all this leads to a negative interaction experience for both of them. In the intervention, the mother is helped, step by step, using the videos, to become aware of the separateness between her own feelings and experiences and those of the child.

Strengthening the Mother's Capacity for Previewing

Previewing refers to the intuitive knowledge that parents have about the next step in their child's developmental zone (Stern, 1985). In at-risk dyads, the parent's capacity to preview the development of the child is often disturbed. The clinician's task is to enhance previewing by offering the mother the mental representations of the next upcoming skill (Trad, 1993). This can happen verbally or by using material provided through the videotaped interaction. The mother is supported in her efforts to facilitate her child's developmental progress or in her "scaffolding" of her child's learning (Cazden, 1983). She is also supported to trust the capacity of the child when help is not needed, as opposed to intrusive and over-directive parenting. Each new developmental step is put in a relational meaning for the mother. For instance, instead of saying "Oh, she is trying to crawl," the clinician will say, "Oh, I can see how she is trying to come after you and crawl when you leave the room." Through this, the clinician shows to the mother two things at the same time: how important it is that these new developmental steps are acknowledged, and the important role the mother has in the child's mind as being the one whom he wants to show these new skills.

Keeping Balance Within the Triad

Through the training, the personnel learn to focus on three relationships: between clinician and mother, mother and child, and clinician and child. This is important, as most of these mothers have difficulty trusting and feeling safe in a relationship. This triangle between mother, infant, and clinician can become intensely painful, and, therefore, the balance between the three relationships must be given much attention. If the clinician gives too much attention to the mother, the infant may remain invisible in the treatment. If the clinician gives too much attention to the infant, this may elicit jealousy in the mother in two different ways: the mother may feel intimidated in her own motherhood, thinking that the clinician is a better mother than she is. Or she may feel jealous about the fact that the child gets the attention that she needs for herself.

Finding the balance in this triangle requires not only keeping the infant visible, but remembering that everything that belongs within the relationship between mother and the infant shall be returned to where it belongs. For example, if the mother turns to the clinician and asks her to take care of her infant while she goes shopping, the clinician will ask the mother, firmly but in a friendly way, to tell her infant how long she will be away and when she will return. Saying this is important, not because the child will yet understand the meaning of the mother's declaration, but instead to encourage the mother to pay attention to and think of her child's experience at that particular moment of separation. It is also a message for the mother, that this is something important happening between the mother and her child, not between the clinician and the child.

■ **RESEARCH DATA**

In the preliminary study, our main interest was to explore individual differences in the situations of these mother–baby pairs, factors related to these individual differences, and the role of maternal mentalizing capacity/reflective functioning in treatment outcome.

Subjects and Procedure

Participants were 34 mother-baby pairs who lived in three of the treatment units described above, and entered the unit during pregnancy or straight after delivery; i.e., within two weeks. All data collection, including the reflective functioning (RF) interviews, was carried out by the treatment unit staffs, except for evaluation of child development, which was made by an outside psychologist. Data collection time points and assessments used are presented in Table 14.1. Scoring of the video measures and RF interviews were made by separate, reliable, and experienced outside raters who were blind to other data and to each others' ratings.

Measure to Assess Maternal Mentalizing Capacity

Maternal RF was assessed in late pregnancy (with those who entered treatment unit during pregnancy) using the Pregnancy Interview (PI) and at four months postpartum using the Parent Development Interview (PDI) (Slade, Bernbach, Grienenberger, Levy, & Locker, 2002, 2005). PI is a 24-item semi-structured interview asking about the emotional experience of this pregnancy; mother's view of the baby and view of the relationship between herself and the baby; and the thoughts, feelings, and changes experienced in relation to her partner and her own mother. Parental Development Interview Revised (PDI-R) (Slade et al., 2002, 2005) is a 40-item semi-structured interview asking about the parent's view of the child, her view of her relationship with the child, her experience of being a parent, childhood experiences of her own parents, the dependence of the child, her experiences of

TABLE 14.1 *Substance-Abusing Mother-Baby Pairs in Residential Treatment (n = 34):*
Procedure and Measures Used in the Study

Pregnancy (n = 24)	Baby 1 month (n = 34)	Baby 3 months (n = 34)	Baby 4 months (n = 34)	Child 1 year	Child 2 years
background	delivery data	BSI	CI	child protection data (n = 34)	child protection data (n = 34)
PI	ED	EPDS	PDI	BSIDII (n = 23)	BSIDII (n = 21)
		IIP	BSIDII	TAQ (n = 23)	

	Type	Name	Abbreviation	Developer
early interaction	videomeasure	Care Index for Infants and Toddlers	CI	Crittenden 2003
mentalizing capacity	interview	Pregnancy Interview Parent Development Interview	PI PDI	Slade et al. 2002, 2005
psychiatric symptoms	questionnaire	Brief Symptom Inventory	BSI	Derogatis 1993
depression	questionnaire	Edinburgh Postnatal Depression Scale	EPDS	Cox et al. 1987
intimate relationships	questionnaire	Inventory of Interpersonal Problems	IIP	Horowitz et al. 1988
early caregiving of the baby	questionnaire	Experienced Difficulties in Early Caregiving	ED	Pajulo et al. 2011
traumatic experiences	questionnaire	Traumatic Antecedents Questionnaire	TAQ	Van der Kolk 2003
child development	standardized test	Bayley Scales of Infant Development	BSIDII	Bayley 1993

separation with the child, and her views of the future. Both interviews are audio-taped and scored from the transcribed narratives by an experienced and reliable coder. A parent's responses to individual questions are scored along a continuous scale (−1–9) with anchor points describing different levels of RF ability described in detail in the manual.

In evaluating parental RF ability from a transcript, three main criteria for true reflectiveness are considered: 1) the parent's awareness of the nature of mental states (e.g., opacity and being susceptible to disguise); 2) the parent's effort to tease out mental states underlying behavior; and 3) the parent's ability to recognize developmental aspects of mental states. The number of signs of true reflectiveness found in the transcribed narrative is the basis in scoring. The more there are specific and different signs of RF, the more positive (higher) is the score, with a score of -1 indicating a rejection of RF, scores of 0–2 indicating very weak ability for RF, a score 3 indicating weak ability, scores of 4–5 representing a normal or close to normal ability, and scores 6–9 representing high or exceptionally high ability for RF. Fresh and spontaneous expressions of specific episodes are especially looked for; the importance of episodic memory is emphasized (Fonagy, Steele, & Steele, 1991; Fonagy, Steele, Moran, Steele, & Higgitt, 1991; Grienenberger, Kelly, & Slade, 2005; Slade, Grienenberger, Bernbach, Levy, & Locker, 2005; Fonagy & Target, 1996). Episodic memory is regarded as the clinically most important memory system, as significant changes in understanding and behavior happen there. General expressions, opinions, or clichés (signs of semantic memory in the left brain hemisphere) are not regarded as signs of RF. For example, a person may tell us that she (cognitively) understands some issue, but is not acting according to this understanding. The RF scale has been validated using samples of ordinary pregnant women and mothers with small children (Fonagy, Steele, & Steele, 1991; Fonagy, Steele, Moran, Steele, & Higgitt, 1991; Grienenberger, Kelly, & Slade, 2005; Slade, Grienenberger, Bernbach, Levy, & Locker, 2005), psychiatric patients and borderline personality disorder patients (Fonagy & Target, 1996).

Results

Background and Other Characteristics of the Group

From the background data, it is evident that this was a group with exceptionally large number of risks in addition to the substance abuse problem per se (see Table 14.2). Most of the mothers were drug users, and their most commonly used

TABLE 14.2 *Background and Other Characteristics of Substance Abusing Mothers in Residential Treatment with Their Babies (n = 34)*

	M	SD	Median	Upper 25%	Lower 25%	Range
Maternal age (years)	25.1	5.8	24.0	28.7	20.2	16–38
Duration of pregnancy at entering treatment (wog)	30.8	5.8	33.0	36.0	26.5	21–39
Age at starting substance abuse (years)	14.7	3.6	14.0	17.0	13.0	6–27
Duration of pregnancy at birth (wog)	39.4	1.7	39.0	40.0	39.0	34–42
Birth weight of the child (g)	3329	456	3285	3590	3012	2130–4410
Child development (BSID II MDI) 4 months	97.5	7.0	98.0	104.5	93.0	85–111
Care Index sensitivity	4.5	2.1	4.0	6.0	3.0	0–9
Care Index unresponsiveness	6.8	4.0	8.0	10.0	4.0	0–14
Length of residential treatment (months)	9.0	4.5	7.0	12.2	6.0	3–18
	n	%				
Single parenting	15	44				
First child	23	68				
Only basic education (max 9 years)	24	71				
Long-term unemployment (> 1 year)	15	44				
Entering treatment unit during pregnancy	24	71				
Unplanned pregnancy	22	65				
Substance use during this pregnancy	27	79				
Child's father having a severe s.a. problem	29	85				
Previous children taken into substitution care	11/11	100				
Primarily a drug problem	20	59				
Poly-substance abuse problem	7	21				
Alcohol problem	7	20				
Excessive smoking	34	100				
Withdrawal symptoms at birth	10	31				
FAE/FAS dg in baby	1	3				

drugs were illegal use of buprenorphine, hashish, and amphetamine. Maternal sensitivity in interaction was found to be on average weak, and unresponsiveness in interaction behavior was common. However, there was also rather large individual variation in both sensitivity and unresponsiveness (Table 14.2). All children were developing within normal limits at four months of age. However, the development scores decreased towards the end of the two-year follow-up. As shown in Table 14.1, child development assessment could be accomplished with only some of the children in follow-up; with 23 at one year of age (68%), and with 21 at two years of age (62%). Among those assessed at the follow-up points, 87% had developed within normal limits at one year of age, and 21% at two years of age. The development had proceeded on average better with those children who had lived with their mother all the time (70%) during the two-year follow-up point.

A high percentage of mothers reported depression and other psychiatric symptoms: over 30% were screened as having postnatal depression, and many mothers received higher scores than the average of Finnish psychiatric outpatient sample (Holi et al., 1998); for example, in anxiety (20%), paranoid symptoms (35%), and psychotic symptoms (32%). The most commonly and highly self-reported trauma experiences, both during the early years (0–6) and during the whole lifetime, were experiences of separation (parental divorce; repeated placements in substitution care; death, illness, or hospitalization of close people) and substance abuse problems within the family.

More detailed descriptions of the results regarding postnatal maternal interaction with the baby, psychiatric symptomatology, experienced trauma, and experience of early caregiving are presented in a separate article (Pajulo et al., 2011).

The treatment had a planned ending with 70%, and the mother went to her own home together with her baby, as the primary caregiver, in 70% of the cases. During the two-year follow-up, 14 children were placed in substitution care either temporarily or more permanently, primarily due to mother's relapse into substance use and/or otherwise insufficient care.

Results Regarding Maternal Mentalizing Capacity/RF

For the mothers participating in this study, the average RF total single score during pregnancy in PI was found to be low (med 2.4), but with individual variation from "lacking RF" to "close to ordinary RF" (0–4.5). Also, at four months postpartum, the average RF total single score was found to be low (med 3.0) but somewhat higher on average, and with individual variation from "lacking RF" to "ordinary RF" level (1.0–5.0). The RF total single score increased during intervention with 63% of the cases, which were assessed at both time points. This increase was also statistically significant. The score decreased with one case and stayed at the same level with the rest (31%). The lowest RF score received by the mother within the different answering paths increased in 20% of the cases, and the highest RF score increased in 70% of cases.

Higher postnatal RF level was associated with higher prenatal RF level. Interestingly, higher postnatal RF was also associated with reporting more experienced family secrets in early childhood. Pre- and postnatal RF levels were not found significantly associated with maternal interaction, amount of psychiatric symptoms, or child development scores.

Change in maternal RF from pre- to postnatal phase was on average 0.6 points in RF total single score (range –2–2.5 points). The amount of change in RF during treatment was found to be associated with two issues: type of substance abuse problem and experienced trauma. Drug abuse problems especially were found to be associated with greater positive change in maternal RF during intervention, compared to alcohol and mixed substance abuse problems. Regarding experienced trauma, physical and emotional abuse in early childhood, family secrets, and total amount of traumatic experiences in their lifetime were associated with less positive change in maternal RF during intervention (Pajulo, Pyykkönen, Kalland, Sinkkonen, Helenius, Punamäki, & Suchman, 2012).

Associations with Later Need for Child Substitution Care

The number of certain types of psychiatric problems in the mother during postnatal period was found to be associated with later need for child substitution-care placements (temporarily or permanently, or both) during the two-year follow-up. These included higher postnatal level of somatization, and hostile and paranoid symptoms in the mother. Global psychiatric symptomatology and phobic anxiety in the mother were also found to be marginally significantly associated with the need for these child-protection actions (Pajulo, Pyykkönen, Kalland, Sinkkonen, Helenius, & Punamäki. 2011).

In addition, lower maternal mentalizing capacity postnatally seemed to predict the need for later child substitution-care placements, both at the child's first and second years (Pajulo et al., 2012). Mothers of the children who had been placed into substitution care by social welfare agency during the two-year follow-up after treatment (Group 1) had on average (had) lower postnatal level of RF and less positive change in RF during intervention than mothers of the children who had not been placed into substitution care (Group 2) (Table 14.3). About 40% of the Group 1 mothers had postnatal RF levels "close to ordinary" or "ordinary" (RF 4–5), compared to 8% of the Group 2 mothers. In this study, the differences in postnatal maternal interaction, prenatal entering in treatment, length of residential treatment, type of substance abuse problem, maternal age, or other sociodemographic background factors were not associated with treatment prognosis in terms of child substitution-care placements.

■ CONCLUSIONS

There is a great need for theoretically driven and accurately focused interventions among psychosocial high-risk groups. We propose that the concept of parental reflective functioning has especially strong relevance for substance abusing mother–baby couples and their treatment. In the model described above, intervention has been designed for mothers who have a particularly severe substance-addiction problems during pregnancy and in the perinatal phase. The mothers are intensively supported in investing in their child instead of substances, with the idea of

TABLE 14.3 *Residential Treatment Intervention for Substance Abusing Mother–Baby Pairs.*

| | Group 1 | | | | | | | | Group 2 | | | | | | | |
| | 1 year | | | | 2 years | | | | 1 year | | | | 2 years | | | |
	n	M	SD	range	n	M	SD	range	n	M	SD	range	n	M	SD	range
PI total RF single score	13	**2.6**	1.4	0–4.5	10	**2.6**	1.5	0–4.5	5	**1.8**	1.0	1.0–3.5	7	**2.0**	1.0	1.0–3.5
PI highest RF score	13	**4.0**	0.9	2.0–5.5	10	**4.0**	1.0	2.0–5.5	5	**3.3**	0.8	2.5–4.5	7	**3.5**	0.7	2.5–4.5
PI lowest RF score	13	**1.5**	1.4	–1.0–3.0	10	**1.6**	1.4	–1.0–3.0	5	**0.9**	1.2	–1.0–2.5	7	**0.9**	1.3	–1–2.5
PDI total RF single score	22	**3.2**	1.1	1.0–5.0	18	**3.2**	1.2	1.0–5.0	7	**2.4**	0.7	1.5–3.0	10	**2.6**	0.8	1.5–3.0
PDI highest RF score	22	**4.8**	1.2	2.0–6.5	18	**4.8**	1.3	2.0–6.5	7	**4.1**	0.8	3.0–5.0	10	**4.2**	0.7	3.0–5.0
PDI lowest RF score	22	**1.0**	0.3	0.5–2.0	18	**1.0**	0.3	0.5–2.0	7	**0.9**	0.6	0–2.0	10	**1.0**	0.5	0–2.0

Descriptive statistics of maternal mentalizing capacity (RF) during pregnancy and at four (4) months postnatally, assessed with PI and PDI interviews. *Group 1* = children not having needed any placements into substitution care during two-year follow-up (neither before 1 year nor by 2 years of child's age). *Group 2* = children having needed one or more placement(s) into substitution care (either before 1 year or 2 years of child's age).

"resetting" the focus of the reward system by intensively facilitating and enhancing the mother's satisfaction with positive interaction experiences with her baby and with being a parent. The individual is supposed to become less focused on her craving for the substance/drug and more on her preoccupation with and investment in the infant. It seems that, with many of the mothers, the intervention has had a significant impact, both in terms of abstinence and the quality of their parenting. With most of the mothers, the intervention seems to have increased at least the mothers' capacity to deal with difficult situations and feelings, and to collaborate with professionals. With some mothers, enough change has not occurred. However, we believe that although the model presented here already contains elements of enhancing maternal RF, described above, there is still a lot that could be done more accurately and systematically with that focus in mind, so that even more mothers could reach transition from the high-risk to the reflective and more sensitive levels in interactions with their children. Our work is continuing with that aim.

■ AUTHOR NOTE

The study has been supported by grants from International Psychoanalytic Association (IPA), National Institute of Drug Abuse (NIDA, NIH), and the Finnish Medical Foundation for the first author.

■ REFERENCES

Ammaniti, M., Candelori, C., Pola, M., & Tambelli, R. (1995). *Maternita e gravidanza. Studio delle rappresentazioni materne.* Manual. Milan, Italy: Raffaello Cortina Editore.

Bayley, N. (1993). *Bayley Scales of Infant Development, 2nd edition (BSID II).* San Antonio, TX: Psychological Corporation.

Beeghly, M., & Tronick, E. Z. (1994). Effects of prenatal exposure to cocaine in early infancy: toxic effects on the process of mutual regulation. *Infant Mental Health Journal, 15*(2), 158–175.

Beeghly, M., Frank, D. A., Rose-Jacobs, R., Cabral, H., & Tronick, E. (2003). Level of prenatal cocaine exposure and infant-caregiver attachment behavior. *Neurotoxicology and Teratology, 25*, 23–38.

Bendersky, M., & Lewis, M. (1998). Arousal modulation in cocaine-exposed infants. *Developmental Psychology, 34*(3), 555–564.

Bion, W. R. (1962). *Learning from Experience.* London: Heinemann.

Burns, K., Chetnik, L., Burns, W. J., & Clark, R. (1991). Dyadic disturbances in cocaine-abusing mothers and their infants. *Journal of Clinical Psychology, 47*(2), 316–319.

Burns, K. A., Chetnik, L., Burns, W. J., & Clark, R. (1997). The early relationship of drug abusing mothers and their infants: an assessment at eight to twelve months of age. *Journal of Clinical Psychology, 53*, 279–287.

Carmichael Olson, H., O'Connor, M., & Fitzgerald, H. E. (2001). Lessons learned from study of the developmental impact of parental alcohol use. *Infant Mental Health Journal, 22*(3), 5–6, 271–290.

Cazden, C. B. (1983). Adult assistance to language development: scaffolds, models and direct instruction. In R. P. Parker & F. A. Davis (Eds.), *Developing Literacy: young Children's Use of Language*. Newark, NJ: International Reading Association.

Cox J. L., Holden J. M., & Sagovsky R. (1987). Detection of postnatal depression. Development of the 10-item Edinburgh Postnatal Depression Scale. *British Journal of Psychiatry, 150*, 782–786.

Crittenden, P. (2003). *Care Index for Infants and Toddlers*. Coding manual. Miami, FL: Family Relations Institute.

Daley, M., Argeriou, M., & McCarty, D. (1998). Substance abuse treatment for pregnant women: a window of opportunity? *Addictive Behaviors, 23*(2), 239–249.

Derogatis, L. R. (1993). *Brief Symptom Inventory (BSI): administration, Scoring and Procedures Manual (3rd ed.)*. Minneapolis, MN: National Computer Systems.

Doan-Sampon, M.-A., Wollenberg, K., & Campbell, A. (1993). Growing: birth to three. Co-operative Educational Service Agency, 5. Portage, WI: Portage Project.

Eiden, R. (2001). Maternal substance use and mother–infant feeding interactions. *Infant Mental Health Journal, 22*(4), 497–511.

Eiden, R. D., Lewis, A., Croff, S., & Young, E. (2002). Maternal cocaine use and infant behavior. *Infancy, 3*(1), 77–96.

Espinosa, M., Beckwith, L., Howard, J., Tyler, R., & Swanson, K. (2001). Maternal psychopathology and attachment in toddlers of heavy cocaine-using mothers. *Infant Mental Health Journal, 22*(3), 316–333.

Fonagy, P., Gergely, G., Jurist, E., & Target, M. (2002). *Affect Regulation,Mentalization, and the Development of the Self*. New York: Other Press.

Fonagy, P., Steele, M., Moran, G., Steele, H., & Higgitt A. (1991). The capacity for understanding mental states. The reflective self in parent and child and its significance for security of attachment. *Infant Mental Health Journal, 13*, 200–217.

Fonagy, P., Steele, M., Steele, H., Leigh, T., Kennedy, R., Mattoon, G., et al. (1995). Attachment, the reflective self and borderline states: the predictive specificity of the Adult Attachment Interview and pathological emotional development. In S. Goldberg, R. Muir, & J. Kerr (Eds.), *Attachment Theory: social, Developmental and Clinical Perspectives* (pp. 233–278). New York: Analytic Press.

Fonagy, P., & Target, M. (1996). Playing with reality: theory of mind and the normal development of psychic reality. *International Journal of Psychoanalysis, 77*, 217–233.

Fonagy, P., Steele, H., & Steele, M. (1991). Maternal representations of attachment during pregnancy predict the organization of infant-mother attachment at one year of age. *Child Development, 62*, 891–905.

Fonagy, P. (2008). The mentalization-focused approach to social development. In Busch N. (Ed.), *Mentalization: theoretical Considerations, Research Findings and Clinical Implications*. New York: The Analytic Press.

Grella, C. E., Joshi, V., & Hser, Y.-I. (2000). Program variation in treatment outcomes among women in residential drug treatment. *Evaluation Review, 24*(4), 364–383.

Grienenberger, J., Kelly, K., Slade, A. (2005). Maternal reflective functioning, mother–infant affective communication and infant attachment: exploring the link between mental states and observed caregiving behaviour. *Attachment and Human Development, 7*(3), 299–311.

Holi, M. M., Sammallahti, P. R., & Aalberg, V. A. (1998). A Finnish validation study of the SCL-90. *Acta Psychiatrica Scandinavica, 97*(1), 42–46.

Horowitz, L. M., Rosenberg, S. E., & Baer, B. A. (1988). Inventory of Interpersonal Problems: psychometric properties and clinical applications. *Journal of Consulting Clinical Psychology, 56*, 885–892.

Jaskari S. (2008) Vauva vanhemman mielessä—kuvia reflektiivisen työotteen kehittämisestä Ensikoti Pinjassa. [Baby in the parent's mind—Description of the process of developing RF working model in residential treatment unit for substance abusing mother–baby pairs.] Ensi-ja turvakotien liiton julkaisu 2008, Nykypaino Oy Helsinki.

Johnson, A. L., Morrow, C. E., Accornero, V. H., Lihua, X., Anthony, J. C., & Bandstra, E. S. (2002). Maternal cocaine use: estimated effects on mother–child play interactions in the preschool period. *Developmental and Behavioral Pediatrics, 23*(4), 191–202.

Kalland, M. (2001). Kiintymyssuhdeteorian kliininen merkitys. Soveltaminen erityistilanteissa [Clinical relevance of attachment theory. Specific situations.] In J. Sinkkonen & M. Kalland (Eds.), *Varhaiset ihmissuhteet ja niiden häiriintyminen [Early Human Relationships and Their Disturbances]* (pp. 198–233). Helsinki: WSOY.

Koob, G. F., & Volkow, N. D. (2010). Neurocircuitry of addiction. *Neuropsychopharmacology, 35*, 217–238.

LaGasse, L. L., Messenger, D., Lester, B. M., Seifer, R., Tronick, E. Z., Bauer, C. R., et al. (2003). Prenatal drug exposure and maternal and infant feeding behaviour. *Archives of Disease in Childhood, 88*(5), 391–399.

Leckman, J. F., & Mayes, L. C. (1998). Understanding developmental psychopathology: how useful are evolutionary accounts? *Journal of American Academy of Child and Adolescent Psychiatry, 37*(10), 1011–1021.

Lester, B. M., & Tronick, E. Z. (1994). The effects of prenatal cocaine exposure and child outcome. *Infant Mental Health Journal, 15*(2), 107–120.

Mayes, L., Feldman, R., Granger, R., Haynes, O., Bornstein, M., & Schottenfeld, R. (1997). The effects of polydrug use with and without cocaine on mother–infant interaction at 3 and 6 months. *Infant Behavior and Development, 20*(4), 489–502.

Mayes, L., & Truman, S. (2002). Substance abuse and parenting. In M. Bornstein (Ed.), *Handbook of Parenting, Vol. 4: Social Conditions and Applied Parenting* (2nd ed., pp. 329–359). Mahwah, NJ: Lawrence Erlbaum Associates.

Mayes, L. C., Magidson, J., Lejuez, C. J., & Nicholls, S. S. (2009). Social relationships as primary rewards: the neurobiology of attachment. In: M. de Haan & M. R. Gunnar (Eds.), *Handbook of Developmental Neuroscience*. New York: Guilford.

Molitor, M., Mayes, L., & Ward, A. (2003). Emotion regulation behavior during a separation procedure in 18-month old children of mothers using cocaine and other drugs. *Development and Psychopathology, 15*(1), 39–45.

Pajulo, M. (2001). *Early Motherhood at Risk: mothers with Substance Dependency*. Doctoral thesis. University of Turku, Finland.

Pajulo, M., Savonlahti, E., Sourander, A., Ahlqvist, S., Helenius, H., & Piha, J. (2001). An early report on the mother–baby interactive capacity of substance-abusing mothers. *Journal of Substance Abuse Treatment, 20*, 143–151.

Pajulo, M., Savonlahti, E., Sourander, A., Helenius, H., & Piha, J. (2001). Prenatal maternal representations: mothers at psychosocial risk. *Infant Mental Health Journal, 22*(5), 529–544.

Pajulo, M., Savonlahti, E., Sourander, A., Helenius, H., & Piha, J. (2004). Maternal representations, depression and interactive behaviour in the postnatal period. A brief report. *Journal of Reproductive and Infant Psychology, 22*(2), 99–98.

Pajulo, M., Pyykkönen, N., Kalland, M., Sinkkonen, J., Helenius, H., Punamäki R-L., et al. (2012). Substance-abusing mothers in residential treatment with their babies: importance of pre-and postnatal reflective functioning. *Infant Mental Health Journal,* vol 33(1), 70–81.

Pajulo M., Pyykkönen N., Kalland, M., Sinkkonen, J., Helenius, H., & Punamäki R-L. (2011). Substance abusing mothers in residential treatment with their babies: postnatal psychiatric symptomatology and its association with mother–child relationship and later need for child protection actions. *Nordic Journal of Psychiatry, 65*(1), 65–73.

Raphael-Leff, J. (1991). Psychological Processes of Childbearing. London: Chapman & Hall.

Rodning, C., Beckwith, L., & Howard, J. (1991). Quality of attachment and home-environment in children prenatally exposed to PCP and cocaine. *Development and Psychopathology, 3*(4), 351–366.

Schechter, D. S., Kaminer, T., Grienenberger, J. F., & Amat, J. (2003). Fits and starts: a mother–infant case-study involving intergenerational violent trauma and pseudoseizures across three generations. *Infant Mental Health Journal, 24*(5), 510–528.

Schechter, D. S., Zeanah, C., & Myers, M. M. (2002). Negative and distorted maternal attributions among violence-exposed mothers of very young children before and after single-session feedback: are maternal psychopathology and reflective functioning predictive? Paper presented at the meetings of the World Association of Infant Mental Health, Amsterdam, The Netherlands.

Slade, A. (2002). Keeping the baby in mind: a critical factor in perinatal mental health. *Zero to Three,* June/July, 10–16.

Slade, A., Aber, J. L., Berger, B., Bresgi, I., & Kaplan, M. (2002). *The Parent Development Interview—Revised.* Unpublished manuscript. New Haven, CT: Yale Child Study Center.

Slade, A., Bernbach, E., Grienenberger, J., Levy, D. W., & Locker, A. (2002, 2005). *The Parent Development Interview and the Pregnancy Interview. Manual for scoring.* New York; New Haven, CT: The City College of New York, and the Yale Child Study Center.

Slade, A., Grienenberger, J., Bernbach, E., Levy, D., & Locker, A. (2005). Maternal reflective functioning and attachment: considering the transmission gap. *Attachment and Human Development, 7*(3), 283–298.

Stern, D. N. (1985). *The Interpersonal World of the Infant. A View from Psychoanalysis and Developmental Psychology.* New York: Basic Books.

Stern, D. N. (1995). *The Motherhood Constellation. A Unified View of Parent–Infant Psychotherapy.* New York: Basic Books.

Suchman, N. E., Mayes, L., Conti, J., Slade, A., & Rounsaville, B. (2004). Rethinking parenting interventions for drug dependent mothers: From behavior management to fostering emotional bonds. *Journal of Substance Abuse Treatment, 27,* 179–185.

Suchman, N. E., Altomare, M., Moller, F., Slade, A., & Mayes, L. (2003). Emotionally responsive parenting: a new parenting intervention for drug dependent mothers. Poster presentation, College on Problems of Drug Dependence Annual Meeting, Bal Harbor, FL.

Suchman, N. E., McMahon, T. J., Slade, A., & Luthar, S.S (2004). How early bonding, depression, illicit drug use and perceived support work together to influence drug dependent mothers' caregiving. *American Journal of Orthopsychiatry, 75*, 431–445.

Swain, J. E., Lorberbaum, J. P., Kose, S., & Strathearn L (2007). Brain basis of early parent–infant interactions: psychology, physiology and in vivo functional neuroimaging studies. *Journal of Child Psychology and Psychiatry, 48*(3/4), 262–287.

Swanson, K., Beckwith, L., & Howard, J. (2000). Intrusive caregiving and quality of attachment in prenatally drug-exposed toddlers and their primary caregivers. *Attachment & Human Development, 2*(2), 130–148.

Trad, P. V. (1993). Previewing: a developmental principal that promotes the therapeutic use of metaphor. *Journal of Clinical Psychology, 49*(2), 261–277.

Truman, S. D., Levy, D., & Mayes, L. C. (2004). Reflective functioning as mediator between drug use, parenting stress and child behavior. Unpublished manuscript.

Van der Kolk, B. 2003. *Traumatic Antecedents Questionnaire. Manual for Scoring.* Brookline, MA: The Trauma Center.

Winnicott, D. W. (1957). *Mother and Child: a Primer of First Relationship.* New York: Basic Books.

15 Attachment and Biobehavioral Catch-up

An Attachment-Based Intervention for Substance-Using Mothers and Their Infants

JOHANNA BICK, KRISTIN BERNARD,
AND MARY DOZIER

Mothers who use illicit substances are nearly three times more likely than non-substance-abusing mothers to abuse or neglect their children (Chaffin, Kelleher, & Hollenberg, 1996; Kelleher, Chaffin, Hollenberg, & Fischer, 1994). Substance abuse appears to represent a specific risk factor, over and above other risk factors such as poverty and mental health problems (Chaffin et al., 1996).

Substance use is associated with a host of problematic parenting behaviors (Hans, Bernstein, & Henson, 1999; Johnson et al., 2002; Molitor & Mayes, 2010; Molitor, Mayes, & Ward, 2003). First, mothers who use substances sometimes neglect their children, failing to provide adequate social stimulation and/or failing to provide a safe, protective interpersonal environment (Hans et al., 1999). Coinciding with their high risk for neglect, many substance-abusing mothers report ambivalence about providing continued care for their children (Mayes & Truman, 2002; Murphy & Rosenbaum, 1999; Suchman, Pajulo, DeCoste, & Mayes, 2006). Second, when engaged with their young children, substance-using mothers are often less sensitive and responsive than non-substance-abusing mothers (Molitor & Mayes, 2010). Third, they are more likely than non-substance-abusing mothers to behave in frightening ways (Hans et al., 1999; Johnson et al., 2002). Each of these issues is associated with challenges for infants and young children, as described below. Therefore, it is not surprising that outcomes for children of substance-using mothers are often less favorable than for other children (e.g., Johnson et al., 2002; Molitor et al., 2003).

We have developed an intervention, Attachment and Biobehavioral Catch-up, that targets substance-abusing mothers' risk for neglect, reduced feelings of commitment and delight with respect to caring for their children, and increased insensitive responsiveness and frightening behavior. This chapter first describes the specific ways in which substance-using mothers often parent differently than other mothers, using case examples that illustrate how the intervention targets each of the specific problematic issues. We will then describe the intervention, and finally present evidence of the intervention's effectiveness.

Risk for Neglect, Reduced Commitment, and Decreased Reward

Maternal substance abuse has been associated with neglect (Cash & Wilke, 2003). Preoccupation with obtaining substances and the effects of substances on mothers' reward and motivation systems underlying parenting are among the factors leading to lower levels of commitment and delight, and the inadequate attention paid to young children.

Case Example 1: Background

Isabel was a 30-year-old heroin-addicted mother. She had two older children who had been taken from her care earlier and eventually adopted by their foster parents. At the point when she was referred to our program, her 10-month-old daughter, Cloe, was living with her. Isabel had a number of childlike and/or dissociative behaviors, including becoming absorbed in her own thoughts while twirling her hair around her finger. She had been using heroin for a number of years; when she had money, she often chose to use it for purchasing heroin, which was readily available in her neighborhood. At such times, she left her child (and sometimes a neighbor's child) with anyone she could find in her apartment. Cloe was left in her crib or in a baby seat for long periods of time, whether asleep or not. A host of children and adults came in and out of the apartment. When Isabel was lucid, and when supported in her efforts, she interacted with her daughter; when she was not lucid, she showed little propensity to interact with Cloe or to protect her child.

Implications of maternal neglect: The primary issue identified in Isabel's parenting ability was her extreme neglect of providing protection and basic care for her child. Although humans have probably evolved to handle a range of caregiving conditions, the experience of neglect is almost certainly outside of the range of experience-expectant conditions (e.g., Greenough, Black, & Wallace, 1987). Human young are born relatively altricial, or dependent upon mothers for help in regulating most aspects of functioning. Therefore, infants whose mothers neglect them may well adapt in ways that prove problematic to long-term functioning. John Bowlby, the architect of attachment theory, first began his study of attachment through observing young boys whom he termed "affectionless thieves" (1944). He found that these boys, who appeared callous and uncaring interpersonally, uniformly lacked a caregiver who had been committed to their well-being. Bowlby suggested that having a committed caregiver, someone who would stand between oneself and danger, was critical to healthy development.

When the substance-abusing mother neglects her young child, the child experiences a world that is highly threatening. Whereas the child is "designed" evolutionarily to depend upon his or her caregiver, he or she must navigate the world without having a caregiver upon whom to rely. Although attachment quality has received extensive attention in the literature, a neglectful or absent caregiver represents a much more fundamental problem for the child than insensitive care. At the level of regulatory functions, the natural progression from a dyadic process to self-regulation is bypassed, with compromises resulting from the child's taking over functions prematurely. For example, the effective caregiver helps buffer the young child from stressors at the neuroendocrine level such that rises in cortisol are not seen in response to challenges; when the child does not have an effective caregiver, cortisol responses are seen (Bernard & Dozier, 2010; Hertsgaard, Gunnar, Farrell, Erickson, & Nachmias, 1995).

■ NEUROBIOLOGY OF NEGLECT IN ADDICTED MOTHERS

The increased rates of neglect found among substance-abusing parents have been attributed to drug addiction's impact on neurobiological systems associated with reward and motivation. Many of the commonly abused substances, such as cocaine or heroin, interfere with the brain systems involved in motivation, joy, and reward (Koob, 1996; Koob & LeMoal, 1997). In the case of mothers with drug addictions, the central reward systems seem to become "rewired"; drug use becomes more highly motivating and rewarding than more natural rewards, such as the parenting of one's child (Suchman, DeCoste, Castiglioni, Legow, & Mayes, 2008). Consequently, mothers with substance abuse problems have been found to express more ambivalence with regard to the continued care of their children, and experience decreased parental motivation, compared to mothers without drug problems (Mayes & Truman, 2002; Murphy & Rosenbaum, 1999; Suchman, Pajulo, DeCoste, & Mayes, 2006).

■ IMPLICATIONS FOR INTERVENTION

Anecdotally, in our work with substance-abusing parents, we have also observed that mothers report reduced feelings of commitment to a long-lasting relationship with their children. Motivated by this observation, we developed a semi-structured interview that systematically assesses the variability in mothers' long-term feelings of commitment and investment in their children. During administrations of this interview prior to the start of our intervention program, we have observed that many mothers admit to having considered placing their children with another caregiver, such as a relative or a foster care provider. When probed further, mothers often reported feeling overwhelmed by the needs of their children, given their struggle with drug addiction, and questioned their abilities to provide a protective environment for their children.

At a behavioral level, we have observed that substance-abusing mothers often seem to show less delight in their young child's behavior, compared with mothers who do not have substance abuse issues. In our previous work with foster mothers and infants, we have found that when mothers display delight toward their children, it elicits delight from the young child, and is highly rewarding to mothers—and certainly to children. Therefore, enhancing mothers' abilities to take delight in their children may be instrumental for addressing the unique parenting issues pertaining to substance-abusing mothers. Because we have found that displays of delight are associated with feelings of commitment

(Bernard & Dozier, 2010), we expect that helping substance-abusing mothers' exhibit delight in their children may also serve to enhance their commitment to their children.

We increase mothers' reward in response to their children primarily in the context of helping mothers learn to follow children's lead. During the Attachment and Biobehavioral Catch-up program, mothers are encouraged to follow along and show delight in their children's actions. For example, when reading a book together, we encourage mothers to allow their children to "lead the dance." If instead their child prefers to play peek-a-boo with the book, we encourage mothers to follow along and celebrate their child's efforts. In addition to praising mothers' efforts, we highlight instances in which children seem delighted by their mothers' involvement and participation. The interventionist comments on these moments of maternal joy and delight as they occur during the session. We also review the moments when mothers successfully take delight in their children to help mothers grasp the powerful influence they have on their children.

Expressing delight or joy in their children's actions is often very difficult for mothers with drug addictions, who may not be used to interacting with their children in this manner. Early on in the intervention, we find that there may only be one or two brief moments in which mothers take delight in their children. However, the gentle support of the interventionist helps mothers to find opportunities in which they can offer praise, encouragement, or positive comments. Illustrating the impact of the mothers' joy on both the children's *and* mothers' mental state becomes a powerful tool for change. By providing ongoing support and encouragement, we find that mothers become more willing and confident in their abilities to express delight in their child's actions. Over time, their delight and enjoyment become more frequent and automatic.

Case Example 1: Intervention

Isabel's parenting behaviors (e.g., leaving her child to obtain drugs, tuning out the child's bids for attention) conveyed a lack of commitment to her child. In discussions with the interventionist, Isabel described how her addiction and strong drug cravings made it difficult to find the energy and motivation to care for her child. She reported that some days, it was even difficult to make sure that Cloe was clothed and fed. When asked what she does when things become too overwhelming, Isabel reported that she often drops Cloe off at a nearby relative's house until she "gets back on her feet." Although it was hard for her to admit, Isabel confessed that she questioned her abilities to be a stable parent for her child, and wondered if her child might be better off being cared for somewhere else.

In Isabel's case, drug addiction clearly reduced her capacity to provide adequate care for her child. She was at risk of neglecting her child's physical and emotional needs, her motivation and confidence in her abilities to care for her child had waned, and her drug use seemed to overtake her ability to perceive her own child as rewarding. One way that the intervention targeted this issue was to increase the number of opportunities in which Isabel could value and enjoy her child during everyday interactions.

During intervention sessions, Isabel was supported in her efforts to take delight in her child. The interventionist highlighted instances, even during mealtime or routine daily activities, in which Isabel could follow her child's lead and take delight in her actions. Importantly, the interventionist praised instances in which Isabel naturally and genuinely took delight in her child during the session. When Isabel reflexively smiled in response to Cloe's giggle, causing Cloe to smile wider, the interventionist commented on how powerful Isabel's expression of delight was for Cloe. Playing back the video clip of this moment helped Isabel see the positive influence of her delight on Cloe. Although Isabel struggled at first, she became less dependent on the interventionist's prompts for help to find opportunities to take delight in her child, and began to do so naturally. Toward the end of the program, Isabel remarked that her interactions with her daughter had become "the best part of her day," and that it made her feel proud that she could have such a positive effect on her child. During a follow-up visit with Isabel, she was proud to tell our research assistant that she had been sober for six months. Although she admitted that on her "difficult days" she sometimes struggled with following Cloe's lead and taking delight in her interactions, she seemed more invested in her role as a mother, more rewarded by her interactions with Cloe, and appeared better able to provide Cloe with a fundamental sense of protection.

Lack of Sensitive, Responsive Maternal Care

Mothers who abuse substances have been found to be less sensitive and responsive than non-drug-abusing mothers (Eiden, 2001; Mayes et al., 1997; Schuetze, Zeskind, & Eiden, 2003). This lack of sensitive care may take several forms. First, mothers may reject their children's bids for reassurance in a number of ways, including actively discouraging the child's bids through making fun of the child (e.g., "Don't be a baby") or chastising the child (e.g., "I told you not to stand on that chair!"), and more passively discouraging the bids through denial (e.g., "You're not really hurt") or distraction (e.g., "Look at the birdie outside"). However different these maternal behaviors appear, they all carry the message that the child should not expect the mother to respond to the child's distress. Second, mothers may be inconsistent in their responsiveness to children's distress. They may be responsive at times and unresponsive at others, or may be rejecting at times and appropriately responsive at others.

Case Example 2: Background

Lenora was a 17-year-old girl who had been using substances (mostly marijuana and alcohol) since she was a young teenager. She was living in an apartment with her two young children when we saw her in our intervention. When her 12-month-old daughter backed away from the interventionist (who was then a stranger to her), Lenora laughed and said, "Don't be stupid, Callie. She's not going to do anything to you." She often told her two-year-old son, Caleb, that he would grow up to be a sissy if he didn't quit crying when he separated from her. When Callie fell off the sofa and was visibly shaken and injured, Lenora said, "Don't you cry—that won't make it hurt any less." While observing Lenora interact with her children during the first few sessions, it became clear to the interventionist that Lenora struggled with providing sensitive, nurturing care at times when her children needed her, especially when they were hurt, frightened, or separated from her. During discussions about her own parenting beliefs, Lenora reported that she believed that too much comfort and affection would spoil her children. She was convinced that providing nurturance would cause her children to be unprepared to deal with a tough world.

Implications of maternal insensitivity: As was the case with Lenora, mothers' own histories of attachment-related experiences significantly influence their parental-related thoughts and behaviors (van IJzendoorn, 1995). Mothers who characteristically idealize their own attachment figures and attachment experiences are those who most often reject their children's bids for reassurance (van IJzendoorn, 1995). Mothers who express extreme anger and seem overly preoccupied with their previous attachment experiences tend to be inconsistent in their availability. Mothers who both value attachment and are open and consistent in their appraisals of attachment experiences tend to be responsive to their infants' signals for reassurance.

Sensitive, responsive maternal care is associated with children's developing secure attachments to their mothers, whereas insensitive care is associated with children's developing insecure attachments (van IJzendoorn, 1995). When children find that their mothers are responsive to them when they need them, they develop "confident expectations" that their mothers will be available to meet their needs. On one hand, if a child's mother typically responds with soothing words and reassurance when the child comes to her distressed, the child will look to her with confidence in her availability when he or she is distressed. On the other hand, if a child's mother typically rebuffs his or her bids for reassurance when distressed, the child will become less likely to turn to her when distressed.

This confidence in maternal availability is assessed in the Strange Situation Procedure, the laboratory assessment of attachment (Ainsworth, Blehar, Waters, & Wall, 1978). In the Strange Situation, children undergo a series of episodes that increasingly challenge them. Of most relevance for classifying children as secure or insecure, mothers are reunited with their children following brief (up to 6-minute) separations. Children classified as "secure" are those who turn directly to their mothers for whatever comfort they need. In the case of a child who has not been very distressed, it might take the form of a smile or verbal greeting following the mother's return; in the case of a child who has been highly distressed, it might be running to the mother and snuggling with the mother for an extended period of time before venturing off to play. Compared with secure children, children classified as "insecure" are less confident that they can be reassured by their mothers. This might be seen in avoidant behaviors such as turning away from the mother upon reunion, or resistant behaviors such as remaining fussy even after the mother has attempted to soothe him or her. (Disorganized behaviors will be discussed in the following section.)

Implications for intervention: Whereas having an insensitive mother is not optimal, it is important to distinguish this from conditions in which the child is not confident that his or her mother will protect him or her (discussed earlier) and conditions when he or she is fearful of the mother (discussed next). Although not optimal, having an insensitive mother is not associated with as problematic outcomes as being unable to trust in the mother's protection or as being frightened of the mother (Fearon, Bakermans-Kranenburg, van IJzendoorn, Lapsley, & Roisman, 2010; van IJzendoorn,

Schuengel, & Bakermans-Kranenburg, 1999). Children with insecure/avoidant or insecure/resistant attachments represent *strategies* for dealing with the mother's unavailability. Children who turn away from their mothers rather than showing their distress are probably minimizing the likelihood of more-significant rejections from mothers who are not comfortable with children's distress. Children who remain resistant and fussy maximize chances of mothers' responding who only respond intermittently. Thus, the behaviors are well-suited to the availability of the caregivers. One of the central targets of Attachment and Biobehavioral Catch-up is to help mothers provide nurturance to their young children. They are helped to provide nurturance even though children may not elicit it (i.e., children have come to not expect it) and even though it may not come naturally to them due to their own beliefs and values regarding attachment.

Case Example 2: Intervention

The intervention targeted Lenora's issues with nurturance in two ways. First, given that Lenora's children had learned to not expect her to be available, the intervention helped Lenora see that her children might need her nurturance even when they did not show it directly. Second, the intervention helped Lenora think through what made it difficult for her to behave in nurturing ways. She was asked to think of the "voices from her past" that she heard when her children cried. Through the help of the interventionist, Lenora explored how her previous experiences were influencing her current parenting. During the video-based feedback, Lenora realized that her son eventually calmed when she soothed him when hurt. She also noticed that he calmed more quickly when she soothed him than if she let him go off on his own. Through discussions with the interventionist, Lenora become convinced that her responsiveness would help her children to grow up more confident and less needy than if they dealt with their struggles alone.

Throughout the latter half of the intervention program, Lenora successfully learned to "override" her automatic response to ignore her children or tell them to stop crying (which was to do what *her* parents would have done), and to respond to her children's distress sensitively. For example, Lenora would remind herself, "my baby needs me to pick her up, even though I hear my mom telling me 'you are going to spoil that child.'" By end of the program, she expressed how much easier responding sensitively to her children's needs had become over time.

Frightening Maternal Behavior

Mothers who use substances have been found to behave in more frightening ways with their infants and young children than non-substance-abusing mothers (Hans et al., 1999; Lyons-Ruth & Block, 1996). The behaviors range from threatening behaviors to hostile, intrusive behaviors, to odd and bizarre behaviors (Johnson et al., 2002; Lyons-Ruth & Block, 1996). For example, mothers may behave in frankly frightening ways, such as yelling at children or hitting them, or may behave in intrusive, overwhelming ways that cause children to recoil. Regardless, these behaviors have the effect of making the child frightened of the mother.

Case Example 3: Background

Bernice had used crack cocaine off and on for the past ten years, and had recently used methamphetamine heavily. During the first session, Bernice remarked that she was under a lot of stress and had very little patience for her children. Being the sole caregiver, Bernice was constantly trying to make ends meet and keep a roof over their heads. As an added stress, Bernice was exhausted from trying to get clean and "had no energy to deal with the trouble her kids were causing." It was clear that Bernice was desperate to keep her children safe, but she often used tactics that were frightening. For example, when her eight-month-old put objects in her mouth, Bernice became fearful that her baby would choke. She yelled loudly, "I TOLD you not to do that! Get that out of your mouth before I smack you." Both the little girl and her three-year-old recoiled in fear. When discussing Bernice's past, it became clear that many of her own experiences with her mother and other caregivers (including her grandmother and foster mother) were characterized by frightening behaviors. For example, Bernice recalled getting a "beating" after she spilled a carton of juice on the kitchen floor when she was trying to pour a glass for her brother. Bernice was aware that such experiences had been difficult for her to deal with but had never thought about the effects on her ability to trust her caregivers. Furthermore, she did not see her own behaviors as frightening except in the most obvious instances.

Implications of frightening maternal behavior: Frightening behaviors like those displayed by Bernice are concerning because of their association with disorganized attachment and dissociative behavior among young children (Lyons-Ruth & Block, 1996). Children's attachment quality is particularly affected by frightening maternal behavior. Main and Hesse (1990) have suggested that when children are frightened of their caregivers, they have an "unsolvable dilemma." Such children are often frightened of the people whom they look to for reassurance and have a dilemma when needing to turn to them. Therefore, children's ability to maintain an organized attachment strategy is disrupted. Indeed, a large proportion of children of substance-abusing mothers develop disorganized attachments (Goodman, Hans, & Cox, 1999; O'Connor, Sigman, & Brill, 1987; Rodning, Beckwith, & Howard, 1991; Swanson, Beckwith, & Howard, 2002).

Disorganized attachment is characterized by odd, anomalous behaviors when children are distressed and in their mother's presence. In the Strange Situation, a number of behaviors have been noted, including the sequential or simultaneous display of contradictory attachment behaviors (such as avoidance and resistance), undirected or misdirected attachment behaviors (such as protesting the stranger's departure from the room), stereotypies, freezing, direct evidence of apprehension of mother, and direct evidence of disorientation (Main & Solomon, 1990).

Implications for intervention. Attachment and Biobehavioral Catch-up targets frightening behavior directly. Mothers are helped to think about experiences from their own past when caregivers frightened them, whether for discipline or teasing, and then helped to monitor their own behaviors with their children, becoming aware of times when they are intrusive or frightening.

Case Example 3: Intervention

Bernice's frightening behaviors were particularly concerning, given their frequency, severity, and noticeable effect on her children. After discussing examples of frightening behavior experienced by other children, the effects of frightening behavior on children's ability to trust their mothers, and Bernice's own experiences of being frightened of her caregivers, Bernice was encouraged to think about her own parenting behaviors that might be perceived as frightening to her children. Because Bernice felt supported by the interventionist and had developed a trusting relationship with her at this stage of the intervention, she openly considered aspects of her parenting that might be overwhelming to her children. She acknowledged that she remembered feeling frightened as a child, but didn't realize that she might be perpetuating what she had experienced.

The interventionist emphasized that becoming aware of her strengths and weaknesses as a parent was an incredible accomplishment. Bernice and the interventionist identified moments in which Bernice responded in a sensitive manner, and observed the positive effect that it had on her children. These moments were compared with instances in which Bernice behaved in a frightening manner. Through this powerful contrast, Bernice began to monitor her behavior and practice alternative ways of responding to her children as a means of keeping them safe.

■ THE ATTACHMENT AND BIOBEHAVIORAL CATCH-UP INTERVENTION

Intervention Development

The Attachment and Biobehavioral Catch-up (ABC) Intervention was first developed for foster mothers. It targeted three key issues that we have identified as important for caregivers of children placed in foster care. First, we found that foster children tended to behave in ways that served to push caregivers away (Stovall & Dozier, 2000; Stovall-McClough & Dozier, 2004). Even when foster mothers were generally nurturing, foster children behaved in ways that served to elicit non-nurturing behaviors. More specifically, children either turned away from caregivers or were fussy and inconsolable. When children turned away from them, foster mothers behaved as if children did not need them; when children were fussy and inconsolable, foster mothers responded angrily in return.

In our clinical work with at-risk birth parents who have high rates of substance abuse, we have also observed that young children often avoid or push their mothers away at times of need. We realized that, similar to foster mothers, these at-risk birth mothers also need to do more than be responsive—they need to actually behave in therapeutic ways, seeing the "need" underlying their children's avoidant or angry behavior. We were aware that this may be especially challenging for birth mothers who are at risk for neglect and often currently struggling with substance abuse problems, but with support and effective scaffolding to increase their parenting, we have found improvements in their children's outcomes (Bernard, Bick, & Dozier, 2012).

The second component of the intervention for foster mothers was helping them provide nurturing care even when it did not come naturally to them (Dozier, Stovall, Albus, & Bates, 2001). Clearly this was an even more critical issue among birth mothers, especially those with substance abuse issues, than among foster mothers, due to the former group's frequent histories of abuse and trauma (Breslau, Davis, & Schultz, 2003; Jacobsen, Southwick, & Kosten, 2001).

The third component of the foster mother intervention was helping mothers follow their children's lead with delight. Foster mothers varied in how well they followed their children's lead and how committed they were to the children in their care (Dozier & Lindhiem, 2006; Lindhiem & Dozier, 2007). Birth mothers who are substance-using very often have difficulty following their children's lead and seem to waver in their feelings that they can provide long-term, stable care for their children (Mayes and Truman, 2002). Related to this, we see deficits in the expression of delight among many substance-using mothers, most likely due to the influence of the drug addiction on their abilities to experience joy and reward in their children (Mayes & Truman, 2002; Murphy & Rosenbaum, 1999; Suchman, Pajulo, DeCoste, & Mayes, 2006)

Finally, we had not identified frightening behavior as a critical issue among foster mothers. When we began intervening with birth mothers, especially those who used substances, this behavior emerged as striking. It was clear that we needed to address this issue.

Intervention Description

Attachment and Biobehavioral Catch-up consists of 10 intervention sessions, each lasting one hour, which are delivered in mothers' homes. The intervention helps mothers provide nurturing care even when children do not elicit it (Sessions 1–2) and even when they struggle to respond to their children's distress with nurturance (Sessions 7–8). This program also increases mothers' delight in their children through following their children's lead (Sessions 3–4, 9), and helps mothers parent in non-threatening or frightening ways (Sessions 5–6).

Although the various sessions target different issues, the interventionist conceptualizes the most challenging issues for mothers after each session and addresses the most relevant issues indirectly or directly in other sessions as well. This is accomplished by carefully observing the mother–child interactions during the first few sessions. For example, if the parent trainer observes that a mother is adept at showing delight in her child, but struggles to respond sensitively, the intervention session may focus more on the importance of nurturing care even when the session emphasis is on following the lead.

Sessions Overview

The intervention is manualized. Although the content is provided in the manual, we expect interventionists to practice the intervention extensively prior to implementing such that they do not need to refer to the manual during their work with mothers.

Sessions 1–2: Providing nurturing care even when the child does not elicit nurturance. Mothers are introduced to the intervention through discussion of their beliefs about a number of aspects of mothering. Several myths of mothering, such as "Babies get spoiled if they get picked up," are discussed, with some of the refuting evidence presented briefly.

Following the introduction, videos of babies who are easily soothed by their mothers are contrasted with videos of babies who either turn away from or are resistant to their mothers. Mothers are helped to see how challenging it is to provide nurturing care in the latter two instances, and yet how critical it is.

Sessions 3–4: Following the child's lead with delight. Mothers see videos of other mother–child dyads in which the mother is following the child's lead or taking the lead herself. She is asked to do several activities with her child, focusing on following the child's lead, such as playing with a book with pull-out shapes, playing with blocks, or making pudding. The interventionist scaffolds the activities, pointing out times when the mother follows the lead, and making suggestions for other ways she might respond to the child. The interventionist particularly stresses the importance of taking delight in the child's efforts.

Session 5–6: Interacting in non-frightening ways. Mothers are shown videos of other mothers who behave in intrusive or overwhelming ways, missing their children's cues of feeling overwhelmed or fearful. Mothers are then asked to play with their children with puppets, but very carefully paying attention to children's signals. Because playing with puppets often elicits intrusive behavior, it is intentionally presented so that mothers will have opportunities to think about how to avoid behaving in intrusive or frightening ways. Mothers are helped to recall times in their own histories when their caregivers were intrusive or frightening, and to recall their own reactions. Finally, mothers are supported in recognizing how they may behave in threatening ways themselves, acknowledging the effects of this behavior on their relationships with their children, and developing strategies for monitoring these frightening behaviors in future interactions.

Sessions 7–8: Voices from the past. Recognizing influences from the past that affect caregiving. Session 6 introduces the importance of mothers' earlier experiences on their caregiving, and Sessions 7 and 8 deal with these issues more explicitly. Mothers are helped to think through experiences with their own caregivers that affect how they react to children's bids for reassurance, and opportunities to follow children's lead. They are helped to become conscious of the "voices from their past" that they hear when parenting.

In so doing, their parenting can become no longer automatic (i.e., driven by their own experiences), but rather consciously chosen. For example, although a mother may think to herself, "Oh, you're such a whiner" when her child asks her to be held, she recognizes that this emanates from her own experiences of asking for reassurance when she was a child. She can then consider the most appropriate (and nurturing) way to respond, "overriding" her natural propensity to turn her child away. The work of Lieberman and colleagues was influential to our conceptualization of these issues (Lieberman, Padron, Van Horn, & Harris, 2005).

Sessions 9–10: Consolidating gains. Sessions 9 and 10 have specific content (encouraging mothers to hold their children more and encouraging mothers to help their children understand, and eventually express, emotions effectively, respectively). For example, mothers are encouraged to engage in a cuddling task with their child in Session 9. During Session 10, mothers are encouraged to "label" their child's emotions throughout the session as a means of helping the child organize different feelings and affective states (Izard, Fine, Mostow, Trentacosta, & Campbell, 2002). However, the primary objective of these sessions is to continue the emphasis on mothers' nurturing their children, following their children's lead with delight, and behaving in non-frightening ways. Interventionists show videos that highlight the progress parents have made in each of the three areas, and celebrate their progress.

Why Intervene in Mothers' Homes?

Although it takes more staff time to intervene in families' homes than in a clinic or office, we consider it critical. Most especially, we want to maximize the likelihood that change in maternal behaviors will generalize to their natural, everyday environment. If mothers come into a clinic, they may well become more nurturing and follow their child's lead better while they are in a session—but they might have difficulty transferring nurturing behavior to the home environment, where perhaps there are more demands and stress. We have intervened with a mother when there were as many as nine additional people in the living room. We find that helping the mother become nurturing, follow the child's lead, and behave in a non-frightening fashion is a very different task when children and adults of different ages and with different needs are present, than if we were to simply intervene with the mother and the child referred for the program.

Why a 10-Session Brief Treatment Model?

There are several advantages to limiting the intervention length, even though we often find that there is still work to be done at the end of 10 sessions. There is a sense of urgency to reach the objectives within the allotted time frame. Interventionists keep in mind how many sessions they have to reach goals, and it provides a structure (as well as a deadline). When, for example, a mother is not following the lead by Session 6, the interventionist thinks of how to incorporate videos that will emphasize the importance in subsequent sessions—but keeping in mind how many sessions remain.

The focus of this intervention differs substantially from longer-term psychotherapy-oriented programs. By exploring their own attachment-related experiences and memories, we help mothers understand their propensities for frightening behavior, and their difficulties with delighting in their child or providing nurturing care. We do this in a supportive context that scaffolds their growth through positive feedback and celebrates their progress. Based on the limited time frame and targeted nature of this program, we place less emphasis on the processing of the mother's mental and emotional state (i.e., feelings of shame, guilt, and anxiety about her parenting or substance abuse issues) during the treatment program, when compared with programs of longer duration. However, we are especially enthusiastic about our effectiveness in changing mothers' behaviors and children's outcomes given the short-term behavioral nature of this attachment-focused program.

What Techniques Are Most Important?

Perhaps the most important component of the intervention is providing "in the moment" feedback to mothers. The interventionist needs to keep in mind the intervention manual content while attending to ongoing interactions between the mother and child. For example, while explaining the importance of nurturance for young children, the interventionist is also attending to the interactions between the mother and child during the session. An interventionist may point out several of mother's displays of nurturance and child's response during the one-hour session. If the mother misses an opportunity to respond sensitively to her child, the interventionist may gently comment, "What do you think about your child's behavior right now? He looks like he doesn't want you, but I wonder what would happen if you rubbed his back anyway."

We also find that it is extremely important to provide supportive, positive feedback to the mother. Even though the interventionist needs to be able to point out weaknesses, this can be accomplished much more readily in the context of a trusting relationship than otherwise. The interventionist needs to "catch the mother being good"—even in the context of the most problematic mothering, there are examples of the mother attending to the child, the child looking to the mother for reassurance, etc.—and is where the interventionist needs to start.

■ EMPIRICAL EVALUATION OF ABC FOR HIGH-RISK PARENTS

The effectiveness of Attachment and Biobehavioral Catch-up among high-risk mothers has been assessed through a randomized clinical trial with 120 birth mothers, many of whom who use substances, and their young children. In this randomized clinical trial, mothers were randomly assigned to receive either the Attachment and Biobehavioral Catch-up intervention or a control intervention. The control intervention, called Developmental Education for Families (Ramey, McGinness, Cross, Collier, & Barrie-Blackley, 1982; Ramey, Yeates, & Short, 1984), targeted cognitive and language development and was selected because it contained the same number, duration, and structure of sessions but did not focus on improving the parent–child relationship quality.

Following the intervention, mothers participated with their children in the Strange Situation so that children's attachment quality could be assessed. Salivary cortisol was assessed prior to and following the Strange Situation. Children whose mothers had received the ABC intervention showed secure attachment more frequently and disorganized attachment less frequently than children in the DEF intervention (Bernard, Bick, & Dozier, 2010). Furthermore, children from the DEF intervention showed cortisol reactivity in the Strange Situation, which was not seen among children in the ABC intervention (Bernard & Dozier, 2010). Cortisol reactivity is typically not seen among young children whose mothers buffer them effectively from stress. Taken together, these results support the effectiveness of the Attachment and Biobehavioral Catch-up intervention in helping children develop secure attachment behaviors and improved behavioral and biological regulation.

We find these preliminary results exciting in that they illustrate the potential for our program to improve parenting outcomes among substance-abusing parents. However, given that the sample of high-risk birth mothers included both substance-abusing and non-substance-abusing mothers at risk for neglect, we are aware of the need for future research. Many mothers with substance-abuse issues participated in drug treatment and relapse prevention programs alongside the ABC program. In recruiting mothers with substance-abuse problems, we found that some mothers had been involved in drug treatment programs for some time, whereas others had just initiated the drug treatment process. In our ongoing work, it seems necessary to address whether intervention effectiveness is associated with stage of recovery and involvement in drug treatment programs. Further, it seems important to explore whether child age and addiction type and severity might be associated with the degree to which mothers benefit from the ABC program. We expect that such questions will be important for delivering treatment programs with maximal effectiveness.

■ CONDUCTING RESEARCH WITH SUBSTANCE-USING MOTHERS

There are many challenges to engaging substance-using mothers in an intervention program and associated research, such as their initial skepticism or lack of interest in participation in research, and difficulty in scheduling due to frequent moves and disconnected phone numbers. We have implemented a range of strategies for recruiting and retaining these mothers as participants in our research. Probably most critical to our research efforts is the relationship we develop with the families, such that mothers do not feel like research "subjects." This begins with the initial phone call and is essential throughout the research visits and intervention sessions. In addition to research staff and interventionists' responding to mothers with a warm and open manner, we encourage staff to bring framed photographs of mothers and their children from earlier visits, send Mother's Day cards and gifts, and give children birthday presents at yearly follow-up visits. Additionally, we maintain as much consistency as possible concerning which staff members make phone calls and conduct follow-up visits. Although these efforts help in engaging mothers in the research, we often still have difficulty scheduling follow-up visits with these families due to frequent transitions in housing and changes in contact information. Thus, we have found it critical to obtain information for several emergency contacts and maintain frequent contact through phone calls and letters. Furthermore, we have several staff members who are racially and socioeconomically similar to our mothers and familiar with the neighborhoods in which the mothers live. They are able to make connections with community members and more easily track difficult-to-reach participants. Although substance-using mothers are challenging to work with for these reasons, we have found working with them to be incredibly rewarding.

■ SUMMARY

Attachment and Biobehavioral Catch-up was developed as an intervention to enhance parenting among high-risk mothers and their young children. The intervention focuses on several issues that have been found to be problems among substance-using mothers. Although the intervention does not address substance use specifically, we think that enhancing mothers' motivation to parent effectively and helping parenting become a more rewarding endeavor serves as a strong motivator for reducing substance use. This intervention has been shown effective in changing children's ability to trust in their mothers and in their ability to regulate physiology in a randomized controlled study.

■ AUTHOR NOTE

Support for this research was provided by NIMH R01 awards 052135, 074374, and 084135 to the first author. We acknowledge the support of the Delaware Division of Family Services and the Philadelphia Department of Human Services; and caseworkers, foster families, birth families, and children at both agencies.

■ REFERENCES

Ainsworth, M. D. S., Blehar, M., Waters, E., & Wall, S. (1978). *Patterns of Attachment*. Hillsdale, N.J.: Erlbaum.

Bernard, K., Bick, J., & Dozier, M. (2012). *Differences in attachment quality among children in the Attachment and Biobehavioral Catch-up intervention and a control intervention*. University of Delaware: Unpublished manuscript.

Bernard, K., & Dozier, M. (2011). This is my baby: Foster parents' feelings of commitment and displays of delight. *Infant Mental Health Journal, 32*, 251–262.

Bernard, K., & Dozier, M. (2010). Examining infants' cortisol responses to laboratory tasks among children varying in attachment disorganization: Stress reactivity or return to baseline? *Developmental Psychology, 46*, 1771–1778.

Bernard, K., & Dozier, M. (2010). *Differences in cortisol reactivity among children in the Attachment and Biobehavioral Catch-up intervention and a control intervention*. University of Delaware: Unpublished manuscript.

Bowlby, J. (1944). Forty-four juvenile thieves: Their character and home-life. *International Journal of Psychoanalysis, 25*, 19–52.

Breslau, N., Davis, G. C., & Schultz, L. R. (2003). Post-traumatic stress disorder and the incidence of nicotine, alcohol, and other drug disorders in persons who have experienced trauma. *Archives of General Psychiatry, 60*, 289–294.

Cash, S. J., & Wilke, D. J. (2003). An ecological model of maternal substance abuse and child neglect: Issues, analyses, and recommendations. *American Journal of Orthopsychiatry, 73*, 392–404.

Chaffin, M., Kelleher, K., & Hollenberg, J. (1996). Onset of physical abuse and neglect: Psychiatric, substance abuse, and social risk factors from prospective community data. *Child Abuse and Neglect, 20,* 191–203.

Dozier, M., & Lindhiem, O. (2006). This is my child: Differences among foster parents in commitment to their children. *Child Maltreatment, 11,* 338–345.

Dozier, M., Stovall, K. C., Albus, K. E., & Bates, B. (2001). Attachment for infants in foster care: The role of parent state of mind. *Child Development, 72,* 1467–1477.

Eiden, D. R. (2001). Maternal substance use and mother–infant feeding interactions. *Infant Mental Health Journal, 22,* 497–511.

Fearon, R. P., Bakermans-Kranenburg, M. J., van IJzendoorn, M. H., Lapsley, A. M., & Roisman, G. I. (2010). The significance of insecure attachment and disorganization in the development of children's externalizing behavior: A meta-analytic study. *Child Development, 81,* 435–456. doi: 10.1111/j.1467-8624.2009.01405.x

Greenough, W. T., Black, J. E., & Wallace, C. S. (1987). Experience and brain development. *Child Development, 58,* 539–559.

Goodman, G., Hans, S. L., & Cox, S. M. (1999). Attachment behavior and its antecedents in offspring born to methadone-maintained women. *Journal of Clinical Child Psychology, 28*(1), 58–69.

Hans, S. L., Bernstein, V. J., & Henson, L. G. (1999). The role of psychopathology in the parenting of drug-dependent women. *Development and Psychopathology, 11,* 957–977.

Hertsgaard, L., Gunnar, M. R., Farrell, M., Erickson, M. F., & Nachmias, M. (1995). Adrenocortical responses to the Strange Situation in infants with disorganized/disoriented attachment relationships, *Child Development, 66,* 1100–1106.

Izard, C. E., Fine, S., Mostow, A., Trentacosta, C., & Campbell, J. (2002). Emotion processes in normal and abnormal development and preventive intervention. *Development and Psychopathology, 14,* 761–787.

Jacobsen, L. K., Southwick, S. M., & Kosten, T. K. (2001). Substance use disorders in patients with post-traumatic stress disorder: A review of the literature. *American Journal of Psychiatry, 158,* 1184–1190.

Johnson, A. L., Morrow, C. E., Accornero, V. H., Xue, L., Anthony, J. C., & Bandstra, E. S. (2002). Maternal cocaine use: Estimated effects on mother–child play interactions in the preschool period. *Developmental and Behavioral Pediatrics, 23,* 191–203.

Kelleher, K., Chaffin, M., Hollenberg, J., & Fischer, E. (1994). Alcohol and drug disorders among physically abusive and neglectful parents in a community-based sample. *American Journal of Public Health, 84,* 1586–1590.

Koob, G. F. (1996). Hedonic valence, dopamine and motivation. *Molecular Psychiatry, 1,* 186–189.

Koob, G. F., & LeMoal, M. (1997). Drug abuse: Hedonic homeostatic dysregulation. *Science, 278,* 52–58.

Lieberman, A. F., Padron, E., Van Horn, P., & Harris, W. W. (2005). Angels in the nursery: The intergenerational transmission of benevolent parental influences. *Infant Mental Health Journal, 26,* 504–520.

Lindhiem, O., & Dozier, M. (2007). Caregiver commitment to children: The role of child behavior. *Child Abuse and Neglect, 31,* 361–374.

Lyons-Ruth, K., & Block, D. (1996). The disturbed caregiving system: Relations among childhood trauma, maternal caregiving, and infant affect and attachment. *Infant Mental Health Journal, 17,* 257–275.

Main, M., & Hesse, E. (1990). Parents' unresolved traumatic experiences are related to infant disorganized attachment status: Is frightened and/or frightening parental behavior the linking mechanism? In M. T. Greenberg, D. Cicchetti, & E. M. Cummings (Eds.), *Attachment in the Preschool Years: Theory, Research and Intervention* (pp. 161–182). Chicago: University of Chicago Press.

Main, M., & Solomon, J. (1990). Procedures for identifying infants as disorganized/disoriented during the Ainsworth Strange Situation. In M. T. Greenberg, D. Cicchetti, & E. M. Cummings (Eds.), *Attachment in the Preschool Years: Theory, Research, and Intervention* (pp. 121–160). Chicago: University of Chicago Press.

Mayes, L. C., Feldman, R., Granger, R. H., Haynes, O. M., Bornstein, M. C. & Schottenfeld, R. (1997). The effects of poly-drug use with and without cocaine on mother–infant interaction at 3 and 6 months. *Infant Behavior & Development, 20,* 489–502.

Mayes, L., & Truman, S. (2002). Substance abuse and parenting. In M. Bronstein (Ed.), *Handbook of Parenting: Vol. 4: Social Conditions and Applied Parenting* (2nd ed., pp. 329–359). Mahwah, NJ: Lawrence Erlbaum.

Molitor, A., & Mayes, L. C. (2010). Problematic dyadic interaction among toddlers and their polydrug-cocaine-using mothers. *Infant Mental Health Journal, 31,* 121–140.

Molitor, A., Mayes, L. C., & Ward A. (2003). Emotion regulation behavior during a separation procedure in 18-month-old children of parents using cocaine and other drugs. *Development and Psychopathology, 15,* 39–54.

Murphy, S., & Rosenbaum, M. (1999). *Pregnant Women on Drugs: Combating Stereotypes and Stigma.* New Brunswick, NJ: Rutgers University Press.

O'Connor, M. J., Sigman, M., & Brill, N. (1987). Disorganization of attachment in relation to maternal alcohol consumption. *Journal of Consulting and Clinical Psychology, 55,* 831–836.

Ramey, C. T., McGinness, G. D., Cross, L., Collier, A. M., & Barrie-Blackley, S. (1982). The Abecedarian approach to social competence: Cognitive and linguistic intervention for disadvantaged preschoolers. In K. Borman (Ed.), *The Social Life of Children in a Changing Society* (pp. 14–174). Hillsdale, NJ: Erlbaum.

Ramey, C. T., Yeates, K. O., & Short, E. J. (1984). The plasticity of intellectual development: Insights from preventative intervention. *Child Development, 55,* 1913–1925.

Rodning, C., Beckwith, L., & Howard, J. (1991). Quality of attachment and home environments in children prenatally exposed to PCP and cocaine. *Development and Psychopathology, 3*(4), 351–366.

Schuetze, P., Zeskind, P. S., & Eiden, D. R. (2003). The perceptions of infant distress signals varying in pitch by cocaine-using mothers. *Infancy, 4,* 65–83.

Stovall, K. C., & Dozier M. (2000). The development of attachment in new relationships: Single subject analyses for ten foster infants. *Development and Psychopathology, 12,* 133–156.

Stovall-McClough, K. C., & Dozier, M. (2004). Forming attachments in foster care: Infant attachment behaviors in the first two months of placement. *Development and Psychopathology, 16,* 253–271.

Suchman, N., DeCoste, C. Castiglioni, N., Legow, N. & Mayes, L. (2008). The mothers and toddlers program: Preliminary findings from an attachment-based parenting intervention for substance-abusing mothers. *Psychoanalytic Psychology*, *25*(3), 499–517.

Suchman, N., Pajulo, M., DeCoste, C., & Mayes, L. (2006). Parenting interventions for drug-dependent mothers and their young children: The case for an attachment-based approach. *Family Relations*, *55*, 211–226.

Swanson, K., Beckwith, L., & Howard, J. (2000). Intrusive caregiving and quality of attachment in prenatally drug-exposed toddlers and their primary caregivers. *Attachment & Human Development*, *2*(2), 130–148.

van IJzendoorn, M. (1995). Adult attachment representations, parental responsiveness, and infant attachment: A meta-analysis on the predictive validity of the Adult Attachment Interview. *Psychological Bulletin*, *117*, 387–403.

van IJzendoorn, M. H., Schuengel, C., & Bakermans-Kranenburg, M. J. (1999). Disorganized attachment in early childhood: Meta-analysis of precursors, concomitants, and sequelae. *Development and Psychopathology*, *11*, 225–249.

16

Psychoanalytic-Attachment-Oriented Group Intervention for Substance-Abusing Mothers and Their Infants

Transference, Secure Base, and Secondary Attachment to the "Group Mother"

RAIJA-LEENA PUNAMÄKI AND RITVA BELT

■ PSYCHOANALYTICAL AND ATTACHMENT PERSPECTIVES: A THEORETICAL FRAMEWORK FOR THERAPY WITH MOTHER–CHILD DYADS

Psychoanalytic and attachment theory emphasizes the actual experiences of mother–infant interaction as the very scene in which earlier vulnerabilities can be transferred to the offspring. Substance abusing mothers often have violent and neglectful pasts and suffer from current emotional problems that together cause heightened risks in their motherhood for themselves and their infants. Interventions involving therapeutic elements that sensitively enrich women's experiences and motivate them for change have the potential to lessen the possibility of, or prevent, mothers from transmitting the traumatic past into interactions with their infants. In this chapter, we first review the central principles of psychoanalytic and attachment theories that guide the development of a mother–infant group intervention with substance abusing mother–infant pairs. This method was created as an integral part of network services for substance-using women in Finland. We then describe the practical issues and therapeutic elements of the group intervention, and discuss specific substance abuse related issues such as regulating difficult emotions and preventing the transfer of traumatic experiences and relapsing into drugs. The group therapeutic- and substance abuse–related topics are illustrated by clinical vignettes from the groups. Finally, we give preliminary results on the efficacy of the mother–infant group intervention to improve dyadic interaction and maternal relational representations and mental health.

Psychoanalytic and Attachment Principles in Group Work with Substance-Using Mothers' Transference

The healing power in psychoanalytic and attachment-oriented interventions lies in the individual's experience of becoming deeply understood and represented in

321

the therapist's mind (Fonagy, Gergely, Jurist, & Target, 2002). In mother–infant group therapy, besides the therapist serving as an object upon whom significant feelings, fantasies, and wishes are transferred, transference also happens between group members and in the dyadic interaction. The therapist listens to "the mother's own cries" and lets her project her unresolved conflicts from experiences with her own early caregivers onto the therapeutic relationship in order to protect the child from the mother's own unmet attachment needs and burdens. This, in turn, allows and encourages the mother to "hear her child's cries," thus protecting her child from the repetition of her own troubled past (Fraiberg, Adelson, & Shapiro, 1987).

According to psychoanalytic group theories, transference can arise, not only between group members and the therapist, but also for the whole group (Bion, 1961; Foulkes & Anthony, 1990). The therapist treats the group as an entity and presents "group as a whole" interpretations. In this way the therapist collects actual group themes. Furthermore, "group as a whole" interpretations are less threatening because every member can take only the part of the interpretation which he/she is ready to accept and can share both positive and negative features.

Activation of Internal Working Models and Integration of Early Experiences

According to psychoanalytic theory, the intimate bodily dialogue between the mother and the infant evokes powerful affects and unconscious and archaic sensations (Fraiberg et al., 1987). If the mother is preoccupied with her own emotional problems, she may easily transfer her distortions and dysfunctional defenses to her interactions with the infant. The aim in the mother–infant group therapy is to link the mother's early experiences of care and nurture to the current interaction between the mother and the infant. The mother's internal working models, created in her early attachment experiences and caregiving relationships, contain perceptions about whether she is a valuable person and worthy of care, other people are benevolent and trustworthy, and the world is predictable and meaningful (Bowlby, 1988).

The attachment system is activated—especially in the face of danger and distress—to help one maintain proximity to nurturing and protective figures. In adulthood, attachment behavior and internal working models are largely dormant, but become activated in traumatic stress and in significant life-transition periods such as becoming a parent (van IJzendoorn & Bakermans-Kranenburg, 1997). Activated working models underlie a mother's perceptions and interpretations of her infant's needs, emotional cues, and signals of distress in mutual interaction (Fonagy et al., 2002; Stern, 1995). These moments of meeting between the mother's representational world and her infant's responses provide valuable material in the mother–infant group therapy. Insightful interpretations, group-created safety, and experiences of being a unique and "good enough" mother help substance-using women to become aware of their significance to the child. They are able to reflect their own early experiences and connect their own past and present mental states to read the mental states of their infant. This new awareness provides them with an opportunity to change the archaic tendencies to deny, split, and project their painful past experiences to others (Klein, 1984), which are common among women with a substance abuse history.

A Secure Base for the Mother and Her Baby

According to attachment theory, the quality of the affectionate bonding between infants and their mothers impacts later human development, personality, and psychopathology (Bowlby, 1975; 1988). Infants use the attachment relationship as a secure base from which they feel both safe and bold enough to explore their environment. Analogously, the therapeutic group can serve as a secure base that provides mothers with a sense of safety and the opportunity to gain new perspectives and the possibility to experience new kinds of human interactions. The safe, therapeutic atmosphere makes it possible for substance-using women to create a "second attachment" relationship with the therapists and the group. The new intersubjectivity, involving shared experience of the new attachment relationship, facilitates their capacity to face abusive and traumatic pasts and transform them into more coherent life histories.

It is of importance that in short-term mother–infant therapies, the focus is on "here and now" dyadic and group interactions, and the therapist regulates and keeps the discussions predominantly in the present. However, the mothers have to feel that they are also allowed to speak about the difficult memories that are activated by the pregnancy and motherhood. The access to and reflection of own past memories within supportive current relationships in the group offer the mothers a secure base for the exploration of both positive and negative feelings (Lieberman & Pawl, 1993; Smith, Cumming, & Xeros-Constantinides, 2010). The comprehensive feeling of being protected herself enables the mother to support her infant to explore the environment and to seek emotional proximity and soothing (Ainsworth, Blehar, Waters, & Wall, 1978; Crittenden, 1997). It creates, in turn, a space for the infant to explore the mother's mental states, which is a precondition to mother–infant intersubjectivity, and this shared experience further encourages them both to "mind-read" each others' feelings, affects and needs (Fonagy et al., 2002). The positive changes in maternal sense of safety can thus, through these newly established dyadic processes, diminish the risk of infants' insecure or disorganized attachment patterns (Bakermans-Kranenburg, van IJzendoorn, & Juffer, 2005), which is common among children of substance-abused women.

The Group "Lap" and Secondary Attachment

The therapeutic processes occur at three levels in the mother–infant group interventions: between the group and the therapist, within the group members, and between mothers and their infants. Integration of emotions and changes in behavior are expected to occur first on the group level, and gradually thereafter on a personal level. The concept of "projective identification" by Klein (1935) is a useful therapeutic tool for observing and interpreting mothers' tendencies to project painful and unacceptable affects within the group. Their activated need for attachment combined with disappointing and terrifying memories is a shared group phenomenon. As described by Bion (1967), the therapist functions as a "container" by ingraining reciprocal responses and affects, thus helping the mother and the group to regulate the projected affects and internalize the regulating function of the therapist.

Stern and colleagues (1998) have suggested that the therapeutic healing power lies in both the implicit nonverbal and explicit verbal communication between the patient and the therapist. In a mother–infant group therapy, this also concerns the communication between the group and therapist and the mothers and their infants. An authentic person-to-person connection is the precondition for the substance abusing mothers' mental integration and thrust in the group and oneself. A therapeutic group forms a medium in which something good, unique, and new is bred, produced, and developed at the group level (James, 2004). Group members may experience the group as "mother's arms safely embracing the participants," making it possible to form "a second attachment to the group mother," and subsequently the members may find lovable aspects within themselves. Similar to a securely attached child, the group members can feel themselves safe and protected, and gradually dare to explore their own thoughts and experiences (Foguel, 1994). This shared sense of safety is finally experienced in interactions between the mother and infant. Group cohesion reflects the extent to which group members and dyads feel safe and protected by the group (Mikulincer & Shaver, 2007), and this holding potential is often symbolized as "group lap" in therapist's interpretations.

Pregnancy as a Critical Period for Change

Pregnancy is a period of preparation for motherhood and includes significant physiological, mental, and social reorganization (Stern, 1995). The prenatal activation of attachment-related working models argues for starting the mother–infant therapeutic interventions already in pregnancy and to continue them, preferably as long as individually needed. This would allow the mother to work on her own early attachment relationships and simultaneously apply these new reflections in forming a relationship with her baby.

In pregnancy, a woman's mind is usually more open to change, and women often have the courage to form a relationship with the baby from early on (Stern, 1995). Winnicott's concepts of transitional space, mirroring and primary maternal preoccupation (1953, 1956) are insightful when helping substance abusing women prepare for motherhood. Pregnancy is a special phase potentiating a close intuitive identification with the future child, and mental preparation is vital for mothers to fulfill the future baby's physical and emotional needs. Maternal drug-abuse increases the fetus' neurobiological vulnerability and may interfere with the infant's adaptation and appropriate regulation of physical and emotional distress (Mayes & Pajulo, 2006). Starting the therapeutic work during pregnancy can therefore function as preventive intervention for the child's well-being and development.

■ THE PSYCHOANALYTIC-ATTACHMENT—ORIENTED GROUP INTERVENTION

In this section, we describe practical aspects, therapeutic elements, and dyadic and group processes of a psychoanalytic-attachment–oriented group intervention model designed for substance-abusing mother–infant pairs. The intervention was developed to provide both mothers and infants with a new way of being together and experiencing mutual interaction. Women's emerging experiences of healing and recovery are described and understood from psychodynamic and attachment theory perspectives. Clinical illustrations are provided to demonstrate how this intervention is conducted and to consider how it could influence the therapeutic change. The clinical vignettes are derived from the therapist's (R. Belt) case notes and session reports, written immediately afterwards. Permission for publication was inquired from each case, and the names of mothers and infants have been changed.

Background

The psychoanalytical-attachment oriented mother–infant group intervention (PGI) was developed originally in a foundation-based, third-sector outpatient care unit in Lahti, a city in Southern Finland with 100,000 residents, where the most jobs are based on service industries, information technology, and education. The intervention was one part of a larger project of the central hospital in Lahti that involved developing a regional treatment model for pregnant substance-abusing women and implementing a systematic treatment referral policy. The development process was supervised by an experienced trainer in group psychoanalysis (Belt & Punamäki, 2007). The group intervention model has since been adopted by the public child welfare sector of social work and is used in the treatment approach and practices in outpatient treatment units in the cities of Tampere and Oulu. The intervention is carried out by several co-therapists who have experience with both groups and substance abusers as clients. The use of this particular method requires specialized therapists who receive systematic training and personal supervision.

Forming and Joining the Group

The group size is kept small, consisting of three or four mother–infant dyads. The small group size has been considered important when the therapists have to work on multiple levels at the same time with high-risk groups such as substance abusers (Field et al., 1998; Moore & Finkelstein, 2001). The work involves practical arrangements, networking, and therapeutic tasks.

The group therapy process starts in late pregnancy, or, in some cases, during the first weeks postnatally, and consists of 20 to 24 weekly three-hour group sessions. Thus, the children are between four and seven months old when the group ends. All mothers participating in the PGI have a history of illegal drug-abuse or polysubstance use and a treatment contact in the addiction clinic of adult psychiatry. The staff refers pregnant women or women with newborn babies to the group therapists for an assessment on a voluntary basis. Mothers who can make a commitment to the intervention plan and have enough motivation to work on both substance abuse problems and parenting are offered participation in the group intervention. The initial assessment consists of three to four meetings, including one home visit, a possible meeting with the child's father, and completion of the Adult Attachment Interview (AAI; George, Kaplan, & Main, 1996) with the mother.

The pre-therapy AAI helps the therapists better understand the working models of mothers' own attachment relations, and to catch up on possible unresolved attachment themes (Baradon & Steele, 2008; Fonagy et al., 2002). Later, during the therapy process, the themes are often activated, and the AAI helps the therapists better recognize and understand each mother's individual reactions and regulate the group discussions. As Baradon and Steele (2008, p. 210) have suggested, using the AAI in parent–infant psychotherapy "can provide an important holding framework in which revisiting in the past and present 'ghosts' can begin."

The first session of the group is structured to give information and make therapeutic plans. Confidentiality concerning discussions and contracting for commitment, drug-screening, etc., are emphasized. Otherwise, the content and structure of the sessions are free and unstructured, being precise only with starting and ending times, and coffee and lunch breaks. The length of each weekly session is three hours.

Group Therapists

Two therapists work with each group. One of the two is a trained group therapist who also has training and experience in working with small children's families and early interaction, as well as with substance abusers. This therapist focuses especially on mothers' reflections about their feelings, behavior, and thinking, and on making connections between maternal mental states and the infant's feelings and behavior. This therapist also uses "group as a whole" interpretations, and engages in "container functions" whenever overwhelmingly painful emotions occur. As in Harwood's psychoeducational groups (2006), the co-therapist in the PGI groups is an experienced addiction clinician and pays the most attention to practical issues and basic needs of both the mother and the baby. She also takes responsibility in communicating with the network of other professionals.

In contrast with more traditional group therapies and in line with parent-infant therapies, the therapists are encouraged to be more spontaneous, vivacious, and engaging, and they actively participate in the group interactions and discussions (Belt & Punamäki, 2007; Flores, 2001). The mother–infant groups of substance abusers are demanding for the therapists, because they encounter women's anger and powerful counter-feelings as resistance is arising from the painful past and often shameful experiences with substances (Lieberman & Zeanah, 1999). The therapist has to be aware of his/her own childhood dynamics and attachment patterns. Therefore the therapist's own psychotherapy and supervision are essential supports to sustain this demanding work.

Centralizing Treatment

Substance abusing women need comprehensive help that is concentrated in one place in order to counterbalance their previous experiences in numerous fragmented services with multiple professionals. Most of the group members have not had stable attachment relations during their childhood and adolescence, which makes them especially vulnerable to the fragmentation of treatment services usually offered to them. Therapeutic work and small, actively engaged social networks make it possible for the mothers to repair previous incoherent attachment experiences (Luthar, Suchman, & Altomare, 2007).

In the early development of this intervention model, the therapists took almost all the responsibility for the well-being of the mother–child dyad. For example, the therapists helped the mothers complete applications and seek social, economic, and health services. They also were available by phone on weekdays. As the model development progressed, a supportive network of other professionals was decisively built around the therapists and mothers, and on-call 24-hour services were established at the outpatient unit. The professional network typically included a social worker from the child protection agency, staff members from the addiction clinic, a public health care nurse, and, if necessary, a local family worker from the social sector. Mothers participated in completing and signing a contract regarding their involvement in the mother–infant group intervention (e.g., commitment, absence, drug screening and consequences of a positive test result, and confidentiality).

The Therapeutic Environment

The group therapy room is designed to be a cozy and child-friendly "holding" environment. It has a large table in the middle that is surrounded by chairs and baby seats, toys, a cradle, rocking chair, mirrors, and mattresses with pillows. There are also videos, a CD player, and books of children's development and fairytales in the room. Recalling of familiar lullabies and cradle songs is an important component of the therapy that invites the mothers' own childhood memories. The mothers are supported in finding pleasure and joy in normal, everyday things like personally served healthy and good-tasting food. The holding environment and nurturing both mental and physical needs have a high symbolic relevance to the therapeutic group work.

The therapists show genuine interest in each mother's specific favorite things, remember babies' and mothers' red-letter days, and always asking them to describe how the food tastes, feels, and smells for them. The therapists provide a peaceful and caring setting for mother–infant dyads so that they can enjoy their mutual interaction. The mother–baby pairs are also often covered or wrapped in a warm blanket. As a sign of relaxation during the sessions, the infants often gradually fall asleep; sometimes the mothers fall asleep as well. The idea is that the mothers are helped first to become in touch with their own needs and expectations for soothing and care, which then makes it possible for them to better understand their children's needs. The therapists also encourage the mothers' fantasies and playfulness.

The Group as Attachment Object

Becoming pregnant and taking care of a small infant does not fit with the drug-abusing culture. In that context, mothers often feel themselves very lonely and abandoned in their preparation for motherhood. They struggle between choosing a new, baby-centered and care-giving lifestyle or continuing the earlier, drug-centered, chaotic life-style (Belt & Punamäki, 2007). A universal phenomenon is that pregnant women seek other mothers' company. The group support is thus especially salient for substance abusing mothers who often have had to leave their previous friends and partners when aiming at abstinence. The group gives them opportunity to feel togetherness, practice new modes of interaction, and share analogous life histories (Flores, 2001; Smith et al., 2010). Women are often relieved to be able to talk about shameful issues, and share feelings of guilt and fear about the possible damage they may have caused to their fetus or infant.

In the beginning of each group session, the mothers often seem preoccupied and troubled with heavy everyday and relational problems, and their minds have to be "emptied and fed"; for example, by having them bring their upsets and news to the group and soothing and consoling them. Then they can better concentrate on feeding their babies, and after that enjoy their own meal. Midway through each session, the atmosphere often becomes calmer, and mothers are better able to concentrate on thinking and discussing themes related to motherhood and babies. In this sense, the attachment to the group provides the security and soothing necessary for the mothers to explore.

It seems of utmost importance for substance abusing women to feel like "ordinary" pregnant and caring women, wishing to help each other with concrete, daily issues. Mothers may spontaneously present each other with clothes that their own baby has outgrown. They also often like to give and receive mutual advice based on their own experiences. The delivery is one of the most central topics in these discussions, with the more "experienced mother" with more children often giving advice and encouraging the "little sister" to physically and psychologically prepare herself for the birth of the child. In all of these ways, the mothers use the group as a second attachment object that provides safe haven for exploring emotions, concerns, and expectations about motherhood and the baby.

Clinical Vignette: Longing not to repeat their parents' patterns

This example illustrates a common topic discussed in the groups: the mothers' constant struggle to avoid repeating their own parents' negative parenting models.

In the group one mother said: "One thought especially terrifies me. I wonder how many generations of alcohol and drug-addicted relatives this child may have from both sides of her parents. Might it be in the genes?" Other group members responded to this: "No, you can change that. But if you allow yourself to continue to use alcohol, you are doing the same to your baby that your mother did to you. Alcohol and drugs get along badly together with a baby!" Then the group discussed how to raise their children to become normal individuals protected against drugs. The women expressed deep worries about the future success of motherhood.

As the group process advances, the mothers become more and more able to tolerate and appreciate observations and comments from the other mothers. They can reflect on each others' parenting behavior and childcare practices and discuss difficult experiences. Topics evoking strong group feelings include a child's illness or developmental problems, threats of placing the child into custody, and partner violence. Groups also have shared joys such as a new baby participating with a mother for the first time in group. Through these sharing processes, mothers form trusting relationships with each other and grow to appreciate the richness of human relationships, in contrast to their previous relationships in the drug culture (Belt & Punamäki, 2007). They may also achieve a more coherent sense of self and identity through reciprocal relations and reflective interpretations. Such experiences are considered essential in launching a renewed attachment process (Fonagy & Bateman, 2006; Harword, 2006).

Clinical Vignette: Finding attachment security

The following is an example of the mothers' recognition of their and their babies' longing for good care. It illustrates that the comprehensive experience of secure place involves both symbolic and practical issues.

During the twelfth session, the mother–infant pairs laid on the mattresses relaxed, and one of the mothers said: "I don't know if I will ever be allowed again to experience anything similar to this group, where even we, the mothers, adults, have been taken care of like little children." Another mother agreed: "It would be wonderful if we could be the sleeping babies and you therapists would be the mothers pushing us in the prams there in the world outside the therapy room." The therapist replied: "Yes, in fact here, momentarily in this room, you are supposed to experience being beloved and taken care of like little babies so that you can then be better able to understand your babies' experience and expectations."

A Secure Base for Multiple Emotions

Analogous to infants who need their mothers to regulate their emotions when distressed, women in the group often need help with their dysregulated emotional states. Substance abusers show both hyper- and hypo-aroused states of mind (Schore, 2003), and the mothers' moods can oscillate strongly within and between sessions. The therapist's task is to act as a container and regulator of these intolerable emotions by helping the mothers to contain simultaneously the "hurt baby-within-her" and her current own baby in her mind (Bion, 1967; Smith et al., 2010). Concerning children, the maternal internalization of mutually regulating interactions is central to their self-regulation and development (Fonagy et al., 2002).

Clinical Vignette: Regulating strong emotions

The following vignette illustrates how normal mood swings in pregnancy may transfer to emotional instability among women who struggle with stopping of the drug abuse. The woman's attempts at emotion regulation are compromised by her living with a drug-abusing partner, and subsequently the therapeutic intervention involves also practical arrangement to guarantee the safety of both the mother and her future infant.

In the third group session, Joan was in her late pregnancy. She described her feelings: "I am so uncertain and deeply scared about how I will cope with the baby after the delivery. My feelings already go so much up and down, poor baby in the womb! I am really ashamed of myself when I cannot control my rage when I'm having a fight with the child's father.... I am afraid I also can relapse back to the drugs. How can I protect the baby?" The mothers and the therapists in the group calmed her down and discussed the life and feelings of her womb-baby. Joan's struggle with strong emotions evoked other mothers' experiences with substance-abusing and violent partners, and Rhea, another group member, gave a bit of advice to Joan: "You have to make your choice between the man and the baby. Otherwise you will lose your child, as it happened with my first child." Members of the group agreed that Joan temporarily needed additional treatment in residential care to protect herself and her baby. Joan felt anxious and insecure, as though she might be abandoned by the group. At the end of the session, she accepted the suggestion and the co-therapist helped her to contact her social worker. Next time she and her child came to the group session from residential interval treatment and told that she was grateful to the group for helping her to make the decision.

Tolerating Emotional Memories

Although the focus in the therapy is on the "here and now," actual problems and pregnancy- and infant-evoked emotions, the substance abusing mothers often show an urgent need to also reflect on their past difficult experiences that have been hidden behind the substances. Mothers simply carry their terrifying earlier experiences and disappointments into the therapy. Therefore, the therapists work to create a safe atmosphere and secure base that allow for the expression of emotions, and for making link between past and present, and integrate the intrusive memories. The choice of interpretation themes and other therapeutic elements accords with the rule that discussions in short-term mother–infant therapies focus mostly on current and actual issues and avoid most painful unconscious conflicts (Broden, 2004; Polansky et al., 2006). Thus, the therapists allow the mothers to tell about whatever bad feelings and memories come into their minds, while controlling and regulating the emotional intensity at a level that is tolerable for the group. Besides, the therapists remind them of the importance of individually tailored follow-up after the group therapy to work on their traumatic experiences as long as necessary.

Transference of the Good Grandmother

Generally the therapists utilize "the transference of good grandmother" and emphasize the mothers' resources and positive assets rather than psychopathologies and conflicts (Stern, 1995). The internalized "good grandmother" provides unconditional acceptance and caring, and can reveal and free the genuine individual needs and decrease projections that have impoverished the mother's mental life (Klein, 1984). However, the therapists also encourage mothers to admit and express their feelings of pain, sorrow, and anger. The mothers can feel safe in the group as the therapists contain their negative and intense feelings and projections. At the same time, the therapists offer the mothers new experiences of benevolence and opportunities for rich and multiple emotional expressions (Bion, 1967; Klein, 1935). These good, reflective, and compensatory experiences can neutralize mothers' anger and enable them to construct more positive or realistic representations of their life histories. Moreover, the therapists aim consciously at serving as a model of a good-enough mothering (Winnicott, 1953) by treating the mothers and babies sensitively and responsively. Mirroring multiple emotions and identification with good sides of human behavior are assumed to result in mothers' new ways of interacting both in the group and with their infants.

Clinical Vignette: Support in tolerating emotional memories

The following example demonstrates how memories of one's own mother activate strong emotions and how group members can attempt to help each other come to terms with a frightening childhood experience. The therapist gives a voice to other, different emotions than those acutely expressed by the women.

In one group, all three mothers had suffered from physically violent behavior of their own mothers. Mothers recalled memories of their childhood families during the third session. They expressed their sorrow in not having had any experience or model of how to be a good woman and mother. Sally told the group: "I used to carry a knife with me since I was four years old because I was so frightened of my mom, particularly at night. You never knew what she might do. She was so unpredictable." Joan said: "My mother used alcohol heavily but she was nice to us." The therapist responded: "Sally, you tell us about the painful experiences you had, whereas Joan, you bring out one way that you used in order to adapt to your mother's behavior. Maybe you are unsure whether we are able to bear your painful experiences and all the badness that has been inflicted on you. Perhaps you think that you have to behave well and tell us only nice stories, or otherwise we shall punish or abandon you?" During the later group sessions, it emerged that these mothers really had learned not to show their own feelings because their mothers could not bear them.

Over time, the mothers give increasing attention to their own feelings and mood and to pondering how they impact their child. They become more aware of the possibility that their drug abuse may have been an attempt to cope with intolerable emotions, and recognize that drugs may have provided for their desire for comfort and consolation.

Soothing and Supporting Mother's Closeness with the Baby

Across the group intervention, the therapists sensitively observe the mothers' body language, signals, and emotional cues, and help them to recognize and express their individual needs and preferences. When possible, sensitive touching is used as a soothing element in the therapeutic process. However, the therapists are very careful about physically approaching the mothers in order not to trigger their traumatic memories. The sensitive interaction between the therapists and the mothers serves also as a model of sensitive and responsive relating to the baby. The modeling and mirroring aim specifically at recognizing the harmful impact of intrusive or unpredictable behavior towards the infant.

Clinical Vignette: Supporting the dyad by soothing the mother

The next vignette demonstrates how the intimate contact of breastfeeding activated women's traumatic memories. Through sensitive listening and reading of the painful signals of shame, the mother, therapist, and group helped reveal a link between the substance abuse and traumatic early experiences.

In the thirteenth session, Lisa mentioned that she felt very relieved about having stopped breastfeeding her baby. She declared that she could not stand the close physical contact with the baby. During the same session, as the infants slept and the mothers lay on mattresses, the therapist cautiously touched Lisa's foot and checked her reaction to it. Lisa replied: "It feels bad, to be touched … when you are sober." Then her eyes filled with tears and she started telling the group about how she had been raped as a young girl. "After that I began the heavy use of amphetamine and continued until the third trimester of my pregnancy." Other mothers joined in the discussion, and some of them shared their experiences of rape and abortion. The therapist verbalized: "Through Lisa, you mothers show how important it is that we therapists read accurately your reactions and not impinge on your bodies. It is the same with your babies." In the next sessions, Lisa was able to consider her feelings about being physically touched, and their connection to her experienced difficulties in physical contact with the baby and feeding her. Mothers brought out in the conversation their conflicting feelings of being a "dirty sexual object" and a mother of an innocent child.

"Group-as-a-Whole" Interpretations

At the end of each group meeting, while serving the group a cup of coffee, the therapists usually presents a "group as a whole" interpretation through collecting issues and themes that have arisen during that particular session. The interpretations aim to express and summarize the emotions and states of minds of both the babies and the mothers. The therapist tries to put into words the desires, despair, and fears that have arisen within the group, in order to help the mothers further explore and recognize those feelings in themselves (Belt & Punamäki, 2007; Foulkes & Anthony, 1990).

Clinical Vignette: Group-as-a-whole interpretation

The next example illustrates the use of a "group as a whole" interpretation at the end of the first group session. It aims at underlining the shared experience and recognizing both pain and difficulties and the potential for a "happy ending."

One of the four mothers participated in the first group session via phone from the maternity clinic with her newborn. Other mothers who were present in the group were in late pregnancy. Mothers in the group were enthusiastic about the first baby born to a group member and discussed the difficulties with their womb-babies and worried how they would be able to cope with their newborns. The therapist stated: "This first group session is also like a newborn child that came into existence well and healthy, although its waiting-time and delivery were long and, in some ways, burdensome. I think we therapists have a wonderful baby who is easy but also challenging with all its different experiences and characteristics that you mothers and your future babies present as individuals."

Including the Infants as Active Participants

When the mothers learn to recognize and respect their own emotions, experiences, and needs, they are more able to see their children's needs, cues, and unique signals and ways of communication. Nevertheless, when treating such needing mothers, there is the risk that the infants will be forgotten. "Where is the infant in infant intervention?" was the title of a review by Lojkasek, Cohen, and Muir (1994) on mother–child early dyadic interventions. It indicated the fact that changes in maternal sensitivity and representations are usually the main therapeutic target, while the infants' role is not explicitly considered.

One important aim in this mother–infant group intervention is to include the infants as full participants in the sessions. As a symbol, the babies have their own seats on the table so that they are always visible. Infants' behavior, unique temperament, and response patterns bring richness to the sessions and fresh material for therapists' interpretations. During the group therapy process, the developing infants (usually from late pregnancy to seven months) begin to receive more and more attention from their own mothers, other mothers, and the therapists, which increases their own active communication. The group shares admiration of the infants' developmental achievements and acknowledges success in mothering the babies. The mothers often comment that their babies are always in a good mood in the group. In fact, they are surprisingly alert and awake, follow intensely what is going on and reacting to the mothers' and therapists' actions. However, the therapists are also aware that some of the children are too vigilant or too stiff because of the prenatal exposure to drugs and/or lack of maternal holding. If necessary, the therapists have to show the child to specific assessment.

Clinical Vignette: Secure base for babies

The babies seem to create their own little group and each has its specific way of being together within the whole group. The next vignette describes the work the therapists do with the babies.

We were playing and singing in a group in which the babies were between two and five months of age. Each baby was enthusiastic to take part in the play. One mother, Kate, who felt that she was not able to play with her son at home, blurted out: "Thomas has waited for this group all week long to have the chance to play again with the other babies." That seemed to be true; four-month-old Thomas had always seemed to cheer up when he saw the other babies. He was often awake during the entire therapy session, had eye contact, and enjoyed the group activities, especially the cheerful play songs. Once, when Kate was extremely anxious and avoidant toward Thomas, the therapist lifted the baby boy in front of his mother. She explained to both of them how important it is that his mother can share her psychic pain with other women, and how grateful Thomas is for his mother bringing him to other children to have fun. Later on, Thomas appeared to have learned to turn on his stomach by following another baby's example. Kate seemed to be a bit jealous that Thomas and other group members enjoyed the playing. After the group intervention ended, however, she also described her relief that the group provided her baby feelings of happiness and pleasure about learning new things when she herself was feeling depressed and unable to do so.

Preventing the Transfer of the Traumatic Past

There is ample evidence for the accumulation of stressors, losses, and traumatic events in the lives of substance abusing women (Nair, Schuler, Black, Kettinger, & Harrington, 2003), combined with dysfunctional coping and insufficient social support (Belt, Punamäki, Pajulo, Posa, & Tamminen, 2009; Burns, Feaster, Mitrani, Ow, & Szapocznik, 2008). From our clinical experience, these external strains can seriously affect women's preparation for motherhood. Mothers need practical help in coping successfully with the chaos in their everyday lives in order to be able to concentrate on their "inner chaos" in therapy.

Many substance abusing women have been victims of physical, sexual, or emotional abuse during their childhood and adolescence (Freeman, Collier, & Parillo, 2002; Medrano, Hatch, Zule, & Desmond, 2002). A traumatic past has been suggested as one reason for reliance on illicit drugs that serve as a defense against painful and shameful memories (Medrano et al., 2002). Within our mother–infant groups, and similar to the observations by Suchman, DeCoste, Castiglioni, Legow, and Mayes (2008), we observed that the substance-dependent mothers often tend to deny or misinterpret the emotional pain arising from childhood memories. The therapeutic task thus is to help women sufficiently recognize the source of their distress or impulsiveness, and to help them integrate the representations of their own mother and childhood with the representations of themselves as a mother.

Maternal unresolved trauma or experiences of violence and neglect are often unconsciously embedded in a mother's intrusive memories and uncontrollable behavior (Hesse & Main, 2000; Scheeringa & Zeanah, 2001). Substance abusing mothers show both over-stimulating interaction patterns with their children, involving intrusive, hostile, and rejecting behavior, and under-stimulation in the form of withdrawal and numbed emotions (Swanson, Beckwith, & Howard, 2000; Tronick et al., 2005). These behaviors may be explained by activation of mothers' early, unconscious, traumatic memories that are triggered by the intimate interaction with the baby. They can lead to frightened and frightening maternal behavior, which in turn elicits fear, confusion, and disorientation in the child (Hesse & Main, 2000). It is therefore essential for the mothers to have a therapeutic relationship that is able to contain the mother's evoked childhood experiences (Belt et al., 2012a). At the same time, the therapists must also remind the mothers of additional opportunities to get help for the theme of trauma after the group ends.

Clinical Vignette: Trauma and attachment to the baby

The following vignette describes how a mother's painful memories are related to her attachment difficulties with her infant. The therapist helps all the mothers in the group become aware of the connection between her past and current feelings of confusion and despair. The therapist acknowledges their helplessness and encourages them to read the infants' emotional cues and listen to their messages in order to prevent the negative burden from transferring onto the infant.

In the third group session, Laura described her relationship to her womb-baby when pregnant: "If I tried to keep off the drugs, I had terrible fears and guilt that I had harmed it [fetus]. After the delivery, I watched the movements of the newborn all the time, afraid of some developmental deficits. I did not dare to get attached to the baby or even have a proper look at him, before someone else had checked him carefully that there were no malformations."

Around the time of the fifteenth group session, Laura was forced to stop breastfeeding after five months, due to a short hospitalization of the child, Andrew. Laura's fear of losing her mind was activated in the group. She felt strongly that she had failed in being a mother to Andrew, and was afraid of having a mental breakdown and losing her baby to foster care. The therapist asked what kind of fantasy Laura had about the way her mother nurtured her in the early months. Laura described the extreme circumstances they lived in: "I was one month old when my mother was losing her mind and she was sent to a psychiatric hospital. My father was an alcoholic, and my sister tried to take care of me. Once I fell off her lap and was then placed in a children's home. Now, I am afraid of repeating the fate of my mother." The therapist summarized the similarities and suggested the multilevel activation: "Laura is carrying every group mother's terrifying feelings of damaging or losing your baby, and losing your mind. On the other hand, Andrew, you may now carry every group baby's feelings of deprivation and that may activate your mother's small baby feelings, especially helplessness. It might be that Andrew's state of mind corresponds to his mother's mood when she was placed in the children's home. What is different, however, is that now you, Laura, are in touch with your emotions and the group is sharing your experiences and emotions. This helps you and the other group members to better cope and control the situation." Laura cried silently and the group mothers and babies listened keenly.

Then the therapist gently encouraged insight about Andrew's experience: "I wonder if we could understand how Andrew is feeling, thinking, and sensing just right now?" Another mother in the group observed and suggested: "I think the baby feels alone when we mothers are drunk or lost in our thought." After receiving attention from the group, the baby boy cheered up. Then the co-therapist took Andrew in her arms and brought her in front of her mother's face and explained to both of them how important it is that the mother can share her psychic pain and grief with the group and get support to give better conditions to Andrew than her mother was able to do. Then Laura burst into tears: "But my mother had no such group to support her!"

During the last group sessions, Andrew showed a strong attachment to his mother, and once Laura held Andrew gently against her breasts and tears were flowing from her eyes. The baby fell asleep and looked happy in his mother's arms, and the mother no longer grew tired of holding and gazing at her baby. All the women in the group, both the mothers and the therapists, wept.

The psychoanalytic-attachment–oriented mother–infant group intervention aims to enhance substance abusing mothers' capacity to examine how their own traumatic experiences may influence their maternal interaction with the baby. Women become more courageous about exploring their inner world, and simultaneously reflecting how it may feel to be a helpless child and how the infant's needs could become best satisfied (Fraiberg et al., 1987). When the mother's mental state becomes more coherent, the door opens for the child to more safely explore the mother's mind (Fonagy, 2001).

Responding to Relapses

Unfortunately, relapses or occasional use of substances are not uncommon during the intervention when the mothers are in a recovery process. When it occurs, it is important to stay and work on the relapse within the whole group and to support the relapsed member. Relapses or other experienced failures are processed in the group as shared disappointments. Every mother in the group has her own lonely struggle between craving for the drugs and caring for the infant, and feels relieved to share it and to receive understanding, advice, and strict guidance. In a successful intervention, the mother's mind and brain reward system are captured from drugs and restored to the child to whom it originally belongs (Suchman et al., 2008). The pleasure of the current, here-and-now mother–infant relationship is one of the aims of the group intervention. At best, the mother falls deeply in love with her infant. The mothers in the intervention groups have called this feeling as a valuable treasure, "deep-lying diamonds."

Fears of relapsing to drugs and losing the child to foster care are strongly present in the group discussions. In most of the groups, one or two of mothers occasionally use alcohol or drugs, and in a few cases, the child has to be taken into foster care or placed in the father's care, at least temporarily. The therapists encourage the mother to complete the intervention without the baby or to arrange for the baby to be brought to the group. In one case, a mother came to the last session with a puppy. The therapist expressed that the puppy might help the mother to keep her baby in mind.

Clinical Vignette: Attachment transition from drug to baby

The next vignette illustrates a mother's struggle between falling back into drug abuse and falling in love with her baby. The group members strongly identified with the mother and provided insightful advice that depicted the significance of the mother–infant relation as an inoculation against relapse.

In a therapy session, one mother admitted that she had relapsed to drinking, and said: "Afterwards, I just couldn't look at the baby at all. I disgusted myself so much. You know how it is; when you start using alcohol or drugs again, you are then thinking about nobody else but yourself." Other group members noticed that her relapse was the first one that happened in this group. The therapist made a group-as-a-whole interpretation by saying that this mother's relapse was actually on behalf of the whole group, and that all knew that it could have happened to the others as well. Another mother replied: "I have learned to recognize the weak moments preceding a relapse. You have to be very alert with those moments, and before you take any alcohol or drugs, just look very deeply in the baby's eyes, and after that you just cannot take any drugs. It's like the baby is the best Antabuse. Actually, the baby gives you better kicks than the drugs."

Completion and Transition

Substance abusing women have often experienced several losses and neglect in their childhood and adolescence, and thus the way of ending of the group therapy is critical (Belt et al., 2012a). Themes of separation are given a lot of attention and time during the therapy process, providing rich material to work through feelings of sadness, insecurity, rage, and abandonment. The group and the therapists often ponder the analogy between the termination process of the therapy and infants' experiences of weaning and separation. The therapeutic interpretations help guide the mothers to observe their infants' reactions and prepare them and the babies for new stages of life and richer human relationships.

Opportunity for Assessment and Referral

The therapy group can also function as an assessment to detect problems and dynamics in the mother, the infant, and their early interaction. It can show how the mother has been cared for in her early childhood. The more deprived the mother has been in her early care, the more central it is that the group offer her safe conditions to learn new ways of interacting and forming a relationship with the baby. The most deprived mothers and their children are also typically referred to follow-up. The group process also reveals the gravity of the mothers' stage of recovery from drug use; for example, her relapses into substances and her keeping company with active abusers. Accordingly, some participants may temporarily need residential or inpatient treatment for substance abusers, during or after the group therapy. During the group process, the mothers themselves become more conscious of their need of psychiatric and/or psychotherapeutic treatment, which facilitates treatments. It is also possible to observe and assess the infant's emotional, sensory-motor, and physical development and to refer him/her to follow-up examinations, if needed. The referrals are more feasible for the mothers, when their increased awareness of their own and children's psychological needs are combined with the thrust in therapeutic support and their own capacity to cope.

Follow-up

In this short-term intervention, most mothers are only in the beginning phase of the recovery from drugs, and each mother–infant dyad has an individually tailored follow-up to ensure a continued beneficial process. After the ending of group therapy sessions, the group therapist arranges for six to ten individual follow-up appointments (across 3–5 months) until the eventual next professional treatment starts. During these appointments, the therapist writes a summary and reviews it with the mother. The idea is to help the mother integrate her personal history with her current life situation, to become more aware of the causes of her substance addiction, and to feel empowered about her life. This work and paper represents a kind of personal "diploma" for being the very subject in one's own life and a success in treatment. The summary also evaluates the dyadic interaction with the infant and gives recommendations for follow-up. Finally, a group follow-up meeting with other members is arranged three to five months after the ending of the group intervention.

■ THE CHALLENGES AND LIMITATIONS OF THE MOTHER–INFANT GROUP INTERVENTION

The psychoanalytic-attachment oriented model is based on time-limited group work with high-risk women in their transition to parenthood. Some problems are inevitable, including the insufficiency of the help, concerns about the child's safety, failure of networking, and the heterogeneity of the group members' psychiatric status and readiness for group work. Mothers in each group express the wish that the group intervention would go on for a longer duration, and indeed, an individually tailored intervention length is preferable. However, so far, the number of personnel and economic issues set limits for the length of both group therapy and individual follow-up.

Also, the need for trauma-focused group or individual therapy in follow-up is often obvious. Although practical help is an integral part of the intervention, it is not always possible to change mothers' everyday stress and living conditions. Sometimes the therapists are highly concerned and fearful that a baby may be in great peril; in particular, if the mother continues to live with a violent and drug-abusing partner. The cooperation with the mother's social network is a crucial part of the intervention in providing her with support in her recovery from illegal drugs, and resources for parenting the child. Therapists work intensively to activate the natural networks of the mothers who are at risk, but the success of this is not in their direct control. Finally, although the therapeutic process begins with a comprehensive assessment, there is inevitable heterogeneity in women's readiness for group work. In cases where a mother uses strong denial and splitting defenses and shows high resistance, she should be referred to alternative treatment, preferable before the assignment to the group. As a group member, a woman with these characteristics is likely to inhibit the group processes and hinder others' opportunities for change.

■ PRELIMINARY EFFECTIVENESS OF THE MOTHER–
INFANT GROUP INTERVENTION

As a part of developing the psychoanalytic-attachment oriented group intervention (PGI), we explored its effectiveness by using two comparison groups: an individually tailored psychosocial support (PSS) intervention, and non-substance-abusing comparison mothers (Belt et al., 2012b; Flykt et al., 2012). The outcomes included improvement in maternal mental health (depressive symptoms) and drug use; quality of mother–child interaction (assessed by Emotional Availability Scales by Biringen et al., 2000); and content of maternal mental representations of the baby and parenting (measured by IRMAG, which is a questionnaire form of the Interview of Maternal Representations; Ammaniti et al., 1992). The research sample consisted of 51 drug abusing (26 in PGI and 25 in PSS) and 50 normative comparison mothers assessed during pregnancy (T1), at four months (T2), and at 12 months (T3) postpartum.

Maternal self-reported abstinence from drugs and treatment completion was high (about 80%) in both intervention groups. Being pregnant was a powerful motive for stopping drug use, as only a few mothers in both intervention groups reported continuing substance use after knowing about their pregnancy. Only four mother–infant dyads (16%) dropped out of PGI, and five dyads (23%) from PSS during 12 months of follow-up in postpartum. Six (20%) and seven (28%) dyads dropped out from the research, respectively. Maternal depressive symptoms decreased linearly from pregnancy to four and 12 months postpartum in both PGI and PSS intervention groups. The depressive symptom levels were, however, significantly higher among PGI than among comparison mothers at each assessment point, PSS being in the middle. We suggest that the high abstinence during the pregnancy may be explained by the effective system used to identify mothers with drug use problems early enough and to guide them to the intervention.

The influence of PGI was substantiated by results showing that maternal hostility in the mother–child interaction was reduced to the same level as that of the non-substance abusing mothers from four to 12 months postpartum. Maternal intrusive interaction responses also decreased in both intervention groups, although especially in PGI. The findings are important, as hostile and intrusive parental interaction patterns are considered the core problems in mother–child relationship among substance abusers (Fraser, Harris-Britt, Thakkallapalli, Kurtz-Costes, & Martin 2010; Johnson et al., 2002) and form a specific risk to child well-being and development (Swanson et al., 2000). Mother–infant inter-action qualities improved in both PGI and PSS groups, as well as in the com-parison group. Mothers became more sensitive and structuring and infants more responsive and involved from four months to 12 months of child's age. Again, the level of problematic mother–child interactions was higher among the substance abusing mothers than non-substance-using comparison mothers at both four- and 12-month assessments.

Finally, mothers in the PGI showed increasingly more optimal representations of themselves as mothers and of their children, from pregnancy to four and 12 months postpartum. In that representational development they came close to resembling the normative comparison mothers. However, mothers in the PSS intervention showed a pattern of idealization and drastic disappointment in their representa-tional change from pregnancy to the child's first year (Flykt et al., 2012).

■ CONCLUSIONS

We believe that "the second attachment" experience of the group intervention makes it possible for drug abusing mothers to find positive resources in themselves and success in being a mother. Mothers have been enthusiastic and have expressed satisfaction about being able to better control their own living and lifestyle, and to regulate their own and their children's feelings and behavior. The psychoanalytic-attachment–oriented mother–infant group intervention seems to help especially the mothers who are motivated to explore the causes for their drug dependence. This positive influence has been shown in the content of the mothers' mental rep-resentations and in the decrease in the high-risk hostile and intrusive interaction style. The activation of the mothers' traumatic childhood experiences within a safe treatment context is an important and vital domain of therapeutic work for these mothers. The group experiences of emotional sharing, putting the infant in the center of attention, and learning dyadic emotion recognition and regulation pro-vides healing elements that can prevent destructive models from being transferred into the next generation.

■ REFERENCES

Ainsworth, M. D. S., Blehar, M. C., Waters, E., & Wall, S. (1978). *Patterns of Attachment: A Psychological Study of the Strange Situation*. Hillsdale, NJ: Erlbaum.

Ammaniti, M., Baumgartner, E., Candelori, C., Perucchini, P., Pola, M., Tambell, R., et al. (1992). Representations and narratives during pregnancy. *Infant Mental Health Journal, 13*, 167–182.

Bakermans-Kranenburg, M. J., Van IJzendoorn, M. H., & Juffer, F. (2005). Disorganized infant attachment and preventive interventions: A review and meta-analysis. *Infant Mental Health Journal, 26*(3), 191–216.

Baradon, T., & Steele, M. (2008). Integrating the AAI in the clinical process of psycho-analytic parent-infant psychotherapy in a case of relational trauma. In H. Steele and M. Steele (Eds.), *Clinical Applications of the Adult Attachment Interview* (pp. 195–212). New York: Guilford Press.

Belt, R., & Punamäki, R-L. (2007). Mother–infant group psychotherapy as an intensive treatment in early interaction among mothers with substance-abuse problems. *Journal of Child Psychotherapy 33*, 202–220.

Belt, R. H., Punamäki, R-L., Pajulo, M., Posa, T., & Tamminen, T. (2009). Transition to parenthood among substance-abusing mothers: Stressors, supports, coping and mental health. *Journal of Prenatal & Perinatal Psychology & Health, 20*(1), 27–48.

Belt, R. H., Kouvo, A., Flykt, M., Punamäki, R-L, Haltigan, J. D., Biringen, Z., et al. (2012a). Intercepting the intergenerational cycle of maternal trauma and loss through mother–infant psychotherapy: A case study using attachment-derived methods. May 8. [Epub ahead of print]

Belt, R. H, Flykt, M., Punamäki, R-L, Pajulo, M., Posa, T., & Tamminen, T. (2012b). Effectiveness of psychodynamic group therapy and psychosocial support in improving dyadic interaction and maternal mental health among drug abusing mothers. *Infant Mental Health Journal, 33*(5), 520–534.

Bion, W. R. (1961). *Experiences in Groups, and Other Papers*. Tavistock Publications, London.

Bion, W. R. (1967). *Second Thoughts*. London: Heinemann.

Biringen, Z. (2000). Emotional availability: Conceptualization and research findings. *American Journal of Ortopsychiatry, 70*, 104–114.

Bowlby, J. (1975). Attachment theory, separation anxiety and mourning. In A. Hamburg and K. H. Brodie (Eds.), *American Handbook of Psychiatry* (pp. 292–309). New York: Basic Books.

Bowlby, J. (1988). *A Secure Base: Clinical Applications of Attachment Theory*. London: Routledge.

Burns, M. J., Feaster, D. J., Mitrani, V. B., Ow, C., & Szapocznik, J. (2008). Stress processes in HIV-positive African American mothers: Moderating effects of drug abuse history. *Anxiety, Stress & Coping, 21*, 95–116.

Crittenden, P. M. (1997). Toward an integrative theory of trauma: A dynamic-maturational approach. In D. Cicchetti & S. Toth (Eds.), *The Rochester Symposium on Developmental Psychopathology, Vol. 10: Risk, Trauma, and Mental Processes* (pp. 34–84). Rochester, NY: University of Rochester Press.

Field, T., Scafidi, F., Pickens, J., Prodromidis M., Pelaez-Nogueras, M., Torguati, J., et al. (1998). Poly-drug using adolescent mothers and their infants receiving early intervention. *Adolescence, 33*, 117–143.

Flores, P. J. (2001). Addiction as an attachment disorder: Implications for group therapy. *International Journal of Group Psychotherapy, 51*(1), 63–81.

Flykt, M., Punamäki, R-L., Belt, R., Biringen, Z., Salo, S., Posa, T., et al. (2012). Maternal representations and emotional availability among drug-abusing and non-using mothers and their infants. *Infant Mental Health Journal, 33*(2), 123–138.

Foguel, B. (1994). The group experienced as mother: Early psychic structures in analytic groups. *Group Analysis 27*, 265–285.

Fonagy, P. (2001). *Attachment Theory and Psychoanalysis*. Other Press: New York.

Fonagy, P., Gergely, G., Jurist, E., & Target, M. (2002). *Affect Regulation, Mentalization and the Development of the Self*. New York. Other Press.

Fonagy, P., & Bateman, A. W. (2006). Mechanism of change in mentalization-based treatment of BPD. *Journal of Clinical Psychology, 62*, 411–430.

Foulkes, S., & Anthony, E. J. (1990). *Group Psychotherapy*. London: Karnac Books.

Fraiberg, S., Adelson, E., & Shapiro, V. (1987). Ghost in the nursery: A psychoanalytic approach to the problems of impaired infant–mother relationships. In L. Fraiberg (Ed.), *Selected writings of Selma Fraiberg* (pp. 100–136). Columbus, OH: The Ohio State University Press.

Fraser, J. G., Harris-Britt, A., Thakkallapalli, E. L., Kurtz-Costes, B., & Martin, S. (2010). Emotional availability and psychosocial correlates among mothers in substance-abuse treatment and their young infants. *Infant Mental Health Journal, 31*(1), 1–15.

Freeman, R. C., Collier, K., & Parillo, K. M. (2002). Early life sexual abuse as a risk factor for crack cocaine use in a sample of community-recruited women at high risk for illicit drug use. *American Journal of Drug & Alcohol Abuse, 28*(1), 109–131.

George, C., Kaplan, N., & Main. M. (1996). *The Adult Attachment Interview Protocol*, 3rd edition. Unpublished manuscript. University of California at Berkeley.

Harwood, I. (2006). Head Start is too late: Integrating and applying infant observation studies, and attachment, trauma, and neurobiological research to groups with pregnant and new mothers. *International Journal of Group Psychotherapy, 56*(1), 5–29.

Hesse, E., & Main, M. (2000). Disorganized infant, child, and adult attachment: Collapse in behavioral and attentional strategies. *Journal of the American Psychoanalytic Association, 48*(4), 1097–1127.

James, J. (2004). Commentary on "Group Therapy with Mothers and Babies in Postpartum Crises: Preliminary Evaluation of a Pilot Project" by Fernanda Pedrina. *International Journal of Group Analysis, 37*(1), 137–151.

Johnson, A. L., Morrow, C. E., Accorno, V. H., Xue, L., Anthony, J. C., & Bandstra, E. S. (2002). Maternal cocaine use: Estimated effects on mother–child play interactions in the preschool period. *Journal of Developmental & Behavioral Pediatrics, 23*(4), 191–120.

Klein, M. (1935). A contribution to the psychogenesis of manic-depressive states. In *The Writings of Melanie Klein* (pp. 236–289). London: Hogarth, 1975.

Klein, M. (1984). *Envy and Gratitude, and Other Works 1946–1963*. London: Hogarth.

Lieberman, A. F., & Pawl, J. (1993). Infant-parent psychotherapy. In C. H. Zeanah (Ed.), *Handbook of Infant Mental Health* (pp. 427–442). New York: Guilford.

Lieberman, A. F., & Zeanah, C. H. (1999). Contributions of attachment theory to infant-parent psychotherapy and other interventions with infants and young children. In J. Cassidy and P. R. Shaver (Eds.), *Handbook of Attachment: Theory, Research and Clinical Applications* (pp. 555–574). New York: Guildford.

Lojkasek, M., Cohen, N. J., & Muir, E. (1994). Where is the infant in infant intervention? A review of the literature on changing troubled mother–infant relationships. *Psychotherapy, 31*, 208–220.

Luthar, S., Suchman., & Altomare, M. (2007). Relational psychotherapy mothers' group: A randomized clinical trial for substance abusing mothers. *Development & Psychopathology, 19*, 243–261.

Mayes, L. C., & Pajulo, M. (2006). Neurodevelopmental sequelae of prenatal cocaine exposure. In D. Bellinger (Ed.), *Human Developmental Neurotoxicology* (pp. 192–229). New York: Taylor & Francis Group.

Medrano, M. A., Hatch, J. P., Zule, W. A., & Desmond, D. P. (2002). Psychological distress in childhood trauma survivors who abuse drugs. *American Journal of Drug & Alcohol Abuse, 28*(1), 761–769.

Mikulincer, M., & Shaver, P. (2007). Commentary on "Attachment, Group-Related Processes, and Psychotherapy." *International Journal of Group Psychotherapy, 57*(2), 233–245.

Moore, J. & Finkelstein, N. (2001). Parenting services for families affected by substance abuse. *Child Wellfare, 80*(2), 221–238.

Nair, P., Schuler, M., Black, M., Kettinger, L., & Harrington, D. (2003). Cumulative environmental risk in substance abusing women: Early intervention, parenting stress, child abuse potential and child development. *Child Abuse & Neglect, 27,* 997–1017.

Polansky, M., Lauterbach, W., Litzke, C., Coulter, B., & Sommers, L. (2006). A qualitative study of an attachment-based parenting group for mothers with drug addictions: On being and behaving a mother. *Journal of Social Work Practice, 20,* 115–131.

Scheeringa, M. S., & Zeanah, C. H. (2001). A relational perspective on PTSD in early childhood. *Journal of Traumatic Stress, 14*(4), 799–815.

Schore, A. N. (2003). *Affect Regulation and the Repair of the Self.* New York: W.W. Norton & Company.

Smith, J. C., Cumming, A., & Xeros-Constantinides, S. (2010). A decade of parent and infant relationship support group therapy programs. *International Journal of Group Psychotherapy, 60*(1), 59–89.

Stern, D. N. (1995). *The Motherhood Constellation. A Unified View of Parent–Infant Psychotherapy.* New York: Basic Books.

Stern, D., Sander, L, Nahum, J., Harrison, A., Lyons-Ruth, K., Morgan, A., et al. (1998). Non-interpretative mechanism in psychoanalytic therapy: The "something more" than interpretation. *Psycho-Analysis, 79,* 903–921.

Suchman, N., DeCoste, C., Castiglioni, N., Legow, N., & Mayes, L. (2008). The mothers and toddlers program: Preliminary findings from an attachment-based parenting intervention for substance-abusing mothers. *Psychoanalytic Psychology, 25*(3), 499–517.

Swanson, K., Beckwith, L., & Howard, J. (2000). Intrusive caregiving and quality of attachment in prenatally drug-exposed toddlers and their primary caregivers. *Attachment & Human Development, 2*(2), 130–148.

Tronick, E. Z., Messinger, D. S., Weinberg, M. K., Lester, B. M., LaGasse, L., Seifer, R., et al. (2005). Cocaine exposure is associated with subtle compromises of infants' and mothers' social-emotional behavior and dyadic features of their interaction in the face-to-face still-face paradigm. *Developmental Psychology, 41*(5), 711–722.

van IJzendoorn, M. H., & Bakermans-Kranenburg, M. J. (1997). Intergenerational transmission of attachment. State of art in psychometric, psychological and clinical research. In I. Atkinson & K. J. Zucker (Eds.), *Attachment and Psychopathology* (pp. 135–170). New York: Guilford.

Winnicott, D. W. (1953). Transitional object and transitional phenomena. *International Journal of Psycho-Analysis, 34,* 1–9.

Winnicott, D. W. (1956). Mirror role of mother and family in child development. In *Playing and Reality* (pp. 111–118). London: Tavistock.

17 Children Exposed to Parental Substance Abuse Who Are Placed in Foster Care

An Attachment Perspective

MIRJAM KALLAND AND
JARI SINKKONEN

■ INTRODUCTION

This chapter will first review empirical literature on the risk and protective factors associated with child placement in foster care, with particular attention to research on children who have been removed from the care of parents due to the parents' substance abuse. Next, findings from a small study examining attachment characteristics and relationships in foster families will be presented, including two case vignettes. Based on these and other, previous findings from this research team, we conclude with specific recommendations for developing optimal foster care services.

Risk Factors Associated with Foster Care

Family foster care can be thought of as an intervention designed to provide out-of-home placement for children living in at-risk home environments. The main objective in foster care is to promote the development of children by providing them an environment that is physically and emotionally safe. Long-term family foster care creates, at its best, possibilities for forming secure and long-lasting attachment relationships that are unlikely to form in institutional care. However, studies regarding the effects of foster care on the development of children show somewhat worrisome results. Children in foster care have higher proportions of emotional and physical problems, higher levels of behavioral problems, lower academic achievement, higher levels of delinquency, and higher mortality compared to other children (Curtis et al., 1999; Rosenfeld et al., 1997; Kalland et al., 2001). A recent study of young people at risk for marginalization in Finland revealed that the risk for being homeless, without education, or unemployed is higher for young people with a placement history. The risk is highest for young men placed in adolescence, and those with several placements (Hämäläinen & Kangas, 2010).

Entry into foster care itself is an atypical event that can be a stressful childhood experience that challenges already vulnerable children. For example, in one study (Lawrence at al., 2006), prospective and longitudinal data were collected on the impact of foster care on child development. The sample included 46 children in foster care. The length of their placements ranged from one to 45 months, and the number of placements ranged from one to 10. Entry into foster care was precipitated by maltreatment in 69% of the cases, and 72% of these cases involved two or more categories of maltreatment. Of the 46 children, 23 were placed in familial foster care (with relatives such as grandparents), and 23 were placed in non-familial foster care (with foster parents outside the family). All children were intermittently or permanently reunified with their biological caregivers. Children in foster care were compared with maltreated children who were not placed into foster care (n = 46) and with children who had a history of neither maltreatment nor foster care (n = 97) but were at risk for other reasons, including poverty or having an unstable home life. Children in foster care showed significantly more behavioral problems in comparison with children who had no history of maltreatment or foster care. Internalizing behavior problems were highest among children exiting non-familial foster care in comparison with children exiting familial foster care, maltreated home-reared children, and adequately cared-for children. Interestingly, greater length of placement was not associated with more behavioral problems.

Children in foster care have often been exposed to a multitude of adversities in their original home environment before placement, such as maltreatment and neglect, family violence, and parental substance abuse. Thus children may have different kinds of attachment disorders already, before entering foster care (Zeanah et al., 2004). Not surprisingly, then, children who have been maltreated in their families of origin before entering foster care are already at exceptionally high risk for poor psychosocial outcomes when they enter foster care (Clausen et al., 1998).

Permanency planning is another important issue facing all children in foster care. Findings suggest that children who reunify with their biological families after a foster care placement show more negative outcomes than youth who do not reunify (Taussig et al., 2001, Lillas et al 2005). A placement history with several brief placements in different foster families contributes negatively to both internalizing and externalizing behavioral problems of foster children (Newton et al., 2000).

An Attachment Perspective on Foster Care

From a developmental attachment perspective (Bowlby, 1969/1982, 1988), it is unlikely that children who have already been exposed to maltreatment will benefit from brief foster care placements. Instead, early separations and losses are thought to have a negative effect on the capacity to build relationships in adult life as well as on the emotional and physical well-being of an individual. Given that children who are attached to a parental figure typically show distress when separated unwillingly from him or her, placement into a strange environment followed by caregiving episodes with a succession of strange people is very likely to be intensely distressing.

Experiences of good-enough caregiving and secure attachment relationships in childhood have been described as the very foundation of healthy individual development. Nonetheless, attachment theory may not be best understood as a linear process, but may be better understood as a theory about the relational context in which child development takes place. For example, anxious attachment does not cause antisocial behavior or depression, but it may represent a developmental context that makes the emergence of such problems more likely (Sroufe, 1988).

From an attachment perspective, missing someone who is loved and longed for is one of the key factors in understanding anxiety. The particular form of anxiety that separation and loss give rise to is not only common, but leads to great and widespread suffering. According to Bowlby (1973, 1988), in order for young children to grow up mentally healthy, they require a warm, intimate, and continuous relationship with their mother or permanent mother substitute. It is therefore not surprising that short-term foster placements seem to contribute to the accumulation of risk of child developmental problems, and multiple short-term placements place children at even greater risk of developing profound relational difficulties (e.g., reactive attachment disorder or other forms of severely disturbed attachment; see Fisher & Kim, 2007; Schofield & Beek, 2005;.Goldman, Fraser, et al., 2010; Newton et al., 2000).

Children, especially those who have been maltreated and neglected, experience challenges as they form attachments with new caregivers. Most children placed into care before about one year of age develop a consistent pattern of responding to their caregivers within one to two weeks (Stovall & Dozier, 2000, Stowall-McClough & Dozier 2004). For older children, this process takes a longer time, because they may have some difficulty trusting new caregivers and behaving in ways that elicit nurturing behavior from them. Even caregivers with an autonomous state of mind may reject these children when they are displaying avoidant or resistant behaviors. Overall, the findings of Dozier and her colleagues regarding the formation of attachments to new caregivers are neither as encouraging as they seem for younger infants, nor as discouraging for older children as might be expected (see Dozier & Rutter, 2008).

■ CHILDREN EXPOSED TO SUBSTANCE ABUSE AND PLACED IN FOSTER CARE

Children are often put in foster care when their biological mother or father has a substance abuse problem, and these children may be especially vulnerable to developmental problems. There is often a strong association between maternal drug use and child maltreatment serious enough to necessitate the removal of children by child protective services (Kelley, 1992). In one study, for example, 94% of young children placed in foster care had biological mothers with substance use problems, and over 80% had developmental, emotional, or behavioral problems (Halfon et al., 1995). In addition to being exposed to adverse caregiving experiences, many children had neurological abnormalities and learning difficulties. Problems were more common in children placed after two years of age and in those with a greater number of placements.

Several studies have confirmed that drug-exposed children in foster care can and do achieve positive educational, emotional, and behavioral outcomes similar to their non-drug-exposed counterparts (Brooks & Barth, 1998; Crea et al., 2008;

D'Angiulli & Sullivan, 2010). As a group, drug-exposed children in family foster care have low average cognitive skills at the time of the placement, but they can make significant improvement in cognitive functioning during the placement. In one study, for example, children with prenatal exposure to drugs scored significantly lower on cognitive skills at the beginning of the placement, but made significantly more progress than the other children during the placement (McNichol & Tash, 2001).

At the same time, drug-exposed children are often more challenging in terms of their health and caregiving needs than children who are not drug-exposed (McNichol, 1999) and can therefore have a marked impact on new caregivers. For example, behavior ratings by foster parents and teachers in one study revealed that children exposed prenatally to drugs had a higher incidence of behavior problems at school compared to their non-exposed foster care peers (McNichol & Tash, 2001).

There is some evidence that the quality of caregiving, rather than alcohol or drug exposure alone, predicts the quality of attachment in children. In a recent study, for example, comparing substance-abusing mothers with mothers matched for other risk factors (except substance use), quality of caregiving and prevalence of attachment security in children were equally low in both groups (Bergin & McCollough, 2009).

Even when children experience adequate care after birth, the cumulative risk factors associated with prenatal substance exposure are still potential contributors to behavioral problems. For example, in a prospective, longitudinal study of children in Norway who were prenatally exposed to poly-substances but otherwise reared under minimal postnatal risk conditions, a continuation of attention problems and specific cognitive deficits commonly associated with attention-deficit hyperactivity disorder (ADHD) was found (Moe, 2002; Slinning, 2004). It appears that the accumulation of biomedical risk factors associated with prenatal substance exposure is still a potential determinant of developmental problems, especially in the area of perceptual and performance functions. It may also be that the behavioral problems in prenatally exposed children have a neurological basis.

The relative impact of maternal substance use versus foster care on child development is complex and not well understood. As mentioned earlier, removal of children often involves multiple and repeated separations during foster care episodes and thereby is a potent threat to the development of healthy attachment and emotional well-being (Goldman, Fraser, et al., 2010; Lillas, Langer & Drinane, 2005). However, in one Finnish study examining the role of the postnatal caregiving environment on the socio-emotional development of prenatally substance-exposed children, placement in foster care at an early age decreased the risk for emotional, social, and neuropsychological problems, as well as the risk for traumatic experiences. Somewhat surprisingly, the number of placements did not increase the risk of problems, and the authors suggested that the benefits of placements, even when somewhat volatile, exceed the negative effects of interruptions in the primary relationship (Koponen et al., 2009).

■ PROTECTIVE FACTORS IN FOSTER CARE

A number of protective factors involving foster care have been identified in empirical research. Most of them are consistent with an attachment perspective that emphasizes the importance of establishing a secure bond between foster parent and child early on. Placement at a very young age (e.g., under 12 months) and a minimal number of placements (preferably one) are protective factors for foster care that coincide with the formation of a secure early attachment (Gauthier et al., 2004; Stovall & Dozier, 2000). Positive outcomes have also been associated with a variety of supports for the foster parent, including training, contact with caseworkers, and stipends (Chamberlain et al., 1992; Fisher et al 2006; Dozier et al 2009).

Two factors seem to be of great importance in predicting the success of the placement: the foster parents' attachment state of mind and their level of commitment. The attachment state can been evaluated with the Adult Attachment Interview (AAI), a semi-structured interview that focuses on childhood relationships and how they are remembered, processed, and understood in adulthood. The transcripts can be classified into three "organized" categories (*autonomous*, *dismissive*, and *enmeshed*), and two "disorganized" categories (*unresolved/disorganized*, and *cannot classify*). An adult classified as "secure" is able to use both cognition and affects, and the discourse is coherent and reflective. Such an adult often has a safe childhood history, but it is also possible that a subsequent psychological processing results in a so-called earned security.

Dozier and her colleagues used the AAI with foster mothers in their important study (Dozier et al., 2001). They showed that the correspondence between foster mother's state of mind with regard to attachment and foster infant attachment quality was similar to the level seen in biological infant-mother dyads. An autonomous state of mind in the caregiver is understandably preferable and suggests that even children older than 12 months can eventually organize their behavior according to the care provided by their new caregiver. The results also indicate a non-genetic dynamic for the intergenerational transmission of attachment.

The foster parents' level of commitment has also been shown to be of crucial importance (Dozier et al., 2007). In fact, highly committed foster parents may succeed even with severely damaged children, whereas less committed parents tend to experience normal children as problematic (Dozier et al., 2007). For the severely neglected and traumatized child, the level of commitment of the caregiver may be even more important than sensitivity to the child's cues (Dozier & Lindhiem, 2006). It has therefore been suggested, instead, that once foster parents have become the psychological parents for a child, it is in the child's best interest to remain with the foster family (Gauthier et al., 2004).

■ FAMILY FOSTER CARE IN FINLAND: BACKGROUND AND PREVIOUS RESEARCH

In Finland, local governments are responsible for both social and health services, including maternity and well-baby clinics that provide regular and cost-free health check-ups and advice about pregnancy, delivery, and care of the child up to seven years of age. According to Finnish law, the child (ages 0–17) must be taken into custody and placed in foster care if his or her development is threatened because of abuse or neglect or by self-harming behavior of the young person (e.g., drug abuse, criminal behavior, school dropout) and if the efforts to support the family or the child within the system of open care (e.g., family counseling, social work, financial support, etc.) have proven insufficient or unsuccessful. About 1.2% of the Finnish children under the age of 18 years grow up in foster care (National Institute for Health and Welfare, Statistics 2010). For many children, foster care will become a long-term solution, and some of them will experience transitions from one home to another. Today, children typically need foster care because of parental substance abuse, mental health problems, and family violence (Kalland & Sinkkonen, 2001).

Even though local authorities are responsible for taking the child into custody and placing the child in foster care, they may use the service of private foster care providers or nongovernmental organizations. In Finland, one such organization that provides foster care is Save the Children, which trains foster parents and searches for suitable foster families for children in need of placement.

As there are only a few studies about the reasons for and effects of foster care in Finland, this investigative team (first and second author of this chapter) started a research project in the late 1990s. The principal investigator (M. Kalland) was recruited from outside the Save the Children Organization. The funding came from the Finland's Slot Machine Association (RAY) which enhanced her independence from the organization. First, we evaluated mortality rates in children registered in the Finnish welfare registry (n = 13,371) and found it to be higher for both females and males placed in foster care than would have been expected on the basis of general population figures or figures for other socially disadvantaged groups (e.g., the working class). Higher mortality was specifically related to deaths caused by substance misuse, accidents, and suicide (see Kalland et al., 2001).

We then examined the reasons for premature dissolution of long-term foster placements in Finland (see Kalland & Sinkkonen, 2001). This study involved 234 children placed in 180 foster families (all siblings in the study sample were placed together). The mean age of the child at placement was 45 months. Common aspects of family histories among placed children included alcohol and drug abuse, mental health problems, single parenthood, and domestic violence. On average, the children had to face seven such environmental risk factors before placement.

During the two-year follow-up, 11% (n = 25) of the children had been moved from their initially assigned placement. We found that foster placements were more likely to dissolve when children had been placed at an older age (the mean age of children at placement was 33 months older in the placement-breakdown group), when they were perceived as difficult by their foster parents, or when the foster parents had biological children of their own. The expected association between breakdown of placement and severity of the child's history of maltreatment was not found. Neither did we find an association between the number of previous placements and placement breakdowns. We also found that family resources, as evaluated by the caseworker, (e.g., good marital relationship, parenting capacity, good physical and mental health, good support from own relatives and training) were associated with permanency of placement. Although risk factors for placement disruption were identified, the reasons for breakdown in placement varied from case to case in a complex way. For example, in four cases, the foster parents wanted to keep the child, but the court decided in favor of kinship care (see Kalland & Sinkkonen, 2001).

■ AIMS OF THE PRESENT STUDY

To learn more about the characteristics of family members involved in foster placements and the relationship between children and their foster parents, we conducted an evaluation of 18 families and 21 children placed with them. We were interested in different factors that might predict the success of the placement, such as the sensitivity of the caregivers, their state of mind with respect to attachment, and possible early traumas they had experienced in their own childhoods. We also wanted to study whether the internal attachment representations of the caregiver are correlated with the child's behavior, and, specifically, whether a caregiver with a balanced state of mind has a greater potential to alter placed children's early trajectories toward dysregulation and disorganization. It must be noted that when this study was designed (1998–1999), none of the seminal papers of Dozier and her colleagues was published yet. Finally, we wanted to use our experiences from this research to train social workers and other professionals in child welfare to understand better the needs of both the children and the foster parents, and to support safe and stable placements.

Participants

Our sample consisted of 21 children, including three pairs of siblings between newly born and four years of age (mean, 2 years 1 month), who were placed with 18 families. The sample was a so-called convenience sample, as it included all children under five placed by Save the Children during the year 2000.

The children came from families in which either one or both parents had a substance abuse problem. The placements were intended to be permanent, as the communities tend to use the help provided by Save the Children only in cases where various interventions in open care have been unsuccessful. The biological parents were considered to be unable to provide a safe home environment for their children due to chronic and difficult mental health problems and/or substance abuse.

The sample of foster parents (18 mothers and 18 fathers) consisted of couples trained by Save the Children and who volunteered to take the 21 children in their families. At the time of placement, the mean age of the foster mothers was 34 years, and of the foster fathers was 40 years. Most of them belonged to the working class (9 fathers, 3 mothers) or lower middle class (5 fathers, 12 mothers). Only three fathers and two mothers had a university degree. Participation in the study was voluntary. There were no refusals—on the contrary, the research was usually welcomed with interest and pleasure. The families were spread over a large area of the country, which necessitated quite a lot of traveling. All the foster children originally came from families in which either one or both parents had a substance abuse problem.

Each child was assessed by the principal investigator during two visits: the first evaluation took place a few weeks after the placement, and the second visit took place approximately one year later. We also did a ten-year follow-up, using only files for the child to evaluate how early interaction and the attachment of the child would relate to permanency of placement.

Methods

Each child was assessed by the principal investigator (M. Kalland) during two visits, the first taking place a few weeks after the placement and the second approximately one year later. In each case, at least two home visits were made, which typically lasted several hours, which allowed for extensive naturalistic observations of the child's home environment. The investigator was shown the child's room, toys, etc., and usually coffee and refreshments were served. The investigator and parents had opportunities to discuss the child's development, his/her relationships with the birth parents, and possible important themes or topics in the child's life (e.g., visits by the biological parents or grandparents, medical problems of the child).

Neglected children are very often (up to 90%) disorganized in relation to their maltreating parents (Cicchetti et al., 2006), which, in turn, is a risk factor regarding future psychopathology (Rutter et al., 2009). We therefore considered it to be important to assess whether foster care might help the children to better affect regulation with their new caregivers. Measuring attachment behaviors of children in foster care is challenging for several reasons. First, these children have a history of neglect and maltreatment of various degrees in their biological families. Despite this, they are often expected to form new attachments with unfamiliar caregivers. In our study, we were not able to assess these children's attachments to their biological parents, but we knew about their lengthy histories with child welfare.

Adult Attachment Interview

All foster and biological parents were interviewed using the Adult Attachment Interview (AAI; George, Kaplan & Main, 1985). The AAI is a well-known and widely used semi-structured interview that focuses on childhood relationships with attachment figures. The interviewer asks questions about attachment relationships, especially in times during childhood when the individual's attachment needs were activated (e.g., times as a child when he/she was sick, injured, or separated from the primary caregiver). The interview typically induces a moderate level of stress in the speaker by asking questions that "surprise the unconscious" (George et al., 1985).

The AAI scoring and classification system originally focused on three "organized" classifications; i.e., secure-autonomous, insecure-dismissing, and insecure-preoccupied categories. Later, two other classifications were added: an unresolved/disorganized, and unorganized/"cannot classify" categories. Narratives in which the adult has lapses in coherence when discussing traumatic experiences or losses are classified as "unresolved/disorganized." If there are not sufficient indicators for the preceding categories or if the scale scores point to contradictory insecure classifications, the transcript belongs to "unorganized/ cannot classify" group (see Hesse, 2008).

In addition to yielding adult attachment classifications, the AAI elicits the individual's self-protective strategy for regulating emotion under increasing stress (i.e., during activation of the attachment system). Adults classified as "autonomous" tend to provide organized, emotionally integrated narratives about their experiences. Those classified as "dismissing" tend to minimize the importance of attachment experiences, often while idealizing their childhood experiences. Narratives in which the adult provides incoherent, affect-laden stories, without an overall, integrated perspective are classified as "preoccupied." Finally, narratives in which the adult has lapses in coherence when discussing traumatic experiences or losses are classified as "unresolved." If there are not enough indicators for the preceding categories, the transcript belongs to "unorganized/cannot classify" group.

The AAI interview was used in the study to compare the foster parent's attachment style with the attachment classification of the child after one year of placement (at the second visit). The AAIs were analyzed with the Main and Goldwyn coding system (Main, Goldwyn, & Hesse, in preparation; see Hesse, 2008). The interviews were classified by a psychologist, trained by an official certified trainer in a two-week institute.

The CARE Index

Separate interactions between the child and the foster mother and foster father, respectively, were videotaped twice at approximately a one-year interval (at the first and second visits). Interactions were coded using the CARE Index (Crittenden, 1979–2005), a play-based system designed to assess the dyadic synchrony and the sensitivity of the caregiver. The Care Index is based on attachment theory and can be used with infants, toddlers, and preschool-aged children. The CARE Index assesses adult sensitivity to the child's signals with two negative endpoints, control and unresponsiveness (Farnfield et al., 2010). The coding system includes a 14-point Adult Sensitivity Scale with suggested points for different interventions. Scores of 0–4 indicate high risk. Scores of 5–6 indicate clear, unresolved interaction problems that warrant intervention. Scores between 7 and 14 are considered "adequate" to "highly sensitive." The coding system also includes a scale for adult unresponsiveness and control. Adults who score fewer than 14 points for sensitivity have inevitably displayed either unresponsiveness or control (or both) in the interaction, which is also coded. An adult with 9 points on the sensitivity scale might therefore get 2 points for unresponsiveness and 3 points for control. The sum will always be 14 points. (Crittenden, 2007).

Attachment Behaviors of the Children

The child's attachment status was assessed one year after the placement with the foster mother, regardless of the child's age. (Since the length of placement was the same, we considered attachment statuses to be comparable across children). In each case, the foster mother was the primary caregiver who spent more time with the child than the foster father, who was working outside the home. In order to examine the child's behavior during separations, we used a procedure whereby the child was separated from his/her foster mother according to the Strange Situation Procedure (SSP; Ainsworth, Blehar, & Waters, 1978). As it was difficult to decide which method should be applied to interpret the findings—one for small children (12–20 months of age) or another for toddlers, our classifications should be interpreted as tentative (see Zeanah et al., 2011).

The Strange Situation Procedure was designed to assess the child's balancing of proximity-seeking and exploration and is considered to be the "gold standard" for systematically identifying patterns of infant–parent attachment. It involves a series of interactions between a 12–20-month-old infant, a caregiver, and a female "stranger." Two brief infant–caregiver separations are included as moderate stressors in order to elicit the child's need for caregiver proximity and support. Differences in how infants organize their attachment and exploratory behaviors, especially during reunion episodes, can be reliably classified as secure, avoidant, ambivalent, or disorganized (Ainsworth et al., 1978; Main & Solomon, 1990).

There are several modifications of the SSP to assess the attachment behaviors of children beyond infancy (see Solomon & George, 2008). We used the Preschool Assessment of Attachment (PAA), developed by Patricia Crittenden (Crittenden, 2004; Farnfield et al., 2010). Both investigators (M. Kalland and J. Sinkkonen) were trained by Crittenden. They coded the tapes separately, and if there were discrepancies in the coding, they looked at the tapes together to reach the final classification.

Results

Many of the foster parents had themselves experienced traumas, loss, and other adverse childhood experiences that probably interfered with their capacity to become adequate parents (see Table 17.1). The number of adverse childhood experiences they reported ranged from none to ten, with an average of three. Twenty-four foster parents (66%) reported having experienced physical punishment as children. Seven (20%) reported having a father who had alcohol problems that, at the very least, triggered marital discord. Five (14%) reported having experienced parental divorce or physical illness in the family. As many as nine (25%) had lost either a father or a sibling during childhood. None of the foster parents reported having been physically maltreated as a child, but one had been reared by his grandmother, and several had experienced some degree of childhood neglect. Importantly, however, all the foster parents reported having felt loved by their parents as children.

TABLE 17.1 *Adverse Childhood Experiences of FosterParents (N = 36)*

	Foster (N = 36)
	N (Percent)
Corporal punishment (mostly non-severe)	24 (66) (mostly non-severe)
Father heavy alcohol user	7 (19)
Father violent toward mother	–
Father ill	5 (14)
Parental divorce	5 (14)
Felt scapegoated	–
Fear of own mother	–
Parental discord	–
Loss of sibling	5 (14)
Parental discord	–
Sibling physically abused	–
Own physical illness as child	5 (14)
Physically abused as child	–
Long-term separation from parent	5 (14)
Death of father	4 (11)
Neglect	3 (8)
	Mean (Range)
Number of adverse events	3 (0–10)

Adult Attachment Interview

The AAI classifications of the foster parents are shown in Table 17.2 together with the attachment classifications of the children. Fourteen foster mothers (88%) were classified as autonomous, and one as preoccupied. One mother was classified unresolved/disorganized (Ud) autonomous, one as Ud dismissing, and one as Ud preoccupied All three were disorganized with regard to a childhood trauma or loss, displaying otherwise an autonomous, dismissing, or preoccupied state of mind. Eleven fathers were autonomous, five were dismissing, and two were Ud autonomous.

CARE Index

As a group, both foster mothers and foster fathers had rather high scores on the sensitivity scale. The mean for the mothers was 8.6 (range 5–12) during the first assessment, and 8.8. (range 3–12) during the second one. The lowest scores at the second visit for a foster mother were associated with the breakdown of a placement in the near future. The fathers had a mean sensitivity score of 7.7 (range 4–12) during the first assessment, and 8.4 (range 5–12) during the second one.

Attachment Behaviors of the Children

Fourteen children out of 21 (67%) were classified as avoidant, three (14%) were classified as secure, and four (19%) as ambivalent after one year of placement in the foster family. Seventeen children had been placed with autonomous foster

TABLE 17.2 *Adult Attachment Classifications for Foster Parents and Attachment Status for Children One Year after Placement*

Family	Foster Mother	Foster Father	Child 1	Child 2
1	F4	F4	Ambivalent	
2	F3	Ud/F4	Avoidant	
3	E2	F5	Avoidant	
4	F4	Ds3	Secure	
5	F1	F2	Avoidant	
6	F3	Ds3	Secure	
7	Ud/E3	Ds1	Avoidant	
8	F5	Ds1	Avoidant	
9	Ud/F5	F3	Ambivalent	
10	F4	F2	Avoidant	Avoidant
11	Ud/Ds1	F4	Avoidant	
12	F3	F2	Ambivalent	Tape damaged
13	F3	Ud/F2	Avoidant	
14	F3	F2	Avoidant	
15	F1	Ds3	Secure	
16	F2	F5	Avoidant	Avoidant
17	F4	F1	Avoidant	
18	F5	F2	Avoidant	Ambivalent

F = Autonomous, Ds = Dismissing, E = Preoccupied, Ud = Unresolved or disorganized with regard to trauma or loss

mothers. All three children who had developed a secure attachment with their foster mother during the placement had autonomous mothers, but 11 (65%) of the children with autonomous mothers had developed avoidant attachment classifications, and four (24%) had developed ambivalent classifications. All children showed a more or less organized pattern of behavior. There were no signs suggesting a disorganized attachment or serious affective dysregulation such as fearfulness, or "silly" or "goofy" behavior.

■ TWO CASE VIGNETTES

To illustrate how risk factors can influence the outcome of foster placement for children of substance abusing parents, clinical material from two contrasting cases involving the biological sons of parents with histories of chronic substance use are presented here. Both boys had histories of *in utero* prenatal as well as postnatal exposure to their biological mother's alcohol use. Each boy was placed in foster care at approximately the same age (between three and four years of age).

Case Vignette 1: Tom

The first boy, Tom (pseudonym), was placed in a family whose parents had experienced the loss of a biological child before they became foster parents. They lived in a flat in an urban area. The mother was classified on the AAI as Autonomous and the father as Dismissive. As both of Tom's biological parents were chronic substance abusers, it was not likely that Tom could ever be reunified with them. Tom was four years old at the time of the foster placement. Tom was described by his foster parents as a very fearful little boy, highly sensitive to different sounds and noises. Whenever he failed or made a mistake, he collapsed by saying "I'll quit." The foster mother also noticed that Tom often remained stuck in his play where two angry animals continued an endless fight. Tom was extremely shy and cautious; he had serious problems in getting sleep and slept initially in the same bedroom with the foster parents.

First visit. The visit took place in the home of the foster parents. The visit lasted for several hours, including coffee and casual discussions with the foster parents as well as formal, semi-structured interviews (AAI) and videotaping of the child with the foster parents (Care Index). The researcher took also notes during the visit regarding the behavior of the child and what the foster parents told her about the child besides the formal interviews. In free-play situations during the first visit of the researcher, the boy was restless and unfocused and showed difficulties in playing in a structured or meaningful manner. He was throwing toys around and showed clear signs of dissociation on several occasions. His communication with the foster mother was often vague and affectless, and he appeared younger than his age. Both parents appeared very dedicated, however, to helping Tom, and showed patience when interacting with him. Both seemed able to accept Tom's anxiety without becoming anxious or irritated, which seemed to help him stay calm enough to engage in simple interactive play.

During the first play assessment, the mother was very sensitive with Tom (scoring 10 out of 14 points on the CARE Index) and was responding to his bids in timely manner, both cognitively and affectively. When he asked her about a toy with a babyish voice in the manner of a one-year-old, she answered with a warm and soft voice, accepting his regression but in a way that brought him up to his own level of development: Tom (holding up a car): "gu-gu?" Mother (with a warm voice): "Yes Tom, it is your favorite car. Shall we play with it together?" There were some occasions when she was unresponsive (scoring 4 points on the CARE Index); for example, a little slow in responding to what he said. During these observed interactions, Tom was usually cooperative, but his efforts were disrupted by his disorganized and somewhat difficult behavior and his apparent dissociation. For example, he sometimes seemed to lose interest when playing with his mother, and would throw things, or cease altogether to have contact with her, just sitting very still and staring with blank eyes, or making some awkward gestures with his hands. On those occasions he did not respond to anything the mother said, and it could take several minutes before she was able to get in contact with him again. At other times, he showed self-soothing behavior (e.g., rocking his body).

Second visit. One year after placement, during the second visit, the mother continued to show sensitivity during the play assessment (scoring 12 points in sensitivity on the CARE Index), and Tom was fully cooperative. The interaction between the two was characterized by reciprocal turn-taking, shared attention, negotiation, and shared eye-contact and joy. To the observer, it seemed like the two of them were in the same world, enjoying the same things and each other. This was in contrast with the scene during the first visit, in which the child disappeared into his own world, and the mother had to make efforts to get him back. The father was also sensitive within the adequate range (scoring 8 points on the CARE Index), but also rather unresponsive (6 points). Tom was less cooperative with the father and became somewhat restless when the father was too passive or did not respond to his bids.

In the assessment of attachment (PAA) with the mother, Tom became regressed during the separation episodes: he used a babyish voice and his play became monotonous. However, although he suddenly appeared to be like a small toddler and shouted for his mother, he managed to control his anxiety and neither cried nor became aggressive. After the reunion he was able to discuss his emotions about the separation with his mother, who was able to answer his questions adequately and with empathy. Tom (with a babyish voice): "Afraid." Mother: "You were afraid when I left the room and you were alone?" Tom nodding. Mother: "You did great. Now I am back, and we can play together, and I am not going to leave again. When we are finished, we go home together." After that discussion, they played together for a while, and then left the room together. Tom did not show anger or anxiety; he seemed to trust his mother.

After the follow-up visit with Tom and his foster parents, researchers were left with a feeling of confidence about his future, as he seemed to be in a process of psychologically and behaviorally reorganizing towards security. A child psychiatrist was consulted who suggested intense individual psychotherapy. Tom began a twice-a-week psychotherapy with an experienced female therapist who collaborated closely with the foster family. A third session was added for a certain period when Tom's biological mother died (Tom was six years old then). Tom's self-esteem was greatly improved and he became much more extraverted. He liked his therapist and never refused to go to his session. The therapy lasted as long as five years due to the child's traumatization and severe fearfulness.

Long-term follow-up. At a recent follow-up visit with a social worker, Tom, at fifteen years of age, was continuing to live with the same foster family, who seemed to be caring for him as if he were their own biological child. He is a handsome young man who takes care of his hygiene as well as his clothes. Girls seem to like him a lot. His strengths are drawing and handicraft, and he is doing well at school. He still likes to be at home with the foster parents; only recently has he got close same-sex friends. He does not smoke, nor has he experimented with alcohol.

Case Vignette 2: Matt

The second boy, Matt (pseudonym), was placed at three years of age with foster parents who were caring for five biological children, in addition to their foster children. The family was living in the countryside in a large house. On the AAI, the foster mother was classified as Enmeshed and the father as Autonomous. Matt's mother was in psychiatric care, had a traumatic childhood history including severe family violence, an adult history of alcohol abuse as well as psychiatric problems, and had physically abused her son. His father had not been in the picture for some time, but was violent against the mother and drug/alcohol-abusing.

First visit. At the first home visit after his placement, the foster mother's contact with Matt seemed quite adequate. However, she seemed to be concentrating on teaching him but did not seem to notice his repeated affective signals. According to the mother, he was not developing normally. He had difficulties remembering things and understanding more complicated sentences, or bids like: "Go and find the football in your room and bring it to me." At three years of age, Matt was a very appealing little boy whose efforts to please his foster parents were heartbreaking. The foster mother was adequately sensitive (scoring seven of 14 points on the CARE Index) but also controlling (scoring 5 of 14 points). Matt was mainly cooperative, but also a bit passive. The father was rather unresponsive in his interaction with the boy.

Second visit. At the second visit one year later, Matt had developed a pattern of avoidance. He seemed to be trying hard to inhibit any display of negative feelings and made almost desperate efforts to please his foster parents. In the CARE Index system, this kind of behavior is classified as compulsive compliance. In the assessment of attachment with his foster mother (PAA), he was classified as having an anxiously avoidant attachment pattern. The foster mother was cognitively oriented during play, but did not respond to his affective bids. In other words, she did the right things but with little emotional warmth.

Follow-up. At follow-up, approximately ten years later, it appeared that Matt's placement had broken down one year previously. According to the social worker, Matt had not become attached to anyone in his foster family, nor did he have many contacts with his biological relatives. His biological father had died, and his biological mother's whereabouts were unknown. During his preschool and school-age years, Matt often behaved in a disruptive way. Later, he was bullied at school and became depressed. He received antidepressant medication and individual psychotherapy, which lasted several years. Despite this, Matt seemed to live in a world of his own and was described by the social worker as having "written his own rules." The foster parents had been active in their efforts to find help for Matt, but the interventions were not effective enough to prevent the breakdown of placement.

■ **DISCUSSION**

Descriptive Data

The foster parents in this study had experienced somewhat more adverse childhood events than we expected. Despite this, many of the foster parents had an autonomous state of mind with regard to attachment. In some cases, at least, they may represent so-called earned-secure individuals (see Crowell et al., 2008, for discussion of this topic). Some of the parents had had painful experiences in childhood, such as a loss of a sibling or an accident that had happened to a younger sibling that they felt responsible for. Dozier and Rutter (2008) have suggested that becoming a foster parent may be a productive way of resolving past traumas or a possibility of changing negative childhood experiences (for example, having felt abandoned) into positive ones with the foster children. Our findings that so many of the parents had emotionally painful experiences in childhood gives support to the idea that becoming a foster parent could be an effort to resolve past traumas. However, it is also possible that using a child as a source of healing one's own unresolved issues could also be hindering the development of a secure attachment relationship.

During the CARE Index assessments, we noticed that many of the foster parents used a very cognitive, educational approach with their foster children as if they had been afraid to experience more emotional aspects of the relationship.

Rather than playing *together* with the child, they taught colors, puzzles, or names of animals, which seemed to maintain an emotional distance between parent and child. The contact was often unilaterally guided and controlled by the adult, thus not responding to the feelings or intentions of the child. In other words, many of the parents were regulating the behavior of the child, but not attending to what happened in the child's mind. Parental mind-mindedness (an ability to read accurately the mental states governing child behavior) has been considered important for secure attachment. However, this ability should be used benevolently in parenting, and concretely in exploring the attentions behind the child's behavior, peeking behind the obvious. Sometimes it can be distorted and go beyond the behavior of the child in a paranoid way: in one case the foster mother described her foster child as violent, abusing her physically and also displaying a severe eating disorder. "I should report him to the police," she said during the interview. The boy was a tiny and shy four-year-old, and after his re-placement into another family, social workers reported that the child has been developing well.

It is possible that a cognitive approach in parenting reflects a fear of losing the child. To maintain emotional distance may protect foster parents from a painful separation. They may even have been warned against becoming too attached to a child who may be removed from their family. Thus, without enough support (e.g., therapy to better understand mixed feelings about becoming close to the child), foster-parenting a child might add new traumatic experiences to both the parent and the child rather than being the productive solution originally intended.

It appears that an autonomous classification for foster mothers was a necessary but not sufficient condition for a child's secure attachment. What is remarkable is that all children seemed to have developed some attachment strategy with their new caregivers. We did not find any disorganized children after one year's placement, although we know from attachment research that most maltreated children form disorganized attachment patterns (Carlson et al., 1989; Cicchetti et al., 2006). In these cases we lack information about the attachment patterns they have had with their biological parents, but we can assume that none of the children have been able to form a secure attachment to a substance abusing, neglectful, and often violent parent. Among the children with dismissing patterns, we found four children who were excessively obedient and compliant, and who even showed signs of emotional role reversal, such as giving care to the foster parent. In Crittenden's classification system, these behaviors are related to compulsiveness (compulsive compliance and compulsive care-giving) (Crittenden, 2004). These children were, however, often described by social workers as emotionally balanced and trusting their parents.

In all, two thirds of the children in the sample were classified as having an avoidant attachment with their foster mother after one year's placement. According to Dozier et al. (2001), the state of mind of the caregiver is important for attachment in foster care. In our study, even the foster mothers who had been classified as autonomous were paired with predominantly avoidant children. Given that many children had experienced various forms of neglect and maltreatment before the placement, they may have met criteria for disorganized attachment prior to the placement. After one year in placement, though, everyone had been able to develop some kind of organized strategy with their caregivers. On the other hand, becoming a foster parent is a challenging task and may activate unresolved traumas or other painful experiences (e.g., questions about one's own infertility and sense of loss of bearing biological children). It is also a complex task, as the foster parents have to deal with the biological parents and possibly grandparents and other relatives, and all the emotions and reactions that these relationships may elicit in the child and in the foster parent him- or herself.

In Finland, alcoholism is the single most important reason for out-of-home placements of the children. Unfortunately, children are often returned to their biological families too soon after abstinence has been achieved, which may be far too early for parents who are vulnerable to relapse. The result may be a troublesome series of dissolved foster placements alternated with unsuccessful unification efforts between biological parents and the child.

Clinical Vignettes: Discussion

In Tom's case, the foster mother behaved initially in a calm or serene manner that seemed appropriate for such a disorganized boy, as it helped to calm him down. We feel that she was able to peek behind the behavior of her son, trying to understand the complex mental states underlying his behavior. Thus she was able to make sense of his behavior, which in turn helped him regulate it. While his mind must have been a mystery for his parents, they were committed to helping him, and used parental reflective functioning and mentalization in order to adapt to and understand him. It seems likely that one of the most important reasons for Tom's successful development and permanent placement was his foster parents' commitment (Dozier et al., 2007), but we think that this commitment was connected not only to their life situation (not having children of their own), but also to their capacity to mentalize: the capacity to reflect on another person's mind makes that relationship meaningful and rewarding.

Matt's foster parents had several biological and foster children in their care at the same time they were caring for him. Differences in commitment have in fact been found to be associated with the number of foster children, with more children being associated with lower levels of commitment (Dozier & Rutter, 2008). Foster parents who do not have biological children (as in Tom's case) seem to be more committed to their foster children (Kalland & Sinkkonen, 2001). Initially, Matt did not seem to be nearly as disturbed a child as Tom had been. His foster parents had been successful with other children, but Matt might have benefited from a warmer and more emotional contact. On the other hand, both of the parents had had traumatic upbringings, and the mother was classified as Enmeshed in the AAI. Although Matt's foster father was classified as Autonomous, he had faced a lot of adversities during his childhood, such as a violent and alcoholic father. It is possible that the foster parents became overwhelmed by the burden of their task, and that Matt for some reason elicited negative responses in them.

As he was lacking emotional warmth, he seemed to have grown up as an unattached child and to have eventually become a loner. His future does not seem to be particularly bright, a fact that could hardly have been predicted from the early assessments.

Implications for Foster Care

One aim of this project was to find implications for foster care and to train social workers to promote safe and stable placements in foster care. Following the research, we started a one- year training program for the social workers. We used the interviews and the tapes in order to illuminate specific attachment and interaction issues. We wanted to train the social workers to identify such issues as avoidance, resistance, intrusiveness, sensitivity, and warmth in interaction. We also gave them an overview of attachment theory and its implications for foster care. The interviews with both foster parents and biological parents were used to develop more understanding and empathy for difficulties in parenting. As a result, some important principles of attachment theory have been used by the social workers in both evaluating, training, and supporting foster parents. Videotapes are being used with new foster and adoption placements.

■ **CONCLUSIONS**

This small-scale study in a natural setting highlights the fact that every foster placement is unique and complex, and the development of the child depends both on his own history and on the history and the capacity of the foster parents. The fact that foster parents may have had severe adversities in their childhood histories has been neglected both in the literature and in social work praxis, and the implications of these adversities are not yet well understood. Given that a child needs a stable placement with foster parents who are ready to invest both time and emotions in the child, there is a great need for empirical research to determine which among myriad foster care arrangements provides a therapeutic experience that is crucial for the child's future. As well, foster parents need and deserve attachment theory–based understanding and training before the placement, and long-term support after the placement from social workers (and possibly other professionals) who understand the complexity of the foster parenting tasks as well as the needs of the child.

We assert that child protection practitioners and foster care services will be enhanced by providers' understanding of attachment theory and its implications for foster care. There is a growing evidence base about attachment-derived relationship-focused interventions that have been shown to be effective (Zeanah et al., 2011). In our understanding, one reason for the fact that foster care seems to have a somewhat worrisome effect on children's development is that the growing knowledge about the complex emotional needs of children has not been brought into practice. In some cases, parent's rights to their children seem more respected in the child protection legislation than children's right to protective and sustainable relationships.

■ **AUTHOR NOTE**

We want to express our gratitude to Emilia Suviala, M.A., for her contribution in analyzing the Adult Attachment Interviews.

■ **REFERENCES**

Ainsworth, M. D., Blehar, M. C., Waters, E., & Wall, S. (1978). *Patterns of Attachment: A Psychological Study of the Strange Situation*. Hillsdale, NJ: Lawrence Erlbaum.

Bergin, C. H., & McCollough, P. (2009). Attachment in substance-exposed toddlers: The role of caregiving and exposure. *Infant Mental Health, 30*, 407–423.

Bowlby, J. (1969/1973/1982). *Attachment and Loss. Vol. I: Attachment. Vol. II: Separation. Vol. III: Loss.* Harmondsworth, England: Penguin Books.

Bowlby, J. (1988). *A Secure Base: Parent-Child Attachment and Healthy Human Development*. New York: Basic Books.

Brooks, D., & Barth, R. P. (1998). Characteristics and outcomes of drug-exposed and non-drug-exposed children in kinship and non-relative foster care. *Children and Youth Services Review, 20*, 475–501.

Carlson, V., Cicchetti, D., Barnett, D., & Braunwald, K. (1989, Jul). Disorganized/disoriented attachment relationships in maltreated infants. *Developmental Psychology, 25*(4), 525–531.

Chamberlain, P., Moreland, S., & Reid, K. (1992). Enhanced services and stipends for foster parents: Effects on retention rates and outcomes for children. *Child Welfare, 71*, 387–401.

Cicchetti, D., Rogosch, F.A., & Toth, S. L. (2006). Fostering secure attachment in infants in maltreating families through preventive interventions. *Development and Psychopathology, 18*, 623–649.

Clausen, J. M., Landsverk, J., Ganger, W., Chadwick, D., & Litrownik, A. (1998). Mental health problems of children in foster care. *Journal of Child and Family Studies, 7*, 283–296.

Crea, T. M., Shenyang, G., Barth, R., & Brooks, D. (2008). Behavioral outcomes for substance-exposed adopted children: Fourteen years post-adoption. *American Journal of Orthopsychiatry, 78*, 11–19.

Crittenden, P. M. (1979–2005). CARE-Index: Infant coding manual. Unpublished manuscript. Miami, FL.

Crittenden, P. M. (2004). The Preschool Assessment of Attachment. Coding manual. Unpublished manuscript. Family Relations Institute. Miami, FL.

Crowell, J. A., Fraley, R. C., & Shaver, P. R. (2008). Measurement of individual differences in adolescent and adult attachment. In J. Cassidy & P. R. Shaver (Eds.), *Handbook of Attachment* (2nd ed., pp. 599–634). New York: Guilford Press.

Curtis, P. A., Dale, G., Kendall, J. C., & Rockefeller, J. D. (1999). *The Foster Care Crisis: Translating Research into Policy and Practice*. Lincoln, NE: University of Nebraska Press.

D'Angiulli, A., & Sullivan, R. (2010). Early specialized foster care, developmental outcomes and home salivary cortisol patterns in prenatally substance-exposed infants. *Children and Youth Services Review, 32*, 460–465.

Dozier, M., Grasso, D., Lindhiem, O., & Lewis, E. (2007). The role of caregiver commitment in foster care. Insights from the This Is My Baby interview. In D. Oppenheim & D. F. Goldsmith (Eds.), *Attachment Theory in Clinical Work with Children* (pp. 90–108). New York, Guilford Press.

Dozier, M., & Lindhiem, O. (2006). This is my child: Differences among foster parents in commitment to their young children. *Child Maltreatment, 11*, 338–345.

Dozier, M., & Rutter, M. (2008). Challenges to the development of attachment relationships faced by young children in foster and adoptive care. In J. Cassidy & P. R. Shaver (Eds.), *Handbook of Attachment* (2nd ed., pp. 698–717). New York: Guilford Press.

Dozier, M., Stovall, C., Albus, K., & Bates, B. (2001). Attachment for infants in foster care: The role of caregiver state of mind. *Child Development, 72,* 1467–1477.

Dozier, M., Lindhiem, O., Lewis, E., Bick, J., Bernard, K., & Peloso, E. (2009). Effects of a foster parent training program on young children's attachment behaviors: Preliminary evidence from a randomized clinical trial. *Child Adolescent Social Work, 26,* 321–332.

Farnfield, S., Hautamäki, A., Norbech, P., & Sahhar, N. (2010). DMM assessments of attachment and adaptation. Procedures, validity and utility. *Clinical Child Psychology and Psychiatry, 15,* 313–328.

Fisher, P., & Kim, H. (2007). Intervention effects on foster preschoolers' attachment related behaviors from a randomized trial. *Prevention Science 8,* 161–170.

Fisher, P. A., Gunnar, M. R., Dozier, M., Bruce, J., & Pears, K. (2006). Effects of therapeutic interventions for foster children on behavioral problems, caregiver attachment, and stress regulatory neural systems. *Annals of the New York Academy of Sciences, 1094,* 215–225.

Gauthier, Y., Fortin, G., & Jéliu, G. (2004). Clinical application of attachment theory in permanency planning for children in foster care: the importance of continuity of care. *Infant Mental Health Journal, 25,* 379–396.

George, C., Kaplan, N., & Main, M. (1985). The Adult Attachment Interview. Unpublished manuscript. University of California, Berkeley.

Goldman Fraser, J., Harris-Britt, A., Leone Thakkallapalli, E., Kurtz-Costes, B., & Martin, S. (2010). Emotional availability and psychosocial correlates among mothers in substance abuse treatment and their young infants. *Infant Mental Health Journal, 31,* 1–15.

Halfon, N., Mendonca, A., & Berkowitz, G. (1995). Health status of children in foster care. The experience of the Center for the Vulnerable Child. *Archives of Pediatrics & Adolescent Medicine, 49,* 386–392.

Hesse, E. (2008). The Adult Attachment Interview. Protocol, method of analysis and empirical studies. In J. Cassidy & P. R. Shaver (Eds.), *Handbook of Attachment. Theory, Research and Clinical Applications* (pp. 552–598). New York: The Guildford Press.

Hämäläinen, U., & Kangas, O. (Eds.) (2010). *Perhepiirissä [In the Family].* National Institute for Health Insurance, Ministry of Education. Helsinki, Finland.

Kalland, M., Pensola, T., Meriläinen, J., & Sinkkonen, J. (2001). Mortality in children registered in the Finnish Child Welfare Registry: a population based study of 13,371 subjects. *British Medical Journal, 323,* 207–208.

Kalland, M., & Sinkkonen, J. (2001). Finnish children in foster care: Evaluating breakdown of placement. *Child Welfare, 80,* 513–527.

Kelley, S. J. (1992). Parenting stress and child maltreatment in drug-exposed children. *Child Abuse & Neglect, 16,* 317–328.

Koponen, A., Kalland, M., & Autti-Rämö, I. (2009). Caregiving environment and socioemotional development of foster-placed FASD-children. *Children & Youth Services Review, 31,* 1049–1056.

Lawrence, C., Carlson, E., & Egeland, B. (2006). The impact of foster care on development. *Development and Psychopathology, 18:* 57–76.

Lillas, C. M., Langer, L., & Drinane, M. (2005). Forced separations and forced reunions in the foster care system *Zero to Three, 23,* 34–40.

Main, M., & Solomon, J. (1990). Procedures for identifying infants as disorganized/disoriented during the Ainsworth Strange Situation. In M. T. Greenberg, D. Cicchetti & E. M. Cummings (Eds.), *Attachment in the Preschool Years* (pp. 121–160). Chicago, IL: University of Chicago Press.

McNichol, T. (1999). The impact of drug-exposed children on family foster care. *Child Welfare, 78*, 184–96.

McNichol, T., & Tash, C. (2001). Parental substance abuse and the development of children in family foster care. *Child Welfare, 80*, 239–56.

Moe, V. (2002). Foster-placed and adopted children exposed in utero to opiates and other substances: prediction and outcome at four and a half years. *Journal of Developmental & Behavioral Pediatrics, 23*, 330–339.

Newton, R. R., Litrownik AJ & Landsverk, J. A. (2000). Children and youth in foster care: disentangling the relationship between problem behaviors and number of placements. *Child Abuse and Neglect, 24*, 1363–1374.

Rosenfeld, A. A., Pilowsky, D. J., Fine, P., Thorpe, M., Fein, E., Simms, M. D., et al. (1997). Foster care: an update. *Journal of the American Academy of Child & Adolescent Psychiatry, 36*, 448–457.

Rutter, M., Kreppner, J., & Sonuga-Barke, E. (2009). Emanuel Miller lecture: Attachment insecurity, disinhibited attachment, and attachment disorders: where do research findings leave the concepts? *Journal of Child Psychology and Psychiatry 50*(5), 529–543.

Schofield, G., & Beek, M. (2005). Providing a secure base: Parenting children in long-term foster family care. *Attachment & Human Development, 7*(1), 3–25.

Slinning, K. (2004). Foster-placed children prenatally exposed to poly-substances—attention-related problems at ages 2 and 4½. *European Child & Adolescent Psychiatry, 13*, 19–27.

Solomon, J., & George, C. (2008). The measurement of attachment security and related constructs in infancy and early childhood. In J. Cassidy and P. R. Shaver (Eds.), *Handbook of Attachment: Theory, Research, and Clinical Applications* (2nd ed., pp. 383–416). New York: Guilford Press.

Sroufe, A. (1988). The role of infant–caregiver attachment in development. In J. Belsky & T. Nezworski (Eds.), *Clinical Implications of Attachment*. Hillsdale, NJ: Lawrence Erlbaum Associates.

Stovall, K. C., & Dozier, M. (2000). The development of attachment in new relationships: Single subject analyses for 10 foster infants. *Development and Psychopathology, 12*, 133–156.

Stovall-McClough, K. C., & Dozier, M. (2004). Forming attachments in foster care: Infant attachment behaviours during the first 2 months of placement. *Development and Psychopathology, 16*, 253–271.

Taussig, H. N., Clyman, R. B., & Landsverk, J. (2001). Children who return home from foster care: A 6-year prospective study of behavioral health outcomes in adolescence. *Pediatrics, 108*, 1–7.

Zeanah, C. H., Scheeringa, M., Boris, N. W., Heller, S. S., Smyke, A. T., & Trapani, J. (2004). Reactive attachment disorder in maltreated toddlers. *Child Abuse and Neglect, 28*, 877–888.

Zeanah, C. H., Berlin, L., & Boris, N. (2011). Practitioner review: Clinical applications of attachment theory and research for infants and young children. *Journal of Child Psychology and Psychiatry, 52*, 819–833.

18 Intervention with Mothers Who Abuse Alcohol and Drugs

How Relationship and Motivation Affect the Process of Change in an Evidence-Based Model

THERESE M. GRANT AND
JANET E. HUGGINS

> *"There were times when I felt like I was going to relapse and my case manager would be there for me, and she'd keep checking on me and I'd get through it. I've learned so much about myself and being responsible again and being a good mother."*
>
> —PCAP Client

■ BACKGROUND

In the mid-1980s, cocaine was at the height of popularity in the United States, and our research team at the University of Washington was awarded a federal grant to study the effects of prenatal cocaine exposure on young children. The research protocol involved enrolling 500 high-risk cocaine-using pregnant mothers, interviewing them, and bringing their babies into our laboratory for periodic neuropsychological testing. Study findings confirmed our hypothesis that prenatal cocaine exposure is not a good thing, but in many ways the most important lessons were those we learned directly from the mothers themselves. We listened carefully as we spent time with them in their cramped apartments, listening to stories of family dysfunction that seemed horrific to young researchers, but were "just the way it is" to the mothers. They wanted to be "good mothers" but were instead giving their babies the same kind of upbringing they had experienced as children. They didn't know any other way.

As the cocaine study came to an end, it seemed to us that a more compelling challenge than studying effects of prenatal substance exposure would be to work in a meaningful way with the high-risk mothers who delivered these babies—to help them take care of the children they already had, and avoid future births of exposed and affected children. Thus began the Parent-Child Assistance Program (PCAP).

■ PARENT-CHILD ASSISTANCE PROGRAM (PCAP)

PCAP began (in 1991 at the University of Washington, Seattle) as a federally funded research demonstration project designed to test the efficacy of a three-year

365

intensive home visitation and case management intervention among substance-abusing pregnant and parenting women, and their children (Ernst et al., 1999; Grant et al., 2003; Grant et al., 2005). PCAP's primary aims are: to help mothers obtain alcohol and drug treatment, stay in recovery, and resolve the myriad of complex problems related to their substance abuse; to assure that the children are in safe, stable home environments and receiving appropriate health care; to link mothers to community resources that will help them build and maintain healthy, independent family lives; and to prevent the births of future alcohol- and drug-affected children.

In their study of outpatient and home visitation parenting interventions for substance-abusing women and their children, Suchman et al. (2006) reviewed published evaluations of quasi-experimental and experimental studies with regard to their impact on drug abuse, maternal adjustment, parent–child interactions, and child outcomes. PCAP (formerly known as the "Seattle Birth to Three Program") was one of six studies that met criteria for the review. Suchman and her colleagues highlighted two fundamental characteristics of PCAP that may account for its high retention and positive outcomes among high-risk mothers: the emphasis on relationship quality between mothers and their case managers/home visitors; and the use of motivational interviewing (MI) strategies that encourage mothers to examine conflicting emotions as they struggle in the process of replacing risky behaviors with healthy, adaptive ones. A third fundamental characteristic of PCAP that may also account for its success is its emphasis on professional supervisory support for the paraprofessionals who deliver the intervention.

■ CRITICAL OBJECTIVES AND COMPONENTS

The PCAP model has been widely replicated in the United States and Canada, and a question often asked is, "What makes the model work?" The purpose of this chapter is to describe the defining principles and key clinical practices that distinguish PCAP. We will explain how PCAP integrates MI strategies into the relational work we do with the clients while taking into account their roles and experiences as mothers. We will also describe PCAP's approach to supporting the paraprofessional case managers in this work that is so often characterized by frustration and burnout. Our intent is to inform interventionists working with this special population of substance-abusing mothers and their children, and to provide guidance to researchers interested in studying this hard-to-reach population.

■ CLINICAL POPULATION

Mothers who enroll in PCAP exemplify the intergenerational nature of familial substance abuse and dysfunction; they were often themselves the neglected and abused children in our communities just a decade or two ago. As children, of the 753 women currently enrolled at nine PCAP sites in Washington State, 90% had substance abusing parents, 68% were physically and/or sexually abused, 64% ran away from home, and 31% had had child welfare services involvement (Grant & Ernst, 2011).

Children who have experienced these kinds of traumatic events are at risk for long-term biological, developmental, and behavioral problems (Atchison 2007; Casanueva et al., 2008; Conners et al., 2003). Their early devaluing experiences can impair the emotional foundations for development by inhibiting self-expression and self-directed action, thus limiting autonomy and intimacy and increasing the risk for future victimization (Jack, 1991; Jack & Dill, 1992; van der Kolk, 2005).

Characteristics of PCAP clients at enrollment reflect the consequences of early trauma on their adult development. At intake, clients are typically in their late twenties, and their life circumstances are almost always grim: most are unmarried (92%), beaten by their partners (77%), have a history of incarceration (76%), and are on public assistance (71%); approximately 69% are homeless or living in temporary housing, including treatment or transitional housing (Grant & Ernst, 2011). All have a history of substance abuse during the most recent pregnancy, and many use alcohol or drugs to self-medicate and cope with the psychological and sometimes physical pain of a lifetime of traumatic events (Gentilello et al., 2000; Kilpatrick et al., 1997; Kilpatrick et al., 1998; Martin et al., 2003; Najavits et al., 1997).

Mothers with co-occurring substance use disorders and trauma symptomatology have been shown to have significant parenting problems (Cohen et al., 2008). Mothers in PCAP, for example, have on average 2.7 biological children, over half of whom are not in their custody. Loss of custody is usually not related to the mother's direct abuse of her child. Instead, it is her substance abuse, involvement in the drug culture, lack of attention to the family, and poor judgment with regard to who she allows to come into contact with her children that lead to potentially dangerous situations and removal of the children from the home. A mother may have provided adequate basic care in the home, but her children are removed because she is arrested and incarcerated for drug use, possession, or sales. In other cases, a mother may continue to be involved in an extremely abusive relationship with a man, placing her and her child at serious risk. Circumstances are complicated by the fact that in either of these situations the mother may lose her subsidized housing, but her housing must be in place in order to regain care of her children.

Paradox of High Risk and Insufficient Treatment

Poor parenting in high-risk mothers with co-occurring disorders contributes to the intergenerational transmission of increased risk for substance use and mental health disorders in their children (Dube et al., 2003). These mothers are often labeled as unmotivated and difficult to reach, and many professionals view them as a hopeless population (Greenhouse, 2000; Nelson & Marshall, 1998; Paltrow et al., 2000; Will, 1999). Consequently, they often become distrustful of and alienated from community resources. *This disenfranchising process results in mothers who are at greatest risk for having children with serious developmental and psychosocial problems being the least likely to seek and receive assistance from community resources.*

■ SNAPSHOT OF RETENTION AND PROMISING OUTCOMES

PCAP's retention rate is nearly 70%. A recent analysis of PCAP outcomes (Grant et al., 2011) found that among 739 mothers who enrolled from January 1998 through December 2004 at five PCAP sites in Washington (King, Pierce, Yakima, Spokane, and Grant counties), 132 (18%) did not complete the program because they disengaged or disappeared (n = 45), moved out of area (n = 37), withdrew (n = 35), died (n = 10), or went into prison long-term (n = 5). An additional 108 (14.6%) participated in PCAP but did not complete the exit interview (reasons include no-shows, could not be located, were too busy, and did not want to end PCAP). A total of 499 (67.5%) participated in PCAP and completed valid intake and exit interviews. In comparison with our approximately 30% attrition rate, Gomby and colleagues (1999) reviewed six home visiting programs and reported attrition rates ranging from 20% to 67%. Katz et al. (2001) reported 41% attrition in a research study including lay home visitation.

Final analyses of this cohort included data from 458 mothers. A total of 41 were excluded for these reasons: had a fetal alcohol spectrum disorder and were enrolled in a separate study, n = 22; exited the program early (< 30 months of PCAP involvement), n = 11; and the index child died or was miscarried, n = 8. Among these 458, 24.9% had a subsequent birth during the three-year PCAP intervention (10.5% were alcohol- or drug-exposed, and 14.4% were alcohol- and drug-free pregnancies). By way of comparison, Ryan and colleagues (2008) found that among 931 substance-abusing women enrolled in a demonstration project, after only 1.5 years of follow-up, 15% of the intervention group and 21% of the control group had a subsequent alcohol- or drug-exposed birth.

At PCAP exit, 71.2% of the mothers were at reduced risk for delivering another exposed child, either because they had been abstinent from alcohol/drugs for at least six months or because they were using a family planning method consistently. Most of the clients had completed inpatient (62.5%) or outpatient (83.2%) treatment (prior to PCAP, 81.4% had attempted inpatient treatment, an average of 3.2 times); at exit, 40% were currently abstinent from alcohol and drugs for at least six months; during PCAP, 77.1% had been abstinent from alcohol and drugs for a period of at least six months. At PCAP exit, 62.8% were using a method of family planning regularly (vs. 12.2% using contraception prior to the target pregnancy), and of these 77.8% were using more reliable methods such as Depo-Provera injections, IUD, or tubal ligation; 30.6% were receiving any income from employment (vs. 4.6% at intake); and 71.8% were in permanent, stable housing (vs. 37.8% at intake).

Our analyses explored the complicated interplay of how maternal risk and protective characteristics and service elements are associated with disrupted parenting and reunification. At PCAP exit, 60% of the mothers were caring for their index child (the child they had been pregnant with at intake). During the intervention, these mothers had more treatment and mental health service needs met, more time abstinent from alcohol and drugs, secure housing, higher income, and support for staying clean and sober. Among women who had multiple psychiatric diagnoses, the odds of regaining custody were increased when they completed substance abuse treatment and also had a supportive partner. Mothers who lost and did not regain custody had more serious psychiatric problems and had fewer service needs met. Their untreated mental health problems may have limited their ability to access mental health services, anticipate and resolve serious problems, and utilize available community services to build a stable home environment and maintain child custody (see Grant et al., 2011, for a full account of study details and findings).

■ **UNIVERSAL PRINCIPLES: THE INTERVENTION BACKDROP**

Before describing the distinguishing aspects of the intervention, we briefly summarize here the important but more universal principles that provide the intervention's foundation: case management, structured implementation, long-term intervention, developmental perspective, and parallel process.

Case Management

The PCAP model incorporates fundamental and well-known components of effective case management (Case Management Society of America, 2010). It is individually tailored, promotes the competence of the client, is community-based and multidisciplinary, and considers the dynamics of the family.

Structured Implementation

The intervention has a well-defined, structured, and manualized protocol for implementation (available at http://depts.washington.edu/pcapuw/) but also involves the practice of continually examining and reflecting on what works and what does not. The manual and structure insure that the principles of the intervention are delivered in practice at a "dose level" that is sufficiently strong.

Long-term Intervention

As a three-year intervention, PCAP offers a realistic length of time during which a woman can form a therapeutic alliance with her case manager and undergo the developmental process of making gradual behavioral changes. The beginning of this process is naturally slow and tentative for most clients, who have never known the steady presence of a trusted parent or other individual in their lives (in fact, many clients state that their own mother first introduced them to drugs). The three-year duration also provides a clear time frame during which clients know they will have assistance; in this way it serves as an external motivator to completing their goals.

Developmental Perspective

The model embraces a developmental approach at multiple levels: the development of the mother as an individual and as a parent; the development of the child; and the professional development of the PCAP case manager. Mothers who grew up with substance-abusing parents experienced insensitive and unreliable caregiving, at best. They knew the emotional pain of having a mother and/or father who did not respond to their distress, and this childhood environment contributes to their fundamental, persistent beliefs that relationships cannot be trusted. Their ability to recognize healthy relationships continues to be compromised. As mothers, this trajectory is evident in their difficulty responding in a developmentally appropriate manner to their own child's emotional cues and distress signals, and in their difficulty in identifying and connecting with healthy individuals who will not pose a threat to the family. PCAP offers these mothers, perhaps for the first time, the opportunity to develop a different kind of relationship. Over the three years, as the case manager works closely with the mother and implements intervention strategies, the woman begins to make positive strides and gradually recognizes that this relationship is a healthy one that allows her to grow. As she trusts the case manager and experiences the reliability of the relationship, she becomes more capable of offering consistent attention and care to her child.

Parallel Process

The attention, care, and support that case managers give to their clients is expected to be reflected in the way the mothers interact with their children. Accepting and supporting the mother in her troubled (and often painful) physical, emotional, and social domains not only helps the mother engage in treatment and avoid relapse, but may also gradually enhance her capacity to care for her child physically, emotionally, and socially. Similarly, the PCAP case managers receive close attention, care, and support from their clinical supervisors, as described below.

■ DEFINING PRINCIPLES AND KEY CLINICAL PRACTICES

In this section, we review the constellation of principles that define PCAP, distinguish it from other programs for high-risk substance-using parents, and are believed to explain its clinical efficacy. These principles place special emphasis on relationship, motivation, paraprofessional role modeling, attending to neurological deficits associated with chronic drug use, harm reduction, preventing harm to the child, being realistic about parenting potential, and developmental supervision. We also explain how each principle is translated into practice, and provide research findings when available.

Relational Focus

Principle

Two relational constructs inform the therapeutic approach with clients and shape the day-to-day case management practices. Relational theory underscores the importance of interpersonal relationships to women as they grow, develop, and define themselves (Miller, 1991; Surrey, 1991). Therapeutic alliance—the process through which a mental health professional builds rapport and engages with a patient in order to help the person achieve desired change (Orlinsky et al., 2004)—is also considered vital. Therapeutic alliance has been well studied by addiction researchers and practitioners and found to be critical to successful outcomes among women with substance-abuse disorders who are in intervention, treatment, and recovery settings (Amaro & Hardy-Fanta, 1995; Finkelstein, 1993). Therapeutic alliance has also been shown to determine the extent of patient compliance and retention in an intervention (Barnard et al., 1988), and it may be more important to treatment outcomes than concrete services received (Pharis & Levin, 1991).

Clinical Practice

The PCAP model puts concepts of relational theory and therapeutic alliance into practice by offering personalized, knowledgeable, and compassionate support from a single case manager who works consistently with her clients for three years. We prioritize hiring paraprofessional case managers who have successfully overcome difficult personal, family, or community life circumstances similar to those experienced by their clients (e. g., substance abuse, single parenting, poverty). Case managers who have undergone difficult change processes and achieved successes (e.g., in education, employment, and relationships) are realistic role models who share their experience of recovery with clients and inspire the hope that it is possible to overcome obstacles.

PCAP clients often present defensively at the start of the intervention; most are ashamed of their substance use in pregnancy and know they have poor parenting skills. The case managers' shared history allows them to literally "get in the door" on home visits—because they are more easily perceived as understanding and empathetic with the client's situation, allowing them to more easily build rapport with those who might be unapproachable. The case managers' sustained empathetic peer guidance, offered in the context of teaching and role modeling, promotes the client's social and emotional development as she learns to trust others, build practical skills, and gradually trust in herself.

PCAP case managers spend an average of approximately two hours of face-to-face time with each client every other week, and an additional 40 minutes per week working with the client's family or service providers. The amount of time spent undoubtedly reflects the complexity of the mother's problems and the personalities involved, but "time spent" may also reflect the extent to which the case manager has developed a successful relationship with her client.

Research Findings

We surmised that more time and more positive and therapeutic relationships with the case managers contribute to clinically relevant maternal outcomes, and data among 458 recent PCAP graduates indicate a moderate "dose–response" effect. When we compared outcomes among clients who spent an average of 30 minutes per week or more with their case managers versus those who spent less time together, we found that those who spent more time were more likely to complete inpatient or outpatient treatment (87% vs. 81%, respectively); to be abstinent from alcohol and drugs for at least six months at PCAP exit (40% vs. 34%); to have had any six-month or longer period of alcohol/drug abstinence during PCAP (85% vs. 70%); and to be using a reliable family planning method (58% vs. 48%) (Grant & Ernst, 2011).

At exit from PCAP, clients are asked to assess the relationship with their case manager using the Advocate-Client Relationship Inventory, a 27-item instrument, adapted with permission from Kathryn Barnard (Barnard, 1998; Sikma & Barnard, 1992). The inventory's four constructs are based on Barnard's conceptualization of the home visitor's role, and PCAP uses the instrument because these constructs reflect PCAP's central principles and the case managers' role. The four constructs include: 1) coach (seven items on the supportive role of a coach, who helps someone reach her potential; 2) ongoing developmental (six items on the role of assisting the mother in her role as an adult, a mother, and a family member); 3) caring (ten items on being emotionally involved, being present, doing for, giving hope); and 4) harmony (four items on harmony among the mother, her family and the case manager).

Among 754 PCAP clients who have completed the inventory, at least 85% agreed or strongly agreed with nine of the ten "caring" constructs, five of the seven "coaching" constructs, and three of the six "developmental" constructs. Fewer clients (68% to 83%) agreed with items in the "harmony" construct, which is perhaps not surprising, because the case managers help clients make major behavioral changes that may create disruption in dysfunctional family systems (Grant & Ernst, 2011).

Stages of Change and Motivational Interviewing

Principle

"Stages of Change" theory recognizes that people will be at different stages of readiness for change at different times, and that ambivalence about changing addictive and other behaviors (e.g., parenting) is normal and should be expected (Prochaska & DiClemente, 1986). Motivational interviewing is a corresponding counseling style developed by Miller and colleagues (1991) that helps clients examine and resolve ambivalence about change and increase intrinsic motivation to change.

MI strategies are based on four basic principles: expressing empathy, developing discrepancy, accommodating to resistance, and supporting self-efficacy (Miller & Rollnick, 1991; Prochaska & DiClemente, 1986; Rollnick & Bell, 1991). The principles embodied in MI naturally complement relational theory, because they call for clinicians to be empathetic and nonjudgmental, to listen closely and respectfully to the client, and to accept and trust in the client's perception and judgment about her own life. The self-efficacy principle of MI complements PCAP clinical practices because a person's self-efficacy (i.e., her belief in her ability to behave in ways that will lead to desired outcomes) will be influenced most powerfully by her own history of accomplishment (Bandura, 1977).

Clinical Practice

PCAP case managers are trained and reinforced in the use of MI strategies. In practice, the most important way in which a PCAP case manager has a positive effect on her client's self-efficacy is by listening carefully to her about what is important and how she thinks about her problems, and valuing this self-expression. Case managers then promote self-directed action by helping clients define and accomplish explicit goals toward behavioral change, and then recognize and celebrate the positive steps they have taken.

PCAP case managers use the "Difference Game" periodically throughout the intervention (Grant et al., 1997) to teach and reinforce the practice of setting and achieving goals. Adapted from a scale developed by Dunst et al. (1988), the game is a card-sort instrument consisting of 31 cards, each of which names a possible client need (e.g., "housing," "safe daycare," "drug or alcohol treatment"). The client sorts the cards into two piles, items that would "make a difference" and those that "would not make a difference." The client selects the five items that represent her most important needs. The case manager then engages the client in a conversation about each card selected ("Tell me about this... ").

For example, one client in PCAP selected the seemingly benign card "Time to get enough sleep." As her story slowly emerged, the case manager learned that the mother did not sleep well because she was (appropriately) worried that someone in her temporary household might sexually abuse her child. After they completed the Difference Game, and using motivational strategies, the case manager worked with her client to identify a few specific, meaningful goals she would like to work on in the next two to four months. Together they agreed on realistic, incremental steps they would each take toward meeting the goals, and who would be responsible for accomplishing each task.

It is critical that some steps, no matter how small, be attainable by the client within the designated period, because it is as she observes herself accomplishing desired behavior that her sense of self-efficacy develops. In the example above, the larger goal was to move into a permanent, safe home, given limited affordable options. The first step was for the case manager to identify two acceptable temporary options and arrange visits so the client could see the spaces, make her own informed choice, and retain a sense of agency.

At the same time, the case manager worked with the client to complete lengthy and detailed applications required for more permanent housing. As they dealt pragmatically with the housing issues, and using strategies of MI (expressing empathy, rolling with the client's resistance to addressing past painful memories of her own abuse), the case manager helped the client understand the value of talking with her mental health therapist about the situation and its relationship to her own past, and the opportunities she had now to respond differently to the potential threat to her own child.

The PCAP goal-setting activity is designed to be dynamic, and is repeated every four months throughout the intervention. This ongoing process allows for the client's gradual development: from initial dependence on the case manager's assistance and support, to interdependence as they work together to accomplish steps toward goals, to independence as the client begins to trust in herself as a worthwhile and capable person, and learns (to the extent she is able) the skills necessary to improve the quality of life for her and her children.

Role-Modeling and Teaching Basic Life Skills

Our clients simply do not have the skills "their mothers should have taught them." They rarely have a mental template for what healthy adult life or parenting might look like, and their bleak backgrounds have done little to prepare them for these responsibilities. In addition, they typically have poor emotional regulation and interpersonal skills, and may respond to problems and disappointments with other adults and with their own children with poorly controlled anger, or withdrawal. The simple approach of consistent support and modeling is a powerful one that has the potential to help women change entrenched family patterns. The comments of a PCAP mother with two children under the age of two illustrate this point: "I really liked working with [case manager]. She was very supportive and taught me to be more observant of my kids. If they do something now, I know they are trying to tell me something so I try to respond. I am trying to reverse the chain. I got beat up as a kid. I didn't get anyone who sang to me or played with me. I am trying to do these things with my kids. [Case manager] taught me how to do this."

PCAP case managers model positive interpersonal behaviors in order to teach the clients how to improve and maintain relationships so they will eventually be able to manage competently on their own. PCAP mothers and their children are typically highly dependent on community providers for a range of comprehensive services. One of the case manager's responsibilities is to meet periodically with members of the client's service provider network with the client present, in order to develop service plans that meet the client's needs while addressing providers' concerns. In preparation for these meetings, the case manager helps the client identify her feelings and organize her thoughts. She then works with the client to practice articulating her views. Over time, the client can learn to speak up in a way that demonstrates self-respect and regard for others, and indicates that she understands how to work more effectively with others.

Attending to Neurological Deficits

Principle

It is essential that case managers consider the impact of alcohol and drug use on neurocognitive functioning among clients, including impairments in attention and concentration, learning, impulsivity, abstraction, and executive functioning (Nordahl et al., 2003; Scott et al., 2007; Vocci, 2008). These problems may not only decrease treatment effectiveness, but they also complicate the client's ability to participate in the goal-setting process, and they impede everyday life functioning in areas such as planning, paying attention to and responding to one's children, and managing a household (Aharonovich et al., 2006; Dean et al., 2009; Henry et al., 2010; Sadek et al., 2007).

Clinical Practice

At PCAP intake, the clinical supervisor administers the Addiction Severity Index (ASI) interview (McLellan et al., 1992), supplemented with additional questions about pregnancy substance abuse, use of community services, and childhood history. Questions include items about the mother's own prenatal alcohol exposure, as well as other indicators of possible neurocognitive impairment (for example, couldn't complete school, difficulty keeping a job, serious head injury). The clinical supervisor conducts the intake interview in a conversational manner in order to elicit the most comprehensive picture of the mother's history, including the ways in which the mother views her problems and copes with them. The supervisor and case manager use this information to identify potential deficits, outline an initial approach to interacting with the client, and develop realistic expectations.

Clients who have neurocognitive limitations may not respond fully to the subtleties of MI counseling. When necessary, case managers modify MI approaches with concrete and explicit activities. They help clients explore choices visually if possible; they accept the client's ideas for solutions, but also offer a few alternative options for the client to consider; they discuss events as soon as possible after they occur in order to maximize the woman's ability to learn from them; they ask more close-ended vs. open-ended questions.

Harm Reduction

Principle

Harm reduction is based on the premise that alcohol and drug addiction and the associated risks can be placed on a continuum, with the goal being to help a client move along this continuum from excess to moderation, and ultimately to abstinence, in order to reduce the harmful consequences of the habit (Marlatt & Tapert, 1993). In this view, "any steps toward decreased risk are steps in the right direction" (Marlatt et al., 1993).

Clinical Practice

Relapse is a well-recognized characteristic of substance-abuse disorders, and PCAP clients are not asked to leave the program because of relapse, noncompliance, or setbacks. Instead, these problems are used as opportunities for clients to learn from their mistakes. This policy is straightforward in theory, but challenging to implement. It requires the case manager to manage her own discouragement (and sometimes anger) about a client's setbacks, renew her commitment to the client's potential, and think creatively about how to re-engage the client. Case managers use clients' relapse experiences to help them examine triggering emotions and events, consider more functional ways of responding to these triggers, and make decisions about how to manage these kinds of situations in the future. When a client is able to successfully rebound from a relapse, she develops self-efficacy as she sees herself coping, repairing the damage done, overcoming a crisis, and moving on.

Preventing Harm to the Child

Principle

Case managers help the client focus her attention not only on reducing alcohol and drug use, but also on reducing other risky behaviors that impact her health and well-being and that of her children. In many cases, clients who are not fully abstinent from alcohol and drugs are parenting their children. When a client is still using substances or is at risk for a relapse, her case manager recognizes and accepts this current situation and at the same time challenges the client to take responsibility for her role as a mother. For example, if a woman has plans to go out with her boyfriend on the weekend, the case manager uses MI to develop discrepancy by asking if she has weekend safety plans for the children. She helps the client think ahead about possible consequences of her weekend activities, and how to plan in order to reduce potential harm. This means they may discuss who will baby-sit, the food and diaper situation, and her birth control plan.

Being Realistic About the Potential to Parent

Principle

The issue of child custody is a recurrent theme in clients' lives because a majority of the women have had children removed from their care by the state. PCAP case managers routinely teach clients about behaviors that are normal and appropriate for their children of different ages, and they model alternative ways of responding to their child's behavior. Clients are often mandated to attend parenting classes (which can vary widely in content and quality) but are reluctant because they have found previous classes to be unhelpful, or because of apprehension about being judged. Case managers talk with their clients about how to conduct themselves in a class, what they might expect, and how they might extract a positive benefit. In some cases, the case manager will accompany her client in the beginning to help her get oriented to the routine and feel more comfortable.

Regaining custody is a common goal stated by clients in their first year in the program, although case managers may not necessarily concur that reunification is in the best interests of the child or children. The turning point for successful resolution of child custody issues occurs when the mother comes to terms with her ability to parent and is willing to consider the best interests of the child. For some mothers, this means deciding to relinquish custody to a foster family who has bonded with the child and would like to adopt. For others, it means staying in recovery and doing whatever is necessary to resume or maintain custody of her child. Regardless of who has custody, case managers work on behalf of the child to secure a safe and stable home environment.

Clinical Practice

As regular home visitors, PCAP case managers are in the unique position to identify problems that may put children at risk in families that would otherwise escape the notice of health and social service providers. PCAP staff members are mandated to report child abuse and neglect. Whenever possible, if case managers believe the child welfare system should be alerted, they let a mother know ahead of time. In many cases, we successfully encourage the mother to call Child Welfare herself to talk about warning signs and difficulties, and to ask for help getting back on track. In this way, the mother conveys to the child welfare worker that she is self-aware and is trying to take responsibility as a parent who wants to improve. Mothers do not generally drop out of PCAP after Child Welfare is called. While they may at first feel angry or betrayed, we challenge them to think about the reality of their behavior and the resulting consequences, always within the context of helping them take responsibility for becoming better parents.

As advocates, PCAP case managers help clients comply with their individual Child Welfare contracts and act as liaisons between the agency and the client. In general, PCAP and child welfare social workers work well together. PCAP case managers keep careful documentation and releases of information so that they can communicate with all parties, verify both client and social worker compliance or non-compliance, and advocate accordingly for the upholding of agreements made in the contract. However, it is not uncommon for a mother to comply with all of her contract stipulations in order to regain custody of her child, only to learn that her social worker plans to recommend that the child be removed for a variety of reasons that can include social worker inexperience and biased attitudes. In these cases, a client may seriously question her own worth and abilities, feel humiliated, and manifest symptoms of depression and anxiety while at the same time suspecting that she has been double-crossed. The PCAP case manager's role is to help her client cope with these complex feelings, and continue to advocate for her by providing documentation, negotiating with child welfare, and helping the client meet demands required as she tries to prove herself again within the system.

■ USING SUPERVISION TO PROMOTE THE PARAPROFESSIONAL CASE MANAGER'S DEVELOPMENT

Closely aligned with the intervention principles described above is the overarching principle emphasizing the personal and professional development of the case manager through intensive and ongoing clinical supervision. Below, we elaborate on this principle and how it is put into practice.

Reflective Stance

PCAP supervisors expect that case managers will progress along a personal developmental trajectory as they work intensively with high-risk families undergoing change. Supervisors support this process by working with the case manager to untangle the intense feelings generated during the work, to help her reflect on her emotional reactions to the client and child, and to examine and understand how these feelings relate to the choices the case manager makes about day-to-day activities with the client (Bertacchi & Norman-Murch, 1999). With ongoing support and training, the case managers can mature in their ability to avoid overreacting, to fully assess situations, and to respond effectively with a balance of honesty, objectivity, and care.

Formalized Approach

A critical element of PCAP has been the development and institutionalization of excellent supervision practices. PCAP supervisors are bachelor's or master's level female clinicians who meet individually with case managers for at least an hour, ideally every week, and at a minimum twice each month. They are available for consultation throughout the week either by phone or in person.

Management of Multiple Roles

The supervisor has diverse roles. As an administrator, she discusses each client's status and reviews paperwork, case notes, and how the case manager allocates her time. As a teacher, she explores with the case manager how case activities are related to client goals and helps her differentiate between crises that need the case manager's intervention and those the client may be ready to handle by herself. As a mentor, the supervisor discusses areas of growth the case manager would like to see for herself and opportunities for additional training.

The supervisor is also in a leadership position that allows her to create a positive, healthy work environment in which case managers can deliver sustained attention and care to their clients. When the parallel process functions well, the supervisor's support of the case manager is reflected in the case manager's attention to the mother, which is in turn reflected in the mother's care for her child. The words of Jeree Pawl come to mind: "Do unto others as you would have others do unto others" (Pawl & St. John, 1998).

Managing Difficult Emotions and Preventing Burnout

Disappointment and frustration are common among service providers who work with high-risk, unpredictable populations. It is critical for the PCAP clinical supervisor to assist case managers in recognizing and understanding these normal responses, rather than reacting to clients in counterproductive ways or ignoring the feelings and increasing the risk of burnout. In a model like PCAP that is based on maintaining long-term trusting relationships between case managers and clients, staff turnover must be kept to a minimum. If burnout results in a case manager leaving, the transfer of a caseload to different staff disrupts the relationship not only with the case manager but also in some cases with the program, and can lead to setbacks for the client.

Monitoring Contact Balance

Supervisors are alert to the particular challenges that arise when case managers work very closely with high-risk women and children in home-based settings. For example, dividing one's time among a caseload of 16 high-risk women can be extremely difficult. (The amount of time spent with clients depends on many factors, and will naturally vary.) *What is important is that the case manager be persistent in trying to find ways to connect and build a relationship with every client.* This is particularly challenging if a client is rude and angry with the case manager, dismissive and harsh with her children, continually misses appointments, or has poor hygiene. On the other hand, clients who are doing well are easier to be with, and it is a natural tendency for case managers to schedule more time with these women.

The supervisor's role is to help the case manager examine and avoid extremes. PCAP case managers complete a form weekly that documents time spent in direct contact with and on behalf of each client. Using this data, the supervisor is able to objectively monitor the time the case manager spends with each client on her caseload. She also provides ongoing training on the key tenets of PCAP—that every mother who has agreed to be in PCAP hopes on some level for a better life, and for some it will take a great deal of time and persistence before a therapeutic alliance can be established and progress can be observed.

Fostering Timely Independence

Supervisors must be attuned to the potential problem of case manager's task-oriented efficiency interfering with the model's goal of helping women achieve healthy independence within the context of a supportive mentoring relationship. For example, a case manager may become frustrated with a struggling client and do the client's work for her, instead of guiding the client in a process that will result in her developing competence and self-efficacy. Alternatively, a case manager may be tempted to leave a "star" client to her own devices, failing to remember the importance of her continued support in helping the client sustain her progress.

Maintaining Healthy Boundaries

Healthy relationships between case managers and clients require that boundaries be articulated and maintained. Early in the development of the PCAP model, we used a focus-group process with case managers to identify essential home visitor boundaries, and we continue to refine these standards based on case managers' field experiences, both good and bad. At present, PCAP has twenty boundaries that case managers review and discuss annually. The boundaries touch, not only on the content of conversations (e.g., "Case managers will role model/discuss aspects of their personal lives they believe are beneficial/relevant to a client's progress and well-being, but will not discuss other aspects of their own personal lives. Ask yourself, 'Whose needs are being met?'"), but also on realistic situations that arise in the course of the work (e.g., "Case managers will not buy goods or services from clients. PCAP staff will not hire clients for any service").

Ongoing Training and Staffing

Comprehensive and ongoing training is essential to building strong staff skills and to helping case managers maintain confidence. PCAP training includes: Initial

80-hour intensive training on program protocols and working with clients; formal training as necessary on topics relevant to the issues case managers encounter; periodic meetings with community agencies to brainstorm about how to work together most effectively and prevent service barriers; annual three-day refresher training on the PCAP model and protocols; annual one-day statewide retreat where PCAP staff members share success stories, problem-solve challenges, and are honored individually for their work.

PCAP sites have weekly, two-hour group staffing/problem-solving meetings where case managers share the highlights of the prior week, examine challenging cases, share community resources, and mentally prepare for the week ahead. This is the only time case managers come together as a group during the week, and the clinical supervisor uses this valuable time to best advantage by gleaning common themes, problems, or service barriers from her individual supervision meetings with the case managers. She then asks case managers to staff specific clients or situations as case study illustrations at the group meeting in order to stimulate brainstorming and discussion. Case managers offer ideas and support, and reflect on experiences with their own clients. Subsequent staffing meetings provide continuity when case managers give updates on client status and on how others' suggestions have worked. A continuing challenge faced by supervisors is maintaining a balance between spontaneity (keeping meetings flexible and interesting) and structure (covering essential business items within time limitations).

Feedback Loop

From a day-to-day perspective, it can be difficult for case managers to see the effect they are having on clients' lives. PCAP has created a dynamic evaluation feedback loop that gives staff the opportunity to examine the data, to see specifically how they are helping clients make gains, and to identify areas for improvement. PCAP staff are trained in data collection methods to assure quality control: The clinical supervisor administers intake interviews using the ASI; the case managers collect data monthly and every six months to track client progress; a research assistant administers exit interviews using the ASI. The program evaluator compiles data and reports trends to staff every six months. This feedback and the accompanying discussion about the meaning of the data give case managers an active role in the evaluation process and help them better understand their work.

Conducting Research with Substance-Abusing Parents and Children

Research with high-risk populations can be challenging, and may include problems with sample recruitment and maintenance, suspicion of researchers' intent, self-report biases, scheduling difficulties and no-shows, transportation and child-care considerations, mandates to report abuse and neglect, and the potential for research records to be subpoenaed. Some of these problems are unavoidable, but none are insurmountable. The most effective way to avoid frustration and failure is to anticipate these issues while writing a grant, and plan realistically for them in the study procedures, the timeline, and the budget.

Taking Time and Showing Interest

To improve the accuracy of data collected and help mothers feel comfortable about revealing personal and sensitive information, it is critical that researchers respect subjects and that subjects trust researchers. This requires *taking time* from the outset to demonstrate sincere interest, to explain the research and how their personal contribution may benefit other mothers and children, and to thank them for being a part of the work. While a consent form may convey some of this information, it is not a substitute for a conversation that conveys honesty, concern, and care. We have found that, for most mothers in PCAP, participating in a university-based research study is a source of pride.

Mandated Reporting and Confidentiality

Researchers must inform clients clearly, both in writing and verbally, that they are mandated reporters. It is advisable to obtain a federal Certificate of Confidentiality in order to protect research records from subpoena (note that this does not necessarily protect case notes or preclude personal testimony). If researchers release confidential data inappropriately, faith in the study or the institution will be undermined, and serious legal consequences can ensue. PCAP has developed an extensive protocol for managing subpoenas that is available to researchers and interventionists. Institutions should additionally seek guidance from their own legal counsel.

▪ CONCLUSIONS AND FUTURE DIRECTIONS

At present, the PCAP model is being fully implemented and evaluated as designed at ten sites in Washington State. Ongoing funding, through state legislative appropriation, is a result of PCAP's positive, sustained outcomes and the state's commitment to serving pregnant and parenting women. SAMHSA has funded three PCAP replication sites that are currently being evaluated, and HRSA has recently funded another. Adaptations of the model are being implemented at over forty sites in provinces throughout Canada, including sites in a number of First Nations communities. The Canadian sites have not yet incorporated a formal evaluation component, which limits our ability to understand the impact of the intervention there and whether cultural adaptations have been effective.

The PCAP model serves as a platform from which to examine research questions regarding prevention and intervention with high-risk substance-abusing pregnant women and their families. For example, we are currently completing a federally funded study exploring the integration of infant mental health (IMH) therapy among PCAP mothers who abused methamphetamine during pregnancy, and their infants. This approach blended individual work with the mother along with IMH dyadic therapy delivered in the home. We recently received a grant that will provide trauma-informed therapy to mothers while they are in long-term residential substance-abuse treatment with their children, and at the same time provide them with specialized training on how to respond to their child's cues and sensory-based needs.

■ CONCLUSION

Substance-abuse professionals recently developed a working definition of "recovery" that resonates with PCAP values because it recognizes that, for a substance-abusing mother, the process of becoming a whole person means far more than achieving sobriety: "Recovery from substance dependence is a voluntarily maintained lifestyle characterized by sobriety (abstinence from alcohol and non-prescribed drugs), personal health (improved quality of personal life), and citizenship (living with regard and respect for those around you)" (Betty Ford Institute Consensus Panel, 2007). PCAP creates an environment in which vulnerable substance-abusing women can achieve recovery and offer their children the possibility of having a better life.

■ REFERENCES

Aharonovich, E., Hasin, D. S., Brooks, A. C., Liu, X., Bisaga, A., & Nunes, E. V. (2006). Cognitive deficits predict low treatment retention in cocaine dependent patients. *Drug & Alcohol Dependence, 81*, 313–322.

Amaro, A., & Hardy-Fanta, C. (1995). Gender relations in addiction and recovery. *Journal of Psychoactive Drugs, 27*, 325–337.

Atchison, B. J. (2007). Sensory modulation disorders among children with a history of trauma: A frame of reference for speech-language pathologists. *Language, Speech & Hearing Services in Schools, 38*, 109–116.

Bandura, A. (1977). Self-efficacy: Toward a unifying theory of behavioral change. *Psychological Review, 84*, 191–215.

Barnard, K. E. (1998). Developing, implementing, and documenting interventions with parents and young children. *Zero to Three, 18*, 23–29.

Barnard, K. E., Magyary, D., Sumner, G., Booth, C. L., Mitchell, S. K., & Spieker, S. (1988). Prevention of parenting alterations for women with low social support. *Psychiatry, 51*, 248–253.

Bertacchi, J., & Norman-Murch, T. (1999). Implementing reflective supervision in non-clinical settings. *Zero to Three, 20*, 18–23.

Betty Ford Institute Consensus Panel. (2007). What is recovery? A working definition from the Betty Ford Institute. Betty Ford Center and the Treatment Research Institute. *Journal of Substance Abuse Treatment, 33*, 221–228.

Casanueva, C. E., Cross, T. P., & Ringeisen, H. (2008). Developmental needs and individualized family service plans among infants and toddlers in the child welfare system. *Child Maltreatment, 13*, 245–258. Epub 2008 May 21.

Case Management Society of America. (2010). *Standards of practice for case management.* Retrieved from http://www.cmsa.org/portals/0/pdf/memberonly/StandardsOf Practice.pdf. Accessed December 5, 2012.

Cohen, L. R., Hien, D. A., & Batchelder, S. (2008). The impact of cumulative maternal trauma and diagnosis on parenting behavior. *Child Maltreatment, 13,* 27–28.

Conners, N. A., Bradley, R. H., Whiteside-Mansell, L., Liu, J., Roberts, T. J., Burgdorf, K., et al. (2003). Children of mothers with serious substance abuse problems: An accumulation of risk. *American Journal of Drug & Alcohol Abuse, 2,* 743–758.

Dean, A. C., London, E. D., Sugar, C. A., Kitchen, C. M., Swanson, A. N., Heinzerling, K. G., et al. (2009). Predicting adherence to treatment for methamphetamine dependence from neuropsychological and drug use variables. *Drug & Alcohol Dependence, 105,* 48–55.

Dube, S. R., Felitti, V. J., Dong, M., Chapman, D. P., Giles, W. H., & Anda, R. F. (2003). Childhood abuse, neglect, and household dysfunction and the risk of illicit drug use: The adverse childhood experiences study. *Pediatrics, 111,* 564–572.

Dunst, C. J., Trivette, C. M., & Deal, A. G. (1988). *Enabling and Empowering Families: Principles and Guidelines for Practice.* Cambridge, MA: Brookline Books.

Ernst, C. C., Grant, T. M., Streissguth, A. P., & Sampson, P. D. (1999). Intervention with high-risk alcohol and drug-abusing mothers: II. Three-year findings from the Seattle model of paraprofessional advocacy. *Journal of Community Psychology, 27,* 19–38.

Finkelstein, N. (1993). Treatment programming for alcohol and drug-dependent pregnant women. *International Journal of Addiction, 28,* 1275–1309.

Gentilello, L. M., Rivara, F. P., Donovan, D. M., Villaveces, A., Daranciang, E., Dunn, C. W., et al. (2000). Alcohol problems in women admitted to a level I trauma center: A gender-based comparison. *Journal of Trauma, 48,* 108–114.

Gomby, D. S., Culross, P. L., & Behrman, R. E. (1999). Home visiting: Recent program evaluation—analysis and recommendations. *Future of Children, 9,* 4–26, 195–223.

Grant, T. M., & Ernst, C. C. (2011). 2009–2011 Biennial Report from the University of Washington Parent-Child Assistance Program to the Washington State Department of Social and Health Services, Division of Behavioral Health and Recovery. Olympia, Washington.

Grant, T. M., Ernst, C. C., McAuliff, S., & Streissguth, A. P. (1997). The Difference Game: An assessment tool and intervention strategy for facilitating change in high-risk clients. *Families in Society, 78,* 429–432.

Grant, T., Ernst, C. C., Pagalilauan, G., & Streissguth, A. (2003). Post-program follow-up effects of paraprofessional intervention with high-risk women who abused alcohol and drugs during pregnancy. *Journal of Community Psychology, 31,* 211–222.

Grant, T., Ernst, C., Streissguth, A., & Stark, K. (2005). Preventing alcohol and drug exposed births in Washington State: Intervention findings from three Parent-Child Assistance Program sites. *American Journal of Drug & Alcohol Abuse, 31,* 471–490.

Grant, T. M., Huggins, J., Graham, J. C., Ernst, C., Whitney, N., & Wilson, D. (2011). Maternal substance abuse and disrupted parenting: Distinguishing mothers who keep their children from those who do not. *Children & Youth Services Review, 33,* 2176–2185.

Greenhouse, L. (2000). Justices consider limits of the legal response to risky behavior by pregnant women. *The New York Times,* October 5, p. A26.

Henry, B. L., Minassian, A., & Perry, W. (2010). Effect of methamphetamine dependence on everyday functional ability. *Addictive Behavior, 35*(6), 593–598.

Jack, D. C. (1991). *Silencing the Self: Women and Depression.* Cambridge, MA: Harvard University Press.

Jack, D. C. & Dill, D. (1992). The Silencing the Self Scale: Schemas of intimacy associated with depression in women. *Psychology of Women Quarterly, 16,* 97–106.

Katz, K. D., El-Mohandes, A., Johnson, D. M., Jarrett, M., Rose, A., & Cober, M. (2001). Retention of low income mothers in a parenting intervention study. *Journal of Community Health, 26,* 203–217.

Kilpatrick, D. G., Acierno, R., Resnick, H. S., Saunders, B. E., & Best, C. L. (1997). A 2-year longitudinal analysis of the relationships between violent assault and substance use in women. *Journal of Clinical & Consulting Psychology, 65,* 834–847.

Kilpatrick, D. G., Resnick, H. S., Saunders, B. E., & Best, C. L. (1998). Victimization, post-traumatic stress disorder, and substance use and abuse among women. In C. L. Wetherington & A. B. Roman (Eds.), *Drug Addiction Research and the Health of Women* (NIH Publication No. 98–4290, pp. 285–307). Rockville, MD: U.S. Department of Health and Human Services.

Marlatt, G. A., Somers, J. M., & Tapert, S. F. (1993). *Harm Reduction: Application to Alcohol Abuse Problems.* NIDA Research Monograph, *137,* 147–166.

Marlatt, G. A., & Tapert, S. F. (1993). Harm reduction: Reducing the risks of addictive behaviors. In J. S. Baer, G. A. Marlatt, & R. McMahon (Eds.), *Addictive Behaviors Across the Lifespan* (pp. 243–273). Newbury Park, CA: Sage Publications.

Martin, S. L., Beaumont, J. L., & Kupper, L. L. (2003). Substance use before and during pregnancy: Links to intimate partner violence. *American Journal of Drug & Alcohol Abuse, 29,* 599–617.

McLellan, A. T., Kushner, H., Metzger, D., Peters, R., Smith, I., Grissom, G., et al. (1992). The fifth edition of the Addiction Severity Index. *Journal of Substance Abuse Treatment, 9,* 199–213.

Miller, J. B. (1991). The development of women's sense of self. In J. D. Jordan, A. G. Kaplan, J. B. Miller, I. P. Stiver, & J. L. Surrey (Eds.), *Women's Growth in Connection* (pp. 11–26). New York: Guilford Press.

Miller, W. R., & Rollnick, S., eds. (1991). *Motivational Interviewing: Preparing People to Change Addictive Behavior.* New York: Guilford Press.

Najavits, L. M., Weiss, R. D., & Shaw, S. R. (1997). The link between substance abuse and post-traumatic stress disorder in women. A research review. *American Journal of Addiction, 6,* 273–283.

Nelson, J., & Marshall, M. F. (1998). *Ethical and Legal Analyses of Three Coercive Policies Aimed at Substance Abuse by Pregnant Women.* Charleston, SC: The Robert Wood Johnson Foundation.

Nordahl, T. E., Salo, R., & Leamon, M. (2003). Neuropsychological effects of chronic methamphetamine use on neurotransmitters and cognition: A review. *Journal of Neuropsychiatry & Clinical Neuroscience, 15,* 17–25.

Orlinsky, D. E., Ronnestad, M. H., & Willutski, U. (2004). Fifty years of psychotherapy process-outcome research: Continuity and change. In M. J. Lambert (Ed.), *Handbook of Psychotherapy and Behaviour Change,* (5th ed., pp. 207–291). New York: John Wiley & Sons.

Paltrow, L. M., Cohen, D., & Carey, C. A. (2000). *Year 2000 Overview: Governmental Responses to Pregnant Women Who Use Alcohol or Other Drugs.* Philadelphia, PA: National Advocates for Pregnant Women of the Women's Law Project.

Pawl, J., & St. John, M. (1998). How you are is as important as what you do. In *Making a Positive Difference for Infants, Toddlers and Their Families*. Washington, DC: Zero to Three.

Pharis, M. E., & Levin, V. S. (1991). "A person to talk to who really cared": High-risk mothers' evaluations of services in an intensive intervention research program. *Child Welfare, 70*, 307–320.

Prochaska, J. O., & DiClemente, C. C. (1986). Toward a comprehensive model of change. In W. R. Miller, & N. Heather (Eds.), *Addictive Behaviors: Processes of Change* (pp. 3–27). New York: Plenum Press.

Rollnick, S., & Bell, A. (1991). Brief motivational interviewing for use by the nonspecialist. In W. R. Miller & S. Rollnick (Eds.), *Motivational Interviewing: Preparing People to Change Addictive Behavior* (pp. 203–213). New York: Guilford Press.

Ryan, J. P., Choi, S., Hong, J. S., Hernandez, P., & Larrison, C. R. (2008). Recovery coaches and substance exposed births: An experiment in child welfare. *Child Abuse & Neglect, 32*, 1072–1079.

Sadek, J. R., Vigil, O., Grant, I., & Heaton, R. K. (2007). The impact of neuropsychological functioning and depressed mood on functional complaints in HIV-1 infection and methamphetamine dependence. *Journal of Clinical Experimental Neuropsychology, 29*, 266–276.

Scott, J. C., Woods, S. P., Matt, G. E., Meyer, R. A., Heaton, R. K., Atkinson, J. H., et al. (2007). Neurocognitive effects of methamphetamine: A critical review and meta-analysis. *Neuropsychological Review, 17*, 275–297.

Sikma, S. K., & Barnard, K. E. (1992). Pilot test of a "nurse-client relationship inventory." Poster session presented at the NCAST Institute, Bellevue, Washington.

Suchman, N., Pajulo, M., DeCoste, C., & Mayes, L. (2006). Parenting interventions for drug-dependent mothers and their young children: The case for an attachment-based approach. *Family Relations, 55*, 211–226.

Surrey, J. (1991). The "self-in-relation": A theory of women's development. In A. Kaplan, J. B. Miller, I. Stiver, & J. L. Surrey (Eds.), *Women's Growth in Connection* (pp. 51–66). New York: Guilford Press.

van der Kolk, B. A. (2005). Developmental trauma disorder: Toward a rational diagnosis for children with complex trauma histories. *Psychiatric Annals, 35*, 401–408.

Vocci, F. J. (2008). Cognitive remediation in the treatment of stimulant abuse disorders: A research agenda. *Experimental Clinical Psychopharmacology, 16*, 484–497.

Will, G. F. (1999). Paying addicts not to have kids is a good thing. *Baltimore Sun*, November 1, p. 15A.

19 Interventions with Adolescent and Young Adult Mothers

JESSICA F. MAGIDSON,
JESSICA L. GARBER, AND
C. W. LEJUEZ

■ INTRODUCTION

Adolescent and young adult women who are pregnant or parenting are at high risk for a host of poor psychosocial outcomes, such as multiple pregnancies, parenting difficulties, disrupted mother–infant interactions, partner violence, and increased rates of psychological disorders (particularly depression), as well as being more likely to face poverty, receive welfare, and face residency instability (Garrett & Tidwell, 1999; Harden, Lynch, Turkheimer, Emery, D'Onofrio, Slutske, et al., 2007; Key, Gebregziabher, Marsh, & O'Rourke, 2008; Lindhorst & Oxford, 2007; Moran, Forbes, Evans, Tarabulsy, & Madigan, 2007; Oxford, Lee, & Lohr, 2010). Difficulties associated with these vulnerabilities are often further exacerbated by the adolescents' and young adults' life inexperience as it relates to their ability to manage responsibilities, such as difficulty managing finances and school responsibilities; indeed, adolescent mothers are less likely to complete high school, attend college, find stable employment, marry, or be self-supporting (Letourneau, Stewart, & Barnfather, 2004). Of particular relevance as a risk factor for poor outcomes is substance use in this population (DiClemente, Santelli, & Crosby, 2009). Adolescent, unmarried pregnant women with less than a high school education have been identified as a group at highest risk for frequent substance use (Ebrahim & Gfroerer, 2003). Although studies have suggested young adults typically "mature out" of substance use (Bachman, O'Malley, & Schulenberg, 2002), substance-using mothers who are in early and mid-adolescence typically continue to use into and following pregnancy; compared to a nationally representative sample of same-aged adolescent women who are not mothers, the prevalence of substance use has been found to be much higher among adolescent mothers (Gillmore, Gilchrist, Lee, & Oxford, 2006).

Substance use among adult mothers, as well as adolescent and young adult mothers, has been shown to be associated with a host of poor child outcomes, from lower birthweight and head circumference (Shankaran, Das, Bauer, Bada, Lester, & Wright, 2004) to infants' acoustic cry characteristics that reflect reactivity, respiratory, and neural control of the cry sound being compromised by prenatal substance use (Lester, Boukydis, & Tworney, 2002). Furthermore, pregnant adolescent and young adult mothers are already at the highest risk for infant mortality and low birthweight compared to all other maternal ages

(Mathews, Menacker, & MacDorman, 2003), and this risk is further exacerbated when the mothers are using substances, as maternal substance use among adult mothers has been shown to have detrimental effects on the mother–infant interaction (Goldman-Fraser, Harris-Britt, Thakkallapalli, Kurtz-Costes, & Martin, 2010).

Despite its high-risk status, the intersection of substance use and teen pregnancy has surprisingly received little research attention, and few empirically based treatment models have been developed to meet the unique needs of substance using adolescent and young adult mothers. Of particular concern is the lack of consideration of developmental context when delivering intervention programs, as targeting adolescent and young adult substance-using mothers' needs is distinct from those of adult populations. Unique factors that must be taken into consideration include social influences (i.e., in relation to peers and parents), demands to juggle personal responsibilities (i.e., related to continued schooling and financial pressures), and issues related to "dual-development" processes (i.e., teenage mothers themselves are in many ways still developing).

In order to address limitations in understanding the treatment needs of substance-using adolescent and young adult mothers and the scarcity of effective treatment approaches to meet these needs, this chapter aims to provide an overview of the specific vulnerabilities of this group, as well as a discussion of components of empirically supported interventions that may provide a potential framework to inform age-appropriate intervention development. The first section outlines specific developmental considerations unique to adolescent and young adult mothers. The second section presents a detailed overview of the very few treatment models designed for pregnant and/or parenting adolescents and young adults with substance use problems. Empirical evidence is presented where available, and particular attention is focused on the specific components of these intervention programs that are tailored specifically to the adolescent and young adult age group. In the final sections, recommendations are provided to guide future directions of work in this area, drawing from the evidence reviewed throughout the chapter, as well as components of integrated parenting and substance use interventions developed for adult mothers that may be useful for future application to younger mothers. Rather than implying that these interventions could be simply extended to the adolescent and young adult populations without modification, the adult interventions are reviewed through a developmental lens, and only components that match the specific vulnerabilities of adolescent and young adult substance using mothers are discussed.

■ ADOLESCENT AND YOUNG ADULT MOTHERS: DEVELOPMENTAL CONSIDERATIONS

Factors that influence parenting as an adolescent or young adult are often distinct from factors that adult mothers typically face, and these factors cut across numerous domains, including family factors, peer influences, and other forms of social support, as well as intra-individual factors related to one's own development, substance use, and psychological comorbidity (Roberts, Roberts, & Xing, 2007).

Stressors related to being a young mother, coping with one's own developmental issues, and the high rates of psychopathology found in this population contribute to high rates of substance use (Black, Nair, Kight, Waschtel, Roby, & Schuler, 1994; Huebner, 2002) which further increase the risk of poor parenting (Nair et al., 2003).

Social Context

Research has suggested the importance of considering the "social context" of adolescent and young adult parenting, given that, particularly for this group, parenting effectiveness is often challenged without appropriate social support (Luster, Bates, & Fitzgerald, 2000). Furthermore, it is also common for adolescent mothers to have a second child before the end of young adulthood; research has found that teenage mothers who have already given birth are five times more likely to have another child before age 20 than are other adolescent girls (Key, Gebregziabher, Marsh, & O'Rourke, 2008). Given that young, substance-using mothers are often single mothers with limited resources and more than one child, effects of social support are crucial in terms of managing multiple responsibilities (Gillmore et al., 2006). Limited psychosocial resources have been shown to be associated with an increased likelihood of harmful parenting practices and other risks to their child's development; however, these threats are often found to be "buffered" by a supportive social network, either family, partner, or professional support (Luster, Bates, & Fitzgerald, 2000; Schellenbach, Whitman, & Borkowski, 1992).

In addition to direct effects on parenting practices, positive social support has been shown to be related to the adolescent and young adult mother's well-being, which has clear implications for parenting abilities and child outcomes. Multiple sources of support (e.g., family, partner, friends) have been shown to decrease rates of depression as well as substance use among adolescent mothers, which in turn improves parent–infant interactions (Stewart, 1993; Stewart, 2000). Support in coping with the daily life of raising a child as a teenager may also reduce rates of relapse for the young mother, given the clearly documented link between stress, as well as parenting stress more specifically, and substance use (Sheinkopf, LaGasse, Lester, Liu, Seifer, Bauer, et al., 2006). Research has shown that specific parental stressors (e.g., infant crying, child deviant behaviors) could be a distinct type of stressor that leads mothers to have an increased desire to use substances (Lang, Pelham, Johnston, & Gelernter, 1989; Pelham, Lang, Atkeson, Murphy, Gnagy, Greiner, et al., 1997). Moreover, mothers who experience high levels of distress may be less effective at responding to their infant, thus worsening the effects of parental stress and further highlighting the importance of support for these young mothers in their daily lives (Sheinkopf et al., 2006).

Lastly, the social context has been shown to change following birth for adolescent and young adult mothers, such that having a baby may "convince" a young mother that she is now an "adult" and can be independent (Morrison, Spencer, & Gillmore, 1998). Thus, in weighing the role of the various forms of social support that may be present in the adolescent's network, it is crucial to consider how the adolescent may receive this support, and what effects this may have on parenting.

The following sections address specific types of social influences and how they may relate to young mothers' needs.

Family Factors

A clear distinction between adolescent/young adult and adult mothers is the role of family involvement. Although not specific to substance users, adolescent mothers tend to rely more on their family for support than do adult mothers. Support from family appears to reduce stress, engender a positive parent–child relationship for the adolescent mother and her child, and promote infant development (Collins, 2005; Logsdon, Birkimer, Ratterman, Cahill, & Cahill, 2001). The child's grandmother has been suggested to be a particularly important source of support for the adolescent mother (Gee & Rhodes, 2003; Dallas, 2004) and may have direct effects on the child's intellectual and linguistic development (Sommer, Whitman, & Borkowski, 2000).

However, it is crucial to note young mothers' "dual role" as both mother and child (Whitman, Borkowski, Keogh, & Weed, 2001; Sadler & Cowlin, 2003). Although adolescents may rate their mothers as the most helpful sources of child-related support, they also often report resentment towards this help; the support may foster a sense of identity confusion for adolescent mothers who are stuck in dual roles, simultaneously acting as a mother and as a child (Morrison, Spencer, & Gillmore, 1998). Conflict with the adolescent's mother may take away from her self-confidence in her parenting abilities and often results in mother–daughter conflict, which has also been shown to have a direct impact on the adolescent's child's functioning (East & Felice, 1996).

Peer Influence

Of particular relevance to adolescents is the role of peer influence. Compared to adults, adolescents are much more affected by peer pressure, peer attitudes and socialization, and peer substance use (DiClemente, Santelli, & Crosby, 2009). Peer substance-using networks are commonly cited as one of the strongest correlates of adolescent substance use (Bauman & Ennett, 1996; Kobus, 2003). However, pregnancy and parenting also force adolescents to alter their social network; adolescent friendships have been shown to change during the postpartum period, as the young mothers are forced to spend more time on childrearing than on social activities (Morrison, Spencer, & Gillmore, 1998). Adolescent mothers often report feeling less support from their peers as a result of inadequate day care services, high rates of school dropout, and increased financial pressures (Collins, 2005). Furthermore, this can contribute to increased substance use as a means to fit in by mimicking peer group use (Lundborg, 2006), or to cope with this distress (Englund, Egeland, Oliva, & Collins, 2008; Fergusson, Horwood, & Ridder, 2007; Shelton & Harold, 2008; Zucker, 2008). Although most pregnant substance-using adolescents stop or at least limit their substance use while pregnant, some do continue into pregnancy (Gillmore, Gilchrist, Lee, & Oxford, 2006). For this latter group, research indicates continued use may be associated with peer substance use as well as school dropout (Gillmore, Butler, Lohr, & Gilchrist, 1992; Haynie, Giordano, Manning, & Longmore, 2005; Spears et al., 2010). Similar factors also appear to influence re-initiation into substance use patterns after giving birth for those who limit their substance use during pregnancy (Gillmore et al., 2006).

Partner Support

In addition to peer influences, romantic partners in particular have been shown to have a significant effect on adolescent and young adult mothers' participation in substance use and other risky behaviors; the more involved the partner tends to be in substance use and risky behaviors, the stronger his influence on the mother (Amaro, Zuckerman, & Cabral, 1989; Spears et al., 2010). Compared to older mothers, adolescent mothers are often single mothers, reducing their likelihood of being involved in reciprocally supportive relationships (Neufeld & Harrison, 1995). In addition to supportive partners' providing resources to young mothers, being in a relationship with reciprocal interaction also may model for adolescents how to meet the demands of child interaction (Letourneau et al., 2004). However, for adolescent and young adult mothers, particularly those who use substances, it is even less likely that these populations will reap the benefits of being in a reciprocal, supportive relationship (Dormire, Strauss, & Clarke, 2006; Neufeld & Harrison, 1995). Indeed, scarce partner support following birth has been shown to be associated with anger and punitive maternal behavior towards the child (Crockenberg, 1987).

Community Support

Community support for childbearing needs is critical to enhance support from friends, family, and partners, particularly when support in these areas is lacking. Among adolescent mothers, professional support from healthcare professionals has been shown to be valued similarly to that of familial support (Burke & Liston, 1994), and was shown to be particularly beneficial when the professional support involved specific skill-building or further parenting education (Schinke, Barth, Maxwell, & Gilchrist, 1986). Although the availability of multiple forms of social support is important for this high-risk, vulnerable group of mothers, access to professional support, as well as appropriate healthcare services, may often be a challenge in this population. For instance, young, low-income substance-using mothers are at high risk for being uninsured at the beginning of their pregnancy; they are often excluded from private insurance agencies due to mental health and substance abuse issues, and Medicaid coverage may not be sufficient for their own as well as child's health care and mental health needs (Aday, 2001). Additionally, fear of stigma and legal implications of admitting to substance use may prevent pregnant, substance-using adolescents and young adults from seeking help in the first place (Fonseca, 2010), which highlights the importance of professionals in the community being sensitive and taking into account the safety of the young mother (Kaiser & Hays, 2005).

Perceived Social Norms

Beyond the practical, financial, and emotional support provided by family and professional support figures, numerous lines of research also suggest the importance of these forms of social support in determining social norms regarding substance use. Exposure to social norms regarding substance use, often dictated by messages delivered by family and professional support figures, has been shown to predict continued substance use and severity of use among adolescent and young adult mothers. Morrison and colleagues (1998) found that adolescent mothers' attitudes and perceived social norms regarding substance use became increasingly less unfavorable in this postpartum period. These attitudes were in line with the messages they were receiving from loved ones and health professionals who stressed the negative effects of substance use during pregnancy but did not continue to stress the negative impact of substance use in the postpartum period. In this way, perceived social norms can be a protective factor when they support positive parenting behaviors, including limiting one's substance use; however, in the same way, they can be a great detriment to those who are surrounded by norms that are less critical of substance use and problematic parenting practices, which may be a particular risk factor in the postpartum period (Morrison et al., 1998).

■ INDIVIDUAL RISK FACTORS AFFECTING PARENTING: "DUAL-DEVELOPMENT HYPOTHESIS"

Unique to adolescent and young adult mothers is the idea that developmental tasks of adolescence may conflict with the tasks of early parenthood; young mothers may face a "developmental crisis" that can lead to a lack of emotional availability to their children (Sadler & Cantrone, 1983). This developmental crisis may consist of identity diffusion, difficulties with trust, lower self-esteem, depressive symptoms, and being less likely to initiate verbal interaction with or show responsiveness to the child, which may all be associated with limited emotional availability and positive affect expressed to the child (Osofsky, Hann, & Peebles, 1993). Adolescent mothers in a developmental crisis are more likely to be punitive with discipline (Garcia-Coll, Vohr, Hoffman, & Oh, 1986), and furthermore, for substance-using mothers, this punitive parenting style may increase the likelihood of problematic conduct and control behaviors in their children (Kandel, 1990). Social support has been shown to help mitigate the effects of this "developmental crisis" on adolescent and young adult mothers' well-being and parenting practice by providing support and resources to make abusive patterns less likely and to promote positive parenting practices. However, this pervasive need for self-identity development remains a key obstacle in successful parenting for young mothers.

The importance of social support for adolescent mothers is particularly relevant when considering these mothers' need to balance their individual needs for treatment and other personal goals with parenting responsibilities. For instance, Fonseca (2010) interviewed adolescent mothers, many of whom were dealing with substance abuse issues, as they partook in a comprehensive, school-based intervention program in order to understand the challenges of adolescent substance-using mothers from both the adolescents' and treatment staff members' points of view. As a result, a few key themes emerged. The need for child care was particularly salient when adolescent mothers were considering their own treatment needs. For instance, adolescent, unwed mothers may not be able to enter into substance abuse treatment, particularly residential programs, if they do not have a familial support network that may be able to take care of the child, often citing the fear of losing their child to child protective services (CPS) as the main concern. Similarly, young mothers without appropriate social support had difficulty juggling parenting with the demands of school, which has clear implications for long-term outcomes of both the young mother and her child. Yet, substance using mothers also reported a renewed interest in returning or completing school after giving birth, as well as other more concrete goals and aspirations for the future compared to pre-pregnancy. Although giving birth may inspire a desire for longer-term changes, young mothers are in a difficult position in having to balance caring for themselves and their own identity development with the need to care for their child. Underlining the importance of social support as delineated in the previous section, without child care or family support to care for the child, the young mother is unable to follow through on her own aspirations and self-development (Fonseca, 2010).

Severity of Substance Use

As indicated in the previous section, some adolescent and young adult mothers may fully desist from substance use upon pregnancy, yet many resume substance use in the postpartum period. Morrison and colleagues (1998) examined substance use, as well as cognitions related to use, among a large sample of pregnant and parenting adolescents from pregnancy to 12 months postpartum. Their findings demonstrated that adolescent mothers tended to reduce rates of substance use during pregnancy; however, they often reinitiated and increased use substantially by six months postpartum and then leveled off to rates similar to pre-pregnancy by 12 months postpartum. Common predictors of greater resumption and/or greater level of substance use included greater history of use before pregnancy, depressive symptoms, partner substance use, childhood abuse, and a longer time period since the child's birth (Morrison et al., 1998; Spears et al., 2010).

Continued use and severity of substance use among teen mothers have numerous implications for the effectiveness of their parenting practices. Particularly among younger, inexperienced mothers, substance users are more likely to provide inappropriate developmental support to meet their child's needs (Spieker et al., 2001). Severity of the mother's substance use, as well as associated stress and health issues, contribute to the quality of her parenting practices and beliefs about parenting, which have direct effects on the mother–infant interaction. Substance using mothers have been shown to be less sensitive and more likely to demonstrate subtly hostile behaviors when interacting with their infants compared with non-substance using mothers (Spieker et al., 2001), and this is a particular risk factor for younger mothers. Adolescent mothers, specifically those who experience rejection and low social support, have also been shown to be more likely to exhibit angry and punitive parenting (Crockenberg, 1987). Compounded by the pharmacological effects of substance use, studies have found a range of negative characteristics common among substance using mothers—ranging from memory and attention deficits, to aggression, impulsivity, depression, and unpredictable behavior—each having the potential to greatly interfere with parenting capability (Clark, Robbins, Ersche, & Sahakian, 2006; Indlekofer, Piechatzek, Daamen, Glasmacher, Lieb, & Pfister et al., 2009; Lori, Akihito, Jason, & Frazier, 2008).

Comorbid Psychopathology

Rates of comorbid psychopathology are high among adolescent mothers (Cassidy, Zoccolillo, & Hughes, 1996), particularly those with substance use problems (Quinlivan, Box, & Evans, 2003). One of the most common comorbid conditions in this population that also has significant effects on parenting is major depressive disorder (MDD). Studies have reported over 50% of substance using teenage mothers experience clinically elevated rates of depression, and these mothers demonstrate less spontaneous, cheerful, proximal, and reciprocal interactions with their infants (Field et al., 1998). Substance use and depression have been shown to have synergistic negative effects on the mother–child interaction and are associated with significant social, emotional, and cognitive deficits for their children (Field et al., 1998). Beyond direct effects on parenting, both depression and substance abuse put children at increased risk for other risk factors, such as exposure to violence, academic problems, and early sexual risk activity and risk-taking (Spears et al., 2010). Adolescent mothers who are younger (16 and under) and those who are depressed represent two high-risk groups who are less responsive and stimulating to their infants and respond poorly to intervention (Letourneau et al., 2004).

Knowledge of Child Development

Lack of experience with parenting practices and knowledge of child developmental progression has been identified as one of the greatest challenges for young substance-using mothers (Fonseca, 2010; Spieker et al., 2001). Adolescent and young adult substance-using mothers have been shown to have unrealistic development expectations about their child's behavior (Spieker et al., 2001) and also have less knowledge of child's developmental milestones (Letourneau et al., 2004). This suggests that young substance-using mothers are often not well prepared or educated in terms of knowledge and expectations about child development, and further education on parenting and basic child developmental processes is needed (Letourneau et al., 2004; Spieker et al., 2001). The mismatch between maternal expectations and realistic child development has been shown to lead adolescent mothers to form negative attributions towards their child as well as themselves as mothers, particularly when comorbid substance use is present (Spieker et al., 2001).

Parenting Distress

Substance using mothers more generally exhibit higher levels of parenting distress than non-substance-using mothers (Sheinkopf et al., 2006), and adolescent mothers, who often have less parental knowledge and even fewer support resources than adult mothers, are even more likely to exhibit high levels of parenting distress (Mollborn & Morningstar, 2009). Teenage and substance-using mothers, representing the intersection of both high-risk groups, may be most vulnerable to experiencing parenting-related distress. Parenting-related distress has been found to explain a significant degree of maladaptive parenting practices among high-risk substance-using adult mothers (Suchman & Luthar, 2001) and is also highly relevant for adolescent mothers who commonly have to juggle multiple responsibilities and also have a less mature understanding of how to effectively cope with distress (Golder, Gillmore, Spieker, & Morrison, 2005).

There are numerous factors that may contribute to the increased parenting stress among substance using mothers, stemming both from actual infant cues as well as mothers' maladaptive cognitions related to child cues. Cocaine-exposed infants often demonstrate increased reactivity compared with non-cocaine-exposed infants (Lester et al., 2002), and these behaviors (e.g., excessive crying, irritability, jitteriness, tone abnormalities, and attention problems) can be considered particularly distressing to mothers (Papousek & von Hofacker, 1998; Porter & Porter, 2004; Nair et al., 2003; Singer et al., 2000). In addition to visible or audible cues that may trigger stress in a parent, an absence of certain cues in cocaine-exposed infants (e.g., times of lethargy, unresponsiveness, lack of enjoyment during play) can also lead to increased frustration and guilt in mothers (Porter & Porter, 2004; Nair et al., 2003; Bendersky & Lewis, 1998). Postnatal effects of drug exposure interfere with an infant's ability to send healthy, positive cues to the mother that normally define the mother–infant attachment, thus feeding the guilt and decreased parenting confidence experienced by substance using mothers (Porter & Porter, 2004; Suchman & Luthar, 2001). Mothers also experience stress from cues related to premature birth characteristics (e.g., low birthweight or irritability) and these often foster maternal cognitions of failure, inadequacy, or guilt (Suchman & Luthar, 2001). Younger mothers may be even more vulnerable to these patterns, given the overall tendency to have lower levels of parenting knowledge, understanding of infant cues, and parenting confidence (Ryan-Krause, Meadows-Oliver, Sadler, & Swarts, 2008; Osofsky, Hann, & Peebles, 1993).

Substance using mothers have reported guilt and shame, not only about the biological consequences of their substance abuse, but also the concomitant lifestyle—often filled with violence and abuse brought on by drug involvement—that their children may face (Suchman & Luthar, 2001; Baker & Carson, 1999), which is often coupled with low rates of school completion and employment among teenage mothers (Hoffman & Maynard, 2008; Bradley, Cupples, & Irvine, 2002). The cognitions of fear, shame, guilt, and frustration associated with parenting for substance using mothers have serious implications, as they are often cited as reasons to not seek external help or resources (Pajulo, Savonlahti, & Sourander, 2001; Suchman & Luthar, 2001; Davis, 1990) and have also been associated with increased parenting stress, depression, hopelessness, and low self-esteem (Porter & Porter, 2004; Kettinger, Nair, & Schuler, 2000).

■ EXISTING TREATMENT APPROACHES

Despite the numerous individual and environmental risk factors facing substance-using adolescent and young adult mothers, there has been surprisingly scarce research attention paid to treatment approaches for this population, particularly those that simultaneously address parenting and substance use. This section outlines the very few interventions that were identified that address both concerns. Given the lack of research specific to this area, the following section also discusses characteristics of successful parenting interventions for adult substance-using mothers that have components that may hold promise for adolescent mothers. Although these components may not be developmentally informed initially, they may be useful starting points to guide future intervention development and to consider which components may be most applicable to the adolescent developmental context.

Integrated Interventions That Address Both Parenting and Substance Use Among Adolescent and Young Adult Mothers

Multicomponent Intervention for Teen Mothers and Their Infants

As one of the few interventions specifically targeting parenting and substance use among adolescent mothers, Field and colleagues (1998) developed an intervention that took place at a vocational school: the intervention was a four-month program that integrated substance abuse treatment, parenting classes, job training, and schooling for poly-substance-using adolescent mothers with infant children. Day care was also provided for infants during schooling. The drug and social rehab program consisted of psychoeducation, frequent urine monitoring, group therapy, Narcotics Anonymous or Alcoholics Anonymous (NA, AA) groups, as well as individual substance-abuse counseling. Individualized treatment plans were developed for each participant based on their substance abuse history, and psychiatric, educational, and vocational evaluations. Psycho-educational material consisted of subjects related to theories of addiction, medical complications, family relationships, male–female interactions, interpersonal and communication skills, assertiveness training, HIV/AIDS and sexually transmitted disease (STD) risk education, spirituality, accessing health care, social and vocational services, as well as additional information on 12-Step programs. The group therapy portion of the intervention focused on themes related to patterns of a substance using lifestyle, such as breaking down denial of substance use, teaching effective problem-solving and coping skills, and focusing on the 12-Step philosophy. Social rehabilitation was conducted two hours per week and addressed problems with daily living, social support, school, parenting, and interpersonal relationships; members of one's support network, such as parents, boyfriends, and friends, were encouraged to attend this aspect of the intervention. Regarding the vocational aspect of the program, mothers had to agree to complete high school or a General Educational Development certificate (GED) in order to participate in program. Mothers attended classes in the morning and received educational counseling. For vocational help, mothers were provided with job counseling, referrals for job training, assistance with placement in vocational training programs, and assistance in finding stable living arrangements and affordable day care at the end of the program.

Although somewhat separate from the substance abuse treatment and vocational and educational rehabilitation, mothers also attended parenting classes two hours per week. The classes were designed to provide education on developmental milestones, child-rearing practices, and exercises for age-appropriate sensorimotor/cognitive development, and to facilitate mother–infant interactions. Infants were in the nursery school day care program while mothers were in school for the majority of the intervention, but mothers also spent one to two hours per day in the nursery school helping, in order to learn how to care for the infants. The nursery was staffed by a head teacher, two teaching assistants, and three mothers, who each served time as teacher-aid trainees. Lastly (having positive implications for both parenting abilities and substance abuse recovery), mothers were also involved in relaxation therapy, which included aerobics, progressive muscle relaxation, music mood-induction, and massage therapy—all techniques that have been previously shown to reduce anxiety, depression, and cortisol reactivity in adolescent psychiatric patients.

Field et al. (1998) examined outcomes among 126 substance using mothers (16–21 years of age) receiving the intervention program compared to a group of non-substance-using adolescent and young adult mothers who participated in the intervention program and a group of substance-using control mothers who did not participate in the program. Mothers of all three groups were similar across the variables of age, education, socioeconomic status, and ethnicity. Six months after participating in the intervention, results demonstrated a differential effect of treatment on numerous positive outcomes related to the mothers' well-being. For instance, by six months, levels of self-reported depressive symptoms in the substance-using mothers' group receiving the intervention approached levels reported by non-substance-using mothers and fell below levels reported by the substance using mothers in the control group. Following participation in the intervention, the substance using adolescent mothers demonstrated lower rates of repeat pregnancy and lower rates of substance use compared to the no-treatment substance using controls. There were also positive effects on education and vocational outcomes: mothers in the program were more likely to receive their high school diploma and obtain employment.

Similar positive effects of treatment were documented for mother–infant interactions and infant outcomes. Mother–infant interactions were videotaped during feeding at the newborn period and during play when infants were three and six months old. The substance using mothers in the intervention demonstrated significant improvements in their coded interactions by three months post-intervention, and by six months, the interactions resembled those of the non-substance-using comparison condition. Regarding infant outcomes, the intervention group's infants demonstrated positive effects on infants' head circumference, developmental complexity of early infant interactions (measured by the Early Social Communication Scales; Seibert & Hogan, 1982; Seibert, Hogan, & Mundy, 1987), and infant mental status development measured using the Mental Status Scale of the Bayley Scales of Infant Development (Bayley, 1969). At 12 months following the intervention, the infants of the adolescent substance-using mothers receiving the intervention had improved Early Social Communication Scales scores and Bayley Mental Scale scores, significantly greater head circumference, and fewer pediatric complications, compared to the substance-using control group.

The intervention program developed by Field and colleagues has numerous strengths, notably its comprehensiveness through addressing education, job training, parenting, substance abuse treatment, social support, and overall mental health and well-being. The techniques are largely derived from empirically supported research and incorporate a developmental perspective; the components are focused on the unique needs of an adolescent/young adult population (ages 16–21). For instance, particular emphasis is placed on school and vocational needs, social rehabilitation and support necessary for adolescents, and relaxation techniques with empirical support specifically in an adolescent population. Parent training focused on basic education that is often deficient in young mothers (e.g., knowledge of developmental milestones).

This intervention program appears to be the most clearly documented integrated approach for substance use and parenting developed specifically for this age group (Field et al., 1998). Meanwhile, it is also important to acknowledge some limitations, such as the potential implications for generalizability and dissemination given the time- and resource-intensive nature of the program. Future research is needed to replicate these findings, to compare the intervention to a closer comparison treatment, as well as to begin to tease apart which components of the multifaceted intervention are the most necessary.

Suchman and colleagues (2006) emphasized in a review of parenting interventions for predominantly adult substance-dependent mothers that the intervention evaluated in Field et al. (1998) demonstrated sustained effects on parent–child interactions—effects that were not found in the other interventions evaluated in the review. Suchman and colleagues suggested that the unique components of the Field intervention that may explain these sustained outcomes include an emphasis on reciprocity, mutual regulation, and harmony in the mother–infant interactions, as the intervention included a significant focus on recognizing infant cues and coaching mothers' sensitive, contingent responses. Suchman and colleagues suggested that "mutual regulatory processes in the mother–child dyad" may be "critical mechanisms" to target in parenting interventions for substance abusing mothers. This may be a particular vulnerability for adolescent mothers, as adolescence is a critical period for the developmental of key brain regions associated with emotion and behavior regulation; furthermore, heightened changes in emotion and arousal associated with puberty may precede full development of these regions, thereby creating a "disjunction" between regulatory abilities and heightened emotional states (Steinberg, 2005), potentially impacting mutual regulatory processes relevant to the mother–child dyad.

Parenting Enhancement Program

One intervention that was developed initially for adult substance-using mothers but has also been evaluated among unwed adolescent mothers (who were not substance users) is Porter's Parenting Enhancement Program (PEP), a program aimed at improving parenting skills and knowledge about infant health, developmental milestones, and safety issues, as well as self-care and relaxation (Porter & Porter, 2004). Studies have adapted PEP for pregnant teens and unwed adolescent mothers, and showed positive effects on maternal and infant health outcomes (Porter & Knicely, 1985). Studies have also evaluated a PEP intervention that combines infant massage, the Blended Infant Massage–Parenting Enhancement Program (IMPEP), and this has been piloted in an adolescent/young adult population. Porter, Bongo-Sanchez, and Kissel (1996) recruited 19 substance-using mothers from a hospital-based Maternal Addiction Program; their sample ranged in age from 14 to 20 years. Half of their sample was assigned to an IMPEP condition (four weekly sessions), and half was assigned to a control condition. The intervention showed perfect treatment retention, which is noteworthy given the high levels of treatment resistance and dropout in this population. Although it was a small sample and results were not statistically significant, the authors argued there was sufficient support to suggest further exploring the gains in attachment-related outcomes, including improved eye contact, more interaction, and active interest in learning more about developmental considerations for parenting.

While the pilot results proved promising, future work is clearly needed to build on an IMPEP intervention for adolescent mothers, specifically those who also are substance users. Research seems only to have continued to build on the efficacy of the IMPEP intervention delivered in adult populations, and interestingly, little differentiation seems to have been made when applying IMPEP to adults versus adolescents. It is unclear whether and how the intervention was modified based on developmental needs of adult versus young adult populations.

■ RECOMMENDATIONS AND FUTURE DIRECTIONS BASED ON PREVIOUS RESEARCH

Numerous studies have pointed to the need to develop interventions for substance using adolescents who are parenting (Morrison et al., 1998; Spears et al., 2010); however, this is a difficult endeavor with a clear need for continued research. This final section outlines recommendations for future intervention-development efforts based on knowledge of both the developmental needs of adolescent substance-using mothers, as outlined above, and on empirically supported interventions that have been evaluated among adult substance-using mothers that have components that may also hold promise for younger mothers. Rather than implying that interventions for adult substance-using mothers could simply be extended to adolescents, which would neglect important developmental considerations, this section focuses on the pieces of available interventions that may best fit the needs of adolescent and young adult mothers described in the previous sections.

Targeting Beliefs Related to Substance Use and Parenting

Given that substance use has consistently been shown to decrease during pregnancy, albeit it often resumes in the postpartum period, researchers have suggested that a desire to protect the baby's health may be a key motivation for reducing substance use during the postpartum period. This is further supported by the fact that adolescents have been shown to respond to clear messages they receive from family and professional support regarding the negative effects on child outcomes of the mother's substance use while pregnant. Researchers have suggested that effective intervention programs may be able to capitalize on these messages in later stages of parenting: efforts must continue to focus on addressing adolescent mothers' beliefs related to how their substance use can also harm the baby in later developmental periods and on the effects of substance use on parent–child interactions and parenting abilities (Morrison et al., 1998). Also related to addressing cognitions and beliefs related to substance use during pregnancy and in the postpartum period, interventions can focus on building relationships with others who are also parenting, which may increase support for resisting substance use during the postpartum period (Morrison et al., 1998). Although research has suggested that cognitive interventions that involve other young substance-using adolescent mothers may be promising, it remains unclear the degree to which these directions have been pursued in intervention-development efforts.

Incorporating Family Involvement

Although not specific to substance using mothers, research has demonstrated that successful parenting interventions with adolescent mothers require family involvement. Family involvement may be incorporated through support groups on how to improve relations with family, as well as interventions that include family members taking part in the treatment process. In this context, educators would work with the mother and family to improve their relations and demonstrate how the young mother can best be supported by family (DiClemente et al., 2009). When a young mother lacks family support or resources, interventions must find ways to creatively incorporate extended family or other means of social support (Letourneau, 2004). Partner-specific support may also play an important role, particularly in relation to the mother's overall well-being, which has key implications for the implementation of effective parenting practices (Gee & Rhodes, 2003). Family and partner involvement may also be crucial in order to allow for young mothers' engagement and entry into the program itself, as daily responsibilities related to school, child care, and access to financial resources may be factors that preclude mothers' ability to participate in intervention programs. However, the incorporation of family into treatment efforts needs to be conveyed to the adolescent in light of her own perception of her developmental stage, as she may view herself as an independent mother not in need of the support of others. In sum, although familial support during parenting has been consistently demonstrated to be important and predictive of better outcomes, this help may not be wholly welcomed, and the indirect conflict and arguments that often result may also be important predictors of adolescent and young adult mothers' parenting confidence and subsequent effects on child outcomes.

Reducing Psychological Barriers to Treatment

A unique challenge to treatment efforts directed at adolescent substance-using mothers is engagement in treatment. Adolescents may perceive intervention efforts as "competing" with peer influences; during a developmental period in which peer influence tends to be most salient, an intervention program must incorporate efforts to address any ambivalence toward change. The Seattle "Birth to Three" program (Ernst, Grant, Streissguth, & Sampson, 1999), although developed for adult populations (mean age = 27 years old), may provide useful strategies to incorporate in an adolescent-focused program. This approach incorporated Motivational Enhancement strategies (Miller & Rollnick, 2002) specifically to target treatment engagement. The approach directly acknowledges maternal ambivalence toward change in substance use and parenting responsibility. Although in the ideal situation an intervention could effectively target ambivalence toward substance use, many adolescents may not be at a stage in which they are ready to change. Moreover, the stigma of being a young, substance-using mother has been reported as a barrier to entry into an integrated substance-use and parenting program (Fonseca, 2010). Efforts targeted at increasing entry into treatment programs must not only incorporate reduction in practical barriers to attendance in intervention programs, but also address the psychological barriers. Research involving adult substance-using mothers has suggested that first engaging an individual in a parenting intervention may also show reductions in substance use behaviors. For example, Suchman and her colleagues (2006) pinpointed reductions in substance use following parenting interventions alone, even when substance-abuse treatment was not a requirement or core focus of the intervention. This is in line with previous theories showing that psycho-education in parenting interventions may also reduce maternal substance use and other maladaptive behaviors by encouraging young mothers to consider how their behavior is harmful to their children, their families, and themselves (Moore & Finkelstein, 2001). Thus, even when comprehensive substance abuse treatment is not available, feasible, or tolerable for adolescent and young adult mothers, openly discussing substance use and other behaviors as they relate to parenting may have positive effects in reducing rates of substance use (Suchman et al., 2006).

Addressing Affect Regulation

An attachment-based approach as a parenting intervention for substance using mothers stresses the importance of accurate perception of and sensitive response to infant emotional cues, as well as the link between misattribution of one's own affective states and insensitive or intrusive parental responding (Suchman et al., 2006). The focus on awareness of affective states, and regulation of these states in particular, has clear relevance to adolescent substance-using mothers, as adolescence is a developmental period in which the "disjunction" between full regulatory capacity and heightened affect during puberty creates a "situation in which one is starting an engine without yet having a skilled driver behind the wheel" (Dahl, 2001; Steinberg, 2005, p. 70). Although an attachment-based framework holds promise, given the heightened vulnerabilities related to affective awareness and regulation in adolescence, continued research is still needed to develop and test an attachment-based intervention tailored to the needs of young substance-using mothers. Preliminary work modifying an attachment-based intervention for adolescent mothers emphasized a particular need to establish rapport with and gain trust from adolescent mothers, to reduce barriers to treatment (e.g., using a home-visiting program; not referring to treatment as an "intervention" or "therapy"), and to carefully consider other factors that may impact the effectiveness of attachment-based interventions, such as a maternal history of trauma or unresolved attachment status (Moran, Pederson, & Krupka, 2005). Future work in this area may consider other developmental modifications to attachment-based interventions, including emphasizing the roles of social influences and dual-developmental processes in contributing to affective distress, as well as a particular focus on strategies to improve self-regulation.

■ CONCLUSIONS

There are clear ways intervention programs can target the specific needs of adolescent and young adult substance-using mothers, incorporating both the powerful social influences on treatment entry and success, as well as the need to balance personal needs and goals related to continued schooling and independence. Intervention programs must focus not only on effective parenting practices, but also on the adolescents' own developmental issues related to self-esteem, identity formation, emotion regulation, relationships, and personal goals as they also may relate to parenting, substance use, and child outcomes. Effective programs must simultaneously address the needs of the developing adolescent together with components of both effective substance use treatment and parenting interventions. However, future research cannot simply extend findings from adults to adolescent and young adult mothers. Rather, a thoughtful consideration of the unique developmental context of adolescence and young adulthood is necessary.

■ REFERENCES

Aday, L. (2001). *At Risk in America.* San Francisco: Jossey-Bass.

Amaro, H., Zuckerman, B., & Cabral, H. (1989). Patterns and prevalence of drug use among adolescent mothers: a profile of risk. *Pediatrics, 84*(1), 144–151.

Bachman, J. G., O'Malley, P. M., & Schulenberg, J. E. (2002). *The Decline of Substance Use in Young Adulthood: Changes in Social Activities, Roles, and Beliefs.* Mahwah, NJ: Lawrence Erlbaum Associates.

Baker, P. L., & Carson, A. (1999). "I take care of my kids": Mothering practices of substance-abusing women. *Gender & Society, 13*(3), 347–363.

Bauman, K. E., & Ennett, S. T. (1996). On the importance of peer influence for adolescent drug use: Commonly neglected considerations. *Addiction, 91*, 185–198.

Bayley, N. (1969). *Manual for the Bayley Scales of Infant Development.* San Antonio, TX: The Psychological Corporation.

Bendersky, M., & Lewis, M. (1998). Prenatal cocaine exposure and impulse control at two years. *Annals of the New York Academy of Sciences, 846*, 365–367.

Black. M., Nair, P., Kight, C., Waschtel, R., Roby, P., & Schuler, M. (1994). Parenting and early development among children of drug-abusing women: Effects of home intervention. *Pediatrics, 94*, 440–448.

Bradley, T., Cupples, M. E., Irvine, H. (2002). A case control study of a deprivation triangle: Teenage motherhood, poor educational achievement and unemployment. *International Journal of Adolescent Medical Health, 14*, 117–123.

Burke, P. J., & Liston, W. J. (1994). Adolescent mothers' perceptions of social support and the impact of parenting on their lives. *Pediatric Nursing, 20*(6), 593.

Cassidy, B., Zoccolillo, M., & Hughes, S. (1996). Psychopathology in adolescent mothers and its effects on mother–infant interactions: A pilot study. *Canadian Journal of Psychiatry, 41*, 379–384.

Clark, L., Robbins, T. W., Ersche, K. D., & Sahakian, B. J. (2006). Reflection impulsivity in current and former substance users. *Biological Psychiatry, 60*(5), 515–522.

Collins, B. (2005). Missing Voices: Teenage Pregnancy and Social Policy. Thesis submitted to Victoria University of Wellington in fulfillment of the requirements for the degree of Doctor of Philosophy in Social Policy.

Crockenberg, S. (1987). Predictors and correlates of anger toward and punitive control of toddlers by adolescent mothers. *Child Development, 58*(4), 964–975.

Dahl, R. E. (2001). Affect regulation, brain development, and behavioral/emotional health in adolescence. *Central Nervous System Spectrums, 6*, 1–12.

Dallas, C. (2004). Family matters: How mothers of adolescent parents experience adolescent pregnancy and parenting. *Public Health Nursing, 21*, 347–353.

Davis, S. K. (1990). Chemical dependency in women: A description of its effects and outcome on adequate parenting. *Journal of Substance Abuse Treatment, 7*, 225–232.

DiClemente, R. J., Santelli, J. S., & Crosby, R. A. (Eds.). (2009). *Adolescent Health: Understanding and Preventing Risk Behaviors.* San Francisco: Jossey-Bass.

Dormire, S. L., Strauss, S. S., & Clarke, B. A. (2006). Social support and adaptation to the parent role in first-time adolescent mothers. *Journal of Obstetric, Gynecologic, & Neonatal Nursing, 18*(4), 327–337.

East, P. L., & Felice, M. E. (1996). Outcomes and parent–child relationships of former adolescent mothers and their 12-year-old children. *Journal of Developmental Behavior Pediatrics, 11*, 175–183.

Ebrahim, S. H., & Gfroerer, J. (2003). Pregnancy-related substance use in the United States during 1996–1998 *Obstetrics & Gynecology, 101*, 374–379.

Englund, M. M., Egeland, B., Oliva, E. M., Collins, W. A. (2008). Childhood and adolescent predictors of heavy drinking and alcohol use disorders in early adulthood: A longitudinal developmental analysis. *Addiction, 103*, 23–35.

Ernst, C. C., Grant, T. M., Streissguth, A. P., & Sampson, P. D. (1999). Intervention with high-risk alcohol and drug-abusing mothers: Three-year findings from the Seattle Model of Paraprofessional Advocacy. *Journal of Community Psychology, 27*, 19–38.

Fergusson, D. M., Horwood, L. J., & Ridder, E. M. (2007). Conduct and attentional problems in childhood and adolescence and later substance use, abuse and dependence: Results of a 25-year longitudinal study. *Drug & Alcohol Dependency, 88*, 14–26.

Field, T. M., Scafidi, J., Pickens, J., Prodromidis, M., Pelaez-Nogueras, M., Torquati, J., et al. (1998). Polydrug-using adolescent mothers and their infants receiving early intervention. *Adolescence, 33*(129), 117–143.

Fonseca, S. (2010). An analysis of discourses within the context of school-linked integrated services for pregnant and parenting young women (Doctoral dissertation, University of Ottawa).

Garcia-Coll, C., Vohr, B., Hoffman, J., & Oh, W. (1986). Maternal and environmental factors affecting developmental outcome of infants of adolescent mothers. *Journal of Developmental Behavioral Pediatrics, 7*, 230–236.

Garrett, S., & Tidwell, R. (1999). Differences between adolescent mothers and non-mothers: An interview study. *Adolescence, 34*, 91–105.

Gee, C. B. & Rhodes, J. E. (2003). Adolescent mothers' relationship with their children's biological fathers: Social support, social strain, and relationship continuity. *Journal of Family Psychology, 17*, 370–383.

Gillmore, M. R., Butler, S. S., Lohr, M. J., & Gilchrist, L. (1992). Substance use and other factors associated with risky sexual behavior among pregnant adolescents. *Family Planning Perspective, 24*, 255–26.

Gillmore, M. R., Gilchrist, L., Lee, J., & Oxford, M. L. (2006). Women who gave birth as unmarried adolescents: Trends in substance use from adolescence to adulthood. *Journal of Adolescent Health, 39*, 237–243.

Golder, S., Gillmore-Rogers, M., Spieker, S., & Morrison, D. (2005). Substance use, related problem behaviors and adult attachment in a sample of high-risk older adolescent women. *Journal of Child & Family Studies, 14(2),* 181–193.

Goldman-Fraser, J., Harris-Britt, A., Thakkallapalli, E. L., Kurtz-Costes, B., & Martin, S. (2010). Emotional availability and psychosocial correlates among mothers in substance-abuse treatment and their young infants. *Infant Mental Health Journal, 31*, 1–15.

Harden, K. P., Lynch, S. K., Turkheimer, E., Emery, R. E., D'Onofrio, B. M., Slutske, W. S., et al. (2007). A behavior genetic investigation of adolescent motherhood and offspring mental health problems. *Journal of Abnormal Psychology, 116(4)*, 667–683.

Hoffman, S. D., & Maynard, R. A. (Eds.) (2008). *Kids Having Kids: Economic Costs and Social Consequences of Teen Pregnancy.* Washington, DC: Urban Institute Press.

Huebner, C. E. (2002). Evaluation of a clinic-based parent education program to reduce the risk of infant and toddler maltreatment. *Public Health Nursing, 19*, 377–389.

Indlekofer, F., Piechatzek, M., Daamen, M., Glasmacher, C., Lieb, R., & Pfister, H., et al. (2009). Reduced memory and attention performance in a population-based sample of young adults with a moderate lifetime use of cannabis, Ecstasy and alcohol. *Journal of Psychopharmacology, 23(5)*, 495–509.

Kaiser, M. M., & Hays, B. J. (2005). Health-risk behaviours in a sample of first-time pregnant adolescents. *Public Health Nursing, 22(6)*, 483–493.

Kandel, D. B. (1990). Parenting styles, drug use, and children's adjustment in families of young adults. *Journal of Marriage & Family, 52*(1), 183–196.

Key, J. D., Gebregziabher, M. G., Marsh, L. D., & O'Rourke, K. M. (2008). Effectiveness of an intensive, school-based intervention for teen mothers. *Journal of Adolescent Health, 42*, 394–400.

Kobus, K. (2003). Peers and adolescent smoking. *Addiction, 98*, 37–55.

Lang, A., Pelham, W., Johnston, C., & Gelernter, S. (1989). Levels of adult alcohol consumption Induced by interactions with child confederates exhibiting normal versus externalizing behaviors. *Journal of Abnormal Psychology, 98*, 294–299.

Lester, B. M., Boukydis, C. F. Z., & Tworney, J. E. (2002). Maternal substance abuse and child outcome. In C. H. Zeanah, Jr. (Ed.), *Handbook of Infant Mental Health* (2nd ed., pp. 161–175). New York: Guilford Press.

Letourneau, N. L., Stewart, M. J., & Barnfather, A. K. (2004). Adolescent mothers: Support needs, resources, and support-education interventions. *Journal of Adolescent Health, 35,* 509–525.

Lindhorst, T., & Oxford, M. (2007). The long-term effects of intimate partner violence on adolescent mothers' depressive symptoms. *Social Science & Medicine, 66*(6), 1322–1333.

Logsdon, M. C., Birkimer, J. C., Ratterman, A., Cahill, K., & Cahill, N. (2001). Social support in pregnant and parenting adolescents: Research, critique, and recommendations. *Journal of Child & Adolescent Psychiatric Nursing, 15*(2), 75–83.

Lori, D., Akihito, U., Jason, M. N., & Frazier, E. (2008). Major depression and comorbid substance use disorders. *Current Opinion in Psychiatry, 21*(1), 14–18.

Lundborg, P. (2006). Having the wrong friends? Peer effects in adolescent substance use. *Journal of Health Economics, 25*(2), 214–233.

Luster, T., Bates, L., & Fitzgerald H. (2000). Factors related to successful outcomes among preschool children born to low-income adolescent mothers. *Journal of Marriage & Family, 62,* 133–146.

Mathews, T. J., Menacker, F., & MacDorman, M. F. (2003). Infant mortality statistics from the 2001 period linked birth/infant death data set. *National Vital Statistics Report, 52*(2), 1–28.

Miller, W. R., & Rollnick, S. P. (2002). *Motivational Interviewing: Preparing People for Change.* New York: Guilford.

Mollborn, S., & Morningstar, E. (2009). Investigating the relationship between teenage childbearing and psychological distress using longitudinal evidence. *Journal of Health & Social Behavior, 50*(3), 310–326.

Moore, J., & Finkelstein, N. (2001). Parenting services for families affected by substance abuse. *Child Welfare, 80,* 221–238.

Moran, G., Forbes, L., Evans, E., Tarabulsy, G. M., & Madigan, S. (2007). Both maternal sensitivity and atypical maternal behavior independently predict attachment security and disorganization in adolescent mother–infant relationships. *Infant Behavior & Development, 31*(2), 321–325.

Moran, G., Pederson, D. R., & Krupka, A. (2005). Maternal unresolved attachment status impedes the effectiveness of interventions with adolescent mothers. *Infant Mental Health Journal, 26,* 231–249.

Morrison, D. M., Spencer, M. S., & Gillmore, M. R. (1998). Beliefs about substance use among pregnant and parenting adolescents. *Journal of Research on Adolescence, 8,* 69–95.

Nair, P., Schuler, M. E., Black, M. M., Kettinger, L., & Harrington, D. (2003). Cumulative environmental risk in substance abusing women: Early intervention, parenting stress child abuse potential and child development. *Child Abuse & Neglect, 9,* 997–1017.

Neufeld, A., & Harrison, M. J. (1995). Reciprocity and social support in caregivers' relationships: variations and consequences. *Qualitative Health Research, 5*(3), 348–365.

Osofsky, J., Hann, D., & Peebles, C. (1993). Adolescent parenthood: Risks and opportunities for mothers and infants. *Handbook of Infant Mental Health* (pp. 106–119). New York: Guilford Press.

Oxford, M., Lee, J., & Lohr, M. (2010). Predicting markers of adulthood among adolescent mothers. *Social Work Research, 34*(1), 33–44.

Pajulo, M., Savonlahti, E., & Sourander, A. (2001). Antenatal depression, substance dependency and social support. *Journal of Affective Disorders, 65*(1), 9–17.

Papousek, M., & von Hofacker, N. (1998). Persistent crying in early infancy: A non-trivial condition of risk for the developing mother–infant relationship. *Child Care Health & Development, 24*, 395–424.

Pelham, W. E., Lang, A. R., Atkeson, B., Murphy, D. A., Gnagy, E. M., Greiner, A. R., et al. (1997). Effects of deviant child behavior on parental distress and alcohol consumption in laboratory interactions. *Journal of Abnormal Child Psychology, 25*, 413–424.

Porter, L. S., Bongo-Sanchez, V., & Kissel, B. (1996). Testing the efficacy of infant massage for enhancing the self esteem of substance-abusing mothers: A pilot study. Unpublished master's thesis by V. Bongo Sanchez & B. Kissel, developed under the direction of L. Porter, Principal Investigator of primary study and Master's Thesis Committee Chair. Florida International University, Miami, FL.

Porter, L. S., & Knicely, B. (1985). A study of the effects of a parenting enhancement program on parents' self esteem, their perception of the infant, and infant health. Unpublished master's thesis by B. Knicely, developed under the direction of L. Porter, Principal Investigator of primary study and Master's Thesis Committee Chair. West Virginia University, Morgantown, WV.

Porter, L. S., & Porter, B. O. (2004). A blended infant massage-parenting enhancement program for recovering substance-abusing mothers. *Pediatric Nursing, 30*(5), 363–372.

Quinlivan, J. A., Box, H., & Evans, S. (2003). Postnatal home visits in teenage mothers: A randomized controlled trial. *The Lancet, 364(9434)*, 582.

Roberts, R. E., Roberts, C. R., & Xing, Y. (2007). Comorbidity of substance use disorders and other psychiatric disorders among adolescents: Evidence from an epidemiological survey. *Drug & Alcohol Dependence, 88*(1), 4–13.

Ryan-Krause, P., Meadows-Oliver, M., Sadler. L., & Swarts, M. (2008). Developmental status of children of teen mothers: Contrasting objective assessments with maternal reports. *Journal of Pediatric Health, 23(5)*, 303–309.

Sadler, L., & Cantrone, C. (1983). The adolescent parent: A dual developmental crisis. *Journal of Adolescent Health Care, 4*, 100–105.

Sadler, L. S., & Cowlin, A. (2003). Moving into parenthood: A program for new adolescent mothers combining parent education with creative physical activity. *Journal for Specialists in Pediatric Nursing, 8*(2), 62–70.

Schellenbach, C., Whitman, T., & Borkowski, J. (1992). Toward an integrative model of adolescent parenting. *Human Development, 35*, 81–99.

Schinke, D. S., Barth, R. P., Gilchrist, D. L., & Maxwell, M. J. (1986). Adolescent mothers, stress, and prevention. *Journal of Human Stress, 12*, 162–167.

Seibert, J. M., Hogan, A. E., & Mundy, P. C. (1987). Assessing social and communication skills in infancy. *Topics in Early Childhood Special Education, 7*, 38–48.

Shankaran, S., Das, A., Bauer, C. R., Bada, H. S., Lester, B., & Wright, L. L. (2004). Association between patterns of maternal substance use and infant birth weight, length, and head circumference. *Pediatrics, 114*(2), E226–E234.

Sheinkopf, S. J., LaGasse, L. L., Lester, B. L., Liu, J., Seifer, R., Bauer, C. R., et al. (2006). Prenatal cocaine exposure: Cardiorespiratory function and resilience. *Annals of the New York Academy of Sciences, 1094*, 354–358.

Shelton, K. H., & Harold, G. T. (2008). Interparental conflict, negative parenting, and children's adjustment: Bridging links between parents' depression and children's psychological distress. *Journal of Family Psychology, 22,* 712–724.

Sommer, K., Whitman, T., & Borkowski, J. (2000). Prenatal and maternal predictors of cognitive and emotional delays in children of adolescent mothers. *Journal of Adolescence, 35,* 87–112.

Spears, G. V., Stein, J. A., & Koniak-Griffin, D. (2010). Latent growth trajectories of substance use among pregnant and parenting adolescents. *Psychology of Addictive Behavior, 24*(2), 322–332.

Spieker, S. J., Gillmore, M. R., Lewis, S. M., Morrison, D. M., & Lohr, M. J. (2001). Psychological distress and substance use by adolescent mothers: Associations with parenting attitudes and the quality of mother–child interaction. *Journal of Psychoactive Drugs, 33*(1), 83–93.

Steinberg, L. (2005). Cognitive and affective development in adolescence. *Trends in Cognitive Science, 9*(2), 69–74.

Stewart, M. (1993). *Integrating Social Support in Nursing.* New York: Sage.

Stewart, M. (2000). *Chronic Condition and Caregiving in Canada: Social Support Strategies.* Toronto: University Press.

Suchman, N. E., & Luthar, S. S. (2001). The mediating role of parenting stress in methadone-maintained mothers' parenting. *Parenting Science & Practice, 1*(4), 285–315.

Suchman, N., Pajulo, M., DeCoste, C., & Mayes, L. (2006). Parenting interventions for drug dependent mothers and their young children: the case for an attachment-based approach. *Family Relations, 55,* 211–226.

Wasserman, G. A., & Brunelli, V. A. (1990). Social supports and living arrangements of adolescent and adult mothers. *Journal of Adolescent Research, 5*(1), 54–66.

Whitman, T. L., Borkowski, J. G., Keogh, D. A., & Weed, K. (2001). *Interwoven Lives: Adolescent Mothers and Their Children.* Mahwah, NJ: Lawrence Erlbaum.

Zucker, R. A. (2008). Anticipating problem alcohol use developmentally from childhood into middle adulthood: What have we learned? *Addiction, 103*(1), 100–108.

20 Mothering from the Inside Out

A Mentalization-Based Individual Therapy for Mothers with Substance Use Disorders

NANCY E. SUCHMAN,
CINDY DECOSTE,
MONICA ROOSA ORDWAY, AND
SUSAN BERS

Does your child ever need your attention? He needs my attention a lot. And he knows how to get it. He comes up and he pulls on me and says "Mommy! Mommy!" when he wants it. *Can you tell me about the last time he needed your attention?* The last time was probably last night at dinner, he was tired. I was cooking and he wanted me to stop what I was doing and put the magnets on the refrigerator, so I did for a minute. *And what's that like for you?* It's a little stressful at times, but you know he can't help when he's feeling needy, so I try to remember that. I felt like finishing cooking and then playing with him, but I tried to have him distracted with other people but it wasn't working, so I stopped for a second. *What do you think it was like for him?* I think it was probably frustrating for him, he just wants what he wants. He's almost two so he doesn't really know how to wait yet [laugh]. *And why do you think he needs your attention?* It's like he feels secure and trusts me. I think I am his main, like the center of his little world. And so he depends on me for a lot of things.

—*Mothering from the Inside Out participant during her exit PDI interview*

◼ OVERVIEW

Mothering from the Inside Out (MIO) is a short-term, supportive, individual psychodynamic therapy for mothers with substance use disorders that emphasizes the development of the capacity for mentalizing. MIO was originally developed for mothers enrolled in outpatient substance-abuse treatment caring for children aged newborn to three in order to (a) provide a positive first experience in a therapeutic relationship, (b) carefully assess the mother's psychological functioning and the child's developmental status, and (c) begin a process of helping mothers make sense of their own and their children's emotional experiences. In this chapter, we describe the MIO intervention and its conceptual basis, review completed research on the intervention's efficacy and mechanisms of change, and discuss implications for future development and dissemination.

■ **BACKGROUND**

Mothers with substance abuse disorders often have long and complicated family histories of substance abuse and psychiatric problems (Choi, & Ryan, 2007; Grant, Huggins, Graham, Ernst, Whitney, & Wilson, 2011; Wilke, Kamata, & Cash, 2005); childhood exposure to physical and emotional neglect and abuse, sexual abuse and other traumas (Cash & Wilke, 2003; Lam, Wechsberg, & Zule, 2004; Minnes, Singer, Humphrey-Wall, & Satayathum, 2008); and, as adults, inconsistent caregiving and exposure to partner emotional abuse and violence (Grant et al., 2011; Marsh, Ryan, Choi, & Testa, 2006; National Center on Addiction and Substance Abuse, 2006). Often bearing children as teenagers or young adults following unplanned pregnancies (Pajulo, Suchman, Kalland, & Mayes, 2006; Rosenbaum, 1981; Taylor, 1993), mothers with substance use disorders commonly begin the psychological and emotional journey into parenthood before or during their psychological and emotional journey into adulthood.

Although quality of caregiving varies widely, in general, mothers who have histories of chronic substance use are at greater risk than mothers with no drug-use history for losing custody of their young children (Choi & Ryan, 2007; Department of Health and Human Services, 1999; Grant et al., 2011). In developmental studies (e.g., Burns, Chethik, Burns, & Clark, 1997; Hans, Bernstein, & Henson, 1999), mothers with substance use disorders have shown lower sensitivity and responsiveness to their infant's cues and marked juxtaposition of withdrawal with intrusive, over-controlling behaviors. From the perspective of attachment theory, the mother's capacity for sensitive and responsive caregiving with young children is likely to reflect in part her own psychological experiences with her own early caregivers. In very simple terms, if her experience with early caregivers was characterized by neglect or abuse, her own psychological representations of the caregiving relationship are likely to be characterized by defensive omissions and/or distortions of painful affect. These defenses serve the important function of protecting her from painful memories and overwhelming affect originating from experiences with early caregivers. They are also likely to interfere with her ability to recognize new psychological and emotional experiences in herself and her child.

Along these lines, Peter Fonagy and colleagues (2002) identified specific patterns of thinking—and developed the concept of reflective functioning—to characterize the narratives of adults who experienced secure and insecure attachments with caregivers during early childhood. They found that adults classified as secure on the Adult Attachment Interview (AAI; George, Kaplan, & Main, 1985) were able to "mentalize"—coherently describe both positive and negative emotional aspects of their experiences with early caregivers and also describe their caregivers' behaviors within an understandable emotional context (e.g., "My father was often worried about work, and so he didn't feel he could spend much time with me when I was young"). Adults who were classified as insecure or disorganized were less able to "mentalize" or identify emotional contexts of relationships with early caregivers (e.g., "My father was never interested in me, that's just how he was"). The experiences of many substance abusing mothers with their early caregivers (in the absence of subsequent secure adult attachments) can predispose them to difficulty in recognizing and understanding emotions (particularly negative emotions) in themselves and their children. With limited capacity to tolerate or make sense of internal affective states (her own or her young child's), the mother often faces unbearable and frightening distress. With only two apparent alternatives at hand—either escaping or combating the distress source—a mother's attempts to withdraw from or over-control a distressed infant becomes more understandable. Mood-altering substances provide another avenue of escape—albeit a self-destructive one—from the inexplicable discomfort.

Chronic maternal drug abuse exacerbates vulnerability to parenting difficulties in at least two ways. First, *in utero* exposure to drugs such as heroin and cocaine can heighten irritability in newborn infants, making it more difficult for them to bond with and be soothed by their parent. Second, chronic drug use probably reduces a mother's capacity to tolerate parenting stress, as follows: Initiation of substance use and subsequent chronic abuse and addiction often begin with an individual's strong desire to regulate internal psychological or emotional distress (Khantzian, 1997). Although drugs and alcohol are very effective and immediate mood changers, over the long term, chronic drug use typically and dramatically reduces stress tolerance (Sinha, 2001) by altering neuroregulatory stress–reward processes in the brain. Under normal circumstances, the human brain will "reward" survival behaviors (e.g., sex, eating, caring for offspring) by releasing dopamine, a neurotransmitter that produces a sensation of pleasure and increases tolerance for stress. Commonly abused drugs typically cause the brain to release very large amounts of dopamine, producing a highly pleasurable and euphoric sensation. Over time, continued substance use causes the brain to adapt to excess dopamine by reducing the number of available dopamine receptors and making it necessary to ingest larger amounts of the substance to achieve the same euphoric effect (Volkow, Fowler, & Wang, 2003). Thus, caring for a baby is likely to be experienced as less pleasurable and more distressing for mothers with chronic substance use histories.

Taken together, the early childhood experiences and neurobiological changes incurred by mothers with addictive disorders, coupled with infant vulnerability to excessive irritability, set the stage for the mother–infant dyad to have great difficulty as regulatory partners (Pajulo et al., 2006). Perhaps because of these multiple vulnerabilities, traditional behavioral parent-training programs have generally failed to improve the quality of relationships of substance using parents with their young children or to promote their children's psychosocial development (for a review, see Suchman, Mayes, Conti, Slade, & Rounsaville, 2004). To begin to address the constellation of vulnerabilities that substance using mothers face in caring for their young children, we have been developing Mothering from the Inside Out (MIO), a supportive, individual, psychodynamic intervention that focuses on supporting the mother's developing capacity to mentalize about or make sense of her own and her child's emotional experiences and understand the child's behavior as being driven by mental states (i.e., thoughts, intentions, wishes, and emotions). MIO is an adjunct intervention offered weekly in conjunction with comprehensive substance-abuse treatment services that include relapse prevention groups, medical and psychiatric care, drug replacement therapy (e.g., methadone, naltrexone, buprenorphine), vocational counseling, transportation, and case management.

From an attachment standpoint, the long-range objectives of MIO are to:

- Support the mother's developing capacity for emotional regulation
- Restore the mother's own capacity to engage in human attachment relationships (replacing attachment to the substance with attachment to the child)
- Promote the mother's capacity to engage with and enjoy her child, tolerate her child's emotional distress, understand her child's attachment needs, and support her child's developing regulatory capacities.

The short-term goals in MIO are to:

- Provide a positive first experience in a therapeutic relationship in which the mother's thoughts and emotions are taken seriously and she feels supported and understood
- Carefully assess the mother's psychological strengths and vulnerabilities, the child's developmental status, and dyadic vulnerabilities
- Begin a process of helping the mother make sense of her own and her child's underlying affective experiences and think about how these experiences are related to individual need, personality, and behavior
- Support the dyad in finding long-term support for their psychological and emotional development.

In 2005, we received funding from the National Institutes of Health to begin developing and evaluating MIO. During the first phase of the research intervention study, we developed the intervention and methods for assessing its efficacy and integrity, and completed a randomized pilot study with 47 mothers. Concurrently, we developed a comparison Parent Education program, also tailored to the individual needs of substance using mothers and children. Preliminary findings from this research demonstrated MIO's feasibility, clinical promise, treatment integrity, and support for proposed mechanisms of change. (For a detailed report on treatment outcomes, see Suchman, DeCoste, Castiglioni, McMahon, Rounsaville, & Mayes, 2010; Suchman, DeCoste, McMahon, Rounsaville, & Mayes, 2011; for a detailed report on treatment integrity and mechanisms of change, see Suchman, DeCoste, Leigh, & Borelli, 2010; Suchman, DeCoste, Rosenberger, & McMahon, 2012.) Subsequently, we received additional funding to begin evaluating MIO in a formal randomized trial that is currently ongoing. Below, we describe the clinical approach used in the MIO and comparison interventions and in conducting research with a very high-risk population of mothers. In our overall approach, the research assessments are incorporated into the clinical program and project staff is involved in intervention delivery and research processes. This approach has allowed the project staff to maintain a perspective that is vital to balancing clinical and research objectives. It also provides a challenging but stimulating mix of tasks that can help prevent the fatigue engendered in working with high-risk populations.

▪ RESEARCH DESIGN

MIO was originally developed and piloted as a 20-week intervention research program (see Suchman, DeCoste, Castiglioni, Legow, & Mayes, 2008; Suchman, DeCoste, & Mayes, 2009). Mothers were eligible to participate if they were caring for a child between birth and three years of age, were actively participating in their substance abuse treatment, and were not actively suicidal or homicidal, nor severely cognitively impaired. The program was initially designed to match the duration of the substance abuse treatment program at the clinic where the study took place. After completing four weekly baseline assessment visits, mothers attended 12 individual weekly therapy sessions followed by four weekly post-treatment assessment visits, a six-week follow-up period, and four weekly follow-up assessment visits. Currently, in a second five-year research phase funded by the National Institutes of Health (NIH), we are evaluating MIO in a randomized clinical trial. We are now including mothers caring for children ages 12 and 60 months of age. The program schedule remains the same except that the follow-up phase is now 13 weeks long (rather than six weeks). Altogether, mothers participate in the intervention study for approximately eight months.

Setting

During the first research phase, the project was housed in the same clinic where mothers were enrolled in treatment for their substance use. During the second phase (currently ongoing), the study has been housed separately in a suite upstairs from the clinic. The suite was designed to be a homey environment with comfortable furniture for adults and small children and fresh pastel-colored painted walls decorated with softly colored child-, family- and nature-themed artwork. Healthy drinks and snacks are always available to participants. Small private offices for the project staff are also comfortably furnished and decorated with folk art and prints of mothers and children. A microwave, changing table, and developmentally appropriate toys are available in the waiting area. A dedicated child care room is available for providing developmentally informed child care while the mother completes assessment visits and counseling sessions. Project staff members provide child care as needed and receive weekly clinical supervision from a developmental specialist. If a child is having difficulty separating from the mother during assessments, the physical space allows the mother to be easily accessible to the child for physical contact, care, and emotional refueling. The entire six-office suite is dedicated exclusively to the project and provides a warm, inviting, and tranquil setting. Mothers often comment about the comfort and enjoyment they and their children experience in visiting the project suite, perhaps in part because it provides an intimate and quiet space away from the hectic clinic and home environments, one where mothers and children can relax and focus.

The project suite was also set up to allow for recording individual sessions, staff trainings, and research assessment interviews with small cameras on miniature tripods in the corner of each room. The child care room has two small cameras that can be used to record activity using wide-angle and close-up lenses. The recording equipment allows assessment of mothers and children to be viewed from other offices, increasing opportunities for live clinical supervision and for therapists to observe clinical assessments.

Project Personnel

Five full-time staff members have offices at the project suite and are available full-time on the project. The Principal Investigator (N. Suchman) has her primary office in the suite, is present on most days to provide "hallway clinical supervision" as needed and weekly formal clinical supervision to MIO therapists and comparison interventions parenting specialists, and is also an MIO therapist. She has primary responsibility for disseminating project information (through publications, seminars, and conferences) and writing grant applications. The Project Director (C. DeCoste), a master's level psychologist, has an office in the suite, manages the day-to-day research and clinical activities, trains and supervises the project staff in assessment methods that include clinical interviews and mother–child interaction, trains the offsite interaction assessment coders, provides clinical supervision to project staff conducting the Parent Education (PE) comparison intervention, and conducts clinical interviews with the mothers.

Three full-time staff members—bachelor's and master's level women with backgrounds in counseling, psychology, or social work—also have dedicated offices in the suite. Each of these staff members serves as a liaison to one drug treatment clinic and guides mothers from this clinic through the study phases (e.g., maintains contact, assists with daily needs, conducts research assessments). They also serve as parenting and child care specialists to mothers from the other drug treatment clinics. As parenting specialists, they provide the individual comparison intervention—PE—for a caseload of two mothers with whom they meet with individually once per week to provide parenting guidance on topics of the mother's choosing, as well as assistance with problems of daily living. They also provide developmentally informed individual child care for young children enrolled in the study and meet weekly with a developmental specialist for clinical supervision of the child care.

Two part-time clinical specialists also have vital roles. The adult specialist—a psychoanalytically trained practicing psychologist (S. Bers) with expertise in adult personality development and psychotherapy—provides clinical consultation to the MIO therapist group and also serves as an individual MIO therapist, carrying a caseload of two mothers at a time. A master's level early childhood specialist from the early childhood team at the Yale Child Study Center conducts developmental screenings with all mother–child dyads and provides weekly developmental and clinical consultation to the project staff who conduct the comparison intervention (PE) and provide child care.

Screening and Recruitment

The drug treatment foundation where the intervention research project is based is housed in three separate locations that are within close commuting proximity.

One project staff member serves as a liaison to each site, attending weekly staff meetings and other functions in order to know the staff and patients served by the clinic. Potential participants can learn about the program from their drug treatment clinician, the project staff, or other mothers who have participated. Each mother in the study has a dedicated project staff member who guides her and her child through each of the assessment phases, starting with informed consent and ending with the follow-up assessment visit. This relationship insures consistent support for the mother and her child as they move through each study phase. This same staff member also works closely with clinic staff to coordinate services for the mother and child. The confidentiality of the personal and parenting concerns discussed by the mother in therapy is preserved, though. As the liaison, the project staff member has a vital role in coordinating care for mothers between the clinic and the parenting program. Her presence in the clinic also helps humanize the research process for clinic staff and patients.

Referral and Consent Procedures

Mothers are typically referred to the study intervention by their drug treatment clinicians or other mothers who have already participated in the program. The drug treatment clinicians usually refer mothers to the study for extra support and individual attention (they typically carry caseloads of 60 patients and do not have time to meet individually with their clients, except to manage crises). Mothers who are interested and eligible then meet with the study liaison to learn more about what their participation would involve before they are invited to consent. During this meeting, the mother learns that the study's purpose is to support mothers in managing the stresses of being a parent by talking with a professional about her parenting experiences. Since mothers are randomly assigned to one of two interventions, both interventions are briefly described (see below) and mothers know there is a 50/50 chance of assignment to each. We also ask mothers' permission for access to their attendance and urine toxicology screen records from the drug treatment clinic so that we can monitor potential secondary benefits of each intervention. Mothers learn that they can withdraw from the study at any time without jeopardizing their status at the clinic. Mothers are informed that they will be compensated financially for completing the research assessments. They also learn about our Certificate of Confidentiality, which provides federal protection to prevent their research records from being subpoenaed by the court system (in the United States, all vulnerable populations are required by law to have this protection when participating in federally funded research).

Alliance Building

Mothers with substance use disorders have many reasons to be wary of a new relationship with research project staff and therapists. Most treatment providers they encounter are part of a treatment system that is closely monitoring their drug use, their parenting, and their illegal activity. Most mothers are likely to have experienced frustration, bitterness, and futility, directly or vicariously, as a result of involvement with the child welfare or court systems. Many of the behaviors involved in maintaining a drug or alcohol habit engender anger, frustration, mistrust, and withdrawal by others, causing the addicted individual to feel angry, bewildered, and dejected. Expectations about being conned, manipulated, neglected, or condescended to make building an enduring and trusting alliance extremely challenging, delicate, and important work. For this reason, much effort during the early stage of a mother's involvement in the intervention project is devoted to assisting the mother in tangible ways that she is likely to perceive as helpful. Mothers are assisted by the program staff in meeting basic needs (e.g., finding housing, food, child care, transportation, legal services), getting supplies (e.g., diapers, food, toys, clothing), and solving everyday problems (e.g., scheduling dilemmas, family conflicts, eviction notices, child welfare visits). Project staff work hard to understand the mother's perspective on personal, parenting, and family problems and to convey to the mother that her beliefs, feelings and wishes are going to be taken seriously in her relationship with the project staff and her research therapist/parenting specialist. A less obvious but equally important component of building a strong alliance involves being very clear and consistent about the boundaries of the relationship between the program and the mother. Mothers learn during consent procedures that program staff have responsibilities as mandated reporters of child abuse and neglect, and about the limitations of confidentiality in circumstances where the well-being of the child or the mother is threatened. Mothers also learn about the program's commitment to communicate clearly about any actions that need to be taken and involve them in any such process. Knowing that the program takes these responsibilities seriously is often experienced as containing and reassuring (knowing that, if she is unable to maintain control, someone will take charge to protect her and her child).

Preliminary Assessment (First Four Visits)

During the mother's first week of enrollment, she meets with her project liaison to begin the initial four-week assessment process. During this phase, the mother will first meet individually with the Project Director, who will gather information about her current living situation, employment and education background, medical conditions and medications, substance use (including during pregnancy), exposure to trauma and psychiatric history, her family's substance use and psychiatric history, and her mental status. During this meeting, she and her liaison will determine her transportation to the program, participation and payment schedule, specific needs for assistance, and specific concerns about parenting her child. Structure and consistency are considered important for both interventions, so the mother is scheduled to visit at the same day and time each week, and, with the liaison, fills in a pocket calendar with all her scheduled appointments to take home with her. After the initial clinical evaluation, the mother is randomly assigned to MIO or PE and is introduced to her individual counselor.

During the next visit, the mother and her child participate together in two brief play sessions in the child care room. These sessions are explained as opportunities to see how the mother and child play and get along together. The play sessions are recorded and also observed by the mother's individual counselor, who will have the chance to talk about the experience with the mother immediately following the session. During the first play session, the mother and child explore a series of novel toys together. In the second session, the mother is asked to teach the child a new task (the Nursing Child Assessment Satellite Training Teaching Scale [NCAST], Barnard & Eyres, 1979; updated 1994) chosen from a list of activities in order of increasing difficulty, and to spend five minutes teaching her child the first task on the list that he/she has not yet mastered (e.g., stringing beads, drawing a circle). Both play sessions are recorded on DVDs and reviewed in clinical supervision to understand how the child communicates his/her emotional needs to the mother and how the mother responds. The sessions are also coded on a number of indices of dyadic adjustment (e.g., maternal sensitivity to child cues, responsiveness to child distress, clarity of child's communication, child's efforts to engage the mother). Following the play sessions, the mother meets with her assigned counselor, who has seen the play session remotely, to begin exploring the mother's interests and concerns that will inform focus of their work together.

During the next two visits, the mother meets with the Project Director to complete two parenting interviews (both require advanced clinical skills), followed by a check-in with her assigned MIO therapist or PE specialist. The Working Model of the Child Interview (WMCI; Zeanah & Benoit, 1993) asks about the mother's experiences with and impressions of her child during instances when most children's attachment needs typically become activated (e.g., at times of separations, illness, or physical injury). The WMCI tends to activate the mother's psychological defenses that protect her from painful early memories and may also distort her representations of her child. The interview typically takes about an hour to complete, but can be divided into shorter sessions if the mother is showing signs of discomfort or fatigue. The WMCI is used clinically to understand how the mother makes sense of her child's emotional needs, personality, behavior, and relationship with her. As a research tool it is coded quantitatively and qualitatively to assess specific characteristics of the mothers' representations (e.g., caregiving sensitivity when the child is distressed, coherence or plausibility, richness of detail about the child, emotional involvement with the child, openness to discovering developmental changes in the child and their relationship, and acceptance of the child's unique characteristics and the caregiving role).

The Parent Development Interview (PDI; Slade, Aber, Berger, Bresgi, & Kaplan, 2003) asks about times that demand parental reflection (e.g., times when the mother felt angry or needy as a parent, times when the mother felt the child needed her attention). Clinically, the PDI is used to understand how the mother makes sense of moments when she herself is distressed as a parent and when she and her child might not be getting along (i.e., whether and how she uses her own and her child's internal states as a guide to understanding the relationship). For research, the PDI is coded for the mother's capacity for reflective functioning, her ability to think about how underlying thoughts and emotions might influence her relationship with her child during a range of difficult moments (e.g., when mother and child were clicking, when the mother was angry as a parent, or when the child needed her attention). The mothers are told that the interviews help us understand their experiences as a mother and how they make sense of their child and their relationship. The interview takes about an hour to complete and can be tiring and difficult for some mothers. Care is taken not to overburden them, by allowing breaks when needed and scheduling meetings with their assigned MIO therapist or PE specialist after the interview session.

The remaining assessment visits focus on the child's developmental status. The developmental specialist meets with the mother and child to complete a developmental assessment (e.g., expressive and receptive language, cognitive and motor development) and to address any concerns the mother might have about the child's developmental progress. To minimize the assessment burden, brief screening tools (e.g., Bayley Screening Test Observational Checklist) are used first; then more extensive assessment is done if developmental problems have been observed during the screening. At a separate visit, the mother and child participate together in the Strange Situation Paradigm (SSP; Ainsworth et al., 1978) to assess the child's attachment classification. Special care is taken to brief the mothers about the purpose of this assessment and what to expect. The day-care room in the suite is used for the baseline SSP since it is not familiar to the child and the mother at this early time point in the study. It is set up to resemble a waiting room. The mother and child navigate several brief episodes of separation and reunion (in the presence and absence of an unfamiliar assistant). Mothers are told that this exercise helps us understand how their child might manage being together and apart in public situations (e.g., the waiting room at the pediatrician's office). If a child becomes very distressed during separations, he/she is quickly reunited with the mother, and the MIO therapist or PE specialist and mother have a chance to talk about the experience immediately following (e.g., the mother learns that the child may be more worried than usual about separations for a few days after the exercise).

Intervention Phase

At the same time as all mothers and children in the intervention study are completing the assessment phase, the MIO mothers are also settling into individual therapy, and the PE mothers into meeting with their individual parenting specialist, while all the children are settling into individual child care. Mothers typically meet with their assigned MIO therapist or PE specialist at the end of each assessment visit, for 30 minutes to an hour. Each child is assigned to an individual child care specialist for one or two hours, depending upon their involvement in the assessments.

Each intervention arm (MIO and PE) provides an opportunity in a weekly meeting for the mother to develop a close relationship with an individual professional (the MIO therapist or the PE specialist) who supports her efforts and helps her meet her needs in providing a stable home life for her child and herself, and works with her—using either the MIO or PE approach—on reducing parenting stress and strain in her relationship with her child. The aim of both interventions is to provide a positive first experience in a supportive relationship in which the mother's thoughts and emotions are taken seriously and she feels supported and understood. In MIO, the focus is on helping the mother enhance her capacity to mentalize or make sense of her own and her child's underlying affective experiences, especially during moments when the mother is stressed and the relationship is strained. In PE, the focus is on helping the mother learn ways to manage stressful parenting situations that she has identified (e.g., bedtime, power struggles, safety, limit setting) by learning new behavioral parenting strategies and receiving relevant developmental guidance. In the two randomized trials, it has been important to develop a strong comparison intervention so that mothers in both arms of the study (MIO and PE) receive an individually tailored intervention that aims to foster a secure alliance and addresses specific personal and parenting concerns. The primary difference between MIO and PE is the emphasis in the former on enhancing the mother's capacity to mentalize about her own and her child's experiences and about their relationship. This allows the research to focus on differences in approach (e.g., education vs. therapy) rather than differences in alliance (which is already known to be a critical ingredient in any supportive intervention; Kazdin, 2007; Shedler, 2010).

Mothering from the Inside Out

The MIO therapist has had the opportunity to observe the client during each of the parenting interviews and interaction sessions with her child and to meet with the mother after each of these activities to talk about them and begin learning more directly about the mother's experiences and concerns. The WMCI provides the therapist a sense of how the mother mentally represents the child and the child's relationship to herself and others—including the amount of richness in detail, emotional engagement, emotional sensitivity, sense of discovery about the child's emerging abilities, and acceptance of the child's unique personality. The PDI provides the therapist a sense of the mother's ability to mentalize across circumstances that vary in stress and arousal levels (e.g., from easy and calm moments to tense moments filled with negative emotions). The mother–child interaction sessions also give the therapist a chance to observe whether and how the mother holds her child's experience in mind as they work and play together and negotiate separations. Above all, these assessments provide important information to the therapist about what she might be able to expect the mother to do and understand in mentalization-based therapy. If a mother is unable to acknowledge details about her child's personality or to identify simple mental states in herself or her child, then the therapist might expect that asking detailed questions about the child or about feelings is likely to elicit anxiety or frustration in the mother. Stated simply, the assessments can provide important information to the therapist about where she can start and how slowly and carefully she will need to proceed in promoting the mother's capacity to mentalize.

Topic Flexibility

In MIO, the mother can talk about a topic of her choosing, and the topics can vary widely. Mothers in our program have wanted to talk about a very wide range of worries and concerns, including power struggles with and between children; frustration with children's willfulness, clinging, dependence, manners, exploration, and safety; strained relationships with partners and family members; problems with cravings and relapse; and frustrations with child welfare case workers or other service providers. The therapist focuses at first on learning about the mother's perception of the situation. The therapist will also suggest that it may be beneficial to explore her experience of the problem. If, for example, a mother expresses frustration about her child's welfare worker keeping her case active and asks for the therapist's help in managing this problem, while learning more about the problem, the therapist will listen for the mother's understanding of the problem, whether she has a sense of her own emotional experience of it, whether she has a sense of what others involved might be thinking and feeling, whether her view has changed over time, and whether she has any sense of the impact of this on her child. The therapist works to manage a balance between supporting the mother in meeting her own goals while encouraging her to explore her own internal experience to the degree that she is able to, and to think about the internal experience of others. So she might say, "I would be glad to think this through with you. It could help to know more about what you are experiencing about this and how you understand her actions and intentions." The therapist adopts a "mentalizing stance" (Bateman & Fonagy, 2006) in which she is interested, curious, and inquisitive about how the mother makes sense of the situation and about the thoughts, expectations, and emotions related to the situation (her own and others'). Generally, the therapy follows a progression in which the therapist and mother focus on an issue that is clearly important to the mother and moderately distressing (without completely overwhelming her). Her concern may not be about the child, yet we have learned that helping the mother mentalize (and thereby become more regulated emotionally) about any number of stressors and their impact on her child is closely related to improvements in her interactions with her child (see Suchman, DeCoste, Leigh, & Borelli, 2010).

Pacing

The therapist tries not to overwhelm the mother with too many questions. For mothers who have difficulty recognizing any aspect of mental experience, the therapist may just ask about her physical experience (e.g., "So what was going on in you when she said that?"). The therapist is genuinely interested in learning more about the mother's perspective and experience and in helping her make sense of her own and others' mental/emotional experience in the situation. She goes at a pace that is acceptable and comfortable to the mother—beginning with making sure she understands the physical reality of what has happened and then slowly learning about the emotional reality and how the mother is making sense of it. She avoids making interpretations or substituting her own thoughts and feelings for the mother's. For instance, the therapist would avoid statements like, "You must be so angry with the child welfare worker" or "Yeah, child welfare workers can be awful sometimes," or "This is the same as the situation we were talking about last week with your probation officer." Instead, she adopts a not-knowing stance toward the mother's experience, creating space for the mother's mentalizing activity by saying something like: "Okay, so let me stop for a moment and make sure

I've got this right. Your caseworker phoned last week and said the supervised visitations are going to be extended. Do you have any sense of why she had decided this?" or "So what went through your mind when she told you this? Did you feel any particular way?" This exploratory process often involves slowing down and encouraging the mother to carefully unpack the details of the interaction that was upsetting, with the ultimate goal of understanding how misunderstandings might have occurred or how her emotions might be intensifying in response to global or distorted assumptions. In other words, the goal is to have a better understanding of her own mind and those of others and how thoughts and feelings influence the relationship.

Inevitably, the mother's perception involves missing alternative explanations or distorting reality. The goal of the therapy is to help introduce flexibility into the mother's thinking and encourage her to imagine alternative plausible explanations of misunderstandings. Sometimes this requires providing developmental guidance about what a child can actually think and do. Other times it involves actively exploring alternative interpretations of behaviors. Generally, an effective progression is to first simply identify breaks in mentalization, then identify affective experiences, and then explore alternative explanations.

Keeping the Child in Mind

The therapist must also continuously hold the child's experience in mind, even if the topic is not directly related to parenting. Not doing so risks losing sight of the child's ongoing dependence on the mother and the mother's responsibility to the child. For instance, the therapist might ask "So, where is [your child] in all of this when you and your husband are arguing? How do you think she might experience or understand this?" A mother might respond that the child is too young to know what is taking place or that the child was not present and so the situation does not affect her. The therapist must pay careful attention to how the mother understands the child's experience and build on this understanding in ways that can help the mother expand her view of her child's mind, little by little. The therapist might say, "Well actually, I'm wondering if—when you get stressed about something, do you think your child might be able to sense this in some way?" and then move on to exploring the mother's understanding of the impact of her own mood or feelings on the child. Another approach to keeping the child in mind involves shifting the focus away from the mother and toward the impact of another significant person or event on the child, making it less threatening for the mother to hold the child's mind in mind. "I know the extended supervision feels very hard for you, and I wonder what it's like for your child. What do you think she experiences with this change? What clues you in to her experiences? How do you keep track of them?" In this way, the therapist is adopting an interested and curious stance, and inviting the mother to join in this stance, too, toward learning how the mother is experiencing and understanding the child. It is another way that the therapist and the mother can give joint attention to the mother's mind while the mother remains active in the "mentalizing shoes" (exploring her own thoughts of the child). If a mother has difficulty recognizing and exploring her young child's mind, an alternative may be to begin exploring the mother's thoughts about the child's physical experiences. "What do you suppose he was sensing then? How do you suppose it might feel in his body? How do you think he experiences this?"

One very important issue for the mentalization-based therapist with mothers is deciding when to focus on the mind of the mother and when to bring the focus to the mind of the child. A unique challenge to MIO, in contrast to dyadic interventions, is maintaining the joint focus on the child despite the absence of the child from the room. MIO was established as an individual rather than a dyadic therapy for substance using mothers because many mothers with chronic substance-use histories, particularly when they first enter treatment and have had only short periods of abstinence, have difficulty regulating strong emotions and require attention to their own regulatory processes before they are able to focus on their children's emotions. Moreover, their children's emotional distress can quickly increase their arousal to intolerable levels, making mentalizing—even in an intervention context—anywhere from difficult to impossible. Children's affective distress may actually serve as a trigger to relapse until the mother's dopaminergic reward system has been reset and the mother has developed the capacity to monitor her own levels of distress (see Rutherford & Mayes, this volume). MIO therefore was conceived as a first step for substance abusing mothers in becoming better regulatory partners with their young children, whereas dyadic interventions are understood to be a vital next step.

Transparent Mentalizing

The therapist also makes her own mentalizing mind available to the mother and does so in a marked manner in which she owns the perspective as her own and acknowledges the inherent limitations of her own insights (Fonagy, Bateman, & Luyten, 2012). If the mother were to say, "I don't need to tell you how I feel! You know me well enough!" the therapist might respond, "Well, it is true that I have been getting to know you better over our last couple of visits. But I can't really know for certain how you are feeling. I know that, in similar circumstances, I would probably feel disappointed and maybe a little mad at first, but I'm wondering if you might be feeling something a little different?" This technique is also helpful when the mother seems to be making assumptions about what the therapist or others think (e.g., in psychic equivalence or teleological mode; see below). For example, if a mother were to say to the therapist, "There is no point in talking about this with the child welfare worker. She thinks I don't care about [my child] and her mind won't change any time soon," the therapist might say, "I'm thinking about the child welfare worker too right now, and I'm wondering how she could be so close-minded and also decide to continue the visitation? It seems to *me*, at least, that being close-minded would lead her to move your case in a different direction. What do you think about that?"

Pre-Mentalizing Modes of Thinking

As the mother talks, the therapist listens carefully for lapses in mentalizing, which can happen quite frequently. These lapses can take many forms, including non sequiturs, lapses in coherence, sudden changes in the topic, silence, or hostility. Lapses can be subtle or obvious as well. A mother might, for example, be talking about the child welfare worker in a frustrated tone and then become distracted by an object in the room: "Oh, I love that photo! Is that your boyfriend?" A subtler shift away from mentalizing might involve a mother's downward glance at her watch. Because lapses in mentalizing can take many forms, it is important that the therapist pay close attention to the mother and get to know her particular strategies for avoiding mental states. When the therapist notes a lapse, she can pause the conversation and ask the mother what happened at the moment of the lapse. "What happened just then when you stopped talking and looked at your watch? Was something on your mind?" or simply, "I was following you up until you changed the topic. Can we go back a moment?"

During mentalizing lapses, mothers may revert to one of three pre-mentalizing modes of thinking that commonly occur in all people to varying degrees (see Bateman & Fonagy, 2006; Luyten, Fonagy, Lowyck, & Vermote, 2012). In *psychic equivalence* mode, the mother has difficulty distinguishing between internal and external reality. She concretely and automatically equates a thought with reality without questioning its veracity, considering alternatives, or having any awareness of being in this mode. She may also be quite confident and certain about her belief. Stated simply, in these moments, if the mother thinks it is so, then it must be so. A mother might say, for example, in response to the therapist's query about the child welfare worker's intent, "She doesn't care about me! She's just looking to get her paycheck!" Even though there is probably a grain of truth to the mother's perception (e.g., perhaps the welfare worker showed haste or insensitivity during a recent visit), the mother's paranoia and certainty serve to thwart any awareness of thoughts or feelings—what the mother imagines to be true is considered true with certainty. This state typically necessitates the use of empathy by the therapist in order to assist the patient in mentalizing.

In *teleological mode*, a mother concretely and automatically equates physical (or external) reality with mental or emotional (or internal) reality. This mode of thinking can be observed in very young children whose rudimentary capacities to represent the mind and intentions of another in their own minds are just developing (see Fonagy, Gergely, Jurist, & Target, 2002). A mother using this mode of thinking might conclude that the child welfare worker must not like her very much because she hasn't returned her calls or hasn't complied with her requests for extra meetings. Quite literally, if the thinking is out of sight, then it cannot exist in the mind. For a mother in teleological mode, it can seem that the only available means to eliminating emotional distress and restoring equilibrium involves taking concrete, physical actions that instill a sense of direct control (e.g., using substances, persuading or coercing a desired response in others).

When the therapist observes the mother to be thinking in psychic equivalence or teleological mode, it is very important to take the mother's experience seriously and to recognize the depth of the mother's feelings of being violated or threatened; it is easy to make light of such thinking when we recognize a patient's thoughts as paranoid and distorted because we may think that making light of them will ease the patient's anxiety about a given situation. It is likely, however, that the reverse is true—by not fully accepting and acknowledging the mother's experience as it is, we are creating a greater distance, and potentially an experience of fright or threat. At the same time, it is important to mirror the affect the mother experiences in a marked fashion so that she can recognize her own experience in the mind of the therapist (not as the experience of the therapist him- or herself). An important part of mentalization-based therapy involves helping the mother develop second-order representations (see Lyden and Suchman, this volume) of affective states. Mirroring the experience (e.g., an intense feeling of threat or fright) even if it is based on a distorted perception of reality, can help the mother feel understood and also to cognitively represent (and regulate) the affective state, a critical first step toward mentalizing.

In *pretend mode*, the patient has seemingly elaborate or intellectual explanations for why things are they way they are, but there is little sense of emotional truth to her story. The mother may blame her problems on her addictive personality or her depression, but the use of psychological terms does not seem to be connected to an authentic emotional experience. It can be difficult to determine when a mother is in pretend mode, especially when her explanations of circumstances make sense intellectually or she uses wordy justifications. For example, a mother might say that her child welfare worker was simply following a prescribed protocol that does not allow her to be sensitive to individual mothers' needs—that the system is the problem. This may be true, but this intellectualization of the problem circumvents an acknowledgement of thoughts and feelings that are instrumental to experiencing a stronger sense of self in the situation and greater ability to regulate emotions. Pseudo-mentalizing can also be intrusive if a mother insists that she "knows" what another is thinking and is unable to recognize the limits of knowing another's mind. With children, especially, intrusive and inaccurate assumptions about their states of mind can compromise the child's developing mentalizing capacities (e.g., inaccurate mirroring of affective states can inhibit second-order representations of affect; see Fonagy et al., 2002; Lyden & Suchman, this volume). Pseudo-mentalizing can seem like reading minds in order to coerce or manipulate others (e.g., "You don't really care how I feel," "If you want Mommy to come home, you'd better do as I say").

Steps Toward Mentalizing

Effective affect mirroring is an important first step toward addressing a mentalizing lapse. Accurate mirroring alone can provide a sense of reassurance and self-recognition that has a regulating effect for the mother and, over time, can promote the development of second-order representations of affective states (Fonagy et al., 2002). Sensing the return to a calm state, the therapist can proceed to encourage the mother's exploration of where and when the breakdown in mentalizing took place. "At what point did you first feel that she was not on your side? What was going on? Who was there? What was going through your mind? Do you remember anything happening just then that upset you?"

Lapses in the moment during a session are also important opportunities for intervention. For example, when a mother begins to describe her frustration with her child welfare worker and then suddenly changes the topic, the therapist can say "Would it be okay if we paused for a moment? because I think something important might have happened just then and that it might be helpful for us to understand it. Just then, when you were describing your frustration with the worker and then asked me whose photo was on my desk—was there any particular thought or feeling you were experiencing just then?" It is important for the therapist to recognize that the mother is probably unaware of the lapse and may not be able to access her thoughts or feelings to describe her experience. For instance, the mother might respond, "Well yeah, the thought running through my mind was, 'Is that your boyfriend in that picture on your desk?!' Nothin' else!" In such instances, the therapist can lend her own mentalizing capacity to the mother, as long as she does so in a marked fashion (Fonagy, Bateman, & Luyten, 2012). For example, the therapist might continue, "Got it! And yes, that is my boyfriend in the photo. But just dialing back a bit, just when you asked me about the photo, I was sitting here thinking that if I were in your shoes, having worked very hard to get an apartment and a job [the things her child welfare worker identified as important goals], to hear her say that my supervision would still need to continue would have me feeling some very strong emotions. And so I was wondering if you might be feeling some strong emotions about this yourself, although it might also feel very hard to talk about them." The mother might then be able to identify the strongest and most defensive emotion—"Well yeah, I was pissed! She had no right to tell me that!" which could be countered by a calm and reassuring, "Okay, that's really good to know." As the discussion ensues, the therapist can explore with the mother the possibility of other emotions or the impact of her anger on her actions. And eventually, if and when the mother is able to focus on her anger in a calm and regulated way, the therapist can explore with her how her child might experience her when she is in an angry state or how her state of mind influences her relationship with her child. But it is important to bear in mind that, for some mothers, simply recognizing the anger will be the most significant therapeutic outcome.

Although mentalizing capacities vary widely across circumstances (with greater arousal associated with lower mentalizing capacity) and individuals (some mothers can mentalize well when not aroused, others may adopt a more concrete stance regardless of arousal level), most mothers whom we have treated are able to recognize very simple mental states (e.g., anger, frustration, happiness, sadness, fear, embarrassment) under relaxed circumstances (e.g., once a comfortable rapport has been established with the therapist). The capacity to recognize even the simplest mental states is a positive sign of the potential to develop better mentalizing capacities, because it indicates the capacity to acknowledge and think about a state of mind (Bevington & Bleiberg, 2010).

As outlined above, the therapist assists the mother in tracking her own thoughts and feelings during stressful situations, as well as the thoughts and feelings of others involved and affected (e.g., her child). Keeping "mind in mind" helps the mother regulate strong negative emotions, distinguish between her own mind and her child's, distinguish between internal and external reality, distinguish between physical and emotional reality, and develop a deeper sense of self. From a psychodynamic perspective, through numerous repeated experiences of focusing on minds during stressful instances in the context of a secure therapeutic relationship, the therapist helps the mother develop and internalize second-order representations of affective experience (which, under normal circumstances involving a secure attachment, would have developed during early childhood in the context of the caregiving relationship) (Fonagy et al., 2002).

Monitoring Burden

The therapist must be mindful not to overburden the patient by expecting her to mentalize at a higher level than she is capable of. Questions about the mother's experience are simple, direct, and exploratory. (e.g., "How was that for you when he started having a tantrum? How do you think it was for him? What was going through your mind just then?") The therapist closely monitors the mother's level of arousal during the conversation, knowing that as arousal increases, the mother's capacity for mentalizing declines. Arousal can be obvious or subtle, and it can take some time for the therapist to know how each individual patient experiences and expresses arousal. So the importance of going slowly and getting to know the patient cannot be overstated. It may be impossible for the mother to join the therapist in thinking about her own mental states or others' when she is highly aroused. The therapist needs to show understanding, support, patience, respect, and calm during these moments helping the patient manage aroused states. The therapist is also careful not to take over the mentalizing function for the patient. If the therapist superimposes her own suppositions about what the patient is thinking or feeling, the patient is likely to become more confused about internal states without having access to a capacity to reflect. Instead, the goal is to bring arousal to a tolerable level so that joint attention to the patient's mind can continue.

Transference and Countertransference

Because MIO is a brief treatment, there are often not many opportunities for mentalizing the transference. When opportunities arise, the therapist might use them to explore with the patient their differences in perceptions. The objective is not to build insight into or explanations for their perceptions, but rather to develop the skill of identifying a puzzling phenomenon that requires focused attention and contemplation in order to restore the patient's mentalizing capacity. For example, if the patient were to say, "You must think this is foolish that I'm even bringing this up," the therapist would be transparent and matter-of-fact with her own perceptions: "That's interesting, the thought of your being foolish didn't even occur to me, but it is clearly occurring to you that I might be thinking that. I was feeling sad just then that this has been such a struggle for you. But I think it might be helpful to talk a little bit more about the thought that you are foolish. Can you say more about that and why you suppose I would have been thinking that?"

Countertransference refers to the thoughts and feelings that arise in the therapist toward the patient during the treatment session. In instances of projective identification (when the therapist experiences during the session what he/she assumes to be the patient's own experience), the therapist will *not* try to give this experience back to the patient (e.g., "it seems that you are feeling angry"). This approach is considered unwise because the patient—and the dyad—are already unstable, and suggesting the patient is having a feeling might be too threatening and destabilizing (Bateman & Fonagy, 2012a). Instead, the therapist acknowledges the difficulty of the current situation by saying, for example, "It is really difficult for us at the moment to work on what is going on"—a statement that is not likely to be too taxing for the patient.

Many other strong feelings can arise in a therapist when working with mothers who have substance using disorders—frustration, hopelessness, powerlessness, disappointment, and annoyance are some common negative feelings. Clinical supervision is critical for maintaining a balanced perspective and for processing one's own reactions. There are times, though, when the therapist, despite good intentions, will become part of an enactment with the patient, reacting to and perceiving the patient in an elicited way. For example, a therapist might convey a mild sense of annoyance or disgust when a mother asks for a letter to the child welfare worker stating that she is fit to have custody. The mother might sense this and comment, "Hey, I'm really not trying to hustle you but...." Then the therapist could try to put into words transparently what just took place. The therapist might say, "You know, I was feeling some pressure that you may or may not have wished me to feel. So I think that pressure made me feel uncomfortable and maybe some annoyance. But I'm wondering if you might be feeling something that is making you feel pressured about this, too." Importantly, the therapist takes responsibility for her own contribution. The therapist is very much in the soup with the patient, monitoring and identifying the lapses in their collaborative mentalizing about the relationship (Bateman & Fonagy, 2012b).

Parent Education Program

In the Parent Education program (PE), the mothers meet individually with a parenting specialist to address the specific personal or parenting concerns that are on the mother's mind. The PE specialist helps the mother identify specific problems to be addressed (e.g., limit-setting, managing separations, finding personal support); provides relevant developmental guidance for understanding the child's behavior (e.g., the cognitive capacities of toddlers); and provides behavioral strategies for addressing the concern (e.g., establishing routines, giving children reasonable options). Over 50 pamphlets providing developmental and behavioral guidance for parents (without emphasizing mentalizing skills) were developed for the parenting specialist to review with the client during individual sessions. For example, to help a mother who has concerns about the child-care worker extending her supervised visits, the PE specialist would help the mother identify her goals (e.g., to talk with the worker or to get a second opinion) and think through the steps toward attaining them (e.g., learning what she must do to comply with the worker's guidelines for reunification) and perhaps role-play a conversation with the Probation Officer (PO). To address a mother's specific questions or concerns about managing bedtime with her toddler, the PE specialist and mother would together review the "Bedtime" pamphlet, which provides specific developmental guidance and parenting strategies and identifies specific strategies for the mother to implement during the week. The pamphlets provide sound suggestions and current information, but do not go into much depth about mentalizing for children (e.g., common emotions experienced by parents and children are mentioned but not elaborated). Mothers may choose any pamphlet to review with the parenting specialist during their session.

Developmental Guidance and Assessment

Because many of the mothers have limited background knowledge about child development (particularly social and emotional development), mothers in both treatment arms (MIO and PE) have access to developmental guidance about their children from a developmental specialist. She is available to provide consultations to all program personnel and mothers as needed throughout the study and regularly meets with each mother–child dyad early in the study to conduct a developmental screening and, if needed, a full developmental assessment. The specialist directly addresses any concerns the mother has about the child's cognitive, language, or motor development and can provide additional assessment, advice, and guidance, as well as help facilitate referrals to child-guidance specialists. The developmental specialist also attends clinical supervision meetings and provides ongoing training. Her consistent presence on the team helps to keep the child in the program staff's mind as they assist the mother with complex case management and clinical issues.

Developmentally informed child care is also provided to children of mothers in both treatment arms (MIO and PE) during the mothers' visits. Program staff receive weekly clinical supervision from the developmental specialist that focuses on developmentally appropriate activities for child care and ongoing assessment of developmental progress in each child participating in the study. Concerns about children that arise during child care and child supervision are also shared with the mother's individual therapist or parenting specialist. In this way, feedback from the child-care team can inform the mother's treatment.

Milieu

Even though the formal interventions involve an individual format, there is a therapeutic milieu component for all mothers participating in the study. The program staff gets to know all mothers well—they guide the mothers and their children through the research assessment component, provide developmentally appropriate child care for all children, and conduct the intervention for mothers randomized to PE. Providing a coherent, supportive milieu that incorporates the clinical and research components and involves all program staff in both components is intended to make participation in the clinical research as comfortable, consistent, and unintrusive as possible. The everyday presence of the Principal Investigator (PI) and Project Director (PD) on site is also intended to lend consistency and coherence to the milieu—for mothers, children, and staff alike.

Clinical Supervision

Working with mothers who have in many cases experienced extensive trauma and loss can be very demanding and emotionally draining—as well as profound and rewarding—for researchers and clinicians alike. As well, the case history for each mother–child dyad is typically very complex (e.g., involving multiple separations and transitions, changes in family configuration and living situations, multiple treatment episodes, problems with daily living, financial and emotional instability, and relapses). Moreover, on any given day, a mother's and child's status can fall precipitously in response to a single event (e.g., job loss, arrest, eviction, theft, argument, relapse, pregnancy, assault). Intensive group supervision in both arms of the study with outside consultants allows full-time team members (e.g., program staff, project director, and principal investigator) to keep track of details, share observations, support one another, receive relevant training, avoid fatigue and burnout, maintain perspective on clinical progress, and identify support and services needed. Each treatment arm—MIO and PE—has a weekly supervision meeting that is attended by one of the outside clinical consultants. The MIO team supervision focuses on clinical cases in the MIO arm and ongoing study of mentalization-based therapy theory and techniques. The program staff meet twice weekly for group supervision—one meeting focuses on clinical cases in the PE arm and is run by the PI (N. Suchman). The second meeting focuses on parenting skills training and child development and is run by the developmental specialist. During this second meeting, the program staff can consult with the developmental specialist about all children in the study who are seen in child care.

Referral and Follow-up

As this is a research intervention, design constraints limit flexibility in the length of delivery. To address this limitation, we begin considering disposition plans during the first assessment phase. The four assessment visits and 12 intervention sessions allow time for a careful, ongoing assessment of the mother's psychological resources, social support, family and economic stability, motivation to engage in therapy, personal stability, and the child's developmental status. Throughout the mothers' involvement in both study arms, the program staff members discuss disposition possibilities. We have identified practices in the community that accept public insurance and work with high-risk clients, and we assist mothers in getting connected with these programs before ending their involvement with our program.

■ SUMMARY OF PRELIMINARY FINDINGS

Sample

The completed randomized pilot study enrolled and randomized 47 mothers of children ages newborn to three. The average age of mothers in the sample was 30.1 years ($SD = 6.5$) and the average child age was 17.7 months ($SD = 13.8$). The majority of mothers were single (64%), Caucasian (70%), high school–educated (79%) and unemployed (81%) at the time of enrollment. At baseline, 60% of the mothers reported having open child welfare cases. Between-group differences on these variables were non-significant except for marital status; significantly more mothers were married in the MIO condition.

Feasibility

On average, mothers assigned to MIO attended 72% of their scheduled meetings with the MIO therapist, 73% of their scheduled assessment meetings, and 82% of their scheduled meetings at the clinics. Mothers assigned to PE attended, on average, 78% of their scheduled meetings with the PE counselor, 78% of their scheduled assessment meetings, and 78% of their scheduled meetings at the clinics (between-group differences were not significant). These attendance records were very encouraging, given the high rate of dropouts reported in previous parenting intervention trials (for a review, see Suchman, Pajulo, DeCoste, & Mayes, 2006).

Treatment Outcomes

Results from the first randomized clinical pilot testing the preliminary efficacy of MIO intervention in comparison with PE sessions generally showed favorable outcomes for MIO mothers at both the post-treatment and six-week follow-up assessments (for complete reports, see Suchman, DeCoste, Castiglioni, et al., 2010; Suchman et al., 2011). Mothers enrolled in MIO showed higher levels of self-focused mentalizing (i.e., capacity to think about their own strong negative emotions in the parenting role and their impact on the child) compared to PE mothers at post-treatment ($d > .50$) and these differences were sustained follow up ($d > .20$). MIO mothers also showed more balanced and coherent mental representations of their children and the caregiving relationship than PE mothers at follow-up ($d > .20$, a delayed effect that suggests that representations may consolidate over time). There were no notable changes in child-focused reflective functioning (RF) (i.e., capacity to think about the child's own strong negative emotions and their impact on the mother) in either group, which may reflect the intervention's primary focus on the mother's mental states.

Even though child-focused RF did not improve, MIO mother–child dyads showed notable improvements in interactive behaviors at post-treatment and follow-up. MIO mothers' behavior during the brief teaching task was more supportive of children's emotional development than PE mothers' at post-treatment ($d > .20$), and this difference was more pronounced at follow-up ($d > .50$). MIO mothers also responded more contingently than PE mothers with their children at post-treatment ($d > .50$) and follow-up ($d > .50$). MIO children's communication and responsiveness to the mother was higher than PE children's at post-treatment ($d > .20$) and follow-up ($d > .50$) and MIO children's contingent response to the mother was also higher at follow-up ($d > .20$).

Mechanisms of Change

We examined the implications of self-focused vs. child-focused mentalizing for maternal caregiving behavior by using pre-treatment data from all mothers (for a full report, see Suchman, DeCoste, Leigh, & Borelli, 2010). We found unexpectedly that maternal self-focused (but not child-focused) mentalizing was associated with maternal caregiving domains, including sensitivity to cues (p <.05), social-emotional growth-fostering (p <.05), and cognitive growth-fostering (p <.05) such that better self-focused mentalizing predicted better caregiving behavior. These findings suggest the importance of targeting mentalization-for-self in the treatment of substance using mothers.

We also tested our proposed mechanisms of change in the treatment model and found that therapist adherence to unique MIO intervention strategies (e.g., exploring mental states and representations), above and beyond promoting a secure alliance (e.g., actively listening, showing genuine empathy and support, normalizing the mother's struggles)—a major component in both MIO and PE—corresponded to improvement from pre-to-post treatment in the mother's capacity to mentalize and the quality of her representations of the child (p <.05) and improvement in the mother's caregiving behavior (p <.05). (For a full report, see Suchman et al., 2012.) We also found that improvement in the mother's capacity to mentalize and the quality of her representations of the child corresponded to improvement in the mother's caregiving behavior (p <.05), even after improvement in substance use was taken into account. Importantly, improvement in maternal depression also corresponded to improvement in maternal caregiving behavior (p <.05). Together, these findings provide the first evidence, to our knowledge, on the mechanisms of change in mentalization-based interventions for parents. They suggest that targeting maternal mentalization in therapy can promote changes at the representation and behavioral levels in women for whom other behavioral and educational interventions have shown more limited efficacy.

■ FUTURE DIRECTIONS

Mentalization-based individual therapy for mothers with substance use disorders is showing clear feasibility and promise. Mothers who have enrolled in our program have often commented on how they liked to come to the program, felt comfortable and safe, were considering issues they had not thought about before (e.g., what their children were thinking and needing emotionally), and felt better when they left. For example, one mother commented during toward the end of her enrolment:

> I think it's been helpful to come here each week. It never occurred to me that [her 11-month-old son] has a mind or thinks about anything. Now I realize that he does and I take his feelings seriously. I also see how you talk to him about what he's thinking and I do that now, too. He seems happier and less frustrated and there's no more head-banging.

Both arms of the research—MIO and PE—have been highly feasible and acceptable in this way. MIO is showing particular promise also for improving reflective capacities, which, in turn, is showing promise for improving caregiving interactions. We are addressing some of the limitations of the first randomized pilot in the current ongoing randomized trial: We are assessing the child's attachment status before and after the intervention, and early results are showing changes from insecure to secure attachment status in all of the MIO mothers' children and some of the PE mothers' children. We are also conducting the follow-up assessment 13 weeks out to further examine the durability of effects.

Beyond testing the efficacy of MIO in a formal, randomized clinical trial, there is a need to examine the best ways to train front-line clinicians in substance abuse treatment clinics to adopt the principles of MIO into everyday clinical practice. Integration of MIO into the treatment clinic has many potential advantages: It would introduce consistency of approach across interventions targeting substance abuse and parenting, allow for tailoring treatment duration and intensity to individual client needs, help to address longstanding interpersonal struggles, and offer new clinical skills for negotiating impasses that otherwise lead to withdrawal from treatment and relapse. Many front-line clinicians will not have had training in supportive psychodynamic therapy or mentalization theory. Methods for introducing this new approach to substance-abuse-treatment providers must be carefully considered and evaluated.

There is also a need to further develop and evaluate the developmental progression of mentalization-based interventions for parents with substance use disorders. Improving the capacity to mentalize strong personal emotions seems to be a critical first step in treating parents. Beyond this step, it will be important to examine how and when dyadic work can be introduced in order to contribute to promoting the mother's interpersonal progress with the child as well as the child's growing capacity for emotional regulation. There is also a need for future adaptation and testing of the MIO model in other substance abuse treatment settings (e.g., residential, home visit) and with other populations (e.g., fathers, young adults, parents of older children).

A mentalization-based approach to psychotherapy is extraordinarily unoriginal in its emphasis on understanding the mind of oneself and others and making sense of behavior in terms of underlying emotions and feelings (Allen, Fonagy, & Bateman, 2008). At the same time, it is revolutionary in its insistence on viewing the patient as the expert on her own mind and the therapist as the assistant who is secondary to the patient's mentalizing process. Most current therapeutic approaches (e.g., cognitive-behavioral, contingency management, motivational enhancement) to treating substance abuse tend to be prescriptive about what a patient should think and feel. While they yield short-term benefits for reducing symptoms, there may be a greater benefit in using approaches that help the patient develop their own minds—and their sense of self. Most important, doing so will probably improve that patient's potential to foster the same psychological and emotional development in the next generation of offspring.

■ AUTHORS' NOTE

The authors wish to thank Carolyn Parler-McRae, Lynne Madden, and the staff and patients of the APT Foundation for their support and participation in this research. We also wish to thank Linda Mayes, Arietta Slade, and our research staff members, Nicole Castiglioni, Laura Donald, Mayra Vega, and

Lourdes de las Heras, for their contributions to this work. Finally, this chapter is dedicated to the memory of Bruce Rounsaville, whose encouragement, open-mindedness, and generous mentorship were vital to this work. This project was supported by the following grants from the National Institutes of Health: K02 DA023584, R01 DA17294 (Suchman); K02 DA023504 (Suchman); T32 NR008346 (Ordway).

▪ REFERENCES

Ainsworth, M. D. S., Blehar, M. C., Waters, E., & Wall, S. (1978). *Patterns of Attachment: A Psychological Study of the Strange Situation.* Hillsdale, NJ: Erlbaum.

Allen, J. A., Fonagy, P., & Bateman, A. W. (2008). *Mentalizing in Clinical Practice.* Washington, DC: American Psychiatric Publishing.

Barnard, K. E., & Eyres, S. J., Eds. (1979). *Child Health Assessment, Part 2: The First Year of Life.* (Publication Number DHEW No. HRA 79-25). Washington, DC: U.S. Government Printing Office.

Bateman. A., & Fonagy, P. (2006). *Mentalization-Based Treatment for Borderline Personality Disorder.* New York: Oxford University Press

Bateman, A., & Fonagy, P. (2012a). *Individual techniques of the basic model.* In A. W. Bateman & P. Fonagy (Eds.), *Handbook of Mentalizing in Mental Health Practice* (pp. 67–80). Washington, DC: American Psychiatric Publishing.

Bateman, A., & Fonagy, P. (2012b). *Borderline personality disorder.* In A. W. Bateman & P. Fonagy (Eds.), *Handbook of Mentalizing in Mental Health Practice* (pp. 273–288). Washington, DC: American Psychiatric Publishing.

Bevington, D., & Bleiberg, E. (2010). *Mentalization-Based Treatment—Families.* Seminar, Yale Child Study Center, New Haven, CT. October 25–27, 2010.

Burns, K. A., Chethik, L., Burns, W. J., & Clark, R. (1997). The early relationship of drug abusing mothers and their infants: An assessment at eight to twelve months of age. *Journal of Clinical Psychology, 53,* 279–287.

Cash, S. J., & Wilke, D. J. (2003). An ecological model of maternal substance abuse and child neglect: Issues, analyses, and recommendations. *American Journal of Orthopsychiatry, 73,* 392–404.

Choi, S., & Ryan, J. (2007). Co-occurring problems for substance abusing mothers in child welfare: Matching services to improve family reunification. *Children & Youth Services Review, 29,* 1395–1410.

Department of Health and Human Services. (April, 1999). *Blending Perspectives and Building Common Ground: A Report to Congress on Substance Abuse and Child Protection.* Washington, DC: DHHS.

Fonagy, P., Bateman, A. W., & Luyten, P. (2012). Introduction and overview. In A. W. Bateman & P. Fonagy (Eds.), *Handbook of Mentalizing in Mental Health Practice* (pp. 3–42). Washington, DC: American Psychiatric Publishing.

Fonagy, P., Gergely, G., Jurist, E., & Target, M. (2002). *Affect Regulation, Mentalization, and the Development of the Self.* New York: Other Press LLC.

George, C., Kaplan, N., & Main, M. (1985). *The Adult Attachment Interview.* Berkeley, CA: University of California at Berkeley, Department of Psychology, unpublished manuscript.

Grant, T., Huggins, J., Graham, J. C., Ernst, C., Whitney, N., Wilson, D. (2011). Maternal substance abuse and disrupted parenting: Distinguishing mothers who keep their children from those who do not. *Children & Youth Services Review, 33*, 2176–2185.

Hans, L.L., Bernstein, V.J., & Henson, L.G. (1999). The role of psychopathology in the parenting of drug-dependent women. *Development & Psychopathology, 11*, 957–977.

Kazdin, A. E. (2007). Mediators and mechanisms of change in psychotherapy research. *Annual Review of Clinical Psychology, 3*, 1027.

Khantzian, E. (1997). The self-medication hypothesis of substance use disorders: A reconsideration and recent applications. *Harvard Review of Psychiatry, 4*, 231–244.

Lam, W. K., Wechsberg, W., & Zule, W. (2004). African–American women who use crack cocaine: A comparison of mothers who live with and have been separated from their children. *Child Abuse & Neglect, 28*, 1229–1247.

Luyten, P., Fonagy, P., Lowyck, B., & Vermote, R. (2012). Assessment of mentalization. In A. Bateman & P. Fonagy (Eds.), *Handbook of Mentalizing in Mental Health Practice.* pp. 43–66. London: American Psychiatric Publishing.

Marsh, J. C., Ryan, J. P., Choi, S., & Testa, M. F. (2006). Integrated services for families with multiple problems: Obstacles to family reunification. *Children & Youth Services Review, 28*, 1074–1087.

Minnes, S., Singer, L. T., Humphrey-Wall, R., & Satayathum, S. (2008). Psychosocial and behavioral factors related to the post-partum placements of infants born to cocaine-using women. *Child Abuse & Neglect, 32*, 353–366.

National Center on Addiction and Substance Abuse. (2006). *Women Under the Influence.* Baltimore, MD: Johns Hopkins University Press.

Pajulo, M., Suchman, N. E., Kalland, M., & Mayes, L. C. (2006). Enhancing the effectiveness of residential treatment for substance abusing pregnant and parenting women: Focus on maternal reflective functioning and mother–child relationship. *Infant Mental Health Journal, 27*, 448–465.

Rosenbaum, M. (1981). *Women on Heroin.* New Brunswick, NJ: Rutgers University Press.

Shedler, J. (2010). The efficacy of psychodynamic psychotherapy. *American Psychologist, 65*, 98–109.

Sinha, R. (2001). How does stress increase risk of drug abuse and relapse? *Psychopharmacology, 158*, 343–359.

Slade, A., Aber, J. L., Berger, B., Bresgi, I., & Kaplan, M. (2003). *The Parent Development Interview—Revised.* Unpublished manuscript, City University of New York.

Suchman, N. E., DeCoste, C., Castiglioni, N., Legow, N., & Mayes, L. (2008). The Mothers and Toddlers Program: Preliminary findings from an attachment-based parenting intervention for substance abusing mothers. *Psychoanalytic Psychology, 25*, 499–517.

Suchman, N., DeCoste, C., Castiglioni, N., McMahon, T., Rounsaville, B., & Mayes, L. (2010). The Mothers and Toddlers Program: An attachment-based parenting intervention for substance-using women: Post-treatment results from a randomized clinical trial, *Attachment & Human Development, 12*, 483–504.

Suchman, N., DeCoste, & Mayes, L. (2009). The Mothers and Toddlers Program: An attachment-based intervention for mothers in substance abuse treatment. In C. Zeanah (Ed.), *Handbook of Infant Mental Health* (3rd ed., pp. 485–499). New York: Guilford Press.

Suchman, N., DeCoste, C., McMahon, T., Rounsaville, B., & Mayes, L. (2011). The Mothers and Toddlers Program, an attachment-based parenting intervention for substance-using women: Results at six-week follow up in a randomized clinical pilot. *Infant Mental Health Journal, 32,* 427–449.

Suchman, N., DeCoste, C., Leigh, D., & Borelli, J. (2010). Reflective functioning in mothers with drug use disorders: Implications for dyadic interactions with infants and toddlers. *Attachment & Human Development, 12,* 567–585.

Suchman, N. E., DeCoste, C., Rosenberger, P., & McMahon, T. J. (2012). Attachment-based intervention for substance using mothers: A preliminary test of the proposed mechanisms of change. *Infant Mental Health Journal, 33,* 360–371.

Suchman, N. E., Mayes, L., Conti, J., Slade, A., & Rounsaville, B. (2004). Rethinking parenting interventions for drug dependent mothers: From behavior management to fostering emotional bonds. *Journal of Substance Abuse Treatment, 27,* 179–185.

Suchman, N. E., Pajulo, M., DeCoste, C. & Mayes, L. C. (2006). Parenting interventions for drug dependent mothers and their young children: The case for an attachment-based approach. *Family Relations, 55,* 211–226.

Taylor, A. (1993). *Women Drug Users: An Ethnography of a Female Injecting Community.* Isle of Wight, United Kingdom: Clarendon Press.

Volkow, N. D., Fowler, J. S., & Wang, G. J. (2003). The addicted human brain: Insights from imaging studies. *The Journal of Clinical Investigation, 111,* 1444–1451.

Wilke, D. J., Kamata, A., & Cash, S. J. (2005). Modeling treatment motivation in substance-abusing women with children. *Child Abuse & Neglect, 29,* 1313–1323.

Zeanah, C. H., & Benoit, D. (1993). Clinical applications of a parent perception interview in infant mental health. *Infant Psychiatry, 3,* 539–554.

21 Working with States of Mindlessness in Substance-Abusing Mothers with Personality Disturbance

TESSA BARADON AND MINNA DAUM

▉ THEORETICAL FRAMEWORK

The clinical work described in this chapter is underpinned by a developmental approach to the acquisition of a capacity to "own" and understand states of mind and to see them as meaningful to ongoing behavior and actions (Fonagy & Target, 1997; Slade et al., 2005). From this point of view, an infant or child's experience of being "held" benignly in the mind of the caretaking adult as a separate, dependent, and developing child is pivotal. Through this process, the child can "look into the eye (mind) of the mother" and see himself as himself—i.e., relatively undistorted by the parent's state of mind or projections (Winnicott, 1971).

It is this experience of safely looking into another person's mind that is often critically missing for children of substance abusing, personality-disordered parents. The model is one of deficit. Poor or tenuous reflective capacities in the parent tend to create similar deficits in the child, with consequent chaos in the mind (lack of connectedness and meaning). Frequently, the parent's state of mind is labile and highly unpredictable—swinging from a position of feeling useless and hating, to feelings of omnipotence and idealized, merged love. Thus, the parent's experience of being with their baby or child is either of being aligned and at one with the child, or persecuted by the child when s/he is seen as separate. As long as the baby is seen as an extension of the mother, the baby can be narcissistically loved. This is a position of safety for the mother. However, whenever the baby creates a separateness—for example, through crying—the baby becomes infused in the mother's mind with malignant "ghosts" from the past (Fraiberg, Adelson, & Shapiro, 1975). This may also be true later on, when the child's budding autonomy emerges in toddlerhood.

For the child, the rigid alternative of either being at one with the mother, or annihilated, is catastrophic. A core problem for the child is the resolution of ambivalence—his/her parallel representations of good mother/self and bad mother/self cannot be integrated. One response to the unpredictable and frightening absence of a containing parent is the development of a persona that diminishes the importance of adult assistance and care. The embodied expressions of these internal positions (Baradon & Broughton, 2010) can be seen in the first vignette of mother and baby. In the second vignette of a mother and a child aged six, verbal and behavioral manifestations of the dilemmas predominate. Presenting the two cases with children of different ages gives a snapshot of the developmental trajectory in response to derailed primary relationships as the child grows older.

■ CLINICAL APPROACH

The concept of *mentalization* is useful as a framework within which to focus the therapist's gaze on the mind-to-mind interactions in the room. What the therapist is working with in the room is a state of "mindlessness" in the mother, in relation to both herself and her baby/child, and the child's attempts to "be" in the face of this mindlessness. Therefore, the overall task is to assist the mother and child to "create" minds of their own—to become more aware of their own mental states, the mental states of the other, and the relationship between the two (for an overview of parental reflective functioning and programmers utilizing this approach, see Nijssens et al.,2012). A central motivating force for the *mothers* we work with is their identity as a mother. What is often lacking is the notion of being a mother to a *specific* child, which implies that the child has needs separate from her own. This is the gap that we are trying to address by giving the mother both the appetite and the tools for thinking rather than not thinking. The therapist's verbal and nonverbal communications to the mother, through which the therapist creates a sense of safety and predictability, are pivotal to helping the mother begin to recognize her feelings, changes in mood, triggers for these changes, and how they relate to her life experiences. Through asking questions, wondering, being empathic, being surprised, and offering his own tentative thoughts, the therapist helps the mother create nuance, texture, and narrative around her experience.

In parallel to working with the mother on reflecting and guessing at meaning (mentalizing), the therapist is attending to the feelings and experience of the *child* and how s/he may be constructing understanding and nascent representations. With infants, the therapist may "mirror" and "mark" the baby's affect (wherein the therapist reflects back to the infant his/her emotional experience, as his own; Fonagy et al., 2002), speak to the baby, or handle the baby (Baradon, Broughton, Gibbs, James, Joyce & Woodhead, 2005). Nonverbal communication and playing with the baby may bypass or supplement verbal communication. With an older child, the experience of being attended to in an age-appropriate way is often unique. The therapist acts as a thoughtful mind, asking questions and being playful, and thus enables the child to become aware of his/her feelings and to begin to make sense of them. For example, children's hypervigilance in relation to unpredictable adults is not a reflective state. Helping a child identify and process his feelings of fear and rage can help free him/her from a frozen state and continue his/her developmental pathway, while remaining mindful of the parent's unpredictability.

Alongside attending to the mind of the parent and the child respectively, the therapist works with *their co-constructed relationship*. Centrally, she relates to each as a separate but related entity. In doing so, she brings the baby/child alive in the mother's mind as a being with a mind of his/her own, and validates the baby/child's own mind. She may question or represent the state of one to the other (to the mother, "I wonder what your child feels when you say you want to kill yourself?" and to the child, "Maybe it's very frightening for you when your mom says she is feeling so terrible, and then you hold onto mummy as tight as you can"). She may invite the mother to join her in wondering about the meaning of the child's behavior. Nonverbal expressions of intersubjectivity are noticed, and moments of pleasurable interaction are highlighted in order to emphasize to them the possibilities of recognition and connectedness between them as two separate people.

■ CLINICAL APPLICATIONS

Setting

The Anna Freud Centre in London serves high-risk populations in terms of parental mental health and consequent risk to children (aged 0–18). Treatments can be long- or short-term, or consist of assessments for the courts. Vignette 1 is taken from the Parent-Infant Psychotherapy program lasting two years. Mother and baby were seen together on a weekly basis by a psychoanalytically trained therapist (T. Baradon). Vignette 2 is taken from a multidisciplinary assessment requested by the court and tasked with making recommendations regarding the risk to the child of remaining in his mother's care. The assessment consisted of 15 individual and family meetings carried out over a period of three months. Family sessions were conducted by a systemic therapist (M. Daum).

Vignette 1

Lena's baby, Sid, was four months old when they were referred for parent–infant psychotherapy by their general practitioner, who was well acquainted with the mother's history. Both her parents were diagnosed with mental health disorders. Lena, emotionally abused by her mother, had started drinking when young and, by her twenties, she "didn't do anything but drink." She reported that she had taken drugs as well, worked as a prostitute, and suffered domestic violence in her brief marriage. Hospitalized for attempted suicide, she was diagnosed with a personality disorder, depression, and obsessive-compulsive disorder. Lena claimed she had stopped drinking and taking drugs when she became pregnant.

In the first session, Lena explained her wish for help not to repeat with Sid her own mother's violence towards her. Her mother was sometimes caring but sometimes "really evil," and it had left her feeling worthless. Lena added that she was afraid of how Sid might treat her in the future. The following vignette occurred 15 minutes into the first session.

Sid is motionless, slumped in Lena's lap, and has a blank expression on his face. Lena offers Sid the bottle. She shifts him so that he is reclining in her arms and places the bottle nipple in his mouth. Feeding is an ordinary occurrence in parent–infant psychotherapy, but the therapist had already been alerted to the mother's concern that Sid did not eat enough, although she (therapist) does not think he looks to be a thin baby.

Sid latches on and draws in the milk noisily. There is a momentary silence. The therapist quickly becomes concerned that the opening in the teat is too big, not adjusted to Ben's physical immaturity, and allowing too much milk through. In the therapist's mind, the milk flow has symbolic meaning—that of the thrust of intergenerational, hostile, and dysregulated emotions.

The initial gusto of the feed is quickly broken as Sid alternates between taking the bottle and coming off it. He generates a sense of discomfort, which is unsettling for both his mother and the therapist.

Lena seems uncertain as to why Sid is not feeding smoothly and what to do to help him. She looks anxiously at the therapist. The therapist responds by leaning forward and looking at Sid, whose gaze locks with hers. With exaggerated facial expression and lilting tone of voice, the therapist mirrors his distressed tone, and then, in a slower and lower voice, suggests that he is taking the milk too quickly and could he slow down a bit? In her nonverbal actions, the therapist matches Sid's heightened physio-affective state and tries to bring it down. Her verbal part of the communication, although spoken to Sid, conveys her thinking to Lena about the possible cause of Sid's irritability in the feed.

There is a moment of silence when both adults gaze at Sid; it feels to the therapist that the adults have joined in the contemplation of his needs.

Lena pulls the bottle nipple gently out of Sid's mouth. The therapist is unsure whether this is a positive incorporation of the therapist's suggestion to slow down—by giving Sid a breathing space through removing the bottle—or a withdrawing and defensive gesture, turning from passive into active (possibly feeling criticized by the therapist about the milk flow and therefore pulling the bottle away from Sid) (Freud, 1934). The therapist watches closely for Sid's response. He pulls his mother's hand towards him in order to latch on again, thereby suggesting that he experiences his mother as collaborative at this point and could express agency in pulling her back into the feed. The therapist's feeling of tension dissipates.

However, after a few gulps, Sid's distress escalates. He pulls away from the bottle, his body tensing, his face puckered and red. His cries express extreme distress. It feels to the therapist that he is approaching a state of "unthinkable anxiety" (Winnicott, 1962), wherein he is in the grip of panic and pain. The therapist feels deep compassion for both Sid and Lena and expresses this, again, both in words and nonverbally. She leans in towards the dyad, body concave as though to embrace and hold, and says in a soft, concerned voice, "Oh dear, Sid, what has happened?" She sympathizes with mother: "mmm..... it's so hard for you, too."

Lena silently seats Sid on her lap facing out and gently pats his back. Although his crying has stopped, he remains unsettled, fretting in a low-key manner. Lena tries the bottle again, asking meekly, "Do you want it?" Sid takes the nipple into his mouth but immediately turns his head away—his body rigid, arms lifted to the side, flapping.

Lena puts the bottle down and looks helplessly at the therapist. The therapist feels that Lena has become a child, too, appealing—like Sid—for a mother who can help. But the therapist is not sure how to helpfully respond and, while she hesitates momentarily, Lena places the dummy (pacifier) in Sid's mouth. He sucks hard, cheeks puffing in and out. His body slumps and his head flops to the side. He gazes blankly, fixedly into space. To the therapist, he appears like a doll—body without a mind.

Reflections on Vignette 1

This clinical sequence illustrates the tension between complex, historically rooted emotions evoked in the mother and the collapse of her capacity for reflective functioning in relation to her baby. In the context of Lena's attachment history, and her unresolved status in relation to it (Main & Goldwyn, 1984; Hesse & Main, 2006; Baradon and Steele, 2008), Sid appeared to represent in his mother's mind trauma and abuse even before he was born. Her anticipation that he might mistreat her when he grows up was played out in her helpless, fearful position in their interactions (Lyons-Ruth, Bronfman, & Parsons, 1999; Melnick, Finger, Hans, Patrick, & Lyons-Ruth, 2008). This role reversal, in which Sid was seen to be more emotionally powerful than she, seemed quite fixed. He was experienced as 'persecutory' in his cries, and, as his screams increased, so did Lena's helplessness. Lena critically failed to reflect on what was happening to Sid in a way that could be experienced by him as containing and regulating of his emotions. The rapid escalation in Sid's negative emotional state was linked to his mother's inability to think about his experience. Consequently, emotional residues from the past held current interactions in their grip and, especially when negative emotions were heightened, interfered with the capacity to experience and represent Sid as a Baby: separate, developmentally vulnerable, and dependent.

With Lena's embedded sense that she was worthless and useless, the bottle was continuously offered over her own body and mind. The therapist hypothesized that the concrete experience of being unable to regulate the current of milk was symbolic of being overwhelmed by her own unbearable feeling states. In the experience of the feed, therefore, physiological and psychological flooding were interwoven.

In parallel, Sid experienced a maternal mind that could not receive his feelings into her reverie (Bion, 1962), and he was forced to make do on his own (see also Crandell, Patrick, & Hobson, 2003). What did he do? Initially, he held onto a (by now) habitual pattern of inhibiting his attachment cues (slumped, blank). When this could no longer be sustained, he sought help by crying—he latched on to the bottle (whether hungry or not) and, when this proved overwhelming, he hung on to the succor of the stranger (therapist in their first session) for as long as possible. Then he fragmented (screaming, his body rigid, arms flapping). Finally he fell into a state of dissociation—a body without a mind.

It is interesting that 'oblivion' was finally resorted to. Dissociation is a final response to terror (Perry, 1997; Schore, 2003, Schore & Schore, 2008). Oblivion was also the defense his mother resorted to through drinking and drugs. The sequence described illustrates the notion of co-construction of defenses between mother and infant through their interactions (Beebe, 2000; Beebe & Lachman, 1998).

The therapist was alerted to Sid's struggle to hold on to himself through his extreme sensitivity to his mother's intrusion (via the bottle), the speed with which his defenses of inhibition and self-soothing collapsed, and the rapid escalation of his distress. In moving closer to Sid, the therapist was trying to use her face, voice, and intonation (Trevarthen, 1979) to regulate his levels of disturbed and disturbing arousal. She was also giving shape to Sid's experience through her body and in words, representing it to his mother, and at the same time modeling a more attuned response (Baradon et al., 2005). Moreover, the therapist's enquiry into Sid's experience—"What has happened?"—modeled the assumptions that his crying was a communication about his state of mind, that there were reasons for the crying—i.e., it was not random, these causes needed to be reflected on; and that she would help his mother respond to her baby's cries with a sense of agency rather than defeat.

The therapist understood that Lena, too, desperately needed to experience a sense of safety with the therapist—of being heard, attended to, and joined with in ways she had not experienced or been able to take in for herself or in relation to Sid. As well as emotional resonance, the therapist offered her mind—the functions of observing, reflecting, linking, and reasoning. It is so interesting that when the therapist's reflective functioning faltered, momentarily filled with emotion herself in the face of Sid's acute distress and Lena's fraught helplessness (see also Hobson, 2002), there was an enactment—Lena plugged Sid with the dummy-drug (pacifier) that induced oblivion. Perhaps the therapist's silence triggered the panic of abandonment and failure in Lena. The sequence ends at this point, but the challenge for the therapist in the session was to regain the position of empathically holding both baby and mother in mind despite their competing claims on her. This entailed managing her concern for the baby, keeping mother on board while attending to him, and attending to mother's helpless distress—thus sustaining the view that two separate people can both have their needs met. Yet she felt that there were sufficient cues from both, even in the first session, that there was potential to use her separate, different mind—her third-ness—in a restorative, creative way.

Vignette 2

William, aged six, and his mother Marina were referred to the Anna Freud Centre Court Assessment Service to assess William's needs and to give an opinion about the risks to his development from remaining in his mother's care. William's parents had separated when he was two years old. He had recently spent some weeks in the care of his elder half-sister, after she raised concerns about her mother hitting William. Further worries were raised by adult mental health professionals about the poor physical state of the home. At the time, Marina was a frequent user of crack cocaine and cannabis.

Marina was of mixed heritage, born in the French colonies. Her mother, a prostitute, had abandoned her to her maternal grandmother's care. She had been close to her grandmother, but was sexually abused as a young child by her maternal step-grandfather over a number of years. She had come to the United Kingdom as an adult; both her mother and her younger half-sister had subsequently committed suicide. At different times following his parents' separation, Marina had made allegations to various professionals that William had been sexually abused by his father as a baby. The substance of her allegations changed over time. William's contact with his father had been intermittent and sometimes withheld by his mother because of her fears that he would be abused again. There were concerns that William was out of his mother's control. She attributed this to his supposed experience of sexual abuse at the hands of his father.

While she refused to discuss her drug use, describing it as a "cultural" issue, the theme of sleep, or oblivion, featured strongly in Marina's narrative. She spoke of being exhausted by William and withdrawing into sleep (or, she implied, intoxication). At these times, she described keeping William next to her, to stop him from doing any damage, or leaving him to himself, locked in the apartment. When asked what gave her the most joy in being a parent, Marina evoked the image of her son asleep. It was apparent that she saw him as an abusive, persecuting figure far more powerful than she.

As part of the assessment, William was seen twice with his mother. The following interaction occurred about an hour into the first session.

Marina has spent the previous few minutes 'monopolizing' the session with the therapist, telling her how exhausting and difficult it is to care for her son. William has distanced himself from his mother, and is playing at another table. After some minutes, at the therapist's suggestion, they join William at the table. Marina, still in her coat, is standing behind William's chair, her head bowed, looking at him, her hands clasping the back of his chair. She has an odd smile on her face, a smile that implies shame, or coyness. William is industriously building a train track on the table. The therapist sits near him, facing both of them to create a triangle. She is aware of anxiety in both William and his mother, and of William's sense of aloneness in the room. The therapist's intention is to assess William's ability to give words to his experiences in his mother's presence, and his mother's capacity to attend to and reflect on what he says.

TH: So do you worry about your mum?

W: I worry about her *so much* (genuinely serious tone)... I forget about it (brittle, peremptory tone).

M: (laughs quietly)

TH: So what do you worry about when you worry about your mum?

W: (cutting off the therapist) I forget about it.

TH: Do you worry your mum's unhappy?

W: Yes.

TH: How do you know when your mum's unhappy?

W: (Theatrical, self-parodying voice, clasps his hands to his heart and throws his head back, closes his eyes) Because I'm so sad of her feelings...

TH: So what does she do when she's unhappy, your mum?

W: (Peremptory voice) She tells me off.

TH: Does she? Does she do anything else?

W: [Singsong tone] Hold on tight, no.

TH: Does she ever go to bed, go to sleep?

W: Hold on tight, no.

M: Yes I do. When I'm very tired I put him to sleep (laughs quietly, something like shame in her expression), isn't it, William?

W: Hold on tight, yes.

TH: And what do you do when your mum's sleeping then?

W: (grins). I creep, and creep, until she's sleeping. Then I steal her phone, delete all her pictures....

M: No, no, he never does that. I don't give him any, my phone (she feels in her pocket to check that her mobile is still there).

TH: Why would you want to delete all her pictures, anyway?

W: (Angry voice) Because I'm so STUPID.

M: (Angry voice) Because he breaks everything. All his toys...

TH: Is that what makes you feel stupid, when you break things?

W: Yeah. I'm so stupid. More stupider than a coward!

M: (Sniggers)

TH: Well maybe it makes you feel stupid when you break things, does it?

W: (Theatrical, self-parodying voice again) It makes me a bit sad... (mimes playing a violin).

William picks up the train track and flings it about. His mother, clearly irritated, grabs his arm roughly and says "Stop it now," her tone hostile. William shrugs her off, then suddenly falls on the floor, writhing, saying his "nuts" hurt, then jumps up. Her voice almost a whisper again, William's mum says he has broken his Nintendo DS. William chats with the therapist about DS games.

TH: So how did you break the DS?
W: (Adopts a loud, declamatory tone, arms stretched wide):
    "Because the PRIME MINISTER TOLD ME TO!!!!"
TH: (To mother): Does William listen to anyone?
M: I hope he listens to his teachers...
TH: Do you find it hard to be strict?
M: I have my rules and I wish he could do, but... he doesn't listen. I avoid hitting him, when I do, it's because I, you know (wipes her brow).
TH: You're desperate?
M: Yes. But then he listens. What do I have to do to get you to listen, William?
W: You have to smack me so much, until, until, until, I HATE.
M: Yeah but I can't do that. Because I'm not allowed to hurt you a lot.
WILLIAM STARTS CRYING, SOBBING, SCREAMING, THEN SMILES.
TH: (To mum): Can you tell when he's really upset?
WILLIAM STARTS SCREAMING AGAIN, SHE PUTS HER HAND OVER HIS MOUTH, HE GIGGLES. MOTHER SMILES.

Reflections on Vignette 2

Throughout this vignette, Marina presented as a depleted, waif-like character quite alone with the task of being a parent. She easily and repeatedly became an observer rather than a participant, regarding William with a kind of awe (when he was being precocious and 'clever') or horror (when he was being impolite or aggressive). She saw herself as the helpless victim in an abusive relationship, as she called attention to William's destructive qualities (see Silverman & Lieberman, 1999). At no point was there a hint of recognition of his young age and consequent vulnerability; instead, she experienced him as persecuting, and sought oblivion through (drug-induced) sleep. At moments when she displayed sudden hostility and loathing towards her son, her tone of voice changed and she resorted to physical means of control. Her hostility had an exhausted quality. Often, while babyhood allows the mother some hope that she can fulfill her baby's and her own needs, as the child grows older, the mother is faced with the terrible loss of that hope.

William, an unusually intelligent child, also presented as a person quite alone, a pseudo-adult and omnipotent. Left in an uncontained, unpredictable situation with a care giver who was alternately withdrawn, disturbed, and hostile, his personality was becoming structured around a denial of vulnerability (what Anna Freud described as "identification with the aggressor"; Freud, 1936). William failed to ask for adult help when he needed it, used words and phrases he did not understand, and defied all authority. He used "forgetting" both to control his panic and to close down any exploration. His use of the phrase "hold on tight" had the quality of a talisman, a defense against meaning as well as an expression of having to hold himself together, and a cue to the therapist that he felt in real danger.

Associated with but going beyond this precocious presentation was William's self-parodying take on emotional expression. The overall impression he gave was of a lack of emotional authenticity. This was understood as both a defensive posture—keeping painful emotions at bay—and an attempt to bridge (through identification) the gap between his mother's gentle words and tone of voice on the one hand, and her palpable hostility on the other.

At an emotional level, Marina made no sense to William and in her non-mentalizing state, she had failed to help him gain any capacity to reflect upon or manage his own emotions (see Hobson, Patrick, Crandell, Garcia-Perez, & Lee, 2005). As a consequence, a simple and straightforward expression of emotion felt impossible, so William resorted to a brittle, pantomimic form of expression whenever the subject of his own or his mother's feeling states was addressed. In adopting this self-parodying tone, William stepped outside of the emotional link with the therapist and demolished it. The therapist felt desperate for him as a vulnerable little boy who could not let himself be touched.

In relation to his mother, William's behavior and words suggested that his attachment was becoming organized into what Lyons-Ruth et al. (1999) have described as a *controlling-punitive stance*. Under threat of abandonment—through her 'oblivion'—by his mother, he maintained his connection with her by humiliating, directing, and controlling her, often in a rather sadistic manner. At the same time, in the face of his own aggressive and uncontrolled behavior and his mother's hostility, William experienced a degree of confusion and self-loathing, and saw himself as "stupid."

■ **DISCUSSION**

The developmental perspective anchors the development of the baby's mind in his/her relationship with an active, adult mind that seeks to understand and scaffold it. This process also underpins the therapeutic work when deficits have occurred. In other words, the therapist's central activity is to notice, try to understand, share, question, and revise her thinking with both the mother and the baby/child. In doing so, she is actively 'scaffolding' emergent reflectiveness in the mother and child, and modeling this process to them. In a sense, it is the therapist's mind that offers a therapeutic space within which this work can take place.

But there are ongoing challenges to the *therapist's stance*. The overwhelming emotion in each of these cases, unmoderated by a thinking mind in the mother or child, requires that the therapist maintain a discipline of self-monitoring and self-regulation in order to sustain her capacity to reflect. First, the pervasive defenses in the parent–child relationship can 'hijack' the therapist into a similar stance. For example, in watching the tape of the interview (Vignette 2), the therapist noted the strong pull towards 'oblivion' or not hearing, such that, at times, she failed to hear important statements by William. Second, holding one's position as equidistant in relation to both mother and child can be challenging, given the needs of each to be merged with the therapist, to the exclusion of the "third." The mother's palpable fear of abandonment and need to feel "at one" with the therapist exerts a pressure to join with the mother in an unboundaried, unthinking way.

In the case of William, the therapist experienced a pull from the mother to view William as she did, and William supported this by pushing the therapist away with his own self-denigrating attitude and behaviors. Fear of losing an often-tenuous connection with a suspicious, labile mother can compromise the therapist's capacity to reflect from moment to moment, and crucially, to keep in touch with the child. In the case of Sid and Lena (Vignette 1), the pull was towards providing protection for the baby. A distressed baby kick-starts the therapist's identifications as well as her own attachment system (Pally, 2005), and thereby she risks losing a sense of the mother's vulnerability. An example of maintaining equidistance was when Sid's cries escalated, and the therapist used her body and tone of voice to reflect both Sid's and his mother's difficulties with sympathy and concern.

Maintaining a Reflective Space

We have found three ideas helpful in addressing the challenge of maintaining a reflective space in the session: the need to de-escalate heightened affect, the importance of not assuming that the mother's mental functioning is the same as the therapist's own, and being as 'real' as possible with the patient.

De-escalating Heightened Affect

Heightened affects comprise not only negative affects, but also excitement, help-lessness, and self-aggrandizement. All negate the capacity to reflect. The therapist might choose to not react (as when William's therapist chats with him in an ordinary, age-appropriate way about his DS [handheld computer] rather than taking up his bizarre behavior), to wonder, to reframe, to move on, or to play. Any of these responses can help de-escalate emotion and open up, in due course, a space to think together about meaning. The main danger, however, is in the use made of the therapist's reflective stance—for example, in the first vignette, the therapist's silence triggered a panicked response in Lena to silence her baby's cries.

Assumptions About the Mind

The assumption that the mind of the other person functions similarly to one's own could be seen as a necessary part of human communication—making links, searching for meaning, seeing cause and effect. In working with these cases, however, one simply cannot assume that these very ordinary processes—which relate to establishing compatibility between the external and internal worlds so that experience makes sense—are taking place. For these mothers, what we see is attribution without reality-checking. There is also an absence of narrative, so that life is experienced by the mother as a series of traumatic events. This model of deficit is addressed by the therapist's constantly offering her own thinking to be examined between mother/child and herself in the room. Anna Freud's (1974) contribution to therapeutic interventions via "developmental help" (Edgcumbe, 2000; Hurry, 1998) addresses the therapist's work with such mental deficits and can be important with mothers as well as children.

Being as 'Real' as Possible

A significant part of offering developmental help to address these deficits is through being as 'real' as one can with one's clients. This involves adapting to their susceptibility to hypervigilance and their tendency to attribute negative intentions to the therapist, as well as sensitivity to non-genuine affect. The therapist will, in all realms of the interaction, make her thoughts and reasoning transparent to the patient. She may, for example, highlight what she has observed and check this with the mother. She may voice her thinking process to the patient to be reflected on together: "I am thinking xxx because of xxx." Another way of being 'real' relates to the realm of nonverbal communication. It is important to recognize how central our bodily communications are to these clients. If words and body language are incongruent, this will be picked up immediately and seen as hypocritical, uncaring, and untrustworthy.

One of the major questions raised in both vignettes is the extent to which there is room for people to be 'alive' in the sense of being a separate person, in a relationship with the other. The therapist's stance of keeping both mother and child in mind, being real in relation to both (adapting to the child's age), and helping them feel that she can contain both of them at the same time, may, over time, address their dilemma around survival despite separation.

■ **SUMMARY**

This chapter has described non-mentalizing states of mind in personality-disordered, substance-abusing mothers as a developmental deficit. Two clinical vignettes—a baby of four months and his mother, and a six-year-old boy and his mother—were presented. These illustrated the to-and-fro between states of mindlessness in the mother, the child's response, and the mother's non-reflective response to the child's behavior—leading to escalating negative affects in each. The therapeutic work is conceptualized as the therapist holding on to and applying her own mind to help mother and child give meaning to (mentalize) their experiences of the self and the other.

■ **REFERENCES**

Baradon, T., Broughton, C., Gibbs, I., James, J., Joyce, A., & Woodhead, J. (2005). *The Practice of Psycho-Analytic Parent–Infant Psychotherapy: Claiming the Baby.* London, New York: Routledge.

Baradon, T., & Steele, M. (2008). Integrating the Adult Attachment Interview in the clinical process of psychoanalytic parent-infant psychotherapy in a case of relational trauma.

In H. Steele and M. Steele (Eds.), *The Adult Attachment Interview in Clinical Context* London: Guilford.

Baradon, T., & Broughton, C. (2010). *Embodied Ghosts in the Nursery.* Plenary paper presented at the Annual Conference of the Association for Child Psychotherapists, London, United Kingdom.

Beebe, B. (2000). Co-constructing mother–infant distress: The microsynchrony of maternal impingement and infant avoidance in the face-to-face encounter. *Psychoanalytic Enquiry, 20,* 421–440.

Beebe, B., & Lachman, F. (1998). Co-constructing inner and relational processes: self and mutual regulation in infant research and adult treatment. *Psychoanalytic Psychology, 15,* 1–37.

Bion, W. R. (1962). *Learning from Experience.* London: William Heinemann.

Crandell, L. E., Patrick, M. P. H., & Hobson, R. P. (2003). "Still-face" interactions between borderline mothers and their 2-month-old infants. *British Journal of Psychiatry, 83,* 239–247.

Edgcumbe, R. (2000). *Anna Freud. A View of Development, Disturbances and Therapeutic Techniques.* London: Routledge.

Fonagy, P., & Target, M. (1997). Attachment and reflective function: Their role in self-organization. *Development & Psychopathology, 9,* 679–700.

Fonagy, P., Gergely, G., Jurist, E. J., & Target, M. (2002). *Affect Regulation, Mentalization and the Development of the Self.* New York: Other Press.

Fraiberg, S., Adelson, E., & Shapiro, V. (1975). Ghosts in the nursery: A psychoanalytic approach to the problems of impaired infant–mother relationships. *Journal of the American Academy of Psychiatry, 14,* 387–421.

Freud, A. (1936). *The Writings of Anna Freud. Vol. II: The Ego and the Mechanisms of Defense.* New York: International Universities Press.

Freud, A. (Ed.) (1974). A psychoanalytic view of developmental psychopathology. In *The Writings of Anna Freud* (Vol. 8, pp. 57–74). New York: International University Press, 1981.

Hurry, A. (1998). *Psychoanalysis and Developmental Therapy.* London: Karnac Books.

Hesse, E., & Main, M. (2006). Frightened, threatening, and dissociative parental behavior in low-risk samples: Description, discussion and interpretations. *Development & Psychopathology, 18,* 309–343.

Hobson, P. (2002). *The Cradle of Thought: Exploring the Origins of Thinking.* London: Macmillan.

Hobson, R. P., Patrick, M., Crandell, L., Garcia- Perez, R., & Lee, A. (2005). Personal relatedness and attachment in infants of mothers with borderline personality disorder. *Development & Psychopathology, 17,* 329–347.

Lyons-Ruth, K., Bronfman, E., & Parsons E. (1999). Atypical attachment in infancy and early childhood amongst children at developmental risk. Part IV: Maternal frightened, frightening, or atypical behavior and disorganized infant attachment patterns. In J. Vondra and D. Barnett (Eds.), Atypical patterns of infant attachment: Theory, research and current directions. *Monographs of the Society for Research in Child Development, 64,* 67–96.

Main, M., & Goldwyn, R. (1984). Predicting rejection of her infant from mother's representation of her own experience: Implications for the abused-abusing intergenerational cycle. *Child Abuse and Neglect, 8,* 203–217.

Melnick, S., Finger, B., Hans, S., Patrick, M., & Lyons-Ruth, K. (2008). Hostile-helpless states of mind in the AAI: A proposed additional AA category with implications for identifying disorganized infant attachment in high-risk samples. In H. Steele and M. Steele (Eds.), *Clinical Applications of the Adult Attachment Interview* (pp. 399–426). New York, London: Guilford.

Nijssens, L., Luyten, P., & Bales, D. (2012). Mentalization-Based Treatment for Parents (MBT-P) with borderline personality disorder and their infants. In N. Midgley & I. Vrouva (Eds.), *Keeping Children in Mind: Mentalization-Based Interventions with Children, Young People and Their Families* (pp. 79–97). London: Routledge.

Pally, R. (2005). A neuroscience perspective on forms of intersubjectivity in infant research and adult treatment. In B. Beebe., S. Knoblauch., J. Rustin, and D. Sorter (Eds.), *Forms of Intersubjectivity in Infant Research and Adult Treatment* (pp. 191–242). New York: Other Press.

Perry, B. D. (1997). Incubated in terror: Neurodevelopmental factors in the "cycle of violence." In J. D. Osofsky (Ed.), *Children in a Violent Society* (pp. 124–149). New York: Guilford Press.

Schore, A. N. (2003). *Affect Disregulation and Disorders of the Self.* New York: W.W. Norton and Company.

Schore J. R., & Schore, A. N. (2008). Modern attachment theory: the central role of affect regulation in development and treatment. *Clinical Social Work Journal, 36,* 9–20. D01 10.1007.D

Silverman, R. C., & Lieberman, A. F. (1999). Negative maternal attributions, projective identification, and the intergenerational transmission of violent relational patterns. *Psychoanalytic Dialogues, 9,* 161–186.

Slade, A., Grienenberger, J., Bernbach, E., Levy, D., & Locker, A. (2005). Maternal reflective functioning, attachment and the transmission gap: A preliminary study. *Attachment & Human Development, 7,* 283–298.

Trevarthen, C. (1979). Communication and cooperation in early infancy: A description of primary intersubjectivity. In M. Bullowa (Ed.), *Before Speech: The Beginning of Interpersonal Communication* (pp. 321–347). Cambridge, UK: Cambridge University Press.

Winnicott, D. M. (1965). The aims of psycho-analytical treatment. In *The maturational processes and the facilitating environment: Studies in the theory of emotional development* (pp. 166–170). London: The Hogarth Press and Institute of Psycho-Analysis. (Original work presented 1962.)

Winnicott, D. M. (1971). *Mirror Role of Mother and Family in Child Development. In Playing and Reality.* London: Tavistock Publications.

22 Fathers Too! Building Parent Interventions for Substance-Abusing Men

THOMAS J. MCMAHON

For much of the past century, men have consistently outnumbered women in populations of substance-abusing individuals (McMahon, Winkel, Luthar, & Rounsaville, 2005), and researchers (e.g., Anglin, Hser, & McGlothlin, 1987; Hser, Anglin, & Booth, 1987; Hser, Anglin, & McGlothlin, 1987) have repeatedly documented gender differences in precursors to addiction, patterns of use, and related problems. Consistently, one of the more striking differences between men and women entering substance abuse treatment involves their status as parents. In general, substance-abusing women are more likely to be the parent of a minor child (McMahon et al., 2005); they are more likely to express concern about the welfare of their children as they enter substance abuse treatment (Gerstein, Johnson, Larison, Harwood, & Fountain, 1997); and they are more likely to seek treatment with minor children in their care (McMahon et al., 2005). Nevertheless, there are actually more fathers than mothers entering substance abuse treatment, because men consistently outnumber women by a ratio of approximately 2:1 (McMahon et al., 2005), and fathers living away from their children appear to be the largest group of parents seeking treatment for alcohol and drug abuse (McMahon et al., 2005).

Despite clear links between substance abuse and disturbance in the psychosocial development of fathers, mothers, and children, relatively little is known about the adjustment of substance-abusing men as parents (McMahon & Rounsaville, 2002). As responsible fatherhood has become the focus of several public policy initiatives (for reviews, see Cabrera, 2010; Cabrera & Peters 2000; Mincy & Pounce 2002), researchers have, on a limited basis, begun to show that alcohol and drug abuse are clearly associated with compromise of responsible fathering (for a review, see Chapter 8). At this point, there is accumulating evidence that paternal substance abuse is associated with (a) problematic attitudes toward parenting, (b) socially irresponsible production of children, (c) poor co-parenting relationships, (d) less positive parenting behavior, (e) more negative parenting behavior, and (f) relatively poorer father–child relationships (for a review, see Chapter 8).

Although alcohol and drug abuse seem to be associated with compromise of fathering, this research also highlights efforts at responsible fathering that are inconsistent with popular stereotypes of substance-abusing men. At this time, there is accumulating evidence that substance-abusing men are frequently present when their children were born, they often acknowledge paternity, they have often lived with their children, they have often made some attempt to provide financial support, and even if not living in the same household, they frequently have ongoing contact with at least some of their children (McMahon, Winkel, & Rounsaville, 2008; McMahon, Winkel, Suchman, & Rounsaville, 2007).

When carefully considered, this research suggests that parenting may be an important, but largely ignored, issue in the treatment of substance-abusing men (McMahon & Rounsaville, 2002). Very few substance abuse treatments used with men clearly focus on enhancement of parenting with an expectation that improvement in their social role performance will contribute to improvement in the psychosocial adjustment of fathers, mothers, and children. Over the years, researchers (e.g., Kelley & Fals-Stewart, 2002, 2007, 2008; Fals-Stewart & O'Farrell, 2003; O'Farrell, Murphy, Stephan, Fals-Stewart, & Murphy, 2004) have shown that marital intervention can improve substance abuse and family outcomes when delivered to substance-abusing men, they (e.g., Catalano, Haggerty, Fleming, Brewer, & Gainey, 2002) have included fathers in clinical trials of comprehensive interventions for substance-abusing parents, and they (e.g., Lam, Fals-Stewart, & Kelley, 2008, 2009) have begun to develop a marital intervention for substance-abusing fathers living with a sexual partner. However, gender differences in the nature of both substance abuse and parenting argue for comprehensive, gender-specific approaches to parent intervention, and researchers (e.g., Luthar & Suchman, 1999, 2000) have begun to develop parent interventions grounded in a clear understanding of the needs substance-abusing women bring to treatment. Although a number of authors (e.g., O'Neil & Lujan, 2010) have argued that parent intervention for men needs to be grounded in contemporary formulations of male gender, there is not yet an empirically validated, gender-specific intervention designed to address the complex needs of substance-abusing fathers.

■ OVERVIEW

Fathers Too! is a semi-structured, gender-specific, individual psychotherapy designed to improve father–child relationships that is currently being developed for men enrolled in substance abuse treatment. Building upon the intrinsic motivation of men to be a better father, the intervention focuses on (a) ways substance use can interfere with self-defined goals to be a more effective parent, and (b) ways fathering can support self-defined goals to establish abstinence. The intervention is based on a developmental-ecological perspective on the parenting of substance-abusing men, and it emphasizes the integration of therapeutic techniques to help men realize their goal to improve their relationship with a specific child.

■ TARGET POPULATION

Although the general approach can be extended to other populations of substance-abusing fathers, *Fathers Too!* is presently being developed for fathers enrolled in methadone maintenance treatment. Only men who express interest in being a more effective father are considered appropriate. Resident and nonresident fathers with biological children are the target population, but men in a position to function as a father figure for other children are also included. Although men involved in a divorce process or men involved with the child welfare system may be enrolled, men with legal mandates that limit access to their children are not considered appropriate. Men must be stable on a maintenance dose of methadone before they begin the program, and men physiologically dependent on another substance must be detoxified before they are allowed to begin. Men with psychiatric or neurological conditions that, even with treatment, would preclude meaningful participation in a semi-structured individual psychotherapy are not considered appropriate participants.

■ RATIONALE

Fathers Too! is currently being developed for men in methadone maintenance treatment because more than 40 years of research indicates that methadone hydrochloride is a safe, effective, long-term treatment for opioid dependence (for a review, see Strain, 2006). Since methadone was first approved as a maintenance treatment, there has also been agreement that psychosocial intervention must complement medical treatment, and researchers (e.g., McLellan, Arndt, Metzger, Woody, & O'Brien, 1993) have shown that methadone maintenance is most effective when offered with intervention designed to address concurrent medical, psychological, family, vocational, and social problems. At this time, 60 to 90 milligrams of methadone daily, two to three clinic visits weekly, and moderate levels of psychosocial treatment appears to be the most efficacious and cost-effective treatment regimen (Rhoades, Creson, Elk, Schmitz, & Grabowski, 1998; Kraft, Rothbard, Hadley, McLellan, & Asch, 1997).

When offered with a therapeutic dose of methadone, complementary psychosocial interventions clearly improve both psychosocial and substance use outcomes. For example, Woody and colleagues showed that individual psychotherapy can be an effective adjunct to the drug counseling typically offered to methadone-maintained patients (Woody et al., 1983; Woody, McLellan, Luborsky, & O'Brien, 1987, 1995). Moreover, Rounsaville and colleagues argued that, to be effective, psychotherapy should be an integral component of the maintenance program that is made available early in the treatment process (Rounsaville, Glazer, Wilber, Weissman, & Kleber, 1983; Rounsaville & Kleber, 1985). More recently, Fals-Stewart and O'Farrell (2003) showed that marital and substance use outcomes can be improved for opioid-dependent men receiving antagonist treatment when family-oriented intervention is added to treatment-as-usual, and Luthar and Suchman (2000) showed that psychological and parenting outcomes can be improved when parent intervention is added to treatment-as-usual for opioid-dependent women receiving agonist treatment. Despite this, most psychosocial interventions integrated into methadone maintenance treatment target the secondary use of alcohol and other illicit drugs so common within this population (e.g., see Rawson et al., 2002). At this time, there are surprisingly few empirically validated psychosocial interventions that target other problems common among opioid-dependent men.

Although intervention to address interpersonal problems is often deferred until after abstinence is achieved, *Fathers Too!* is being developed for use with men who have completed an orientation phase of methadone maintenance treatment. This is being done for several reasons. First, even if they are still using alcohol and illicit drugs, substance-abusing men may have ongoing contact with their children. Second, enrollment relatively early in a course of treatment when their distress about their inability to function as a father is likely to be highest may actually facilitate their engagement and make it easier to highlight ways that continued use of alcohol and illicit drugs compromises father–child relationships. Third, *Fathers Too!* targets men who may be actively using, because, even after they are enrolled in methadone maintenance treatment, use of alcohol and other illicit drugs is very common, and there is a need for creative intervention that targets this secondary use of alcohol and other illicit drugs. Although other approaches to psychosocial treatment target the substance abuse directly (e.g., see Rawson et al., 2002), *Fathers Too!* attempts to link compromise of fathering with continued use in an effort to promote retention in treatment and accelerate movement toward abstinence. Finally, *Fathers Too!* targets men who are actively using because, when dealing with secondary substance abuse and interpersonal issues of this nature, there is no evidence that there are advantages associated with waiting for a period of sustained abstinence. In fact, there is some evidence that treatments that address substance use and family problems simultaneously may be more effective than approaches that focus only on the substance use (e.g., see Fals-Stewart & O'Farrell, 2003).

In addition to targeting men early in the treatment process, *Fathers Too!* targets men with a child from birth to 21 years of age because research indicates that men enter substance abuse treatment with children of all ages (McMahon et al., 2005). Although children differ developmentally, there are common themes in father–child relationships that justify focusing on the nature of these relationships from birth through early adulthood. By focusing on the common dimensions of father–child relationships with attention to ways developmental issues differ for children of different ages, *Fathers Too!* has the potential to meet the needs of most fathers entering substance abuse treatment.

■ PRIMARY GOAL

The primary goal of *Fathers Too!* is to improve father–child relationships while decreasing the use of alcohol and illicit drugs.

■ CONCEPTUAL FRAMEWORK

From the beginning, *Fathers Too!* has been grounded in a developmental-ecological perspective on parenting that conceptualizes fathering as a complex, dynamic process with profound implications for fathers, mothers, and children (for discussion, see Belsky, 1984, 1993; Belsky & Jaffee, 2006; Cicchetti & Lynch, 1995; Cicchetti & Valentino, 2006). *Fathers Too!* builds on this work by acknowledging the validity of developmental-ecological models of fathering that allow for dynamic modeling of ways substance abuse compromises ability to function effectively as a father and ways inability to function effectively as a father may contribute to the perpetuation

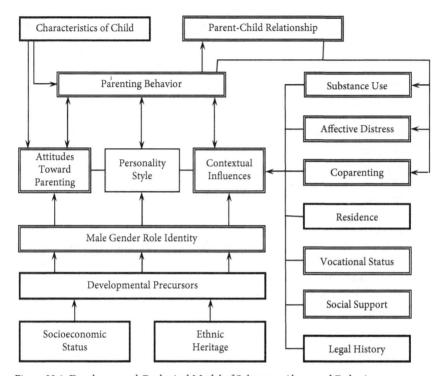

Figure 22.1 Developmental-Ecological Model of Substance Abuse and Fathering.

of alcohol and illicit drug use. Figure 22.1 outlines the conceptual model that has guided development of the intervention. Constructs double-outlined represent constructs targeted by *Fathers Too!*

Within a developmental-ecological model of substance abuse and fathering, there are nine broad conclusions grounded in empirical data that must be carefully considered in the development of a parent intervention designed to address the complex needs of substance-abusing fathers.

- Any parent intervention designed to meet the needs of substance-abusing men must acknowledge that patterns of pair-bonding, procreation, and parenting vary with socioeconomic status and ethnic heritage (for reviews, see Garcia Coll & Pachter, 2002; Hoff, Laursen, & Tardif, 2002).
- Any parent intervention designed to meet the needs of substance-abusing men must acknowledge that, when compared with men who have no history of substance abuse, substance-abusing men report greater exposure to childhood adversity known to heighten risk for compromise of parent–child relationships across generations (e.g., see Dube et al., 2003).
- Any intervention designed to meet the needs of substance-abusing fathers must allow for ways traditional ideas about the nature of masculinity influence the parenting behavior of men (for a review, see O'Neil & Lujan, 2010).

- Any intervention designed to meet the need of substance-abusing fathers must acknowledge that parenting behavior and substance abuse are both influenced by personality style (for reviews, see Belsky & Barends, 2002; Verheul, van den Bosch, & Ball, 2009).
- Any intervention designed to meet the needs of substance-abusing fathers must acknowledge that (a) values, attitudes, and beliefs about parenting play an important role in determining actual behavior (for reviews, see Bugental & Happaney, 2002; Holden & Buck, 2002; Siegel & McGillicuddy-De Lisi, 2002) and (b) substance-abusing men often demonstrate values, attitudes, and beliefs about parenting that represent risk for compromise of parent–child relationships and poor developmental outcomes in children (for a review, see Chapter 8).
- Any intervention designed to meet the needs of substance-abusing fathers must acknowledge that situational factors consistently influence the nature of father–child relationships (for a review, see Carlson & McLanahan, 2010). The existing literature suggests that there are seven contextual influences likely to affect the fathering of substance-abusing men: (a) ongoing use of alcohol and illicit drugs, (b) psychological distress, (c) quality of the co-parenting relationship, (d) residence with children, (e) social support for parenting, (f) employment status, and (g) legal history.
- Any intervention designed to meet the needs of substance-abusing fathers must acknowledge that characteristics of the child also influence the quality of parent–child relationships, particularly the age and gender of the child (for a review, see Parke, 2002).
- Any intervention designed to meet the needs of substance-abusing fathers must acknowledge that there is a reciprocal relationship between the psychosocial adjustment of men and participation in family life. The psychosocial adjustment of men influences participation in family life, and participation in family life influences the psychosocial adjustment of men (for a review, see McMahon & Spector, 2007).
- Finally, any intervention designed to meet the needs of substance-abusing fathers must acknowledge that fathers, mothers, and children stand to benefit from positive father–child relationships. Even when the sexual partnership has ended, mothers receive more emotional, instrumental, and financial support when fathers are involved with their children (e.g., see Carlson & McLanahan, 2010); and even when not living in the same household, children may benefit when fathers are present in a positive way (for a review, see Carlson & Magnuson, 2011).

■ DEFINING CHARACTERISTICS

Fathers Too! is defined by six distinguishing characteristics: (a) a focus on fathering, (b) a relational focus, (c) a focus on self-defined goals, (d) the matching of therapeutic technique to therapeutic task, (e) attention to male gender, and (f) a focus on both fidelity and flexibility. When integrated into a coherent *gestalt*, these six dimensions distinguish *Fathers Too!* from other psychosocial interventions that target either substance abuse or problems with parenting.

A Focus on Fathering

As noted above, *Fathers Too!* focuses on the fathering of substance-abusing men. The intervention is designed to actively engage men around their interest in being a more effective parent and then link that goal with the need to remain in substance abuse treatment, establish abstinence, and avoid relapse. More than anything else, this effort to consistently link effective parenting with sustained abstinence is the characteristic of *Fathers Too!* that differentiates it from both other substance abuse treatments and other parent interventions. Once men are engaged around their desire to be a more effective parent, the goal is to build positive father–child relationships and decrease the risk for continued substance use by increasing positive parenting behavior and decreasing negative parenting behavior.

A Relational Focus

Fathers Too! is grounded in a relational approach that emphasizes the assessment and treatment of each father in a dynamic process involving fathers, mothers, and children unfolding across generations. As suggested by Suchman, Mayes, Conti, Slade, and Rounsaville (2004), behavioral approaches to parent training have not proven very efficacious when used with substance-abusing mothers. Given the ways chronic substance abuse compromises parent–child relationships, Suchman et al. (2004) have argued that parent intervention designed to better meet the needs of substance-abusing mothers may need to focus more on the emotional quality of the parent–child relationship. Consistent with this, *Fathers Too!* builds on contemporary ideas about the need for comprehensive, systemic approaches to clinical intervention that acknowledge the complex nature of relational difficulty common among men and women with serious psychopathology that may be related to personality disturbance (for further discussion, see Magnavita, 2005). Rather than focusing on the development of parenting skills designed to promote more effective management of challenging behavior in the child, *Fathers Too!* focuses on helping men develop more satisfying dyadic (father–mother and father–child) and triadic (father–mother–child) relationships within their family of procreation. The focus is more clearly on the development of the father's relationships than management of the child's behavior.

A Focus on Specific Goals

Consistent with other approaches to psychosocial intervention (Miller et al., 1994; Miller & Rollnick, 2002; Weissman et al., 2000), *Fathers Too!* is characterized by a focus on the definition and pursuit of personal goals. Before beginning treatment, each client is asked to identify specific goals involving (a) their alcohol and drug abuse and (b) their relationship with a child. From the beginning, the focus of the treatment is defined by a mutual understanding of the client's personal goals.

Matching of Therapeutic Technique to Therapeutic Task

In an effort to match the therapeutic strategy with the focus of the treatment at each step in the behavior change process, a broad range of acceptable therapeutic techniques is used to address the multidimensional nature of parenting behavior. That is, the therapeutic technique is matched to the therapeutic task being pursued within a specific treatment session. Acceptable, proven therapeutic techniques are integrated into a coherent *gestalt* designed to address the different dimensions of parenting behavior. Consequently, motivational, expressive, cognitive, interpersonal, and behavioral exercises are used at different points in the treatment to (a) provide structure, (b) maintain interest, (c) promote participation, (d) examine different dimensions of parenting behavior, and (e) implement plans for behavior change. This is done because, although some technical approaches focus more exclusively on one specific dimension of a problem like motivation for change (e.g., see Miller et al., 1994, Miller & Rollnick, 2002), other approaches to clinical intervention acknowledge the need for attention to the different dimensions of a problem when working toward lasting behavior change (for further discussion, see Norcross, 2005). Given that substance-abusing men are likely to present with (a) limited motivation, (b) problematic attitudes toward parenting, (c) traditional definitions of gender, (d) feelings of guilt and shame, (e) difficulty in co-parenting relationships, and (f) negative parenting behavior, no single therapeutic approach is likely to adequately address the problems they face as parents.

Figure 22.2 illustrates how motivational, expressive, cognitive, interpersonal, and behavioral techniques are integrated during delivery of the intervention to promote movement through a behavior-change process. Early in the treatment,

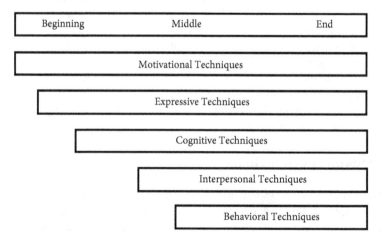

Figure 22.2 Stages of Treatment and Integration of Therapeutic Techniques.

when clients are more likely to be considering change, the emphasis is on the use of motivational and expressive techniques. As treatment continues, cognitive and interpersonal techniques are introduced to facilitate preparation for change. Toward the middle of treatment, the emphasis shifts more clearly to the use of behavioral techniques designed to promote initial change in actual parenting behavior, and toward the end of treatment, motivational techniques are again used to enhance motivation for maintenance of initial change and continued pursuit of treatment goals.

Attention to Male Gender

As a psychosocial intervention for men, *Fathers Too!* is also grounded in current understanding of male gender. There are four ways this is done. First, research concerning the nature of male gender (for a review, see Levant, 1996) informs thinking about this population of men *as* men. Next, research documenting gender differences in the nature of substance abuse (e.g., see Anglin et al., 1987; Hser, Anglin, & Booth, 1987; Hser, Anglin, & McGlothlin, 1987) informs thinking about this population of men as substance-abusing men. Third, research concerning the nature of fathering, particularly socially and economically disenfranchised populations of fathers (for reviews, see Carlson & Magnuson, 2011; Carlson & McLanahan, 2010), informs thinking about this population of men as fathers. Finally, the growing literature on men in psychotherapy (e.g., see Brooks, 1998) informs delivery of the intervention to substance-abusing fathers.

Fidelity with Flexibility

Within specific parameters, *Fathers Too!* allows the clinician to structure the treatment so that it meets the needs of an individual client. Working within the conceptual framework outlined here, the clinician has license to use motivational, expressive, cognitive, interpersonal, and behavioral techniques in a creative, flexible manner to move the client toward realization of his specific treatment goals. A modular approach to the selection and organization of treatment sessions that does not require that all treatment sessions be delivered to each client allows the clinician to tailor the treatment to the needs of a specific client.

■ THERAPEUTIC STANCE

Clinicians delivering *Fathers Too!* are expected to take an active, empathetic, and flexible therapeutic stance in an effort to create a positive helping relationship within which to deliver the intervention. Throughout the treatment, clinicians are expected to (a) provide structure, (b) communicate understanding of targeted problems, (c) convey a sense of acceptance, (d) facilitate discussion, (e) emphasize personal responsibility for change, (e) accept responsibility to be the change agent, and (f) provide support and assistance. Within each session, they take an active, directive stance designed to keep the client remain focused on the realization of his personal goals without being prescriptive. Rather than simply providing information, teaching skills, and prescribing solutions, clinicians are expected to (a) encourage clients to explore their thoughts, feelings, and behavior; (b) promote consideration of alternatives; (c) provide information; (d) help generate plans; and (e) facilitate the development of new skills in ways that allow the client to "own" the work done within the intervention.

■ THERAPEUTIC TECHNIQUES

Fathers Too! allows for the thoughtful, creative use of motivational, expressive, cognitive, interpersonal, and behavioral techniques to promote behavior change in fathers. Table 22.1 contains a listing of specific techniques drawn from different approaches to clinical intervention that can be used in the delivery of *Fathers Too!*. Given the multidimensional nature of parenting behavior, no single technical approach is viewed as wholly adequate. The challenge for clinicians is to effectively integrate specific techniques in a way that works for both the clinician and the client. As noted above, clinicians match the therapeutic technique to the stage of treatment and the therapeutic task being pursued within each session to effectively address a specific dimension of parenting behavior. This does not mean, however, that multiple techniques are integrated into each treatment session. In fact, they are not. Instead, a specific therapeutic technique guides delivery of each session or block of sessions.

For example, if the client and the clinician are exploring beliefs about the effective discipline of children, cognitive techniques would be the primary strategy for the treatment session. If the client relates his belief system to childhood experiences within his family of origin, it might be appropriate to acknowledge the continuity in parenting behavior across generations, but it would not be appropriate to abandon exploration of the client's current belief system to encourage expression of emotion about having been physically abused as a child. Ideally, that would have been done earlier in the treatment during a session that addressed the developmental dimension when encouraging expression of emotion would have been more consistent with both the stage of treatment and the focus of the session.

Similarly, the utilization of diverse therapeutic techniques does not mean that clinicians simply choose those they find the most familiar or the easiest to use. For example, it is not appropriate for a clinician with extensive training in motivational intervention to use motivational strategies later in the course of this treatment when the goal is to help a client develop more effective ways of communicating with a teenage daughter. To be delivered in a manner consistent with the conceptual model, that treatment session would have to involve the use of behavioral techniques. Consequently, during the course of a full treatment, clinicians are expected to utilize many, if not most, of the techniques outlined in Table 22.1. Most of these techniques are routinely used in other forms of substance abuse intervention, and they are familiar to many clinicians. The challenge for the clinician who has not done similar work is to apply them creatively to address the parenting issues the client brings to treatment.

TABLE 22.1 *Integration of Therapeutic Techniques in* Fathers Too!

Motivational Techniques
  Share the evidence
  Highlight discrepancy: Link fathering and substance use
  Elicit motivational statements
  Emphasize self-efficacy
  Undermine resistance
  Develop treatment goals
Expressive Techniques
  Encourage emotional expression
Cognitive Techniques
  Explore belief systems
Interpersonal Techniques
  Take a relationship inventory
  Resolve parenting role disputes
  Plan for new parenting roles
  Explore strategies to build better co-parenting relationships
  Involve significant others
  Build social support
Behavioral Techniques
  Monitor alcohol and drug use
  Examine co-parenting and parenting behaviors
  Reinforce positive parenting behavior
  Identify negative parenting behavior
  Explore alternatives to negative parenting behavior
  Rehearse new behaviors
  Encourage *in vivo* testing of new behaviors
Gender-Specific Techniques
  Challenge common myths of masculinity
  Explore alternative gender role behavior
  Explore continuity across generations
  Use visual representation
  Develop action plans
  Build in rituals

■ BUILD IN RITUALS

Rituals can be important in psychotherapy pursued with men (Brooks, 1998). Consequently, *Fathers Too!* incorporates a simple ritual involving a handshake that is used consistently by both male and female clinicians. At the beginning of each treatment session, the clinician greets the client with a handshake to say "Hello." At the end of each session, the clinician ends with a handshake to both indicate agreement about the plan for continued treatment and say "Goodbye." Other simple rituals (e.g., talking over a cup of coffee) can also be integrated into the sessions.

■ PROSCRIBED TECHNIQUES

Aggressive confrontation, argument, labeling, lecturing, simple education, excessive use of clinical interpretation, and behavioral contracting are not allowed in the delivery of *Fathers Too!*. Although participation in 12-Step programs is not discouraged, discussion of 12-Step philosophy and encouragement of enrollment in self-help groups is also not allowed, unless it is somehow directly related to a parenting issue (e.g., having children attend a Nar-Anon group). Use of other approaches to the development of parenting skills (e.g., a filial approach where the clinician works with parent and child together) and use of techniques drawn from other approaches to family intervention (e.g., structural family therapy) are also prohibited.

■ OUTLINE OF THE TREATMENT

Fathers Too! has five critical components. Typically, the intervention comprises 16 to 24 treatment sessions conducted over the course of 16 to 20 weeks. Each intervention consists of (a) a pretreatment assessment, (b) four mandatory evaluative sessions, (c) 12 to 16 treatment sessions, (d) a maximum of four supplementary treatment sessions, and (e) a mandatory termination session. The four evaluative sessions begin the treatment for everyone in the same manner, and the mandatory termination session ends the treatment for everyone in the same manner. The other treatment sessions are drawn from a menu of thematic sessions developed to address problems common within the target population, and they are selected to address the different dimensions of parenting that must be addressed to help each client realize his treatment goals. Up to four supplementary sessions may also be used to facilitate evaluation, communication, or treatment planning with significant others. All sessions are approximately 60 minutes long, but when indicated, supplementary sessions may be longer.

■ INITIAL ASSESSMENT

The initial assessment of each client enrolled in *Fathers Too!* is comprised of a pretreatment assessment and four evaluative sessions. Before seeing his clinician, each father completes a pretreatment evaluation designed to generate information about (a) initial treatment goals, (b) current family system, (c) ongoing substance use, (d) personality disturbance, (e) quality of co-parenting relationships, (f) positive and negative parenting behavior, (g) quality of parenting received from biological parents, and (h) childhood trauma. This pretreatment assessment also includes information about positive and negative parenting collected from the child, and information about the emotional-behavioral adjustment of the child collected from both father and child. A summary of this pretreatment assessment is provided to each clinician when the first treatment session is scheduled. As treatment begins, the clinician uses this information to inform completion of the four evaluative sessions. The four evaluative sessions are listed in Table 22.2. This initial

TABLE 22.2 *Mandatory Initial Assessment to Begin* Fathers Too!

1. Genogram
2. Linking Fathering and Drug Use: The Fathering and Drug Abuse Timeline
3. Ghosts from the Past: Things Adults Taught Me about Being a Parent
4. Personal Feedback: Clarifying Goals

series of treatment sessions culminates with a discussion of the results, refinement of the client's treatment goals, and development of a treatment plan.

■ THEMATIC TREATMENT MODULES

After the goals of treatment have been defined, the clinician selects the thematic treatment modules needed to help the client realize his goals. The thematic treatment modules that have been defined thus far are listed in Table 22.3. Each module is composed of two to five treatment sessions. Once the most appropriate treatment modules have been chosen, they are ordered for delivery to the client following the developmental-ecological hierarchy outlined in Table 22.4, with examples of thematic sessions that might be used at each step in the treatment process.

TABLE 22.3 *Thematic Treatment Modules within* Fathers Too!

1. Confronting Ghosts from the Past
2. Men and Emotions: Shame and Guilt
3. Thoughts About Being a Father
4. Who Can Help? Building Social Support for Fathering
5. Working with Mom: Co-parenting with the Mother of Your Child
6. Staying Clean = Being a Good Father, Being a Good Father = Staying Clean
7. You and Your Child: A Relationship Inventory
8. How Old Is Your Child? Developmental Concerns of Childhood and Adolescence
9. Just Being There: On Being Available and Consistent
10. Talk to Me: Communicating with Children
11. My Thoughts, His Thoughts, My Feelings, Her Feelings
12. Doing Things with Children
13. Who? When? Where? Why? More About Doing Things with Children
14. Hitting Hurts: Disciplining Children
15. Just Do What You Want: Not Disciplining Children Hurts
16. Can You Do the Math? Helping with School
17. Not Being There
18. What About the Money? Financial Support of Children

TABLE 22.4 *Developmental-Ecological Hierarchy for Ordering of Thematic Treatment Modules*

Address the developmental dimension
  Confronting Ghosts from the Past
Address the affective dimension
  Men and Emotions
Address the cognitive dimension
  Thoughts About Being a Father
Address the interpersonal dimension
  Who Can Help? Building Social Support for Fathering
  Working with Mom: Co-parenting with the Mother of Your Child
Address the behavioral dimension
  Just Being There: On Being Available and Consistent
  Talk to Me: Communicating with Children
  Doing Things with Children

Consistent with general guidelines for delivery of the intervention, this initial listing of thematic sessions is considered tentative. As the treatment evolves, specific sessions can be dropped, and additional sessions can be added to better address the parenting issues of the client as they unfold over time. Outlines of the treatment sessions were developed to serve as examples of ways specific issues might be addressed in a manner consistent with the treatment protocol. When indicated, clinicians and supervisors can collaborate on modification of specific sessions to better meet the needs of the client, as long as the modification is consistent with general guidelines for delivery of the intervention. Modification to make them more relevant to children of different ages is always considered.

Moreover, this listing of thematic treatment sessions is not exhaustive. If a client presents a treatment issue that cannot be addressed by a specific session or cluster of sessions, the clinician and supervisor collaborate on the development of a thematic session that will address the parenting issue in a manner consistent with the treatment protocol. The treatment manual includes a template to guide development of a new thematic treatment session, and as new thematic sessions are developed, they are added to the treatment manual.

■ SUPPLEMENTARY TREATMENT SESSIONS

Supplementary sessions are used to facilitate communication and treatment planning with a third party. Consultations with (a) father and child, (b) father and mother or other caregiver, (c) father and drug abuse counselor, and (d) father and some other source of social support are all acceptable. Supplementary sessions can also be used to secure consultation with a child and adolescent clinician. For example, there may be need to clarify the extent to which a child may be having serious psychiatric difficulty. Even if trained as a child and adolescent clinician, it would not be appropriate for the *client's* clinician to do that evaluation. Similarly, a clinician who is not a child psychologist may want assistance from a child psychologist to help a client understand the results of a special education evaluation completed with his child and plan for the client to participate in the special education planning process.

When a decision is made to conduct a supplementary treatment session, there is always careful planning for that session with the client. When considering the use of a supplemental session, the clinician works with the client to (a) clarify the need for the session, (b) secure agreement that the session will be potentially helpful, (c) define the goal of the session, (d) clarify expectations for each of the participants, and (e) consider ways the session should be structured. Whenever a supplementary session is held, there is also always a review of the meeting during the next scheduled session with the client.

■ MANDATORY TERMINATION SESSION

When clients complete 16 to 20 weeks of *Fathers Too!*, there is a mandatory termination session where clinician and client review the course of the client's treatment,

TABLE 22.5 *Structure of* Fathers Too! *Treatment Sessions*

1. Greeting ritual
2. Review of the week
3. Review of previous session
4. Evaluative or thematic activity
5. Development of an action plan
6. Ending ritual

review the extent to which he realized his treatment goals, and identify goals he can continue to pursue.

◼ STRUCTURE OF TREATMENT SESSIONS

Each treatment session is delivered following the structure outlined in Table 22.5. Although the amount of time devoted to each component of the session may be adjusted, each element should occur within each treatment session. As noted, every session begins with a handshake as the clinician greets the client for the session. If not spontaneously initiated by the client, this greeting is initiated by the clinician. After the greeting, the next 10 to 15 minutes of every treatment session are devoted to a brief review of important events that have occurred since the last session from the perspective of the client's treatment goals. The next five to 10 minutes of each session are then devoted to a review of salient material from the previous treatment session and the outcome of any action plan initiated at the end of that session. The outcome of any action plan is always reviewed to highlight the logical progression of the intervention and the client's movement toward his treatment goals. The last 30 to 40 minutes of each session are devoted to completion of the evaluative or thematic activity planned for that day.

As each treatment session comes to a close, the clinician briefly introduces the evaluative or thematic activity that will be the focus of the next treatment session. Again, the intention is to highlight the logical progression of the treatment and the relevance of each session to the client's treatment goals. When the course of a session raises questions about what the focus of the next session should be, the clinician can share the question with the client, and they can collaboratively decide what the focus of the next session should be. Every session then ends with a handshake. If not spontaneously initiated by the client, it is always initiated by the clinician.

◼ SPECIAL CONSIDERATIONS

Delivery of a parent intervention to substance-abusing men is likely to involve some challenges, both challenges that are common in the delivery of any substance abuse intervention and challenges that are specific to the delivery of a parent intervention. Experience with delivery of the intervention thus far suggests that there are five challenges clinicians need to be prepared to actively address: (a) problems with attendance, (b) other pressing concerns, (c) acute intoxication, (d) recurrent substance use with signs of physical dependence, and (e) potential child abuse or neglect. Within *Fathers Too!*, an effort is made to anticipate these challenges and respond in a proactive manner within established guidelines for management of the challenge.

■ EVALUATION

Over the past 10 years, the systematic, goal-oriented approach to the development of psychosocial treatments outlined by Rounsaville and his colleagues has been used to conceptualize, manualize, and document the potential efficacy of this individual psychotherapy (e.g., see Carroll, 1996; Carroll et al., 2000; Carroll & Nuro, 2002; Rounsaville, Carroll, & Onken, 2001; Rounsaville, Chevron, & Weissman, 1984; Rounsaville, O'Malley, Foley, & Weissman, 1988). At the time this chapter was prepared, there had been two preliminary evaluations of *Fathers Too!* In a psychotherapy development study (McMahon, Suchman, Carroll, & Rounsaville, 1999), the psychotherapy was outlined in a treatment manual and procedures were established for selecting and training counselors and rating videotaped treatment sessions for adherence to the treatment protocol and quality of delivery. A pilot study comparing the potential efficacy of *Fathers Too!* when added to standard methadone maintenance treatment suggested that the fathers who received *Fathers Too!* as a supplemental treatment demonstrated potentially meaningful declines in secondary substance use and high-risk parenting behavior (McMahon, 2009).

In a second study of potential efficacy (McMahon et al., 2005), *Fathers Too!* (McMahon, Giannini, & Maccarelli, 2006) was recently compared with individual drug counseling (Mercer & Woody, 1999) when added to treatment-as-usual for men receiving methadone maintenance treatment. Both treatments were also combined with the low-cost approach to contingency management with reinforcement of attendance at treatment (Petry & Martin, 2002). The goal of the project was to explore the comparative efficacy of the two approaches to psychosocial intervention in the context of the best attendance at treatment possible. The results of that comparative study were being evaluated at the time this chapter was prepared.

■ CONCLUSION

Although fathers, more than mothers, are likely to be quickly, and inaccurately, labeled the incompetent, indifferent, irresponsible, potentially dangerous parent as they enter substance abuse treatment (McMahon & Giannini, 2003), existing data on the nature of substance abuse and fathering highlight the need for family-oriented intervention designed to minimize the harm associated with paternal substance abuse (for a review, see Chapter 8). As suggested previously (McMahon et al., 2008), the emerging literature indicates that clinicians should be prepared to engage men in a dialogue about parenting issues as they enter substance abuse treatment, because (a) they will all be at risk to become fathers under difficult circumstances, (b) many of them will already be fathers, (c) many of the fathers will demonstrate positive parenting behavior that should be supported as much as possible, and (d) many of the fathers will demonstrate negative parenting behavior that needs to somehow be addressed. Moreover, men enrolled in substance abuse treatment should be engaged in a dialogue about parenting issues because (a) they are interested in parent intervention (McMahon et al., 2007), (b) they can be engaged in family-oriented intervention (Andreas, O'Farrell, & Fals-Stewart, 2006; Fals-Stewart & O'Farrell, 2003; Kelley & Fals-Stewart, 2002), (c) family-oriented intervention can have positive effects on both substance use and family functioning (Fals-Stewart & O'Farrell, 2003), and (d) family-oriented intervention can have a positive effect on the psychosocial adjustment of other family members, even if they do not participate in the treatment (Andreas et al., 2006; Kelley & Fals-Stewart, 2002).

■ AUTHOR NOTES

Support for the development of *Fathers Too!* has been provided by the National Institute on Drug Abuse (Grants P50 DA09241 and R01 DA020619). Some of the material presented in this chapter was taken from *Fathers Too! A Parent Intervention for Drug-Abusing Fathers* (McMahon, Giannini, & Maccarelli, 2006).

The author would like to offer this chapter in memory of Bruce Rounsaville, M.D., who generously helped him secure the funding needed to develop this parent intervention for substance-abusing fathers. The author would also like to thank Francis Giannini, L.C.S.W., Lisa Maccarelli, Ph.D., Nancy Suchman, Ph.D., Nancy Petry, Ph.D., Kathryn Nuro, Ph.D., and Kathleen Carroll, Ph.D., for their contributions to the development of this intervention.

Correspondence concerning this chapter should be addressed to Thomas McMahon, Ph.D., Yale University School of Medicine, Connecticut Mental Health Center, West Haven Mental Health Clinic, 270 Center Street, West Haven, Connecticut 06516. Electronic mail may be sent to thomas.mcmahon@yale.edu.

■ REFERENCES

Andreas, J. B., O'Farrell, T. J., & Fals-Stewart, W. (2006). Does individual treatment for alcoholic fathers benefit their children? A longitudinal assessment. *Journal of Consulting & Clinical Psychology, 74,* 191–198.

Anglin, M. D., Hser, Y., & McGlothlin, W. H. (1987). Sex differences in addict careers. 2. Becoming addicted. *American Journal of Drug & Alcohol Abuse, 13,* 59–71.

Belsky, J. (1984). The determinants of parenting: A process model. *Child Development, 55,* 83–96.

Belsky, J. (1993). Etiology of child maltreatment: A developmental-ecological analysis. *Psychological Bulletin, 114,* 413–434.

Belsky, J., & Barends, N. (2002). Personality and parenting. In M. H. Bornstein (Ed.), *Handbook of Parenting. Vol. 3: Becoming and Being a Parent* (2nd ed., pp. 415–438). Mahwah, NJ: Lawrence Erlbaum.

Belsky, J., & Jaffee, S. (2006). The multiple determinants of parenting. In D. Cicchetti & D. Cohen (Eds.), *Developmental Psychopathology. Vol. 3: Risk, Disorder, and Adaptation* (2nd ed., pp. 38–85). New York: Wiley & Sons.

Brooks, G. R. (1998). *A New Psychotherapy for Traditional Men*. San Francisco, CA: Josey-Bass Publishers.

Bugental, D. D., & Happaney, K. (2002). Parental attributions. In M. H. Bornstein (Ed.), *Handbook of Parenting. Vol. 3: Becoming and Being a Parent* (2nd ed., pp. 509–535). Mahwah, NJ: Lawrence Erlbaum Associates.

Cabrera, N. J. (2010). Father involvement and public policies. In M. E. Lamb (Ed.), *The Role of Father in Child Development* (5th ed., pp. 517–550). New York: John Wiley & Sons.

Cabrera, N. J., & Peters, H. E. (2000). Public policies and father involvement. *Marriage and Family Review, 29*, 295–314.

Carlson, M. J., & Magnuson, K. A. (2011). Low-income fathers' influence on children. *Annals of the American Academy of Political & Social Science, 635*, 95–116.

Carlson, M. J., & McLanahan, S. S. (2010). Fathers in fragile families. In M. E. Lamb (Ed.), *The Role of Father in Child Development* (5th ed., pp. 241–269). New York: John Wiley & Sons.

Carroll, K. M. (1996). Integrating psychotherapy and pharmacotherapy in substance abuse treatment. In F. Rotgers, D. S. Keller, & J. Morgenstern (Eds.), *Treating Substance Abuse: Theory and Technique*. New York: Guilford Press.

Carroll, K. M., Nich, C., Sifry, R. L., Nuro, K. F., Frankforter, T. L., Ball, S. A., et al. (2000). A general system for evaluating therapist adherence and competence in psychotherapy research in the addictions. *Drug & Alcohol Dependence, 57*, 225–238.

Carroll, K. M., & Nuro, K. F. (2002). One size cannot fit all: A stage model for psychotherapy manual development. *Clinical Psychology: Science & Practice, 9*, 396–406.

Catalano, R. F., Haggerty, K. P., Fleming, C. B., Brewer, D. D., & Gainey, R. R. (2002). Children of substance-abusing parents: Current findings from the Focus on Families Project. In R. J. McMahon & R. D. Peters (Eds.), *The Effects of Parental Dysfunction on Children*. New York: Kluwer Academic/Plenum Publishers.

Cicchetti, D., & Lynch, M. (1995). Failures in the expectable environment and their impact on individual development: The case of child maltreatment. In D. Cicchetti & D. J. Cohen (Eds.), *Developmental Psychopathology. Vol. 2: Risk, Disorder, and Adaptation* (pp. 32–71). New York: Wiley & Sons.

Cicchetti, D., & Valentino, K. (2006). An ecological-transactional perspective on child maltreatment: Failure of the average expectable environment and its influence upon child development. In D. Cicchetti & D. J. Cohen (Eds.), *Developmental Psychopathology. Vol. 3: Risk, Disorder, and Adaptation* (2nd ed., pp. 129–201). New York: Wiley & Sons.

Dube, S. R., Felitti, V. J., Dong, M., Chapman, D. P., Giles, W. H., & Anda, R. F. (2003). Childhood abuse, neglect, and household dysfunction and the risk of illicit drug use: The Adverse Childhood Experiences Study. *Pediatrics, 111*, 564–572.

Fals-Stewart, W., & O'Farrell, T. J. (2003). Behavioral family counseling and naltrexone for male opioid-dependent patients. *Journal of Consulting & Clinical Psychology, 71*, 432–442.

Garcia Coll, C. T., & Pachter, L. M. (2002). Ethnic and minority parenting. In M. H. Bornstein (Ed.), *Handbook of Parenting. Vol. 4: Social Conditions and Applied Parenting* (pp. 1–20). Mahwah, NJ: Lawrence Erlbaum Associates.

Gerstein, D. R., Johnson, R. A., Larison, C. L., Harwood, H. J., & Fountain, D. (1997). *Alcohol and Other Drug Treatment for Parents and Welfare Recipients: Outcomes, Costs, and Benefits.* (Available from the U.S. Department of Health and Human Services, Office of the Assistant Secretary for Planning and Evaluation, 200 Independence Avenue, S. W., Washington, D.C. 20201).

Hoff, E., Laursen, B., & Tardif, T. (2002). Socioeconomic status and parenting. In M. H. Bornstein (Ed.), *Handbook of Parenting. Vol. 2: Biology and Ecology of Parenting* (2nd ed., pp. 231–252). Mahwah, NJ: Lawrence Erlbaum Associates.

Holden, G. W., & Buck, M. J. (2002). Parental attitudes toward childrearing. In M. H. Bornstein (Ed.), *Handbook of Parenting. Vol. 3: Becoming and Being a Parent* (2nd ed., pp. 537–562). Mahwah, NJ: Lawrence Erlbaum Associates.

Hser, Y., Anglin, M. D., & Booth, M. W. (1987). Sex differences in addict careers. 3. Addiction. *American Journal of Drug & Alcohol Abuse, 13*, 231–251.

Hser, Y., Anglin, M. D., & McGlothlin, W. H. (1987). Sex differences in addict careers. 1. Initiation of use. *American Journal of Drug & Alcohol Abuse, 13*, 33–57.

Kelley, M. L., & Fals-Stewart, W. (2002). Couples- versus individual-based therapy for alcohol and drug abuse: Effects on children's psychosocial functioning. *Journal of Consulting & Clinical Psychology, 70*, 417–427.

Kelley, M. L., & Fals-Stewart, W. (2007). Treating paternal alcoholism with Learning Sobriety Together: Effects on adolescents versus preadolescents. *Journal of Family Psychology, 21*, 435–444.

Kelley, M. L., & Fals-Stewart, W. (2008). Treating paternal drug abuse using Learning Sobriety Together: Effects on adolescents versus children. *Drug & Alcohol Dependence, 92*, 228–238.

Kraft, M. K., Rothbard, A. B., Hadley, T. R., McLellan, A. T., & Asch, D. A. (1997). Are supplementary services provided during methadone maintenance really cost-effective? *American Journal of Psychiatry, 154*, 1214–1219.

Lam, W. K., Fals-Stewart, W., & Kelley, M. L. (2008). Effects of parent skills training with behavioral couples therapy for alcoholism on children: A randomized clinical pilot trial. *Addictive Behaviors, 33*, 1076–1080.

Lam, W. K., Fals-Stewart, W., & Kelley, M. L. (2009). Parent training with behavioral couples therapy for fathers' alcohol abuse: Effects on substance use, parental relationship, parenting, and CPS involvement. *Child Maltreatment, 14*, 243–254.

Levant, R. F. (1996). The new psychology of men. *Professional Psychology: Research & Practice, 27*, 259–265.

Luthar, S. S., & Suchman, N. E. (1999). Developmentally informed parenting interventions: The Relational Psychotherapy Mothers' Group. In D. Cicchetti & S. L. Toth (Eds.), *Rochester Symposium on Developmental Psychopathology. Vol. X: Developmental Approaches to Prevention and Intervention* (pp. 271–309). Rochester, NY: University of Rochester Press.

Luthar, S. S., & Suchman, N. E. (2000). Relational Psychotherapy Mothers' Group: A developmentally informed intervention for at-risk mothers. *Development & Psychopathology, 12*, 235–253.

Magnavita, J. J. (2005). *Personality-Guided Relational Psychotherapy: A Unified Approach.* Washington, DC: American Psychological Association.

McLellan, A. T., Arndt, I. O., Metzger, D. S., Woody, G. E., & O'Brien, C. P. (1993). The effects of psychosocial services in substance abuse treatment. *Journal of the American Medical Association, 269*, 1953–1959.

McMahon, T. J. (2009, June). *Fathers Too!*: A parent-intervention for drug-abusing men. In N. E. Suchman (Chair), Interventions for Parents with Substance Use Disorders: New Findings from Clinical Research. Workshop presented at the annual meeting of the College on Problems of Drug Dependence, Reno, NV.

McMahon, T. J., & Giannini, F. D. (2003). Substance-abusing fathers in family court: Moving from popular stereotypes to therapeutic jurisprudence. *Family Court Review, 41*, 337–353.

McMahon, T. J., Giannini, F. D., & Maccarelli, L. M. (2006). Fathers Too! A Parent Intervention for Substance-Abusing Men. Unpublished treatment manual, Department of Psychiatry, Yale University School of Medicine, New Haven, CT.

McMahon, T. J., & Rounsaville, B. J. (2002). Substance abuse and fathering: Adding Poppa to the research agenda. *Addiction, 97*, 1109–1115.

McMahon, T. J., & Spector, A. Z. (2007). Fathering and the mental health of men. In J. E. Grant & M. N. Potenza (Eds.), *Clinical Guide to Men's Mental Health* (pp. 259–282). Arlington, VA: American Psychiatric Publishing.

McMahon, T. J., Suchman, N. E., Carroll, K. M., & Rounsaville, B. J. (1999). Relational parent intervention with drug-abusing fathers. In B. J. Rounsaville (PI), *Psychotherapy Development Research Center* (National Institute on Drug Abuse Grant P50 DA09241). Yale University, New Haven, CT.

McMahon, T. J., Suchman, N. E., Petry, N. M., Pruett, K. D., Carroll, K. M., & Rounsaville, B. J. (2005). *Parent Intervention for Drug-Abusing Fathers* (National Institute on Drug Abuse Grant No. R01 DA020619). Yale University, New Haven, CT.

McMahon, T. J., Winkel, J. D., Luthar, S. S., & Rounsaville, B. J. (2005). Looking for Poppa: Parenting responsibilities of men versus women seeking drug abuse treatment. *American Journal of Drug & Alcohol Abuse, 31*, 79–91.

McMahon, T. J., Winkel, J. D., & Rounsaville, B. J. (2008). Drug-abuse and responsible fathering: A comparative study of men enrolled in methadone maintenance treatment. *Addiction, 103*, 269–283.

McMahon, T. J., Winkel, J. D., Suchman, N. E., & Rounsaville, B. J. (2007). Drug-abusing fathers: Patterns of pair-bonding, reproduction, and paternal involvement. *Journal of Substance Abuse Treatment, 33*, 295–302.

Mercer, D., & Woody, G. E. (1999). *Individual Drug Counseling* (Therapy Manuals for Drug Addiction Series, NIH Publication No. 99-4380). Rockville, MD: National Institute on Drug Abuse.

Miller, W. R., & Rollnick, S. (2002). *Motivational Interviewing: Preparing People for Change* (2nd ed.). New York: Guilford Press.

Miller, W. R., Zweben, A., DiClemente, C. C., & Rychtarik, R. G. (1994). *Motivational Enhancement Therapy Manual: A Clinical Research Guide for Clinicians Treating Individuals with Alcohol Abuse and Dependence* (Project MATCH Monograph Series, NIH Publication No. 94-3723). Bethesda, MD: National Institute on Alcohol Abuse and Alcoholism.

Mincy, R. B., & Pounce, H. W. (2002). The responsible fatherhood field: Evolution and goals. In C. S. Tamis-LeMonda & N. Cabrera (Eds.), *Handbook of Father Involvement: Multidisciplinary Perspectives* (pp. 555–597). Mahwah, NJ: Lawrence Erlbaum Associates.

Norcross, J. C. (2005). A primer on psychotherapy integration. In J. C. Norcross & M. R. Goldfried (Eds.), *Handbook of Psychotherapy Integration* (2nd ed., pp. 3–23). New York: Oxford University Press.

O'Farrell, T. J., Murphy, C. M., Stephan, S. H., Fals-Stewart, W., & Murphy, M. (2004). Partner violence before and after couples-based alcoholism treatment for male alcoholic patients: The role of treatment involvement and abstinence. *Journal of Consulting & Clinical Psychology, 72,* 202–217.

O'Neil, J. M., & Lujan, M. L. (2010). An assessment paradigm for fathers in therapy using gender role conflict theory. In C. Z. Oren & D. C. Oren (Eds.), *Counseling Fathers.* New York: Routledge.

Parke, R. D. (2002). Fathers and families. In M. H. Bornstein (Ed.), *Handbook of Parenting. Vol. 3: Becoming and Being a Parent* (2nd ed., pp. 27–73). Mahwah, NJ: Lawrence Erlbaum.

Petry, N. M., & Martin, B. (2002). Low-cost contingency management for treating cocaine- and opioid-abusing methadone patients. *Journal of Consulting & Clinical Psychology, 70,* 398–405.

Rawson, R. A., Huber, A., McCann, M., Shoptaw, S., Farabee, D., Reiber, C., et al. (2002). A comparison of contingency management and cognitive-behavioral approaches during methadone maintenance treatment for cocaine dependence. *Archives of General Psychiatry, 59,* 817–824.

Rhoades, H. M., Creson, D., Elk, R., Schmitz, J., & Grabowski, J. (1998). Retention, HIV risk, and illicit drug use during treatment: Methadone dose and visit frequency. *American Journal of Public Health, 88,* 34–39.

Rounsaville, B. J., Carroll, K. M., & Onken, L. S. (2001). A stage model of behavioral therapies research: Getting started and moving on from stage I. *Clinical Psychology: Science & Practice, 8,* 133–142.

Rounsaville, B. J., Chevron, E. S., & Weissman, M. M. (1984). Specification of techniques in interpersonal psychotherapy. In R. L. Spitzer & J. Williams (Eds.), *Psychotherapy Research: Where Are We and Where Should We Go?* (pp. 160–172). New York: Guilford Press.

Rounsaville, B. J., Glazer, W., Wilber, C. H., Weissman, M. M., & Kleber, H. D. (1983). Short-term interpersonal psychotherapy in methadone maintained opiate addicts. *Archives of General Psychiatry, 40,* 629–6363.

Rounsaville, B. J., & Kleber, H. D. (1985). Psychotherapy/counseling for opiate addicts: Strategies for use in different treatment settings. *International Journal of Addictions, 20,* 869–896.

Rounsaville, B. J., O'Malley, S. S., Foley, S., & Weissman, M. M. (1988). The role of manual-guided training in the conduct and efficacy of interpersonal psychotherapy for depression. *Journal of Consulting & Clinical Psychology, 56,* 681–688.

Sigel. I. E., & McGillicuddy-De Lisi, A. V. (2002). Parent beliefs are cognitions: The dynamic belief system model. In M. H. Bornstein (Ed.), *Handbook of Parenting. Vol. 3: Becoming and Being a Parent* (2nd ed., pp. 485–508). Mahwah, NJ: Lawrence Erlbaum Associates.

Strain, E. C. (2006). Methadone dose during maintenance treatment. In E. C. Strain & M. L. Stitzer (Eds.), *The Treatment of Opioid Dependence* (pp. 89–118). Baltimore: John Hopkins University Press.

Suchman, N., Mayes, L., Conti, J., Slade, A., & Rounsaville, B. (2004). Rethinking parenting interventions for drug-dependent mothers: From behavior management to fostering emotional bonds. *Journal of Substance Abuse* Treatment, *27*, 179–185.

Verheul, R., van den Bosch, L. M. C., & Ball, S. A. (2009). Substance use. In J. M. Oldham, A. E. Sodol, & D. S. Bender (Eds.), *Essentials of Personality Disorders* (pp. 361–378). Arlington, VA: American Psychiatric Publishing.

Weissman, M. M., Merkowitz, J. C., & Klerman, G. L. (2000). *Comprehensive Guide to Interpersonal Psychotherapy.* New York: Basic Books.

Woody, G. E., Luborsky, L. L., McLellan, A. T., O'Brien, C. P., Beck, A. T., Blaine, J., et al. (1983). Psychotherapy for opiate addicts: Does it help? *Archives of General Psychiatry, 40,* 639–645.

Woody, G. E., McLellan, A. T., Luborsky, L., & O'Brien, C. P. (1987). Twelve-month follow-up of psychotherapy for opiate dependence. *American Journal of Psychiatry, 144,* 590–596.

Woody, G. E., McLellan, A. T., Luborsky, L., & O'Brien, C. P. (1995). Psychotherapy in community methadone programs: A validation study. *American Journal of Psychiatry, 152,* 1302–1308.

23 Behavioral Couples Therapy for Substance-Abusing Parents

MICHELLE L. KELLEY,
KEITH KLOSTERMANN, AND
JAMES M. HENSON

Parental substance use can affect children in many ways. First, exposure to maternal alcoholism and illicit drugs *in utero* may cause physical and central nervous system insult to the developing fetus that may result in long-term developmental consequences (e.g., Glantz & Chambers, 2006). Second, some behaviors such as alcohol abuse appear to be moderately heritable (e.g., see Boris, 2009). Finally, considerable research has shown that family contexts characterized by parental drug or alcohol use may lead to ineffective parenting practices (e.g., poor discipline: Barnard & McKeganey, 2004; Leonard et al., 2008; Suchman & Luthar, 2000; Young et al., 2007). In some cases, parental substance use may result in impaired parent behavior or discipline, and in other instances, inadequate child-monitoring (Widom & Hiller-Sturmhofel, 2001). Although not mutually exclusive, the focus of this chapter is on children who reside with one or more substance-abusing parents for part or all of their childhoods and who often experience concomitant family factors associated with parental substance abuse.

■ CHILDREN RESIDING WITH CAREGIVERS WHO ABUSE ALCOHOL OR DRUGS: EPIDEMIOLOGICAL EVIDENCE

Alcoholism and drug addiction are among the most harmful social, legal, and economic problems for individuals and families in the United States and across the globe. The World Health Organization (2010) estimated that 76.3 million individuals worldwide have an alcohol-use disorder, and 5.3 million individuals have drug-use disorders. Approximately 25 percent of youths under the age of 18 experience alcohol abuse or dependence in the family (Grant et al., 2006). Combined data from the 2002–2007 National Household Survey on Drug Use and Health (NHSDUH) estimated that 8.3 million children (11.9%) under the age of 18 lived with at least one parent who was dependent on or abused alcohol or an illicit drug in the past year. More specifically, approximately 7.3 million (10.3%) children lived with a parent who was dependent on or abused alcohol, and about 2.1 million (3.0%) lived with a parent who was dependent on or abused illicit drugs. The NHSDUH estimates that 5.4 million children under 18 years of age lived with a father who met the criteria for past-year substance dependence or abuse, whereas 3.4 million lived with a mother who met the criteria (Substance Abuse and Mental Health Services Administration [SAMHSA], 2009a).

■ EFFECTS OF PARENTAL SUBSTANCE ABUSE ON CHILDREN IN THEIR HOMES

Although children of substance abusers (COSAs) have considerable resiliency and often become successful adults, as a group, youths who live with a substance-abusing parent are at-risk for higher levels of depression and anxiety (Billick et al., 1999; Kelley et al., 2010; Klostermann et al., 2011a; Stanger et al., 1999), poor self-concept (Rangarajan, 2008), externalizing symptoms (Catalano et al., 2002; Wilson et al., 2004), academic problems (Blanchard et al., 2005), and negative health outcomes (Christoffersen & Soothill, 2003; Osborne & Berger, 2009). In a sample of cocaine- and opiate-addicted mothers, Luthar et al. (1998) found that nearly 66% had at least one major psychiatric diagnosis by the time they were 12 years old. Similarly, Wilens et al. (2002) showed that 59% of children of opioid-dependent parents had at least one psychopathological condition as compared to to 41% of children of alcohol-abusing parents and 28% of controls.

Parental substance use is also a major risk factor for offspring alcohol and drug use and abuse (Braitman et al., 2009; Chassin et al., 2002; Coffelt et al., 2006; Hicks et al., 2010; King et al., 2003). For instance, Biederman and colleagues (2000) found that 53% of children who were exposed to parental substance use disorders during adolescence had substance use disorders themselves, compared with 15% of those who were not exposed during adolescence.

■ TREATMENT OPTIONS FOR SUBSTANCE-ABUSING PARENTS AND THEIR CHILDREN

In response to this clear and growing awareness of the needs of these youth, Tommy Thompson, who at the time was the U.S. Secretary of Health and Human Services, undertook a comprehensive initiative to create programs within substance abuse treatment agencies throughout the country to help children cope with the effects of their parents' addiction. This effort included very strong encouragement of substance abuse treatment agencies in the United States to implement a program developed by SAMSHA and the National Association of Children of Alcoholics, described in the Children's Program Kit (CPK; SAMHSA, 2003), which was sent to all the American agencies.

In addition to the CPK, there has been a proliferation of interventions that target a combination of parent and child outcomes. Although intergenerational risk for substance use disorder can, in part, be attributed to genetic factors (e.g., see Dick & Agrawal, 2008; Glantz & Chambers, 2006; Hasin et al., 2006; Merikangas, 2002; Prescott et al., 2005), it is now acknowledged that concomitant sequelae associated with substance use by parents (e.g., poor parenting, high inter-parental conflict and violence, neighborhood violence, poverty) are often the primary contributory factors in the emotional and behavioral problems observed in COSAs (see Glantz & Chambers, 2006; Jacob et al., 2003; Slutske et al., 2008). Moreover, the cumulative effects from multiple risk factors increase the possibility that child development will be compromised (e.g., Sameroff et al., 1987).

From this vantage point, much of the existing research operates from the belief that child outcomes will improve by providing effective services to parents. Therefore, interventions for these parents often include working with parents and children to improve children's outcomes (Greenberg et al., 2008). Toward this end, a number of programs that address both parent and child needs have been developed (e.g., Catalano et al., 1999; Dawe & Harnett, 2007; Luthar & Suchman, 2000; Schuler et al., 2002); however, these programs are typically designed to treat methadone-maintained mothers of infants or young children.

Directly involving children of COSAs in treatment may be optimal, but it is important to recognize that many substance-abusing parents may be reluctant to allow their children to receive direct services or may not be aware that their children have mental health needs. Although drug-using mothers often report concern about how their drug use will affect their children (e.g., McMahon et al., 2002; Woodhouse, 1992), their fear of involvement with the child welfare system may prevent substance-abusing parents from seeking treatment (Kearney et al., 1994; Wilson et al., 2007). Specifically, some parents may not want their school-aged children involved in the treatment process, because they are concerned that this will raise concerns about their suitability as parents. Also, youths in these homes may be aware of the stigma associated with substance abuse and may not want to be identified as the child of a substance-abusing parent. For example, 15- to 19-year-olds viewed children of alcoholics as more deviant than typical teenagers and similar to "mentally ill" teenagers (Burk & Sher, 1990).

It is also important to recognize the diversity in parents who experience substance abuse. Although the vast majority of research and programs for substance-abusing parents focus on substance-abusing mothers and the needs of their families (e.g., Colby & Murrell, 1998; Glantz & Chambers, 2006; Redelinghuys & Dar, 2008), men are more likely to abuse or be dependent on alcohol or drugs than women. For instance, in 2008, 12 percent of men age 18 or older indicated substance abuse or dependence in the previous year, and 6.3 percent of women met criteria for abuse or drug dependence (SAMSHA, 2009b). Thus, residing with a substance-abusing father may be a more likely scenario for youth to experience parental substance abuse, and along these same lines, fathers may be less likely to seek treatment for family problems (including parenting). Parenting programs are often focused on the role of mothers, and men are much more difficult to engage and retain in "parenting" programs (Fabiano, 2007); thus, programs that address substance abuse by parents and support family and child functioning, but do not necessarily target parenting, may be key for some families.

■ BEHAVIORAL COUPLES THERAPY FOR SUBSTANCE-ABUSING PARENTS

Considering that it may be difficult to treat some COSAs directly, a promising approach is Behavioral Couples Therapy [BCT] for alcoholism and drug abuse. BCT is a comprehensive psychosocial intervention for substance abuse that focuses on reducing addiction severity, improving dyadic adjustment, reducing interparental conflict and violence, and improving the family environment and parent adjustment. As we explain below, BCT may have benefits for the psychological adjustment of youth in these homes.

Origins of Behavioral Couples Therapy

Behavioral Couples Therapy (BCT) was originally developed for martially distressed couples (see Byrne et al., 2004; Jacobson, 1979). In response to the desire to meet the diverse needs of clients and their partners, the standard BCT model has evolved into several offshoot approaches in the general psychotherapy treatment arena, including Enhanced Cognitive Behavioral Therapy (ECBT), Self Regulatory Couples Therapy (SRCT), and Integrative-Behavioral Couples Therapy (IBCT; Kelly & Iwamasa, 2005).

Behavioral Couples Therapy for Alcohol and Drug Abuse

In recent years, BCT has been revised for use as a conjoint treatment for substance use. BCT for alcohol and drug abuse is a theoretically based, manualized, comprehensive psychosocial intervention that focuses on reducing addiction severity, improving dyadic adjustment, reducing interparental conflict and intimate partner violence, and improving the family environment and parent adjustment (Klostermann et al., 2011b; McCrady et al., 2009; O'Farrell & Fals-Stewart, 2006).

BCT operates on the fundamental premise that alcoholism and drug abuse by one partner often contributes to relationship problems between substance abusers and their partners (e.g., relationship dissatisfaction, instability, dyadic conflict, psychological distress, violence). In fact, relationship conflict often accompanies alcohol (e.g., McKinney et al., 2010) and drug use (O'Leary & Schumacher, 2003). In a meta-analytic study of the relationship between alcohol use/abuse and violence, Foran and O'Leary (2008) found a small-to-moderate effect size for the association between alcohol use and male-to-female partner violence; the effect size for female-to-male partner violence was small. However, there was a larger association of alcohol and violence when comparing clinical versus non-clinical samples and when measures assessed more severe alcohol problems.

Similarly, both laboratory and survey studies have shown that cocaine use is associated with aggression. Because cocaine is a powerful central nervous system (CNS) stimulant that causes hyperarousal symptoms (e.g., a tendency to become irritable or angry, exaggerated startle responses, sleep disturbance), cocaine use may have a pharmacological effect or aggression-promoting effect that increases violence (Parrott et al., 2003). It is also possible that illegal drug use may reduce behavioral disinhibition so that physical aggression is more likely to occur (Fillmore, 2012). or that greater impulsivity, which may be higher among cocaine-dependent individuals as opposed to alcohol abusers, may in turn relate to higher levels of partner physical and emotional abuse (Parrott et al., 2003).

In a laboratory study, individuals who ingested a low dose of cocaine displayed higher levels of physical aggression than participants in a placebo condition (Licata et al., 1993). Using data from the National Family Violence Survey and the National Survey of Families and Households, O'Leary and Schumacher (2003) found the odds of severe male-to-female physical aggression were higher on days of cocaine use.

Other reasons to address relationship issues in substance abuse treatment are that dyadic factors play a critical role in the maintenance and exacerbation of drinking and drug problems, as well as relapses after treatment for both men (e.g., Emmelkamp & Vedel, 2006; Maisto et al., 1988) and women (e.g., Connors et al., 1998; Epstein & McCrady, 1998; Grella et al., 2003; Sun, 2007). Thus, substance use and relationship problems appear to reinforce each other, thereby creating a "vicious cycle" for many couples.

Based on the awareness of the interrelationship between substance abuse and family interactions, BCT attempts to actively involve a spouse or partner in treatment so that the partner can be involved as a coach in the process of behavior change, disorder-specific relationship issues can be addressed, and general relationship functioning can be addressed (Kelley et al., 2009; Powers et al., 2008). Thus, the goal of BCT is to create a harmonious cycle between substance use recovery and relationship functioning by using interventions designed to address both sets of issues concurrently and reinforce positive behaviors.

■ **PRIMARY BCT TREATMENT ELEMENTS**

In the early sessions of treatment, therapists delivering BCT concentrate on shifting the focus from negative feelings and interactions about past and possible future alcohol or drug use to positive behavioral exchanges between partners. In later sessions, emphasis is placed on communication skills training, problem-solving strategies, negotiating behavior change agreements, and continuing recovery strategies.

BCT Methods Used to Address Substance Use

As the name implies, the therapist treats the substance-abusing patient with his or her intimate partner and works to build support for abstinence from within the dyadic system. The therapist, with extensive input from the partners, develops and has the partners enter into a "recovery contract" (also called a "sobriety contract"). As part of the contract, partners agree to engage in a brief, daily "sobriety trust discussion," in which the substance-abusing partner states his or her intention not to drink or use drugs that day. In turn, the patient's partner verbally expresses positive support for the patient's efforts to remain sober. Couples record their sobriety trust discussion on a daily calendar (used as a visual and temporal record of problems) provided by the therapist. As a condition of the recovery contract, both partners agree not to discuss past drinking or drug use or fears of future substance use between scheduled couple therapy sessions. Rather, disagreements regarding past substance use and fears of future use are reserved for the couple therapy sessions. Many contracts also include specific conditions for partners' regular attendance at self-help meetings (e.g., Alcoholics Anonymous, Narcotics Anonymous).

BCT Methods Used to Enhance Relationship Functioning

BCT also seeks to increase positive feelings, shared activities, and constructive communication through the use of standard couples-based behavioral assignments that are conducive to sobriety. *Catch Your Partner Doing Something Nice* (Turner, 1972) has each partner notice and acknowledge one pleasing behavior performed by the other each day. In the *Caring Day* assignment (e.g., Liberman et al., 1980), each partner is asked to surprise their significant other with a day of special things that show that they care for their partner. Because years of alcohol and drug abuse often result in a decrease in shared enjoyable activities, the focus of *Shared Rewarding Activities* (O'Farrell & Cutter, 1984) is to help the couple plan and engage in a mutually agreed-upon activity. Each activity must involve both partners, either as a dyad or with their children or other adults, and can be performed either at or away from home. Teaching *Communication Skills* (e.g., Gottman et al., 1976) such as paraphrasing, empathizing, and validating can help the substance-abusing patient and his or her partner better address stressors in their relationship and in their lives as they arise, which also decreases the risk of relapse.

Couples-Based Relapse Prevention and Planning

Relapse prevention occurs during the later stages of BCT. In this phase, the partners develop a written plan (i.e., Continuing Recovery Plan) designed to support abstinence (e.g., continuation of a daily Sobriety Trust Discussion, attending self-help support meetings) and list contingency plans should a relapse occur post-treatment (e.g., re-contacting the therapist, re-engaging in self-help support meetings, contacting a sponsor). A key element in creating the Continuing Recovery Plan is the negotiation of the post-treatment BCT activities. For example, the substance-abusing partner typically does not want a life that involves the structured exercises and homework that are part of BCT, whereas the non-substance-abusing partner is often suspicious of progress made in treatment (i.e., relationship improvement, abstinence) and advocates for continued participation in some activities (e.g., self-help meeting attendance, Sobriety Trust Discussions). In the Continuing Recovery Plan, partners develop a mutually agreed-to, long-term gradual decrease in the frequency of the various BCT activities until they are terminated. In the case of problems with any of the planned transitions, partners are encouraged to contact their BCT counselor.

Session Structure and Treatment Duration

BCT is moderately to highly structured. Each BCT session consists of three objectives: 1) review of relationship problems, any substance use, and home practice; 2) introduction of new material; and 3) assignment of home practice. A typical BCT session begins with an update on any alcohol or drug use that has occurred since the last session. Next, compliance with the Recovery Contract is reviewed and any impediments to compliance are addressed. The session then transitions to a review of any home practice from the previous session. This is followed by a discussion of any relationship or other difficulties that may have arisen since the last session, with the goal being problem resolution. Next, new material (e.g., instruction in and rehearsal of skills to be practiced at home during the week) is introduced and modeled in front of the therapist to ensure the activity is conducted correctly. Finally, at the end of each session, partners are given specific home practice assignments involving the material learned in session to complete before the next scheduled session.

■ EVIDENCE FOR COUPLES-BASED TREATMENT FOR SUBSTANCE ABUSERS AND THEIR PARTNERS

During the last three decades, couples therapy for substance abuse has received extensive empirical scrutiny, with most research focusing on BCT. In general, these studies have compared BCT to some form of traditional individual-based treatment for substance abuse (e.g., coping skills therapy, 12-Step facilitation).

In a sample of male alcoholics and their female partners, O'Farrell et al. (1985) randomly assigned participants to alcoholism counseling (e.g., 12-Step facilitation, disulfiram encouragement), alcoholism counseling plus interactional couples group therapy, or alcoholism counseling plus BCT. Clients in the BCT condition continued to report relationship benefits during the two-year follow-up; however, men in all conditions improved significantly, as indicated by non-drinking days.

McCrady et al. (1986) examined the impact of spouse involvement in behavioral interventions for alcoholism. This investigation compared minimal spouse involvement (MSI), alcohol-focused spouse intervention (AFSI), or BCT in a sample of 37 alcohol-abusing patients and their partners. Findings revealed that BCT was superior to AFSI and MSI in reducing alcohol use and increasing relationship satisfaction at post-treatment and at the 18-month follow-up phase of the study.

In a sample of problem drinkers, Walitzer and Derman (2004) compared individual, cognitive behavioral treatment (CBT), AFSI, and BCT. Although participants in both the BCT and AFSI interventions outperformed the CBT condition in terms of drinking outcomes at post-treatment and follow-up, BCT did not produce significantly better relationship satisfaction than AFSI.

Vedel, Emmelkamp, and Schippers (2008) enrolled 64 alcohol-disorder patients (male and female) and their partners in BCT or CBT. Drinking outcomes were similar at post-treatment for clients in each condition; however, participants in the BCT condition reported greater relationship satisfaction. Powers et al. (2008) showed that couples who attended BCT for substance abuse were less likely to experience relationship dissolution (e.g., separation, divorce).

A study of veterans who received BCT for substance use disorder found those with and without post-traumatic stress disorder showed improved from pretreatment to post-deployment. Regardless of whether or not the veteran had PTSD, improvements were noted in dyadic satisfaction, and decreases were found in alcohol use, alcohol consequences, male-to-female violence, and psychological distress symptoms (Rotunda, O'Farrell, Murphy, & Babey, 2008). These results suggest that BCT may benefit those with alcohol use disorder and comorbid PTSD.

Importantly, improvements in specific objectives of BCT (i.e., positive communication, shared activities, and negotiation of agreements) have been positively correlated with marital satisfaction in couples taking part in BCT for alcohol abuse. In addition, compared to baseline levels, BCT has been associated with a 60 percent reduction of intimate-partner violence (IPV) prevalence and frequency among alcohol- and drug-abusing men and their non-substance-abusing female partners (O'Farrell et al., 2004) during the year after treatment. Reducing IPV is critical, given that among couples who enter treatment for substance abuse, the vast majority (i.e., more than 95%) report instances of partner violence in the year prior to treatment (Klostermann & Fals-Stewart, 2006).

Collectively, research has shown that BCT results in equal or greater likelihood of client abstinence. Moreover, with few exceptions (see Walitzer & Derman, 2004), BCT has been shown to result in superior outcomes in terms of relationship functioning.

■ WHY BCT MAY HAVE SECONDARY BENEFITS FOR CHILDREN IN THEIR HOMES

Although the relationship between parental substance abuse and children's risk has been well established (e.g., Stanger et al., 1999), we know less about the mechanisms of action underlying this risk. Although parental modeling of alcohol or drug use presents a certain degree of risk for youth substance use (Abar, Abar & Turrisi, 2009), a growing body of research has demonstrated that interparental conflict, particularly partner violence, has a direct and corrosive impact on children's emotional and behavioral development (e.g., Grych & Fincham, 1990). As we explain below, partner conflict and violence may be an indicator of an aggressive interpersonal interaction style that a parent is likely to use, not only with his or her partner, but also in parenting children. Thus, it is plausible that substance abuse treatments that attempt to reduce parental substance use and improve dyadic functioning may have dual benefits for children in these homes.

Parental Substance Abuse, Interparental Conflict, and Children's Emotional Security and Behavior

Exposure to severe interparental conflict has been linked to children's feelings of terror and helplessness; fears for their own and their parents' safety (Levendosky & Graham-Berman, 1998); and children's depression, anxiety, somatic complaints, and sleep disruptions (Kitzmann et al., 2003; Lewis-O'Connor et al., 2006; McFarlane et al., 2003). Davies and Cummings (1994) contend that children evaluate marital conflict in terms of its implications for their emotional security and respond accordingly. IPV may affect children's emotional security, and, in turn, may increase risk for adjustment problems (Cassidy & Shaver, 1999).

Exposure to IPV, and the victimization that children experience from their exposure to IPV, may also increase children's proneness to bullying and aggressive, violent, and delinquent behavior (Baldry, 2003; Lemmey et al., 2001; McFarlane et al., 2003; Moretti et al., 2006). Although there is variability in the causes of anti-social behavior, early externalizing problems with a pattern of aggressive behavior by middle childhood are related to a developmental trajectory of highly stable and intensifying aggression during adolescence that may persist into adulthood (Moffitt et al., 2002; Nagin & Tremblay, 1999). For instance, Huesmann et al. (1984) found that eight-year-old boys identified as "aggressive" were more likely to commit serious criminal acts, abuse their spouses, and drive while intoxicated as adults.

Moreover, adolescent boys exposed to IPV are more likely to believe that use of aggression is acceptable in romantic relationships (Kinsfogel & Grych, 2004) and engage in more aggressive behaviors with their romantic partners (Heyman & Slep Smith, 2001; Kinsfogel & Grych, 2004). Violent men are less effective problem-solvers, exhibit more negative communication, and are more hostile during con-flict with female partners (e.g., Anglin & Holtzworth-Munroe, 1997). Young men who have witnessed interparental conflict may bring ineffective conflict manage-ment skills into adult relationships, and their poor conflict management skills may mediate relationship violence (Skuja & Halford, 2004).

■ PARENTAL SUBSTANCE ABUSE, INTERPARENTAL CONFLICT, AND FAMILY PROCESSES

In recent years, there has also been a growing awareness that interparental conflict is intrinsically and empirically linked to family processes and parenting (Bradford & Barber, 2005; Krishnakumar & Buehler, 2000). Although there are different forms of interparental conflict (Krishnakumar & Buehler, 2000), the overtly hos-tile style (Ahrons, 1981; Camara & Resnick, 1988) that involves frictional con-flict in which couples display verbal aggression and physical violence (Buehler et al., 1997) is characteristic of many substance-abusing couples (Klostermann & Fals-Stewart, 2006). In these couples, poor communication is hypothesized as the mode by which partners communicate and work through everyday disagreements that "spill over" into parent–child interactions and parenting behaviors (Erel & Burman, 1995).

More specifically, Krishnakumar and Buehler (2000) have argued that parents in aggressive relationships may try to control their children by exhibiting coercive-ness and harsh discipline. Coercive parent–child interactions are characterized by inconsistency, poor monitoring, little warmth, harsh discipline, and frequent neg-ative verbalizations toward children (Reid et al., 2002). Coercive parenting has been related to children's noncompliance, stealing (Anderson et al., 1996), and aggression (McFadyen-Ketchum et al., 1996).

■ SUMMARY

Children who live with a substance-abusing parent often manifest emotional and behavioral problems (e.g., Luthar et al., 1999) and many risks to healthy develop-ment. Given the heterogeneity among substance-abusing families, it is important to recognize that different types of empirically validated treatments are available to support children in these homes. One such treatment that has considerable empirical support is BCT (Powers et al., 2008). In particular, BCT may be appropriate for families in which one parent is substance-abusing and the other is not, for parents who do not want their children to receive direct treatment or for children who do not want to receive direct treatment, and for couples who display chronic interparental conflict in addition to alcohol or drug abuse. It is plausible that the mechanisms presumed to change during BCT treatment (e.g., communication skills, problem solving) may transfer to other family interactions such as parent–child interactions (e.g., reduce parental over-reactivity, improve problem-solving), which, in turn, affect child behavior.

It is also important to recognize that BCT appears to be a flexible treatment that can be modified to meet the specific needs of families. Thus, it is possible that additions to the standard BCT approach can be made to address the particular needs of COSAs. In fact, results of a pilot study in which we integrated parent skills training with BCT yielded very promising effect sizes and trends that suggest that the addition of parent skill training to BCT is feasible and may enhance the effects of BCT for internalizing behavior in preadolescent children (Lam et al., 2007). Although modifications to BCT may be necessary, BCT holds promise for benefiting youth behavior despite not being directly administered to children in these homes.

However, in order to provide an empirically supported BCT option for agencies who work with these families, a clear understanding of the treatment's potential secondary benefits (i.e., "trickle down" effects) across youth behaviors and across children's developmental stages, as well as the mechanisms through which the program works (i.e., mechanisms of action), is critical. For instance, a focus of BCT is developing clear, non-critical, supportive communication. It is possible that this type of communication may also benefit parent–child interactions. Moreover, couples learn ways to support each other, and engage in fun activities they enjoyed prior to the development of the client's substance use problem (O'Farrell & Fals-Stewart, 2006). We believe improving communication, learning to support one another, and shifting family energy away from the client's drug and toward other enjoyable activities may extend to the larger family. In fact, it is important to examine whether BCT has important benefits for children in their homes and parent–child interactions (i.e., more positive family interactions and less negative behavior for children [depression, anxiety, aggressive behavior and so forth] and better relationships between parents and their children).

Also, many couples who enter substance abuse treatment engage in intimate-partner violence (e.g., Klostermann & Fals-Stewart, 2006). Although couples in which one partner is a batterer (e.g., Johnson, 2002) or engages in severe physical violence, or in which one or both partners fear physical reprisal from their partner (e.g., O'Leary, 1993) are not considered appropriate for couples therapy, it is possible that BCT for substance abuse may benefit couples who engage in infrequent partner aggression and lesser forms of partner violence (e.g., pushing or slapping). Although the decision to engage in BCT should be weighed carefully and with many factors considered (e.g., relationship commitment, couple safety, therapist training), it is possible that BCT may work to reduce both parental drug use and interparental aggression. Thus, BCT has the potential to reduce interparental violence. Importantly, both parental drug use (Luthar et al., 1999) and interparental violence (Kitzmann et al., 2003) have been linked to negative child outcomes. Clearly, the question of if the reduction of parental drug use, the reduction of parental violence, or both will benefit youths in these homes is important to address.

We would also appeal to investigators to examine the relative effectiveness of BCT for different family forms. For instance, Osborne and Berger (2009) found that the risk of health and behavior problems in children living with a substance-abusing parent was not moderated by parent gender. However, to date, there have been no studies of the effectiveness of BCT for children of substance-abusing mothers. Globally, there is also a need to see if BCT can be adapted for different family types. For instance, it is possible that BCT can be adapted for single parents and other family members (e.g., grandparents) or close friends. This is especially important as the 2010 American Communities Survey estimated that 5.4 million grandparents were living with grandchildren in their homes (U.S. Census Bureau, 2011).

Although the question of whether BCT has positive influences on children in their homes warrants greater attention, we know that the indirect effects of BCT on children are limited. For instance, the effectiveness of BCT may vary as a function of the severity of parental drug use and as a function of children's developmental stage and gender. For instance, it is possible that adolescents who reside with a substance-abusing parent have spent more years in homes characterized by low emotional support (Miller et al., 1999). In turn, prolonged exposure to this type of corrosive family environment may result in higher levels of negative affect, more insecurity, higher acceptance of aggression, and a greater likelihood of serious negative behaviors (e.g., aggression, delinquency, violence, and substance abuse). Thus, for some youth, individual treatment may be warranted. At present, however, it is important to examine the secondary effects and potential mechanisms of action associated with BCT. Once these mechanisms are understood, it may be possible to refine or modify the treatment (as needed) to address youth with different family and clinical needs.

■ **AUTHOR'S NOTE**

This chapter was supported in part by a grant from the National Institute on Drug Abuse (R01 DA024740).

■ **REFERENCES**

Abar, C., Abar, B., & Turrisi, T. (2009). The impact of parental modeling and permissibility on alcohol use and experienced negative drinking consequences in college. *Addictive Behaviors, 34*, 542–547.

Ahrons, C. R. (1981). The continual co-parenting relationship between divorced spouses. *American Journal of Orthopyschiatry, 51*, 415–428.

Anderson, C. A., Hinshaw, S. P., & Simmel, C. (1996). Mother–child interactions in ADHD and comparison boys: Relationships with overt and covert externalizing behavior. *Journal of Abnormal Child Psychology, 22,* 247–265.

Anglin, K., & Holtzworth-Munroe, A. (1997). Comparing the responses of maritally violent and nonviolent spouses to problematic marital and non-marital situations: Are the skills deficits of physically aggressive husbands and wives global? *Journal of Family Psychology, 11,* 301–313.

Baldry, A. C. (2003). Bullying in schools and exposure to domestic violence. *Child Abuse & Neglect, 27,* 713–732.

Barnard, M., & McKeganey, N. (2004). The impact of parental problem drug use on children: What is the problem and what can be done to help? *Addiction, 99,* 552–559.

Biederman, J., Faraone, S. V., Monuteaux, M. C., & Feighner, J. A. (2000). Patterns of alcohol and drug use in adolescents can be predicted by parental substance use disorders. *Pediatrics, 106,* 792–797.

Billick, S., Gotzis, A., & Burgert, W. (1999). Screening for psychosocial dysfunction in the children of psychiatric patients. *Psychiatric Annals, 29,* 8–13.

Blanchard, K. A., Sexton, C. C., & Morgenstern, J. (2005). Children of substance abusing women on federal welfare: Implications for child well-being and TANF policy. *Journal of Human Behavior in the Social Environment, 12,* 89–110.

Boris, N. W. (2009). Parental substance abuse. In C. H. Zeanah, Jr. (Ed.), *Handbook of Infant Health* (3rd ed., pp. 171–179). New York: Guilford Press.

Bradford, K., & Barber, B. K. (2005). Interparental conflict as intrusive family process. *Journal of Emotional Abuse, 5,* 143–167.

Braitman, A. L., Kelley, M. L., Ladage, J., Schroeder, V., Gumienny, L. A., Morrow, J. A., et al. (2009). Alcohol and drug use among college student adult children of alcoholics. *Journal of Alcohol & Drug Education, 53,* 69–88.

Buehler, C., Anthony, C., & Krishnakumar, A. (1997). Interparental conflict and youth problem behaviors: A meta-analysis. *Journal of Children & Family Studies, 6,* 223–247.

Burk, J. P., & Sher, K. J. (1990). Labeling the child of an alcoholic: Negative stereotyping by mental health professionals and peers. *Journal of Studies on Alcohol, 51,* 156–163.

Byrne, M., Carr, A., & Clark, M. (2004). The efficacy of behavioral couples therapy and emotionally focused therapy for couple distress. *Family Therapy: An International Journal, 26,* 361–387.

Camara, K. A., & Resnick, G. (1988). Interparental conflict and cooperation: Factors moderating children's post-divorce adjustment. In E. M. Hetherton & J. D. Arasteh (Eds.), *Impact of Divorce, Single Parenting, and Step-parenting on Children* (pp. 169–197). Hillsdale, NJ: Lawrence Erlbaum Associates.

Cassidy, J., & Shaver, P. R. (1999). *Handbook of Attachment: Theory, Research, and Clinical Applications.* New York: Guilford Publications.

Catalano, R. F., Gainey, R. R., Fleming, C. B., Haggerty, K. P., & Johnson, N. O. (1999). An experimental intervention with families of substance abusers: One-year follow-up of the focus on families project. *Addiction, 94,* 241–254.

Catalano, R. F., Haggerty, K. P., Fleming, C. B., Brewer, D. D., & Gainey, R. R. (2002). Children of substance-abusing parents: Current findings from the focus on families project. In R. J. McMahon (Ed.), *The Effects of Parental Dysfunction on Children* (pp. 179–204). New York: Kluwer Academic/Plenum Press.

Chassin, L., Pitts, S. C., & Prost, J. (2002). Binge drinking trajectories from adolescence to emerging adulthood in a high-risk sample: Predictors and substance abuse outcomes. *Journal of Consulting & Clinical Psychology, 70,* 67–78.

Coffelt, N., Forehand, R., Olson, A. L., Jones, D. J., Gaffney, C. A., & Zens, M. S. (2006). A longitudinal examination of the link between parent alcohol problems and youth drinking: The moderating roles of parent and child gender. *Addictive Behaviors, 31,* 593–605.

Colby, S. M., & Murrell, W. (1998). Child welfare and substance abuse services: From barriers to collaboration. In R. L. Hampton, V. Senatore, & T. P. Gullotta (Eds.), *Substance Abuse, Family Violence and Child Welfare—Bridging Perspectives* (pp. 188–219). London: Sage.

Connors, G. J., Maisto, S. A., & Zywiak, W. H. (1998). Male and female alcoholics' attributions regarding the onset and termination of relapses and the maintenance of abstinence. *Journal of Substance Abuse, 10,* 27–42.

Davies, P. T., & Cummings, E. M. (1994). Marital conflict and child adjustment: An emotional security hypothesis. *Psychological Bulletin, 116,* 387–411.

Dawe, S., & Harnett, P. (2007). Reducing potential for child abuse among methadone-maintained parents: Results from a randomized controlled trial. *Journal of Substance Abuse Treatment, 32,* 381–390.

Dick, D. D., & Agrawal, A. (2008). The genetics of alcohol and other drug dependence. *Alcohol, Research, & Health, 2,* 111–117.

Emmelkamp, P. M., & Vedel, E. (2006). *Evidence-Based Treatment for Alcohol and Drug Abuse.* New York: Routledge, Taylor, & Francis Group.

Epstein, E. E., & McCrady, B. S. (1998). Behavioral couples treatment of alcohol and drug use disorders: Current status and innovations. *Clinical Psychology Review, 18,* 689–711.

Erel, O., & Burman, B. (1995). Interrelatedness of marital relations and parent–child relations: A meta-analytic review. *Psychological Bulletin, 118,* 108–132.

Fabiano, G. A. (2007). Father participation in behavioral parent training for ADHD: Review and recommendations for increasing inclusion and engagement. *Journal of Family Psychology, 21,* 683–693.

Fillmore, M. T. (2012). Drug abuse and behavioral disinhibition. In J. C. Verster, K. Brady, M. Galanter, & P. Conrod (Eds.), *Drug abuse and Addictions in Medical Illness: Causes, Consequences and Treatment* (pp. 25–34). New York: Spring Science + Business Media.

Foran, H. M., & O'Leary, K. (2008). Alcohol and intimate partner violence: A meta-analytic review. *Clinical Psychology Review, 28,* 1222–1234.

Glantz, M. D., & Chambers, J. C. (2006). Prenatal drug exposure effects on subsequent vulnerability to drug abuse. *Development & Psychopathology, 18,* 893–922.

Gottman, J., Notarius, C., Gonso, J., & Markman, H. (1976). *A Couple's Guide to Communication.* Champaign, IL: Research Press.

Grant, B. F., Dawson, D. A., Stinson, F. S., Chou, S. P., Dufour, M. C., & Pickering, R. P. (2006). The 12-month prevalence and trends in DSM-IV alcohol abuse and dependence. *Alcohol, Research, & Health, 29,* 79–91.

Greenberg, R., Bonifacio, A., & Werner, D. (2008). Children of substance abusers: COSA resource list. Retrieved on September 1, 2010, from http://womenandchildren.treatment.org/documents/cosa-resource-508v.pdf.

Grella, C. E., Scott, C. K., Foss, M. A., Joshi, V., & Hser, Y. I. (2003). Gender differences in drug treatment outcomes among participants in the Chicago Target Cities Study. *Evaluation & Program Planning, 26,* 297–310.

Grych, J. H., & Fincham, F. D. (1990). Marital conflict and children's adjustment: A cognitive-contextual framework. *Psychological Bulletin, 108,* 267–290.

Hasin, D., Hatzenbuehler, M., & Waxman, R. (2006). Genetics of substance use disorders. In K. M. Carroll & W. R. Miller (Eds.), *Rethinking Substance Abuse: What the Science Shows, and What We Should Do About It* (pp. 61–80). New York: Guilford Press.

Heyman, R. E., & Smith Slep, A. M. (2001). Risk factors for family violence: Introduction to the special series. *Aggression & Violent Behavior, 6,* 115–119.

Hicks, B. M., Iacono, W. G., & McGue, M. (2010). Consequences of an adolescent onset and persistent course of alcohol dependence in men: Adolescent risk factors and adult outcomes. *Alcohol: Clinical & Experimental Research, 34,* 818–833.

Huesmann, L. R., Rowell, L. D., & Lefkowitz, M. M. (1984). Stability of aggression over time and generations. *Developmental Psychology, 20,* 1120–1134.

Jacob, T., Waterman, B., Heath, A., True, W., Bucholz, K. K., Haber, R., et al. (2003). Genetic and environmental effects on offspring alcoholism: New insights using an offspring-of-twins design. *Archives of General Psychiatry, 60,* 1265–1272.

Jacobson, N. S. (1979). Increasing positive behavior in severely distressed marital relationships: The effects of problem-solving training. *Behavior Therapy, 10,* 311–326.

Johnson, R. L. (2002). Pathways to adolescent health: early intervention. *Journal of Adolescent Health, 31*(6 Suppl), 240–50.

Kearney, M. H., Murphy, S., & Rosenbaum, M. (1994). Mothering on crack cocaine: A grounded theory analysis. *Social Science & Medicine, 38,* 351–361.

Kelley, M. L., Cooke, C. G., Neff, J. A., & Doane, A. N. (2010, July). *Characteristics Associated with Days of Attendance and Treatment Compliance Among Clients in Substance Abuse Treatment.* Melbourne, Australia: International Congress of Applied Psychology.

Kelley, M. L., Platter, A. J., & Fals-Stewart, W. (2009). Behavioral couples therapy for substance abuse: Treatment components, efficacy, and effectiveness. In G. Fisher & N. Roget (Eds.), *Encyclopedia of Substance Abuse Prevention, Treatment, and Recovery* (pp. 15–18). Thousand Oaks, CA:.Sage.

Kelly, S., & Iwamasa, G. Y. (2005). Enhancing behavioral couple therapy: Addressing the therapeutic alliance, hope, and diversity. *Cognitive & Behavioral Practice, 12,* 102–112.

King, K. A., Vidourek, R. A., & Wagner, D. I. (2003). Effect of parent drug use and parent–child time spent together on adolescent involvement in alcohol, tobacco, and other drugs. *Adolescent Family Health, 3,* 171–176.

Kinsfogel, K. M., & Grych, J. H. (2004). Interparental conflict and adolescent dating relationships: Integrating cognitive, emotional, and peer influences. *Journal of Family Psychology, 18,* 505–515.

Kitzmann, K. M., Gaylord, N. K., Holt, A. R., & Kenny, E. D. (2003). Child witnesses to domestic violence: A meta-analytic review. *Journal of Consulting & Clinical Psychology, 71,* 339–352.

Klostermann, K., Chen, R., Kelley, M. L., Schroeder, V. M., Braitman, A. L., & Mignone, T. (2011a). Coping behavior and depressive symptoms in adult children of alcoholics. *Substance Use & Misuse, 46,* 1162–1168.

Klostermann, K., & Fals-Stewart, W. (2006). Intimate partner violence and alcohol use: Exploring the role of drinking in partner violence and its implications for intervention. *Aggression & Violent Behavior, 11*, 587–597.

Klostermann, K., Kelley, M. L., Mignone, T., Pusateri, L., & Wills, K. (2011b). Behavioral couples therapy for substance abuse: Where do we go from here? *Substance Use & Misuse, 46*, 1502–1509.

Krishnakumar, A., & Buehler, C. (2000). Interparental conflict and parenting behaviors: A meta-analytic review. *Family Relations, 49*, 25–44.

Lam, W. K., Cance, J. D., Eke, A. N., Fishbein, D. H., Hawkins, S. R., & Williams, J. C. (2007). Children of African-American mothers who use crack cocaine: Parenting influences on youth substance use. *Journal of Pediatric Psychology, 32*, 877–887.

Lemmey, D., McFarlane, J., & Wilson, P. (2001). Intimate partner violence: Mothers' perspectives of effects on their children. *The American Journal of Maternal/Child Nursing, 26*, 98–103.

Leonard, N. R., Gwadz, M. V., Cleland, C. M., Vekaria, P. C., & Ferns, B. (2008). Maternal substance use and HIV status: Adolescent risk and resilience. *Journal of Adolescence, 31*, 389–405.

Levendosky, A. A., & Graham-Berman, S. A. (1998). The moderating effects of parenting stress on children's adjustment in women-abusing families. *Journal of Interpersonal Violence, 13*, 383–397.

Lewis-O'Connor, A., Sharps, P. W., & Humphreys, J. (2006). Children exposed to intimate partner violence. In M. M. Feerick & G. B. Silverman (Eds.), *Children Exposed to Violence* (pp. 3–28). Baltimore, MD: Paul H Brookes Publishing.

Liberman, R. P., Wheeler, E. G., de Visser, L. A., Kuehnel, J., & Kuehnel, T. (1980). *Handbook of Marital Therapy: A Positive Approach to Helping Troubled Relationships*. New York: Plenum Press.

Licata, A., Taylor, S., & Berman, M. (1993). Effects of cocaine on human aggression. *Pharmacology, Biochemistry & Behavior, 45*, 549–552.

Luthar, S. S., Cushing, G., Merikangas, K. R., & Rounsaville, B. J. (1998). Multiple jeopardy: Risk/protective factors among addicted mothers' offspring. *Development & Psychopathology, 11*, 117–136.

Luthar, S. S., & Suchman, N. E. (2000). Relational Psychotherapy Mothers' Group: A developmentally informed intervention for at-risk mothers. *Development & Psychopathology, 12*, 235–253.

Maisto, S. A., O'Farrell, T. J., McKay, J., Connors, G. J., & Pelcovitz, M. A. (1988). Alcoholics' attributions of factors affecting their relapse to drinking and reasons for terminating relapse events. *Addictive Behaviors, 13*, 79–82.

McCrady, B. S., Epstein, E. E., Cook, S., Jensen, N., & Hildebrant, T. (2009). A randomized trial of individual and couple behavioral alcohol treatment for women. *Journal of Consulting & Clinical Psychology, 77*, 243–256.

McCrady, B. S., Noel, N. E., Abrams, D. B., Stout, R. L., Nelson, H. F., & Hay, W. M. (1986). Comparative effectiveness of three types of spouse involvement in outpatient behavioral alcoholism treatment. *Journal of Studies on Alcohol, 47*, 459–467.

McFadyen-Ketchum, S. A., Bates, J. E., Dodge, K. A., & Pettit, G. S. (1996). Patterns of change in early childhood aggressive-disruptive behavior: Gender differences in predictions from early coercive and affectionate mother-child interactions. *Child Development, 67,* 2417–2433.

McFarlane, J., Groff, J., O'Brien, J., & Watson, K. (2003). Behaviors of children who are exposed and not exposed to intimate partner violence: An analysis of 330 black, white, and Hispanic children. *Pediatrics, 112*:e202–e207

McKinney, C. M., Caetano, R., Rodriguez, L. A., & Okoro, N. (2010). Does alcohol involvement increase the severity of intimate partner violence? *Alcoholism: Clinical and Experimental Research, 34,* 655–658.

McMahon, T. J., Winkel, J. D., Suchman, N. E., & Luthar, S. S. (2002). Drug dependence, parenting responsibilities, and treatment history: Why doesn't mom go for help? *Drug & Alcohol Dependence, 65,* 105–114.

Merikangas, K. R. (2002). Genetic epidemiology of substance-use disorders. In H. D'Haeren, J. A. den Boer, & P. Willner (Eds.), *Biological Psychiatry* (pp. 537–546). New York: Wiley.

Miller, B. A., Smyth, N. J., & Mudar, P. J. (1999). Mothers' alcohol and other drug problems and their punitiveness toward their children. *Journal of Studies on Alcohol, 60,* 632–642.

Moffitt, T. E., Caspi, A., & Harrington, H. (2002). Males on the life-course-persistent and adolescence-limited antisocial pathways: Follow-up at age 26. *Development & Psychopathology, 14,* 179–207.

Moretti, M. M., Obsuth, I., Odgers, C. L., & Reebye, P. (2006). Exposure to maternal vs. paternal partner violence, PTSD, and aggression in adolescent girls and boys. *Aggressive Behavior, 32,* 385–395.

Nagin, D., & Tremblay, R. (1999). Trajectories of boys' physical aggression, opposition, and hyperactivity on the path to physically violent and nonviolent juvenile delinquency. *Child Development, 70,* 1181–1196.

National Household Survey on Drug Use and Health. (2009). Children living with substance-dependent or substance-abusing parents: 2002 to 2007. Retrieved on September 13, 2010, from http://www.oas.samhsa.gov/2k9/SAparents/SAparents.pdf.

National Institute on Alcohol Abuse and Alcoholism. (1993). Genetic and other risk factors for alcoholism. In *Alcohol and Health: Eighth Special Report to the U.S. Congress* (NIH Publication No. 94–3699, pp. 61–83). Washington, DC: National Institutes of Health.

O'Farrell, T. J., & Cutter, C. S. (1984). Behavioral marital therapy couples groups for male alcoholics and their wives. *Journal of Substance Abuse Treatment, 1,* 191–204.

O'Farrell, T. J., Cutter, H. S. G., & Floyd, F. J. (1985). Evaluating behavioral marital therapy for male alcoholics: Effects on marital adjustment and communication from before to after treatment. *Behavior Therapy, 16,* 147–167.

O'Farrell, T. J., & Fals- Stewart, W. (2006). *Behavioral Couples Therapy for Alcoholism and Drug Abuse.* New York: Guilford.

O'Farrell, T. J., Murphy, C. M., Stephan, S. H., Fals-Stewart, W., & Murphy, M. (2004). Partner violence before and after couples-based alcoholism treatment for male alcoholic patients: The role of treatment involvement and abstinence. *Journal of Consulting & Clinical Psychology, 72,* 202–217.

O'Leary, K. D. (1993). Through a psychological lens: Personality traits, personality disorders, and levels of violence. In R. J. Gelles & D. R. Loseke (Eds.), *Current Controversies in Family Violence* (pp. 7–29). Newbury Park, CA: Sage.

O'Leary, K. D., & Schumacher, J. A. (2003). The association between alcohol use and intimate partner violence: Linear effect, threshold effect, or both? *Addictive Behaviors, 28,* 1575–1585.

Osborne, C. & Berger, L. M. (2009). Parental substance abuse and child well-being: A consideration of parents' gender and co-residence. *Journal of Family Issues, 30,* 341–370.

Parrott, D. J., Drobes, D. J., Saladin, M. E., Coffey, S. F., & Dansky, B. S. (2003). Perpetration of partner violence: Effects of cocaine and alcohol dependence and post-traumatic stress disorder. *Addictive Behaviors, 28,* 1587–1602.

Powers, M. B., Vedel, E., & Emmelkamp, P. M. G. (2008). Behavioral couples therapy for alcohol and drug use disorders: A meta analysis. *Clinical Psychology Review, 28,* 952–962.

Prescott, C. A., Maes, H. H., & Kendler, K. S. (2005). Genetics of substance use disorders. In K. S. Kendle & L. J. Eaves (Eds.), *Psychiatric Genetics* (pp. 167–196). Washington, DC: American Psychiatric Publishing.

Rangarajan, S. (2008). Mediators and moderators of parental alcoholism effects on offspring self-esteem. *Alcohol & Alcoholism, 43,* 481–491.

Redelinghuys, J., & Dar, K. (2008). A survey of parents receiving treatment for substance dependence: The impact on their children. *Journal of Substance Use, 13,* 37–48.

Reid, J. B., Patterson, G. R., Dishion, T., & Snyder, J. (2002). *Antisocial Behavior in Children and Adolescents: A Developmental Analysis and Model for Intervention.* Washington, DC: American Psychological Association.

Rotunda, T. J., O'Farrell, T. J., Murphy, M., & Babey, S. H. (2008). Behavioral couples therapy for comorbid substance use disorders and combat-related post-traumatic stress disorder among male veterans: An initial examination. *Addictive Behaviors, 33,* 180–187.

Sameroff, A. J., Seifner, R. J., Barocas, R., Zax, M., & Greenspan, S. (1987). Intelligence quotient scores of four-year-old children: Social environmental risk factors. *Pediatrics, 79,* 343–350.

Schuler, M. E., Nair, P., & Black, M. M. (2002). Ongoing maternal drug use, parenting attitudes, and a home intervention: Effects on mother–child interaction at 18 months. *Developmental & Behavioral Pediatrics, 23,* 87–94.

Skuja, K., & Halford, W. K. (2004). Repeating the errors of our parents? Parental violence in men's family of origin and conflict management in dating couples. *Journal of Interpersonal Violence, 19,* 623–638.

Slutske, W. S., D'Onofrio, B. M., Turkheimer, E., Emery, R. E., Harden, K. P., Heath, A. C., et al. (2008). Searching for an environmental effect of parental alcoholism on offspring alcohol use disorder: A genetically informed study of children of alcoholics. *Journal of Abnormal Psychology, 117,* 534–551.

Stanger, C., Higgins, S. T., Bickel, W. K., Elk, R., Grabowski, J., Schmitz, J., et al. (1999). Behavioral and emotional problems among children of cocaine- and opiate-dependent parents. *Journal of the American Academy of Child & Adolescent Psychiatry, 38,* 421–428.

Substance Abuse and Mental Health Services Administration. (2003). Children's Program Kit: Supportive Education for Children of Addicted Parents. Rockville, MD: National Clearinghouse for Alcohol and Drug Information.

Substance Abuse and Mental Health Services Administration. (2009a). *Results from the 2008 National Survey on Drug Use and Health: National Findings* (Office of Applied Studies, NSDUH Series H-36, HHS Publication No. SMA 09-4434). Rockville, MD: SAMHSA.

Substance Abuse and Mental Health Services Administration. (2009b). Office of Applied Studies. (2009). *Results from the 2008 National Survey of Drug Use and Health: National Findings.* Rockville, MD: SAMHSA.

Suchman, N. E., & Luthar, S. S. (2000). Maternal addiction, child maladjustment and socio-demographic risks: implication for parenting behaviors. *Addiction, 95,* 1417–1428.

Sun, A. (2007). Relapse among substance-abusing women: Components and processes. *Substance Use & Misuse, 42,* 1–21.

Turner, J. (1972, October). *Couple and Group Treatment of Marital Discord.* Paper presented at the Sixth Annual Meeting of the Association for Advancement of Behavior Therapy, New York.

United States Census Bureau. (2011). 2010 American Community Survey: Table B10001. Retrieved from http://factfinder2.census.gov/faces/nav/jsf/pages/searchresults. xhtml?refresh=t.

Vedel, E., Emmelkamp, P. M. G., Schippers, G. M. (2008). Individual cognitive-behavioral therapy and behavioral couples therapy in alcohol use disorder: A comparative evaluation in community-based addiction treatment centers. *Psychotherapy & Psychosomatics, 77,* 280–288.

Walitzer, K. S., & Derman (2004). Alcohol-focused spouse involvement and Behavioral Couples Therapy: Evaluation of enhancements to drinking reduction treatment for male problem drinkers. *Journal of Consulting and Clinical Psychology, 72,* 944–955.

Widom, C. S., & Hiller-Sturmhofel, S. (2001). Alcohol abuse as a risk factor for and consequence of child abuse. *Alcohol Research & Health, 25,* 52–57.

Wilens, T. E., Biederman, J., & Bredin, E. (2002). A family study of the high-risk children of opioid- and alcohol-dependent parents. *The American Journal on Addictions, 11,* 41–51.

Wilson, J. J., Beckmann, L., & Nuñes, E. V. (2007). The identification, prevention, and treatment of vulnerabilities among children of alcohol- or drug-dependent parents. In V. Panos (Ed.), *Mental Health Interventions and Services for Vulnerable Children and Young People* (pp. 203–232). London, England: Jessica Kingsley Publishers.

Wilson, J. J., Nuñes, E. V., Greenwald, S., & Weissman, M. (2004). Verbal deficits and disruptive behavior disorders among children of opiate-dependent parents. *The American Journal of Addictions, 13,* 202–212.

Woodhouse, L. D. (1992). Women with jagged edges: Voices from a culture of substance abuse. *Qualitative Health Research, 2.* Retrieved September 25, 2007, from http://qhr. sagepub.com/cgi/content/abstract/2/3/262.

World Health Organization. (2010). Facts and figures. Retrieved from http://www.who.int/ substance_abuse/facts/en/index.html.

Young, N. K., Boles, S. M., & Otero, C. (2007). Parental substance use disorders and child maltreatment: Overlap, gaps, and opportunities. *Child Maltreatment, 12,* 137–149.

24 Family-Based Interventions for Children with Prenatal Substance Exposure

CYNTHIA V. HEALEY,
PHILIP A. FISHER,
AMANDA VAN SCOYOC, AND
ANGELA M. RELLING

■ INTRODUCTION

As noted elsewhere (see Salo, Chapter 10, this volume) and in a burgeoning scientific literature, children with prenatal substance exposure (PSE) face a multitude of risks. These include an increased likelihood of developmental delays, emotional and behavioral disorders, psychiatric diagnoses, academic difficulties, substance abuse, and juvenile justice system involvement (Delaney-Black et al., 1998; Hellemans et al., 2010; Lester et al., 2009; Levine et al., 2008; Seifer et al., 2004; Sood et al., 2001; Streissguth et al., 2004). Because these children typically experience many known environmental risk factors for poor outcomes (e.g., poor parenting, poverty, and increased family stress), it is difficult to determine which poor outcomes result from PSE, other risk factors, or some combination of risk factors.

Due to the interplay between PSE and complex family and environmental factors, individual children with PSE are likely to struggle with a constellation of difficulties in their everyday functioning. While some children with substance-using parents can demonstrate normal functioning, researchers have shown that there is a considerable variation in the effects of PSE and that individual children and adolescents with PSE are likely to experience one or more of the following difficulties: externalizing/internalizing behavior problems, social competence deficits, oppositional behavior, language delays, fine motor deficits, academic under-achievement, memory deficits, inattention, hyperactivity and poor impulse control, poor executive function, sleep difficulties, cognitive inflexibility, learning difficulties, delinquency, inappropriate sexualized behavior, and substance abuse (Acra, Bono, Mundy, & Scott, 2009; Goldschmidt, Richardson, Cornelius, & Day, 2004; Hellemans et al., 2010; Janzen, Nanson, & Block; T. J. Linares et al., 2006; McLaughlin, Williams, & Howard, 1998; O'Leary et al., 2009; Olson, Feldman, Streissguth, Sampson, & Bookstein, 1998; Streissguth, Barr, Kogan, & Bookstein, 1997; Streissguth et al., 2004).

Further complicating research on the effects of prenatal exposure is the extent of heterogeneity in maternal substance use. It is increasingly common for substance abusers to use multiple substances (Rounsaville, Petry, & Carroll, 2003; Staines et al.,

2001). Research on the comorbidity of alcohol dependence and other substance use indicates that the majority of women admitted to alcohol-abuse treatment programs report using another substance at least once a week in the year preceding treatment (Caetano & Weisner, 1995), and two-thirds of individuals entering treatment have used another substance within 90 days of beginning treatment (Staines et al., 2001). Estimates of specific drug-use among alcoholics are strikingly high. In the general population, alcoholics report abusing cocaine (30%–60%), marijuana (20%–50%), and benzodiazepines (12%–20%; Petry, 2001).

Given the high incidence of polysubstance use in the general population, it is likely that infants prenatally exposed to an identified substance have been exposed to other substances *in utero*. However, prenatal polysubstance exposure has not adequately been addressed in the current literature, which tends to focus on the *in utero* effects of substance-specific exposure. Heterogeneity of substance exposure might explain, in part, the varied constellation of symptoms found among infants and children with PSE.

It is also becoming apparent that children with PSE manifest not only psychological difficulties but also neurodevelopmental deficits. Although the nature and extent of these deficits can vary, there appears to be a coherent behavioral endophenotype involving neurobehavioral disinhibition among children with PSE (Chapman, Tarter, Kirisci, & Cornelius, 2007; Kirisci, Tarter, Reynolds, & Vanyukov, 2006; McNamee et al., 2008). Neurobehavioral disinhibition may reflect difficulties in executive functioning, alterations in reward sensitivity, and difficulties with stress regulation (Lester & Padbury, 2009). Prior studies have found alterations in underlying neural systems (e.g., prefrontal cortex function, hypothalamic-pituitary-adrenal axis) in children with PSE (Fisher, Kim, Bruce, & Pears, 2012; Fisher, Lester, et al., 2011).

Behavioral difficulties that can indicate poor neurological functioning include increased symptoms of attention deficit hyperactivity disorder (ADHD), emotion dysregulation, deficits in executive functioning, and poor response-inhibition and impulse control as evidenced by increased rates of conduct disorder and oppositional defiant disorder (Kirisci et al., 2006; Tarter et al., 2003). Given the breadth of these difficulties, underlying neurodevelopmental deficits might explain why conventional mental health services have limited utility in addressing the multifaceted needs of this population.

Because of the neurodevelopmental effects of PSE and the complexity of the environments in which children with PSE typically live, effective treatments should be more comprehensive and intensive than those for children without PSE. Of particular importance when identifying effective interventions is a focus on decreasing risk factors and increasing protective factors, maintaining stable home placements and positive parent–child interactions, and providing services that are developmentally and age-appropriate (Bertrand et al., 2004; Streissguth et al., 1997). Family-based interventions may be a particularly promising approach for children with PSE because they address individual and environmental factors.

Parenting children with PSE is highly challenging. For biological parents managing their own addiction and recovery, the added stress of parenting a special-needs child can be overwhelming. Higher levels of parenting stress and maladaptive parenting practices (e.g., abuse and neglect) have been observed among mothers who used drugs during pregnancy (Kelley, 1998). Parenting stress has been shown to predict externalizing and internalizing behavior problems in children regardless of drug exposure (Accornero, Morrow, Bandstra, Johnson, & Anthony, 2002; Bagner et al., 2009).

Additionally, high rates of maternal distress coupled with substance abuse during pregnancy have been shown to negatively impact children's cognitive functioning (Singer et al., 1997). Johnson, Nusbaum, Bejarano, and Rosen (1999) found that maternal stress and a lack of social support interfered with a mother's emotional availability and responsiveness, predicting, in turn, poorer functioning in toddlers with PSE. Conversely, children with PSE have been shown to demonstrate improved functioning in multiple developmental domains when placed with kinship or foster caregivers (who exhibited significantly less parenting stress) compared to children with PSE who lived with their biological parents (Brown, Bakeman, Coles, Platzman, & Lynch, 2004).

Additional environmental risk factors commonly associated with substance abuse (e.g., maternal depression, negative life events, psychiatric problems, and incarceration) are likely to increase overall stress, potentially decreasing effective parenting practices and increasing the likelihood of abuse and neglect (Nair, Schuler, Black, Kettinger, & Harrington, 2003).

As noted above, when providing family-based services for children with PSE, there is likely to be a host of contextual risk factors that must be considered. Hutchins and Dipietro (1997) found that women who had used cocaine during pregnancy were more likely to suffer from depression and to have family histories of substance abuse, personal histories of abuse (particularly sexual abuse), less social support, partners who are currently using substances, and less stable living conditions. Many concomitant environmental factors can contribute to or exacerbate the prevalence of sociobehavioral and mental health problems for children with PSE (e.g., living with a parent who has a substance abuse problem, early parental death, maternal depression, maltreatment, transient living, child welfare involvement and subsequent out-of-home placement, and being raised by foster or adoptive parents; O'Connor & Kasari, 2000; Streissguth et al., 2004).

Among children with PSE, potentially diverse developmental challenges, heterogeneity of problems, and potentially diverse caregiver risk factors make treatment selection increasingly complicated. These complexities highlight the need for comprehensive, multidimensional treatment modalities to address skill development across several domains and settings in this population. Early intervention is particularly important for these children. Consistent with diathesis–stress formulations (Zuckerman, 1999), early adversity can cause individuals to be highly vulnerable to later stressors, which mediate poor outcomes. These vulnerabilities sensitize children to environmental stressors that are more prevalent for children with PSE. This increased vulnerability to stressors negatively influences neurophysiological and socioemotional-behavioral development (Gutman & Nemeroff, 2003; Jutras-Aswad, DiNieri, Harkany, & Hurd, 2009). Furthermore, the fact that the developmental windows during infancy and childhood in which integral skills can be remediated are potent, but limited, increases the need for targeted and effective intervention.

In the following section, we describe a number of family-based interventions. Some of these programs were designed specifically for children with PSE and their caregivers. We also present several evidence-based therapies that are likely to be effective with, but were not originally designed for, this population; these are discussed because they target salient outcomes and the methods of treatment delivery are suitable to the needs of this population.

Family-based interventions are emphasized over child-only treatments for several reasons. First, children are more likely to generalize skills that have been practiced in a naturalistic setting. By training a family in therapeutic techniques, the child can be immersed in a learning environment that fosters skill development and a positive parent–child dynamic. When children receive therapy or training in a removed context (e.g., in an individual therapist's office), they are less likely to transfer skills to the intended settings (e.g., home, school, and community). Secondly, given the extant risks, comorbid factors, and familial issues noted above, it is imperative that families be included in the treatment process. Parents play an unparalleled role in developing and maintaining skills and behaviors in their children by their use of encouragement and limit-setting. Without parents' inclusion in the therapeutic process, children might not sustain their gains and master new skills and behaviors. Third, family-based interventions allow parents to voice their values and priorities in treatment planning. Such participation is likely to increase parents' ownership of their roles in treatment and increase their involvement.

There is a paucity of interventions developed specifically for children with PSE and their families. In fact, there are very few comprehensive and ecologically informed intervention approaches that have been designed for this population. Of those that are available, many have only been field-tested, and few have been studied with methodological rigor. Most of the programs described below were not developed specifically for children with PSE but were developed for children with similar prevalent, significant social-behavioral problems. These programs generally target issues germane to this population: social-behavioral deficits, self-regulatory deficits, effective parenting practices, family wellness, and parenting stress. Not every program addresses each issue; similarly, not every child with PSE or their caregiver needs treatment across all of these domains. Treatment selection must be guided by the child and family's unique needs. Although several of the programs discussed below were not explicitly studied with children with PSE, there is reason to believe that they would have similar positive outcomes. Ultimately, these should be empirically examined. In the meantime, however, children with PSE, their families, and their treatment providers must make decisions in good faith regarding care from the options currently available.

In the following section, we describe family-based intervention programs that involve the parent and child in treatment and/or utilize the parent as a therapeutic agent for change. These programs range in age and intervention targets and are categorized into two primary types: home-based programs for children living with their biological caregivers, and child welfare programs for children living in kinship or foster care.

■ **HOME-BASED PROGRAMS**

Children's Friendship Training

Although initially developed for children with autism spectrum disorders (Frankel & Myatt, 2003; Frankel et al., 2010), Children's Friendship Training (CFT) was adapted for use for children with fetal alcohol spectrum disorders (FASD) due to a prevalence of social skill deficits in both populations. CFT is rooted in social learning theory and is a manualized, evidence-based social skills intervention that has demonstrated efficacy with children who have autism spectrum disorders, ADHD (Frankel, Myatt, Cantwell, & Feinberg, 1997), and oppositional defiant disorder (Frankel & Myatt, 2003). In modifying the program, researchers took into account the neurocognitive deficits typical among children with FASD (e.g., poor language performance, problems with memory, poor executive functioning, and inadequate play skills) and addressed them by adapting the treatment delivery process without changing the core content or intervention components (Keil, Paley, Frankel, & O'Connor, 2010; Laugeson et al., 2007). Adaptations to address language deficits included breaking down content into smaller components, increasing opportunities for exposure and rehearsal of new material, presenting information in multiple formats, and emphasizing the use of simpler and repetitive language appropriate to children's developmental levels. Adaptations to address memory and executive functioning deficits included increased use of verbal prompts, increased use of role-playing, and requests of parents to increase rehearsal and review of homework assignments. Behavioral issues were addressed in the adaptation by regularly reviewing the group rules and expectations for behavior, utilizing positive reinforcement techniques to increase prosocial behavior and minimize behavior problems, and providing children who demonstrated significant problem behaviors with more intensive individualized supports, such as incentives for targeted behavior goals. Lastly, to accommodate deficits in play skills and limited peer networks, the parents were asked to schedule regular game times to provide additional practice selecting and playing games the children would be likely to play with a peer. Parents were also encouraged to enroll children in extracurricular activities with children of a similar developmental (not chronological) age to increase the likelihood of social success and acceptance (Laugeson et al., 2007).

The intervention consists of 12 concurrent child and parent group sessions that occur once weekly for 90 minutes and are designed to teach 6- to 12-year-olds specific social skill behaviors (e.g., social communication, reciprocal peer interactions, and conflict resolution) and to encourage parents to facilitate prosocial peer-relationship development by coaching children in navigating social situations and facilitating relationship development with potential playmates. Examples of group topics for children include having a conversation, joining a group of children at play, being a good sport, and handling bullies and conflict situations. Parents explore topics such as supporting child friendships and play dates, and handling teasing. Key features are taught through simple rules of social behavior, modeling, rehearsal, and feedback during intervention sessions and through home-based rehearsal and practice assignments.

Researchers have examined CFT's impact on social skills development and maintenance over time (O'Connor et al., 2006) and changes in social information processing, focusing specifically on the impact of social information processing on hostile attribution (Keil et al., 2010) in a sample of 100 children with FASD. The results showed that, three months after receiving CFT, the intervention children demonstrated significantly improved social skills and decreased hostile attribution compared to the control children who also had documented prenatal alcohol exposure (Keil et al., 2010). The results were not observed, however, by the children's regular teachers in the school setting (O'Connor et al., 2006), indicating the need for further research and strategies to improve the generalization of skills to other settings.

Families Moving Forward

Families Moving Forward (FMF) is a low-intensity behavioral consultation intervention carried out by local mental health providers with specified FMF training that lasts from nine to 11 months and provides the parents of children with FASD at least 16 bimonthly sessions. FMF, based on social learning theory, is designed to help caregivers learn new behavioral strategies to increase positive parental behavior when confronting challenging child behavior. FMF consists of basic training concepts and a host of additional topics for individualization. The core concepts include providing information regarding FASD, altering caregiver negative thoughts about his/her child by increasing their knowledge of how the neurodevelopmental effects of FASD influence a child's acting-out behaviors, advocating for certain accommodations that a child might need, increasing access to community resources, and addressing caregiver-related issues (e.g., addiction, recovery, and self-care). The parents can also have consultations on behavior management, medical issues, coping, and relationship issues.

The program is currently being studied at the University of Washington and Seattle Children's Research Institute, but some preliminary evidence of the program's efficacy is available. In a small randomized control trial, 52 families with children (ages 5–11 years) were assigned to either the FMF intervention group or a standard-of-care group that received available community services (Bertrand, 2009). All children had FASD diagnoses and externalizing and/or attention problems. After participating in FMF, the parents in the experimental group had significantly improved parenting-related self-efficacy and increased self-care behaviors compared to the control parents. The FMF parents also reported that their family needs were being met more frequently, they had higher satisfaction with service providers, and their children had decreased disruptive behavior problems. Parental social satisfaction with FMF was also extremely high: parents reported that the intervention included the right amount of services.

Parent Management Training

Parent Management Training (PMT) is an individual- or group-based intervention designed to educate parents in effective practices for improving parent–child interactions, decreasing child inappropriate or problem behaviors, and increasing child prosocial behavior (Kazdin, 2003). PMT is built upon the principle that parent–child interaction is central to shaping child prosocial or antisocial behavior (Patterson, Reid, & Dishion, 1992; Reid, Patterson, & Snyder, 2002).

The dynamics underlying the coercive family process (Patterson, 1982) have particularly influenced the treatment components of PMT. Coercive parent–child processes serve to interfere with the development of prosocial behavior due to ineffective, harsh, or inconsistent discipline practices from parents that tend to reinforce children's negative behavior. In PMT, families are taught to condition the desired prosocial behaviors through contingency management (reinforcement balanced with limit-setting) and reconceptualizing problem behaviors as shaping and teaching opportunities. The parents are encouraged to think of problem behaviors as skill deficits and are taught to provide a high rate of encouragement and feedback toward the development of prosocial behaviors, in balance with setting predictable and consistent limits on inappropriate behaviors. A typical example might include establishing a token-economy or sticker-chart system that encourages a desired behavior and giving the child a brief time-out or removing a privilege for a problem behavior.

PMT Oregon (PMTO), a variation of PMT that is highly structured and based on social learning theory and interaction principles (Forgatch, 1994), is intended for use with the parents of children who have severe and chronic behavior problems. In PMTO, the parents learn how to reduce problem behaviors and prevent subsequent escalations through encouragement, discipline, positive involvement, monitoring, and problem-solving (Forgatch & Martinez, 1999).

PMT is one of the best-investigated interventions for children and adolescents and has been studied in scores of randomized controlled trials with children (ages 12–17 years; Kazdin, 1997). Clinically significant improvements have been observed in up to two-thirds of children with disruptive behavior disorders (Kronenberger & Meyer, 2001). Forgatch and DeGarmo (1999) discussed the positive impact that PMTO has been shown to have on parenting practices. Furthermore, other researchers examining PMTO have shown parenting practices to mediate long-term child outcomes such as noncompliance, delinquency, and internalizing and externalizing behavior problems (DeGarmo & Forgatch, 2005; DeGarmo, Patterson, & Forgatch, 2004; Martinez & Forgatch, 2001). The principles of PMT have been integrated into numerous program variations to address particular populations.

Although there is no literature on PMT and its effectiveness specifically in children with PSE, several principles of PMT could be highly effective with this population. PMT asks parents to give clear and specific directions when making requests. This is particularly salient for children with cognitive difficulties and developmental delays, as the parents are encouraged to identify their child's unique learning and understanding capabilities and modify parenting accordingly. Similarly, PMT guides parents to identify meaningful targets for child skill development and utilize encouragement and limit-setting methods that the child will be most responsive to. This highly individualizable approach is ideal for children with PSE due to the heterogeneity of behavioral concerns. Lastly, PMT emphasizes structuring the environment to increase predictability, using therapeutic parenting approaches consistently, and providing many practice opportunities. For children with cognitive and learning deficits, this approach is integral to shaping skills and increasing the likelihood of generalization across settings.

Parent-Child Interaction Therapy

Parent–Child Interaction Therapy (PCIT; Eyberg & Boggs, 1998) is an evidence-based, behavioral parent-training model designed to decrease child behavior problems. Originally designed for preschool-age children, PCIT has been studied with the parents of children up to 12 years old with positive outcomes. PCIT's intervention targets include improving the quality of the parent–child relationship, decreasing child behavior problems, increasing child prosocial skills, and establishing parental use of positive discipline practices. The PCIT therapist observes the parent and the child interacting in a clinic setting and coaches the parent on using effective parenting techniques via a headset or earbuds. The intervention is short-term, typically lasting 12 to 16 weeks (one-hour weekly sessions). Similar to PMT, PCIT is a highly individualizable intervention that readily adapts to variety of presenting problems that are typical for children with PSE and their parents. The intensive *in vivo* coaching available to parents has a great deal of utility when working with high-risk families such as those with histories of substance abuse problems; these families are likely to struggle with numerous extraneous stressors and have difficulty adopting new parenting practices, and could benefit from intensive feedback.

The theoretical underpinnings for PCIT identify the root of child behavior problems as being within the parent–child relationship. The intervention model posits that improving the parent–child dynamic will result in reductions of externalizing behavior problems (Eyberg, Nelson, & Boggs, 2008). The treatment is characterized by two distinct phases. Phase 1, Child-Directed Interaction, is focused on relationship enhancement: strengthening parent–child attachment and increasing child prosocial skills and positive parenting practices. Phase 2, Parent–Child Interaction, is focused on the use of effective discipline practices to reduce child noncompliance and other problem behaviors and on supporting parents in developing appropriate expectations for the child.

To date, there has only been one study examining the effects of PCIT in children with PSE (Bertrand, 2009). Bertrand reviewed a study from the University of Oklahoma Health Sciences Center in which researchers compared a group version of PCIT to a less intensive parenting support and management intervention comprising components from other effective behavioral interventions. No attempts were made to modify PCIT for this population. Children with FASD were randomly assigned to the treatment groups, and both groups demonstrated significant reductions in problem behavior, though not significantly differing from each other.

In addition to this study, the results from a number of other studies lend credence to implementing PCIT with this population; the effectiveness of PCIT has been examined in children who demonstrate many of the comorbid issues present among children with PSE. Bagner and Eyberg (2007) examined the effectiveness of PCIT for treating disruptive behavior problems in children with mental retardation through a small randomized control trial. Their results indicated fewer disruptive behaviors, increased compliance, decreased parenting stress, and increases in positive parent–child interactions post-intervention. More extensive exploration is warranted, however, to examine whether the different etiologies of comparable problem behaviors among children with mental retardation and children with PSE underscore inimitable treatment needs.

Further, although McDiarmid and Bagner (2005) did not explicitly study children with developmental disabilities, they argued that a number of critical features in the PCIT program map onto the learning needs of such children, and that, with slight modifications (i.e., word simplification), PCIT could effectively reduce disruptive behaviors among this population.

In another study, Bagner, Sheinkopf, Vohr, and Lester (2010) examined the effects of PCIT with children born prematurely, a common occurrence among infants with PSE. Their results indicated that, compared to the families that did not receive the intervention, the PCIT families reported fewer attention problems, decreased aggression, decreased internalizing and externalizing problems, and increased compliance among their children. In addition, the parents were observed to engage in more positive parenting practices and reported lowered stress related to child behavior problems.

Nixon (2001) found that, compared to their same-age peers, the behavior-disordered children of parents who received PCIT demonstrated significant decreases in hyperactivity and exhibited more temperamental flexibility. These changes were sustained at a six-month follow-up.

PCIT has also been found to be effective at improving parent–child interactions and discipline practices among families with histories of physically abusing their children (ages 4–12; Borrego, Urquiza, Rasmussen, & Zebell, 1999; Chaffin et al., 2004). This is particularly meaningful given the co-occurrence of maltreatment among many families with substance abuse problems. In fact, some of the families in the study by Chaffin et al. reported prior and/or current substance abuse problems. Although these reports do not indicate that the children in the study were prenatally exposed to substances, there is an increased likelihood that some may have been. In an alternate child welfare context, PCIT foster caregivers have reported lower levels of parenting stress and high rates of satisfaction with the intervention model (McNeil, Herschell, Gurwitch, & Clemens-Mowrer, 2005; Timmer, Urquiza, & Zebell, 2006).

To be modified effectively for use with the PSE population, additional consideration must be given to developmental principles. Children with PSE are likely to demonstrate inattention (Leech, Richardson, Goldschmidt, & Day, 1999), and their parents will probably need guidance in giving clear directions and using frequent prompts and redirection. Such children might also be struggling with receptive and expressive language delays (Morrow et al., 2004), necessitating that parents emphasize clear and repetitive wording for commands or prompts. Lastly, PCIT therapists might need to provide additional guidance regarding a parent's expectations for growth and behavior change: the trajectories of children with PSE often differ from children with more typical development.

The Incredible Years

The Incredible Years parent-training program is rooted in social learning theory and the principles of negating the coercive family process; it is one component of a three-part series (which also includes teacher- and child-training modules) designed to promote parenting competencies and strengthen families with children (ages 0–12 years; Webster-Stratton & Reid, 2003). The parent-training module targets parental nurturance and self-confidence regarding parenting, positive and therapeutic discipline practices, problem-solving, communication, support, school involvement, and collaboration with teachers. The program is delivered via basic or advanced curricula, and the number of group-based training sessions varies by age range.

The Basic curriculum is completed across eight to 20 group-based sessions that occur weekly for two hours. These sessions include brief videotape vignettes modeling parenting skills focused on social learning and child development principles. The group facilitator discusses the vignettes, which serves to stimulate problem-solving and collaborative learning. The Advanced curriculum (completed after the Basic training) includes additional vignettes to be viewed and discussed over nine to 12 sessions and targets the complex personal and interpersonal risk factors salient to families at greater risk (e.g., parental depression, marital discord, lack of social support, poor problem-solving, and environmental stressors) that contribute to coercive family processes and inhibit the use of positive parenting practices. The Advanced curriculum provides training on four domains: personal self-control, communication skills, problem-solving skills, and strengthening social support and self-care.

Although training programs exist for children as old as 12 in The Incredible Years, the developers focused primarily on ages three to eight for several reasons (Webster-Stratton & Reid, 2003). First, the beginnings of oppositional defiant disorder and conduct disorder can be seen as early as age four. Second, early intervention is more effective at preventing subsequent maladjustment at home and at school. Third, school readiness and a positive early school experience predict greater achievement over time. Fourth, young children with significant conduct problems frequently go untreated, which results in a negative developmental trajectory.

The Incredible Years has been researched extensively, including six randomized control trials designed by the developer and colleagues (Webster-Stratton, 1981, 1982, 1984, 1990, 1994, 1998; Webster-Stratton & Hammond, 1997; Webster-Stratton, Hollinsworth, & Kolpacoff, 1989; Webster-Stratton, Kolpacoff, & Hollinsworth, 1988). Several independent replication studies have also been conducted (Brotman et al., 2003; Jones, Daley, Hutchings, Bywater, & Eames, 2007; Larsson et al., 2009; J. Patterson et al., 2002; Scott, Spender, Doolan, Jacobs, & Aspland, 2001; Spaccarelli, Cotler, & Penman, 1992; Taylor, Schmidt, Pepler, & Hodgins, 1998), and effect sizes have been moderate to strong. Compared to the control groups, the children of parents using this program have been shown to exhibit significant reductions in aggressive and destructive behavior, decreased oppositional and defiant behavior, increased prosocial behavior and social competence, and improved problem-solving. Further, compared to the control groups, the parents using this program have been shown to exhibit decreased harsh and inconsistent discipline practices, increased use of effective discipline practices, and improved marital problem-solving as compared to controls. In addition, all of these studies have indicated long-term effects that were not differentially affected by child gender, parental ethnicity, socioeconomic status (SES), or level of parental education.

Although the program has been studied as a prevention strategy with high-risk populations (Barrera et al., 2002; Brotman et al., 2003; Gross et al., 2003; Webster-Stratton, 1998; Webster-Stratton, Reid, & Hammond, 2001), no studies have been conducted using The Incredible Years specifically with the parents of children PSE and little attention has been paid to examining the effectiveness of the program with special-needs children. However, some level of generalizability for children with PSE can be argued.

Linares, Montalto, Li, and Oza (2006) piloted The Incredible Years as a co-parenting training program for foster caregivers paired with mandated biological parents. Their results indicated increased positive parenting in the foster and biological parents and increased collaborative co-parenting in the treatment condition. Similarly, the program was piloted with 136 families who had open child welfare cases; the results indicated significantly decreased levels of parenting-related stress and child behavior problems compared to baseline measures (Webster-Stratton & Reid, 2010). McIntyre (2008a, 2008b) adapted the program for children with intellectual and developmental disabilities. The results indicated reductions in negative parent and child behavior after receiving the intervention. Lastly, Jones et al. (2007) found that The Incredible Years program resulted in significant reductions in ADHD symptomatology. These findings held even after controlling for post-intervention changes in rates of defiance.

Nurse-Family Partnership

The Nurse-Family Partnership (NFP) program is an evidence-based community intervention that supports the health care needs of low-income, first-time mothers. The mothers are enrolled in the program early in their pregnancy and begin receiving home visits from a NFP-registered nurse no later than their twenty-eighth week of pregnancy. Approximately 64 home visits are conducted until the child is two years old. The NFP nurse works with the mother from a strength-based perspective to provide education regarding preventive health and prenatal care practices (e.g., diet and substance use); emotional support to prepare for motherhood; education regarding child development and positive parenting practices; and life coaching for the mother and her family regarding self-efficacy, economic self-sufficiency, and personal future-oriented goals.

Ongoing research has been conducted on the NFP program for over 30 years based on three large-scale randomized control trials with almost 20 years of longitudinal follow-up. The program has been shown to improve prenatal health–related behavior (Olds, Henderson, Chamberlin, & Tatelbaum, 1986), reduce rates of child abuse and neglect, decrease unintended subsequent pregnancies, increase intervals between pregnancies, reduce welfare dependence, decrease maternal criminality, decrease maternal substance abuse, reduce the rate of child intellectual impairment due to tobacco exposure *in utero*, reduce childhood injuries, reduce juvenile criminality and antisocial behavior, reduce juvenile substance use, and increase child school readiness and academic achievement (Eckenrode et al., 2000; Eckenrode et al., 2010; Kitzman et al., 2000; Kitzman et al., 2010; Olds, Henderson, Chamberlin et al., 1986; Olds, Henderson, Tatelbaum, & Chamberlin, 1986; Olds, Henderson, & Tatelbaum, 1994a, 1994b; Olds et al., 1997; Olds et al., 2004). Moreover, the NFP program has been shown to significantly reduce government spending as compared to matched controls, even after accounting for the program cost (Olds et al., 2010).

Although the NFP program's effectiveness for at-risk families has been well demonstrated, no specific information regarding children with PSE in the treatment or control groups or differential effects has been reported. However, a number of the program's components might be well suited to this population. First, the program is highly individualizable, allowing unique child and family-related factors to be addressed in treatment. Second, the program's strong emphasis on development and health-related factors is essential for the parents of children with PSE. Third, the program relies on the early identification and recruitment of mothers for enrollment and treatment, enabling intervention during crucial early development.

SafeCare

SafeCare, an evidence-based parent-training model rooted in social learning theory, is designed for families who are at risk for, or who have already been reported for, child maltreatment (Lutzker & Bigelow, 2002). Based on an ecobehavioral approach, the SafeCare treatment components were derived from the understanding that maltreatment arises in combination with individual parental factors, parent–child interactions, family factors, and greater societal and cultural factors (Edwards & Lutzker, 2008). The program has four primary modules: Health (e.g., preventing and treating common illnesses), Home Safety (e.g., identifying and eliminating safety hazards in the home), Parent–Child or Parent–Infant Interactions (e.g., training parents to promote development, increase positive interactions, and manage difficult behaviors), and Problem-Solving/Counseling (e.g., offering solution-oriented problem-solving and counseling techniques to be used across the three content modules and to address parent needs that fall outside the range of the SafeCare model). The intervention is delivered via home visitors who work with the parents until they reach a set of skill-based criteria for each module.

Compared to the control families, the SafeCare families have been shown to be less likely to have an initial child maltreatment report or recurrence or to have a child removed from their home (Gershater-Molko, Lutzker, & Wesch, 2002).

High rates of accuracy in skill demonstration have also been observed. Further, the SafeCare children have demonstrated 85% compliance with parent requests (compared to 69% compliance at baseline), and the SafeCare parents have demonstrated at least 85% reductions in overall hazards in the home (Edwards & Lutzker, 2008).

Due to the complex and multifaceted risks of families with substance abuse problems and children with PSE, the risk for maltreatment is high. Although this program could be an excellent targeted prevention measure for families with histories of substance abuse and children with PSE, no researchers have examined the effectiveness of SafeCare in this population.

■ CHILD WELFARE PROGRAMS

Children with PSE come to the attention of child protective service agencies for variety of reasons (e.g., identification at birth, community referral identifying a potential for child abuse or neglect, and parental criminal activity). Out-of-home care for these children is not uncommon. In one sample of 415 individuals with FASD, 80% were not raised by their biological mothers (Streissguth et al., 2004). Related to this, in a study reviewing the case records of 639 children in out-of-home care (kin or foster care placements), 79% of the caregivers met the criteria for substance abuse (Besinger, Garland, Litrownik, & Landsverk, 1999). Being a foster caregiver for children with emotional and behavioral difficulties is nothing short of challenging; these children often have significant social and behavioral difficulties that can lead to a multitude of negative outcomes (Brooks & Barth, 1998; Bruce, Fisher, Pears, & Levine, 2009; Clausen, Landsverk, Ganger, Chadwick, & Litrownik, 1998; Fisher, Stoolmiller, Gunnar, & Burraston, 2007; Landsverk & Garland, 1999; Zima et al., 2000). Adding the developmental complexity typical of children with PSE makes the task exponentially more difficult. The factors leading to out-of-home placements for children with PSE (e.g., abuse and neglect) serve to significantly elevate risks to a child's overall functioning and well-being. Foster children with PSE exhibit higher rates of social, thought, and attention problems; delinquency; and aggression than those being cared for by their biological mothers or kinship caregivers (Linares et al., 2006; Minnes et al., 2010). Effective family-based services for foster caregivers are critical for addressing child behavior problems and stabilizing placements, as placement disruptions are correlated with a host of negative outcomes (Albus & Dozier, 1999; Courtney, 1995; Proch & Taber, 1985). Although not all of these programs were developed for the PSE population, their efficacy in stabilizing placements and fostering behavior change suggests that they are appropriate for this population.

Support and Training for Adoptive and Foster Families

There is evidence to suggest that many children with PSE will be placed in foster care within months of birth (Eiden, Foote, & Schuetze, 2007), yet foster caregivers rarely receive the type of education and support necessary to care for such infants (Burry, 1999; Zukoski, 1999). The Support and Training for Adoptive and Foster

Families (STAFF) Project was developed in response to this need (Burry & Noble, 2001). The STAFF Project focuses on securing permanency for infants (ages 0–2 years) by providing training and support services to foster and adoptive caregivers. The curriculum elements were derived from a comprehensive review of the literature and feedback from 132 adoptive families of children with PSE regarding developmental needs and special parenting considerations. The six-hour curriculum includes five modules: 1) Introductory Activities; 2) Information on Substance Abuse, Addiction, Attachment, and Confidentiality; 3/4) Information on Caregiving for Infants With PSE Specifying Effects of Both Alcohol and Drugs; and 5) Long-Term Resources for Information Gathering, Support, and Assistance.

In a non-randomized quasi-experimental study, the participants demonstrated significant increases in content knowledge after participating in the intervention and reported high levels of social satisfaction (Burry & Noble, 2001). More methodologically rigorous research is needed to study the effectiveness of this program and to confirm these promising preliminary results.

Safe Babies Program

The Safe Babies Program was also developed in response to the need for specialized foster care for infants with PSE and is implemented as part of the Vancouver (Canada) Ministry of Children and Family Development (D'Angiulli & Sullivan, 2010). It was modeled after a pilot project aimed at providing specialized education and support to the foster families of infants with PSE and working with families to maintain an optimal caregiving environment (Marcellus, 2004). The Safe Babies Program provides support to foster caregivers via the following: a community health nurse; resource workers; an advisory committee; six training sessions addressing developmental considerations, health-related issues, safety, respite, and permanency planning; monthly meetings with a support group; and biannual newsletters.

In a non-randomized, quasi-experimental study of the program (with a small sample of pre-term and full-term foster infants with PSE), the results indicated an association between the program and positive developmental outcomes and physiological regulation (D'Angiulli & Sullivan, 2010). Additional research is needed to further examine the program's effectiveness.

Multidimensional Treatment Foster Care

The Multidimensional Treatment Foster Care (MTFC) program is an intensive, comprehensive intervention for foster children (Chamberlain, Leve, & DeGarmo, 2007; Chamberlain & Reid, 1991). The program was developed as an alternative to regular foster care, group or residential treatment, and incarceration for children with pervasive, chronic behavior problems. Derived from principles of social learning theory and ecological theory, MTFC coordinates multiple treatment components to address the needs of children, their foster caregivers, and their biological parents across settings. The children receive individual therapy and behavioral skills training. In the preschool adaptation of the program (MTFC-P), the children also participate in weekly therapeutic playgroups to develop school readiness (Fisher, Ellis, & Chamberlain, 1999). The foster caregivers receive ongoing training and support in PMT and are trained to participate as members of the clinical team by implementing therapeutic interventions with a high rate of consistency in the home under the direction of a clinical team. The biological parents receive ongoing family therapy and consultation to improve parent–child interactions while the child remains in care to prepare for reunification. The MTFC children also benefit from school consultation and case management with other service providers (e.g., social workers, physicians, legal representation, and speech/language therapists).

Several randomized trials and numerous other studies have been conducted with the MTFC programs, yielding a robust evidence base for the program's feasibility and effectiveness. The outcomes for Juvenile Justice youth in MTFC have been examined for males and females, with the results indicating higher rates of program completion, fewer days in locked settings, and significant decreases in criminal or delinquent activity compared to children in group care settings (Chamberlain & Reid, 1998; Eddy, Whaley, & Chamberlain, 2004; Leve, Chamberlain, & Reid, 2005). Furthermore, Juvenile Justice girls in MTFC have been shown to have higher rates of homework completion and school attendance during treatment (Leve & Chamberlain, 2006) and fewer pregnancies (Kerr, Leve, & Chamberlain, 2009).

The results from the MTFC-P randomized control trial demonstrate increased effective parenting practices in the foster home, reduced child behavior problems, improved physiological regulation, and improved attachment behaviors among MTFC-P children (Fisher, Gunnar, Chamberlain, & Reid, 2000; Fisher & Kim, 2007; Fisher et al., 2007). In addition, the MTFC-P intervention has been shown to significantly decrease risk for subsequent placement failures irrespective placement history (Fisher et al., 2000), thus increasing the odds of a successful permanent placement.

Project KEEP

Project KEEP is a group-based, 16-week, manualized intervention of training, supervision, and support for foster and kinship caregivers (ages 5–12 years; Price, Chamberlain, Landsverk, & Reid, 2009). It integrates training content from MTFC and PMTO and emphasizes the use of positive reinforcement, effective discipline, and monitoring. The foster parents attend a training/support group session for one hour weekly to learn strategies for reducing child problem behavior and stabilizing the current foster placements. The session topics include contingency and reinforcement systems, limit-setting, power struggles, school success, and self-care. Home practice assignments are assigned each week and are reviewed the subsequent week.

The effectiveness of the original Project KEEP intervention was tested using a randomized control trial design with 700 families (Price et al., 2008). The authors examined the impact of the Project KEEP intervention on the likelihood of positive or negative placement changes among foster children and whether the intervention moderated the relationship between the number of prior placements and permanent placement failure. The families were randomized to treatment and control groups. For the control participants, the number of prior placements predicted negative exits from the current placement. Specifically, children with higher numbers of placement disruptions were more likely to experience a negative exit. The Project KEEP intervention, however, was shown to mitigate the risk of negative exits despite a history of multiple placements, and to increase the likelihood of a positive exit (e.g., reunification). The KEEP children also demonstrated significantly fewer behavior problems than the control group (Chamberlain, Price, Reid, & Landsverk, 2008).

■ CURRENT AND FUTURE DIRECTIONS

Children with PSE exhibit extremely high levels of risk given their co-occurring individual and contextual factors that interfere with healthy development. Without effective intervention, the trajectories for these children are fraught with difficulties. Many of the interventions discussed above, although not initially designed for children with PSE, may be effective with this population. However, the theoretical underpinnings of most family-based interventions posit that the crux of child behavior change lies within the parent–child interaction dynamic, wherein behaviors are maintained or discouraged. By contrast, children with PSE evidence behavioral difficulties that result in part from the neurological damage caused by PSE. Although the parent–child interaction pattern is an important influencing factor, it does not explain the entirety of the behavioral phenomenon demonstrated in this population. This highlights the importance of population-specific interventions or adaptations.

Interventions designed to address the unique and specific needs of this population are necessary. These interventions must be thoughtfully developed with consideration of the scope and diversity of factors salient to the treatment of children with PSE, their caregivers, and the relevant settings. A universal approach will not be capable of addressing all issues, but there are several key features that should be included in intervention development. First, treatment approaches that recognize the need for individualizing methods based on the ever-changing developmental and social-behavioral needs of the child are imperative to improving treatment outcomes. Treatment models must emphasize using developmentally appropriate instructional methods for the child-directed components of an intervention that support skill acquisition and generalization. Similarly, family-based interventions should address a caregiver's understanding of the child's unique developmental needs. Equipping a caregiver with the tools necessary to be proactive and responsive to the rapidly changing developmental and behavioral needs of the child is more likely to engender long-term success. Second, reducing environmental risk factors (e.g., substance use, lack of safety, and placement instability) is vital for overall success. Third, increasing protective factors (e.g., positive parent–child interactions, peer networks, academic success, and social support for parents and caregivers) is an important counterpoint to risk reduction. Fourth, providing parents and caregivers with strategies to mitigate stress, parenting-related and otherwise, is integral to effectively utilizing therapeutic parenting strategies and maintaining a positive and responsive approach. Without the necessary coping skills for dealing with the contextual risk factors germane to this population, parents struggle to make good use of even the most well-designed and effective methods.

These interventions must then be tested using rigorous methodological designs to establish a clear evidence base for their use. Randomized trials are also needed to examine existing interventions that are likely to be effective but were not originally intended for this population. Interventions such as MTFC-P, which have been shown to impact underlying neural systems affected by PSE such as the HPA axis, may be especially promising. Furthermore, it is likely that some of children with PSE were included in the studies noted above. In many cases, however, this has not been explicated in the literature; and a small number of children with PSE in a larger mixed sample would not prove sufficient. When possible (and in cases where the samples included a sizeable portion of this population), secondary analyses of the data are needed to examine the unique effects of the intervention on children with PSE. Specifically, for treatment utility and external validity, it is integral to examine whether children with PSE made differential gains and whether relevant meditating and moderating factors can explain the resulting variance in treatment outcomes.

As discussed above, therapeutic techniques and interventions that can be highly individualized might be most appropriate, given the heterogeneity and varying intensity of behavioral and developmental concerns among this population. One such technique is called *Marte Meo* (which translates as "on one's own strength"), which has been field-tested worldwide. Given its limited empirical basis, *Marte Meo* was not included in the review of family-based interventions above. However, it has the potential to be highly efficacious with this population.

Developed in the Netherlands by Maria Aarts and colleagues, *Marte Meo* focuses on the observed strengths of a child and his/her parent or caregiver as a means of potentiating development (Aarts, 2008). In *Marte Meo*, a trained therapist works with a parent or caregiver, whose child may be of any age, to identify an aspect of the child or parent–child dynamic that needs improvement. Child social, emotional, linguistic, and cognitive developments are potential targets. The therapist then takes a short film of the child in a naturally occurring setting or activity and proceeds to carefully edit the film to illuminate the strengths observed in the child or parent–child interactions relevant to the identified need. These brief, edited films are then shown to the client with a microanalytic narration from the therapist, highlighting the frame-by-frame sequence of events that foster the child's development. In this way, the *Marte Meo* therapist facilitates a shift in the parent's perceptions of self and of their child and enables the parent to be more engaged and responsive to the child's developmental processes. In total, the *Marte Meo* therapist might record five or six films for a treatment time of approximately three months.

Marte Meo has been field-tested with infants and children who struggle with attachment, irritable temperament, ADHD, autism, intellectual disability, communication delay, and mental health problems. It has been used with biological parents, foster caregivers, teachers, and other professionals and has been in practice in 30 countries for over 20 years. In a non-randomized control trial, *Marte Meo* was used for the early detection and intervention of externalizing behavior problems in a school setting with children (ages 4–12 years; Axberg, Hansson, Broberg, & Wirtberg, 2006). The *Marte Meo* children demonstrated significant decreases in problem behavior at home and school compared to the control children. These results were found to have been maintained at a two-year follow-up assessment.

Lastly, innovative techniques that might facilitate enhanced neurological functioning or promote plasticity also warrant examination. Therapies such as attention training (Amir et al., 2009; Rueda, Rothbart, McCandliss, Saccomanno, & Posner, 2005; Wells, 2007) or mindfulness training (Heywood, Fisher, & Tang, 2011) might help remediate deficits in self-regulation, attention, and cognitive flexibility. In addition, there are promising new approaches for using nutritional supplementation to facilitate neural plasticity and neurogenesis that might help improve outcomes (Thomas, Abou, & Dominguez, 2009). All of these approaches could prove to be appropriate adjunct therapies for enhancing the effectiveness of more comprehensive treatments for children with PSE and their parents and caregivers. Again, relevant scientific investigations into these approaches are needed.

At present, attempting to determine the best ways to address the needs of children with PSE leads to a multitude of unanswered questions. However, we should be encouraged by the numerous avenues opened for exploration, including risk-prevention efforts with women in high-risk groups, prenatal and postnatal treatment options, school- and home-based contexts for care and treatment, and long-term support systems for adolescents and adults with PSE. As we move forward, it is paramount that scientists conscientiously examine these approaches with methodological rigor and that practitioners refer children and families to treatments that are ecologically informed, developmentally sensitive, and focused on outcomes relevant to their unique needs.

▪ REFERENCES

Accornero, V. H., Morrow, C. E., Bandstra, E. S., Johnson, A. L., & Anthony, J. C. (2002). Behavioral outcome of preschoolers exposed prenatally to cocaine: Role of maternal behavioral health. *Journal of Pediatric Psychology, 27,* 259–269.

Acra, C. F., Bono, K. E., Mundy, P. C., & Scott, K. G. (2009). Social competence in children at risk due to prenatal cocaine exposure: Continuity over time and associations with cognitive and language abilities. *Social Development, 18,* 1002–1014.

Albus, K. E., & Dozier, M. (1999). Indiscriminate friendliness and terror of strangers in infancy: Contributions from the study of infants in foster care. *Infant Mental Health Journal, 20,* 30–41.

Amir, N., Beard, C., Taylor, C. T., Klumpp, H., Elias, J., Burns, M., et al. (2009). Attention training in individuals with generalized social phobia: A randomized controlled trial. *Journal of Consulting & Clinical Psychology, 77,* 961–973.

Aarts, M. (2008). *Marte Meo: Basic Manual.* Harderwijk, The Netherlands: Aarts Productions.

Axberg, U., Hansson, K., Broberg, A. G., & Wirtberg, I. (2006). The development of a systemic school-based intervention: *Marte Meo* and coordination meetings. *Family Process*, *45*, 375–389.

Bagner, D. M., & Eyberg, S. M. (2007). Parent–child interaction therapy for disruptive behavior in children with mental retardation: A randomized controlled trial. *Journal of Clinical Child & Adolescent Psychology*, *36*, 418–429.

Bagner, D. M., Scheinkopf, S. J., Miller-Loncar, C., LaGasse, L. L., Lester, B. M., Liu, J., et al. (2009). The effect of parenting stress on child behavior problems in high-risk children with prenatal drug exposure. *Child Psychiatry & Human Development*, *40*, 73–84.

Bagner, D. M., Sheinkopf, S. J., Vohr, B. R., & Lester, B. M. (2010). Parenting intervention for externalizing behavior problems in children born premature: An initial examination. *Journal of Developmental & Behavioral Pediatrics*, *31*, 209–216.

Barrera, M., Jr., Biglan, A., Taylor, T. K., Gunn, B. K., Smolkowski, K., Black, C., et al. (2002). Early elementary school intervention to reduce conduct problems: A randomized trial with Hispanic and non-Hispanic children. *Prevention Science*, *3*, 83–94.

Bertrand, J. (2009). Interventions for children with fetal alcohol spectrum disorders (FASDs): Overview of findings for five innovative research projects. *Research in Developmental Disabilities*, *30*, 986–1006.

Bertrand, J., Floyd, R. L., Weber, M. K., O'Connor, M. J., Johnson, K. A., Riley, E. P., et al. (2004). *Fetal Alcohol Syndrome: Guidelines for Referral and Diagnosis*. Atlanta, GA: Centers for Disease Control and Prevention.

Besinger, B. A., Garland, A. F., Litrownik, A. J., & Landsverk, J. A. (1999). Caregiver substance abuse among maltreated children placed in out-come-home care. *Child Welfare*, *78*, 221–239.

Borrego, J., Jr., Urquiza, A. J., Rasmussen, R. A., & Zebell, N. (1999). Parent–child interaction therapy with a family at high risk for physical abuse. *Child Maltreatment*, *4*, 331–342.

Brooks, D., & Barth, R. P. (1998). Characteristics and outcomes of drug-exposed and non drug-exposed children in kinship and non-relative foster care. *Children & Youth Services Review*, *20*, 475–501.

Brotman, L. M., Klein, R. G., Kamboukos, D., Brown, E. J., Coard, S. I., & Sosinsky, L. S. (2003). Preventive intervention for urban, low-income preschoolers at familial risk for conduct problems: A randomized pilot study. *Journal of Clinical Child & Adolescent Psychology*, *32*, 246–257.

Brown, J. V., Bakeman, R., Coles, C. D., Platzman, K. A., & Lynch, M. E. (2004). Prenatal cocaine exposure: A comparison of two-year-old children in parental and nonparental care. *Child Development*, *75*, 1282–1295.

Bruce, J., Fisher, P. A., Pears, K. C., & Levine, S. (2009). Morning cortisol levels in preschool-aged foster children: Differential effects of maltreatment type. *Developmental Psychobiology*, *51*, 14–23.

Burry, C. L. (1999). Evaluation of a training program for foster parents of infants with prenatal substance effects. *Child Welfare*, *78*, 197–214.

Burry, C. L., & Noble, L. S. (2001). The STAFF Project: Support and training for adoptive and foster families of infants with prenatal substance exposure. *Journal of Social Work Practice in the Addictions*, *1*(4), 71–82.

Caetano, R., & Weisner, C. (1995). The association between DSM-III-R alcohol dependence, psychological distress and drug use. *Addiction*, *90*, 351–359.

Chaffin, M., Silovsky, J. F., Funderburk, B., Valle, L. A., Brestan, E. V., Balachova, T., et al. (2004). Parent–child interaction therapy with physically abusive parents: Efficacy for reducing future abuse reports. *Journal of Consulting & Clinical Psychology, 72,* 500–510.

Chamberlain, P., Leve, L. D., & DeGarmo, D. S. (2007). Multidimensional treatment foster care for girls in the juvenile justice system: Two-year follow-up of a randomized clinical trial. *Journal of Consulting & Clinical Psychology, 75,* 187–193.

Chamberlain, P., Price, J. M., Reid, J., & Landsverk, J. (2008). Cascading implementation of a foster and kinship parent intervention. *Child Welfare, 87,* 27–48.

Chamberlain, P., & Reid, J. B. (1991). Using a specialized foster care community treatment model for children and adolescents leaving the state mental hospital. *Journal of Community Psychology, 19,* 266–276.

Chamberlain, P., & Reid, J. B. (1998). Comparison of two community alternatives to incarceration for chronic juvenile offenders. *Journal of Consulting & Clinical Psychology, 66,* 624–633.

Chapman, K., Tarter, R. E., Kirisci, L., & Cornelius, M. D. (2007). Childhood neurobehavior disinhibition amplifies the risk of substance use disorder: Interaction of parental history and prenatal alcohol exposure. *Journal of Developmental & Behavioral Pediatrics, 28,* 219–224.

Clausen, J. M., Landsverk, J., Ganger, W., Chadwick, D., & Litrownik, A. (1998). Mental health problems of children in foster care. *Journal of Child & Family Studies, 7,* 283–296.

Courtney, M. E. (1995). Reentry to foster care of children returned to their families. *Social Service Review, 69,* 226–241.

D'Angiulli, A., & Sullivan, R. (2010). Early specialized foster care, developmental outcomes and home salivary cortisol patterns in prenatally substance-exposed infants. *Children & Youth Services Review, 32,* 460–465.

DeGarmo, D. S., & Forgatch, M. S. (2005). Early development of delinquency within divorced families: Evaluating a randomized preventive intervention trial. *Developmental Science, 8,* 229–239.

DeGarmo, D. S., Patterson, G. R., & Forgatch, M. S. (2004). How do outcomes in a specified parent training intervention maintain or wane over time? *Prevention Science, 5,* 73–89.

Delaney-Black, V., Covington, C., Templin, T., Ager, J., Martier, S., & Sokol, R. (1998). Prenatal cocaine exposure and child behavior. *Pediatrics, 102,* 945–950.

Eckenrode, J., Campa, M., Luckey, D. W., Henderson, C. R., Jr., Cole, R., Kitzman, H., et al. (2010). Long-term effects of prenatal and infancy nurse home visitation on the life course of youths: Nineteen-year follow-up of a randomized trial. *Archives of Pediatrics & Adolescent Medicine, 164,* 9–15.

Eckenrode, J., Ganzel, B., Henderson, C. R., Jr., Smith, E., Olds, D. L., Powers, J., et al. (2000). Preventing child abuse and neglect with a program of nurse home visitation: The limiting effects of domestic violence. *Journal of the American Medical Association, 284,* 1385–1391.

Eddy, J. M., Whaley, R. B., & Chamberlain, P. (2004). The prevention of violent behavior by chronic and serious male juvenile offenders: A two-year follow-up of a randomized clinical trial. *Journal of Emotional & Behavioral Disorders, 12*(1), 2–8.

Edwards, A., & Lutzker, J. R. (2008). Iterations of the SafeCare model: An evidence-based child maltreatment prevention program. *Behavior Modification, 32,* 736–756.

Eiden, R. D., Foote, A., & Schuetze, P. (2007). Maternal cocaine use and caregiving status: Group differences in caregiver and infant risk variables. *Addictive Behaviors, 32*, 465–476.

Eyberg, S. M., & Boggs, S. R. (1998). Parent–child interaction therapy for oppositional preschoolers. In C. E. Shaefer & J. M. Briesmeister (Eds.), *Handbook of Parent Training: Parents as Co-Therapists for Children's Behavior Problems* (2nd ed., pp. 61–97). New York: Wiley.

Eyberg, S. M., Nelson, M. M., & Boggs, S. R. (2008). Evidence-based psychosocial treatments for children and adolescents with disruptive behavior. *Journal of Clinical Child & Adolescent Psychology, 37*, 215–237.

Fisher, P. A., Ellis, B. H., & Chamberlain, P. (1999). Early intervention foster care: A model for preventing risk in young children who have been maltreated. *Children's Services: Social Policy, Research, & Practice, 2*, 159–182.

Fisher, P. A., Gunnar, M. R., Chamberlain, P., & Reid, J. B. (2000). Preventive intervention for maltreated preschool children: Impact on children's behavior, neuroendocrine activity, and foster parent functioning. *Journal of the American Academy of Child & Adolescent Psychiatry, 39*, 1356–1364.

Fisher, P. A., & Kim, H. K. (2007). Intervention effects on foster preschoolers' attachment-related behaviors from a randomized trial. *Prevention Science, 8*, 161–170.

Fisher, P. A., Kim, H. K., Bruce, J., & Pears, K. C. (2012). Cumulative effects of prenatal substance exposure and early adversity on foster children's HPA-axis reactivity during a psychosocial stressor. *International Journal of Behavioral Development, 36(1)*, 29–35.

Fisher, P. A., Lester, B. M., DeGarmo, D. S., LaGasse, L. L., Lin, H., Shankaran, S., et al. (2011). The combined effects of prenatal drug exposure and early adversity on neurobehavioral disinhibition in childhood and adolescence. *Development & Psychopathology, 23*, 777–788.

Fisher, P. A., Stoolmiller, M., Gunnar, M. R., & Burraston, B. O. (2007). Effects of a therapeutic intervention for foster preschoolers on diurnal cortisol activity. *Psychoneuroendocrinology, 32*, 892–905.

Forgatch, M. S. (1994). *Parenting Through Change: A Programmed Intervention Curriculum for Groups of Single Mothers*. Eugene, OR: Oregon Social Learning Center.

Forgatch, M. S., & DeGarmo, D. S. (1999). Parenting through change: An effective prevention program for single mothers. *Journal of Consulting & Clinical Psychology, 67*, 711–724.

Forgatch, M. S., & Martinez, C. R., Jr. (1999). Parent management training: A program linking basic research and practical application. *Tidsskrift for Norsk Psykologforening, 36*, 923–937.

Frankel, F., & Myatt, R. (2003). *Children's Friendship Training*. New York: Brunner-Routledge.

Frankel, F., Myatt, R., Cantwell, D. P., & Feinberg, D. T. (1997). Parent assisted children's social skills training: Effects on children with and without attention-deficit hyperactivity disorder. *Journal of the Academy of Child & Adolescent Psychiatry, 36*, 1056–1064.

Frankel, F., Myatt, R., Sugar, C., Whitham, C., Gorospe, C. M., & Laugeson, E. (2010). A randomized controlled study of parent-assisted children's friendship training with children having autism spectrum disorders. *Journal of Autism & Developmental Disorders, 40*, 827–842.

Gershater-Molko, R. M., Lutzker, J. R., & Wesch, D. (2002). Using recidivism data to evaluate Project SafeCare: Teaching bonding, safety, and health care skills to parents. *Child Maltreatment, 7*, 277–285.

Goldschmidt, L., Richardson, G. A., Cornelius, M. D., & Day, N. L. (2004). Prenatal marijuana and alcohol exposure and academic achievement at age 10. *Neurotoxicology & Teratology, 26*, 521–532.

Gross, D., Fogg, L., Webster-Stratton, C., Garvey, C., Julion, W., & Grady, J. (2003). Parent training of toddlers in day care in low-income urban communities. *Journal of Consulting & Clinical Psychology, 71*, 261–278.

Gutman, D. A., & Nemeroff, C. B. (2003). Persistent central nervous system effects of an adverse early environment: Clinical and preclinical studies. *Physiology & Behavior, 79*, 471–478.

Hellemans, K. G. C., Sliwowska, J. H., Verma, P., & Weinberg, J. (2010). Prenatal alcohol exposure: Fetal programming and later-life vulnerability to stress, depression and anxiety disorders. *Neuroscience & Biobehavioral Reviews, 34*, 791–807.

Heywood, C. V., Fisher, P. A., & Tang, Y. -Y. (in press). Mindfulness training: A promising approach for addressing the needs of child welfare system children and families. In J. A. Jaworski (Ed.), *Advances in Sociology Research* (Vol. 8, pp. 1–29). Hauppauge, NY: Nova Science Publishers.

Hutchins, E., & Dipietro, J. (1997). Psychosocial risk factors associated with cocaine use during pregnancy: A case-control study. *Obstetrics & Gynecology, 90*, 142–147.

Janzen, L. A., Nanson, J. L., & Block, G. W. (1995). Neuropsychological evaluation of preschoolers with fetal alcohol syndrome. *Neurotoxicology & Teratology, 17*, 273–279.

Johnson, H. L., Nusbaum, B. J., Bejarano, A., & Rosen, T. S. (1999). An ecological approach to development in children with prenatal drug exposure. *American Journal of Orthopsychiatry, 69*, 448–456.

Jones, K., Daley, D., Hutchings, J., Bywater, T., & Eames, C. (2007). Efficacy of The Incredible Years Basic parent training programme as an early intervention for children with conduct problems and ADHD. *Child: Care, Health & Development, 33*, 749–756.

Jutras-Aswad, D., DiNieri, J. A., Harkany, T., & Hurd, Y. L. (2009). Neurobiological consequences of maternal cannabis on human fetal development and its neuropsychiatric outcome. *European Archives of Psychiatry & Clinical Neuroscience 259*, 395–412.

Kazdin, A. E. (1997). Parent management training: Evidence, outcomes, and issues. *Journal of the American Academy of Child & Adolescent Psychiatry, 36*, 1349–1356.

Kazdin, A. E. (2003). Problem-solving skills training and parent management training for conduct disorder. In A. E. Kazdin, & J. R. Weisz (Eds.), *Evidence-Based Psychotherapies for Children and Adolescents* (pp. 241–262). New York: Guilford Press.

Keil, V., Paley, B., Frankel, F., & O'Connor, M. J. (2010). Impact of a social skills intervention on the hostile attributions of children with prenatal alcohol exposure. *Alcoholism: Clinical & Experimental Research, 34*, 231–241.

Kelley, S. J. (1998). Stress and coping behaviors of substance-abusing mothers. *Journal of the Society of Pediatric Nurses, 3*, 103–110.

Kerr, D. C. R., Leve, L. D., & Chamberlain, P. (2009). Pregnancy rates among juvenile justice girls in two randomized controlled trials of multidimensional treatment foster care. *Journal of Consulting & Clinical Psychology, 77*, 588–593.

Kirisci, L., Tarter, R. E., Reynolds, M., & Vanyukov, M. (2006). Individual differences in childhood neurobehavior disinhibition predict decision to desist substance use during adolescence and substance use disorder in young adulthood: A prospective study. *Addictive Behaviors, 31*, 686–696.

Kitzman, H. J., Olds, D. L., Cole, R. E., Hanks, C. A., Anson, E. A., Arcoleo, K. J., et al. (2010). Enduring effects of prenatal and infancy home visiting by nurses on children: Follow-up of a randomized trial among children at age 12 years. *Archives of Pediatric & Adolescent Medicine, 164*, 412–418.

Kitzman, H. J., Olds, D. L., Sidora, K., Henderson, C. R., Jr., Hanks, C., Cole, R., et al. (2000). Enduring effects of nurse home visitation on maternal life course: A three-year follow-up of a randomized trial. *Journal of the American Medical Association, 283*, 1983–1989.

Kronenberger, W. G., & Meyer, R. G. (2001). *The Child Clinician's Handbook* (2nd ed.). Boston: Allyn & Bacon.

Landsverk, J., & Garland, A. F. (1999). Foster care and pathways to mental health services. In P. A. Curtis, G. Dale, Jr., & J. C. Kendall (Eds.), *The Foster Care Crisis: Translating Research into Policy and Practice* (pp. 193–210). Lincoln: University of Nebraska Press.

Larsson, B., Fossum, S., Clifford, G., Drugli, M. B., Handegård, B. H., & Mørch, W. -T. (2009). Treatment of oppositional defiant and conduct problems in young Norwegian children: Results of a randomized controlled trial. *European Child & Adolescent Psychiatry, 18*, 42–52.

Laugeson, E. A., Paley, B., Schonfeld, A. M., Carpenter, E. M., Frankel, F., & O'Connor, M. J. (2007). Adaptation of the children's friendship training program for children with fetal alcohol spectrum disorders. *Child & Family Behavior Therapy, 29*(3), 57–69.

Leech, S. L., Richardson, G. A., Goldschmidt, L., & Day, N. L. (1999). Prenatal substance exposure: Effects on attention and impulsivity of six-year-olds. *Neurotoxicology & Teratology, 21*, 109–118.

Lester, B. M., Bagner, D. M., Liu, J., LaGasse, L. L., Seifer, R., Bauer, C. R., et al. (2009). Infant neurobehavioral dysregulation: Behavior problems in children with prenatal substance exposure. *Pediatrics, 124*, 1355–1362.

Lester, B. M., & Padbury, J. F. (2009). Third pathophysiology of prenatal cocaine exposure. *Developmental Neuroscience, 31*, 23–35.

Leve, L. D., & Chamberlain, P. (2006). A randomized evaluation of multidimensional treatment foster care: Effects on school attendance and homework completion in juvenile justice girls. *Journal of Social Work Practice, 17*, 657–663.

Leve, L. D., Chamberlain, P., & Reid, J. (2005). Intervention outcomes for girls referred from juvenile justice: Effects on delinquency. *Journal of Consulting & Clinical Psychology, 73*, 1181–1185.

Levine, T. P., Liu, J., Das, A., Lester, B., Lagasse, L., Shankaran, S., et al. (2008). Effects of prenatal cocaine exposure on special education in school-aged children. *Pediatrics, 122*, e83–e91.

Linares, L. O., Montalto, D., Li, M., & Oza, V. S. (2006). A promising parenting intervention in foster care. *Journal of Consulting & Clinical Psychology, 74*, 32–41.

Linares, T. J., Singer, L. T., Kirchner, H. L., Short, E. J., Min, M., O., Hussey, P., et al. (2006). Mental health outcomes of cocaine-exposed children at six years of age. *Journal of Pediatric Psychology, 31*, 85–97.

Lutzker, J. R., & Bigelow, K. M. (2002). *Reducing child maltreatment: A guidebook for parent services.* New York: Guilford Press.

Marcellus, L. (2004). Developmental evaluation of the Safe Babies Project: Application of the COECA model. *Issues in Comprehensive Pediatric Nursing, 27,* 107–119.

Martinez, C. R., Jr., & Forgatch, M. S. (2001). Preventing problems with boys' noncompliance: Effects of a parent training intervention for divorcing mothers. *Journal of Consulting & Clinical Psychology, 69,* 416–428.

McDiarmid, M. D., & Bagner, D. M. (2005). Parent–child interaction therapy for children with disruptive behavior and developmental disabilities. *Education & Treatment of Children, 28,* 130–141.

McIntyre, L. L. (2008a). Adapting Webster-Stratton's Incredible Years parent training for children with developmental delay: Findings from a treatment group–only study. *Journal of Intellectual Disability Research, 52,* 1176–1192.

McIntyre, L. L. (2008b). Parent training for young children with developmental disabilities: Randomized controlled trial. *American Journal on Mental Retardation, 113,* 356–368.

McLaughlin, T. F., Williams, B. F., & Howard, V. F. (1998). Suggested behavioral interventions in the classroom to assist students prenatally exposed to drugs. *Behavioral Interventions, 13,* 91–109.

McNamee, R. L., Dunfee, K. L., Luna, B., Clark, D. B., Eddy, W. F., & Tarter, R. E. (2008). Brain activation, response inhibition, and increased risk for substance use disorder. *Alcoholism: Clinical & Experimental Research, 32,* 405–413.

McNeil, C. B., Herschell, A. D., Gurwitch, R. H., & Clemens-Mowrer, L. (2005). Training foster parents in parent–child interaction therapy. *Education & Treatment of Children, 28,* 182–196.

Minnes, S., Singer, L. T., Kirchner, H. L., Short, E., Lewis, B., Satayathum, S., et al. (2010). The effects of prenatal cocaine exposure on problem behavior in children 4–10 years. *Neurotoxicology & Teratology, 32,* 443–451.

Morrow, C. E., Vogel, A. L., Anthony, J. C., Ofir, A. Y., Dausa, A. T., & Bandstra, E. S. (2004). Expressive and receptive language functioning in preschool children with prenatal cocaine exposure. *Journal of Pediatric Psychology, 29,* 543–554.

Nair, P., Schuler, M. E., Black, M. M., Kettinger, L., & Harrington, D. (2003). Cumulative environmental risk in substance abusing women: Early intervention, parenting stress, child abuse potential and child development. *Child Abuse & Neglect, 27,* 997–1017.

Nixon, R. D. V. (2001). Changes in hyperactivity and temperament in behaviorally disturbed preschoolers after parent–child interaction therapy (PCIT). *Behaviour Change, 18,* 168–176.

O'Connor, M. J., Frankel, F., Paley, B., Schonfeld, A. M., Carpenter, E., Laugeson, E. A., et al. (2006). A controlled social skills training for children with fetal alcohol spectrum disorders. *Journal of Consulting & Clinical Psychology, 74,* 639–648.

O'Connor, M. J., & Kasari, C. (2000). Prenatal alcohol exposure and depressive features in children. *Alcoholism: Clinical & Experimental Research, 24,* 1084–1092.

O'Leary, C. M., Nassar, N., Zubrick, S. R., Kurinczuk, J. J., Stanley, F., & Bower, C. (2009). Evidence of a complex association between dose, pattern and timing of prenatal alcohol exposure and child behavior problems. *Addiction, 105,* 74–86.

Olds, D. L., Eckenrode, J., Henderson, C. R., Jr., Kitzman, H., Powers, J., Cole, R., et al. (1997). Long-term effects of home visitation on maternal life course and child abuse and neglect: Fifteen-year follow-up of a randomized trial. *Journal of the American Medical Association, 278,* 637–643.

Olds, D. L., Henderson, C. R., Jr., Chamberlin, R., & Tatelbaum, R. (1986). Preventing child abuse and neglect: A randomized trial of nurse home visitation. *Pediatrics, 78,* 65–78.

Olds, D. L., Henderson, C. R., Jr, Tatelbaum, R., & Chamberlin, R. (1986). Improving the delivery of prenatal care and outcomes of pregnancy: A randomized trial of nurse home visitation. *Pediatrics, 77,* 16–28.

Olds, D. L., Henderson, C. R., Jr., & Tatelbaum, R. (1994a). Intellectual impairment in children of women who smoke cigarettes during pregnancy. *Pediatrics, 93,* 221–227.

Olds, D. L., Henderson, C. R., Jr., & Tatelbaum, R. (1994b). Prevention of intellectual impairment in children of women who smoke cigarettes during pregnancy. *Pediatrics, 93,* 228–233.

Olds, D. L., Kitzman, H., Cole, R., Robinson, J., Sidora, K., Luckey, D. W., et al. (2004). Effects of nurse home-visiting on maternal life course and child development: Age six follow-up results of a randomized trial. *Pediatrics, 114,* 1550–1559.

Olds, D. L., Kitzman, H. J., Cole, R. E., Hanks, C. A., Arcoleo, K. J., Anson, E. A., et al. (2010). Enduring effects of prenatal and infancy home visiting by nurses on maternal life course and government spending: Follow-up of a randomized trial among children at age 12 years. *Archives of Pediatric & Adolescent Medicine, 164,* 419–424.

Olson, H. C., Feldman, J. J., Streissguth, A. P., Sampson, P. D., & Bookstein, F. L. (1998). Neuropsychological deficits in adolescents with fetal alcohol syndrome: Clinical findings. *Alcoholism: Clinical & Experimental Research, 22,* 1998–2012.

Patterson, G. R. (1982). *Coercive Family Process.* Eugene, OR: Castalia.

Patterson, G. R., Reid, J. B., & Dishion, T. J. (1992). *Antisocial Boys: A Social Interactional Approach* (Vol. 4). Eugene, OR: Castalia.

Patterson, J., Barlow, J., Mockford, C., Klimes, I., Pyper, C., & Stewart-Brown, S. (2002). Improving mental health through parenting programmes: block randomised controlled trial. *Archives of Disease in Childhood, 87,* 472–477.

Petry, N. M. (2001). A behavioral economic analysis of polydrug abuse in alcoholics: Asymmetrical substitution of alcohol and cocaine. *Drug & Alcohol Dependence, 62,* 31–39.

Price, J. M., Chamberlain, P., Landsverk, J., & Reid, J. (2009). KEEP foster-parent training intervention: Model description and effectiveness. *Child & Family Social Work, 14,* 233–242.

Price, J. M., Chamberlain, P., Landsverk, J., Reid, J., Leve, L. D., & Laurent, H. (2008). Effects of a foster parent training intervention on placement changes of children in foster care. *Child Maltreatment, 13,* 64–75.

Proch, K., & Taber, M. A. (1985). Placement disruption: A review of research. *Children & Youth Services Review, 7,* 309–320.

Reid, J. B., Patterson, G. R., & Snyder, J. (Eds.). (2002). *Antisocial Behavior in Children and Adolescents: A Developmental Analysis and Model for Intervention:* Washington, DC: American Psychological Association.

Rounsaville, B. J., Petry, N. M., & Carroll, K. M. (2003). Single versus multiple drug focus in substance abuse clinical trials research. *Drug & Alcohol Dependence, 70,* 117–125.

Rueda, M. R., Rothbart, M. K., McCandliss, B. D., Saccomanno, L., & Posner, M. I. (2005). Training, maturation, and genetic influences on the development of executive attention.

Proceedings of the National Academy of Sciences of the United States of America, 102, 14931–14936.

Scott, S., Spender, Q., Doolan, M., Jacobs, B., & Aspland, H. (2001). Multicentre controlled trial of parenting groups for childhood antisocial behaviour in clinical practice. *British Medical Journal, 323,* 194.

Seifer, R., LaGasse, L. L., Lester, B., Bauer, C. R., Shankaran, S., Bada, H. S., et al. (2004). Attachment status in children prenatally exposed to cocaine and other substances. *Child Development, 75,* 850–868.

Singer, L., Arendt, R., Farkas, K., Minnes, S., Huang, J., & Yamashita, T. (1997). Relationship of prenatal cocaine exposure and maternal postpartum psychological distress to child developmental outcome. *Development & Psychopathology, 9,* 473–489.

Sood, B., Delaney-Black, V., Covington, C., Nordstrom-Klee, B., Ager, J., Templin, T., et al. (2001). Prenatal alcohol exposure and childhood behavior at age six to seven years: I. Dose-response effect. *Pediatrics, 108,* e34.

Spaccarelli, S., Cotler, S., & Penman, D. (1992). Problem-solving skills training as a supplement to behavioral parent training. *Cognitive Therapy & Research, 16,* 1–17.

Staines, G. L., Magura, S., Foote, J., Deluca, A., & Kosanke, N. (2001). Polysubstance use among alcoholics. *Journal of Addictive Diseases, 20*(4), 53–69.

Streissguth, A. P., Barr, H., Kogan, J., & Bookstein, F. (1997). Primary and secondary disabilities in fetal alcohol syndrome. In A. P. Streissguth & J. Kanter (Eds.), *The Challenge of Fetal Alcohol Syndrome: Overcoming Secondary Disabilities* (pp. 25–39). Seattle: University of Washington Press.

Streissguth, A. P., Bookstein, F. L., Barr, H. M., Sampson, P. D., O'Malley, K., & Young, J. K. (2004). Risk factors for adverse life outcomes in fetal alcohol syndrome and fetal alcohol effects. *Journal of Developmental & Behavioral Pediatrics, 25,* 228–238.

Tarter, R. E., Kirisci, L., Mezzich, A., Cornelius, J. R., Pajer, K., Vanyukov, M., et al. (2003). Neurobehavioral disinhibition in childhood predicts early age at onset of substance use disorder. *American Journal of Psychiatry, 160,* 1078–1085.

Taylor, T. K., Schmidt, F., Pepler, D., & Hodgins, C. (1998). A comparison of eclectic treatment with Webster-Stratton's parents and children series in a children's mental health center: A randomized controlled trial. *Behavior Therapy, 29,* 221–240.

Thomas, J. D., Abou, E. J., & Dominguez, H. D. (2009). Prenatal choline supplementation mitigates the adverse effects of prenatal alcohol exposure on development in rats. *Neurotoxicology & Teratology, 31,* 303–311.

Timmer, S. G., Urquiza, A. J., & Zebell, N. (2006). Challenging foster caregiver–maltreated child relationships: The effectiveness of parent–child interaction therapy. *Children & Youth Services Review, 28,* 1–19.

Webster-Stratton, C. (1981). Modification of mothers' behaviors and attitudes through a videotape modeling group discussion program. *Behavior Therapy, 12,* 634–642.

Webster-Stratton, C. (1982). Teaching mothers through videotape modeling to change their children's behavior. *Journal of Pediatric Psychology, 7,* 279–294.

Webster-Stratton, C. (1984). Randomized trial of two parent-training programs for families with conduct-disordered children. *Journal of Consulting & Clinical Psychology, 52,* 666–678.

Webster-Stratton, C. (1990). Enhancing the effectiveness of self-administered videotape parent training for families with conduct-problem children. *Journal of Abnormal Child Psychology, 18,* 479–492.

Webster-Stratton, C. (1994). Advancing videotape parent training: A comparison study. *Journal of Consulting & Clinical Psychology, 62*, 583–593.

Webster-Stratton, C. (1998). Preventing conduct problems in Head Start children: Strengthening parenting competencies. *Journal of Consulting & Clinical Psychology, 66*, 715–730.

Webster-Stratton, C., & Hammond, M. (1997). Treating children with early-onset conduct problems: A comparison of child and parent training interventions. *Journal of Consulting & Clinical Psychology, 65*, 93–109.

Webster-Stratton, C., Hollinsworth, T., & Kolpacoff, M. (1989). The long-term effectiveness and clinical significance of three cost-effective training programs for families with conduct-problem children. *Journal of Consulting & Clinical Psychology, 57*, 550–553.

Webster-Stratton, C., Kolpacoff, M., & Hollinsworth, T. (1988). Self-administered videotape therapy for families with conduct-problem children: Comparison with two cost-effective treatments and a control group. *Journal of Consulting & Clinical Psychology, 56*, 558–566.

Webster-Stratton, C., & Reid, M. J. (2003). The Incredible Years parents, teachers and children training series: A multifaceted treatment approach for young children with conduct problems. In A. E. Kazdin & J. R. Weisz (Eds.), *Evidence-Based Psychotherapies for Children and Adolescents* (pp. 224–240). New York: Guilford Press.

Webster-Stratton, C., & Reid, M. J. (2010). Adapting The Incredible Years, an evidence-based parenting programme, for families involved in the child welfare system. *Journal of Children's Services, 5*, 25–42.

Webster-Stratton, C., Reid, M. J., & Hammond, M. (2001). Preventing conduct problems, promoting social competence: A parent and teacher training partnership in Head Start. *Journal of Clinical Child Psychology, 30*, 283–302.

Wells, A. (2007). The attention training technique: Theory, effects, and a metacognitive hypothesis on auditory hallucinations. *Cognitive & Behavioral Practice, 14*, 134–138.

Zima, B. T., Bussing, R., Freeman, S., Yang, X., Belin, T. R., & Forness, S. R. (2000). Behavior problems, academic skill delays and school failure among school-aged children in foster care: Their relationship to placement characteristics. *Journal of Child & Family Studies, 9*, 87–103.

Zuckerman, M. (1999). Diathesis–stress models. In M. Zuckerman (Ed.), *Vulnerability to Psychopathology: A Biosocial Model* (pp. 3–23): Washington, DC: American Psychological Association.

Zukoski, M. (1999). Foster parent training. In J. A. Silver, B. J. Amster, & T. Haecker (Eds.), *Young Children and Foster Care: A Guide for Professionals* (pp. 473–490). Baltimore, MD: Paul H. Brookes.

INDEX